THE APOCALYPSE LIKE NEVER INTERPRETED BEFORE,
CHANNELED AND NARRATED BY YESHUA (JESUS) AND THE ASCENDED MASTERS,
REVEALING THE PARALYZING MISINTERPRETATION BY THE CHURCH.

THE ASCENDED MASTERS ON THE APOCALYPSE

TERRY L. NEWBEGIN

NEC
PRESS

Published by NEC Press
Tennesee, USA

Copyright © 2021 by Terry L. Newbegin
All rights reserved.

No part of the book may be reproduced by any mechanical, photographic, or electronic process, or in a phonographic recording. The book will not be stored in a retrieval system, transmitted, or otherwise copied for public or private use other than for "fair use" as brief quotations embodied within the book without prior written consent from the author.

The author does not dispense medical advice nor prescribe the use of any technique as a form of treatment for physical or medical problems without the advice of a physician, either directly or indirectly. The author is only offering information as a unique nature to help in your quest for clarity, health, abundance, and joy. If you use the information or techniques in this book for yourself, which is your constitutional right, the author and the publisher assume no responsibility for your actions or any of its results.

Book Cover and Interior Design by Monkey C Media
Edited by Nancy Salminen

First Edition
Printed in the United States of America

ISBN: 978-1-7356947-0-2 (Trade Paperback)
ISBN: 978-1-7356947-1-9 (Ebook)

Library of Congress Control Number: 2020918916

The Apocalypse Like Never Interpreted Before, Channeled and Narrated by Yeshua (Jesus) and the Ascended Masters, revealing the paralyzing misinterpretation by the Church

CONTENTS

Prelude..01
A Message Statement...12
Consciousness..20
Christ Consciousness 33
We Are a Sanctioned Christ...41
The Seven Churches & the Seven Spirits Before the Throne...................50
The Alpha and The Omega..63
The Physical Body and the Seven Gold Lampstands 69
Reviewing the Seven Layers of Our Consciousness 81
Understanding thE Physical Body 86
Understanding the Astral Body..96
Understanding the Emotional Body...102
Understanding the Etheric-Mental Body...110
Understanding the Intuitive Body..121
Understanding the Mind and Soul Body of Responsibility................131
Understanding The Spirit Body..139
Understanding Polarity Energy (Positive and Negative) 144
Summarizing of the Mind & Physical Body, and How it Relates to
    Revelation 4:4-11 153
Memory and How It Works..166
The Opening of the Seals 181
The Sealing of the Thousands 196
The Twelve Tribes of Israel and How They Relate to the Physical Body
    (12,000 X 12,000 = 144,000)...205
The Return to Higher Consciousness...221
Total Recall 227
The Realization of Our Dark Creations 239
Moving from One Incarnation to the Next......................................250
How Crystal, Cosmic & Earth Energies Work with Our Divine Plan...270

Moving from A Three-Density to a Four-Density Consciousness 280
You Are a Divine Being..303
The Conflict Among Consciousness, Our Mind, & Ego-Personalities...316
The Beast and the Anti-Christ Revealed..328
Overcoming the Separation of Our Mind..344
Our Mind (Anti-Christ) Becomes the Savior 359
Tapping into Our Memories 369
Hell Converts to Heaven..385
How We Became a Slave to Our Ego, the Mind, & the System.................419
Why Do We Feel We Fell from Grace? 440
Coming into Our Awakening 455
The Coming of Christ 466
Salvation Comes to Those Who Seek It...479
Our Journey Through Time and Space..487
The New Heaven and New Earth 504
We Are Eternal, Indestructible and Unchangeable 520
The Christ Return is Now Fulfilled..524
ACKNOWLEDGMENT..541

PRELUDE

I would like to share a vision I had a few years ago where I was standing on a hillside overlooking a valley. And, as the sun rose and filled the valley with light and warmth, I began to feel a violent wind blow across the valley, rocking the trees back and forth with such force, everything began to fall to their demise. And, when the wind picked up even more, I noticed the land making up the valley shifted as if it was gushing waves moving across an ocean. Then, in the twinkling of an eye, the intense wind and the gushing wave movement of the land suddenly changed. And, that is when I saw a new valley appear right before my eyes.

This new valley contained colors and trees of such grandeur it would put to shame the colors and trees exhibited today in our three-dimensional world. When I saw this distinctive and unusual majestic landscape unfold before my eyes, an incredible feeling of peace and unconditional love came over me, and that is when I heard a voice say: "Now the "Old Earth" has passed and a "New Earth" has come."

From this vision, I realized that it represents the year 2020 (completion), where everything looks scary. But, by the end of 2020, the vision shown is to inform us about those of us (trees) dealing with the dark (old earth, old system) will fall, and those of us (trees) dealing with the light will move forward and upward to a fifth-dimensional consciousness (New Earth/New System). And that is when everything will change!

From this vision that I experienced is of the same New Heaven and New Earth that John the Apostle experienced in his vision over 2000 years ago. Therefore, the time for the ascension (rapture) is here, and the apex of this new energy coming onto earth will happen between now and December 21, 2020. In other words, (12 + 21 + 20 + 20 = 73, and as we break this number down into the primary numbers (7 + 3 = 10), it represents completion.

The completion of an "Old World" system and the beginning of a "New World" system where people's vibrational signature (DNA) will rise to a consciousness awakening to where they come to realize that they have been played by those of the dark for centuries. This completion is for those that are ready, as it was for John, in declaring their sovereignty as a Christ also, and then letting go of their old, dogmatic beliefs about the Tree of Knowledge of Good and Evil.

The awakening is about letting go of this three-dimensional polarity world of suffering (the old valley in my vision) to meet up with a new world consciousness and energy of four (the new valley), where our divine plan is revealed to us as something, we each created for ourselves to work toward. It is an awakening in spirit that we are the Christ mentioned in the Book of Revelation. All the chaos we are seeing and experiencing in this polarity energy (old world) is about to end for those ego-personalities that have been manipulating the system for their own benefit.

So rejoice, the time has come to bring out within humanity all that we harbor as good and evil. It has been centuries that we, on a third-dimensional level, have been playing with a force that keeps us separated into groups where we fight each other over control, power, and greed. We, the people of the world, have forgotten that the Book of Revelation depicts the relationship between our mind-soul, our "I AM" Christ spirit, and our self-absorbed physical consciousness.

However, even though we have been self-absorbed for many lifetimes, it has led some of us to a New Consciousness where we are about to become free of all that is of polarity and fear living. And, once the message is understood at a realization consciousness, we will welcome in this New Energy of Four and become a Christ in our own right. Then our deliverance and ascension (rapture) are assured by us moving from a three-dimensional consciousness to a fourth and fifth-dimensional consciousness where we can now experience the magic of healing, peace, and true freedom.

I know the Book of Revelation has been played with for centuries, where many scholars and religious leaders have tried to make sense of the extreme symbolism behind the written text. And now, Yeshua and the Ascended Masters are willing to present to you a "New Voice" on Saint John's highly debated and difficult book to read and understand, the "Apocalypse."

We all have, including most religious organizations, assumed that God's vision to Saint John is about "soon to emerge conditions," including World War III, an asteroid hitting the earth, having great storms, the death of one-third of the population, and the framework where the Anti-Christ emerges to take on Jesus and his army of angels. Therefore, the "Apocalypse" has become a universal cosmic wonder that requires the right examiners to unlock its mystery and its wisdom. And, who are these master examiners?

They are those highly known Ascended Angels from beyond the physical veil, and they are experts when it comes to Biblical writings. In fact, one could not ask for worthier commentators then these well-known angels to bring out the wisdom behind the "Apocalypse." And, according to these grandmasters, the true prophecy and wisdom behind "Apocalypse" is not what we have been taught it to be at all.

Meanwhile, or until you finished reading the book, let's eliminate your confusion, your fear, and the unrest caused by such a prophecy as the end of the world. Oh, you may hear of an asteroid or two coming close to the earth. But be assured, the future of the earth, and those that love humanity, is going to be golden.

As difficult as the Book of Revelation is to read and understand because of its extreme symbolism, these captivating Ascended Masters from behind the physical veil will help us understand what we have been taught about the Bible's version of the Beast and Anti-Christ is actually about a "New Beginning" for us all, and not what we have been led to believe as something terrifying.

As a child between the ages of eight and ten, I witnessed and saw what people would describe as apparitions. And, when I learned of their identity in my older years, my first impression was to kneel and honor them as Gods. But, once I heard one of them speak to me about who we indeed are at our core, all I could do was stand in awe without saying a word. That was when these angelic beings introduced themselves to me as Yeshua Ben Joseph (known as Jesus), Mother Mary, Mary Magdalene, Tobias, Melchezidek, Moses, Kuthumi Lal Singh, Adamus Saint Germain, Abraham, Methuselah, and Saint Dominic.

However, it wasn't until 2004 when I witnessed a prophetic event where I was lying in bed staring at a huge rustic brownish wooden door that looked like a big bank vault, having three extended metal straps connected to three metal hinges about four inches wide that went across the top, middle, and bottom of the door. And, when the large wooden door opened, I noticed the door appeared about eight feet high and three feet thick. That is when I saw these angelic beings sitting around a wooden picnic table.

Then, like a blink of an eye, I went from lying in bed to standing in the entranceway of this impenetrable vault looking door, staring right at these angelic beings watching me. And, as I observed them, I heard: "*Welcome to the wisdom of the Bible.*" That was when I first met Lord Melchizedek, as he informed me, he would be the group leader in the writing of my books. Standing there in awe, Lord Melchizedek asked me to enter the room. And, when I stepped across the entranceway of this vault looking doorway, his words were, "*We are here to help you* (me) *with the forgotten wisdom of the Bible, as we* (they) *are experts on the subject.*"

Then Lord Melchizedek followed up by saying that "*I was a person that always enjoyed being in the front line when it comes to matters of the Divine.*" And yet, still, in awe, Lord Melchizedek finished by saying that *"I was a priest under the order of Melchizedek."* It was from this experience I later learned how to channel these grand Ascended Masters, including Jesus. It was also the time where Jesus informed me that he prefers to be called "Yeshua Ben-Joseph" or just "Yeshua."

It was from that time forward these Ascended Masters now work and speak through me as one unit, although at times, one or two may come in to speak with me separately. And now, it has been about sixteen years working with them in the writing of my books. And, from working with them, Lord Melchizedek and the group are indeed *"experts on the subject of the Bible."* And, if you read this book, you will see for yourself.

According to the Masters, there is no "divine will" to follow like the Church mentions. But there is a "divine plan" that we created for ourselves to go out and discover who we are as an extension of the Spirit of One.

In reference to my birth name, it is Terry L. Newbegin, and I am a channeller and teacher of New Energy and New Consciousness. And, I work with a group of Ascended Masters from the angelic realm that goes far beyond the physical veil and what surrounds us as only Crystal, Cosmic, and Earth Energy. One of the biggest surprises I have learned from channeling these angelic beings was when I asked Yeshua (Jesus) about his role as being our Lord and Savior. And, to my surprise, his reply was, *"That belongs to those that dare to awaken from their sleep to a 'knowing' that they are their own savior."*

That was when I was awakened to religions misleading us when it comes to "knowing the real Christ." For, the man who walked upon the earth over two thousand years ago in planting the Christ seed was Yeshua Ben Joseph and not a man named Jesus. The second biggest surprise I learned! The Father God that Yeshua mentioned when he walked the earth was not about a single-minded super father deity that created earth and humanity but is the makeup of all souled beings that use a "universal omnipresent mind field of pure unbiased energy" for their creations.

Channeling of the Ascended Masters on the Apocalypse

For example, Yeshua informed me, *"God is like a vast ocean and us humans are the drops of water making up that ocean; and, if we took away all the drops, then there would be no ocean, therefore no God."* It is, therefore, because of forgetting, that we humans together are the ocean, thus the God we week. It is just that we have forgotten that we are the "I AM That I AM" who met up with Moses atop Mount Horeb, Exodus 3:1-17. And, as the church proclaims in the final days of God's judgment, 1 Thessalonians 4:16-17, and I paraphrase here, *"for the Lord will descend from heaven, and the dead in Christ will rise first, then those who are on the earth will be caught up together with them in the clouds to meet the Lord in the air."*

As you can see here, the church interpretation of this "caught up together with them in the clouds to meet the Lord in the air," is all based on their study about Jesus coming to earth in the end days to rapture up those who worship him and give their allegiance to him. However, before examining the church's understanding of this misleading reference, the Ascended Masters want to remind us that in the early days, before Yeshua, the Hebrew definition of God was not Jesus or Yeshua, but was "Yahweh" (YHWH), meaning "I AM THAT I AM."

The name "Yahweh" is the proper name for God and the Goddess, or as known as our higher consciousness (Oversoul) at work, and not that it is referring to a God of sin and punishment, for that God is a false God. Therefore, with the help of Yeshua and the Ascended Masters from the angelic realm, and by my remembered name, "I AM That I AM" a Christ also, we are working together in the writing of this book to uncover the extreme misunderstanding of the Church prophecies tied to "Apocalypse," and that of the "Rapture."

Because of many lifetimes on earth, we all have forgotten our real name in favor of our human name. And with it, we have forgotten that our "I AM" is the only thing absolute, having no beginning or end and that our "I AM" is a self-governing souled being that depends only on its own consciousness acts in creating our world. We have forgotten that our Oversoul is constant, compassionate, unchangeable, and we have the authority to do as we please, as long as we do not interfere with our fellow souled beings.

Therefore, the profound messages found in this book go far beyond what the churches of the world teach and believe, for they teach us that we are all sinners and that we are less than God, thus no Christ. Therefore, Yeshua and the Ascended Masters are hoping this book will open the gates of your soul memories, revealing to you the hidden truth (wisdom) behind the "Apocalypse" compared to the Church's interpretation where Jesus, the man, comes to earth for your salvation.

With any in-depth study of the "Apocalypse" that fails to consider the human body and how it functions with our Oversoul, our mind-soul consciousness, our memories, and our physical consciousness would be contrary to any idea of Christ coming soon for our salvation. Notwithstanding the many lifetimes of our past, religions have overlooked the "human body" and its value in interpreting the Book of Revelation because they assume humankind was created to live out one lifetime to become balanced with God's divine plan.

As we study the wisdom behind the "Apocalypse," we will discover that my book is not based on religious views about Yeshua (Jesus) coming into a rapture. Instead, the book is centered upon balancing our three-dimensional body, our masculine/feminine identity, and transforming it into "one body of consciousness" to meet up with our own "I AM" Christ consciousness, thus opening us up to our own magic and freedom. Therefore, the first message from these Ascended Masters is to open up and discover your many cycled lifetimes that you have experienced, and have recorded in memory since the time you left the first creation eons ago (Garden).

If the terminology and jargon used by Yeshua and the Ascended Masters in the interpreting become challenging, just relax, keep reading, and do not fear the message, because everything will become more evident by the time you finish the book in its entirety. Also, the aspirations of the Ascended Masters are not to change anyone's mind about Yeshua (his real Hebrew name). They are here to demonstrate that we long ago dived deep into polarity energy and materialism to answer the question, "Who am I?" And, with that question, we all get to learn the wisdom behind our choices. However, in that quest, we all have become stuck in a belief we have only one lifetime to get things right.

From this message given by the Ascended Masters, we hope to open the gateway of your soul memories, revealing your many-layered lifetimes where you have played upon the earth trying to define your "I AM's" purpose. Yeshua came to earth to illustrate the Christ Principle and to remind us who we are, but we did not listen, and therefore we lost our freedom (free will) to those who love to control us through power, fear, money, race, chaos, and confusion. This message, as it was back in Yeshua's time on earth, will help many to remember who Christ is, who God is, who the Anti-Christ is, who the Beast is, and to reveal the truth behind the "Tree of Knowledge of Good and Evil."

Channeling of the Ascended Masters on the Apocalypse

From the study of this book, you will learn there is nothing to fear with God, Satan, and the Anti-Christ because, if you allow yourself to awaken from your sleep, you have already been ordained as a high priest destined to higher consciousness and understanding, even if you have committed atrocities called sin. It is not sinning! It is that we have been merely learning the wisdom behind our choices and how we have played them out in many lifetimes.

When fear and the belief in sin are removed from our consciousness, we are then ready to open ourselves up to the hidden wisdom (manna) behind the Book of Revelation, Yeshua, Christ, the Beast, the Anti-Christ, and how they relate, not to the ending of the world as we know it, but to the end of our suffering.

When Yeshua allowed himself to be crucified by those who believed in polarity energy (tree of good, evil, sin, and punishment), it represents the acceptance of our own trials and tribulations as something that we all chose for ourselves to experience to complete our own divine plan. Everything we experience in life, no matter what that is, cancer, health, richness, poorness, always wanting or not wanting, comes from what we have set up for ourselves to experience in any given lifetime. And, we will continue to suffer if we are afraid to change our minds and let go of the old dogmatic ways of thinking about sin, Satan, Christ, and who Christ is.

By letting go of the old doctrine about sin, Satan, Christ, free will, the belief in a God that punishes, and religious traditions, we will find it is the most beneficial thing we could ever do for ourselves. The "tree of knowledge of good and evil" is nothing more than the splitting of our consciousness and this "universal omnipresent mind field of pure God energy of Light" into conflicting energies (positive and negative, polarity), so we could use it to experience opposites. And, since polarity energy was unknown to us in the early stages of our creations, we have been experiencing fear, control, and power on a vast scale.

How can we create freedom and work from "free will" if we are lied to every time we attend church and watch television? The churches of the world, and all of what we see and hear on television, especially the media, our politicians, and our religions, are all about division and fear. And, the more they divide us into different belief systems, the more they can keep us from ever knowing that we are all a sovereign Christ in our own right.

It is time to take back our life, free will, power, and become conscious creators like our brother Yeshua. When we fail to look at ourselves as one human race, and as a divine spark coming from the Spirit of One, we become a slave to those that love control, fear, money, and power. Just listen to our politicians, our religions, and our educators, pay attention to their motives, and you will notice that whatever they are saying, none of it is in our best interest. They say what we want to hear for them to maintain their power and control over us.

Today, we are not Americans or even one human race; we are called out by our nationality, and then as Republicans, Democrats, Independents, Green Party, Socialist Party, the Left, the Right, Communist, and Constitution Party, etc. It is the same with Religion, as they too have many, many variations of faith to keep us in fear. And now, the challenge is for us to find the courage to question the status quo. Yeshua did, and it cost him his life! Even the belief that some God created us is a lie. Thus, our "free will" becomes "their will be done" and not ours. Most all of us want the same things, peace, harmony, health, and the freedom to be left alone without anyone interfering.

Therefore, the question to ask yourself! Were you created with "free will and as a free agent of God or not?" If you believe you are exercising your "free will," then why do we continuously die, suffer, live in need, have bad relationships, and choose illnesses that challenge us physically and financially? The answer is with our Oversoul, for she (feminine) has a deep passion for experiencing many things, and it takes many lifetimes to achieve them. One lifetime, no matter how long we live, cannot come close to what our Oversoul desires to experience. And this is why it is so easy for those in power to keep us separated. It is all about maintaining their power.

However, that ends when we become awakened to "who we truly are at our core essence." If a child dies only hours, days, months, or years after birth, what has their Oversoul learned, other than what it is like to die young? There can be many things the Oversoul learned in that short lifetime. And, by setting aside our dogmatic beliefs about why the child died young, our Oversoul calls out to the "universal omnipresent mind field of pure neutralized unbiased energy of light (God)" to have us learn that we are following our Oversoul's "divine plan." And we do it by using fear, power, control, and polarity energy as the source. (Tree of Knowledge of Good and Evil (Genesis 2:9))!

Our Oversoul's objective is to learn "all that there is to know about polarity energy, positive and negative, good and bad, right and wrong, male and female," and life in general. Our Oversoul does not care, while we are in human form, what we are experiencing; illness, poorness, richness, good or bad, life or death. Why is that? Because those experiences come from our own choices, as they are all part of our own "Divine Plan." All that our Oversoul is concerned about is for us to learn the wisdom from the experiences, which is why there is no such thing as sin.

It is not meant for our Oversoul to interfere with our choices, and, at the same time, she does not want to get stuck in a human body forever. In other words, if the human ego is not willing to move forward in the understanding of one's Oversoul's purpose to learn wisdom through experiences, then one's Oversoul will take over and create the situations that will help move one along in the journey of discovering one's acts and choices. Hence, here comes the accidents, illnesses, etc.! Actually, our Oversoul right now has a whole different outlook from our human idea about how to accomplish this purpose.

Now, it sounds like our "Oversoul" has a different identity than our human identity, and yet, they are the same. It is just that our consciousness is layered into having different frequency waves, and our higher consciousness vibrates at a very high rate than our human consciousness. I know this can be hard to comprehend, but coming from the human ego, it comes down to understanding our Oversoul's purpose, because eternity is eternity.

For example, our human consciousness looks at our politics, religion, hunger, diseases, death, suffering, separation, poverty, bad relationships, anger, greed, and the belief in right or wrong, and sin and punishment as real; while our "Oversoul" sees only these experiences as expansion and growth, and no sin committed. Our "Oversoul" sees these things experienced as learning wisdom, as our human ego sees them as problems, sin, and as of right and wrong.

When we use this "universal omnipresent mind field of pure neutralized god energy of light" for our choices and acts, and how it is brought to our mind-soul for interpreting, then it becomes our mind's agenda on an intellectual scale to judge them as either good or bad, right or wrong. What happens when we stop this pure god energy of light with our views of good and evil, or right and wrong, or being a Democrat or Republican as being who we are? It takes the shape of whatever our human consciousness is focused upon. And, if we are focused on these things, then those are what our Oversoul will give life to for us to experience. It is that simple!

You have, along with certainty and belief, a human body made up of flesh, cells, bones, and many other components. But you also have multiple physical bodies where you have lived upon the earth before, and you are unaware of them in this lifetime. These other ego-personality aspects of you are inter-dimensional bodies not in the flesh anymore; they are multiple, unrefined, and refined life bodies that exist in a nonphysical state where you have lived these lifetimes in the past.

However, there are some of these inter-dimensional bodies that never did live on earth in a physical body, and yet many have. And, these ego-personality aspects (lifetimes) of you are unrefined and refined bodies where you are working out your Oversoul's divine plan to express and expand in consciousness to gain wisdom. And, since consciousness activates energy and energy potentials around us, it also states that we are hungry or that our body is in pain. And, since our consciousness is much more focused on this limited physical dimension, then what do we think we will experience?

Healing comes when we perceive these many ego-personality aspects (lifetimes) from the past and accept them as our creations. Instead, we fear these ego-personality aspects so much we pretend by believing we have only one lifetime. The reason we think this way is because our mind-soul focuses only on our present lifetime. When one swears that their politics is the right way to go and another swears the opposite, then know in a past lifetime, one has already played out the opposite.

We have locked up in memory these many ego-personality aspects (lifetimes) of our past (unrefined and refined). And, because of it, we have suppressed our Oversoul from reaching our ego-consciousness of today. Thus, we blocked up our energy to where our body becomes ill, just like a dam blocks the flow of the water. Because we believe in separation, the energy we use collapses on itself to gain a higher understanding of why it is stuck. Thus, answering the question of why the Book of Revelation associates itself more with the physical body and our journey through many lifetimes than with Yeshua coming to earth for our salvation.

It is not about Yeshua coming to save us. It is about Christ within the self coming to save the self. It is through memory and our past ego-personality aspects (lifetimes) where we get to know the real Christ. Therefore, it takes a wise person to let go of their religious and political beliefs that have resulted from experiencing pain and suffering. To look only at earth and man and what it is like to be in chaos right now is to overlook the Oversoul's divine plan to bring in awakening, higher understanding, and New Expansional Energy for us to experience a new freedom. Freedom that only comes from the Christ consciousness within the self, where this consciousness only deals with Crystalline Energy.

This consciousness understanding does not judge or take sides or determine what is right or wrong or creates chaos. This understanding of consciousness and energy only provides infinite order and neutrality in all things that we create for ourselves to experience.

Channeling of the Ascended Masters on the Apocalypse

The Book of Revelation is exploring the cellular memories of the physical body and its makeup, right down to our personal history. Therefore, please bear with Yeshua and the Ascended Masters, as they present this material to you. If they occasionally repeat things, it is due to the layout of the chapters and their verses.

A MESSAGE STATEMENT

With the interpretations of Apocalypse, also known as the Book of Revelation in the Bible, the Churches of the world desire us humans to believe that the author of the Book is, in fact, God and or Jesus, his son. However, the message goes far more in-depth than Jesus giving a narration on what becomes of us and our sinful ways. In fact, the whole Bible of today has been rewritten by the dark forces, including the Book of Revelation. Therefore, the wisdom behind the message given by the Ascended Masters is for those that are ready to be uplifted to a higher consciousness frequency where they become awakened to the real truth behind John's vision.

From channeling the Ascended Masters from beyond the physical veil, the man Jesus, as described by religions, was not the same man who walked the earth over two thousand years ago. However, there was a Jewish man that carried a Hebrew name of "Yeshua Ben Joseph" that was very out spoken about the Christ Consciousness and how energy works. So, where did religions come up with the name Jesus? We all know that this holy man was born a Jew and not as a Greek, for the name Jesus comes from the Greek dictionary of the New Testament, referenced under the name "Jehoshua."

Referenced in the Hebrew and Chaldee Dictionary, the name "Jehoshua," or the name "yehowshua" was later interpreted to being the "Lord's" name, "YAHWEH." Meaning, free, save, deliver, help, defend, having salvation, having a savior, and having a victory! Even the name Christ is derived from the name "YAHWEH." The word "saved" is a translation of the Hebrew word "Yasha." And this is the root word from which the name Jesus came from.

Channeling of the Ascended Masters on the Apocalypse

However, the "J" sound used to pronounce the name Jesus did not even exist in Hebrew during "yehowshua" time on earth, that later was translated to "Yeshua." Even Archaeologists have found the name Yeshua Ben Joseph carved into 71 burial caves in Israel, dating from the time Yeshua was alive. Therefore, the answer to the question about Yeshua's name comes down to translation. It was precisely this interpretation by the Greeks given to Yeshua Ben Joseph that finally evolved into the modern name, Jesus of today.

When the New Testament was written in Greek, before it was in English, the authors used the Greek "s" sound instead of the "sh" sound in Yeshua and then added the final "s" to the end of the name to make it sound masculine. Maybe Catholics remember the version where Jesus did not have brothers and sisters, and yet, Yeshua did have brothers and sisters. Yeshua just was the firstborn.

Thus, in this presentation, and since Yeshua's name is the real name of the holy man that walked the earth over two-thousand years ago, the Ascended Masters and I will continue the usage of his real name, Yeshua, and not as Jesus. And, according to Yeshua, there are thousands of Jesus' on the other side of the veil, as there is a Jesus that fits every dimensional religious belief.

The book you are about to read may be the most important book you will ever read, as it is a channeled book offering many insights into the "Apocalypse" from beyond the physical veil, narrated by Yeshua himself and the Ascended Masters. It is a book that reveals the long-awaited truth about Christ and how the church has kept us in the dark about the significance of Christ's importance. As known in western society, there are many people, especially church-going, that do not believe in communicating with spirits from beyond the physical veil, let alone hearing messages from the angelic realm. Therefore, they may not accept this presentation. And because of it, I feel sad for their loss!

Most religious people believe that God speaks only through his church and his scholars, and yet, there are many throughout the world today that do communicate directly with spirits beyond the grave (both high and low). And, because of this belief by the church and their followers, it has been centuries where they, and the God they describe in the Bible, have taken over our "free will" and "spiritual training" into knowing our Oversoul, the real God, Christ, Satan, and the Bible in its true wisdom.

With this message, then know the author of the Book of Revelation is not so much as John, the human; it was his own "I AM" Christ consciousness in representing John. My friends, it was John, the Apostle himself, coming into the remembrance of his real name, "I AM THAT I AM." The confirmation to this is uncovered in the wisdom behind Revelation 1:1: *"The revelation of Jesus Christ, which God gave to him, to show his servants what must happen soon. He made it known by sending his angel to his servant John."*

From speaking with the angelic realm, the Ascended Masters proclaim the human mind is nothing more than a center for mental impressions based on polarity (opposing energy), sin, judgment, and thought patterns that carry within them a dense intellectual vibrational energy frequency (signature) that only perceives us, humans, as unworthy of being a Christ also. For example, it comes hard for us to see ourselves as a divine expression of the Spirit of One. Why? It is because of guilt and shame tied to many past lifetimes that are part of our DNA today.

We all have forgotten this dense impenetrable intellectual energy signature (DNA) carries within it a mental identification that only deals with rational thought, analyzing, polarity, judgment, emotions, and the belief that academic intelligence is the highest order of things when it comes to the flesh. Through time, space, and the journey of many lifetimes, we have lost our awareness in what we perceive as our mind-soul, the intelligence it holds in memory, and how they are both a mental version of us where we have learned to characterize polarity (good and evil) as something real.

During my study of polarity, I realized that I am the creator of energy and how it serves me through my spirit, my mind-soul, my beliefs, my intelligence, my thoughts, and my choices. And, when I came to this realization, that is when I surrendered my judgments about polarity and sin in favoring myself to ascend (caught up) from merely being a human on earth to a "divine-human consciousness knowing" that I am the supreme creator Goddess of my experiences.

And, once I forgave myself, gave up judging others, and letting go of the narrative of my mind-soul holding a God and a Satan in fear. My energy flowed freely throughout my physical body, breaking down my old way of thinking to where I am now communicating with my remembered name, "I AM THAT I AM." This change of thinking afforded me an infinite flow of "Expanded Pure Neutralized Crystalline Energy of Light" (symbolic of the real God) to come into my life. Thus, changing "all that I thought was the truth" to appreciate that I was a slave to my many-layered beliefs, and to a system in what religion represented as truths (lies) for many lifetimes.

It was religion that taught me that the "mind of reason" is our tool in discerning God, Satan, what is ethical, and what is immoral. Or, otherwise,

I would be destined to hell forever! However, in creating such a fear-based approach to what I understood about God, I became locked into a consciousness that good comes from God, and what is evil comes from the devil. Thus, I created a belief within me so strong that I must be good or otherwise, hell was knocking on my door. It was through beliefs like this that religions realized they could join up with kings, queens, rulers, and governments to control us, using mind control, thus controlling everything we believe about religion and God.

As religions and governments led us all down a path of destruction and the takeover of our minds and bodies, making our choices and actions for us, we have become their slaves and their food to gain power. However, once we learn to open our hearts and minds and allow ourselves to remember this massive takeover by those in power, we will learn to open up to the true God-Goddess, Christ, and our own "I AM THAT I AM" consciousness. Thus, taking back our own power and revealing to ourselves our connection to Christ and our Oversoul, the feminine.

Also, in this revealing, we can unveil our many, many ego-personality aspects from past lifetimes to our present self in this lifetime if we so chose. Thus, it is time to integrate our many personality-aspects of our past as "one body of consciousness." That is when we will be lifted, as in a Rapture, to become a Christ-like being in our own right, as Yeshua did. What we are seeing and experiencing today has nothing to do with God's laws, sin, the end days, or Yeshua returning to earth to save us. It is about our own awakening to the real Christ, the Oversoul. For every one of us is a Christ in our own right.

The facts remain! Religion, science, humankind, and governments have always made everything complicated and mysterious when it comes to our true identity and how we should be controlled and managed. And, the best way to control us is for us to be obsessed with a false God that created us and that we must worship; to be obsessed with fear, sin, guilt, shame, and a God of judgment and punishment (polarity). And that is how they play us against each other so as for the system to maintain their power.

To step into the consciousness of mastering your own life is to understand who you are at your core essence. From there, you get to know who God is and who God is not. And, that is when you get to realize that you, all of us, gave up "free choice (will)" a long time ago to the church, the media, our governments, and to our family and friends in favor of following a false God and those that love power.

Yes, without realizing it, we have tied "free will" to our thoughts about a God that holds an energy of polarity as real. And the results! We follow the human system to the end, no matter what is said to be the truth. As long as religion can present us with a devil after our soul, a God of sin and punishment, heaven and hell, and politicians that do nothing for us, they can tie up our mind, soul, and our energy almost forever without us even realizing they are controlling us through fear, and by way of our thoughts and beliefs. It is to realize that our leaders know that our mind knows how we believe and think, which then sets up who we think we are all day long, just a human needing a savior.

We are all asleep to the church, the media, and our politicians being our savior and our salvation without realizing they are leading us more and more away from whom we indeed are, and more into their hands as slaves. Our leaders know we believe with all our hearts in polarity (positive and negative), and a God of sin and punishment; thus, we give away our "free will" and our connection to our own "I AM" Christ consciousness to them so they can do with it as they please. And, in doing so, we allow them to create our experiences and reality according to their beliefs and what they feel is best for us.

This is happening today all around the world, as everyone is pitted against each other in order for the system (harlot) to maintain their control over our health, our money, our thoughts, our choices, our actions, and our experiences. Therefore, the purpose for writing this book using the Apocalypse as a guide is to uncover the false narrative about ourselves, about sin, about punishment, about the Anti-Christ and the Beast, and what is behind the Rapture.

The first message specified by Yeshua and the Ascended Masters, "we humans are the Absolute 'I AM' Creator of energy and the bringer of our many physical bodies," and no one else. God did not create us! We created ourselves! Thus, we are the only ones responsible for what we create. Therefore, this God of judgment, sin, and punishment is not the real God because the God of the Bible has been replaced with a God that holds us as weak humans, and the system knows that.

It was our governments and churches throughout history that gave rise to this false god and a system we would die for. And, they continue today in giving this God of the Bible power to fit their narrative of a God we must worship. This false narrative of a conditional God works hard to keep us asleep to the real truth when it comes to our freedom, our sanity, and Christ's return. We have forgotten that our consciousness is "Christlike," and it has been that way since our awakening back in the first creation.

We are eternal-everlasting, omnipresent (everywhere at once), all-powerful, all-knowing, and we are the supreme creator of our mind-soul, our many ego physical bodies, our experiences, and our reality. And, when

Channeling of the Ascended Masters on the Apocalypse

I learned of this, my Oversoul (the Supreme Christ within) reminded me of my real name; "Yahweh," as in "I AM That I AM," a Christ also. And, when you come into this realization, then your remembered name will be shown to you as an "I AM" because, at your core, you are the same.

Know that your purpose for coming to earth was not about God being outside of you or part of a book that you must follow and worship. But it is about your consciousness, choices, belief systems, and your experiences using opposing energy to gain wisdom when it comes to "who you are at your core level." It is about remembering that your consciousness must shift from perceiving who you believe you are from a mental and ego level to looking within yourself to find the real you, for you to are the "I AM THAT I AM," you are Yahweh, and you are a Christ also, as you are all three.

My friends, it was us souled beings and not some God outside or above us, that set-in motion a challenge of discovery long ago that led into multitudes of belief systems that eventually led to what is believed today as a male God who created us, male and female. And, when speaking of this, the time has come for some of us to learn the real truth about who we indeed are when it comes to the rapture, as the rapture is nothing more than our ascension to a higher and much wiser consciousness where energy rises to a frequency where we leave behind the old ways of thinking and believing in a God of sin and punishment.

There is nothing outside of us that exists, not our mind-soul, physical body, the illness we believe we suffer, the earth we believe we live upon, the sin we believe we committed, and the judgments to which punishment comes. Know these things, and more, are all part of and inside of our consciousness. Therefore, all of what we believe about God and Satan are just projections and the interpreting of the energy we use for creating our experiences, no matter what that is, good or bad.

What is forgotten is that there is only "one energy," and this energy is ours, no one else's but for each of us to use for our creations. So, be careful how you use it! What to remember is that you own the energy that surrounds you, for it is in infinite supply, and it belongs to no God, no Satan, no person who acts as a mediator, no political party, or Church outside of you. And, since you, your consciousness, is the source of your energy, then you are the source of your experiences and reality.

Also, the energy that surrounds you right now has no power, no influence, and no opposite to it, for at its core, it is neutral, absolute, motionless, nonviolent, and is at your disposal for you to command, direct, and implement using your consciousness and beliefs. When this is understood and remembered, this then changes your perception of reality (beliefs) where you learn to manage your energy in knowing you are the Christ, the Messiah, Yahweh, and the "I AM THAT I AM," in creating your experiences instead of seeing yourself as a created human wandering through time and space floundering.

The remembering of your real name (Yahweh) sets you free from using polarity energy by neutralizing it before your next creations. Thus, setting you up from having to go out and steal energy (power) from others just to get high on life or to be right on what you are presenting to others. "Examples are:" putting others down, blaming others for your failures, looking at yourself as a failure, killing someone for pleasure or gain, thinking it brings you life, or being drawn into drama where you need to be right, or speaking to others where you only see yourself as the expert.

When releasing this egotistical dual thinking and blaming, even to the point of feeling guilty and ashamed about how you live your life, you set yourself up to freeing yourself from having to be a slave to your ego and to those that love to steal your energy. It is about coming into a knowing where you have forgotten that power and polarity energy is just a perception, therefore not real. There is only neutral energy, and it is always there waiting for you to activate it with your consciousness to serve you as a creator, and not as a slave. Not even the COVID-19 is real to those that vibrate at a higher level than the disease itself.

Not only are we a Master, a God, a Goddess, a Christ, the "I AM THAT I AM," we are also the Beast and the Anti-Christ simultaneously. Why? It is because it was us souls who decided what to do with our energy and consciousness that surrounds us in serving our divine plan to "know all that there is to know about life, light, dark, and polarity." And this is why Yeshua and the Ascended Masters give the message, *"Consciousness and energy, together, are what makes up your creations and reality in what you experience."* Thus, remembering who we are becomes very important for having a new relationship with our consciousness and the energy that surrounds us.

When we only see ourselves as a mind-soul in a physical body having to deal with positive and negative, good and evil, and right and wrong (polarity) as to all that is, then that is the relationship that will develop our reality to experience. And, like heaven and hell, when we feel and believe that God is punishing us, or that we are undeserving, unworthy, and feeling guilty, ashamed, and unholy, then that is when we become a slave to the system (Harlot). Also, that is when the elements of cosmic (mental) and earth energy (polarity) bring to us what needs releasing before forgiveness and grace can become part of our mental consciousness. Otherwise, our life here on earth never changes.

Channeling of the Ascended Masters on the Apocalypse

By way of guilt, shame, and not letting go of our belief in polarity energy, that is what keeps us playing with karma. Therefore, to understand God's wisdom in Revelation, John 1:1, we first must understand "who God and Christ are" and "who we are at our core essence." And, when we utter the "words" as a Christ also, they carry a specific vibrational sound or energy signature to them that emits a frequency that will respond to our consciousness and physical body in a more loving way. Then our convictions, our attitudes, and our beliefs expressed become our experiences.

Therefore, we, in its purest definition, are expressing our authority as a "divine being" in bringing about the "energy" that surrounds us in a neutral divine state that descends to polarity energy when it is believed to be our reality to experience our deepest convictions. And, if we believe that "all that is, is positive and negative, that we are just a human, and that we are a creation of an outside God above us," then we will experience this energy in the same way.

It is because of how our "words" engage the mind and soul memories, and how we process our definition of them intellectually and with emotions that determine our reality and how we will experience our choices. Therefore, to appreciate *"the Word was with God,"* Revelation, John 1:1, it might be necessary to look into understanding our own words and the energy put behind them to serve us, opposing or Christ-like.

And with that, Yeshua and the Ascended Masters will do their best to help you remember that your consciousness is the source of life, and the energy you draw toward you is what serves you, and what gives your beliefs animation and form to experience them. And that is when your perception of energy, consciousness, and your suffering can change to a new understanding where healing becomes part of your reality, giving you health, abundance, great relationships, and understanding.

Chapter 1

CONSCIOUSNESS

If you have a desire to know and understand the Apocalypse, then you have to look at "consciousness." Because, from my channeling with Yeshua and the Ascended Masters, "consciousness" is the state of being aware of yourself as the creator.

From working with the Ascended Masters, I have learned that God did not favor his priests, pastors, ministers, sheiks, evangelist, or any of his institutions over me (or anyone) in identifying God or my "consciousness" as part of the "I AM" Christ handiwork. By proclaiming my consciousness as a Christ also and letting go of the God of judgment, sin, and punishment, as portrayed throughout the Bible, I have awakened to the most debated and challenging book in the Bible; the Book of Revelation, written and narrated by the Apostle John.

Most people have no idea that the component elements of our mind-soul, ego-personality, the flesh body, earth, the universe, and the celestial realms have always been sanctioned with cosmic and vibrational energy, also known as positive and negative (or the Tree of knowledge of good and evil). Therefore, knowing this, we have the power to eliminate our karmic suffering whenever we are ready to let go of this God of sin, punishment, and judgment that keeps us in chains like a slave working on autopilot.

The reason most are blind to this wisdom is because of the way our parents taught us, their parents taught them, and by our religious leaders lacking the courage to recognize God as not a single-minded personality consciousness that holds us in contempt or judgment because of sin. It is not about a single-minded God that created us or gave us rules to follow. It is, however, about a "universal omnipresent mind field of pure neutral energy of light" that, according to the Ascended Masters, have been called

Channeling of the Ascended Masters on the Apocalypse

God out of ignorance. How often have we heard that God is light? Well, God is light! But, not in the light as you think.

According to Yeshua and the Ascended Masters, the fitting way to appreciate God, and our passion for him, is to associate God, not as a supreme being who created us or is over us, but with this "universal omnipresent mind field of pure neutral god energy of light" that we souls use to animate our creations to feel our experiences. Therefore, God is not a single-minded deity that created us and needs worshipping. God is this "universal omnipresent mind field of pure neutral energy of light" that we souled beings use to manifest our creations.

The church and their scholars have always made consciousness, God, Satan, earth, and the "tree of knowledge of good and evil" (Genesis 2:17) complicated. And, the best way to hide this truth is by having us be obsessed with confusion, sin, punishment, and having us believe in the concept of fearing a God of judgment. This causes our consciousness to lock into traditional thinking about God as a punishing God that hates sin, good, and evil as if it is something real.

Thus, all structured systems, like the God of the Bible, governments, religions, and the media, maintain their power by establishing the ground rules that create the conditions in what we will choose to experience in life and then make it as if we choice the experience. However, there is a new and exciting consciousness arising that puts to rest fear, rigid traditions, and a ruling God of sin, judgment, and punishment forever. And, this consciousness comes from the channeling of the Ascended Masters and how they will demonstrate, using the Apocalypse as a guide, that we can change our consciousness and energy frequency where we can override this polarity vibrational energy signature (DNA) of positive (good) and negative (bad) to a New Expansional Energy of Four.

For example, with our own consciousness being the source of life and the Goddess that created God (energy), our mind-soul, our ego, and our physical existence, as we know it today, can become an awakening consciousness that knows we are the Christ on earth. What is forgotten, and needs reminding, is the component elements of the earth in using positive and negative energy as the primary source for our choices have ended up as the testing ground for our soul growth. It was from the mind (Adam) and our soul consciousness of responsibility (Eve), and not our spirit consciousness, that first led us to experience polarity energy (positive and negative) here on earth.

It has been with our many lifetime's past that has kept us stuck, emotionally, and in a mental perception that some God created us, male and female, to work with an energy that vibrates lower than our Christ consciousness. Therefore, the ascended masters and I aspire to contact any part of your ego consciousness to help reconnect you to your own Oversoul's memory about how positive and negative energy came about (tree of knowledge good and evil), and how it works with your everyday choices in life.

Most of us are asleep when it comes to the understanding of our consciousness and the energy we use for our choices. It is with these choices that lead to what we are experiencing today, including our suffering and death, and why it exists in our life. Know that everything we experience in life today is delivered to us, not only through religion, but based on our beliefs, perception, reason, and that of our intellectual thinking about some God above us that we must worship.

As our church leaders have taught us that man was created in the image of God, after His likeness, male and female (Genesis 1:26-27), we are to believe that man was physically created in the image of God. Thus, making God as a male deity with all power to himself. And this is why man believes himself better than a woman. However, with Yeshua and the Ascended Masters, these verses have been much misunderstood for centuries, purposely. Therefore, despite what we were taught about God's male identity and power, I would like to bring to your attention Genesis 1:1; *"In the beginning, when God created the heavens and earth."*

In traditional thinking, or what religions would want us to believe, Genesis 1:1 is speaking of the beginning of physical *earth* and *heaven*. But on the contrary, Yeshua and the Ascended Masters relate Genesis 1:1 to higher understanding (Heaven) and that of form (Earth). Religions overlook the full wisdom behind *"heaven and earth"* because everything they understand about these things is coming from intellectual thinking. Thus, they look at creation solely as something outside of them and having a literal meaning.

Therefore, before any beginning of the earth, the universe, energy, animals (wild and tame), the fish of the sea, the cattle, all the creatures that crawl on the ground, and even our physical body, it first has to begin with "consciousness and end with energy." Because without the "act of consciousness," there would be no you, no me, no awareness, no God, no energy, no universes, no stars, no planets, no earth, and no creatures of all kinds, nor all that earth contains. There would not even be light, dark, positive, or negative!

The churches of the world need to look deeper into the wisdom behind the Book of Genesis before describing God and his creations. And, the first thing they have to look into is the existence of the Spirit of One because her consciousness is what gave God life (energy)! It was not that God was "all that was" in the beginning, it was with the consciousness of the "Spirit of One," for she was (and still is) the unprecedented self-governing "I AM" consciousness, complete unto herself. And, from the wisdom behind the text in Genesis, the Spirit of One knew nothing other than her self-governing "I AM" consciousness.

Therefore, *"heaven and earth"* are not about a literal place where we go when we die, or a place we live upon, but is descriptive of the Spirit of One's "I AM" consciousness and the universal mind field of pure energy that she uses for her creations. My friends, it takes consciousness and the energy of light (god) first, before any materialism or form can appear as something of a literal nature; otherwise, it remains unknown and formless.

It was in the beginning, if you want to call it the beginning, this unprecedented self-governing Spirit of One asked herself, "Who am I?" And, it was from the perspective of this question that she instantly created a "universal mind field of pure Crystalline energy" to serve her. For example, when the Spirit of One awakened to her "I AM" consciousness, she gave notice *(the word)* and uttered *(expressed)* to herself, "I exist, and if I exist, then 'I AM' a spirit that is aware of my infinite consciousness as being the source to make things known, either as dense energy or transparent energy. Hence, if I can do all of that, then, "I am the architect, originator, sculptor, and the executor for my consciousness acts" and what expands from it.

And, since she was the architect and executor for her consciousness acts, she had the full authority (power) to manifest anything she desired, even this universal mind field of pure energy of light (God) that appeared as a transparent form to serve her, for nothing could stop her. And, as Yeshua and the Ascended Masters reveal, she had all the authority of a Goddess, for she was, and still is today, "all that there is/was" from the very beginning, and not this God of the Bible that religions proclaim created man, male and female.

From what the Masters channeled through me, then know, nothing can exist outside of the Spirit of One's omnipresent consciousness, not energy (light) nor darkness (unknown), not even positive and negative. Thus, *"heaven"* is not a place of residency but is illustrative of the Spirit of One's omnipresent consciousness at its highest level, known as "all that was/is now, for she is absolute, transparent, solid and present everywhere at once."

The beginning was not the physical creation of "heaven and earth." It is the Spirit of One coming to an awareness where "her consciousness" is all that was and is today, even before time, space and physicality. Not even light, dark, positive, negative, right, and wrong were known to her, for those things came much later. It was a moment in consciousness where the Spirit of One shaped and formed a "universal omnipresent mind field of pure unbiased energy" that generated an ethereal-celestial dimension that gave the appearance of a structured composition that appeared as "light." And, "light" itself, when studied in spirit, has form, and therefore is symbolic for God and Earth in Genesis.

When we look deeper into the wisdom behind Genesis', Revelation, the Bible, and humankind, and then beyond their literal meanings (since Earth and Humanity are of form), it represents this "universal omnipresent mind field of pure unbiased god energy" appearing as "light." And this "light" is a dominion unto itself that caused spirit clarification to show that ignorance (darkness) was overcome by exerting "consciousness" and "awareness" to form matter. And, by transforming energy (symbolic of God) into form (light) to experience life (like earth and one's physical body), then energy also became symbolic in Genesis and Revelation as signifying earth, dust, soil, sand, and that of light (God), just to mention a few.

However, the biggest symbology was given to this "universal omnipresent mind field of pure unbiased god energy," and it came to be understood as the "God of light." Therefore, the wisdom found here is that it took a "consciousness act" on behalf of the Spirit of One (Goddess) to bring into existence this "universal omnipresent mind field of pure unbiased god energy of light," that happens to be misunderstood as some God outside of us giving animation to her expressions, ideas, beliefs (words), and to her aspirations to answer the question, "Who am I?" And, along with it, having form attached to the experience.

This is like a transparent prototype of you, and yet it can be found in the physical as your mind-soul and the body, the earth, the universe, the moon, and the stars. All of these forms are components that come from this universal God of light that Yeshua called Father. Hence, the story of the beginning is not about physical earth, humankind, or heaven in a literal sense as first taught. It is the creation of God as signifying this "pure energy of light." Thus, transparent, and not a God as a single-minded super personality.

Therefore, it was "consciousness," the "I AM" of the Goddess that created God as being energy! Thus, giving form (some structure) to the Spirit of One's ideas and desires to know and see herself. Hence, Yeshua and the Ascended Master's passion is to remind us that God, as we understand God, is not of a single-minded supreme personality. God is a "universal omnipresent mind field of pure unbiased energy" structured as "light" that we spirit's use for our creations.

The Spirit of One's consciousness is the ultimate source for all with animation and consciousness, including being the source for this energy of light (God). Thus, the Spirit of One's consciousness is vast, infinite, immeasurable, absolute, and is the unquestionable consciousness that created God (pure universal energy of light) for the purpose to formulate her ideas, desires, and creations into matter. It was the Spirit of One, in the beginning, that knew of herself but was not conscious of having the ability to see herself, like looking into a mirror and seeing nothing.

Therefore, her consciousness, at the beginning of awakening, was void of ideas, thoughts, and desires, let alone having any form to see herself in the mirror. Thus, this is the meaning behind Genesis 1:2, and the *"darkness covered the abyss."* This also can have the definition of "unknowingness" or "unawareness." The bottom line, "darkness" is nothing more than the Spirit of One's ignorance, in the beginning, not having any awareness of her own consciousness as being the source, the architect, and the designer of energy to serve her in bringing about form to see herself. Thus, energy (God) was created in the form of light to accommodate her in her creations.

And, when applying the wisdom behind Genesis 1:6-7, separating one body of water from the water above and below the dome, it is referring to the Spirit of One's consciousness coming to an awakening where she now understands that she is the source and the all-prevailing and ever-present consciousness that is present everywhere at once. Therefore, the water *"above the dome"* is of her Spirit and the source of life; and the *"water below"* the dome is the "I AM" omnipresent consciousness in full awareness that she is the principal source for all that lives, including pure energy (God), we souled beings, and all that is physical and non-physical.

It was the "consciousness act" of the Spirit of One (the Goddess) initially that gave life to God (energy) and not the other way around as religions declare. And with this act, she became both the Father-Mother God-Goddess that Yeshua spoke about when he walked the earth over two-thousand years ago. However, religions changed the phrase "Father-Mother God-Goddess" to just "Father-God" to prevent any confusion among the populist at the time. This also concludes that man (Adam) is not above woman (Eve) or that man has more power than a woman. With this understanding about man and woman, then the belief that positive is better than negative is misjudged, for they are both the same since they come from the same God energy of light.

Allow me to use a car battery, for example. The car needs positive and negative to start the engine. Therefore, it isn't that positive was higher than negative, or visa versa, it is that it took them both to start the engine. We have forgotten that we can take on any form we desire, male, female, or both. And Yeshua and the Ascended Masters are here to remind us of this! To verify this, the Ascended Masters ask you to look deeper into the wisdom behind Genesis 1:20-25, where it speaks of the *"great sea monsters and the swimming creatures of all kinds with which the water teams."*

To know and understand the wisdom behind *"with which water teams,* is the totality of the consciousness of the Spirit of One lining up her consciousness to expand it by giving life to many parts and pieces of her consciousness. And, who are these many parts and pieces of her? They are the gazillions upon gazillions of us souled beings, for we are the composition of the Spirit of One's consciousness in action; thereby, we are her "I AM" consciousness as much as her consciousness is our consciousness.

It was soon after the Spirit of One became awakened and aware of her ability to be a Goddess, that she transformed her consciousness into many parts and pieces of herself to experience life. And, we souled beings are the parts and pieces of her. Thus, we are all the same, carrying the same creative power, no one higher or lower than anyone else, not even Yeshua. We, together, are the Goddess consciousness in action forming energy into matter.

We spirit's, all gazillions upon gazillions of us, are what gives God (energy) animation so we can experience life. Thus, Genesis 1:26-27 is not about humankind was given life as a male or female. It is about we souled beings inheriting a consciousness and a mind of polarity and became the source of life for our creations as a Goddess unto self. And this is seen in Genesis 1:20-25, as every one of us possesses a masculine and feminine side of self that works with positive and negative energy. This is why we all can be incarnated as a male or female in different lifetimes.

The act of consciousness gave the Spirit of One the avenue to move past her infinite and unchanging divine consciousness, by way of her fragments (we souled beings), to experience energy (God of light) and life in opposite to her divine absoluteness. Therefore, the Spirit of One's divine plan found in Genesis was for us souled beings (humankind) to be wrapped up in an illusionary energy role where we could play opposite to our "I AM" Christ consciousness, thus becoming the Anti-Christ. This is in the very image of the Spirit of One because of us being her consciousness, and hers ours.

Channeling of the Ascended Masters on the Apocalypse

The wisdom and the gift behind this act were for us souls to maintain our divineness since we are part of the Spirit of One's consciousness. And this was accomplished by awakening within her, the individualization of our souled being as part of this "universal omnipresent mind field of pure neutralized god energy of light," to use in bringing about polarity energy where we, acting on her behalf, could learn "all that there is to learn" about creating multitudes of potentials, good and bad, for us to experience and learn wisdom. Thus, the question, "Who she is?" became our question when we souled beings awakened as her consciousness.

Again, we souled beings together, are her extensions and the "I AM THAT I AM" that gave animation to the "God of light" (energy). And, not only that! We also gave life to many ego-personality aspects (lifetimes) of ourselves to play out opposite roles as to whom we are as a Christ. Thus, our mind becomes the Anti-Christ when in the flesh, or until we overcome the flesh as Yeshua did.

To accomplish this act, we souled beings worked together as the Goddess and acted as one consciousness, giving life to planets, universes, stars, birds, animals, insects, rocks, plants, and everything else that is seen, felt, heard, tasted, and smelled or otherwise perceived by using this "universal mind field of pure God energy of light" to give those creations form and animation.

Remember, in our awakening in the first creation (higher consciousness), we had no form! We were, and still are, just an "I AM" consciousness, the actual image of the Spirit of One, the Goddess, and we use energy (light) in giving our creations structure (form) and animation to experience life in the way we so choose. And, once we realized we could create a form (like a physical body) using energy, that is when we said, *"how good this was,"* because we became amazed and filled with excitement. So much so, we created billions and billions of potentials and lifetimes, good and bad, to bring about animation and form so we could experience both sides of the coin to learn wisdom. And, we continued until we finally became lost in our animated creations.

At the beginning of our infant spirit stage, we became so inspired by our connection with this *"universal omnipresent mind field of unbiased god energy of light"* that it led us to mimic the Spirit of One and fragmented our "I AM" Christ consciousness into a likeness called our mind-soul (Adam-Eve) and ego-personality consciousness (Serpent-Beast). And, this is where we all created many physical and non-physical ego-personality aspects (lifetimes) of ourselves where we ended up becoming a companion with our own "I AM" Christ consciousness to learn about life and polarity energy. Thus, we gain overwhelming wisdom while simultaneously taking responsibility for our choices.

This is the true wisdom behind Genesis's story of creation, as we souled beings became aware and conscious of ourselves as an extension of the Spirit of One, and not that we were some creation of a single-minded male God above us. Thus, Genesis 1:26 has nothing to do with the creation of humankind as we understand it as male and female. It is about us souls fragmenting our own "oneness of consciousness" by mimicking the Spirit of One and creating within us a new layer of consciousness called our mental mind-soul (Adam/Eve) and an ego-personality consciousness (Serpent) that now holds an energy source of positive and negative as something real.

It was with this belief in the positive and negative energy of long ago that we lowered our consciousness frequency so we could play in a reality of opposites, like good versus evil, male versus female. Yet, all of it is an illusion. It was the creation of our mind-soul (male-female) and our ego-personality consciousness (the serpent) that took on the position as the Son of God (mind) and the Son of Man (ego). And then later, they became known as the Anti-Christ and the Beast found in the Book of Revelation. And, that is when we souls, from the mind-soul and ego level, became the Lord of Lords, the King of Kings, and the ruler and creator of our many lifetimes, choices, and experiences.

The wisdom behind *"God creating man in His divine image, male and female"* in Genesis 1:26, has nothing to do with a male supernatural God creating male and female. And this is indicated by how we, as an extension of the Spirit of One, had the authority to manipulate this *"universal omnipresent mind field of unbiased god energy of light"* and transform it, where one side of this energy rotated clockwise (positive-male) and the other side of this same energy rotated counter-clockwise (negative-female). Thus, we were the ones who generated a rotational energy spin called polarity, or an opposing energy that plays opposites. This is also known as positive (male) and negative (female).

The "tree of knowledge of good and evil" found in Genesis came about within our own "oneness of consciousness" (Garden) before we ever moved our mind-soul, our ego-consciousness, and our energy outward into a cosmic mental energy field. The energy rotating clockwise produced a positive rotation while the energy rotating counter-clockwise produced a negative spin or rotation, and yet neither positive (male) or negative (female) are good or bad.

Also, with this creation, and without us realizing it, all of it is an illusion, for we, all spirits, are neither male nor female, for we are both.

Channeling of the Ascended Masters on the Apocalypse

Consciousness is just consciousness, and energy is just energy to be used for our creations, no matter if we desire to be a planet or human. And, as I mentioned, the poles on a battery have positive and negative cells to produce an electrical current to start the engine of a car, and yet, this does not make the battery good or bad or that it is a male or female.

Therefore, the "Christ Consciousness," as we understand it, is not about one man. It is the "seal/mark" of the Goddess (or the "I AM" within us, and everyone else), for we are the source, the "I AM" Christ, Goddess, and the God for our manifested creations. We, all souled beings together, acting as "one body of consciousness," are the totality of the Spirit of One's "I AM" Christ consciousness, and therefore the God-Goddess in action. Even our many parallel ego-personality aspects of many lifetimes in the past, present, and future are part of the Spirit of One's Consciousness.

Hence, we humans are Christ, just like Yeshua! And, this is why the wisdom behind, *"so it is with Christ"* in Corinthians 12:12 means, everything possessing consciousness is part of the Christ consciousness; because nothing can exist outside of the Spirit of One's "I AM" omnipresent consciousness, not even we souled beings because we are her and she is us. Therefore, all is ONE! Not even this "universal omnipresent mind field of pure unbiased god energy of light" can exist without we souled beings giving it a command to transform nothingness into somethingness for us to experience.

The God of the Bible, the Devil, the Anti-Christ, the Beast, Religion, and our governments, as we understand them, only get their life and energy (power) from us. Religions steal our life-giving energy from us by convincing us that we are sinners and that we are not Christ, and the government steals our energy by convincing us they know what is best for us. Thus, they maintain their power and control over us.

This God of the Bible, the Devil, the Anti-Christ, Religion, and Governments are false mandates and need to be released if we hope to move beyond the mind of ignorance (clouds) to meet up with our own "I AM" Christ consciousness and our true freedom. Realize it is impossible to know Christ using the mind because the mind was created to reason with our choices and to play with opposing energy.

Traditional religions and governments know this, and they use that knowledge to control our minds. Remember, in my father's house, there are many mansions (consciousnesses) (John 14:2). Therefore, revisiting what was written about Genesis 1:26-27, our mind, the masculine-Adam-positive side of us, and our soul-Eve, the feminine-negative side of us, are not about gender. They represent that both man and woman carry a mind and a soul consciousness of responsibility where polarity energy is generated as the source for our creations while in the flesh.

By the Spirit of One fragmenting her total consciousness to where we souled beings acted on her behalf, the act allowed her, by way of her extensions (we souls), to venture independently outside of her absoluteness of a neutralized Energy and consciousness to learn all there is to know about positive and negative. And, with that, she delivered to us souled beings' complete authority (free will) over what we choose as a divine plan to follow to accomplish this act.

Therefore, it was you, and all souled beings, working together as one body of consciousness, receiving this authority that allowed us all to come up with an idea to manipulate this *universal omnipresent mind field of pure unbiased god energy of light;* to do as we pleased with no interference coming from the Spirit of One (our "I AM" consciousness). And, since the Spirit of One became us souled beings, or our "I AM" Christ consciousness, then the first thing we did as a Goddess was split our oneness of consciousness into two parts. Thus, giving us an outer mental consciousness and an inner mental soul sub-consciousness of responsibility.

The outer consciousness became known as our mind (male-Adam) of a mental nature that took on a positive energy rotation while, in contrast, the inner feminine-Eve part of that same consciousness took on a negative energy rotation. Thus, we all now produce energy that takes on opposite roles, and now, since we created it, we must take responsibility for our consciousness acts and how we use that energy. Hence, the energy of positive (signified by Adam-male) and negative (signified by Eve-female) were created from out of this *"universal omnipresent mind field of pure unbiased god energy of light"* that religions call God, the Father.

The creation is not about male and female per se, but mental energy that carries opposite, positive and negative, good and bad, right and wrong, male and female, that the churches give literal meaning to a woman coming from the rib of man, and therefore beneath the man. It comes down to realizing that consciousness and energy, at its core, have no gender or that consciousness is made of energy. It is consciousness that uses energy (male-positive and female-negative) to manifest form in establishing us humans to be seen and witnessed either as a male or female to experience life. Yet, our consciousness has no form or gender until it commands energy to take on some structure of a form and gender.

My friends, the time to remember who we are is now! We souled beings, acting as one Goddess, set up our own divine plan eons ago for us to follow. Thus, this allowed us souled beings to take on the answerable acts (choices) of our outer/inner mind (signified by Adam-Eve) in what we desired to express to this universal god energy of light in giving animation for us to feel and experience our choices to learn wisdom.

Know this, we all wanted to be perceived as something tangible where we could see, touch, smell, hear, and taste our experiences rather than exist as only in consciousness and light. Therefore, *"after our likeness"* is not about you, and all souled beings, taking on the looks of a single-minded male God or that of a physical male or female but is about your "mind-soul consciousness" coming from out of your own "I AM" Christ consciousness in order to experience life. And, the polarity energy we use for our creations come from out of this pure universal energy of light that we souls manipulated to take the form of duality, positive and negative.

It took all souled beings to come up with an imagination so wild that we, as an individual, soon followed the divine plan of the Spirit of One, causing us to come up with a divine plan or our own to explore all possibilities known today as positive (male) and negative (female) to learn the wisdom behind our choices. And, we do it by generating many ego-personality aspects, male and female, having many energy vibrational signatures (DNA) to play out on earth as something real, and yet it is all an illusion.

What made this divine plan unique is the mind of the masculine (Adam) acting on a more profound sensation that made us feel emotional instead of the mind keeping its knowingness of being part of the Christ consciousness. Thus, making us feel separated from our own "I AM" Christ consciousness, separate from our mind-soul consciousness of responsibility (Eve), and even separate from our many ego-personality aspects (lifetimes).

However, even though we felt this emotional state of vulnerability, our soul consciousness of responsibility (Eve) was there to record all the choices made by the masculine side of the mind (Adam). Thus, we allowed our "I AM" Christ consciousness to stay authentic, divine, and untouched. We purposely altered our focus from our "I AM" Christ consciousness to a mental consciousness to create whatever we desired, using the energy of positive (Adam) and negative (Eve) that is to this day not real.

Therefore, when religions speak of *"God created man (male and female) in his divine image,"* it has a deeper meaning than what religions give it. It is about how we, as extensions of the Spirit of One, from out of our own "I AM" Christ consciousness, are the ones that shaped and fashioned the second level of our consciousness (second creation) composed of having a mental-mind (male) and a soul consciousness of responsibility (female) where the energy rotates in two different directions, creating a rotational energy of opposites to deal with our creations.

It was from this mental consciousness that the birth of our ego-personality took over the power of the mind-soul to control the mind in creating what we want to experience. Thus, separating our ego from our mind-soul and spirit, the "I AM." Whatever our mind (son-Adam-husband) and ego (the serpent) expressed to act on, the soul (daughter-Eve-wife) recorded those expressions, either as positive and negative, good and bad, right and wrong, male and female, and then fed them back to our mind to choose one to experience. Whatever our mind acted on, it is then recorded within our soul to be delivered back to our mind and ego when we are ready to experience the choice. From there, the experience turns into wisdom where it is passed on to our "I AM" Christ Spirit.

My friends, know that our choices in life respond to where our energy frequency is vibrating. Therefore, God (energy of light) does not recognize our wants, desires, needs, or prayers. God only understands the frequency in which our consciousness is vibrating at. Thus, this is why most of us are not healed from a disease because we, in spirit, have had this experience before coming to earth.

For example, if we lose sight about ourselves, vibrating in an energy frequency of fear, sin, guilt, and shame, we are, without doubt, going to attract things of a similar energy vibration (like a false God or a disease). If we are vibrating with an energy frequency of unconditional love, joy, and abundance (God of light), we will attract things that support that energy frequency (health, abundance, and joy).

And, as given in my other books, it would be like tuning our consciousness into a radio station where there are many false Gods (energy, low/false to high/true) to serve us. It is about tuning into the harmony frequency (energy (real-God)) that we want to listen to, just like we have to tune into the energy (real-God) we wish to manifest for us to experience.

Chapter 2

CHRIST CONSCIOUSNESS

Now that we have established that we are only "consciousness" and have been since our awakening back in the first creation. Then, the ideal book to describe "consciousness" and "Christ" actually comes from the most misunderstood book in the Bible, the Book of Revelation, written by Apostle John. When reading and studying the Bible's Apocalypse through the eyes of an Ascended Master, the book has nothing to do with the end days or any rapture prophesied by religion. And, as expected with clerics like priests, pastors, and evangelists, they use the Bible in literal terms to keep us in fear and confusion to maintain their control over us.

The Apocalypse is more than just words construed to keep us in waiting for the Rapture to meet Jesus in the air. It is a guide in revealing that we no longer need to see ourselves as a sinner because the book helps open up the gates to our soul memories to uncover our divine plan to become a sovereign Christ in our own right. In other words, Yeshua is not our savior, or that he is coming to be our savior. Our savior is our own, "I AM," Christ consciousness! What do I mean by this? Well! Through the "awakening of consciousness," we get to understand the "Christ Consciousness" as the self.

Not that the Apocalypse has always been a mystery because of its extreme verbiage. In fact, the human individual is a mystery. And, when fear, confusion, and the belief in polarity energy (opposites) are resolved within us, that will be the time when we are ready to open up to the hidden wisdom behind Yeshua, Satan, and the Christ Consciousness. Humanity has forgotten the history of God, Himself, Earth, and who Christ is, and how these things have been documented, interpreted, and passed down to us by our religion and government leaders.

According to Yeshua and the Ascended Masters, the Bible's Genesis is the "Alpha," where the first awakening of the Christ consciousness occurred. And, the Book of Revelation is the "Omega," where our journey through many lifetimes ends because of the opening up of our soul memories (seven seals). Thus, revealing to us that we are a Christ also. Religions have taught that Yeshua is the only Christ and that he came to earth to take away our sins. However, the Christ mentioned in the Apocalypse is not about Yeshua or Jesus coming to save or rapture us. It is that Christ is the divine logo found within us all, expressing our authority as a Christ once we are awakened.

The Apocalypse, in its highest wisdom and its acute metaphors, is about our story and journey from the time we were all awakened in spirit as a Christ to where we are now ready to become a witness to our soul-fulfilling its mission in answering the question, "Who am I?" And, it took many lifetime physical forms to accomplish the task. We all know there is no set date or time for the rapture because the day and time are only reserved for the individuals that are ready to raise their mind and physical frequency to where they come into a knowing they have completed their karma. And now, some are prepared to remember that they are the Christ and the savior.

The *"lifting up to heaven,"* like in a rapture, is symbolized by our awakening as a Christ also. It was not the creation of the universe or earth that was the first explosion. It was the Spirit of One breaking up into gazillions upon gazillions of pieces of herself. And, within each piece, her consciousness became our consciousness. Hence, if her consciousness is the Christ, then our consciousness is a Christ also. For our "I AM" Christ consciousness is in the divine image of the Spirit of One. Therefore, we are a Christ as much as Yeshua!

According to Yeshua and the Ascended Masters, the composition of our spirit consciousness is that of the Spirit of One as being our "I AM." Hence, within each souled being, no matter if one is good or evil, there contains the divine essence of the "I AM" Christ consciousness. No one is left out, not even the smallest of life! An excellent example is found in 1 Corinthians 12:12, where Paul states, *"A body is one though it has many parts, and all the parts of the body, though many, are one body, so also with Christ."*

Paul was not only referring to the human body, but he was also relating to the wholeness of all gazillions upon gazillions of souled beings and more that are the "many parts" of the Spirit of One's consciousness. Thus, making you, me, and all with life, a Christ also. Therefore, the real Christ is not with just one man. The true identity of Christ is that of our divine logo (mark), "I

AM That I AM." Thus, we carry the seed of the Christ consciousness as our true identity, no matter if we are practicing good or evil.

When we learn to integrate the essence of our "I AM" with all lifetimes we have ever lived, along with our many ego personality-aspects that were not given a flesh body, that is when we become a real embodied Christ walking on earth just as our brother Yeshua did over two thousand years ago. The "harvest" many speak of, and what Yeshua mentioned in Luke 10:2, can take place at any given moment in one's life. All that we have to do to experience the rapture is to lift our consciousness frequency, stop judging, let go of dualistic beliefs, and be willing to accept the simple truth we are a Christ also, without doubting it.

Know that the harvest is not about a group of religious people being taken up to heaven in a rapture. It is better to release that belief because most of us here on earth are "following a God of judgment, sin, and punishment." Thus, missing the boat for ascension, all because of being stuck in a consciousness of a God that hates, judges, and believes we must worship him. When Yeshua said, *"the harvest is abundant, but the workers are few"* (Mathew 9:37), he was referring to those of us on earth that refuse to open up to being a Christ in their own right. We refuse because we only see ourselves as a human that needs saving.

Yeshua's suffering and his death on the cross is a metaphoric description of our journey through time and space incarnating into many lifetimes, sowing, reaping, and then forgetting who we are as a Christ. We have forgotten that we are an extension of the Spirit of One (Goddess), and we have been given everything the Mother/Father had, including the total freedom to express, love, experience, and choose our divine plan to awaken to the Christ consciousness within us. We could even turn our back on our Christ consciousness because we knew, from a deeper level, that we will eventually return to our divine oneness again.

It was after we felt our separation from the Spirit of One, and having the same authority as her, we instantly mimicked the Spirit of One and created the ability to see ourselves through the manifesting of many like images of ourselves (lifetimes) to explore the question, "Who am I?" And, we did it by creating billions upon billions of potentials to experience on earth (good and bad) as the means to answer the question, "Who am I?"

And, the first image created, before coming to earth in the physical, was our mind-soul and an ego-personality to help create a psychological consciousness where we would act through the mind and ego in an emotional and reasoning way to expose our thoughts, our idea of polarity energy, and the perception held in memory about free will and choice. Along with this creation, we inspired an ego-personality consciousness that made us feel unique and separate from our "I AM" Christ consciousness.

Because of being a God-Goddess also, we worked it out for us souls to move in many directions all at once, using polarity energy to shape and materialize our beliefs, potentials, and creations having either a positive or negative quality to it. This process helped us learn about our choices by experiencing them when operating out of a physical and non-physical realm. Therefore, it is not about sin and punishment, as the Church describes. It is about being magical, divine, and perfect because it has given our own "I AM" Christ consciousness the avenue to learn the wisdom behind our choices.

The manifesting of our mind-soul consciousness of responsibility and our ego-personality of defiance (the second creation) has allowed our "I AM" Christ consciousness to learn, feel, expand in wisdom, using polarity energy. This is for us to absorb and understand all things rather than just be in a state of incompleteness. Hence, the beginning of a new mental, ego, and emotional consciousness has been shaped and formed within us, as this correlates with Genesis' six days of creation.

This act of working out of our mind-soul consciousness was where our Christ consciousness gave life to many ego-personality aspects (lifetimes) of us to learn the wisdom behind the "tree of knowledge of good and evil" (which is just polarity-energy). It was the only way for us souls to become a complete sovereign God-Goddess and a Christ in our own right. Hence, the symbolism of our mind became Adam, our soul consciousness of responsibility became Eve, our defiant ego-personality became the serpent, and the Garden became known as our total consciousness, and the three together became known as our three-dimensional consciousness.

From out of our higher consciousness, in the beginning, it was based only on us souls being in a consciousness state but holding no wisdom, no understanding of life, or what it means to be alive and make choices. Therefore, the creation of our three-dimensional consciousness helped us explore all possibilities of life, both good and evil. It helped us get lost, not only in our own consciousness but in our creations until such a time when we would finally let go of the belief in dual-polarity energy and that we are only human.

Know that in the beginning stages of our consciousness, we were non-active because our consciousness held no energy. For example, when a baby is born, it knows nothing of itself. The baby has consciousness but is not aware of itself until it evolves (grows) to where the baby can "act in consciousness" on its own. It was the same for us souls at first. We all were part of the "one consciousness," and we had to grow and expand in consciousness before coming to an awareness where we could "act in consciousness" and bring about some type of form to experience life. And, this form that we souled beings created was a *"universal omnipresent mind field of pure unbiased god energy of light"* that we all decided to call God.

That is when our individualized "I AM" Christ consciousness allowed us souls to express and formulate a mind-soul consciousness of responsibility and an individualized ego-personality to feel our separateness from the Spirit of One's Christ consciousness. And, once our "I AM" allowed us to feel our separateness from our Christ consciousness, that is when we felt a deep urge to move outside of it and explore beyond the boundaries of our "I AM" consciousness (Garden). And, because of our "I AM," not knowing what fear was, we souls, from our mind-soul and ego level, said farewell to our Christ consciousness, and then we explored the questions, "Who am I?" and "What is our purpose?"

The choice led us down a road of emotions and nervousness never felt or experienced before. This caused us souled beings' uncertainty, doubt, and the fear of losing our awareness of being a unique spirit that holds a Christ consciousness. This fear drew us into creating an energy source called positive and negative, polarity energies, which Yeshua and the Ascended Masters call the "wall of fire."

Once we souled beings entered into this polarity energy (or wall of fire), considerable fear and confusion set in at our mind-soul level of consciousness. Why? Because we found it was ripping our mental consciousness and this polarity energy into billions upon billions of pieces that ended up being our many potentials and lifetimes for us to experience. This does not mean we have billions and billions of lifetimes, even though we could. It means we all have created billions and billions of potentials, good and bad, to experience, physicality and non-physicality.

Therefore, the creation story of Genesis is not about Adam, Eve, and the Serpent being kicked out of any Garden. It is symbolic of our mind (Adam), our soul consciousness of responsibility (Eve), and our ego-personality (Serpent) being a metaphor for creating and choosing polarity energy as a source for our journey through time and space playing with power, the belief in sin, and that we would take on opposite roles to learn wisdom.

Adam became illustrative of our outer mental consciousness of a positive nature, Eve became representative of our negative soul side of responsibility to record everything that our mind, the masculine, chose to experience, and our Ego personality became the defiant one (Serpent) in misleading us into believing we are only human. Thus, the energy frequency of positive and negative became far less than the "pure god energy of light" we used in the first creation. But, with our Adam and Eve side working together as one body of consciousness, like the battery starting an engine, the polarity energies used for our creations are where we can accomplish magic and many things. All we have to do is keep this dual-energy balanced.

However, we forgot our magic because of not keeping this dual-energy balanced! Thus, it was the beginning of forgetting about our "I AM" Christ consciousness. It was our ego-personality (serpent-beast) that became the metaphor for our rebellious and overexcited nature in playing opposite roles in the flesh dealing with polarity energy, good and evil, right and wrong, male and female. In other words, it took the ego to move us souled beings outside of our Christ consciousness, even though it is an illusion, and into an ego-personality consciousness that became the experiencer (warrior) for our mind and soul consciousness of responsibility.

It was our ego (the Beast) that pushed our mind-soul consciousness acts toward using these polarity energies (positive and negative) for our creations. The Bible depicts it as the Tree of Knowledge of Good and Evil (Genesis 2:17). And, once our mind-soul and ego-personality lowered its frequencies to enter into the polarity of "two," we souls rebelled, not only within ourselves but against each other about who was right and wrong about who Christ is. That was when we, because of focusing out of our mind-soul and ego consciousness, actually rebelled against our own "I AM" Christ consciousness. Thus, our perfection as a divine being became lost to us through the forgetting of who we are at our core level.

That was when we took on an independent ego-personality that made us feel fear, separated, free, and unique because of a reasoning mind, compelling us to convince us that some God created us and that we must be good or else. This rationalizing uniqueness gave way to where we souled beings eventually played opposite roles to whom we indeed are at our core. Thus, this "act in consciousness" by our mind-soul consciousness caused a lot of chaos deep within us because we, for the first time, experienced ignorance (darkness) to this polarity energy, for it was unknown to us at the time. Even today, we all still fight against our own "I AM" Christ consciousness because we look at ourselves as unworthy of being Christ.

Religions, governments, and the Media are the biggest culprits because they keep us in fear by having us stick to the belief that some Christ outside of us will come down out of the clouds, with his army of angels, and save us through a Rapture. Because of religious beliefs, this polarity energy (positive and negative), through time and space, built up within us such fear that it eventually led us to create many, many ego-personality aspects called lifetimes. However, it was necessary for us to experience positive and negative, good and bad, right and wrong, because it allowed us to understand its lack of clarity to what we were feeling.

From this polarity energy, it created within us a consciousness of desire to explore a course of action that created everything we now experience today as something of an astral-etheric-and earthly realm. The Bible explains them as "there are many mansions in God's Kingdom" (John 14:2). It was our Oversoul who gave life and manifested many ego-personality aspects of us (lifetimes), both light and dark, to come to earth to slow down our energy frequency so we could experience our choices in a physical body of denseness and forgetting.

This creation helped us eventually learn everything there is to know about polarity energy, because it was through our mind and soul consciousness of responsibility (Adam-Eve), giving birth to our many ego-personality aspects (lifetimes) that enabled us to explore the dark recesses of our mind and soul consciousness to answer the question, "Who am I?" It was then when we stopped trying to remember who we were, and that is when we finally learned to let go of the idea and belief that we are a Christ also. And now, here we are working out karma to get to a consciousness frequency where we can once again remember we are Christ.

Because of our great desire to experience our choices associated with positive and negative, we, over time, ran and hid from our Christ consciousness because we felt unworthy because of the way we used this neutralized and unbiased God energy of light. And, it doesn't help either when religions preach that we will never be worthy of being a Christ. And, because of this teaching, we developed a fear of God and Satan so much that we now carry a deep feeling not to disappoint this false God, so we worship Him. All because of our choice to rebel against our true nature, symbolized by the Adam-Eve taking the bite of the apple (Genesis 2:16-17), we souls eventually lost our awareness of being an extension of the Spirit of One, a Goddess and a Christ in our own right.

However, know that Adam and Eve literally did not take a bite of an apple or that they ever lived, or that they were kicked out of any garden. It is really about us souled beings lowering our consciousness and energy to such a low frequency, we ended up lost (asleep) in our many beliefs, ego creations, and to whom we are from a higher level. It was us souled beings who chose a long time ago to descend from a higher state of consciousness (heaven) to a lower place in consciousness that translated into judgment, sin, positive and negative, male and female, good and evil, God and Satan (duality). Hence, sin then only exists as part of our mind and ego levels of consciousness and has no part with our divine nature or "I AM."

We have forgotten that our mind-soul and our ego-consciousness have many parallel phases to them. Remember, we have a super-subconsciousness, or an (i) "I AM" Christ consciousness part of us that is united with this "universal omnipresent mind field of pure unbiased god energy of light" (Mother-Father) that we used in creating polarity energy for our creations. We also have an (ii) mind-soul taken up as our sub-consciousness, and we have an (iii) outer ego-personality consciousness taken up as our many physical consciousnesses (lifetimes), all riding the rails of karma. Thus, we are a multi-dimensional being playing in many parallel realities.

The differing functions of our consciousness (spirit, mind, and ego aspects) is to call attention to the different realms of our soul's development through time and space as we learn more about this unknown polarity energy of positive and negative. And, each stage of our soul's development manifested through the physical realm, is the testing portion of the universal vibrations of polarity. From this idea, we sooner or later come to learn that we are responsible for developing our soul and the energy we use for our creations. However, we will also discover that we can ask our "I AM" to forgive us because, at the "I AM" level, we have never sinned or done any wrong. We suffer because we believe we are not Christ.

By studying Revelation, and the Bible, from the standpoint of seeing ourselves as a spiritual being's rather than holding to a physical viewpoint that we are only human, we can learn of our total layering of consciousness from somewhere beyond the physical world. Maybe now we can understand that most people are not aware of their beginnings and how they came to live upon the earth. And that is because most people are on different energy and consciousness frequencies because of personal choice in knowing who Christ is.

Chapter 3

WE ARE A SANCTIONED CHRIST

Since our beginning on earth, it has been all about "thinking" in terms of our human existence. For example: Have you ever heard about René Descartes, the French philosopher and a mathematician? He was credited as a foundational thinker in developing western philosophies and science when he made the statement, "I think so therefore I Am." Yeshua and the Ascended Master's approach to this philosophy is not so much "I think," because that statement alone binds us to only experiences with polarity energy (good and evil).

Therefore, it is not, "I think, so, therefore, I am!" It is "I AM THAT I AM Consciousness; so, therefore, 'I exist'" only as Consciousness!" Thus, what is outside of "Consciousness" is just an illusion, including the mind, polarity energy, and even "what I think about philosophy," and our human body. When "thinking" becomes our judgment for "therefore, I Am," that is the beginning of our suffering because all thoughts come from a mental perception that polarity energy (good and evil) is real. From the deepest level of our existence, it is not about "thinking" or "who we are in the physical," it is about our "consciousness acts" that created the philosophy, "I think so therefore I AM."

Hence, ninety-seven percent of the world population remains part of the matrix philosophy that "I Am" my thoughts, and therefore, "I am" my mind, my body, and what I judge as real is what makes me as to who "I am." Know that our ability to clarify complex concepts in life is not through "I think" but through "consciousness" because all that comes from "thought" is controlled by the belief in polarity energies.

This creates a philosophy deep within us that we faithfully follow others, which is why we suffer.

We may think and believe we are following Jesus because of "free will," and yet, we are following a system (matrix-harlot) tied to the mind and its opposing view on every thought we think. It is not "free will," as we all believe it to be! Why? Because "Free Will" is always measured (judged) by the emotions of the mind and one's belief system. Thus, we, as "I AM Consciousness," have forgotten that we created a "divine plan" to follow what our "I AM Consciousness has set up from the beginning of our awakening eons ago to fulfill our undertaking and become a "consciousness" of unlimited wisdom.

This is why we put little thought about who we are from a consciousness of a higher nature. This happens because of our beliefs, the way we think, and how we look at ourselves as a sinner. We are not sinners, and we never were sinners! However, we are experiencers of energy and members of the Christ Consciousness. We have forgotten that thinking/thought is all about the mind (anti-Christ) and the ego-personality (beast) being controlled by the polarity forces of dual-energy (the tree of knowledge of good and bad). Remember, our mind (Adam) and soul (Eve) were deceived through "thought" and that of emotions.

If you search for spiritual truth using the church, their rituals, your parent's beliefs, and your mind filled emotions and ego-personality, then know you are hypnotized to groundless thinking where you are a slave to endless memories and the beliefs of others, all because of following a God that deals in worship, good, evil, sin, and punishment. And, so you suffer! You were born into this world of polarity, but with having no awareness of you being trapped in an emotional perception where you use cosmic and earth energy as the source to experience life instead of using crystalline and crystal energy.

And, like a prison, if you fight to get out of your emotional mind, then you are treating the mind as to whom you are from a physical understanding. It is like a dog chasing its tail! Therefore, you will be chasing your mind, Christ, and truth forever because of the emotional trap of believing in polarity energy. So, no matter what and when you go out to find Christ or "who and what you are from the core level," your emotional beliefs will always be there to remind you "who you are only from a mental level," which is why you are a slave to your mind and ego personalities.

It is not about getting rid of your emotional ties to the mind and your many ego personalities, or hiding from them, like Adam and Eve hiding from God, it is about an awakening to the illusion of it all. Remember, the mind and your many ego-personalities (the beasts) are always about polarity thinking (good vs. evil) and emotions. And this is true just by observing how we all are experiencing different realities. We have forgotten that the mind and ego need to be servants to our heart center, where the "I AM" Christ Consciousness resides.

It is about dropping the labels behind good, bad, punishment, sin, and judgment about who we "think" we are to where it becomes easier to awaken to a "knowing who we are," consciousness only. We are the "I AM" that is part of the Christ Consciousness (Goddess). The philosophy of needing a savior is nothing more than our unwillingness to recognize ourselves as a Christ also. And, once awakened to our consciousness, as "I Exist as a Christ, we are no longer to look at a person, or ourselves as a sinner because we have accepted our cross (karma) and have done our sowing and reaping. All that is left is "letting go" and "allow."

The time has come for us to ascend to a higher state of consciousness without any reservation and in acceptance and love to whom we indeed are as a Christ that created our mind for us to experience life. The time has come to let go of all limitations of our human existence and integrate all parts and pieces of ourselves, for we, like all souled beings, are a sanction Christ in our own right. The example of this is with Revelation 1:1, *"the Revelation of Jesus Christ,"* and *"God giving John, his servant, what must happen soon."*

Revelation 1:1 is not about Yeshua coming to earth or showing John what is to happen soon to Mother Earth and us. It is about our "I AM That I AM" Christ consciousness conveying a message to us and to our human ego-personality (the experiencer) what would happen if we would just awaken to our existence as a Christ. Many would agree that Yeshua walked the earth over two thousand years ago, but many are unwilling to admit he fulfilled his mission when he left earth.

Therefore, the real author of the Apocalypse is not Yeshua. It is the sanction "I AM" Christ consciousness within John, and within human consciousness. The error in our thinking is caused by forgetting that Apostle John is an outer expression taken up as his mind-soul and ego-personality. Thus, John, the individual, is an aspect and a servant to his own "I AM" Christ consciousness. This means it is the same for us humans here on earth!

Just in the phrase *"God gave to him,"* verifies John's own "I AM" Christ consciousness is about to enlighten him, while in physical form, about his true identity as a sanction Christ in his own right. Therefore,

Yeshua, the man, is just symbolic for John's Christ consciousness, and not that Yeshua is speaking to John as a Christ. Therefore, Revelation 1:1 shows that John, the Apostle, was ready to meet up with his own "I AM" Christ consciousness. It is the same for all of us once we are ready to allow it.

The wisdom found behind Revelation 1:1 is that our Christ consciousness, the "I AM," is trying to inform us, while in physical form, that we too are a sanction, Christ. It is that we have forgotten there are many concepts of Christ, what it is, and what it does. Religions love to assign human values and reasoning thoughts to it through the icon of a perceptional and emotional God who lives in a book that portrays good and bad as real, instead of us being a Goddess (Christ too) that uses God (Energy) for our creations.

We have forgotten that we have been operating for a long time on the concept of a single-minded God that created us in a limited way, such as a male and female, without realizing we can be many things all at once; all because of how we "think" about Christ and how the title is assigned to one man. To this day, we continue to fail and understand our "I AM" is a real-life Christ consciousness and the divine spark (logo) within us that was awakened eons ago.

Failing to understand comes from our trained emotional mind and ego-personality working in a three-dimensional world where duality, high and low, light and dark, good and bad, right and wrong, are the dominant directives with our thinking with polarity energy and how it is used for our creations. The reason we never think or move past our mind and ego in the search for Christ, as the Apocalypse is the great example, is because Yeshua's return, like in a rapture, will never come about in anyone's lifetime if we continue using the mind and ego as our search engine.

Once we learn to move beyond the mind and ego and move into our heart center, that will be the time when our Oversoul will open us up to the "secrets" of Christ and how Christ has already returned to earth as us humans. Thus, if we continue to ignore and misunderstand who we are, who Christ is, and who God is, then we will always be exposed to experiencing opposites. Yeshua knew who he and Christ were when he walked the earth, but we failed to listen to him. Instead, we worshipped Yeshua as the only Christ, and then we made him responsible for our mistakes by saying he died for our sins.

This belief is why we today continue to misunderstand Yeshua's miracles as something that only comes from a God outside of us, and is why our prayers go unanswered. By continuing to look at our human ego-personality as a creation from a God outside of us, we, without realizing it, will never get to know the real Christ. Thus, our suffering continues! It was mass consciousness and you who gave life to a belief system where we all fell into a trap that such things as light and dark, good and bad, right and wrong, God and Satan, and positive and negative are "all that is real."

We have forgotten, because of our mind and ego beliefs about the oneness of our "I AM," that the Christ consciousness (the tree of life) is part of a three-dimensional consciousness (spirit, mind-soul, and ego consciousness). If we have a strong belief that we are only human, then our mind and name are all that we are because of that belief. You "think," so therefore, you are what you think." Thus, we placed ourselves in creating a God outside of us, and we have become limited to a reality that only deals in controlled energy known as opposites, where war, power, sickness, judgment, envy, perception, sin, punishment, deprivement, suffering, indulgence, and immorality are played as real.

It is with the belief in a God outside of us, and a God that created us, that keeps us playing with karma; thus, keeping us stuck in a mental consciousness where we play with many lifetimes, suffering. It is our mind and ego that will forever work under the rules presented by the "tree of knowledge of good and evil, duality until we awaken to this process, and how it is all an illusion placed there by all us souls, to learn the wisdom behind our choices.

Eons ago, believe it or not, our mind and ego were flawless, blameless, and perfect. But, once the mind-soul allowed our beastly nature (ego) to open up to polarity thinking (the bite of the apple), believing, and expressing, we began to fill our soul memories with multitudes of lifetimes believing in good, bad, and a God that created us. This method helped layout our divine plan about how to deal with these many lifetimes from a three-dimensional consciousness. And now, we are exposed and privy to all kinds of beliefs (revelations) that found their way into our "I AM" Christ consciousness as wisdom. Thus, giving us the gift of understanding life and who we are at a higher level.

However, it seems like we have a hard time remembering because of the firm belief in sin and fear. This is why we have come up with the concept of karma (sowing and reaping) to understand our choices from a physical level. It is through karma, where we reveal to the world our hidden dark secrets. And, by failing to realize that our Christ consciousness is not susceptible to belief systems such as good, evil, right, wrong, power, control, sin, and punishment, we demonstrate our ignorance in knowing the real Christ.

And, since John in the Book of Revelation was in physical form during his vision, he then represents our human ego-personality consciousness or the name we hold in this lifetime, becoming the servant who can deliver to the self (by way of the mind, the king of kings) the knowledge, understanding, and the wisdom of what we have learned journeying through many lifetimes playing with karma. Know that we all have portrayed many names, personalities (servants), and stories (lifetimes) that caused us to experience light (good) and dark (evil) incarnations. And, because of it, our ego-personalities, the names held in many lifetimes past, have become the sacrificial lamb as Yeshua did in his time.

Thus, some of us have borne our cross, learning about this polarity energy. And now, we can become a true sovereign being in our own right, just like our brother Yeshua. The "Revelation of Christ" is us becoming a Messiah and Savior for our own many ego-personality aspects that are now spread throughout the omniverse, and not that Yeshua is coming to save us as humans. Yeshua has done his part, and now it is up to us to do the same.

The vision of John, since he was in physical form, is symbolic for those of us on earth that have done our time going through many incarnations learning, understanding, and taking responsibility for our choices. And now, we are ready to rise in consciousness and out of our ignorance (clouds) to meet up with our "I AM" Christ consciousness. And, once we have finished our work on earth after many incarnations playing with polarity, we may awaken to the wisdom of letting go of guilt, shame, suffering, and feeling separate from our Christ consciousness, especially the belief that we have sinned.

Once we release these things, including thinking about good and evil as real, then we will come to a knowing we are a sanction, Christ. Therefore, Yeshua represents the divine Sonship within us all, as we move through our trials and tribulations here on earth. And, we have been doing it ever since we left the first creation eons ago (higher consciousness-Garden).

The phrase "to show his servants" in Revelation 1:1 is not the church moving into a rapture, but it is referring to our many ego personality-aspects (lifetimes) of light (good) and dark (evil) incarnations that are now ready to experience what is to happen soon, which is their ascension. This will happen if we, from the mind-soul and ego level, allow these incarnated ego-personality aspects (servants) to integrate and become one with the self and our "I AM" Christ consciousness.

If we allow ourselves to awaken to the mind and ego as the Anti-Christ and the Beast, then the "happening" is our ascension in this lifetime where we can come into the wisdom of knowing we are Christ. Thus, the word "soon" implies, if we are ready to awaken as a Christ also and let go of everything that is not real, then we are ready to act like a Christ here on earth.

Note: In prophecy, there is no such thing as "time and space!" Therefore, "soon" has the representation of measuring our mind-soul and the many ego-personality consciousnesses (lifetimes) we are tied too, and the wisdom found in understanding who Christ is. Thus, the word "soon" is pointing toward us in identifying ourselves as a sanction Christ. Then, the question becomes, do we believe we are Christ or just a human looking for salvation through the man Jesus? However, keep in mind that only we remember that question.

By Christ making "it known by sending his angel to his servant John," the reference is not about how we look and understand angels or servants. It is about our perceptive ability to conclude that our memory to "all that we are," since our awareness in consciousness, can be found within the mind and our soul consciousness of responsibility (angel). And, the "servant" is us humans working out of our ego-personality in this lifetime, and our many ego-personalities of many lifetimes' past are servants for our "I AM" Christ consciousness in expression.

When we in the flesh are on the expansional track in developing our mind-soul and ego, and knowing we are a sanction, Christ, then those many light and dark ego-personality incarnations we have experienced on earth become our directing and guiding light to higher consciousness, to higher understanding, and the wisdom found in all our choices. Know that we cannot have Yeshua be a Son of God unless we are also. Once this is realized from the human mind and ego levels, then the fear of Satan and hell dissolves.

It is us humans who embrace the total energy of "all that is, was, and ever will be for each of us," because, in its principle form, we are an extension of the Spirit of One. Thus, we are her, and she is us, and that we are not a child of the Spirit of One. How can we be a child of her if we are her? It is us humans in the flesh, as an ego-personality aspect, that is a child of our "I AM" Christ consciousness. We are one with our mind, our spirit, the mass consciousness, and with our many ego-personality aspects spread throughout many-dimensional physical and non-physical realms. And, if we are all that, then why do we fight each other over power and belief systems?

We all have a "spirit consciousness," which is our true nature. We have a "mind-soul consciousness" that comprises of polarity energy. And, we have an ego-personality consciousness made up of many physical bodies that are the children of our own Oversoul, the "I AM." And yet, they are all one! Just as they are many parts of the Christ consciousness, so it is with us and our ego incarnations.

Therefore, who is giving John the message in Revelation 1:1-3? It is his own "I AM" Christ consciousness moving through his mind-soul (the angels), and then passing the message down to his human ego-personality (the servant, John). Therefore, the Rapture for John was in the lifetime he played as an Apostle. It will be the same for you and me when we are ready to open up to the Christ within ourselves. It is time to make this known to our many personality aspects of us, and then let go of our beliefs about sin, punishment, good, bad, right, wrong, and that some God created us.

According to Yeshua and the Ascended Masters, the measuring of human consciousness was taken upon the earth, and some of us are now ready to end our trials, tribulations, and mental variations of polarity thinking in this lifetime. And, like John in his time, are we prepared to lift our consciousness in a whole new way of understanding who Christ is and that of polarity energy? Maybe the time has come for some of us, if we so choose, to put away our old dogmatic beliefs in sin, limitations, and Yeshua coming to save us. For this is confirmed in Revelation 1:2, as our "I AM" (Oversoul) bears witness and gives testimony to our many incarnations, by forwarding to memory, what our soul consciousness of responsibility has recorded, good and bad.

Therefore, the "word of God" is the awakened self, in this lifetime, having the ability to understand the mystery of God, Satan, and Christ as to whom we all are part of "all that is life and non-life." And, from this awakening, this puts us, and those who become awakened, on a level where biblical symbology, including the Apocalypse, is understood as something where we and our ego-personality aspects of many lifetimes come together to find the answers to the questions "Who am I?," "Who is Christ?," and "Why am I here?"

Since John the Apostle symbolizes our ego in this lifetime coming from a literal understanding of Christ to an awakened state of who Christ is, then the "word of God" is our capacity to understand the written language (tongue) of our soul memories and how we have worked them out in the physical realm over many lifetimes. We become the creative authority and the sanction Christ on earth, and not Yeshua because it is we who suffered our revelations throughout many lifetimes playing on earth. And now, we have the authority, strength, wisdom, and the skills to bring forth those memories (reporting) that will support our declaration of being a Christ also. All that is left is for us to accept this revelation (message), as John, the Apostle, did in his time!

And, as said in Revelation 1:3, if we can acknowledge, understand, and accept ourselves as a sanction Christ also, and with no reservation or trying to hide (aloud) from the mystical importance of our lessons learned throughout many lifetimes (prophetic message), then we are at the threshold of ascension (rapture). If we trust (heed) in ourselves as a Christ, then what is being expressed (written) in this book becomes the agreed time (appointed) for our awakening. The only thing left is for us to allow and accept it.

If we confront our fears of old, dogmatic beliefs about being kicked out of the garden, which is nothing more than a higher consciousness, then we come to a realization that we voluntarily took on the concept of polarity long ago (the Tree of Knowledge of Good and Evil) to learn the wisdom behind our choices. Once adhered too, then suddenly, out of the blue, like a thief in the night, we will have the "ears to hear" (feel) and the "eyes to see" (understand) the real meaning behind the book of Apocalypse.

Chapter 4

THE SEVEN CHURCHES AND THE SEVEN SPIRITS BEFORE THE THRONE

When Yeshua and the Ascended Masters channeled about the "creation of the earth and the physical body," they referenced Revelation 1:4 and 1:11, where John, the Apostle, speaks of the "Seven Churches in Asia" and the "Seven Spirits before the Throne." Since John represents those of us on Earth, *"who is, who was, and who is to come"* into a knowing that the physical body embodies the "Seven Churches in Asia" and how the body relates to the "Seven Spirits Before the Throne," then know that our physical body embodies these "seven churches" as the "Seven Chakra Centers also," known as the "Seven Endocrine Glands,"

It is the "Seven Chakra Centers (Endocrine Glands)" within the physical body that is characterized by the *"Seven Churches in Asia,"* which makes us a Christ in physical form. We have an ego-personality consciousness, a spirit consciousness, and a mind-soul consciousness, and all these levels of consciousness contain the "Seven Divine Attributes," symbolized by the "Seven Spirits Before the Throne."

The word "Asia" in Revelation 1:4, represents the physical body and its "seven chakra centers." And, because we all chose the flesh and earth to experience life in an opposing way, then our physical body and ego-personality have become the avenue to grow in spirit and in consciousness using the "seven chakra centers (endocrine glands)." Each gland (chakra-angel) plays a fantastic role in the awakening to the "Seven Divine Attributes" of the Oversoul ("I AM" Christ consciousness), symbolized by the Spirits before the Throne." Please bear with me, and I will amplify on this shortly.

The extreme symbology tied to Apocalypse using metaphors, like the Anti-Christ, the Beast, and its number, including spirit, mind-soul, ego, the physical body, and its seven glands, a spiritual code is revealed to those of us who are ready for the harvest that Yeshua mentioned over two thousand years ago. When we learn to understand that we all create our own reality from a small and limited part of our total consciousness, that is when we will begin the groundwork for awakening to a knowing we are Christ, God, Goddess, the Anti-Christ, and the Beast all rolled up as "one body of consciousness."

Remember, in the beginning, when we all first left higher consciousness, our mental consciousness (the mind-soul) was pure and neutral, having no defining features of light or dark to it because we, in our purest of consciousness, are not made of energy. It is how we use energy for our creations!

In the beginning of our awakening to consciousness, we were without a form of any kind, even before creating anything to experience. But once we acted from out of an emotional and mental consciousness (the mind), it eventually led us to where we took on an identity with whatever we were thinking and believing, good (light) or evil (dark). Thus, it became our reality. From the moment our mind-soul consciousness of responsibility took on an obscured form of denseness, and the belief in separation is where we felt a solidness, comparatively nothing at first, to what the physical body's heaviness is today.

But, once our beliefs became more entangled with the forces of polarity thinking, we became part of a system that dealt with choices of good (light) and evil (dark), right and wrong, as something real. Thus, the heaviness of the physical body was formed, even though everything is an illusion since we are only energy and consciousness. And, once we believed the heaviness of the physical body was real, because of it feeling real, our good (light) and bad (dark) thoughts merged into a weighty, single, solid, physical body where each gland within the endocrine system became its distinctive function to carry out.

Because of our thought patterns and expressions being of light and dark, we all took on a belief that caused us to descend into a material body, taking on many light and dark ego-personalities (lifetimes) in exploring this heartfelt polarity energy as something real. And now, Apocalypse is about having the potential to ascend out of that belief in polarity energy (the Tree of Knowledge of Good and Evil (Gen. 2-9)) to a place in consciousness where we can understand that we are neither light nor dark, good or bad because we are only energy and consciousness.

Because we, at our core, are only pure, unconditional, and neutral, having only a spirit consciousness that has no form to it. It has always been our belief in polarity that has kept us locked into a mental, emotional consciousness where we seem only human. Therefore, to bring out the implication of the *"seven churches in Asia"* and the *"seven spirits before the throne,"* Yeshua and the Ascended Masters refer us to examine Revelation 1:10-11.

The "I" in Revelation 1:10 represents us, the self, the one who set in motion an undying change in consciousness where we can now choose our future events based on our consciousness actions and how we unfold our memories since the beginning of our incarnations. For example, all acts of consciousness come from our expressions, thoughts, beliefs, and ideas *(words)*; thus, we become our testimony *(revelations)* in playing them out on Earth in many physical bodies. And now, while in a physical body *(the servant)*, we can reveal those past lifetimes, through memory, as we have been playing them out sowing and reaping. Thus, we can now express in a loud voice that they, too, are part of the Christ consciousness.

Hence, we get to recognize the meaning of Revelation 1:11, *"write on a scroll what you see and send it to the seven churches."* The metaphoric meaning is about us, or the self, from the beginning of our awakening eons ago, putting to memory *(scroll)* every thought, idea, belief, and desire that we have ever breathed life into and manifested here on earth, good and bad. And, from the ruling tendencies written below, and in the way we played them out in many physical bodies, we have transmitted and conveyed *(sent)* what we have learned about the "seven building blocks" of the physical body back to the higher self.

These "seven building blocks" have become known as *the "seven churches in Asia."* They are:

1. *Ephesus*, the first church, represents the root chakra of the physical body and is part of the gonads level (ovaries, females and testes, males). This center deals with survival and your relationships to the physical world, such as your attitudes, feelings of attachments, and the process about how you learn wisdom in each lifetime played out. This then determines your future. Purification of this chakra opens up your ability to become the "I AM" for your spirit

(Oversoul), mind-soul, ego personalities, and the physical body. It also allows you to focus and develop on a soul mental level. The color associated with this chakra is red.

2. *Smyrna*, the second church, represents the root chakra of the physical body and is associated with the Leyden center, navel, or lower abdomen area of the body. It is also known as the seat of the soul. This is the area where you build up choices and then give them substance to experience them in the physical, either now or in the future. It also represents your creativity using the life forces. Also, it is this area where you have suffered many hardships, poverty, the feeling of need, and false ideas because of the belief in light and dark and mystical practices. The color associated with this chakra center is orange. This area is especially sensitive to guilt and repression.

Remember, fear and feelings of unworthiness can trap our energy in these lower chakras, preventing us from creative expression and the full use of our mental abilities. Stuck or trapped energy in this area can bring about destructive energy in ways it will bring in physical problems.

3. *Pergamum*, the third church, represents the root chakra of the physical body and above the navel. It is the bridge between your upper and lower areas of the body and relates to the intestines, pancreas, liver, and kidneys. It is also known as the solar plexus. This chakra is your body's battery, storing your vital energy. It also represents your digestion and absorption of food (ideas, thoughts, beliefs, etc.). It is the lower seat of your intuition or your gut feelings and instincts. Purification of this chakra helps eliminate the disease from your body and brings clear thinking to your mind. The color associated with this chakra is yellow.

Our solar plexus chakra is the joyful center of being, the carefree responsive child within us. It is like the rays of the sun, the joy of life spreads out from this center, elevating our moods, creating optimism, thoughts of wisdom, and inspiration. This center is also associated with intellectualizing everything that comes into our physical body, even memory.

4. *Thyatira*, the fourth church, represents your heart chakra, sometimes called the love chakra, located in the center of the chest. This chakra relates to the heart, lungs, shoulders, and back. The heart chakra is the chakra of all love, both for the self and others. This includes the ability to give and receive or give and take. The

purification of this chakra brings you to the perfect balance or alignment of your body, mind, and attunement with your spirit. The color associated with this chakra is green.

A healthy heart chakra pumps vital life force energy to every cell in our physical body, via the blood and energy. Self-love and self-acceptance of being a Christ radiate outward and then reflect back to us as love and acceptance of others. When we criticize and judge ourselves and others, we deny our "I AM" Christ-spirit and its love for us, blocking our vital pathway to our body. We can clear these pathways by releasing anger, resentment, guilt, judgment, and allowing the love and acceptance of our "I AM" Christ to enter our human body.

5. Sardis, the fifth church, represents the throat chakra, sometimes called the artist's chakra and is the chakra of creative expression located at the center of your throat. This chakra relates to the throat and neck, vocal cords, and your thyroid gland, as this chakra relates to your communication center and higher center of creativity. It represents self-expression, creative expression, and your success in the material world. Purification of this chakra releases tension and anxiety, allowing full self-expression, higher understanding, and intelligent thoughts that come in from the wisdom learned because of your many lifetimes. The color associated with the throat chakra is blue.

The throat chakra deals with speaking up for ourselves and speaking out about unconditional love and compassion for ourselves and others. There is no need to be afraid, no need to compare ourselves with others, or worry about what they might think, have, or say about us just because we say we are a Christ. The throat chakra is very sensitive to repression, and if it becomes blocked, our energy cannot flow. Thus, our creativity and the way we express ourselves is repressed. Therefore, intimacy and close personal relationships are affected.

6. *Philadelphia*, the sixth church, relates to your pineal gland, also known as your crown chakra. This chakra center located deep within the brain refers to that part of you that is dedicated and devoted to expressing unconditional love, friendship, and your relationships toward yourself and others, which is holy and pure.

Channeling of the Ascended Masters on the Apocalypse

This is the place where you can find the [1]"Key of David. The "key" represents divine or unconditional love and is the key in connecting yourself to your "I AM" Christ/Oversoul. The color associate with the crown chakra is indigo.

The pineal gland is considered to be one of the holiest centers in the physical body. According to [2]Edgar Cayce, it is the place of "the mount of God." If we illuminate this chakra center by devoting our thoughts and feelings for friends, family, and relationships toward others, as unconditionally and with compassion, then our Christ consciousness will draw our lower earthly centers up to a higher understanding (mountain) and unite our lower chakra centers with our "I AM" (crown chakra).

Our Christ consciousness acknowledges the works of this center, saying we know the truth of our spiritual nature despite how weak we have become from our materialistic struggles. However, deep within, we retain the truth of our real identity, nature, and purpose for life. Therefore, our "I AM" Christ consciousness finds no fault with us. There is nothing our pineal gland has to do except continue searching for the truth.

7. Laodicea, the seventh church, represents your pituitary gland, also known as your third eye; it is sometimes called the chakra of responsibility and intuition and is located between your eyebrows at the center of the forehead. This chakra relates to your brain, heart, lungs, and blood. Your third eye chakra represents the ability to perceive beyond your five physical senses and to intelligently interpret the information being seen beyond the limits of time, space, and matter, and to understand higher levels beyond duality or a three-dimensional world. Purification of this chakra means taking full responsibility for your creations, good and bad, which then stimulates your divine, mental, and physical senses, thus

---

1 David was the youngest son of Jesse, and he became a king of Israel in Saul's stead (1 Samuel 17:12, 23:17). David is often referred to as a forerunner of one becoming a more perfect man, like Jesus Christ. Therefore, David represents the divine love (unconditional) individualized in man or you coming into connection with your own Christ-being.

2 Edgar Cayce was born in 1877 on a farm in Hopkinsville, Kentucky, and he died in 1945. Edgar Cayce's psychic abilities began as early as his childhood when he first talked to his dead grandfather as well as with other spirits. Mr. Cayce was the most documented psychic of the 20th century, for he gave more than 40 years of his adult life to giving psychic messages to thousands of seekers while in an unconscious state, diagnosing illnesses and revealing past lives, as well as prophecies to come to earth. Mr. Cayce's work is part of the A.R.E. center in Virginia Beach, Virginia.

calming the ego-personality, which then increases your spiritual awareness. This also has a balancing effect on your past and karmic conditions. The color associated with this chakra is violet.

When we quiet our mind before deciding, like in deep breathing-meditation, our physical body and ego-personality become free of stress. Thus, opening up the opportunity in not allowing unworthiness and doubt to creep into our mind. This allows our third eye (spirit) to open and feel intuitive about what is beyond our physical senses. Hence, the seventh church, *Laodicea*, is the master gland (angel), while in a physical body, helping us move past our mind and the five physical senses. And, when we do not allow this, our Oversoul or Christ within, becomes saddened over this center because it is *"neither cold nor hot"* (Rev. 3:15-16).

By not quieting our mind before a choice, it comes down to where we, on a mental-soul level of consciousness, become unconcerned *(lukewarm)* about our spiritual progress. Thus, creating within us an avenue where our "I AM" Oversoul consciousness *"spit us out of its mouth."* Therefore, we may think we are rich with knowledge, understanding, and need nothing because of our religious beliefs, faith, and rituals. But our Oversoul challenges those beliefs, rituals, and our faith because they are *"appalling, depressing, poor, blind, and naked"* to the hidden wisdom behind whom we are deep within our soul.

How this center has no redeeming qualities and no virtue of acknowledging our true identity because our Christ Oversoul consciousness gives none, as this center is stagnant and lukewarm, contributing nothing to the overall spiritualization of the body. Our Oversoul, therefore, warns us, saying, "We will sooner or later find the real truth, but only after we have gone through the trials of fire (sowing and reaping)." That is when we will wear the white garments of purity *(truth)*, covering our nakedness of vulnerability, and that is when we will anoint our eyes to see the real self as a Christ.

In a backhanded way, our Christ consciousness (Oversoul) acknowledges its love for this center, crying out: *"Those whom I love, I reprove and discipline"* (Rev. 3:19). And, this my friends, are us humans incarnating into many lifetime ego-personality aspects sowing and reaping. Therefore, if this center will rise within us and conquer the self first, then our "I AM" will grant us, from the human level, to sit with the Christ consciousness on the throne of wisdom as Yeshua did (Rev. 3:21).

We are the power that rearranges and directs what we desire to experience in our reality. What we <u>believe</u> produces our thoughts; our <u>thoughts</u> create our feelings (passion), and upon those <u>feelings</u> are our life <u>actions</u>. Thus, this determines our <u>reality</u> and how we experience life.

Channeling of the Ascended Masters on the Apocalypse

The universe is all-serving! It observes what we classify as our reality and gradually rearranges itself to support our beliefs. Hence, *we*, from the mind and ego level, are the witnesses and the servants for our Oversoul-Christ consciousness. Thus, we have to take full responsibility for everything that happens in our life; everything, nothing is left out.

When Yeshua and the Ascended Masters speak of "Asia" in Revelation 1:11, they are addressing it according to the Metaphysical Bible Dictionary. This refers to those souled beings taking on a physical body and becoming part of the earth to play out as many potentials, good and bad, as possible to learn wisdom. But, before addressing the *"seven spirits before the throne"* in Revelation 1:4, allow me to uncover what Charles Fillmore and his Metaphysical Bible Dictionary have done to help in our awakening.

Charles Fillmore (1854-1948) was an innovative thinker, a pioneer in metaphysical thought when most religious beliefs in America were with mainstream thinking. Charles Fillmore was a lifelong advocate and writer about the inquiring mind. He took pride in keeping up-to-date with the latest scientific and educational discoveries and theories when it came to religious, spiritual thinking. The ideas presented by Charles Fillmore's Metaphysical Bible Dictionary are based on the teachings of Jesus Christ. They are presented in a cross-denominational format, which makes the book perfect for this presentation.

Remember, Asia was supposed to be the site of the Garden of Eden and the birthplace of humankind. Not only that, but the birthplace of many churches! Therefore, Charles's metaphysical meaning to Asia is that of the physical body and how it became part of the physical Earth. Since Asia was part of the Eastern Hemisphere of the earth as a continent, it, therefore, brings out the importance of its metaphoric meaning as referred to in Charles Metaphysical Bible Dictionary as the physical body.

Thus, when looking into the wisdom behind the *"seven churches,"* John is not referring to seven literal churches in Asia, even though these churches were real. He is referring to the "seven spiritual centers" within the physical body as the Endocrine Glands and with each gland (angel) playing a fantastic role in awakening us to our Christ consciousness, as it did for John.

According to Yeshua and the Ascended Masters! When we learn to study "Genesis and Revelation" through the sensitivity of our ego-personality as the experiencer for our Oversoul rather than through the mind of reason, logic, and judgment, we do discover who God and the Christ are, as we get to understand that the creator is self, becoming an active Christ force in all things made. This includes the DNA frequency of our physical body, the earth, stars, moon, animals, insects, etc.

Therefore, the *"seven churches"* in Revelation 1:4 are parts of our physical body, known as the "seven endocrine glands," and are also known as the "seven chakra centers." When we chose the path of polarity energy, or what is known in the Bible as the Tree of Knowledge of Good and Evil, we chose from an ego-consciousness and illusionary energy and reality where we came to believe that our layered mind-soul consciousness is the source for our intelligence, our physical body, and our good and bad manifestations.

Because of this action, we have forgotten that our Christ-consciousness is part of our Oversoul, mind-soul, and our many ego-personality aspects (lifetimes) and creations. This is why our Christ consciousness becomes the holder of all of what we act on, good and bad. You know, Christ taking on the sins of the world, as this is a metaphor in us taking responsibility for our own creations, and what we do not want to accept as our responsibility, we place it with our "I AM" Christ consciousness.

Therefore, it is our Christ consciousness that holds all of our dark creations, and they will remain until we are ready to face them as our creations. Sometimes we can feel those dark creations around us, and we take it as the Devil or evil spirits, and all the time, it is our Christ Consciousness trying to remind us of those dark creations that we refuse to accept as our creations.

Through the "seven spiritual attributes" of the Spirit of One, symbolized by the *"seven spirits before the throne"* in Revelation 1:4, there sit the "seven days of creation" found in Genesis, Chapter One and Chapter Two. Thus, the *"seven days of creation"* is not to be taken literally but as a metaphor for the "seven divine attributes that make us all a Christ also. And, also what is mentioned as the "Seven Spirits Before the Throne" in Revelation 1:4, as the "seven chakra centers."

Therefore, without realizing it, our Christ consciousness feels our thoughts, beliefs, desires, and experiences (good and bad) through the layering of our consciousness. And, it feels it through the "seven endocrine glands (chakra centers)" of our physical body. Our Christ consciousness feels them through the wavelengths (frequencies) that are measured through our many ego incarnated personalities.

These "seven endocrine glands" are energy centers that relate to our vital organs and the glandular functions of the physical body. Each center also corresponds to the colors of the rainbow; red, orange, yellow, green, blue, indigo, and violet. Color is a vibration just like sound, though it vibrates at a higher or faster level, so we cannot hear it. For instance, red has the longest wavelength in the visible spectrum, while violet has the shortest. Also, not only are these seven endocrine glands part of our physical body only, but they are also related to the *"seven seals"* found in Revelation 6, 7, and 8.

When relating to Revelation's 1:4 about *"grace to you and peace,"* it refers to our evolution in consciousness, journeying through many physical lifetimes learning the wisdom behind playing opposite roles to whom we are at our core. And, when finished, we refine *ourselves* to where we can set the stage to open our mind-soul to a state of mental calmness and serenity *(peace)* where we can finally become the faithful observer *(witness)* to what we create while in the flesh.

Therefore, we humans are a Christ *who is, who was, and who is to come* like a thief in the night. The second coming is not about Yeshua, for he has finished his work. It is the Christ within all of us, allowing ourselves, from the mind-soul and our many ego personalities (lifetimes), to come together as "one body of consciousness." This consciousness vibrates at a much higher frequency than ever before, while in the flesh.

Therefore, when we look at *"the seven spirits before his throne,"* and how it relates to the "seven divine attributes of the Spirit of One" (the seven days of creation), it calls to memory the wisdom and the stimulation of our Christ consciousness, the comforter, to come forth and help us raise our mind-soul and many ego-consciousnesses to a higher frequency. Thus, we awaken to where we have always been Christ.

It is our soul consciousness of responsibility (symbolized by Eve) that holds the memories and wisdom of our choices, actions, and the many ego-personality aspects (lifetimes) that we played out in a three-dimensional physical world using polarity energy as the source. And now, the redemption we seek can come from the Oversoul, the "I AM" Christ within the self, and not from Yeshua coming to earth to save us.

It takes our Christ consciousness to stimulate our soul memories into action so we can experience our choices, sowing, and reaping, to where we can *"bring all things to our remembrance even from the foundation of the world"* (John 14:26). Thus, the *"seven spirits before the throne"* refer to the *"seven angels."* And, these angels take up the "seven divine attributes" found in the "seven days of creation" in Genesis Chapter One and Chapter Two. The wisdom found in these first two chapters in Genesis is the makeup of our total consciousness, for we are a Christ, a God-Goddess, the Son of Man, the Son of God, the Anti-Christ, and the Beast all rolled up into one body of consciousness.

Therefore, allow Yeshua and the Ascended Masters to introduce you to the *"seven spirits before the throne"* and how they relate to the *"seven days of creation"* in Genesis 1:1-30; as they are:

1. The "first day of Creation" represents the first divine attribute of the "seven spirits before the throne" (angels) in Revelation 1:4. It refers to us, in the beginning, as an "I AM" Christ desiring to become conscious and aware of the self, accepting the conscious act about being an extension of the Spirit of One.

In other words, our "spirit-Oversoul or "I AM" Christ consciousness" is the individualized portion of the greater whole, and it is a higher version of us rather than of our mind-soul and our many ego physical consciousnesses. Therefore, the *"first spirit (angel) before the throne"* is the self coming into an awareness of being an individualized portion of the Spirit of One (Goddess), where we, in physical form, come to know that we are a Christ also.

2. The "second day of Creation" is the second divine attribute of the *"seven spirits before the throne"* (angels) in Revelation 1:4. We, on a subconscious level, possess a high level of intelligence because it is tied to *"universal consciousness"* (or the wholeness of all consciousnesses, all souled beings), meaning we all can tap into this higher universal intelligence when we are ready to do so.
3. The "third day of Creation" is the third divine attribute of the *"seven spirits before the throne"* (angels) in Revelation 1:4. We, on a subconscious level, possess a consciousness that always desires to grow and expand by way of experiencing choices; thus, we gain a wealth of wisdom and understanding about who we are, for we are a Christ also.

The composition of our "I AM" Christ consciousness is absolute divine love, for we all possess, at a deeper level, a well-balanced, harmonious, and compassionate masculine (positive) and feminine (negative) energy and consciousness that is unchanging, neutral, and pure. Thus, we, from a deeper level, cannot sin! We can only experience this polarity energy by forming our thoughts into something that feels real but is not, as our physical body.

4. The "fourth day of Creation" is the fourth divine attribute of the *"seven spirits before the throne"* (angels) in Revelation 1:4. Where we, on a super subconscious level, are divine and have the free will to do as we please, as long as we do not interfere with the intentions of another soul.

5. The "fifth day of Creation" is the fifth divine attribute of the *"seven spirits before the throne"* (angels) in Revelation 1:4. We, on a super subconscious level, have a spirit that is the essence of all life energy, both positive and negative, in all time, space, and dimensions (astral realms, including Earth).

Our spirit is the "I AM" divine spark and the source that gives all our creations lifelike multiple ego-personality lifetime aspects with which to play. And then, we, from the divine level, spread them throughout many dimensions, as the earth is just one of them. And, this applies to everyone, as all members are equal to God-Goddess because all is God-Goddess. It is that we all have forgotten!

6. The "sixth day of Creation" is the sixth divine attributes of the *"seven spirits before the throne"* (angels) in Revelation 1:4. We, on a super subconscious level, enjoy absolute divine love that is unconditional and unchangeable.

We all have a divine passion and an oneness of purpose about us that was set in place deep within our consciousness long before we ever left higher consciousness (Garden), and it remains today. That is why we cannot sin! Sin only comes from the misunderstanding about who we are at a higher divine level. Regardless of what we believe, all spirits/soul members are in the image that reflects everyone as a God, Goddess, and a Christ also, with having only pure, neutral, and universal energy to use until our spirit activates it into what seems as form.

This means that we all can create or use this pure unbiased god energy of light for whatever purpose we choose, good or bad, because it makes no difference to our Christ consciousness. Remember, it is our human ego and mind consciousness (the Son of Man and the Son of God) that holds the authority of our "I AM" Christ consciousness because we are the master and the Lord of Lords over all influential forces in the manifesting of all possibilities of life and what we experience as our reality.

7. The "seventh day of Creation," referred to in Genesis 2, is the seventh divine attribute of the *"seven spirits before the throne"* (angels) in Revelation 1:4. We, on a conscious level, need to associate our intuitive feelings and emotions with the silencing of our mind before making choices; otherwise, we will always choose from a place of polarity energy.

Learn to calm your mind down before choosing what you desire to experience, or your emotions will get the best of you. If you do not learn to silent your mind before deciding, the chances of you experiencing low energy frequency become typical with your creations. Thus, your experiences on earth become adventures you may not want. Remember, no one knows the Father (pure unbiased energy) and the Son (the mind) better than you because you are the Father, the Mother, and the Son.

Chapter 5

THE ALPHA AND THE OMEGA

When the Ascended Masters referred to the *"faithful witness, the firstborn of the dead,"* Revelation 1:5 and 1:10-11, they were not speaking about Yeshua, they were speaking of the Christ consciousness within us all. At the beginning of our awakening long ago, we souled beings ultimately learned of our "I AM" as the Christ consciousness. However, it was through the measuring and our expansion *(evolution)* of our consciousness when we reckoned with the question, "Who am I?" And, that is when we became dead *(asleep)* to our real name. Therefore, the firstborn of the dead is our "I AM" Christ consciousness, as Yeshua (Jesus) symbolizes this act.

When Yeshua was born on earth, he did not realize he was a Christ until later in life, which is why he symbolizes the Christ within all of us. We all have been playing in many physical lifetimes, not knowing we are a Christ. And, like Yeshua before us, we too will come to a place in consciousness where we will evolve to a knowing we are a Christ in the flesh.

If we invite in our "I AM" consciousness (the firstborn) to enter our mind-soul and ego-personality physical consciousness (the second-born), the likelihood we will uncover what we have forgotten since the activation of our many ego-personality aspects, our "I AM" will become the "faithful witness" to all of what we have placed in memory since leaving higher consciousness. And, if we allow ourselves to awaken, from the mind-soul and ego levels, and see ourselves as the *"the firstborn of the dead,"* that is when we will finally understand why we have been asleep since the time we lowered our consciousness frequency long ago.

If we can learn to accept the Christ consciousness as to whom we are at our core, that will be the time to integrate and raise our consciousness frequency, like in a rapture, and rule over our ego-personality aspects of many *(kings of the earth)*, and place them into "one body of consciousness," as to whom we indeed are, a Christ also. When done, we do open up to all the lies, like thinking we are a sinner. As Yeshua and the Ascended Masters proclaim, we cannot sin from the "I AM" Christ level because that part of our consciousness is absolute and unchangeable. Therefore, in a sense, we are perfect already!

For example: In 1 Corinthians 15:47, *"The first man was from the earth, earthy; the second man, from heaven."* Religions use this verse to indicate Adam as the first man on earth and Yeshua as the second man on earth. Yet, this is a prime example of the inconsistency for interpreting the Bible from a literal viewpoint. To keep the viewpoint consistent, then the word "second" in 1 Corinthians 15:47, according to religion, should have the same literal meaning as the first. Therefore, Cain is the second born that came "from heaven" since he was the firstborn of Adam and Eve.

However, according to Yeshua and the Ascended Masters, Adam and Eve were not real people; the names given as Adam and Eve are to represent our mind and soul consciousness of responsibility. In contrast, Cain represents our individualized ego-personality incarnated in the flesh playing with the belief of polarity energy (sin). Thus, *"heaven"* is signified as our Oversoul, or "I AM" Christ consciousness, and "all that we are within consciousness." Therefore, we are not only our minds and physical body, as they are not real.

The firstborn is signified as to the positive-masculine and negative-feminine side of our mind and soul consciousness of responsibility, while the second-born is that of our individualized ego-personality (represented by Cain). By decoding the Bible, and the raising of our consciousness frequency, we get to learn there never was a separation between our Christ consciousness (represented by Yeshua) and our higher awareness (represented by Abel). Therefore, we are already the Christ we seek!

By accepting ourselves as the creator and a Christ, without feeling guilty or unworthy, because of our physical state, or what we believe we have done right or wrong, we ascend (like in a rapture) to an understanding where we come to realize our consciousness is multi-dimensional. The physical dimension is one of them. The wisdom in raising the frequency of our layered consciousnesses (lifetimes) to a knowing that we are a Christ is where our ego-personality (second born-Cain) becomes one again with our mind-soul (firstborn of the dead) and our Oversoul.

Therefore, we souls are the first and the second born! We came from higher consciousness (heaven-Adam), and we had to lower our consciousness before entering the earth, which is why Cain represents that lowering of consciousness. However, before we could lower our consciousness frequency, we had to hide (kill) our higher awareness (Abel) to whom we truly are. Otherwise, we would have always known we are Christ.

By allowing ourselves to move back into the knowing as a Christ, we not only learn about our real identity and how we lowered our consciousness, we also get to understand God's status as a "universal mind field of pure unbiased neutralized energy of light" that we souls use for our creations. It is not that some God is our creator. We all have been hypnotized by the "Tree of Knowledge of Good and Evil (duality), and it has kept us in this hypnotic state for many lifetimes. And, with this hypnotization, it keeps us from tapping into the wisdom gained in each of our lifetimes.

This explains why most everyone on earth, at their level of understanding, has no clue when the time of the rapture comes, because it all depends on when we are ready to let go of the old way of thinking. Ezekiel 21:24: *"Therefore, thus says the Lord God, 'Because you have made your iniquity to be remembered, in that your transgressions are uncovered so that in all your deeds your sins appear because you have come to remembrance, you will be seized with the hand.'"*

This remembrance comes to us, after many lifetimes, evolving and peeling away from our hypnotic state while we believe polarity energy is real. When we realize that we are the creator and the Christ, we awaken where we can tap into our memories and journey back in time by expanding our consciousness and seeing through the layers and layers of our consciousnesses where we have played them out in many lifetimes.

For example, this is how I able to write this book. By expanding my mind-soul and ego-consciousness with the other parts and pieces of my total consciousness, including my human consciousness, I can reconnect with my higher "I AM" consciousness and gather the wisdom gained in each of my many lifetime memories, and then present those memories in a book. The same is true for you if you desire to learn the history of Earth and how man has come to forget about himself. By looking into our beliefs, that of others, and how our spiritual leaders have hypnotized us using the icon of a false god, we learn that God-Goddess, the Anti-Christ, and the Beast are us all. Once this is known, how can we follow a false God?

Many have asked, "If I have lived in a physical body before, then why can't I remember?" The reason we cannot remember past lifetimes is that each ego-personality aspect of us only limits itself to what they see, touch, smell, taste, feel, and believe in that particular dimension they happen to reside. We do not realize that our mind-soul is programmed to perceive and relate to a three-dimensional reality. Thus, leaving out any awareness that our consciousness can expand and retrieve information from other parts of our total consciousness, including the time before we left higher consciousness (Garden).

According to Yeshua and the Ascended Masters! We alone are responsible for our Christ consciousness, our mind-soul, our ego, our body, and our many lifetime experiences, whether we think we created them or not. If we are experiencing an illness, an accident, or a stroke of good or bad luck, we have created it somewhere along the line in our many lifetimes. If someone hits a golf ball and it lands in front of you or hits you, then you have created the experience. Otherwise, the ball or you would not be there.

Look at what we have accomplished by taking the symbolic bite of the apple (unknown principles of polarity energy, positive and negative). We do not only learn the wisdom of our choices but also the wisdom found in each positive and negative choice. Thus, we are becoming a much wiser God-Goddess in the process then when we were before leaving Higher Consciousness (Garden). Hence, how can religions call this sin? When we volunteered to be in service to our Oversoul, the "I AM" Christ within, learns all the limiting factors of polarity, both good (light) and evil (dark).

The ascension (religion calls the rapture) is not just the physical you coming into new and safe energy; it is also the expression of you are Christ in the flesh. This awakening brings you the true meaning behind the second coming. The churches teach that Yeshua is the only Christ, but this belief assures them that we all will follow a false prophet, meaning them. Thus, we remain in a mental state, believing we are a sinner forever. So, now you know the metaphoric unpardonable sin!

Remember, when a prophet or church speaks stating you are not God, you are not Christ, you are not the Son of God, you are not the Messiah, and you are not a church scholar, because that is reserved for the church elites, that is when you know you are dealing with a false prophet. A false prophet will always preach to you that you must worship and follow Yeshua (Jesus) when, in truth, they are telling you to follow and support them. Yeshua said, "you are all Gods" (John 10:34), so act like one. Be wise and understand the real wisdom here. *"If they say to you, 'look, he is in the desert,' don't go out. Or he is in the inner rooms, don't believe it"* (Matt. 24:25–27).

Channeling of the Ascended Masters on the Apocalypse

Why would you follow someone who claims to be Christ if you are Christ? So, follow no one but your own Christ-spirit. Know that the second coming of Christ is a very personal experience for those who are ready to move beyond the belief in good and evil (or light and dark) and let go of the old, dogmatic polarity energy of the Bible. If our leaders believe in good and evil, then they are not to be followed. Especially, when they speak of light and dark. Therefore, the second coming of Christ happens within the self. It does not come from polarity thinking or believing, or from any church, or political party, because everything connected to polarity energy and thinking is an illusion. It happens when we learn to go inward (east) and discover Christ is already there.

In 2 Peter 3:10: *"The day of the Lord will come like a thief in the night, and then the heavens will pass away with a mighty roar, and the elements will be dissolved by fire, and the earth and everything done on it will be found out."* In retrospect, this means, suddenly, perhaps at the most unexpected time, (like a thief in the night), something awakens you from the darkness of your ignorance and brings you into a new awareness where God, the Goddess, and Christ is you. Then, as portrayed in the rest of the verse, all the foundations of your reality built on light and dark will crumble, allowing you to come alive in a whole new consciousness and new energy of oneness (New Earth).

To become the Lord of Lords and the Alpha and Omega, Yeshua demonstrated his actions, while in the flesh, by showing only unconditional love and compassion for everything and everyone. Therefore, when we all have mastered the influences of the polarity energy within the self, we place our rebellious ego nature (serpent) in harmony with the law of compassion and oneness. Thereby, we become the Alpha (the Christ we were in the beginning) and the Omega (the Christ we are in the end).

Many people throughout the world today have not gotten to where they will accept themselves as a Christ, and because of it, they live minimal lives. Not that I am making a judgment on them. It is only to point out that they do not believe they are more than just a human mind and body. They just cannot believe they are the true essence of God and the Goddess in human form.

"The almighty" in Revelation 1:8 is the all-powerful, all-supreme, and the unquestionable *you* as the Father-Mother and Christ in the flesh. And, when you reach out to this wisdom, you come to an understanding that it was your mind-soul and ego-personality that was the first (Alpha) to leave higher understanding (the Garden). And now, the mind (Anti-Christ) and your ego personalities (the beasts) are the last (Omega) to return or

remember. However, this does not mean you are done learning, but you are on the way to balancing and filling yourself with the wisdom of knowing your true identity as a Christ, a God, and Goddess in human form.

Revelation 1:9, the reference to John is our ego-personality in this lifetime, learning to take responsibility for our thoughts, choices, and creations of our past, present, and future. And now, with our many past lifetime experiences, good and bad, they *"share"* with us their memories of what they have mentally suffered *(distress)*. It is up to each of us to accept this, forgive ourselves, and then allow ourselves to have compassion for our many ego-personalities spread through many dimensions.

Patmos in Revelation 1:9 is the island to which John was banished. It is a rocky island in the Aegean Sea and the place where John received his vision. The symbology is that "Patmos" is a place within our consciousness where we realize, through memory, that we are in the flesh, producing suffering because we lack the understanding that we are worthy of being a Christ. Also, Patmos symbolizes our human body and mind and how they can be an island of limitations. And, because of it, our Christ consciousness is isolated from its real environment, which is why we find ourselves in a limited mind and physical body today (Island of Patmos).

It is through memory, awareness, and accepting ourselves as the alpha and the omega where it becomes the place in consciousness where we can release ourselves from the pain of suffering. Because of our many lifetimes past, our ego-personality aspect of today may be ready to share the memories of why we suffer. Throughout our many lifetimes, we have persistently endured our hardships. And now, the time has come to look at ourselves with great honor and admiration as having value because we are worthy of Christ since we are Christ no matter what we believe we have done in life.

When we choose to see ourselves as a Christ, we then move from out behind the clouds of our ignorance (darkness) to where we can experience our divinity in a more profound and enlightened way.

Chapter 6

THE PHYSICAL BODY AND THE SEVEN GOLD LAMPSTANDS

The deep state that John was caught up in Revelation 1:12, as he turned to see whose voice it was that spoke to him was when he observed the *"seven gold lampstands."* He found it was his own "I AM" Christ consciousness speaking to him. And, as John (the Apostle) turned away from the outer world of polarity energy (the letting go of the belief in it), John, his "I AM" Christ, and all his ego-personality aspects of past lifetimes, became "one body of consciousness" again. And, from his physical state of consciousness, John assessed this sudden higher understanding of his multidimensional self, and the world around him. That is when John witnessed his own journey of lifetimes being played out before him. And, that is when he wrote down what he saw and heard.

We, too, from the mind and ego levels of consciousness, are a witness to our journey, and we, like John, have written what we observed, heard, and experienced by recording these experiences deep within our soul as memories. And know, all that we have to do is tap into those memories for wisdom and understanding. It was John, and not Yeshua, who perceived his spiritual evolution. And, that is when John understood it to be the same for all souls who, by their evolution, can sense the true meanings of their personal stories (lifetimes) and strange metaphors tied to their revelations.

John used the experience he was witnessing to help benefit the journey of many others by writing his experience down for all of us to examine and figure out later, just as we do with dreams. And what John wrote down for us to explore was the story behind the Apocalypse. For example, the words of John when he *"turned to see whose voice it was that spoke to him,"* is symbolized by the self in a physical lifetime finally coming into a new awareness where we can allow it to move within our heart center. And, if we do, then complete understanding can be revealed about why we are here on earth.

John's writings, *"spoke to me,"* Revelation 1:12, is symbolic of our "I AM" Christ consciousness expressing a desire to the physical part of us, asking if we are ready to awaken to a new vibrational frequency movement that will soon direct our focus to let go of all things outside of us, including our belief in polarity energy, that we are a sinner, and that someone is higher than us. The wisdom behind John's words is about allowing our Christ consciousness to commune with us directly like it is talking to us in a loud voice. Therefore, the time is now for the communion with our own "I AM" Christ consciousness and how it is determined to awaken us from our sleep.

So, we can now become a witness *(saw)* to what we have experienced while journeying through time and space incarnating in many physical bodies. We have gained exceptional treasures of wisdom (gold) along the way, and these treasures (wisdom) are found within our consciousness, sub-consciousness, and our super-subconsciousness. It was long ago when we submitted our:

1. "I AM" Christ consciousness, the source of life, and our;
2. Mind-soul, as the center of consciousness and the generator of our beliefs, thoughts, feelings, ideas, and the perception of truth. And then, we allowed our;
3. Ego-personality, the Beast, help us arrive at a position of being God-Goddess and a Christ in our own right.

Therefore, when John speaks of the *"seven gold lampstands,"* in Revelation 1:12, he is referring to his "I AM" Christ consciousness and how he understood the causes that transformed him from a human to a divine-human who now understands the interactions between his various levels of consciousnesses, portrayed by the *"seven gold lampstands."*

John is giving us the message; we, too, can transform ourselves from being only human to being a divine-human. And, we do it through the "seven (churches) endocrine glands" of the physical body. For instance:

1. The church of Ephesus is not only part of the level of the gonads, but it is also where our desires set in; because we have, without

realizing it, a great passion for learning, even though we are in the physical denying that passion.
2. The Church of Smyrna is not only associated with the Leyden center, navel, or lower abdomen area of the body, and the seat of the soul, it also is connected to *substance,* like our etheric body.

Compare this to our neutralized consciousness as in a state of having a spirit, a mind-soul, and an ego-consciousness that helped us choose "form" (like a physical body) as the vehicle for evolution and learning wisdom. Our etheric body then helped us move into many physical and non-physical forms, and then spread them throughout multiple dimensions to feel and experience our choices. This attitude then helped us feel:

3. *Independent* and *intelligent,* for which the Church of Pergamum is symbolic of our solar plexus chakra. This chakra is our body's battery for storing energy. This is the level where we can rationalize our creations on an intellectual, emotional basis. As this gave us:
4. A consciousness of *growth* and *expansion;* represented by the Church of Thyatira, also called the love chakra, located in the center of the chest. It was by way of false faith and our mental perception about a God outside of us instead of having the confidence we are God, the Goddess, and the Christ. This false faith then set the stage for our intuitive body that led to:
5. *Free will* and *dominance,* for which the Church of Sardis represents as the throat chakra, and sometimes called the artist's chakra, where it relates to our vocal cords in speaking out. This speaking out led to control and power and losing our free will by:
6. *Expressing* our *love* and *friendship* from a mental perception of polarity, as this center relates to the Church of Philadelphia and the pineal gland, also known as our crown chakra. We all base our truths on the principles of good and evil, right and wrong, light and dark, God and Satan, all mind-controlled. This directed us into a belief of:
7. *Judgment* and *taking responsibility* for our choices and actions, as the Church of Laodicea relates to our pituitary gland, also known as our third eye. We live out of our mental and physical consciousness where we get to feel our choices of good and evil, right and wrong first hand.

One of the most misunderstood verses in Apocalypse is Revelation 1:13, *"In the midst of the 'seven lampstands' one like a son of man, wearing an ankle-length robe, and a gold sash around his chest."* This relates to us souls, creating many ego-personality lifetime aspects playing with polarity energy. Therefore, we have created a 'super personality aspect' that carries the source and the power *(lamp)* of the "I AM." Thus, placing our mind and ego into the position *(stand)* to remember who we are and how we have transformed ourselves from a human to being a divine-human.

Because of our desire to experience life in the flesh, we gave substance to our consciousness that now provides structure to our spirit-Oversoul, mind-soul, and our many ego personalities aspects that are spread throughout many dimensions. This "act in consciousness" gave us the feeling of being independent from the rest of the cosmos and other souled beings. Thus, giving us the feeling of having great power that sets the stage for control and dominance over others. However, deep within our subconsciousness, we have a real identity ("I AM") that holds love and compassion for whatever we did in the past and what we do now.

Revelation 1:13, *"wearing an ankle-length robe,"* represents our connection to our higher self. The ankle bone connects the leg bone to the highest bone in our foot, symbolized by our ego-personality that is the lowest form in a physical lifetime. The highest bone in our foot signifies the ego-personality that is connected to our "I AM" Christ consciousness, and to all other ego-personality aspects of us from different lifetimes. Remember, we all have a higher ego-personality; it is just that we have killed that personality in favor of focusing out of an ego-personality that loves to play with polarity energy.

The *length* of the robe symbolizes how we have been distancing ourselves from our many light and dark personality aspects of our past, and from our "I AM" Christ consciousness for a long time without realizing it. But, since some of us humans have paid the price for our so-called sins through sowing and reaping (bearing our cross), we now can wear the "robe" of purification. Meaning, we can become a true master in our own right in this lifetime if we so choose. All that it takes to get this robe is to let go of the belief in polarity energy (light and dark), the belief in sin, and then trust ourselves as the master of our fate and reality.

The *"gold sash around his chest,"* Revelation 1:13, has the meaning of the "treasures" (wisdom) we have gained and learned while journeying through many incarnations; and this "wisdom" is locked up within our super-subconsciousness. This wisdom *(gold)* can be found by searching our hearts and then feel the real truth. Know that "all that we are," and is, is infinite and everlasting concurrent action. This means everything happens at once, and though there is a type of sequence to it, there is no beginning and no end.

Channeling of the Ascended Masters on the Apocalypse

We all are the creator God, the Goddess, and Christ, who manifested a super personality in this lifetime to help awaken us to whom we are, for we are the witness in integrating our "I AM" Christ.

As the Ascended Masters look into Revelation 1:6, *"who has made"* is about us as humans. By moving our consciousness focus from knowing we are a Christ to a consciousness of only being human, we all have created many potentials and possibilities in which to explore and experience the energy of polarity, positive and negative. This includes the forming and shaping of our many ego personalities that have become unbalanced as well as balanced. However, in that creation, we also created a physical dimension (Earth-Kingdom) where sowing and reaping (wall of fire) have become the avenue back to balancing our consciousness and the energy used for our creations.

The choices we made long ago to consume our mind-soul consciousness with memories of opposing-energy (good and bad lifetimes) have gained us enormous understanding and wisdom today. By playing in duality, we have finally reached a consciousness where we can free ourselves from being a slave to our mind (Anti-Christ) and to our many ego-personalities (beast) that are spread throughout many dimensions.

Look at what we all have accomplished by taking the symbolic bite of the apple (duality). We not only learned the wisdom behind our choices, but we also learned to become a very wise Christ and God-Goddess in the process. Therefore, again, how can religions call this sin? We all volunteered to be in service to the Spirit of One and our own "I AM" Christ consciousness to learn all the limiting factors of opposing energy, light, and dark.

How often have we heard religions say, *"no one shall come unto the Father but by Christ" (John 14:6)?* When we understand Christ as to whom we are at our core, then we get to know who the Father is, a "universal mind field of pure, infinite, and unadulterated neutral energy of light" that we souls use for our creations to experience life. Therefore, God is not a person, or is he white and supreme. God is an energy that we souled beings, together, created to use with our consciousness in bringing about whatever we decide to experience, materialness or non-materialness. In other words, God's energy of light is part of our Beingness as if consciousness and energy are one.

According to Yeshua and the Ascended Masters, *"the hair on his head was as white as wool or as snow,"* Revelation 1:14. This is metaphoric of our physical nature operating more on an intellectual scale than on a spiritual one. The *"head"* is symbolic of our minds! Thus, our thinking and belief systems come from our rational thought patterns instead of spiritual thought patterns. Hence, because of us souls operating rationally through many lifetimes, we have gained a lot of wisdom (which the *"white hair"* represents).

Even now, ninety-seven percent of the population allow themselves to be ruled by their rational mind, the five physical senses, and what their ego-personality (beast) drives them to do with their beliefs. This is why we believe so much in our politicians and the system they represent. However, at some point or lifetime, the ego-driven physical part of our beastly consciousness will transform itself to higher consciousness, and that is when we will finally accept the "I AM" Christ consciousness as to whom we are at our core level.

The *"white hair"* not only represents wisdom, but it also represents the "I AM" Christ within us all and how it can become available to the mind-soul if our ego-personality allows it to come into our total consciousness. However, as long as we operate from intellectual nature, the ego-personality (beast) will not allow it.

"His eyes were like a fiery flame" represents how we look at and understand authority, or power, as something real. As we express our choices to the mind (Anti-Christ), our ego (beast) then sets judgment upon those choices according to the belief in polarity energy as being real. And, because of our passionate nature inflaming our choice to grow in wisdom and understanding, the experiences will eventually bring us to a "knowing" that we are God, the Goddess, Christ, and Satan all rolled up into one "body of consciousness." Still no sin here!

From the very beginning, when we all left higher consciousness (first creation-garden) and moved into the second creation (astral-physical consciousness), we manifested an everlasting force of potentiality, understanding, intelligence, and wisdom into an active "I AM" Christ present in our life. And, because of this act in consciousness, we must accept the responsibility for everything we have chosen and will bring into our lives to experience. We are the creator God-Goddess who brings the experienced conditions into our life, whether we believe it or not. Again, we create our accidents, illnesses, abundances, joys, and sorrows.

For example, each light bulb sheds its own light, and therefore, each light (spirit) is responsible for its own darkness. Thus, consequently, we all have:

1. *Fire*, representing the passionate elements of our energy that surrounds us (positive and negative). We have:
2. *Water*, representing the lifeblood (spirit) of creation, followed by:
3. *Air*, which fills the spaces between the polarity energy of our soul (fire) and spirit (water), as the air represents our mind/mental.

Channeling of the Ascended Masters on the Apocalypse

Then we have:
4. *Earth*, dirt, (representing form, thoughts, belief systems, concepts, and desires); and where our defiant ego-personality consciousness (Satan) will hold us as a slave for many lifetimes because of our strong belief in polarity energy, good, evil, and power until we become awakened to whom we are as a Christ.

Fire represents the dual-energy that we use for our creations, as it takes polarity energy to experience our creations either as good or bad. Fire also represents the purification of our soul choices, as we journey through hell using karma. Air represents the space (freedom) between our "I AM" Christ identity and our consciousness of a mental nature. It takes the breath of life (air-mental and spirit-water) in giving animation to our physical body to experience this polarity energy in the flesh. Water represents the lifeblood that connects us to our spirit and physical body. And Earth is the holding place for our many ego-personality consciousnesses in a physical body.

These are the four elements of the Earth. And, since the feet are the foundation for our physical body, while on earth, then the feet of Yeshua in Revelation 1:15 represents our ego-personality (Son of Man) at work in a physical body playing with polarity energy as the source for our creations. Revelation 1:15 is identifying our light-good and dark-bad creations, and it is what carries our ego-personalities of many to integrate with our consciousness of today.

Because of the "fire of justice" (furnace-hell), we have in memory everything we have ever expressed, thought, believed, and experienced throughout our many lifetimes. Thus, we have guaranteed our deliverance (salvation) from our sins playing in polarity. The process of karma (trial by fire-furnace) helps us clear out all memories of corruption, belief in duality, and a God that judges and punishes us. Thus, releasing us from our stuck and limited energy. All that is left for us to do is let go of the belief in sin and dual-energy. And, the sooner we do, then the sooner we will arrive at the gates of heaven (higher understanding).

When we speak of Revelation 1:16, Yeshua and the Ascended Masters are referring to the "seven layers of our consciousness," as those layers are taken up as the *"seven stars."* Therefore, we, as an individual or group consciousness, hold all power, authority, and with it, the responsibility to accept the concept that we are an extension of the Spirit of One. Thus, making us a divine being that is equal to God, Goddess, and Christ in all ways.

The secret behind Apocalypse is that we are all a Christ in expression. It is and has always been our "I AM" (holy) spirit, for which Yeshua represents, that embraces and supports everything we do, good and bad, right and wrong. And, it is our mental soul (Eve) and the Christ within us that holds the memories of everything we have ever thought, expressed, carried out, and manifested throughout time and space, physically and non-physically.

Therefore, the most effective way we found in becoming a sovereign and complete God-Goddess in our own right was to split our Oneness of Consciousness into what the *"seven stars"* symbolize, as each layer of our consciousness has become a consciousness of its own. And yet, they are all one. These layers of consciousness consist of us having a:

1. Spirit body,
2. Mind-body,
3. Intuitive body,
4. Etheric/soul body,
5. Emotional body,
6. The astral body, and many ego-driven
7. Physical bodies

It was and has always been us humans (to whom John represents) that allowed ourselves to be overwhelmed by the desire to learn the wisdom behind the principle of polarity (light and dark, good and bad). Therefore, the only way we could hide the real self ("I AM") from the false selves (ego personalities) was to explore this dual-energy by layering our consciousness many times over, like an onion. It was our mind, the Son principle (Adam), that took on the belief of duality, positive and negative, that brought about the artificially induced condition of our soul being less than God that led to the belief in sin, and that we are only human.

We purposely volunteered to enter the void/abyss and earth in physical form (second creation). And, by implementing polarity energy as being part of our "seven layers of consciousness," we allowed ourselves to evolve, grow, and expand in consciousness. Thus, giving us awe-inspiring wisdom.

However, when we first came to earth, we agreed to lower our vibrational frequency signature to where we felt like it was a "fall in consciousness." And, with this fall, it left us susceptible to the influences of polarity energy because it surrounded us like a plaque. That is when we brought in the attributes of our physical nature, known as the "seven deadly acts in consciousness," as they are called sins. They are:

1. Sadness
2. Anger

3. Lust for power
4. Envy
5. Pride
6. Greed
7. Laziness

From these "seven deadly acts," all other sins committed fell under them. And, once we introduced ourselves to these "seven deadly sins (acts)," after leaving higher consciousness, we became the exact opposite of our Christ consciousness. And now, we have been playing in a multi-layered consciousness where we forgot that we are Christ and a God-Goddess. The polarity of light and dark, good and bad, right and wrong, God and Satan, sin, and punishment became real to us through the means of our layering consciousness *(the seven stars)*. But remember, it is still all an illusion put in place by us souls to feel independent and to experience our choices as either good or bad.

The *"sharp, two-edged sword coming out of his mouth,"* Revelation 1:16, represents the justice of sowing and reaping (karma) mentioned in the Bible. We souls, since we are a Goddess, are responsible for giving the breath of life to a mind-soul that holds thoughts, ideas, beliefs, and desires as to good and evil, as we journey through many lifetimes expressing them. We are the creator of our world and the karmic conditions we experience.

Therefore, it is you, and the mass consciousness, and not Yeshua, who carries the *"two-edged sword"* of karma, and therefore you are the only one that can take away your so-called sins. Your "I AM" Christ consciousness was the gateway through which you have come forth from the invisible (spirit) to the visible (physical). And, it is through the invisible where you come to a knowing you are the creator of your illnesses, bad luck, and poverty (karma). But, at the same time, you are also the God-Goddess that can change those creations to health, good luck, and richness.

The *"mouth,"* Revelation 1:16, represents the face, as it denotes our outward appearance right now is physical. By coming into physical form, we opened the doorway for our Christ consciousness to discover the wisdom behind the value of polarity energy. Not only that, but we also gave our Christ consciousness the gift of feeling what it is like not being Christ, God-Goddess. How else could God-Goddess (the composite of all souled beings) get to know "all things?"

We, like Christ, are infinite, and our Oversoul has a great desire to know all things. And, to accomplish this task, we put on many false faces (layered consciousnesses (lifetimes)) to explore this unknown polarity energy. And because of it, we have become a better and wiser God-Goddess than before leaving higher consciousness. However, because of having many lifetimes, some of us are in the process of remembering who we are.

In other words, Revelation 1:17-18! *"When I caught sight of him, I fell at his feet as though dead. He touched me with his right hand and said, 'Do not be afraid. I am the first and the last, the one who lives. Once I was dead, but now I am alive forever and ever. I hold the keys to death and the netherworld.'"*

John is reminding us, as he did to himself in his day, that maybe some of us are ready to remember who we are, while in physical form, that we are more than just human. There are some of us who are beginning to awaken to the Christ within without doubt. We can observe this just by seeing what is going on around the world today, as it looks like everything is in chaos. But it is not about chaos! It is that some of us here on earth are beginning our transitions from a three-density energy frequency consciousness to a four-density frequency consciousness (fourth-fifth dimension). And, from the viewpoint of our mind and ego-personality consciousness in this lifetime, the time for our metaphoric rapture is in the making.

If we allow ourselves to awaken to where our layered consciousness can reveal what we have gone through in many lifetimes (revelation), then our consciousness will rise in frequency. We can catch sight of our Christ consciousness *(caught sight of him)*. However, we must be ready to let go of the belief in polarity energy. And then, we can invite in our "I AM" into our life, and it will reveal to us the many past lifetimes where we have played out using opposing-energy.

With this revelation at hand, we can understand who carried out the physical actions that embraced a movement in consciousness that took us from knowing we were Christ to a lower vibrational frequency *(fell)* that locked us into "all that we are is human." It is from this lower vibrational frequency where we believe we are only an ego-personality in human form *(feet)*. Thus, we fell asleep to ever being Christ *("fell at his feet as though dead)."*

The idea of *"he touched me with his right hand and said,"* represents our "I AM" consciousness, giving us souls a unique fingerprint *(touched)* that identifies us as the servant and the authoritative power *(right hand)* that long ago sent us off on a long journey to play out our "divine plan" and become a unique and sovereign God-Goddess in our own right. And, *"do not be afraid. I am the first and the last,"* represents that we souls were the *first* to send ourselves on a journey of discovery. And, we will be the *last* with the authority and power of a God-Goddess to bring us back to a knowing we are Christ again.

So, why would we fear Christ? Most of us do fear our "I AM" Christ consciousness because of not wanting to take responsibility for our choices.

Channeling of the Ascended Masters on the Apocalypse

This is why most of us will not take the time to discover who Christ/God is and who we are at our core. We are *"the first Christ and the last Christ,"* and we always have been. But instead, most of us rely on our religious teachings, our mind, our ego, and our faith in a false God to tell us who we are and who we are not. Therefore, our faith in this God of the Bible is nothing more than fear-based because we are afraid to study the self.

When we all began our journey outside of higher consciousness (Garden), we were like a child having the understanding of an eight-year-old. We had no parents to guide us, not even a good friend, and yet we had the power of a Goddess. Can you imagine having no beginning or end, having the wisdom and understanding of an eight-year-old, having no one to answer to or guide us, but we have the power of a Goddess? Believe it or not, that was our reality at the beginning of our activeness of consciousness long ago.

Revelation 1:18, *"I hold the keys to death and the netherworld."* We all became dead to our "I AM" Christ consciousness because of our journey playing with polarity energy as if it is real, but now some of us are ready to awaken from our first death (asleep) about what is real and what isn't. And, since we are the ruler and king over all our ego-personality aspects (lifetimes) spread throughout multidimensions in this lifetime, we have, believe it or not, overcome hell and death just by journeying through many dimensional realms *(netherworld)*, sowing and reaping. And because of it, we have created for ourselves the remembrance of "who we truly are at the physical level."

All that is left to remember is who we are and to allow and choose it from a conscious level. It is that simple! Once we learn we are a Christ also, we then can speak plainly, *"I was once dead, but now I am alive, and that is forever."* Know that once we remember who we are, we overcome the first death (forgetting we are Christ) to where we will always remember who we are as Christ also. When this happens, we become a sovereign God-Goddess and a Christ in our own right.

Maybe now you can understand where, in Revelation 1;19, you are to *"write down, therefore, what you have seen, and what is happening, and what will happen afterward."* As for me! I am writing down what I have seen, what is happening, and what will happen all because of allowing myself to move beyond my mind and ego creations as being real. My books written are the testimonies and revelations of my awakening to the Christ within myself.

Our ego and mind, like John's, are servants to our own Oversoul in recording our thoughts, beliefs, and desires to memory. The name given us in this lifetime is that we are rationalizing and reasoning with what we understand about God, Jesus, and our Christ consciousness. Thus, our mind-soul and ego-personality, here and now, are the means for us to experience life in the physical world. Therefore, the revelations that Yeshua experienced here on earth over two thousand years ago, which was revealed to him by his Christ consciousness, actually has become our revelations here on earth. And, because of it, our Christ consciousness is ready to reveal to us our revelations (many lifetimes sowing and reaping) if we so choose to awaken to them.

Since John symbolizes that part of us that rationalizes and reasons with what we see, feel, taste, smell, hear (five physical senses), and understand about physical life, then reason and logic have become the means of carrying out our journey through many lifetimes, sowing and reaping (revelations). Therefore, the act of reincarnation has set the pattern for us to become a Christ of wisdom and responsibility, using consciousness and evolution as the vehicle to remember who we are at our core.

Chapter 7

REVIEWING THE SEVEN LAYERS OF OUR CONSCIOUSNESS

To help with any misunderstanding about what was said in the last chapter, Yeshua and the Ascended Masters asked me to review Chapter Six, the last chapter, by referencing Revelation 1:20 here in Chapter Seven. *"We are shown the secret meaning of the seven stars in the right hand, and of the seven gold lampstands: the seven stars are the angels of the seven churches, and the seven lampstands are the seven churches."*

When looking into the wisdom behind the *"right hand,"* it represents our authority (power) as a Christ that has also chosen the most effective way for us to express our divine plan to feel our experiences. Remember, in the first creation, our consciousness was pure and formless (symbolized by the Garden), and the energy we generated was of pure transparent, weightless light. Thus, we could not feel, taste, smell, touch, or see our chosen experiences.

But, when we souled beings lowered our consciousness frequency to a mind-soul mental consciousness, symbolized by leaving the garden (the second creation), our consciousness and energy of pure transparent, weightless light body, took on a denser form where we souls, as a collective Goddess, made it feel real. And, once we souled beings moved our focus from pure energy to more solid energy, symbolized by the abyss and the second creation of nothingness, we created out of the belief in it, polarity energy, which was unknown to us at the time.

In other words, our Crystalline Neutralized God Energy of Light condensed into an etheric type of energy where we formed new energy called Crystal Energy. This Energy is not as pure as Crystalline Energy, and therefore, it can give off a "dualness" to it when not used properly. However, through the measuring of our consciousness (time-evolving and playing with "Crystal Energy)," we souls transformed our mental consciousness into creating "Cosmic energy" that ended up as intellectual and perceptual energy where we souls created many multidimensional and emotional realms that led us into "Earth Energy" of a real denseness without us realizing we even did it.

Therefore, it has been, and still is, our ruling and defiant ego-personality nature, along with our mind-soul consciousness, that ultimately continues to shape and structure the Crystal Energy, the Cosmic Energy, and the Earth Energy into a physical body of such denseness, all that what we experience today is only polarity energy. Through this action, our revolutionary three-dimensional consciousness has become the chosen vehicle capable of holding polarity energy (Crystal, Cosmic, and Earth Energy) in such a way that it isolated us from the Crystalline Energy and from our "I AM" Christ consciousness.

This action then separated us from being aware that we have created other lifetimes to be played out in different dimensions, using Crystal, Cosmic, and Earth Energy as our source and all having a dualness to them, other than Crystalline Energy. However, through this isolation, it enabled us to grow, learn, and evolve through many lifetimes and experiences (good and bad) with no interference coming from our "I AM" Christ consciousness.

And, as our many ego-personality consciousnesses hold our energy in isolation, it clothed our formless consciousness into *seven subtle bodies of consciousness*. Although, at our core essence, we only contain a Christ-like consciousness and a Crystalline Energy of absolute light and neutrality. Therefore, these "seven subtle bodies" are symbolic of the *"seven stars,"* along with the *"seven churches"* (endocrine glands) and the *"seven gold lampstands"* (purpose), and they are all part of our total consciousness. Thus, we became and are a three-dimensional being. And, within each layer of consciousness, we clothed *(hid)* ourselves with:

Channeling of the Ascended Masters on the Apocalypse

Seven Angels/Stars	Seven Churches/Glands	Seven Gold Lampstands
1. Spirit-Body	1. Laodicea/Pituitary	1. Responsibility
2. Mind-Body	2. Philadelphia/Pineal	2. Relationships
3. Intuitive-Body	3. Sardis/Thyroid	3. Control/Power/Free Will
4. Etheric-Body	4. Thyatira/Thymus	4. Growth/Expansion
5. Emotional-Body	5. Pergamum/Adrenals	5. Memory/Intellect
6. Astral-Body	6. Smyrna/Leyden	6. Substance
7. Physical-Body	7. Ephesus/Gonad	7. Desires

Embedded within each layer of our consciousness, there are many belief patterns or, as Master [3]Tobias calls, networks. I call them the seven subtle bodies of our consciousness *(stars)* formed from out of our Oneness of Consciousness desiring to experience itself through many different directions, and yet all at once.

However, we had no schedule to follow, so our ruling ego-personality (the serpent) became the motivating force behind our purpose to experience life. Why? Because our ruling ego-personality had us feel separated from the wholeness of our total consciousness. Because of the purpose to feel and experience life, our "I AM" established a movement in consciousness where we eventually activated a three-dimensional consciousness: our spirit, our mind-soul, and our many ego forms (physical and non-physical). And, once we established ourselves as a three-dimensional consciousness, our "I AM" handed all authority over to the masculine side of the mind (the Son).

That is when we began to intellectualize and sensor our purpose and belief systems to where our soul mental consciousness of responsibility (Eve) stored those perceptual, sensory beliefs away as memories to be retrieved later. Know that our mental soul consciousness of responsibility (Eve) is always tied to our Oversoul when it comes to memories. It was our ruling ego-personality (Beast), working with our mind (Anti-Christ) that implemented this polarity energy (positive and negative) for differing views when it came to our purpose in life. This gave our ruling ego-personality (serpent) the power to be the judge and jury of our choices instead of our mind-soul and spirit.

---

3 Tobias was an energy or spirit channeled by Geoffrey Hoppe which has since been reincarnated. Tobias was part of a spiritual group called the Crimson Council, which has since been taken over by Adamus Saint-Germain. This council has the spiritual purpose of teaching the use of energies on the planet and other places in creation. Tobias and Adamus Saint-Germain of the Crimson Council bring energy of wisdom and love and a perspective from the other side of the veil. (More information about on the Crimson Council and the Crimson Circle can be found on the web at www.crimsoncircle.com.)

Through judgment, using an ego-consciousness of defiance, we souls condensed *(clothed)* our pure god energy of light into several layers of consciousnesses and energies, giving us the means to cultivate, grow, and expand our consciousness to where we could learn "all that there is to know" about polarity energy. This allowed us to serve our mind-soul consciousness of responsibility and our many ego personalities in a false concept about someone having control, dominion, and power over us (which the church of Sardis symbolizes).

Helped by our own "I AM" Christ consciousness, we souls found the means to hide our "I AM" deep within the "seven subtle bodies" *(seven angels)* and within the "seven ductless glands of our endocrine system of the physical body" (symbolized by the seven churches). These seven angels *(stars)* became our hidden companions to express love and friendship (the church of Philadelphia), and to express a consciousness of judgment and responsibility (the church of Laodicea), all based on polarity, right and wrong, good and bad, light and dark, God and Satan.

And, once we have learned to take full responsibility for our judgments and actions, we can become a much wiser God-Goddess than what we were before we left higher consciousness. From these seven angels *(stars)* and the *seven churches* (endocrine system), we had the means to feel and experience good and evil, helped by our ruling ego-personality (Beast). Thus, we would gain the wisdom of our choices and experiences. This helped us become a much wiser God than before leaving higher consciousness.

Remember, everything is an illusion, except when working out of our core essence, the "I AM"! These illusions seem real because we still believe and are living them. Belief systems are powerful, strong, and inviting! They can hold us in a frame of mind where the only way out is for us to bring some disease or accident into our life so a different direction can be taken. This is where unexpected accidents and illnesses in people's lives come from. It is because they have a deep desire to move in a different direction to become awakened. But they do not know how to do it, so they use this method of diseases and accidents to change course. Once we become awakened to being a Christ also, we can release those methods.

"*The seven gold lampstands,*" Revelation 1:20, represent the generating of the source of life (spirit) and our energy toward a movement in consciousness, where we (from the mind) submit our pure god energy of light in supporting a structure (physical form) that would endure endless growth and wisdom for our "I AM." Therefore, the *seven stars* mentioned in Revelation 1:16 became the *seven angels*. The *seven gold lampstands* mentioned in Revelation 1:12 became the *seven churches*, as they both represent the "seven building blocks" of our mind and physical level of consciousness in Revelation 1:11-12, 20.

Therefore, the church that Yeshua mentions in the Bible is not some church outside of us; it is our physical body, so take good care of it. Remember, it is within our physical body (the church) where we meet Christ and not in some building.

"Do you not know that you are the temple of God and that the Spirit of God dwells in you? If anyone destroys God's temple, God will destroy that person; for the temple of God (you) is holy" 1 Corinthians 3:16–17. *"For in one Spirit, we were all baptized into one body, whether Jews or Greeks, slaves or free persons, and we were all given to drink of the one Spirit"* 1 Corinthians 12:13. Also, *"If (one) part suffers, all the parts suffer with it; if one part is honored, all the parts share its joy. Know you are the Christ's body, and individually parts of it"* 1 Corinthians 12:26–27.

Paul is telling us we are the totality of our own consciousness, and yet the wholeness of us is more than the sum of its parts, as all is ONE. What does all this mean? If we look at ourselves as a God-Goddess and a Christ also in our own right, then it means that God is not one individual but rather the composite of all souled beings. And, it takes us all to ignite this God's energy of light in bringing forth our manifestations to experience. It is, therefore, from this massive universal mind field of pure unbiased god energy of neutrality and light that Yeshua called Father, is a telepathic grid of continually expanding (growing) consciousness where the mass consciousness creates universes, galaxies, planets, moons, animals, trees, insects, etc.

Therefore, it was you who created your mental and physical consciousness and then placed in time and space, given intuitive understanding, intelligence, and the eternal power in creating your passion for experiencing life. This God energy of light and neutrality surrounds and forms your many ego-personality aspects of light (good) and dark (evil) lifetimes. And, at the same time, creates universes, planets, rocks, trees, galaxies, insects, animals, meadows, air, and anything else that has structure, form, and identity, which affect the body of Christ!

Chapter 8

UNDERSTANDING THE PHYSICAL BODY

To understand Apocalypse, you have to speak about the human body and how it relates to your uniqueness as a souled being. Yeshua was acknowledged as having a physical body, and with that physical body, he became the example for bringing in the Christ consciousness into perfect expression. Thus, revealing that we, too, while in a physical body, can bring in our Christ consciousness. Because of this "universal omnipresent mind field of pure unbiased god energy of light," we, like the mind and body of Yeshua, are made up of the same mind and body. Therefore, we are already perfect, as was Yeshua when he walked the earth.

Our human body is transitory, limited, and weak, but as a divine-human, we are assured, limitless, secure, and strong. The twelve disciples sent forth by Yeshua to preach, teach, and heal, signify the twelve faculties of the mind and the twelve metaphorical meanings of their names. These represent the right brain hemisphere but function under the direction of our Christ consciousness (Matthew 10:5). The twelve tribes of Israel, along with the twelve metaphorical meanings of their names, represent the left-brain hemisphere.

The words, *"he is not here, for he has risen,"* (Matthew 28:6), is speaking of the human ego consciousness resurrecting the physical body into a divine physical body, which continues to be crucified today because of the belief in sin. And, once we let go of the belief in sin, the physical body will then restore itself into its uniqueness, holding a consciousness wide awake to whom it is, a divine being in the flesh.

Channeling of the Ascended Masters on the Apocalypse

"Go quickly and tell his disciples, he has risen" (Matthew 28:7), which is symbolic of us humans, while in human form, proclaiming our "I AM" Christ consciousness to the right brain hemisphere. Saying the time to awaken from our sleep (death) is now. And, by Yeshua saying, *"follow me"* in Matthew 8:22, he is inviting us all, while in the flesh, to overcome this old belief in polarity energy and have our physical body become like his. Thus, freeing us from sowing and reaping!

By believing in sin and polarity is to follow our overpowering ego (Beast), giving us the ultimate reality that causes our outward physical manifestations to feel real. And yet, none of what we are reflecting outward with our thoughts and beliefs are real. Therefore, we are dead to the authentic self as a Christ. When temptations arise from our memories because of our many past lifetime beliefs in sin and polarity, we create building blocks within our physical body that lead to energy becoming stuck in the areas of the endocrine system of the body. And, the only way we can release this stuck energy is by journeying through many lifetimes, sowing and reaping.

Once we finish with this belief in a God of judgment and polarity energy as being real, then a lifetime will come when we will eventually let go of this old belief in sin and punishment. Those who believe in sin, rational thinking, and everything needing to be explained in a logical format (left and right brain activity) are not masters of their ego nature. Instead, they are like beasts in their mind and consciousness, trying to feast on everything that is physical-driven. These people become slaves to their physical body, their mind, and ego-personalities, causing polarity energy, positive and negative, vibrational frequency, to move in a direction that brings in their karmic conditions.

As long as these outward beliefs in polarity energy rule our thoughts, we will always remain a slave to them. And, when we allow our Christ consciousness to flow freely through our mind, ego, and physical body without interfering, a new belief generates within us that becomes very multidimensional and expansional. This opens up *(come alive)* the pathways of those blocked areas in the endocrine system of the physical body. Thus, we become healthier and live longer.

Shown in Revelation 1:12, the *"church of Ephesus"* on a metaphysical level represents desire, from which a movement took place in consciousness that led to the general belief of there being a beginning and, therefore, an end. And, when we look at this beginning from a mental level of consciousness, then the church of Ephesus symbolizes we, from the ego-personality, taking on a physical body that resulted in us creating many like images (lifetimes) of ourselves to play out in a physical body to answer the question, "Who am I?"

It is from the physical level; Ephesus takes into consideration all three levels of our consciousness through the gonad level. This is where we, the creator, produce "like images" of ourselves, and then spread them throughout multi-dimensional physical realms to learn and grow through the means of experiencing our beliefs and choices to gain wisdom.

Ephesus was a City of Asia Minor and the capital of Ionia, and at one time, it was a center of learning and commerce. It was noted for its beautiful temple, built for worshipping the goddess Diana. The metaphysical meaning for Ephesus is the central building block of our desires and how they became part of our multi-consciousnesses in materializing our spirit, mind, ego, and our multiple ego-personality aspects of light (good) and dark (evil) into a physical body to be played out on earth.

It takes a desire to help spark consciousness into taking action that eventually led to structuring our consciousness into multi-ego personality consciousnesses. Yet these many consciousnesses are still *one*, which is also why we feel separated from our Christ consciousness. Thus, from the gonad level, we take up a physical body as a male or female. And, it is at this level where we meet and create all situations to be played out in any particular lifetime.

And, once we moved outside of the first creation (higher consciousness) and created other lifetimes, these ego-personality aspects (lifetimes) of good and evil became the cause of our confusion, fear, and suffering, as they moved in and out of consciousness without us even realizing it. Therefore, the meaning of the "*'one' who holds the 'seven stars' in his right hand and walks in the midst of the seven gold lampstands,*" Revelation 2:1, and is the angel within us that supports the gonad level of consciousness. Why? Because our (i) spirit body, (ii) mind-body, (iii) intuitive body, (iv) etheric body, (v) emotional body, and the (vi) astral body are under the control of the (vii) physical body without us even realizing it *(the seven stars)*.

We have layered our "oneness of consciousness" like an onion, with many different-sized spheres of detaching skin. And, each detaching skin represents an ego-personality aspect (lifetime) that is evolving *(walking)* through the process of (i) desire, (ii) substance (physical body), (iii) memory, (iv) growth, (v) choice, and (vi) relationships. Thus, we are learning to take (vii) responsibility for it all (symbolized by the *seven golden lampstands*).

We are a spiritual being first, and we are a God-Goddess because we are the Christ giving life to "all that we are in consciousness." We have descended from a higher understanding (heaven) into physicality and onto this earth to experience the belief in polarity energy (light and dark). And now, we have taken hold of a belief system about a single solitary white male God who created us and is separate from us being as real. Therefore, the Church of Ephesus reflects that separateness and lost feeling of not being a Christ in our own right. Now, we must reverse our focus on polarity and sin, and realize that our beginning is only about our human body, and not our spirit or Oversoul.

When we look at our "I AM" allegorically as our Christ consciousness, we are participating in this "universal omnipresent mind field of pure unprocessed neutral energy of light (God)" that Yeshua called "Father." Thus, we set the stage for our spirit to become an active force in all things created. We are the ones who, in Revelation 2:3, *"knows our works, labor, and endurance."* We are also the ones who *"cannot tolerate wickedness"* because it was us who *"tested"* ourselves by creating many ego-personality aspects *(apostles)* of light (good) and dark (bad). And now, we have *"discovered"* that all ego-personality aspects of ourselves are *"impostors."* However, knowing they are impostors do help us learn to accept our "I AM" Christ much easier when in human form.

Our Christ consciousness knows that we feel ashamed, embarrassed, and guilty because of putting up with our appalling and unspeakable past lifetimes. But, if it weren't for us examining, choosing, and experiencing those self-appointed ego-personality aspects *(self-styled Jews* can mean apostles too*)* to play out in any lifetime, we would have never discovered those lifetimes of ours as impostors. And this is why there is no such thing as sin, good or bad.

We all have journeyed through many lifetimes of long-suffering (endurance and suffering) on behalf of our "I AM" Christ consciousness *(for my namesake)*. Therefore, do not *"grow weary"* (Revelation 2:3) or feel hopeless, because we have brought great understanding and wisdom to our Christ consciousness and to the whole of creation, including all of what we have given life to. Know, at the beginning of our awakening in spirit, our "I AM" did not know about life or itself until we gained enough courage to leave our "oneness of consciousness (Garden) and give birth to a lower version of ourselves to explore what we created as polarity energy (the Tree of Knowledge of Good and Evil).

And, once we felt separated from our Christ consciousness, we then brought in a new conscious feeling of time, space, and having many lifetimes. Thus, in its true meaning, it was only us souled beings that moved outside of the Garden of Eden or that of our higher understanding of consciousness. This outer, external consciousness became known as the abyss mentioned in the Bible, for this consciousness was nothingness, a complete void, because "all that was" turned aside from our early love for this oneness, purity, and compassion for the sake of exploring the question, "Who am I?" Thus, *"we have lost the love we had at first,"* Revelation 2:4.

Because of what we did long ago, it is time for us to give this God of the Bible a new name; a name where this white male false creator dissolves, and the "love we had at first" for our "I AM" consciousness can come back into our awareness. After what we have done and experienced through countless incarnations sowing and reaping, we have now given ourselves the avenue to let go of this single white male false God of the Bible and move into a spiritual understanding of being the Christ we seek.

Know, as we played in our newfound mind-soul and ego-consciousness of uniqueness, individuality, and separation, we became a hunter and an explorer creating multitudes of positive and negative ideas, potentials, and ego-personality aspects of ourselves, good and bad, to experience. We filled the abyss of endless nothingness with many forms and dimensions, physical and nonphysical. And now, "all that was" as an "oneness of consciousness" (heaven/garden, God) no longer exists because that oneness has now filled the abyss of nothingness with "all that is now," polarity energy and physicalness.

We souls became seekers in trying to find what used to be "all that was," was the oneness of consciousness, and we have been doing it by seeking the principle of polarity energy to find it. We simply played and devoured all the energy we could, without realizing or knowing the consequences of our actions (symbolic of Adam and Eve's bite of the apple). Even though we missed the love and oneness of our own "I AM" Christ consciousness, we felt the exhilaration of discovering our real identity. This new feeling was where we created our first story (ego-personality) in which our other ego-personality aspects (*self-styled apostles*) of good and evil have been built.

Even in today's world, everyone, including those who play the game of evil, has this great urge to return home, and it is felt at the core of their heart center. This urge to go back to their "I AM" Christ consciousness (home) goes way back to when they first left their higher consciousness (Garden) long ago, for they can feel this strongly within their hearts. Therefore, they, fearing never to return home (heaven) because of what they did, fall victim to their belief of not being part of the Christ consciousness. Thus, hell is assured for them! It is because of this fear of not returning home again that these defiant souls play the game of annihilating everything around them.

Channeling of the Ascended Masters on the Apocalypse

Man has always thought of heaven as a religious place where there is a supreme being who is a white, a male deity with long white hair and a beard, sitting on a golden chair, judging and deciding about who is allowed into heaven and who is not. Most people believe that heaven is a perfect dwelling in some unspecified place where they go after death, but while they are on earth, they must suffer and somehow justify their existence. Of course, we can give this "heaven of perfect dwelling" credit for one thing. It allows us to recognize and learn about the real heaven because it is not out there in some space or sky, but it is part of our Christ consciousness.

Some of us have been very persistent with our convictions, belief systems, and unwavering courage that has brought us unlimited wisdom and understanding when it comes to soul growth. And some of us have no idea of the wisdom we hold within memory because of our many lifetimes, including us humans being a unique and grand angel. My friends, according to Yeshua and the Ascended Masters, we were the ones, not Adam and Eve, who set the pattern of separation a long time ago, and now we carry the Christ-seed, the "I AM" within us. Now, can you see how far *"you (we) have fallen?"* Revelation 2:5.

However, do not feel bad because of it. This also refers to those people that feel they have done horrendous acts against their brothers and sisters. Please do not feel unwelcome in the house of Christ. Know that it was a perfect divine plan that you, yourself, set up a long time ago. Therefore, you never made a mistake or that you have sinned. And, when you come into that awareness, you set the stage for atonement to take place within your heart, mind-soul, and body.

When we begin to re-think *(repent)* our stand on this long-time belief in polarity energy, positive and negative, good (light) and evil (dark), right and wrong, God and Satan, and being separate from our Christ consciousness (Goddess), we will find ourselves at the gate of higher understanding (heaven). If we do not allow ourselves to re-think *(repent)* about what we believe to be real, like polarity and a God outside of us that is of singularity, then the incomparable treasures of wisdom that can be found within our soul memories will remain behind the clouds of our ignorance until we learn to let go of these old dogmatic beliefs.

Remember Revelation 1:12, where John *"sees whose voice it was that spoke to him, and as he turned, he saw the seven gold lampstands?"* John is referring to his own "I AM" Christ consciousness and not Yeshua. Therefore, if we so choose, we can comprehend and understand the causes that can transform us from being only a human to a divine-human in the flesh. This is where we can choose the interactions between our various layers of beliefs depicted by the *"seven gold lampstands"* that can be removed from its place (Revelation 2:6).

Without realizing it, our memories have been trapped in limited polarity energy through what we have formed as our physical body, and now the time has come, if we so choose, to allow our memories to surface. And, we need not die to free our memories of old; we only need to step out of the limiting, dualistic beliefs that have kept them trapped. As long as they (aspects of our past lifetimes in other dimensions) are part of our energy, still unaware of being more than human, we cannot understand or meet our Christ consciousness deep within.

Because the "I AM" operates at a frequency much higher than our many past lifetime aspects. And, when we try to define Christ by human standards, we limit the very nature of who we are at our core consciousness. Yeshua, our brother, has told us that the Kingdom of Heaven is already here because true salvation comes from trusting in ourselves as a Christ and not for us to look for Yeshua to save us. It is about embodying "all that we are" as a Christ. And, the moment we accept ourselves as a Christ also, we will discover what it means to let go of a belief that causes pain and suffering.

When we remove our notion of God as a single white male God who created us, and stop trying to define Christ as only accepting those who are good, then we will discover God, Goddess, Christ, Satan, and ourselves as being more than human. Since we have journeyed through time and space, taking on many behavior patterns (lifetimes) that led to us following dogmatic religious beliefs, we, in this lifetime, *"have much in our favor"* (Revelation 2:6). Because now, we have come to a place in consciousness where we can feel our Christ consciousness today, encouraging us to open up to the words written in our Book of Life (memory) and see the true meaning behind John's words.

Believe it or not, we humans have traveled the road of religious beliefs and their teachings for a long time, many lifetimes. And now, there are some of us about to awaken to whom we indeed are. And maybe, now, we are ready to release those old belief systems of light and dark creations. Why? Because we do reach an understanding where we cannot bear those teachings of religions any longer. Therefore, *"you detest the practices of the Nicolaitans, just as I do"* (Revelation 2:6).

Nicolaitans is a Greek word that coincides with the Hebrew name Balaam. And Balaam was the son of Beor, a native of Pethor in

Mesopotamia. Balaam was also a prophet for the Midianites. He was hired by Balak, king of Moab, to curse the Israelites; instead, he obeyed the voice of Jehovah (a false god) and blessed them (Numbers 22:5–24:25). Though Balaam did not curse Israel, he did counsel Balak to lead the Israelites into idolatry (worshipping false gods) and fornication (using pure energy of light (God), so it defiles their true core essence as they might forsake their own "I AM" Consciousness (Goddess) and be destroyed (Revelation. 2:14; Numbers 25, 31:16).

In the spiritual sense, Balaam belongs to the mental phase of our mind. And, since Balaam was a foreigner as far as the Israelites were concerned, he represents our mental consciousness and how we are likely to experience disagreements and disputes between new truths and letting go of old religious beliefs (Israelitish) about what we have been taught by religion and their false God of judgment and punishment (Jehovah). Even though we, from a mental consciousness, strive for power or dominion in keeping to our religious teachings alive, our mind-soul reaches no higher in its expression than where we are in our stage of evolution or soul growth. So, please keep that in mind when arbitrating was right or wrong.

Many do not realize or understand the human mind will always seek to understate our judgments, the undercutting ourselves, and us polluting our thoughts with polarity thinking. Thus, we eventually destroy our religious beliefs (all pertaining to the Israelites) and how they continually struggle to gain a perfect understanding of new truths about a God named Jehovah, who understands good is good and evil is bad. However, know that there is a real God that is the "I AM That I AM," Yahweh, a Goddess of neutrality.

In the end, all of what the human mind believes to be true are indeed overcome in some lifetime, and its powers of selective judgments, according to good and evil, are then lifted (ascend) to a higher consciousness of neutrality. We can see this using the Moabites and Midianites as they were defeated. And, Balaam, who was fighting with them against the Hebrews, was also slain (Numbers 31:8).

In closing this chapter, we find in Revelation 2:7, where *"let them,"* clearly states that it is our choice to pay attention to our feelings because it is only we humans who can perceive *(hear)* the vibrational frequency of our "I AM" Christ consciousness giving us the means to open our eyes, heart, and mind. We can do this by way of our "I AM's" *(spirit's)* pledge *(word)* to the "seven endocrine glands" *(churches)* of our physical body, and it is nothing more than allowing our individualized ego to explore the ruling tendencies of our belief systems. The purpose! It is to see and understand how we transmit and convey what we have learned about the "seven building blocks" of our physical body.

It is these seven building blocks *(churches)* that are part of the *"seven spirits before the throne"* (Revelation 1:4), the *"seven stars"* (Revelation 1:16, 2:1), and the *"seven golden lampstands"* (Revelation 1:12). So, put no other Gods before us, not this God of the Bible, or even Yeshua, for he simply served as a manifestation and example of how we, as a Christ also, move and live through the flesh using a physical body.

The *"victor,"* Revelation 2:7, are those of us moving past the belief in polarity, good and bad, right and wrong, light and dark, sin, judgment, and God and Satan as two beings at war. The conflict between God and Satan is nothing more than a metaphoric meaning taking place within each individual and has nothing to do with two characters battling each other over our soul.

Once we move past these old, dogmatic beliefs, we then move into a new expansional energy (non-duality) where we share or partake *(eat)* from what we have learned from our many lifetimes and stories. Also, since we lived out those lifetimes in a physical body, we can tap into the wisdom just by choosing to do so. And, once we learn how to tap into our soul memories, the roots of the "tree of life," our higher consciousness becomes centered within our physical consciousness, connecting us to the wisdom of the wholeness of our total consciousness.

The *"victors"* are those of us who have come to earth and have endured a lifetime after lifetime under the veil of ignorance or through spiritual amnesia but have persisted. We were the ones, along with Yeshua, a long time ago, who planted a seed deep within our consciousness, knowing that the seed would not sprout immediately but would have a veil (physical consciousness) wrapped around it to protect it until we were ready to sprout (grow). All that has happened is that we have forgotten about the seed placed deep within our consciousness and the knowledge that not all of the seeds would sprout at once.

Therefore, *"Spirit's word"* is nothing more than an idea being born deep within us to explore this polarity energy, and that of a physical body to forget who we are for a while. It is also a metaphor for the consciousness of the mass (all souls). For example, in Genesis 1:1, *"In the beginning when God created,"* signifies our capacity, utilizing the universal omnipresent mind field of pure neutral god energy of light to move us souls into a manifested physical body. Therefore, the word of God is the perfect result generated by our own "I AM" Christ consciousness working through our desire to learn about life and this polarity dual-energy.

And, as we acted upon our desires for learning wisdom, it produced a belief system that set the framework in which we activated this pure universal energy of light to manifest a belief in a God separate from us that partakes in a belief of polarity energy. Hence, the word of God comes from us, and it was made active by the movement of our consciousness and desire to manifest the activity of our divine plan to learn wisdom.

The word of God is metaphoric for our own Christ consciousness and is the gateway through which we have come forth from the invisible (within) to the visible (outside). It is through the invisible that we know that we are God, Goddess, Christ, and Satan, all rolled up into "one body of consciousness." But to understand this, we have to journey through many lifetimes of sowing and reaping before we awaken to it.

Chapter 9

UNDERSTANDING THE ASTRAL BODY

In Chapter Seven, I wrote, "to understand the Apocalypse, we have to mention the human body and how it relates to our uniqueness as a souled being." However, to understand all layers of consciousnesses, we have to relate our uniqueness not only to our physical body, but we also need to pay attention to our Astral Body (symbolized by the Church of Smyrna). Therefore, to clarify what John was saying in Revelation 2:8-9, he was not only speaking of himself as Christ, but all souled beings are Christ.

When John spoke about the *"first and the last who once died but now lives,"* Revelation 2:8-9, he was talking about the Christ within us all where we were once much aware *(alive)* of our "I AM" Christ consciousness before we focused out of a lower emotional consciousness (leaving the Garden). And, once we took on the belief of polarity energy, we became dead to any knowing of "who we were at our core essence." However, after journeying through many lifetimes sowing and reaping, there are many of us here on earth who are becoming more and more aware *(alive)* of being a Christ also.

This becomes more understood when our "I AM" Christ consciousness turns its attention to our Astral Body, along with its partner, the Leyden Center of the Physical Body, where our choices form into matter (symbolized by the Church of Smyrna) to experience. It is from our Astral Body where we can identify ourselves as "the first" and "the last," as we were unaware *(once dead)*, and now we are becoming aware again *(alive)*. However, only if we choose!

Channeling of the Ascended Masters on the Apocalypse

It comes from the Leyden Center (Smyrna) in the physical body, the navel or lower-abdomen chakra area, where we have suffered many hardships, lack of understanding, poverty, and many false ideas because of the belief in sin. We have not only held false beliefs about sin and punishment, throughout many lifetimes as our truths, but we have also housed and worshipped the many ego-personalities we have created, good and bad *(members of Satan's assembly)*.

And, since the Leyden Center, symbolized by the Church of Smyrna, is the "seat of our soul," according to [4]Edgar Cayce, then it is associated with our subconsciousness or the Astral Body. Thus, our "I AM" Christ consciousness knows our soul memories and the hardships we have suffered in the physical. When we primarily work with our many ego-personality aspects from the past, and with our consciousness of today (the Beast), then our mind-soul (Adam and Eve) will suffer and starve for more spiritual understanding. This is why many of us leave religions because not enough is given to us about who Christ is other than him being a God we need to worship. Christ is more than just a person to worship.

However, notwithstanding the suffering we experience, our "I AM," Christ consciousness says that our soul is rich with wisdom because of holding the memories of our experiences, good and bad. Therefore, we should never fear our trials and tribulations felt by the physical body because when we learn to let go of our dualistic opposing beliefs, our "I AM" Christ consciousness will crown us with full awakening and understanding. And yet, our "I AM" warns us by saying, if this center allows fear and dual beliefs, such as sin, light, dark, good and bad, to take hold of the seat of our soul (Smyrna), then the energy within our physical body will become stuck.

That is when illnesses become part of our life. Why? Because our "I AM" Christ consciousness promises that if we would stop fearing our existence as a Divine Being, then we will not suffer a second death. Therefore, the second death occurs only when we follow old traditions, habits, a belief in duality, sin, light and dark, and a belief that God created us. Remember, we created ourselves as a God-Goddess also! If this spiritual center, represented by the church of Smyrna, releases within us the belief in the dual principles of opposing energy, like light and dark,

---

4 Edgar Cayce was born in 1877 on a farm in Hopkinsville, Kentucky, and he died in 1945. Edgar Cayce's psychic abilities began as early as his childhood when he first talked to his dead grandfather as well as with other spirits. Mr. Cayce was the most documented psychic of the 20th century, for he gave more than 40 years of his adult life to giving psychic messages to thousands of seekers while in an unconscious state, diagnosing illnesses and revealing past lives, as well as prophecies to come to earth. Mr. Cayce's work is part of the A.R.E. center in Virginia Beach, Virginia.

and our ability to generate fear, then we will never fall short of knowing Christ. Thus, we will never suffer a second death (forgetting) even if we are part of the physical world.

We will always have before us the possibility of falling back into a belief system of good and evil, right and wrong, positive and negative, God and Satan, and life and death, duality because of our upbringing. Therefore, Yeshua and the Ascended Masters ask us to choose our thoughts and beliefs wisely. Know that our Christ consciousness will always strive to bring us the truth about duality and the illusion of sin. Why? It is because we are always in fear, doubt, and blame that result in death. Therefore, for the "I AM" Christ to know our pain, suffering, and tribulations, we must know and learn that we are the Christ experiencing them.

Our divinity allowed us souls to descend *(fall)*, dropping all parts and layers of our consciousness frequency to a level of limitations *(poverty)* to experience life and what is known today as light and dark (opposing energy). Even though we had an exceptional understanding before we left the oneness of "all that was" *(rich)* in the beginning, the abuses we endured by entering nothingness resulted in generating multiple ego-personality aspects of light and dark *(self-styled Jews)*, and how they became our many lifetimes and realities here on earth. As we can see, these ego-personality aspects from past lifetimes can cause us much chaos and confusion if we allow it.

From our many lifetimes past, we have produced a falseness *(slander)* about us that gave way to a lie that became part of our belief system today, and now we claim the lie as our truth. When we blame others for our misfortunes and turn away from taking responsibility, we create belief patterns of good and evil, right and wrong, God and Satan as being real. Thus, we become our description of how we form our many components of multiple personalities *(Satan's Assembly)* clothed in the finest garments *(physical bodies)* of self-deceit. But these aspects of us will be subjected to and examined by the scales of time and space, sowing and reaping, to find the real truth.

And, in Revelation 2:10, *"have no fear of the sufferings to come. The devil will indeed cast some of you into prison to put you to the test; you will be tried for ten (10) days. Remain faithful until death, and I will give you the crown of life."* If we learn to awaken to our Christ consciousness and let go of our dogmatic belief patterns of duality, including our religious traditions, then we too would have no fear because of what we are experiencing with karma today. Why? Because once we awaken to whom we are at our core, we learn to accept what we are experiencing as something that we chose to experience, rather than asking why we are experiencing the condition.

Channeling of the Ascended Masters on the Apocalypse

If we can allow ourselves to come to the awareness that the *"devil"* in Revelation 2:10 is nothing more than the self in our Astral body, introducing *(casting)* ourselves to a physical body that feels like a *"prison"* because of its limitations. That is when we will realize that all we are doing is examining *(testing)* every potential we can imagine experiencing the principle of polarity energy.

In our beginning stages of evolution, or when we first left the oneness of our consciousness (garden) long ago, we had no fear because fear was an unknown product to us at the time. But once we moved our focus and mindfulness (symbolized by Adam and Eve) to an ego-personality consciousness (beastly nature), we took on the belief in sin and that of polarity energy, which causes us to suffer. Because we took on these dual beliefs, fear became the foundation of our focus, and that is when we felt separated from our Christ consciousness.

This newfound fear-consciousness caused you to feel like it was some "devil" banishing *(casting)* you from your "I AM" Christ consciousness, the Goddess. But you were never cast out of any garden (higher consciousness) because, in reality, you are still in the garden today! Why? Because you are always as one consciousness. It is that you just have layered that oneness of consciousness with a host of many ego-personality aspects that feel separate from you.

Please note: Yeshua and the Ascended Masters channeled this message: "Your Christ consciousness, the Goddess, has not banished you from higher consciousness (Garden) like religions teach. It is only the ego-personality side of your consciousness (Satan side) that makes you feel separated, deceiving you into believing you are only human." Therefore, because of this firm belief, it becomes difficult for you to remember who you are, why you are here on earth, and why you are confined to a three-dimensional body *(prison)*. And, a limited one at that!

How do we know when the day comes to step off the incarnating and karmic wheel? We know, by inviting in our own "I AM" Christ consciousness to become one with our human consciousness. Thus, we leave behind the "faith principle that is fear-based" and take up a "knowing trust principle" where we all are God, Goddess, and a Christ rather than looking for Christ. This knowing then sets the pace where we finally integrate all that we are and ever have been and become one again with our own Christ consciousness.

Therefore, the *"period of ten (10) days,"* Revelation 2:10, is symbolic of us experiencing a cycle of many nonphysical and physical lifetimes, learning the wisdom behind our choices by using the Tree of Knowledge of

Good and Evil (polarity energy). Once understood, we then return to our oneness again, but this time we are filled with wisdom and understanding.

The *"remain faithful until death"* (Revelation 2:10) are those series of lifetimes we all have played out while repeatedly journeying through the opposing energy cycle of physical earth, being unaware *(death)* that we are God, and a Christ also. This was our first death! But now, if we so choose, we can create the process where we can become aware *(alive)* that we are God, the Son, Christ, and Satan, all rolled up into being the Almighty. It is symbolic of God-Goddess, and the Christ within us all overcoming our many ego personalities (Satan's assembly) and all that is tied to polarity energy.

Therefore, the time has come to inherit all of what you have learned journeying through time and space, which is an excellent understanding of wisdom. Know that a lot of credit has to go to your rebellious and unruly ego personalities playing in duality because it gave you the freedom to become a sovereign Goddess and Christ in your own right *(the crown of life)*.

In Job 1:12, *"And the Lord said to Satan, 'Behold, all that he has is in your power; only do not lay a hand upon his person.' So, Satan went forth from the presence of the Lord."* The "Lord" is you becoming aware that you are a master and a Christ in your own right. When the Lord, relating to your mind, says to your ego-personality of defiance (Satan), *"all that he has is in your power,"* it comes apparent that your mind is telling you that you are the creator of your many ego-personality aspects of good and evil. Therefore, you have the power (authority) to forgive all personality aspects of your past and present self, and integrate them with your ego-personality of today, symbolized by Job.

When we look at the metaphor of Job and his family, we will find that Job's family was taken down by Satan because the Lord (his mind) expressed (said) to his ruling ego (Satan) that he could not touch his ego of today (Job). Therefore, Satan (our defiant ego of today) went after Job's family (our many ego-personalities or lifetimes past). And, according to scholars, Job's family, including his wife, suffered dearly under the hands of Satan.

Therefore, the symbology here is that Job's family represents our many good and bad ego-personality aspects from past lifetimes, where we suffered dearly because of playing in duality. But now, Job (our ego-personality of today) has reached consciousness where we have the understanding to integrate our past ego-personalities of good and evil as one forgiven. And, when we do, our mind becomes "Lord of Lords" and a God in our own right.

Channeling of the Ascended Masters on the Apocalypse

Once this is understood and realized by us while in the flesh, our Satan consciousness (our ego-personality of today) cannot touch our many past ego-personalities; however, if we do not come to this realization, then like Job's family, all of our many past lifetimes will continue to work from duality. Thus, causing us more pain, suffering, and more lifetimes to be played out here on earth.

Therefore, you are equal to Christ and have the same authority as Christ. And, if you have the same power, then there is no way your rebellious ego nature (Satan) can ever again lead you down the road to destruction even after you've awakened from the mind and ego levels. Therefore, take no fear of Satan trying to steal your soul. "Satan" is just a term used to label your personality lifetimes of past blindness when you were hypnotized to the real truth about the Tree of Knowledge of Good and Evil, being nothing more than polarity energy that is not real anyway.

We all have been suffering for many lifetimes based on a false message. And, by our Christ consciousness, *"not laying a hand upon"* our unruly ego-personality consciousnesses (Satan), we, by way of our mind, have allowed our false ego personalities (Satan assembly) to feel separate from our Christ consciousness. That is when we fell asleep to us having mastership over the mind *("went forth from the presence of the Lord")*.

Now, I am not writing this book to bring you fear, only love. However, if you fail to let go of the illusion of not being a Christ also, then you risk journeying through more lifetimes. How many more lifetimes will it take before you allow yourself to awaken? Well, that is up to you! Understand who you are, and understand that it was you who moved your consciousness through multiple lifetimes, playing with polarity energy, positive and negative. And now, it is up to you, from the mind-soul and physical ego level, to turn loose those old, dogmatic belief systems and return to your Christ consciousness.

Once you do, you become the champion *(victor)* to those who are still asleep in their first death. Therefore, the second death cannot harm you if you learn to let go of sin, Satan, and all of the dualistic thinking, and look at yourself as equal to Christ because you are a Christ in expression. It comes down to trusting in yourself as Christ, the Son, and the Creator, leaving behind any concept of a God above you that created you or a Satan coming to battle Christ for your soul. I know this can be difficult, but I also know it has been done by many others, including Yeshua.

Chapter 10

UNDERSTANDING THE EMOTIONAL BODY

When looking into the *"presiding spirit of Pergamum,"* Revelation 2:12-13, it represents the intellectual-emotional center of the physical body. This is where we, from the adrenal gland (solar plexus chakra), unwisely guard against any doubt that there is a God who will use trial by fire for sinning (karma). All this happens without us realizing that the process is based on the memory of like-minded religious written words to uphold a deceitful set up in a false God to keep us stuck in an emotional consciousness of polarity as being real. Thus, stealing from us the memory of being a Christ.

This is the price we pay for refusing to consider the study of the mind-soul consciousness, *"the one with the sharp, two-edged sword"* (opposing-energy), and how our emotional consciousness keeps us stuck in moving forward in our quest for spiritual enlightenment. It is our mind-soul and emotional consciousness found in Revelation 2:12-13, acknowledging that the solar plexus chakra center of the physical body is where we hold to faith and conviction, on an intellectual level instead of a spirit level, where both God (light) and Satan (dark) feel real to us.

Therefore, this center can be the most dangerous and the most powerful chakra center in the human body. Why? The energy of the solar plexus level (adrenal glands) is where we find the *"two-edged sword"* of justice (karma) for needing to take responsibility for our choices. If the balance is maintained within our emotional consciousness, then the life forces freely cross the solar plexus level each time they pass from our higher to lower consciousness.

Channeling of the Ascended Masters on the Apocalypse

Through this center, we separate the emotional consciousness from our higher Christ-like consciousness. Thus, our emotional consciousness is the deliberator for our mind and defiant ego-personality consciousness. That is why we experience the two-edged sword of justice (law of sowing and reaping). And, it will continue until we finally let go and move past our emotional beliefs in a God that created a Satan that is after our soul. Also, related to Revelation 2:12-13, our mind-soul consciousness is always communicating with our ego-personality, as this center is the birthplace for our anger, impulsive reactions, and evil urges.

All this happens because of our emotional ties to a belief in God that we think created us, is above us, a God to worship, and a God that will send us to hell if we do not do as he says. Therefore, our adrenal area of the physical body is our weakest link when it comes to the enlightenment of our spirit. However, the adrenal gland (solar plexus), symbolized by the Church of Pergamum, is essential to our soul growth.

When we repress or control our gut (intuitive) feelings in this area of our body on any subject built upon polarity energy, positive and negative, we automatically transfer our feelings and thoughts to an intellectual and emotional mindset so powerful that the outcome slows down in rejoining with our Christ consciousness. Thus, we experience more lifetimes.

From Revelation 2:12-13, *"I know you live in the very place where Satan's throne is erected,"* or more known as our emotional consciousness. It is from the Adrenal area of the physical body where we operate from while making choices and decisions when it comes to new truths about spirit. Therefore, we need to be careful about what we accept as truths, for this is the place where polarity energy forces are built upon. Thus, from the seat of our emotional consciousness *(Satan's throne)*, we place all our beliefs about God, Satan, good, bad, right, and wrong into a concept of a reasoning mind. This is where ninety-seven percent of the world population is today in understanding God versus spirit.

Because of the way we act emotionally, using reason as our moral directive, our ego-personality consciousness operates independently from our spirit and mind-soul. Thus, our faith has changed from knowing we are Christ and has been replaced by fearing God. This is signified by *"Antipas"* in Revelation 2:13! It was, and still is today, our intellectual concept of a God who created us, and is outside of us, that makes up the symbolism of Antipas' martyrdom given in Apocalypse. This is also why our faith in God is fear-based, which is very strong with our emotional consciousness. We have so much fear when it comes to God, and is why religions and governments can keep control of us with much ease. And that makes it hard to let go or move forward with new truths.

Antipas was a faithful follower of Yeshua during his days on earth, and despite his ideas in what Yeshua taught about Christ, Antipas did not measure up to those who controlled the earth. These individuals, like most people today, believed in the principle of the intellectual and reasoning mind as the standard for one's faith, power, intelligence, reality, and the truth about Yeshua as the only Christ. Therefore, those who put all faith in a God or a Christ outside of themselves become, without realizing it, part of the Antichrist movement, all because of fear being the default.

As mentioned in Revelation, 2:5–6, *Nicolaitans* is a Greek word that coincides with the Hebrew name Balaam, which belongs to the mental phase of the mind. Since Balaam was a foreigner to the Israelites, the name represents our mental consciousness and how we are likely to experience disagreements and disputes when learning new truths about God-Christ and what is right. This all happens because of us being so obsessed with old, dogmatic, religious beliefs and rituals that we have been taught and have been accepted by our stubborn ego-personality consciousness, symbolized by Israelitish.

When we, from a mental consciousness, strive to keep our religious beliefs and government teachings because of a two-party system, our mind reaches no higher in its expression than the level of our human intellect and reasoning. No person can reach any higher than where he or she has evolved, which is why it may be hard for a person to understand what I am writing here unless that person has reached the consciousness beyond the mind of reasoning. If some of you have come this far and have some understanding of what is written, then you are further along in your evolution than you think.

When we *"follow the teaching of Balaam,"* symbolized by our false need to make God a mystery, we sacrifice our mental and ego consciousnesses of many personalities of light and dark (lifetimes) to worshipping idols, like this God of the Bible, money, power, and politicians.

Balak was the king of Moab, and he was frightened because of Israel's victories. So, he hired Balaam to curse the Israelites, so he might finally defeat them. Therefore, the spiritual significance is that Balak symbolizes the destructive waste of our mixed-up emotional thoughts and errors *(practice fornication)* that rule over the physical mind because of our false dogmatic beliefs.

Remember, we all lost sight eons ago of the human mind refusing to awaken even though it seeks pleasurably understated judgments to undermine, adulterate, and destroy our Israelitish ego thoughts when it comes to knowing the Christ we are. Thus, we follow a false God instead of self as a God and a Goddess! And, it is from this belief in this false God that we continue to struggle to gain a perfect comprehension and realization of new truths about God and Christ.

And, since *Nicolaitans* coincides with the Hebrew name Balaam, it represents our mental phase of the mind that is a foreigner to our many ego-personalities of other lifetimes, symbolized by the Israelites. We, from the emotional level of consciousness, are the guilty ones who cause our pain, sorrows, illnesses, poverty, and lack (always needing) all because of fear. This all happens because of the way we hold to old, dogmatic, religious, and governmental beliefs with God, Satan, and our politicians.

Most of us fail to understand the beliefs we hold today about this God of the Bible, and how it has been rewritten often by kings (governments) and religious leaders of old. And now, these uncompromising teachings are part of our heritage and belief systems. These uncompromising traditions have been taught to us by our parents, their parents before them, our church, and our politicians, as these groups represent again our "Israelitish" side of our ego-personality consciousness. We all cause our happiness, good relationships, abundance, health, and joy, along with our unhappiness, illnesses, and the poverty we experience.

We are the cause by allowing our emotional mind to have control over our lack of trust in the higher self as a Christ. Instead, we continue to see our minds needing help, guidance, and healing from a force outside of us, such as Yeshua. There is no healing we need other than to awaken from our sleep! There is only energy and beliefs that seek release and resolution so we can serve the self in a new way as a Christ also.

We work hard to control our situations, thoughts, and old beliefs because of our upbringing, which creates chaos in our life. We do not realize the many burdens, limitations, and responsibilities we put on ourselves because of the way we were brought up. We even try to control the image of God (who and what God is), and yet, all we are doing is limiting the very nature of who we are as a Christ. Therefore, *"repent"* in Revelation 2:16, is not about going to church, or joining one, or falling to our knees to a false God asking for forgiveness. It is about changing our minds or rethinking our beliefs for control, fear, good and bad, God and Satan, and polarity energy in general.

Repentance is nothing more than choosing thoughts of harmony, unconditional love, being non-judgmental, and accepting ourselves as a Christ and a God-Goddess displaying only compassion for others and yourself, no matter how offensive someone can be toward us. Yeshua did it to the point he was crucified! We adulterate our Christ consciousness and the Crystalline Energy we possess by thinking in dualistic terms when we judge what is right (light) and wrong (dark). And, when we judge another over who is right or wrong, good or bad, democrat or republican, then we are in the intellect and in a reasoning mind.

Therefore, we are not manifesting our life experiences from our "I AM" divine consciousness. We are manifesting them through fear and emotions. Thus, most of the energy that comes into our life is then controlled by the way we think and what we believe to be our truths. Therefore, most controls are based on our past experiences (lifetimes) because of the belief in duality, light, and dark. All of what we experience in life today has been set up in a series of controls that we have put on ourselves because of the way we look at God and Satan as two opposing energies. Thus, controlling the very nature of what we think is right and wrong.

Therefore, to repent is to rethink our position with God, Christ, Satan, and how we control our lives through the means of dual thinking as being real. When we hold onto our human identity as only a name, male, female, and that we are only a democrat or republican, we are trying to control God and our beliefs by restricting our pure energy and preserving our life stories through the physical senses instead of opening ourselves up to our divine senses.

And, as in Revelation 2:16, *"if we do not, our Christ consciousness '(I)' will come to us soon and fight against them with the sword of my mouth."* The words in Revelation 2:16 have nothing to do with God coming after those who do wrong or evil. The real God is unchangeable and unconditional; therefore, the real God never uses power or energy to fight anything. Why, two-fold; First, there is no such thing as power, and second, the real God is actually the Goddess, the "I AM," and she is forever forgiving, having no judgment against you or any soul, even if that soul is forever evil. However, evilness will always catch up to those that use it over others because of the agreed "law of karma."

In the eyes of a real and loving Goddess consciousness, there is no such thing as sin, power, or light versus dark. It is just the "I AM" within you, understanding itself (you) as an extension of the Spirit of One just out playing with polarity energy to learn wisdom and responsibility. We all continue to forget that we have moved into the land of the Tree of Knowledge of Good and Evil, opposing energies, (dimensions), not realizing that we (the mass) have created this polarity dimension to learn wisdom and responsibility through our creations.

Therefore, the religions of the world are selling us a bill of goods when it comes to this God who judges, fights, and acts against us if we disagree with him and his scholars (priest, evangelist, preacher, etc.). Thus, the God of the Bible is no more than an icon and idol, put in place by those in authority to maintain their power and control over us. The word God itself in the new Bible is derived from the word *Jehovah*, a name that came from the reptilian race eons ago.

The name Jehovah is one of God's names in the Bible, and in the Authorized Version, it is improperly translated as "the Lord" (Exodus 6:2–3; Psalm 83:17). In the American Standard Version, the name Jehovah is given where "Jah" occurs in the Hebrew text. Moses said in Exodus 3:14–15 that "Yahweh" is God's name, and he told Moses his name means "I Am That I AM." Hebrew students say that the original God is JHVH (Yahweh), which means the ever-living, male-female energy and consciousness within us all.

In the Old Testament, the "I AM that I AM" is symbolically describing Yahweh, and yet the name was changed in the Bible to Jehovah because of highlighting good versus evil. In the New Testament, Jehovah is called Christ. However, according to Yeshua and the Ascended Masters, the God named Jehovah was changed by us long ago to control the narrative of a God of polarity by advocating the belief in judgment, sin, punishment, love, hate, and good and evil to maintain their power over us.

However, Moses said God was the "I AM That I AM, meaning, this is my name forever, and this is my memorial unto all generations. Therefore, your real name, my real name, and everyone else's real name is Yahweh, the "I AM That I AM," for we all have no other name than "I AM That I AM." Therefore, the expression *"I will come to you soon and fight against them with the sword of my mouth,"* Revelation 2:16, is not about Yeshua or Yahweh is the God of the Bible. It is how we all express in words our belief in a false God named Jehovah, a God of polarity and power as our truth.

Although without realizing it, it all comes from our emotional consciousness and dogmatic religious beliefs, we must reap what we have sown because our "I AM" Christ consciousness cannot fight against anything or anyone. Why? It is because of our "I AM" is forever unchangeable, forgiving, and unconditional, even to those who commit great evils against us.

"Fighting against them with the sword of my mouth" is nothing more than us experiencing karma because we are following a false god. Through karma, we set the stage a long time ago to bring in the "universal law of destiny," which is represented by the name Seth in Genesis. Thus, it

was our own "I AM" Christ-spirit that set this law into action because, from a higher level, we knew down deep that someday we would follow a false God. Remember, the real God-Goddess is the self at a higher understanding. The higher self knows that polarity energy is false and is not real, where this God of the Bible is all about duality, therefore false.

It was all souled beings who placed this law of destiny (karma) in our path of evolution to help expand our understanding, wisdom, and consciousness. And, we accomplished this task by splitting our ego side of our consciousness into billions and billions of potentials and false personality aspects of good and evil to experience our choices. Therefore, it is always our stubborn ego-personality consciousness that is the judge and jury of what we desire to experience in each lifetime and not our mind-soul.

Know that you have given yourself a name, an occupation, and a story to follow in each lifetime that you have had on earth to learn wisdom and responsibility for your choices. Thus, you become a much wiser God-Goddess than before you left higher consciousness. Therefore, the Beast found in Apocalypse, in its sincerest form, is you in the flesh playing out of a personality to learn wisdom and responsibility. It is our stubborn beastly nature, our beliefs, and controls causing our heartaches, and not some devil outside of us.

Once we understand this, we will be ready to receive our inheritance (being a sovereign God in our own right) and feel the throne of our "I AM" descending into our physical consciousness in this lifetime. The *"hidden manna"* in Revelation 2:17 is our long-lost forgotten "I AM" Christ consciousness and the Crystalline energy of neutrality that arises with it, as being our solution consciousness. The Ascended Master Tobias called it, "Dei un Gnost," or simply Gnost.

This Gnost consciousness, along with its pure neutral Crystalline energy, is a collection of creative solutions to our many explored experiences, good and bad, that comes into our physical consciousness when we move to a higher energy frequency and consciousness. This solution (Gnost) consciousness is useful for bringing in healing for our mind, physical body, and our many ego-personalities of the past. We have a spirit (Christ) consciousness, a mind-soul consciousness, and an ego-personality consciousness, and all layers are part of our physical body of today.

And now, when awakened, we can bring in our solution consciousness for healing, represented by the *"hidden manna."* This solution consciousness is the merlin (miracle) part of our consciousness that brings us solutions from beyond the limitations of our emotional mind and ego personalities that keep us stuck in the belief that good and evil, right and wrong, are real. By tapping into our solution (Gnost) consciousness, we come to a knowing, and not a belief, that we are a Christ also. And, from that knowing comes healing, abundance, and joy.

We can find more about this Gnost consciousness in Revelation 7:1, where it relates to the *"four angels standing at the four corners of the earth."* However, for now, let us examine Revelation 2:17, *"I will also give him a white stone upon which is inscribed a new name, to be known only by him who receives it."* Yeshua and the Ascended Masters are speaking about the trust we need in ourselves as a Christ rather than the need to have faith in something that cannot be understood from the mind level. That is when we will learn to tap into our solution (Gnost) consciousness and learn about "timelines," as the meaning is also called "past life regression." Thus, healing begins!

According to Master Tobias, our solution (Gnost) consciousness is the fourth component of our total beingness, alongside the body, mind-soul, and our spirit. It is the part of us that never forgot the solutions to everything we created, good and bad. Therefore, built within our own consciousness, there is a divine solution to every situation we created and experienced in the physical. But before we can bring in this solution (Gnost) consciousness of magic back into our lives, we first must move beyond the belief about some God outside of us created us.

Chapter 11

UNDERSTANDING THE ETHERIC-MENTAL BODY

When it comes to the *"angel of the church in Thyatira,"* Revelation 2:18, the reference is to our thymus gland in the physical body and how it signifies growth and expansion. This area of our body calls out to us to intensify our work since we are a Christ. By trusting in ourselves as a Christ, we remove what is "faith" from our mind and replace it with "trust" and "no fear." Understand, when reconnecting to the divine solution (Gnost) consciousness, we have the vision and the knowing of being Christ because we have been tested in the furnace of justice (incarnations). And now, our thymus gland (angel), the heart chakra, has charity, trust, patience, service, and compassion, with the most recent works being greater than the first.

We cannot employ our solution (Gnost) consciousness using the mind of old energy and beliefs. Why? Because the mind and ego right now are not functioning with the Christ realm. Our solution (Gnost) consciousness can be used only through the "I AM" Christ consciousness. And, we bring it into our earthly consciousness when we accept ourselves as a Christ. Thus, our three-dimensional consciousness becomes "one body of consciousness," where our *"new name,"* like Moses, is "I AM that I AM" (Yahweh). Once we open up to who we are at our core, our new name, the "I AM That I AM," then establishes itself as part of our mind and ego-personality consciousnesses as the chosen one.

However, knowing this and being accompanied by our new name, "I AM," we are still part of the earth realm simultaneously. But we can become our energetic signature because we know now about our solution consciousness and our new expansional energy for liberating our good and evil creations. It is learning that the concept of evil (dark) and good (light) has been only a form of control by others, and now we can see it for what it is, an illusion put in place by our mind and by others so as for us to experience life and learn about our choices.

And, from this *"new name,"* "I AM That I AM Christ," we get to understand the mystery and the wisdom behind God, Goddess, Christ, and Satan, as did Moses, Yeshua, and John. However, this means nothing to anyone still playing with the polarity energy of good and evil (old earth) as being real. It is about you, the one who will say, "I AM the Christ" that have dedicated yourself to sowing and reaping through many lifetimes, taking responsibility for your actions.

So now, if you so choose, you can integrate your many-layered personality consciousnesses into "one body of consciousness." Thus, establishing *(inscribed)* within you an awareness of introducing yourself to a New Expansional Energy of Four (New Earth) as something that will be ever-changing *(evolving)* daily. However, your "I AM" has one major issue with your thymus center (gland), referenced by Revelation 2:19. *"I know your deeds, love, faith, service, and your patient endurance."*

If you live life without an understanding that love is unconditional, then you risk understanding that love is only gratification and pleasure from this center. And this is represented by the false prophet Jezebel in Revelation 2:20, whose motto is to get all you want no matter how you obtain it, even though it is false love. Living through your four-lower vibrating consciousnesses with no thought of any spiritual principles that deny the existence of sin and opposing energy as an illusion, then your "I AM" gives a warning.

If we do not look at the heart center about rethinking *(repent)* our beliefs about polarity energy, then we will experience great suffering each time we journey through more lifetimes. Again, understand that we are a Christ also! Meaning, everything needs to be looked at as unconditional love and neutralized energy, without exception, even if we believe it is wrong for a person to create evil. By not understanding sin, punishment, good and bad, or anything of duality, to be a mere illusion created by us souls eons ago to learn wisdom, then we will experience a greater tribulation because we believe in duality as being real. No wonder everything we experience seems so real, and yet it is an illusion.

Therefore, as we pass through the cycle of lifetimes, there does come a time when we will seek the throne (Christ within). And, when we do, our

"I AM" (Yahweh) promises us that if this center changes, it will bring us the *"morning star"* to help balance our energy and beautify our life. And, of course, the "morning star" is referenced by Satan or the Devil. Does this surprise you?

As our "I AM" moves us toward the truth of being created in the divine image and likeness of the Spirit of One (Father-Mother God-Goddess), we awaken to this truth within our heart chakra of balance (the morning star). Then our spirit, mind-soul, ego, and our long-lost solution Gnost consciousness, along with our many ego-personality aspects (the beast), become balanced. Thus, we become a body of "oneness" living out of the highest of consciousness.

The Apocalypse is about you, from a physical understanding, moving beyond your mind, emotions, polarity energy, and into accepting yourself as the source and giver of the message. Always know your mind right now is the Anti-Christ and your ego is the Beast (Satan) until you awaken to whom you indeed are as a Christ in this lifetime. Once you learn of the message, then your ego (the Beast) is transformed from being the "Son of Man" in Revelation 2:18 to where you, from the mind-soul, become the Son of God and a Christ in the flesh, who now understands your authority as a creator.

When we express our choices and bring judgment upon what we manifest by journeying through many lifetimes working with polarity energy as our fundamental belief system (tree of knowledge of good and evil), we do become passionate about our sowing and reaping *(blaze like fire)*. Thus, fulfilling our desire to grow in wisdom and to understand why we experience karma *(trial by fire)*. Therefore, the symbolization of *"feet"* in Revelation 2:18 represents our many ego-personalities, physical and non-physical, and how we have been evolving *(polished)* in consciousness each time we come to earth.

And because of it, we do reach a place in consciousness where we become self-assured *(brass)* that we have been purified *(refined)* by fire, and we learn to let go of our old dogmatic belief in polarity energy (sin and punishment, good and bad). Maybe some of us feel we are not moving forward in a spiritual sense, but we are moving forward steadily, gaining ground with every breath we take.

Therefore, who knows our work (revelations) better than our own "I AM" consciousness? Hence, who knows *"your deeds, your love and faith,"* and to whom you have *"served"* better than our "I AM" Christ-spirit? It is you who knows you better than anyone else. Not even Yeshua (Jesus) knows you better than you know yourself. Think of it this way: Each time you have completed a lifetime and have come around again to experience another lifetime, you continuously (without realizing it) have expanded your consciousness to where you can recognize the Christ as you.

Also, our "I AM" knows how we have been patient and how much we have endured over many lifetimes, which is why now, we can let go of our mental perception of a God and Christ outside of us that created us. Thus, know then that some of us are on the verge of awakening. The only thing holding us back is that we are afraid to let go of our heritage, traditions, and family roots. Know that we have been incarnating into the same ancestry bloodline for lifetimes, which means we have known our parents, children, aunts, uncles, and cousins before.

The DNA bloodline of our ancestors attracts and pulls us right back into the family tree when we are ready to incarnate. And this is why we act, look, think, and believe like our family members. However, even though some of us have carried the family DNA for many lifetimes, some of us are ready to step out of the family tree and move forward with different beliefs. We know these family members because they act, think, and behave differently than their siblings.

By awakening to whom we are as a Christ also, we do reach a lifetime where we release our karma of the family bloodline, which then frees us from our debts and obligations to our family tree and everyone else. Therefore, if you are ready to let go of the family beliefs, then trust yourself as a Christ. Know that you have persisted and endured your journey through many lifetimes sowing and reaping. And now, you have gained the ability to override your barriers of dual thinking, the family bloodline, and your obligations to them and the world.

Trust yourself and move into the wisdom of expansional energy where your last works are greater than they were before you left higher consciousness (garden). Make a clear choice and give yourself permission to free yourself and become a sovereign Christ-like being in your own right. Remember, the limitations you are experiencing right now are due to your family beliefs and the fear generated from those beliefs. And when you transform these old beliefs and fear, you change your past by healing your past, thus creating new potentials for yourself that will bring you joy, abundance, health, and happiness in your present lifetime.

Many of us have gone through lifetimes releasing and integrating, and yet, are we ready for a new understanding of Christ? For some of us, it may happen in this lifetime. But for others, it may happen in another lifetime before they can complete the cycle of polarity energy and move to a higher frequency. Once we accomplish this in the flesh, then the ego-personality aspect of today becomes greater than the first ego-personality aspect when we first moved out of our higher consciousness frequency (Garden) long ago (Revelation 2:19).

The cross of Yeshua is a divine symbol of us humans becoming balanced and a sovereign God/Christ in our own right in this lifetime if we are ready to let go of old DNA beliefs and the fear attached to them. The cross is a sacred symbol where we have placed part of ourselves in the flesh (ground) and the other parts and pieces in other realms. However, religions use the cross as a symbol of suffering where we reason with sin as something real instead of understanding it as our divine plan to become sovereign. Even today, most of us believe we must suffer to get to heaven. Don't you think it is time to take yourself off the cross and let go of this old idea?

Religions use the symbol of the cross to show how much Yeshua suffered for our sins, and that keeps us emotionally tied to our family, the belief in sin, and suffering. We cannot reconnect to our "I AM," our solution (Gnost) consciousness, and higher understanding if we keep on believing in sin, suffering, death, and punishment. It is time for us to realize that the "I AM" within is unconditional and unchangeable when it comes to love, and compassion for our many created ego-personality aspects playing with the polarity energy. The real Christ, the higher you, has no desire to see your ego or body suffer. So, take yourself down off the cross and let go of your fear-based faith.

As far as Yeshua and the Ascended Masters are concerned, when religions still show Yeshua on the cross, it represents man refusing to let go of his suffering and struggling with the belief in sin, punishment, and polarity energy. And this is why the Ascended Masters mention in Revelation 2:20, symbolically speaking, of us maintaining our way of life through the process of rational thinking and the perception of polarity energy as being real. Know that we became the founder (prophet) of the life we now are living today and not some God above us.

For example, the *"woman Jezebel, who calls herself a prophetess"* in Revelation 2:20, symbolizes our consciousness acts, the feminine side of us, giving life to what we are experiencing today, good and bad. We are not just one physical body or that we have only one life to live. We all are a multidimensional being having many bodies of consciousnesses.

The *"woman Jezebel"* was the daughter of Ethbaal, king of the Sidonians and wife of Ahab, king of Israel (I Kings 16:31). Jezebel was an adulterer, representing the uncontrolled and raging passions of the ego side of one's consciousness. And, when the ruling tendencies of our many ego-personality aspects (lifetimes) are blended in the intellect (represented by King Ahab), the unchecked desires of the ego-personality become widespread to the point of adulterating our own pure energy and creating multiple ego personalities (lifetimes) to experience life. Thus, our soul consciousness of responsibility (Eve) is then involved in giving us lessons *(teaching)* in sorrow, struggle, and suffering.

Therefore, we are deceiving *(misleads)* ourselves into a belief that we are only human males or females. And this is nurturing *"an altar for Baal in the house of Baal"* (1 Kings 16:32). Jezebel can also symbolize the ruling emotions on the physical level, deceiving us into believing in a God and a Satan outside of us as being real. Jezebel met a violent death in her time, which represents our passion and appetite for an ego nature, and these aspects eventually burn themselves out because of karma (II Kings 9:30–37). These unchecked ego-personality aspects of immorality, which have played in the dark as our past lifetimes, continue to deceive us today without even realizing it is happening. Fear indicates that we are being played with by others.

To *"play the harlot"* in Revelation 2:20 does not, as we might think, involve adultery or fornication. The word *harlot* means we have mixed our pure god energy of light through our mind and soul consciousness of responsibility (the feminine) with ideas and beliefs using polarity energy (light and dark, good and bad). And, because of it, we have had many lifetimes and experiences playing with the forces of positive and negative as a belief. The complaint coming from our "I AM" is how we use our energy of neutrality and adulterate it by involving ourselves so profoundly with the mental processes of emotional and rational thinking; thus, creating for ourselves many false beliefs (represented by Ahab).

We have consistently brought to life and manifested what we believed as our truths even as far back as our first belief in the bite of the apple. Therefore, the *"eating of foods"* (like the apple, for example) in Revelation 2:20 is symbolic of us humans giving life to many thoughts and lifetimes carved out of false images *(idols)*; and then worshipping them as something real. And this is why we worship this God of the Bible as a supreme deity and why we fear him, not realizing he comes from the beliefs of all these worn-out ego-personality aspects from past lifetimes. And this is also why we need time *"to repent"* (Revelation 2:21).

This means we need to give ourselves a time to reach an understanding as to why it takes many incarnations to rethink our position with duality (tree of knowledge of good and bad). By thinking or reconsidering this polarity energy as a creation for us to acquire wisdom, and not that it was created for punishment, we begin to accept unconditional love and compassion for ourselves and others as the root of our consciousness.

However, if we refuse to rethink our position on the use of polarity energy, we will continuously manifest and experience suffering, such as diseases, poverty, and bad relationships, all because we are following a consciousness *(her harlotry)* of dogmatic beliefs. The word "harlotry" comes from the word "harlot," which is not really about women of bad character; rather, it represents human consciousness. Nowadays, the word refers to a particular woman, but at one time, it was used to refer to all of humankind. The word "harlot" also was called a juggler or jester of either gender. But, by the close of the seventeenth century, its usage had disappeared.

That is when the meaning of "harlot" came to be associated only with females. Then it was moved on and used for a system or policy by which a political unit is governed. Never the less, the word "harlotry" now represents the whole human race and how all organized groups, including religions, use dual-energy, fear, and judgment to create acts that defy what the human race considers moral standards, such as stealing, killing, and not caring about doing wrong. And this is also tied to the kings (governments) of the earth, for they are the ruling ego-personalities who play out the collective belief systems and the moral standards of the people.

Therefore, "harlotry" speaks of the judgment or the rebalancing (repentance) of our dogmatic and unbending beliefs that emotionally create unending conditions of positive and negative experiences for us to follow. And it is also why most of the population supports and follows the Anti-Christ and the Beast represented in the Apocalypse.

Know what determines the power of any government, dictator, or religion is its people. For example, if the people (human consciousness) did not support the political system, the Cabal, or religion, then it would not exist. Once human consciousness awakens to the truth, one is Christ, then the political system, to whom we know as the Cabal, and religion, as we know it, will fall. Thus, we would gain back our power and authority as a Christ in our own right.

Have you ever heard the expression, "You made your bed, now lie in it"? Well! Revelation 2:22-23, is the proficiency of our many past personality aspects, good and bad, and they are about lifetimes where we played with the dark forces. And now, our "I AM" Christ consciousness promises to give us the time and space to work out our karmic conditions. Therefore, time, space, and incarnations have become the avenue for us to measure the choices we have made in each lifetime. Thus, helping us understand our choices and the purpose of taking responsibility for them.

Let it be known it was our "I AM" Christ consciousness that encouraged us to move from a higher frequency consciousness to a lower one. And then, to adulterate the Crystalline God Energy of Light purposely so we could experience our choices to learn wisdom. And, to accomplish this activity in consciousness, we all created and took on the belief in polarity energy, fear, sin, and punishment as a divine plan. Not that we had to experience intense suffering (sowing and reaping); we just chose it because of the wisdom we would gain from our choices.

It was because of our strong belief in vibrational energy, positive and negative, where we humans, from the rational mind and ego level, continued to adulterate this pure universal neutral god energy of light in complete defiance. We did it by creating more ego-personality aspects *(children)* of ourselves to play in the dark until we, the creator, put an end to it *("put her children to death")*.

We all have journeyed through many lifetimes, placing our lost stubborn and disobedient lifetimes in the shadow of our divine consciousness. And today, we encounter them as our thoughts because they live within us, even after their death in the physical. And this is why most of us fear Satan: because we are running from our past lifetimes. We all have personality aspects of ourselves from which we have done some terrible things, and we are not willing to admit it. These dark personality aspects are dead to us because we are not willing to allow ourselves to let them into our consciousness today.

Therefore, these ego-personality aspects of other lifetimes are still in the land (realm) of darkness, and they are again playing their games because we will not accept them as our creations. We deny them because we cannot believe that we would do anything that would defy our place with God. Some of these dark ego-personality aspects seek us out, requiring that we take responsibility for them. They are our creations, and all they are seeking is for us to accept them as our creations.

Then we can release them with love, honor, and compassion.

We also deny them because of the teachings of today are never to include the dark to be part of our life. And yet, no one seems to ask the question, "How can God be only light if darkness exist?" When churches teach that God is light and Satan is dark, we will always express our beliefs and judgments in the same manner. We forget that light and dark need each other, as do positive and negative because nothing light or dark could exist without the depth they both bring to our understanding and experiences.

An excellent example of this is how we use the poles of a battery (positive and negative) to bring us pleasure and discontentment. Therefore, the light (positive) and the dark (negative) work together to help us all. Light and dark work under the same principle as a battery, where positive and negative work together to benefit experiencing something. By observing light and dark and the way they balance and complement each other through time and space, it becomes apparent that the light (good) and dark (bad) creations we have expressed through many lifetimes have given us the wisdom and balance we hold in memory right now.

Thus, through the measuring of our consciousness, our choices, and our incarnations, we gain complete freedom. And, by denying or rejecting our dark creations, we suffocate our energy, putting it out of balance. When we are not willing to rethink *(repent)* our belief in a God of judgment, sin, and punishment, then the forces of our human nature and our choices and actions must be brought to bear through the application of incarnations (trials and tribulations).

Therefore, it was the mass consciousness (all souls) that chose to test the fire of justice using the physical body, polarity, and earth as the vehicle for purification. It is a system where we souls will come to reach a new level of understanding where we move our mental consciousness beyond the dual forces of light and dark and into a new neutralized consciousness.

It is our "I AM" Christ consciousness that explores *(searches)* all the response patterns of our memories, getting to know the essence of all that we have created. Whether these thoughts, beliefs, ideas, and desires were good or bad made no difference to our "I AM" because all that mattered was that we played them out. We have transmitted and conveyed what we have learned as the seven building blocks (all the churches) of our total consciousness and our physical body, and these building blocks are:

1. Desiring
2. Choosing
3. Reasoning
4. Growth
5. Belief in power
6. Relationships
7. Responsibility, which unblocks our belief in light and dark, and then brings balance while we are still part of the flesh.

Therefore, *"I am the searcher of hearts and minds,"* written in Revelation 2:23, that created the purpose behind whatever I do in life, good and bad. And I, myself, am the creator of my many personality aspects (children), and I sentence *"each of them what their works deserve"* throughout many lifetimes. However, this does not mean we are saved by our incarnations or what we do here on earth in this lifetime. It is about what we do with the influences that we have created during our many lifetime choices, beliefs, and actions.

In other words, we will be given precisely what we have built up in memory as we journey through time and space incarnating; whether it is sowing or reaping, it makes no difference to our "I AM."

When looking into Revelation 2:24-29, Yeshua and the Ascended Masters are speaking of our mental consciousness, symbolized by the Church of Thyatira and that of our Thymus Gland in the physical body. That is where our growth and expansion of our consciousness come from. It is our mind level of consciousness where we *"uphold the teachings"* of polarity energy, good and evil, as being real, and placing us in the position where we *"know nothing of the deep secrets of Satan* (our ego-personality)." Thus, this is where the relationship to our "I AM" Christ consciousness *"places no further burden"* on our mind and ego consciousness.

It is because our "I AM" *"holding fast to what we have"* in memory, good and evil until we are ready to face ourselves as a Christ. And, once we are prepared to meet our good and bad choices, our "I AM" will redeem them as not real, releasing us from the belief in sin and punishment. Thus, this is the true meaning behind Yeshua (our own Christ consciousness) taking on the sins of the world. Yeshua was the example of the Christ within us all taking on our choices (sins) and holding them until we are ready to release them as experiences to learn wisdom and not as committing sins. The sins of humankind are not so much what we did in life but rather what we continue to believe in now, a God who judges and only loves when worshipped.

The *"deep secrets of Satan"* is not about a single character outside of us or about an angel that fell from grace. It is what has been chosen as polarity energy and applying it to our past lifetimes to our present moment. It has been our inharmonious, dogmatic belief system, or what we call sins, that has given us tremendous growth, wisdom, and the expansion of our consciousness to a higher frequency, and not the worshipping of Yeshua or God as we believe.

As we journey through time and space, lifetime after lifetime, learning about the forces of polarity, our soul consciousness of responsibility (the Eve principle) holds onto what we have declared our truths. And then, at a suitable time, the wisdom of what we have learned is fed right back to us, our mind, for resolution. Therefore, the time will come when we realize that our truths and lies are tied to our mind of reason. And, when we recognize that our dark creations (lifetimes of doing bad) carry the same energy as our light creations (lifetimes of doing good) and that our mind rejects our dark creations as if we have done something wrong, then we can release that tied-up blocked energy within us.

Thus, the law of cause-and-effect is fulfilled; therefore, we will no longer be under its jurisdiction. And this is when we can release our diseases, poverty, and our bad relationships and accept ourselves as worthy of health, money, and good loving relationships. Once we become victorious and move beyond the belief in good and evil, we expand our consciousness to the point of letting go of those old, dogmatic beliefs and the memories tied to them, symbolized by the word, *nations* in Revelation 2:26-28. And that is when we will be ready to let go of any guilt or shame associated with our memories of good and evil. And then, healing can come into our life.

We *"will rule them with an iron rod,"* when we come into our Mastership while in the flesh. And this happens when we, from the mind level, overcome the belief in polarity energy and how we look at our light and dark creations as real. By letting go of our old, dogmatic beliefs and our dual thinking, we inherit the authority of our "I AM That I AM" identity, which places us in a position to heal ourselves from all illness and poverty.

When we awaken to the wisdom of our successes *(smashed)* that we have held for so long within our memories, as failures, we will feel our divinity come into our life. And that is when the mysteries of God, Christ, and Satan will open up to us. As this is *"the morning star,"* the Satan within us, allowing us to reconnect with our "I AM" Christ consciousness once we complete our work here on Earth. Therefore, *"whoever has ears ought to hear what the Spirit says to the churches"* (Revelation 2:29). If we have an open mind and heart about who God is and or isn't, we will eventually discover that God is here in the flesh as the self.

Therefore, put no other Gods before you, not even Yeshua, because you are part of the Spirit of One (Godhead) that gave Yeshua life. Your ego personality of today (who you think you are) becomes fulfilled when you know that you are part of the great, infinite energy that Christ represents and that you are not limited to only your human self. If you confront your fears and your belief in what is not real, then out of the blue, you will have ears to hear (feel) and eyes to see (understand) the real meaning behind the Book of the Revelation.

Chapter 12

UNDERSTANDING THE INTUITIVE BODY

In Revelation 3:1, the "*angel of the Church of Sardis*" writes this: *"the one who has the seven spirits of God and the seven stars says this: 'I know the works that you have the reputation of being alive, but you are dead.'"* The Church of Sardis is not only about the thyroid gland and the intuitive body, but it also relates to the consciousness of communications, dominion, the activity of free will (control), and how we carry out the belief structure of power as being real.

Because of our strong belief in power, we use our free will and communication skills to measure our importance; spiritually, intellectually, along with our ideals and how they rank in life. When we left Higher Consciousness (first creation-Garden) long ago for the first time, we felt a sense of uniqueness. Hence, from that point, we felt a sensation deep within that is understood today as power. And, this power belief is enlightened even more, all because of the belief that free will is something real. And yet, power and free will are only mere illusions.

Therefore, the *"angel of the church in Sardis"* is the thyroid gland or throat chakra, sometimes called the artist's chakra. This chakra of creative expression is located at the center of the throat, and it relates to the neck, vocal cords, and thyroid gland. And the throat area of the body is the communication center and the higher center of creativity because it represents self-expression, creative expression, purpose, and our successes in the material world. By balancing this chakra center, we can release tension and anxiety; thus, allowing full expression, higher understanding, and intelligent thoughts to flow through us without blocking the energy because of judgment. The color associated with the throat chakra is blue.

Also, since this chakra center relates to the throat, speech, and our free will, it is associated with our divine plan (will) as well. The throat chakra is very sensitive, and if it is kept down by force because of our dualistic beliefs, it becomes blocked, and our energy cannot flow freely. This means our creativity and expression become inactive or chaotic.

"The one who has the seven spirits of God and the seven stars" in Revelation 3:1 is symbolic of our total consciousness and the seven energy centers given in Revelation 1:11, as the seven building blocks of the physical body. These seven building blocks (chakras) are controlled by the endocrine system in the body with the belief in having free will. Our Divine Plan (Will) is the motivating force that keeps us expressing and expanding. And, it will always concede and acknowledge our free will (even though an illusion) as having great qualities because of it tied to all levels of our consciousnesses, including the physical body.

The illusion of free will helps to express our dogmatic beliefs linked to the mind as something powerful and intelligent. Therefore, without realizing it, we are acting upon them in keeping ourselves in line with our "divine plan" (will) to know all there is to know about duality. Because of our intellect and how strongly we believe in free will, it becomes ranked as the controlling factor in our life. And, because of it, we believe that our activities in life are not corrupt, tainted, or dishonored.

But this center (throat chakra) is dead to the real truth and is imperfect because of the belief that "divine will" comes from a God outside of us. Well, it doesn't! Our "divine plan" comes from our higher consciousness because it desires to know all things about polarity energy (playing opposites) and how it becomes wisdom. Thus, this center needs to awaken to the real truth because it is and has been closer to death than we realize. Now, how to strengthen and awaken the throat chakra to the real truth is to understand that "free will" and "divine will" are the same, for they work together, helping us learn how to awaken from our sleep.

Once we realize that "free will" is part of the forces of duality, and that divine will is the trust center of the "I AM," then our Christ consciousness will declare to us, while in the flesh, that we are the Creator, the Father-Mother, the Son, and the Christ, and that all of our past ego-personality aspects (lifetimes) of good and bad are the angels that bring us closer to the real truth. The words from our mouth, the thoughts that come from our mind, and our feelings within our heart center need cleansing of self-exaggeration, self-glorification, and self-exaltation. Why? Because everything we speak comes from dualistic thinking.

Channeling of the Ascended Masters on the Apocalypse

Thus, if we desire to commune with our "I AM," we must allow the channeling of our "divine plan (will)" to flow through all seven endocrine glands without the deceptiveness of our illusionary "free will" of the mind blocking its message because of dual thinking. The throat center is the projector of our words, and these words can heal or harm us because of a deep belief that "free will" and duality are real. This center, acting in unison with our "divine plan" (will), can transform the vibrational polarized energy of the seven church centers (endocrine system) to an expansional energy of four where we lead ourselves to our divine consciousness.

Remember, once we asked the question, "Who am I?" And, when doing so, we birthed an outer masculine consciousness with an ego (no matter if male or female) that became the explorer, adventurer, and creator of everything that has been created since we left higher consciousness. And this includes our many dark creations as well and what we judge as wrong or evil.

Man (male or female) has been taught that God is an all-powerful male entity that sits in a place called heaven, waiting for the day to judge us. My friends, according to Yeshua and the Ascended Masters, there is no such God. This male entity, the God of the Bible, has been so imprinted within our minds that we now believe he holds all energy of creation to himself. Well! There is no such God that holds all judgment, or power over us, or who governs our life. No such God is separate from us or has forgotten us, but there is a God-Goddess within us all who has sparked our consciousness to explore all possibilities of life. Therefore, the God we seek is self.

From our mind-soul level of consciousness, the second creation, where "all that was," was once "one consciousness," we then transformed it into "all that is today," a consciousness of multiple parts and pieces of the self that are spread throughout the omniverse. Therefore, "all that was" *(heaven)* exists no longer because we souled beings have transformed the Spirit of One and this universal God energy of light into "all that is today."

Because of this "act in consciousness," we had brought our "I AM" Christ consciousness to new places, heights, and dimensions that never existed before we left higher consciousness (home). And this is why our higher consciousness (heaven) is no longer the way it was.

This second creation brought about by our mind-soul and ego-personality consciousness of many, it is what the Bible describes as the abyss. However, Yeshua and the Ascended Masters call it our playground where we come to experience polarity energy of good and evil to appreciate the question, "Who am I?" Also, the second creation became a place where we souled beings entered into our creator-ship training in the flesh to meet every situation in life, good and bad, that we could imagine. And, we have been doing this since we left our higher consciousness (Garden) long ago.

We have been in creator-ship training, playing with opposing energy in various ways that give us the feeling of having power, a free will, and an intelligent center second to none. This power, and the illusion of free will, felt so strong that we souls created stars, galaxies, universes, planets, and even the Earth. We used this power, free will, and our intelligent center, not only to create but to control and destroy. And, because of this intuitive feeling, we became addicted and exhilarated to where we wanted more and more of it.

This feeling of more, as represented by Adam and Eve's biting the apple, became our downfall as we souls stole energy from one another no matter what it took to get it. And this is why we have war, murder, theft, manipulation, rape, lying, blame, judgment, greed, envy, and lust for power. I could go on and on! However, no matter what we did, our 'I AM," divine Oversoul holds the memory of all our choices, actions, power, intelligence, and our redemption. And this is why it takes our free will (that comes from our mind) to allow our divine plan (will) to move those memories down to our physical level.

And now, because of our strong belief in free will, it takes us, from the "I AM," to stimulate our soul memories into action where we, from the mind and physical level, can remember that power, free will, intelligence, and the secret of energy that is universal and everlasting. Therefore, we can never run out of energy. And yet, we try so hard to steal it. Why do we steal it? The answers lie within the message of this book. And all we have to do to tap into the message is to allow free will to integrate with our divine plan without any interference coming from our beliefs, mind, and ego-personalities.

Knowing our work by our reputation represents our life in this physical world, coming into the knowledge that everything outside of us is an illusion, including our physical body, sin, polarity energy, intelligence, and how we look at power and our position in the church. And this is why humankind has been battling the illusion of power and their intellect for so long.

We all have fallen into a human belief that we must destroy everything that is not understood from a reasoning level. For example, the teaching of religion and how one practices his/her beliefs is always in conflict with others who strongly believe that their faith is the correct religion. It is the same with politics! Therefore, they will always try to discredit or destroy one another, even to the point of killing in the name of God and Country.

Fear of the unknown or misunderstanding God has been pushed aside as being dark and evil, which is why people will not open their hearts or minds to other possibilities. We stay with old thinking without realizing we do evolve. Even God and the Universe cannot remain stagnated; they too must grow and expand. So, most of us continue to fight the light and the dark (unknown-ignorance) as something real, and all that it does is create the barriers that prevent us from integrating our Christ consciousness with our human identity.

When we separate the good (light) and the bad (dark) within ourselves, because of the fear of not going to heaven, this prevents us from experiencing the joys and the miracles of life and heaven. Therefore, when the darkness of night falls upon us, we have become afraid of the dark, and what we cannot understand generates more fear. This fear of the dark is nothing more than our soul memories bringing out the activities and dramas that have led us into creating many lifetimes of doubt, limitations, guilt, and shame over the actions we have chosen. And this is the metaphoric presentation of the apple and being kicked out of the garden. The result is the creation of blame onto others for what we feel deep within ourselves.

The symbol of the apple became the icon for sin, fear, and the darkness that we felt inside, without realizing it came from our rebellious ego nature, known as our Satan personality. This blame game grew larger and larger through time, and that is when we hid from what we did not understand or like about ourselves. We have never sinned from higher consciousness because it was our "I AM" carrying out the Christ-idea to hold onto our negative baggage of hate, jealousy, greed, sadness, pride, laziness, and lust for power (the seven deadly sins) to help with wisdom. And this is why our Christ consciousness knows us better than anyone else.

It knows our revelation is about coming into an intellectual awareness of what we have been calling evil, sin, punishment, and darkness. And, it was our "I AM" consciousness that took on the role of being the storehouse for this distorted polarity energy we call light and dark, good and bad. The real truth is playing out our beautiful and challenging lifetimes in physical form because it has allowed us to play with the energies of positive and negative in a way we could never do before leaving higher consciousness (first creation).

The whole idea was to slow down our energy frequency to experience flesh. Thus, it was never a mistake done by our "I AM"! It was a way for us to become a conscious creator, to understand creation itself, and to discover who we are by experiencing our choices. Now, our biggest challenge is to face up to trusting ourselves as real creators. And because of karma, all energy seeks resolution. How else will we learn the results of our choices?

We are casting our pure unbiased God energy of light and our "I AM" consciousness under the lens of our beliefs to understand the energy of light and dark. Hence, as for most of us, our work playing in dual-energy is not yet done in the eyes of our "I AM." And, once we have emphasized the light and dark enough to understand their real importance in becoming a self-governing Christ also, we awaken to the real truth. However, how many lifetimes will it take for us to come to this realization?

Some people have had a taste of this real truth through the choices they made while journeying through many lifetimes, sowing, and reaping. And now, they are awakening to their "I AM" Christ consciousness. These people realize that truth, like God and energy, is universal, and it expands through time and space. However, others still ignore the fact that God and energy are universal, and them being Christ because all they see and understand about themselves is their humanity. And this is why these people have not found their work complete in the eyes of their "I AM" Christ consciousness. Including why they do not see themselves as worthy and equal to Christ.

These people are alive and well, breathing the air that keeps their bodies active, but they are dead (asleep) to the real truth. There are individuals, religious and non-religious, who have opened up to deeper truths about spirit. But still, once they feel uncomfortable with the norm, they quickly revert back to their old, dogmatic training to interpret their experiences.

An excellent example of this is when a person hears about a brutal murder. He or she cannot accept that a person committing such a crime has not sinned against God and is deserving punishment in hell forever. Therefore, theoretically, some of us may say we are living in the spirit of God, but in actuality, we are not. And this is because the idea of sin, darkness, forgiveness, aggressiveness, mental intelligence, and evil will always put us in a limited state for knowing who Christ and we are. The reason is that we believe in a God who is good and a Satan who is evil. We have forgotten that our core essence is not of good or bad, nor is it light or dark, or that we are from this world. Thus, everything outside of our core essence is just an illusion.

How can God, or our sovereign self, punish what is classified as an illusion? Sometimes we dream at night that we killed someone, and then we say in the morning, "Thank God, it was only a dream." Realize all that we have been doing here on earth is playing in a dream state of physicality to learn and understand duality and our choices. And, once polarity energy and our choices are understood from a spirit level, then our "I AM" state holds onto that understanding and the wisdom of the experience until we can tap into the memories of the experience and find that it was all for the purpose consciousness expansion.

This enables us to become a master over our belief patterns, multiple images, and everything that we bring into a structure. Know that the mind and the free will cannot ever know the Father-Mother God-Goddess, or the "I AM" Christ consciousness because the mind cannot comprehend how the true God-Goddess can exist beyond light and dark (duality). And this is why we always look at God of judgment and condemnation as the true God.

When we allow our lives to be regulated by our belief systems, emotions, and free will, according to opposing concepts, we are living our life from the choices generated from the mind. And this creates beliefs that cause us to suffer because of our emotional ties to them. From this meaning, we are not exercising the mystical forces over the Beast (rebellious ego nature). Instead, we remain asleep *(dead)*, continuing to develop whatever keeps us from knowing that our divinity is the place and part of us that holds our dark creations until we are ready to face them. This dark side is what makes us so fearful of an Antichrist.

By not having trust in ourselves as Christ or God, we push our divinity, and those dark creations, even further away. And this is why many of us turn our backs on good things because we feel unworthy of them. Many of us, without realizing we are doing it, actually set up circumstances where we do not allow ourselves to enjoy life or ever learn the real truth. Hence, when we get angry, excited, or confused about situations, and then base our choices on the emotions they carry, we are living from out of our mind and the intellect, and all because of duality beliefs. This prevents us from being silent before making choices, which keeps us out of touch with our divinity (divine plan).

However, by allowing our free will to integrate with our sovereign divine plan (will), we can bring balance to our emotions, which in the end leads us beyond the existence of light and dark. And, when we learn to accept who we are at our core, we come to know who we are as a Christ and God-Goddess. Know that our core essence is spirit, and our consciousness is pure, universal, and neutral, meaning we are complete and perfect already. But we do not believe it! Thus, we continue to strive for perfection.

This perfection is found in Revelation 3:3, as this verse is simply about some of us coming to know who we are at our core. And this is why in Revelation 3:3 it is about some of us here on earth returning to higher consciousness and understanding where we again come to know that we are Christ in the flesh. And, Revelation 3:3 calls this to mind, for our makeup is of a:

1. Universal Omnipresent Mind Field of pure neutralized God energy of light, and a consciousness of a Christ nature
2. We have an outer Mind-Soul that is the playground to act out our dual opposing beliefs, for it is all mental
3. We have an Ego-personality of rebelliousness that has taken on the role of learning responsibility for our choices
4. And, we have a Physical Body that has become the vehicle (church) for experiencing it all

From this perfection, our primary reality is spirit consciousness, and we use energy for our creations, and not that we, in spirit, are made of energy. It is our physical body that is made of energy. Our secondary reality is our outer mind-soul that partakes in positive and negative, good and bad, right and wrong, light and dark, God and Satan, and is where we create judgment as to the means to learn responsibility. Then the third reality generates these good and bad lifetimes where we live them out in the physical to feel and experience our choices using polarity energy.

Because of accepting our dualistic beliefs and how they are based on what we have heard and been taught, we continue to experience the painful emotions of power and control as something real, rather than reexamining or rethinking *(repenting)* those beliefs. If we did, we could awaken *(rouse)* to our "I AM" Christ consciousness, the true essence of who we are at our core. If we all could allow for awakening and learn to reexamine what we believe as good and evil, we would not be confused or overwhelmed when the "I AM" Christ consciousness comes from out of the blue to inform our lower vibrating physical consciousness of its great power *(authority)*.

When we do not allow for the rethinking of our old dogmatic dual beliefs, we will more than likely go through some unpleasant and unwanted experiences. Through our challenges in life, and the way we deal with them, we will find our true essence, the "I AM" Christ within, giving us space away from others to contact our divine plan (will). And this is what our "I AM" consciousness means by calling to mind how we accept things so easily by others (religions). It is to remind us that our lower vibrating consciousness of many light and dark creations is where we perceive problems because at the reality of our "I AM," there is no such thing as lifetimes or issues where we created evil. They exist only in the mind and physical level.

Therefore, it is the lower vibrating consciousnesses (mind, ego, and physical levels) that need to rethink our position, and in doing so, we will change our understanding about having problems. Without learning to trust in ourselves as Christ *(not watchful)* and allow ourselves to rethink *(repent)* our beliefs (empty that glass), then the things we still believe in, such as having problems and the existence of a devil, will mislead us like a thief in the night when we least expect it (at a time you cannot know).

If we are not watchful to our beliefs and the reactions toward them and what we are experiencing in life, then sowing and reaping will come upon us with a vengeance, and it will feel as if God has sent his wrath upon us. All things we do in life must be remembered and met by ourselves. Therefore, things can happen to us unexpectedly, like a thief in the night, that seems to have no cause or purpose but are directly related to the choice already made in this lifetime or some past lifetime. However, in Revelation 3:4-5, we *"have a few people in Sardis who have not soiled their garments; they will walk with me dressed in white because they are worthy."*

Even though we have many memories and many ego-personality aspects of light and dark (lifetimes), symbolized by the word *people*, most of those chosen memories are connected to old belief systems of judgment, good and bad, God and Satan; duality in general. We also have within our chosen memories many ego-personality aspects that have not played out any lifetimes in duality or even tasted *(soiled)* the flesh *(garments)*. Therefore, these ego-personality aspects that have not yet tasted the flesh can evolve *(walk)* along with those ego-personality aspects that have moved beyond the belief in polarity, because they too are worthy of integrating with their creator, *you.*

When we have journeyed through enough lifetimes playing in polarity energy and have purified ourselves from the illusions of sin and punishment, fashioned and formed by our mind-soul, that is when we can transform and integrate our mind-soul, ego, and all of our many ego-personalities of the past back to "one body of consciousness." And this includes those personality aspects that never been in the flesh because we are the Master *(victor)* of our consciousness (house).

Know that God, Yeshua, and Satan are not our masters, because only we can be the Christ master and the God-Goddess of ourselves. Once we overcome our intellect and the belief in power, control, and duality, our defiant ego-personality will release our outlook on opposing energy. At the same time, we are still part of the physical body *("garment")*. And once done, we evolve in consciousness to where we can clothe ourselves with the new truth *("dressed in white")* of us all being a Christ also.

And, in Revelation 3:5, *"never erase his name from the book of life but will acknowledge his name in the presence of my Father and his angels."* Our many chosen memory lessons and the wisdom we had learned about how to be a better God-Goddess than before we left higher consciousness is the name we hold in this lifetime. Thus, this name (your name) will never be erased from memory (Book of Life), and that our many other ego-personality aspects of light and dark *(angels)* will be acknowledged forever in the presence of our "I AM" Christ consciousness (Father-Mother).

With having an open mind about God, Yeshua, and Satan, we will always find that God, Yeshua, and Satan are metaphorically about us being in the flesh working out our Divine Plan (will) in becoming a sovereign God-Goddess in our own right. Therefore, put no other God before you, not even Yeshua, for he simply served as a manifestation and an example of how the Christ consciousness moves through you and your many ego personalities (lifetimes). And, this is the agreement (covenant) that we all made with our own "I AM" Christ consciousness long ago, which is depicted in Revelation 3:6.

When referencing Revelation 1:3: If we acknowledge, understand, and accept *(read)* who we are with no doubt or attempting to conceal or hide *(aloud)* the mystical importance *(prophetic message)* of our lessons because of our many lifetimes, and, if we have paid attention *(heed)* to what has been expressed and written in this book, then the agreed *(appointed)* time we have specified for our awakening is now suddenly upon us. Are you ready?

Chapter 13

UNDERSTANDING THE MIND AND SOUL BODY OF RESPONSIBILITY

In reviewing Revelation 3:7, *"to the angel of the church in Philadelphia, write this: 'The holy one, the true, who holds the key of David, who opens and no one shall close, who closes and no one shall open, says this.'"* You are the living angel that expresses unconditional love, friendship, and the relationship toward yourself and others when awakened, as all of it is based on the Mind-Soul and the Pineal Gland in the physical body. Therefore, you are the *"holy one"* who holds the *"key of David."*

Philadelphia was a small border town without a garrison founded by the people from Pergamos. It had an open-door policy to spread Greek ideas throughout the area. Philadelphia was also a City of Lydia in Asia Minor. Therefore, the *Church of Philadelphia* represents the love faculty in consciousness where everything is tied to duality, polarity energy, and to the Mind-Soul mental level. As this City was in Asia Minor, it can also represent old, tired, worn-out belief systems that we should have left behind long ago. However, because of the City of Lydia, it means we do eventually undergo a change in beliefs after a while, which then gives birth to a new spiritual understanding.

The *"key of David"* comes from this new spiritual understanding because of our love center *(Philadelphia)* that can reach its highest quality in connecting us to our Christ consciousness. The "key of David" can also refer to our memories of being the Father-Mother God-Goddess in expression. It is those memories that can be the forerunner of our movement into a Christ-like mind. Therefore, the name David itself signifies divine love that is individualized deep within while we are still part of physicality.

When David was in his youth, he daily communed daily with God, meaning he reflected only unconditional love from out of his mind-soul mental level. But when he developed his character as a king in dominion over men, David manifested the limitations of his mind and ego to a more significant degree (rise in frequency). And, as the Bible states, David was anointed king of Israel in Saul's stead because Saul became insane.

Because of David's skill on the harp, he was summoned to play before King Saul to soothe him with music. Thus, David won the affection of Saul because his music proved very useful in quieting the out-of-control monarch. This illustrates and symbolizes the power of unconditional love and how it can harmonize the most challenging and unpredictable mind. Therefore, the symbolism is about our beliefs and thoughts of duality and how they are withdrawn from the head (mind/Saul) and then gradually transferred to our heart center (David), where we can display unconditional love. Thus, we find fault with no one, not even our worst enemy.

In Isaiah 22:22, *"I will place the key of the House of David on his shoulder; when he opens, no one shall shut, when he shuts, no one shall open."* The real "key" is our hidden chosen memories of being Christ, the Father-Mother God-Goddess in expression. Whether we have been pretending to be someone else, we are still God and the Goddess. Therefore, the memory of us being God-Goddess, Christ, and Satan cannot be shut out by another person. However, we can shut ourselves out by moving deep within our controversial mind and ego, fixating on old dogmatic beliefs in polarity energy, good and bad, as being real. Therefore, the only one who can open us up again is our mind, for it is the Lord of Lords and the Son of Goddess. It is just that our mind is sound asleep to whom we are.

When Yeshua walked upon the earth over two thousand years ago, he learned the workings of his mind, ego, energy, and how memory works. Therefore, Yeshua represents, at the mind level, where we can understand the workings of our ego, energy, and how memory works while in physical form. Memory is our soul history, a history that concerns this universal omnipresent mind field of pure unbiased god energy of light that surrounds every one of us where each of us owns that part of God to do with as we please. Thus, God is not a person! God, as we all understand God to be, is pure unbiased energy of light that we use to form our creations to experience them.

Within our memory, even though we are in the flesh, we already know the workings of polarity, positive and negative, the influences they project, and how opposing energy works throughout our spirit, mind, and physical body. Since we are the only ones who know our desires, beliefs, passion, and sins when it comes to memories and how we manifested numerous lifetimes throughout the multidimensional realms to play, then we are the only ones that can save ourselves. Yeshua (Jesus) cannot save you. Only you can save you!

Therefore, consider Revelation 3:8: *"I have left an open door before you, which no one can close"* other than yourself. For this open door is your subconsciousness and is the doorway to your already chosen memories of the past. And, you can tap into these memories through deep breathing at least up to fifteen to thirty minutes a day. No man, religion, government, or teacher, not even Yeshua, can shut off the operations of your memories or prevent you from tapping into them. Not even you can shut yourself off from receiving the memories of the past, but you can block them out for a while. Yet, they will eventually work through to our conscious mind because of sowing and reaping.

Our memory consciousness may have little strength to force us to act, but it does have enough strength to hold, within our soul mental body, what we have believed throughout our many lifetimes. Thus, when the time is right, because of sowing and reaping, we cannot deny our "I AM" Christ consciousness any longer.

Remember Simon Peter denying Yeshua? It refers to our outer-ego personality in this lifetime, denying those memories of us being Christ. And, the triple denial represents how we reject and deny our "I AM" Christ-spirit, our mind-soul, and all of our ego personality forms as being "one body of consciousness," without realizing they are all under the umbrella of our own "I AM" Christ consciousness.

This limited strength is related to our entrance into the second circle of creation (abyss) long ago, where we measured our creations along the lines of positive and negative viewpoints as being real. We used a two-dimensional corresponding consciousness system because it gave the energy that we used for our creations the same character when it comes to quantity, origin, structure, and function in the second circle. The difference between the first circle was our soul recording our creations by using a two-dimensional system where our mind gave the perception that time, space, and limitation were real.

Do not confuse this two-dimensional system with our three-dimensional consciousness just because we brought a large but limited amount of energy into the second circle with us (astral/physical realms) to use for our creations. The only difference was the energy coming into the two-dimensional system was limited. It had the same character and the same function as in the first creation, but in the second creation, the energy had a positive and negative blueprint to it. Thus, it made it limited!

It has been since leaving the first creation of neutrality; we have been restructuring and reorganizing that limited amount of energy into positive and negative patterns to play with. Yeshua and the Ascended Masters compared it to having "the same amount of sand in the sandbox." Therefore, look at the sand in your sandbox as the limited energy you brought with you into the second circle (mind-soul) to play with. You can create several sandcastles, but then you have to destroy them (rearrange the energy) to build more castles.

It has always been a considerable, but limited, amount of energy we have been playing within the second circle that keeps us stuck in our mind (two-dimensional corresponding consciousness). All of what we have created with this limited energy had to be held somewhere for our mind (Adam) and soul consciousness of responsibility (Eve) to have the freedom to continue to move forward, to create, and to grow. Thus, everything we created was placed in memory as being part of our dark-negative personality aspects. This created karma or cause-and-effect, which is referred to in the Bible as sowing and reaping. We gave ourselves space and the freedom to develop and explore our unlimited interests and individuality.

We are the head God-Goddess (Oversoul) waiting for us to forgive ourselves and our many ego-personality lifetimes and then integrate them as part of our total consciousness *("and yet you have kept my word and have not denied my name")* Revelation 3:8. And, it is our mind-soul consciousness that works with polarity energy along with the connection to our many ego personalities that claim their purpose is to work from a belief in dual-energy *("those that are the assembly of Satan"* in Revelation 3:9).

Therefore, each of our many ego-personality aspects (lifetimes) carry within them the memories of all that we did. And now, we can tap into those memories at will because we are the creator of each lifetime. Those *"who claim to be Jews and are not but are lying"* in Revelation 3:9, are those repeated belief patterns where we believe that we are virtuous, honest, honorable, respectable, upright, and blameless. But hidden deep within our memories is a falseness that can be recognized by our mind.

Remember, we cannot fool ourselves! We can, however, through our disruptive ego-personality aspects (a physical lifetime), claim to be all those things. But in reality, we are more than who we think we are as a human. We cannot fool our memories about what choices we have made, and yet have never taken responsibility for, at least from the subconscious level. Oh, we can lie to ourselves and others, but we cannot lie when it comes to our memories. Thus, the mind-soul *"will make them come and fall prostrate at our feet,"* Revelation 3:9.

We know deep within we are the God-Goddess and the creator of our beliefs. We just are not ready to admit it. And, because of this knowledge, and before leaving our Oneness of consciousness, we all stretched and expanded *(prostrate)* our consciousness to where our lower vibrating physical consciousness *(feet)* engaged in actions that brought our chosen memories of duality to the forefront of our consciousness. And, from this mind of duality, we, from our physical nature, will always measure those already chosen memories with an agreement of sowing and reaping until it eventually awakens us to whom we are at our core.

This means that all of our light and dark ego-personality aspects (lifetimes), since the time we left higher consciousness (garden) long ago, have been deliberately measured and judged by a mind that has not as of yet been awakened. It was through this measuring or judging of our mind that helped slow down our energy enough to adjust the effectiveness of what we give life to for soul growth. These ego-personality aspects of light and dark (lifetimes) are still part of our oneness of consciousness even now, but in parallel levels of existence.

The only thing that separates our past lifetimes from our present, other than awareness, is the awakening of trust in the self, being a Christ also. The phrase, *"And they will realize that I love you,"* in Revelation 3:9, symbolizes the sacrifices of our hidden memories. They have been taken up in all those light and dark ego-personality aspects of our past lifetimes when we were a predator, journeying through many earthly lifetimes, sowing, and reaping.

It is through these light and dark ego-personality aspects from the past that we gain the means for spiritual growth, expansion, and responsibility for our choices. Therefore, the "I" in Revelation 3:9 is relating to our Christ consciousness that loves us unconditionally, regardless of our many past self-indulgence or self-gratitude lifetimes, and even when we reject, our "I AM" Christ's love because we see ourselves as unworthy. In the end, every ego-personality aspect of us shall bow to its creator, the self as a Christ. Let this not be forgotten!

If you learn to keep to the messages by Yeshua and the Ascended Masters here in this book, then Revelation 3:10 *"will keep you safe in the time of trial that will come to the whole world."* And, who is the "whole world?" It is the wholeness of all memories about you choosing many lifetimes in expressing your love for life to learn the wisdom behind your choices. It is learning the relationships you have had with your creative mind and filling your soul with memories of many experiences based on the illusion of dual-energy.

In partaking with the Tree of Knowledge of Good and Evil, we became the sacrificial lamb in bringing in the wisdom of duality, and in the end, we become a sovereign God-Goddess in our own right. Also, in this choosing of polarity energy, we have helped introduce what we have created, good and bad, to our angelic family that has not chosen the flesh, teaching them what to do and what not to do.

We have been journeying from one state of consciousness (lifetimes) to another, learning the wisdom of those experiences via sowing and reaping *(time of trial)*. And today, we have taken on an intellectual belief that our mind, rather than our spirit, is the lifeblood that keeps alive the wholeness of who we are and the memories of physical and nonphysical lifetimes *("the whole world")*. Because of our sacrifice coming to earth, we now have the authority to *"test"* the physical senses, and what we see as materialism becomes the means to move us into the next level of our evolution.

Therefore, do not fear your dualistic beliefs or thoughts, or what you did or didn't do because your "I AM" Christ consciousness will keep you safe from falling back to the old ways of looking at duality once you awaken to the real truth. Because of memory, you possess the key to your many ego-personality aspects, physical and nonphysical *("inhabitants of the earth")*. This key can open the door of your subconsciousness, telling you to take account of your trials and tribulations, which will catapult you into new energy and new consciousness.

Thus, *"hold fast"* for *"I am coming quickly,"* in Revelation 3:11, is that of our "I AM" Christ consciousness is ready to open the doors of our physical consciousness if we are prepared to receive it. The term, *"so that no one may take your crown"* in Revelation 3:11, refers to you, in this very moment, trusting in yourself as a Christ also. And, if you have doubt, then you will give away your "crown" (freedom) to those around you and your memories of dogmatic beliefs.

The crown is a symbol of our wisdom and the freedom that we have accumulated in memory through the process of evolution. If we do not allow ourselves to awaken to our wisdom soon, then our crown (freedom) has been stolen by our belief in things that are not real. Many of us have said, even though we cannot remember, we are waiting for the day when we can become one body of consciousness again. The time is now for some of us to open up to remembering and feeling everything again while in the flesh.

Channeling of the Ascended Masters on the Apocalypse

Do not wait until you die to recall who you are, who you were, or why you are here. The wording of *"the victor I will make into a pillar in the temple of my God"* in Revelation 3:12 is about your most powerful and effective memories retained while journeying through many lifetimes, sowing and reaping. Know that your memories have become an enduring body of consciousness that identifies you in this physical life as the Godhead, the king, and the Lord of Lords. For your physical body is *"the temple of God."* You just have forgotten!

It was you, along with the mass, that has created time, space, and all material things in nature, including earth. And, you and the mass defined it the evolution of your belief systems, attitudes, and experiences. You have been using time, earth, and duality to help you, as a God-Goddess, to place your events into a defined objective to understand your choices. You have been working linearly, following a belief that you are a creation of some God outside of you. And, you have been merely following a support system *(pillar)* defining your consciousness by responding to ideas and beliefs you have been taught for centuries.

"On him, I will inscribe the name of my God and the name of the city of my God" (Revelation 3:12), which is referenced by Exodus 3:14-15, where Yahweh said to Moses that His name was "I AM That I AM." Meaning, in Hebrew: "JHVH" or "Yahweh," the ever-living male-female God-Goddess in the Old Testament. And, in the New Testament, it is the "I AM Christ." Therefore, in the name of the *"city of my God"* sits the living memory of the "I AM" God and the Goddess.

According to the metaphorical dictionary, "the presiding thought or meaning of a city is found in the significance of its name, combined with that of man, a country or nation with which it is mentioned." Therefore, the *"city of my God"* symbolizes the highest importance you possess in memory where you understand that you are the living God-Goddess, the creator, the builder, the maker of your physical body, and experiences. It is through trusting in you as God-Goddess that brings these memories into manifestation while you are still in the flesh. And, with *"the new Jerusalem"* in Revelation 3:12, it signifies a redeemed or awakened you (male or female) coming into a realization that you are the "I AM."

Jerusalem is the City of David and symbolizes the great nerve center in the back of the heart. It is from this point where our "I AM" Christ transmits a high vibrational wavelength to our many ego-personality aspects from past lifetimes. However, this happens only if we are ready to receive a higher knowing and understanding of the "I AM," and how much it has accumulated in memory from the time we all left higher awareness (Garden), until this very moment in our physical life. Through multiple lifetimes, where we reaped what we sowed, great understanding and wisdom have come to all parts of us as a God-Goddess *("which comes down out of heaven from my God,"* or higher self). Therefore, our *"new name"* is "I AM That I AM."

Truth is first conceived in the heart center (not the mind) symbolized by Jerusalem, but because of intellectual reasoning and dominance, it drifts to a mind of sleep. You could say, when Paul was taken to Rome in chains, it became a fitting symbol of truth, captured by the intellect and confined to the bonds it had placed upon you (Acts 28:14–20).

Chapter 14

UNDERSTANDING THE SPIRIT BODY

When Yeshua and the Ascended Masters looked into Revelation 3:14, *"to the angel of the church in Laodicea,"* they are speaking of those that are beginning to take responsibility for everything they have created journeying through many lifetimes sowing and reaping. Because of our mental and physical bodies, we only believe and understand things from a state of dual consciousness. Hence, judgment and dual thinking become our energy signature (DNA)! If we would only realize that when in the flesh body, ninety-seven percent of our thoughts and beliefs come from all that is mental and physical, which is why we have to come into a realization of being more than just human before we can move forward to our Spirit Body of Consciousness.

There are many throughout the world, and beyond physicalness that has been faithful in following their desire to experience everything there is to know about physical life and the tree of duality. And because of it, some of us are ready to immerge as a *"witness"* to all of what we have created as an individual and as a human group consciousness.

Throughout our journey, having many lifetimes playing with polarity energy, the time has come for some of us to redeem those ego-personality aspects (physical (living) and the non-physical aspects (those that died)) by calling in our "I AM" Christ consciousness to lift them to a higher energy frequency. And this is the meaning behind the *"faithful and true witness"* in Revelation 3:14, because some of us have taken full responsibility for our creations in this lifetime, good and bad.

And, this is why in Revelation 3:15-16, our "I AM" Christ consciousness *"knows our works"* in what we have expressed and chosen to experience since the time we all left higher consciousness (Garden) eons ago. Our "I AM" knows that we have been learning about polarity energy and taking responsibility for what we have created by using it. It even knows that everything we have created, good and bad, has been put to memory for us to work out lifetime after lifetime until we come into some realization that we are more than just human.

Our "I AM" even knows the enthusiasm and support we gave initially by stepping off the road of "neutrality" so we could learn everything there is to know about polarity energy. And, because of it, we have been discovering that this road of duality is paved with karmic conditions, all according to what we have chosen and believed in since the time we left higher understanding (first creation). And now, those beliefs have become our anchor for staying in our mind and how we acted so strangely toward our ego.

However, with some of us coming into the realization that we are the "I AM" Christ, we are learning it was our "I AM" that gave us, from the mind-soul level, the same creative abilities as it had. Hence, we inherited the throne a long time ago. But we are asleep to this truth! We even came to a place where we believed the intelligent center of the mind was the place of our many creations, not realizing these creations came from the separated ego-personality. This is where our "I AM" knows and *"wished that we were either cold or hot,"* for we are just *"lukewarm"* with this unwavering understanding about who we are at our core consciousness.

Know that our "I AM" desires us to know that we are equal to Christ because we are Christ in all of consciousness, including the flesh. The reason we do not believe it or remember it is because we still feel separated from our "I AM." This is like having a feeling that God is separate from us, and yet we are one and the same, Christ. Not realizing this stops us from taking full responsibility for our acts in consciousness, like creating many lifetimes playing in polarity energy. And this is why we must say to ourselves, "I, not Yeshua, am responsible for my creations, for everything I experience in life, good and bad comes from me."

Therefore, my friends, you will never figure out God or Spirit using the mind. You cannot ever know God by placing rules, rituals, and structures on yourself and others. Religions do that, which is why someday their so-called truths will tumble down around them. Religions try to define God through reason, rules, rituals, and calling you a sinner. This type of teaching, and you accepting, only bottles up the energy within your physical body. Thus, creating illnesses! And the only way to release it is through letting go of old religious beliefs.

And this is why Revelation 3:16, your "I AM" will *"spit you out of its mouth"* by having your many ego-personality aspects balancing their energy through sowing and reaping. This will then bring you to the appropriate place within the heart center where you will someday release the ideas of polarity energy and the illusion of sin. Therefore, take a deep breath and release everything that is of dual-energy and see yourself rise in consciousness to a New Energy of Neutrality. It is up to you whether or not you have a passion for taking the first step in becoming a Christ while in the flesh or wait until another lifetime.

Because of our mental and physical nature, we understand God only from a state of polarity energy, which then brings in judgment, sin, and worship. Then we say we are deep in keeping (rich) with God's laws, and because of it, we expect God to enlarge our life with health, joy, and prosperity. It is because of this belief; we do not know or understand how we can lose ourselves when it comes to knowing Christ. How can we know God or Christ if we do not know how "pitiable," "poor," and "blind," stripped *"naked"* of any idea about who we are in the scheme of things?

We always define life the way we think it should be, all based on a duality mindset with God being a mystery, rather than accepting what life can be based on in a new mindset of neutrality. We sometimes wonder why things are not changing in our lives and yet, we pray and pray to God, but all that we seem to do is struggle and worry about a virus, our next fill-up at the gas pump, and where the money will come from to buy food, clothing, and to pay the rent.

So, I ask you, what do you have to lose by opening up to some new ideas about God? If we could look into Revelation 3:18, to open up our heart center, then our "I AM" will advise, support, and counsel us to accept *(buy)* those memories of experiences of wisdom where we have been tested and tried by the fires of justice *(gold)*. And, with some of us coming into realization, we learn that our choices and experiences through many incarnations, sowing, and reaping, have removed our impurities *(refined)*, and all that is left now is to awaken to a knowing we are the "I AM" Christ walking the earth.

Through many incarnations journeying through the physical and non-physical astral realms, we have filled our soul with many potentials to play out here on earth. And now, we can lead a life with overwhelming proportions of health, joy, great relationships, and prosperity *(rich)* if we like. Due to our sowing and reaping, we can now display and express our divinity *(wear the white garment,* the Christ) outward using our physical body, our mind, and ego consciousness without feeling appalled or shameful.

It is you, and not Yeshua, with authority to forgive your sins, or what you *think* are your sins, and to forgive those who hurt you. And then, you can heal yourself of poverty, sadness, and illnesses using the spiritual *ointment* of Crystalline energy. And, you have only to open your heart and mind and, for the first time in your life, consider truth to be something that evolves instead of something that remains stagnant and inactive *(eyes to see)*. Once you learn to understand using your heart center, knowing you are Christ, then it becomes a great desire for the "I AM" to join you in the flesh, and then give birth to those belief patterns that will lead you back to a "knowing" that you are more than just human.

By allowing ourselves, to rethink *(repent)* our position about our ego-personality aspects of light and dark, that we have loved, criticized *(reprove)*, and disciplined *(chastise)*, using the law of duality, we have set up "all that we are" free from sin evermore, including the original sin (Revelation 3:19-20). By allowing our "I AM" to take its position *(stand)* at the doorway of our mental and physical consciousness, we allow the recurring trumpet of Gabriel's horn *(knock)* calling us to open our eyes, mind, heart, and physical body *(house)* to a whole new consciousness and understanding where we take delight *(dine)* in our new freedom.

Most of us have been looking at our journey here on earth through the eyes of a human. That was fine for a while because we forgot that we created our divine plan (will), but instead, we followed our human plan. And that is, when things did not work out, as we became lost, angry, and frustrated, along came religion, saying we are sinners, and we believed them. This caused us to say we were imperfect. And, because of this belief, we spend most of our time praying, attending church, giving away our money, and asking a God of judgment for forgiveness.

How often have we prayed to God, asking repeatedly, what should we be doing, or what do you want me to do? Then we wait and wait for an answer until we come to a belief that God is supposed to be a mystery because of faith. Then we do what we believe God wants us to do anyway. My friends, our "I AM" does not care what we do, because it is just the passion of our soul desiring to experience everything, that's all. Know that our divine plan (will) changes all the time because we have changed it every time we have lived a lifetime on earth.

Know that our divinity embraces our past lifetimes, good and evil, and all the potentials of the future we have not even chosen yet. Know that our divinity has a great desire to integrate with our human plan right now to bring fulfillment of spirit where we, from the physical level, can work in unison with our "I AM." And, according to Revelation 3:21, our human consciousness can feel the flow of new energy coming from our "I AM," not in words that are written in some scripture because there is no lack or illness in our life, only the illusions of them.

Therefore, according to Revelation 3:22, *"those who have ears ought to hear what the Spirits say to the churches."* These seven churches are the building blocks that relate to the seven endocrine glands within the physical body given in Revelation 1:11. It is not about hearing what God or Christ has to say in some building. It is addressing those of us who have the "ears" to listen to the Christ within ourselves, telling each gland in our physical body to work in unison or as "one body of consciousness." And, if we allow this, we become the grandmaster and the Christ coming to rescue the self.

Chapter 15

UNDERSTANDING POLARITY ENERGY (POSITIVE AND NEGATIVE)

According to Yeshua and the Ascended Masters, Chapter Four of the Apocalypse may be the most challenging chapter to comprehend. The chapter is filled with multiple themes of discussion running through it, verbalizing it as rather complex to read and interpret. Chapter Four of the Apocalypse not only deals with the forces of positive and negative, but it also deals with the human body and its endocrine system, the left and right brain activities, the five physical senses, and the twelve major systems of the physical body.

Most people fail to consider the human body and its makeup when it comes to Christ and the Apocalypse. For example: By looking into Revelation 4:1, the vision of John is referring to us in the here and now so we can understand the concept of opening up our physical consciousness to feel into the polarity energy impulses of our soul memories that are beginning to come alive deep within. Thus, lifting our ignorance where we, on a conscious level, can realize we have a sub and super-consciousness that is filled with memories about who we are, where we come from, what we have done since our awakening, and that we are a Christ also.

Thus, *"open door to heaven"* in Revelation 4:1 is about you, and if you so choose, you can open your consciousness to a higher frequency, to higher understanding, and then recognize that you are Christ in the flesh.

Channeling of the Ascended Masters on the Apocalypse

Know that you must eventually remember from whence you came, and your memories are the means of getting you there. Your memories are vital because, without them, you would not know the wisdom of your experiences, or retain anything of your past, nor remember what you did yesterday. How else could anything be possible?

Journeying through many lifetimes, playing with polarity energy, positive and negative, is the process we use for soul growth, building memories, and building wisdom. Without memory and soul growth, we would never reach our heavenly state of mind mentioned in Revelation 21:1: "*I saw a new heaven and a new earth.*"

If John represents us in ego form here on earth, then some of us here and now are beginning to see some of our old ideas, old truths, and our dogmatic opposing beliefs being replaced by a higher consciousness of neutrality, where we understand now that we have been working out of vibrational energy that moves back and forth. This causes us to create unpredictable variations between two extremes, such as good and evil.

Therefore, if John is correct in what he saw in Revelation 4:1, then the New Earth (representing our higher consciousness) will carry a configuration unlike the variations between two extremes. It will replace it with a consciousness that processes our creations with a "new arrangement" about how atoms work with New Expansional Energy of Four. Yeshua, in his day, healed the sick, and he did it by understanding energy and how it works with consciousness and with the physical body. This is why Chapter Four of the Apocalypse refers to the physical body and of the polarity energy more than the other chapters, even though they all deal with the material or matter in general.

From my understanding of the atom, and I am no expert, it is a basic unit of matter consisting of a dense, central nucleus surrounded by a cloud of negatively charged electrons. The atomic nucleus contains a mix of positively charged protons and electrically neutral neutrons. The electrons of an atom are bound to the nucleus by the electromagnetic force. An atom containing an equal number of protons and electrons is electrically neutral; otherwise, it has a positive or a negative charge to it. Therefore, an atom is classified by the number of protons and neutrons in its nucleus. The number of protons determines the chemical element, and the number of neutrons determines the geometric pattern of energy and how it relates to the earth and the physical body.

In this case, it is positive or negative. When we souls were working from a higher consciousness frequency back in the beginning, and from which all creation came into expression, there was no such thing as positive and negative. The only thing that existed was an "omnipresent universal mind field of pure neutralized unbiased energy of light." In other words, just consciousness and energy!

And, back in the first creation, we souled beings had never heard of the word, God. From channeling Yeshua and the Ascended Masters, the God taught to us today as a white self-contained male deity who confines all power to himself is nothing more than this "omnipresent universal mind field of pure unbiased harmonized energy of light." This means all souled beings back in the first creation (first circle), you and me, we're only in a consciousness state of neutrality.

But once we souls animated (or activated), this neutralized energy to help with the understanding of the question, "Who am I?" it produced an increase in rapid vibrations that became unpredictable and slightly different from what was neutralized before. This act caused the atom to split into vibrational energy of two, causing the energy to vibrate between two extremes, one rotating to the right and the other to the left, causing a resistance between the two that opposed each other. Today, this vibrating energy is called positive and negative.

Therefore, what John observed was the play with the polarity energy of positive and negative ever since he (we) left the first creation, or what is called his oneness of consciousness. Religions call this force the Tree of Knowledge of Good and Evil. However, now the time has come for some of us to move into a New Energy (New Earth) that takes us way beyond this opposing force of two. This New Energy is called "New Expansional Energy of Four," which is symbolic of the "New Earth" that John saw replacing the "Old Earth" (or old vibrational opposing energy of two).

Just imagine a circle representing the Oneness of our spirit consciousness, and we are using the Universal Mind Field of Pure Neutralized Energy being generated from it. Our consciousness is what generates this pure energy of light into action and not the other way around. It takes passion, desire, imagination, focus, and belief systems to trigger our consciousness into action. Therefore, we must take full responsibility for whatever we are experiencing and stop blaming others for what we are experiencing, even if we believe it is not our fault. Just look at it as something that we created in some previous lifetime.

Also, when we lowered our consciousness and this pure energy of light to this vibrational frequency of opposing energy, we allowed our higher consciousness to remain pure and neutral. In contrast, it split our consciousness and this pure energy of light into two parts, as one became our subconsciousness and the other our outer consciousness. That is when the circle of one split into two circles, along with the energy, one rotating clockwise and the other counterclockwise. Thus, positive and negative was created!

It comes from these two circles, symbolized by our Christ consciousness and our mind-soul consciousness, where we turned our oneness of consciousness into generating polarity energy that caused duality. And each circle, spinning in the opposite direction from the other, causes resistance that produces the forces of positive and negative as feeling real.

Now, after eons of time, a change is taking place at the center of our Beingness. And, since all things we have ever experienced resulted from the second circle spinning in opposing directions, we now have the opportunity where we can prepare to meld the two circles back together as "one body of consciousness" again. Instead of the two circles or the energies spinning opposite each other, they come together to form an oneness of a "New Expansional Energy of Four" that begins at the center of our heart center instead of from our mind-soul and ego consciousness.

In Revelation 4:1, *"I heard the trumpet like a voice that had spoken to me before,"* also refers to Revelation 1:10, in which the *"trumpet sound"* is you, and not Gabriel, proclaiming to yourself to integrate your "I AM" Christ consciousness, your mind-soul, your solution Gnost consciousness, and all of your many ego-personality aspects and memories from every lifetime you have spent on earth into "one voice" and "one expansional impulse." Thus, rewiring yourself here in the flesh to the fullness of you as Christ. Therefore, know that your divinity carries the memory of truth. And, this truth is always there, ready and waiting for you to acknowledge it.

It is our "I AM" Christ consciousness, and not Yeshua, that is sending out to all our ego-personality aspects of us, including our human ego of today, a multidimensional frequency, asking us, *"Come up here, and I will show you what must happen afterward,"* Revelation 4:1. *"Coming up here"* represents how we move from a lower vibrating frequency consciousness to a higher frequency consciousness where we can acknowledge our past lifetimes, whether or not we acted them out positively or negatively makes no difference to our "I AM" (Oversoul). The only important thing is what wisdom we have gained from playing them out in the physical.

Once we allow this truth to enter our physical consciousness in the here and now, then these past lifetimes of many can be revealed to us through memory. After all, it has been these lifetimes of our past that have been our revelations. And this is why *"afterward,"* in Revelation 4:1, refers to how we needed to know the workings of polarity energy, positive and negative, and how we used it to experience our choices to learn wisdom and responsibility. Our divine plan was to incorporate the belief in opposing energy as real for our human consciousness to understand what it means to take responsibility for our acts through time and space.

Therefore, before you can recall the wisdom of what you have learned throughout your many lifetimes, you first must learn to let go of the belief in polarity energy, good and bad, right and wrong, as if it is real. The symbolism of *"happen afterward,"* in Revelation 4:1, has no reference to any prophecy of a future event other than you admitting and acknowledging your memories of old and how you played them out using polarity energy in many lifetimes.

From this explanation, we can see why this polarity energy principle, good and evil, is not the pattern of our "I AM," for the geometric design of our "I AM" is pure, unbiased, absolute, unchangeable, and neutral. Why? Because it is the actual image of the "Spirit of One," the Goddess. In our desire to become a sovereign Goddess in our own right, the opposing energies have become the means to generate many branches of positive and negative belief systems and ego-personality aspects of ourselves to explore and experience on behalf of our "I AM" Christ consciousness. Remember, John 15:6, and I paraphrase. *"The branch that separates itself from the tree withers away and dies."*

Therefore, we humans represent the branch that set ourselves up a long time ago to separate ourselves from our own "I AM" Christ consciousness (the root of the tree). It is not that we have sinned against God; we just volunteered to cut ourselves off from the source of neutralized energy and our "I AM." And once we cut ourselves off from the source, we began to swirl in a mental reality where the dominant attitudes and thoughts were only good, evil, light, dark, negative, positive, birth, and forgetfulness (death). So, there is the meaning behind being kicked out of the Garden (higher consciousness) at its simplest terms. We kicked ourselves out of the Garden to learn wisdom, and not that some God above us decided for us.

As we grew in consciousness, we created a false belief in separation from the Source of Life, our "I AM." Thus, forgetting that we, each member, is the Source of Life. And, as a human group, we engaged in different belief systems where we became involved in many power struggles, trying to manipulate each other through power and the belief in polarity energies. That is when our energy became so entwined and tangled that everything slowed down around us. From that energetic bottleneck, planet Earth became the ideal place to express and live out our belief in polarity energy to help awaken us from it.

Channeling of the Ascended Masters on the Apocalypse

When we entered earth long ago, living out many lifetimes, we felt the pain of our creations. And this provided us with an understanding of what we created in the astral realms before we ever came to earth. But, once we entered the earth, sowing and reaping, we learned quickly to take responsibility for our good and evil creations, all due to the belief in polarity as being real. We all became so stuck in a consciousness belief that we separated (dead) ourselves from the lifeline of our own "I AM" Christ-identity without realizing we were even doing it.

It was from this strong belief in polarity that we brought in the perfect set-up for the creation of a single-minded God having all knowledge, power, and wisdom all to himself. And, in the attempt to find the ultimate truth and the return to our true nature, we fought one another over the very truth we were seeking. And, because of it, the earth is now the home for many belief systems and religions, each claiming they have the exclusive path back to God.

It was because of energy coming to a standstill that led us to become so inflexible with our beliefs that we now have forgotten why we are here on earth. We created so many belief systems about being separated (dead) from the source of life, we created the illusion of a God above us as being our creator. However, when we look into the meaning of Revelation 4:2-3, we can see the "I" conveys to us humans to become awakened to being Christ in this lifetime.

Both verses, Revelation 4:2-3, are not really about John's vision. They are symbolic of those of us humans that are ready to open our mental state and hear this small voice deep within, asking us to empty our minds of old dualistic beliefs about some God creating us to a mind of knowing we are the creator. These verses are telling us to learn how to expand our physical consciousness to where we can intuitively feel our "I AM" Christ consciousness conveying to us a message that the time has come for us to choose to become awakened.

My friends, Revelation 4:2-3, reveals that we can live in a place of awareness, acknowledgment, and a knowing who we are at our core consciousness. Or, we can stay in a place of ignorance. Once we move away from the belief in polarity and the dogmatic beliefs tied to them, we will come into a place of knowing we are a Christ also. This is where we can remove ourselves from the power and control of others and their dogmatic opposing beliefs. This is also a place where we can take back our power as a Christ and Goddess in our own right.

Hence, the *"throne"* set in *"heaven"* indicates that we humans have the authority to open up to our "I AM" once again and know that we are the authority of our creations, and that is when we will be shown the seat of our soul and the memories held within.

Heaven is not somewhere out there. It is a place deep within consciousness where we finally learn of our soul memories and our many ego personality aspects of light and dark (lifetimes). These ego-personality aspects are spread throughout the multi-nonphysical dimensional realms with the assigned qualities learned in each lifetime, including what we have understood as power. Therefore, the best thing that comes from the seat of our soul memories is learning the wisdom of our experiences.

Once we souled beings moved from our oneness of consciousness and into a physical body long ago, we lost our awareness of being a Christ. And now, since we walked through many incarnations, sowing and reaping, some of us evolved from being a disaster to being an ornamental *(jasper and carnelian)* where we (while still in the physical) now can sense our progress by way of energy frequency, color, and intuition. Therefore, from our intuitive feelings and deep breathing, we can open up our third eye and move beyond the five physical senses.

Through color and our third eye, we will receive information that goes far beyond the limits of our mind, time, space, and matter. The colors that are part of the rainbow *(jasper and carnelian,* for example), and their meanings, refer to the quality of our conscious awakening. The color indigo refers to that part of us that is devoted to expressing unconditional love and friendship in our relationships with the self and others. The color blue refers to the part of us dedicated to our purpose, communication, and higher creativity centers. Blue also represents self-expression, creative expression, and successes in the material world.

The color green refers not only to soul growth from gratification, but to love, both for the self and others, and the ability to give and receive or give and take. The color yellow refers to the bridge between our upper and lower areas of the physical body and how it relates to what feeds our mind and body. You can also say the color yellow in the rainbow represents the lower seat of our intuition or our gut feelings and instincts in the physical.

The color orange refers to the seat of our soul, as this is the area where we build up our choices and then give them the energy needed to experience them in the physical world. The color orange also represents the many hardships we have suffered because of our belief in positive and negative as the basis for our choices. Finally, the color red refers to our survival consciousness and our relationship to the physical world through our desires, attitudes, feelings of attachments, and the training we acquire in each physical lifetime that we spent upon the earth.

Channeling of the Ascended Masters on the Apocalypse

The word *carnelian*, according to the Wikipedia Encyclopedia, means "a hard, reddish, translucent, semiprecious stone that is a variety of chalcedony" (a grayish stone that is a variety of banded quartz). This means that once we become awakened to being a Christ, we have an appearance of a glowing and soft nature, like a light body, not in weight, but in a feeling of divineness resonating from the physical body. It is about us allowing universal truth to filter through our mind (translucent) without applying the intellect and reasoning principles to exploit the value (semiprecious stone) of what we have learned in wisdom journeying through lifetimes experiencing many varied ego-personality consciousnesses.

Sometimes we may feel or think that our choices are coming from the mind. But I assure you, many are coming from the soul memories of our past lifetimes. Remember, while we are incarnated in a physical body, our thoughts and beliefs of the present are generally produced more from our previous lifetimes than from our present one. Our mind (Adam) is part of our soul consciousness of responsibility (Eve), and they (the self) were both deceived by our defiant ego nature (the Beast), all because they have assumed the role of judge, jury, and decision-maker in what we believe to be our truths.

It is as if our ego-personalities, of past lifetimes (Satan's assembly), are having an affair with our soul consciousness of responsibility (inner feminine self), and our mind (the masculine) is supporting this affair without it realizing what is happening to it. We are blind to the relationship because we are focused on our dogmatic opposing beliefs as our only truth. Because of this, our ego has produced many other ego-personalities that are considered our past lifetimes. Our ego-personality today is considered our beastly nature, and the assembling of Satan's warriors are our many past lifetimes because we still carry within us their belief systems.

It is our mental soul and our divinity that holds our memories to what we have done, positive and negative, and they feed them back to our mind to choose what kind of story (lifetime) we will experience. Once we enter the physical realm, our stubborn ego (Satan) interferes and judges our choices as right or wrong, good (light) or evil (dark), true or false, positive or negative, God or Satan. Thus, we fight with our "I AM" Christ consciousness as if it is a dark place to go. Therefore, until we awaken to this practice, every decision we make on earth is artificial and untrue. And, every decision is a lie because it is tied to these opposing dualistic beliefs. We lie to ourselves and others all the time, just by saying we are a sinner.

Further into Revelation 4:3, "*throne was a halo as brilliant as an emerald,*" indicates our connection to higher understanding where we, if we so choose, can be shown the seat of our soul memories. Again, it is about some of us that are coming into some remembrance of being a Christ also. The *"halo"* of the rainbow and its colors become our distinct, crystallized colors being a Christ in action, while we are in the flesh. The precious stone of green *(emerald)* becomes the symbol for our growth in consciousness.

Chapter 16

SUMMARIZING OF THE MIND AND PHYSICAL BODY, AND HOW IT RELATES TO REVELATION 4:4-11

Revelation 4:4, the *"twenty-four other thrones on which twenty-four elders sat, dressed in white garments and with gold crowns on their head."* Yeshua and the Ascended Masters are speaking of the twelve left-brain and twelve right-brain activities in the physical body. Not only that, but they are also telling us the physical body consists of having "seven nerve centers" or "endocrine centers" that lead from the brain to the "five outer senses." The *"throne"* is again us humans in this lifetime as the headmaster and the Christ who created many ego-personality aspects (lifetimes) of ourselves to play upon the earth. Therefore, it was not some God above us who created us. It was the self that created the self!

The *"twenty-four other thrones"* are not about the literal number twenty-four (24) either. It is where the masters bring in the study of "numerology," as numbers carry a specific power and influence to them when it comes to spirit, the Bible, and creation. In the science of "numerology," numbers are reduced to its lowest value, except for 11 and 22, known as master numbers. Because of the mathematical geometry of shapes and numbers that affect our everyday life, Yeshua and the Ascended Masters ask you to be patient in discovering what these numbers mean when it comes to the Apocalypse.

As known, we cannot go any higher than number nine (9). Therefore, in the study of numerology, we will find number ten (10) will always come back to itself, back to the number one (1) again when reduced to its primary value after each cycle (zero). And, since we are playing in the second cycle, then numerology, and the study of sacred geometry, is connected to the physical body and the world. Thus, there is no place where numbers do not affect us.

When we understand how the "omnipresent universal mind field of pure neutralized god energy of light" works with our "I AM," our mind-soul, our solution Gnost consciousness, and our many ego personalities, and how they are translated into numbers, we will get to understand how our dualistic ideas and desires in the physical relate to the "law of attraction." In the beginning, before time, space, polarity, and materialism, our "I AM" brought nonexistence into existence. And, it was done by our Christ consciousness, also known as our Oversoul, by manipulating *(arousing)* this "universal omnipresent neutralized god energy of light" using sacred geometry.

And this is why the Bible is full of numbers; they represent the geometric pattern of turning nothingness (abyss) into somethingness (all that is today). Without mathematics or sacred geometry, there would be no physical body, earth, stars, universes, planets, rocks, trees, animals, or anything that has form. Therefore, the building blocks of space, time, earth, and all physical life and manifestation come from the geometric configurations of our Christ consciousness.

Therefore, God, in the most real sense of the word, is not a single white male individual having all power to himself. God is the composition of the Spirit of One, our "I AM" Christ consciousness and this "omnipresent universal mind force of pure neutralized energy of light" that we souls use to create our desires to bring into form, like a physical body. And this is where we get the symbology of the essence of a Father-God, the Mother-Goddess, and where it comes from. Yeshua called this essence of this "omnipresent universal mind field of pure neutralized energy of light," Father (God) to keep it simple during his time on earth.

It is the combination of the two that represents the "I AM" Christ consciousness within all of us. Thus, we too are the Father-Mother, God-Goddess playing out of a three-dimensional consciousness; (i) spirit, (ii) mind-soul, and (iii) an ego-personality. And, this is why we symbolically say that God is in the middle of everything, because, in the most real sense, he is.

Because of our Oversoul's strong desire to expand in consciousness to know "all that there is to know about life and polarity," then passion has become the key to move our expressions in consciousness to the imaginational level where our Christ Spirit can arouse this "god energy of light," thus, turning our thoughts and desires into form (like a physical body). For example, the masters will break down the influential aspects named in the Book of Genesis that represent the "six days of creation" found in the Bible, Genesis 1:1–31, to help with the understanding of "who we truly are."

The "six days of creation" has nothing to do with the creation of physical earth or days of the week. Why, because they represent the "I AM" in the first creation where our Oversoul structured us souled beings as a Goddess, and because of our desire to see ourselves as a living creator, we transformed into "six major divine attributes" to identify ourselves as a living Christ, God-Goddess. Then later, we realized that these six divine attributes needed another significant quality added, called "silence" before expressing choices to be manifested (symbolized by the seventh day in Genesis), all because of free will. Therefore, Genesis' seven days of creation are symbolic of the "seven divine attributes" found as part of our Oversoul. And they are as follow:

1. We all have an Infinite consciousness that is forever active, cannot die (first day)
2. We all are tied to universal Intelligence, where we, all souled beings, can tap into (second day)
3. Our Consciousness, since we are an extension of the Spirit of One, was conceived for soul growth and expansion (third day)
4. We souls, eons ago, developed a Divine Plan (will) where we would learn all that there is to know about all energy, including polarity, and that we are a Goddess in our own right (fourth day)
5. We souls have a spiritual essence about ourselves that is the essence of life where we can give the breath life to; thoughts, beliefs, ideas, and many ego-personality aspects (fifth day)
6. We souls also have a "Christ consciousness" that is absolute, unchangeable, and unconditional when it comes to our creations because our true essence is always in a divine unconditional love state (sixth day)

It is with these "six divine attributes" that make us the chairperson and the monarch (God-Goddess) mentioned in the Bible and not some God outside of us that we cannot touch, smell, hear, taste, and see. And, since this number six (6) represents us, humans, as a living God and a Christ also, then it also represents the first six (6) found in the number (name) of the Beast ((6)66) given in Revelation 13:18; as this will be explained further in Revelation 13:3.

The amazing thing about the *"gold crowns"* in Revelation 4:4 is about the wisdom and understanding we all have gained because of journeying through many lifetimes playing with the belief of polarity as being real. Thus, we create for ourselves lots of sowing and reaping because of those beliefs. However, it is through sowing and reaping, where we feel firsthand our trials and tribulations in learning the wisdom behind our choices. Therefore, once awakened to this truth, we have earned the *"white garments"* of freedom from this belief in opposing energy.

It is through the freedom of the belief in opposing energy where we become a sovereign God-Goddess in our own right, while we are still part of the flesh. We are recognizing that there is no supreme being over us, for we, together, are the supreme being and creator of everything that we experience in life. The suffering comes from us humans believing in good and evil, that we are separate from God, and that we need a savior. Salvation and the forgiveness of sins come to us when we awaken to the truth that we are God, the Goddess, Satan, and the Christ, just as Yeshua did in his time.

There is a perception in Revelation 4:4, about the number twenty-four (24), and yet the number is really forty-eight (48), as this is where the wisdom of Yeshua and the Ascended Masters comes to light. Because of the structured position we hold to positive and negative as being real, we, the mass-consciousness, created the mind as having twelve left-brain and twelve right-brain activities. Not only did we, the mass, fashion the mind-soul having these twelve left-right brain activities, we also created twelve endocrine system senses and twelve major systems to the physical body. When putting all this together, it adds up to "forty-eight" (48) and not twenty-four (24).

When we study Revelation 4:4, it appears to be "twenty-four" because of the mentioned *"twenty-four elders."* However, because of the two halves of the mind (left-right) and how each side senses things in different modes of perception, it must also then be for each hemisphere, giving us all twelve left (outer) and twelve right (inner) activities of the mind. When we look at the physical body, there are "seven nerve centers" (endocrine centers) leading from the brain to the "five outer senses," adding up to twelve. Then, we have twelve major systems of the human body. When added to the left and right brain activities, it gives us forty-eight (48), and not twenty-four (24) as assumed.

Revelation 4:4 is the beginning of the wisdom where we could, if we so choose, become complete in this lifetime as far as karma. It is all about opening up to a new understanding of who we indeed are, who God is, and who Christ is. Therefore, the answer to the puzzling Revelation 4:4 is the wholeness of our total consciousness and how it comprises of us having a super-subconsciousness that contains the six (6) divine attributes of our "I AM" mentioned above. And, it is through these six (6) divine attributes that nourish the "twenty-four (24) thrones" in the physical body.

It is also the seven (7) nerve centers (endocrine centers) that leads from the brain to the five (5) physical senses, and the twelve (12) major systems of the human body, that makes us completed as a three-dimensional consciousness, which is symbolized by the *"twenty-four (24) elders sit upon."* Thus, our three-dimensional consciousness composition comprises of us souls having the six (6) divine attributes of spirit. We all experience the twelve (12) left and twelve (12) right-brain activities. We have seven (7) nerve endocrine centers leading from the brain to the five (5) physical senses, and we have twelve (12) major systems of the human body, all working together as one. Together, the total is the sacred geometric number of fifty-four (54), then reduced to nine (9).

To clarify, 6 + 12 + 12 + 7 + 5 + 12 = 54! When broken down to its lowest value of 5 + 4, it equals 9. The next step is to come into completion because the only thing that comes after 9 is 10. Thus, having a meaning where we, in this lifetime, can come back to our state of "oneness" again. However, this will not be the same "oneness" from when we first left higher consciousness (Garden) but a "new oneness" where we are a wise and sovereign God-Goddess in our own right. Thus, we no longer have to be part of anyone else's sovereignty.

Also, these *"twenty-four elders"* in Revelation 4:4, symbolize the "twelve tribes of Israel (left hemisphere)" and the "twelve disciples of Yeshua (right hemisphere)," along with the twelve metaphorical meanings of their names. Allow Yeshua and the Ascended Masters explain!

Since we are a three-dimensional consciousness, when in the flesh, the "six divine attributes of spirit" found in Genesis 1:1–31 are referring to the six days of creation; thus, they need to be added to the *"twenty-four other thrones"* and the *"twenty-four elders,"* and how they are all part of each dimensional level of consciousness. We have a (i) spirit, (ii) mind-soul, and (iii) ego-personality (physical levels), adding up to a sacred geometric pattern totaling fifty-four (54) angels that are *"dressed in white garments and with gold crowns on their heads."* And, not just the twenty-four mentioned in Revelation 4:4!

I know this can be confusing, but when we put this all together, we are the Alpha and the Omega, the first and the last, for we are the Father-Mother, God-Goddess, the Son, and the holy one that sits upon the throne. Therefore, put no other god before you, not even Yeshua. All of this represents that we are journeying through cycles of activities in a three-dimensional existence playing with polarity energy as the framework of our existence and reality. Then, when we are finished with our work playing with opposites, we return once again back to the sacred number of 10 (1 + 0 = 10), back to our oneness of consciousness where we move on to a new cycle filled with wisdom and sovereignty.

In this completion, we are bringing with us the wisdom of everything that we have learned while playing in this polarity energy. We also bring with us all the wisdom of the wholeness of the mass (all souled beings) from whatever they and you have played out in the second cycle (zero), including the wisdom we inherited while in the first cycle (zero). When we reach this awareness and understanding, we become a true creator God-Goddess (Spirit of One) in our own right who has found the way back home (heaven) by home (heaven) finding us.

By studying the chart below, Yeshua and the Ascended Masters hope to clarify Revelation 4:4 in more detail. When looking at the charts below for what the *"twenty-four elders"* characterize, we will see that they represent the "twenty-four activities of the mind" (the left and right hemispheres). Then, followed up with the chart for the *"twenty-four other thrones,"* characterized by the "seven endocrine glands," the "five physical senses," and the "twelve major systems" of the physical body. We hope a little understanding comes through.

First, let's look at the mind and its left and right brain hemisphere and how these activities relate to the "twelve tribes of Israel" and the "twelve disciples of Yeshua." Please note; Dan, a son of Jacob, was named as one tribe of Israel, and yet, Dan is not mentioned in the Apocalypse. For this reason, I placed his name in italics at the bottom of the list. The reason for leaving Dan out of the book of the Apocalypse is because of the mass having a hard time moving past what the name characterizes.

Know that judgment is one's testimony within memory that we if we so choose, can move into our completeness, "four-square" (1 + 3 = 4), which will be mentioned later in the book. However, for now, let us look at the "twelve left and right brain activities," and how they relate to the "twelve tribes of Israel" and the "twelve disciples of Yeshua."

Then we will follow up with the "seven endocrine system senses," including the "five physical senses" and the "twelve major systems of the physical body," which characterize the *"seven thrones."* And, they are not in any particular order.

Channeling of the Ascended Masters on the Apocalypse

L/Brain Activity	12 Tribes of Israel	R/Brain Activity	Disciples
1. Sight/Understanding	Reuben	Justice/Emotions	James Zebedee
2. Hearing/Following	Simeon	Desires Suffer/Form	Judas
3. Love/Service	Levi	Reason Intellect	Thomas
4. Spirit-Intelligence	Judah	Free Will/Expression	Matthew
5. Forgetfulness	Manasseh	Courage/Responsibiity	Andrew
6. Strength/Power	Naphtali	Choice/Substance	James Alphaeus
7. Fortune	Gad	Power/Passion/Speech	Philip
8. Spirit Ideals	Asher	Duality in Action/Growth	John
9. Hidden/Wisdom	Issachar	Purging/Elimination	Thaddeus
10. Abundance	Zebulun	Universal Intelligence	Simon
11. Authority/Power	Joseph	Imagination	Bartholomew
12. Faith/Trust	Benjamin	Compassion/Belief	Peter
13. Judgment	Dan		

We will now follow up with the "seven endocrine systems senses," along with the "five physical senses" and the "twelve major systems" of the physical body, characterized by the *"seven thrones."* They are not in any particular order.

Terry L. Newbegin

Endocrine System/ Outer Five Senses	Seven Churches	Major Systems of the Physical Body
1. Gonads	Ephesus	Reproductive (male/female)
2. Leydig	Smyrna	Circulatory
3. Adrenal	Pergamum	Digestive
4. Thymus	Thyatira	Respiratory
5. Thyroid	Sardis	Immune
6. Pineal	Philadelphia	Skeletal
7. Pituitary	Laodicea	Endocrine
8. Taste		Muscular (front & rear)
9. Smell		Integumentary
10. Touch		Nervous
11. Sight		Lymphatic
12. Hearing		Urinary

The twenty-four mind activities *(elders)* and the twenty-four physical attributes *(thrones)* are, and have always been, part of our mind and ego-personality aspects from which we, in the physical form, have been playing the game of duality. When we reunite these twelve inner (left) and outer (right) brain activities of our mind with our twenty-four (24) physical attributes, defined above, we see ourselves, and everyone else, as a sovereign God-Goddess in our own right.

It is with the unity of consciousness; each personality aspect of us is where we finally move our human consciousness to a knowing that the kingdom of heaven is at hand, right at our fingertips. Therefore, no person, not even the worst of the worst, can be rejected or left behind as religions proclaim. It comes down to the lifetime where we move beyond belief in polarity, and that we are equal to Christ because we are a Christ and the God-Goddess in human form. .

When we learn the wisdom behind Revelation 4:5, it comes alive because, from the seat of our soul (the Leydig center), our "I AM" Christ consciousness becomes the *"flash of lightning,"* the "twinkle of an eye," emitting a repetitive vibrational frequency to our mind-soul and our ego physical consciousness, revealing to us, that we are complete. All that is left is for us to do is open up to the message. It is not Christ Yeshua coming to save us. It is you saving you! The message is not about disasters coming to earth, even though it could because of the mass reflecting outside of themselves what is inside to deal with.

It is about our "I AM" Christ consciousness trying to get us to open up to the secrets in the Book of Revelation, revealing to us our journey as souled beings and as a Christ also. Even in the word "apocalypse," it does not mean destruction, day of reckoning, or the end of the world; the true meaning of the word is "to reveal." Religions interpret the word of God as to "revealing" his anger toward us because of our wicked ways and, therefore, God will destroy us. Revelation/the Apocalypse is a message to us, while in physical form, where we can begin our awakening and completion as a God-Goddess in our own right.

Many among us have worked out our karma over many lifetimes. And now, some of us are ready to receive sudden flashes of thought patterns that will reflect our resolve to studying beliefs about polarity energy that will free us from our chains of dual beliefs. Think of it this way! Many are beginning to suddenly have deep urges of wanting to examine their beliefs when it comes to the God of the Bible.

Like the *"rumblings and peals of thunder"* in Revelation 4:5, as some of us are having flash thoughts rising up within us, and we are getting excited about the memories of our many lifetimes flaming up within us wanting to come home to their creator. And, this excitement is found in the *"seven flaming torches burning in front of the throne"* in Revelation 4:5 as the "Seven Divine Attributes" of the "I AM" Christ consciousness. These seven attributes are also tied to Genesis "seven days of creation." And, they are again:

1. Spirit/Christ consciousness – Our "I AM" is a very <u>active consciousness</u>, cleaning and purifying our Oversoul and the many light and dark pieces of us (lifetimes). And once completed, our (i) "I AM" spirit, (ii) mind-soul, and (iii) ego personalities of many begin to integrate into "one body of a sovereign consciousness, while we are part of a physical body.

In Hebrew 12:29: *"For our, God is a consuming fire."* Thus, know that our "I AM" consciousness is the prevailing fire bringing about integrating our mind-soul and our many ego personalities of good and evil.

2. We all have a Spirit <u>Intelligence</u> of a universal nature, having authority, enormous understanding, exceptional wisdom, and a notable truth about ourselves deep within.

3. Our "I AM" Christ consciousness is filled with <u>multitudes of experiences</u> because we volunteered to allow our "oneness of consciousness" to expand and grow to a level where;
4. We have a <u>Divine Plan</u> and Free Will that have become the means for our purpose to "know all that there is to know" about polarity energy and life.
5. We have a Christ consciousness that is the essence of all life energy. Therefore, our "I AM" gives life to <u>multiple ego-personality aspects</u> of light and dark. Hence, we create many lifetimes playing with potentials lined with good and evil to learn responsibility and wisdom.
6. Since our core essence is of a divine unconditional love state, our "I AM," Christ consciousness is <u>unconditional</u> and <u>unchangeable</u>, having compassion for all that we create, good and bad.
7. Before deciding, we need to learn to <u>silence</u> our mind before choosing, since we are dealing with polarity energy. Better yet, it is best to take deep breaths before choosing. Deep breathing and silencing the mind will help us tap into the treasures of wisdom lying dormant within our Christ's memory.

Referencing the phrase *"sea of glass like crystal"* in Revelation 4:6, we have a super sub-consciousness where our "I AM" Christ consciousness resides. And, it is protected by our subconsciousness (mind-soul) and our outer ego physical consciousness. Therefore, our true essence, the "I AM," resides within a three-dimensional consciousness. And, in the center, our subconsciousness is the seat of our soul *(throne)* where our "I AM" placed within it unlimited unexpressed thoughts, potentials, ideas, and unstructured beliefs about positive and negative, good and bad, right and wrong, for us to partake and experience here on earth in a physical body to learn wisdom.

From our subconscious *(center)* and the seat of our soul *(throne)*, we long-ago set-in motion a belief in the law of cause-and-effect *(justice)*, because that forms and shapes this polarity energy in the direction we assign our physical body to play upon the earth. It is through our outer ego physical consciousnesses (many faces or personalities) that we acknowledge our memories of many past lifetimes where we played them out in the physical. Therefore, we unconsciously assist our mind-soul in expanding and growing in consciousness. And this is done by the *"four living creatures"* in Revelation 4:6-7.

These four creatures are symbolic of the four lower elements of our physical body here on earth. They are mostly known as the four natural urges of (i) courage, (ii) reproduction, (iii) sustenance, and (iv) gratification.

However, without us realizing it, most of us here in the physical, live our life using our beastly urges coming from our many past lifetimes mentioned in Revelation 4:6.

For example: *"covered with eyes in front and back"* is referring to our many past lifetimes, where each eye ("I") have lived upon the earth experiencing the four lower elements playing with polarity energy as the means for our source of creations. It is through these four lowering forces of (i) fire, (ii) earth, (iii) water, and (iv) air, that we, on a conscious level (front), experience the impulses of our past lifetime ego-personality aspects of light and dark (back); all without realizing that ninety-seven (97%) percent of our beliefs and choices made in our present lifetime come from past lifetimes.

Today, we identify ourselves more with our past life experiences than what we believe we are today, which is why most of our expressions, fears, and manifestations come from the beliefs of our past lifetimes. Also, this may answer questions about why some of us experience life-threatening diseases.

When we get into Revelation 4:7, the first, second, third, and fourth creatures, we are speaking of our beginning, when we left higher consciousness and moved into an emotional, mental consciousness, and created an astral-physical realm. At first, we displayed great courage and had no fear in what we were manifesting to experience. However, once we allowed our beastly ego-personality to take over the creation process, we clarified that we were becoming a skilled predator of immorality. It was with this skilled predator ego that we forgot about our Christ consciousness.

The lion is the king of the beasts, which is why we dared to move outside of our "I AM" Christ consciousness long ago and into a three-dimensional consciousness using polarity energy, as this protected our divinity from this coarser consciousness. At the same time, we journeyed through many lifetimes, working out karmic justice based upon our predatory choices. This is why the adrenal area of the body is part of our memory, for it is the storehouse of all our predatory lifetimes where we reaped what we sowed.

It took a great deal of courage for us to enter earth and move into many physical bodies (lifetimes) to experience this unknown polarity energy, positive and negative. However, we did it to benefit learning wisdom and taking responsibility. Courage alone was not enough to remember our "I AM" Christ consciousness again. So, we needed memory to note our passion and commitment to experiencing everything of duality; otherwise, we would not be where we are today in the understanding of spirit.

The *"second was like a calf,"* Revelation 4:7, represents us souls having the courage to leave our Christ consciousness and move into the second creation. Thus, our mind-soul and ego consciousness, where we formed our consciousnesses into a dualistic and opposing solid energy, is where we gave ourselves the means to create the physical universe, earth, our physical bodies, animals, birds, fish, the plant kingdom, and much more. The calf here in Revelation 4:7 is also associated with the Church of Ephesus.

Also, *"the third had a face like a human being,"* represents sustenance (or supporting life), water, temptation, and choices. It is the life of humanity and what we desire to manifest and accomplish in the physical. Therefore, what do you wish to achieve in the physical? Do you wish to become a divine-human that only needs to trust in yourself as God-Goddess, or are you looking for a Christ outside of you to do it for you? The *"human being,"* Revelation 4:7, is also associated with the Church of Smyrna.

"The fourth looked like an eagle in flight," Revelation 4:7, represents air or our etheric mental consciousness reflected through our many gratifications, incarnations, love, good and evil; and, most of all, growth. This is where our self-indulgence and predatory ego nature come from. It comes from our personality aspects of past lifetimes, where we played with the forces of the intellect and reasoning. The eagle is also associated with the Church of Thyatira.

Creatures	Physical Nature	Mind	Spirit	Physical Forces	Church
1. Lion	Courage	Justice	Memory	Fire	Pergamum
2. Calf	Reproduction	Form	Desire	Earth	Ephesus
3. Man	Sustenance	Being	Choices	Water	Smyrna
4. Eagle	Gratification	Incarnation	Growth	Air	Thyatira

To clarify this, I will associate the "four living creatures" with the basic principles of our "I AM" spirit, mind-soul, physical levels of consciousness, and the four lower elements of life, along with the four churches associated with them.

In recapping, Revelation 4:8, *"the four living creatures"* and *"each of them having six wings"* and *"covered with eyes inside and out;"* are the attributes of the divine self as a Christ and a God-Goddess having the authority in governing all the influences that we put on each level of our three-dimensional consciousness (spirit, mind-soul, and ego physical nature).

Channeling of the Ascended Masters on the Apocalypse

The *"eyes inside and out"* are associated with the *"four living creatures"* tied with our expressions, ideas, beliefs, thoughts, and how we give them life by using many ego personalities of light and dark (lifetimes) to learn about life, gain wisdom, and take responsibility. We, from the soul level, judge ourselves based upon our courage in the physical, fair dealings (justice) that come from the mind, and how we pay our debts (sowing and reaping) using the memory of spirit.

Within each level of our three-dimensional consciousness, inside and out, our ego, physical personality, mind-soul, and our "I AM" Christ-Spirit carry within them the six divine attributes, giving us, while in physical form, the authority to govern all influences coming from all multiple layers of our consciousness. These *"six wings,"* Revelation 4:7, are associated with the portrayal of the "perfection of the 'six divine attributes'" given in Genesis 1:1-31, as the six days of creation in Revelation 4:4.

It takes the "six divine attributes" of our "I AM" Christ consciousness *(six wings)* to express that we are an infinite, everlasting creator of perfection. And, the polarity energy (good and evil, right and wrong, light and dark) was created to learn the wisdom behind our choices. Therefore, in the deepest of truth, we are perfect, constant, unchangeable, and without sin. It is only from a mind and an ego that is asleep, and that is where we believe we have sinned.

Also, please note, these "six divine attributes" *(six wings)* of our "I AM" Christ consciousness denote the first six (6) contributed to the number of the beast found in Revelation 13:8. It is our "I AM" Christ consciousness *"who was, who is, and who is to come"* in Revelation 4:8, and not Yeshua. Know that it is our many ego personalities of past lifetimes that cry out to us in this lifetime *"day and night, for they do not stop exclaiming"* their voices as our creations. Remember, we sit on the throne forever and ever.

The "twenty-four elders" that *"fall before the one who sits on the throne and worships,"* Revelation 4:10-11, represent the twelve left and right brain activities, the twelve tribes of Israel, and all of what they represent. It is the "twelve left and right brain activities" that fall under the one who sits on the throne, *you*. It is you who chooses to believe in polarity energy as being real. Thus, the pure Crystalline energy that surrounds us then flows through our left and right brain hemispheres, changing the way we respond to this energy.

"Worthy are you, Lord your God-Goddess, *to receive glory, honor, and power,* for you, as a living God-Goddess, created your world of reality" using many ego-personality aspects (lifetimes) in fulfilling your mission to learn wisdom.

Chapter 17

MEMORY AND HOW IT WORKS

When we look into the wisdom, Revelation 5:1-14, when it speaks of the *"scroll,"* Yeshua and the Ascended Masters are referring to memory and how it works, both consciously and unconsciously *(both sides)*. It is through memory where we bring to life our soul's activities (divine plan) and how we played them out in each lifetime. The example of how memory works would be like a book, as a chapter out of many would represent a lifetime on earth collecting memories. Therefore, how many chapters (stories) have you played out on the stage of the earth?

The *"right hand,"* Revelation 5:1, represents us, from the mind-soul level, learning that we are more than human. We enlighten ourselves through memory. Therefore, no one can enlighten us about Christ other than ourselves because we are the Christ that holds all memory in choosing the way we learn about polarity energy.

By *"writing on both sides and was sealed with the seven seals,"* Revelation 5:1, represents the memory as the key in revealing to us how our outer physical consciousness (the ego) and inner subconsciousness (the mental) play a big part in our awakening to the Christ within. Therefore, we not only *"sit on the throne"* as a living Christ, but we also sit in judgment for every thought and choice we made.

Revelation, Chapter Five, is about us humans accepting the memories of our polarity creations, good and bad. And, if we judge these memories as sin, then the justice of karma that we will receive will be based upon those judgments.

Channeling of the Ascended Masters on the Apocalypse

In Genesis 2:25, *"the man and his wife"* represents our mind (Adam) and our soul region of responsibility (Eve). Our mind-soul consciousness represents the outer positive-masculine and inner negative-feminine side of us, where, in the beginning, our mind-soul *"felt no shame"* in what we created. It was during the measuring of our mind-soul consciousness millions and millions of years later is where we felt our exposed (*nakedness*) creations of unworthiness, shame, and guilt. And now, we have exposed all that we have created, good and bad, leaving our energy and consciousness unbalanced.

In the beginning, when our focus moved from higher consciousness to a mental consciousness, we had no faults or memories of sin or wrongdoings. However, once we manipulated the polarity energy and used it as power, that is when we exposed ourselves by dominating others. It was in our dominating of others where we all agreed to a belief in good and evil, right and wrong, judgment, power, and weakness. However, it was necessary to have this experience because, if we were going to move away from the awareness of a Christ also, then we needed something that would remind us later who we are.

Therefore, we placed in memory the law of cause and effect (karma), and the belief in an evil spirit (Satan) that would take us on a journey of discovery. Whatever we thought, believed, or acted upon (good and bad) became part of our soul memories. Thus, in time, those memories became our reality to experience in the flesh. Yeshua and the Ascended Masters call these memories the Book of Life, for this book is nothing more than our soul record of everything we have done since the time we left higher consciousness (Garden). Some people call this the Akashic Records.

Everything that we do in this now moment or have done in past lifetimes, and everything we think and feel right now in our heart, all have been part of our soul memories played out on earth. We cannot escape from what we have ever thought, judged, or done. But we can heal what we have done simply by acknowledging and taking responsibility for it. Our Christ-spirit comes to us with the acceptance of everything that comes into our path, whether we feel it is our fault or not.

Revelation 5:2, the *"mighty angel proclaiming in a loud voice,"* is about us and our actions taking hold of the polarity in such a way it isolated us from remembering our Christ consciousness and our ego personality aspects (lifetimes) that are part of our total consciousness today. However, this isolation was a good thing because it enabled us to grow and evolve using polarity energy to learn wisdom without interference coming from our Christ consciousness.

Therefore, no one is worthy to open the seven seals other than the self. Once we have journeyed through the process of our emotional body, the adrenal, solar plexus area, we learn and recognize what we have taken in as our belief systems. And, that is the time where we will learn the language of the right brain hemisphere in Revelation 4:4.

From the seven angels in Revelation 1:20, the one who shouts the loudest was the influential force between our outer ego, physical consciousness, and our inner subconsciousness. This is indicated by the division of the right and left-brain hemispheres, where there are no direct communications between the two, other than through memory. Therefore, no man or woman, including Yeshua, is worthy to open the seals of our memories (book of life) until we awakened to our own Christ consciousness, like our brother Yeshua did.

No human or religion, not even you, can ever be worthy to open the seven seals unless you finally overcome the emotional belief that a God outside of you created you, judges you, and one that you must worship. As long as we continue to believe that Yeshua is coming for our salvation, then we will never be worthy to open our memories *(scroll)* to our past lifetimes. No one can save us but ourselves because everything must be met on an individual scale. Not even our free will is strong enough to free us from our bondage playing with polarity energy. Why? Because our free will is joined to our emotional, mental level of understanding to whom Christ is.

Religions teach their followers it was because of Eve (woman) that man was thrown out of the Garden, and, if we buy into that story, it demonstrates the point of our unawakened mind (Anti-Christ) becoming the testing portion for our emotional body. Remember, Genesis 1:27, *"God created man in his divine image, male and female."* Therefore, both male and female are created equally, as male and female just represent the masculine-feminine within us. Thus, we can take on a male or female body.

What is overlooked is our many ego-personality aspects (lifetimes) comes from the emotional part of our feminine consciousness, signified by Eve, rather than coming from our masculine side of the mind, signified by Adam. Thus, this gives our masculine side (male or female) the feeling of more importance than our feminine soul side, even though it is the same mind (person).

It was our masculine side of the mind (Adam) that began appropriating the idea of two powers, positive and negative, and not our feminine soul side of that same mind. The result was that our mind, the masculine, fell away from its true spiritual nature of "one pure energy" and into a belief of two opposing energies as being real. This belief then produced the idea of a God of good and a Satan of evil. That was when our masculine side of the mind ignored the feminine side of us as less important, not knowing it was totalness of our mind all along. This action is where we began to focus using our ego, the beastly personality consciousness, and to whom we were in the scheme of things.

To confirm this interpretation! Yeshua and the Ascended Masters refer us to Genesis 2:18, *"It is not good for man to be alone. I will make a suitable partner."* And, in Genesis 2:21, *"the Lord God cast a deep sleep on the man, and while he was asleep, he took out one of his ribs and closed up its place with flesh."* First, when Yeshua and the Ascended Masters speak of the Lord God, they are talking about our mind, since all authority was passed down to the son-the masculine, the master of creation, the mind. And, when our masculine side (Adam side) went into a *"deep sleep,"* we became unaware of the soul side of self (Eve side) recording everything that our masculine side chose to experience, and how it is our masculine side of the mind that must take responsibility for the choice.

Therefore, the symbolization of *"taking out one of his ribs"* is where our mind (Adam side), when we began to focus out of mental consciousness, started to use this "omnipresent mind field of pure neutralized god energy of light" to manifest an energy of two. Thus, *"bone of my bone"* symbolizes this opposing energy where one side carries a masculine-positive side and the other side of that same energy carries a feminine-negative. And this is where the verse references *"closing up its place in the flesh,"* meaning that it represents consciousness coming from consciousness and energy comes from energy.

We took our "oneness of consciousness," the "I AM" Christ, and our "energy of oneness" and created a new layer of consciousness called the mental or the imaging consciousness. And then, we split our "energy of one" to having an "energy of two" where the two opposed each other. Thus, giving life to a feminine soul side of self that became the holder (concubine) for whatever the mind acted on, good or bad. And this why Eve, the soul side of our mind, became the responsible keeper for all our thoughts, ideas, desires, and choices.

The story of God, Adam, Eve, and the Serpent in the Garden is a metaphoric myth that helps us understand our "I AM," our mind-soul, our ego, and our many ego-personalities playing with polarity energy, learning responsibility for those choices and the wisdom that comes from them. The name Eve symbolizes feeling, life, expression, and she represents our soul region of responsibility for the masculine mental side of us. Thus, giving us, in any given lifetime (male or female), the feeling of existence.

Our Eve (soul) consciousness is only responsible for recording (or taking in the seed of memory) everything that our mind (the masculine) chooses and experiences. Therefore, our mind, the masculine side of us, is the author and writer of whatever we act on in consciousness to experience. Now, maybe we can understand why women have the babies, for our soul side of the mind gives life to whatever our mind desires and chooses to experience.

If the Adam side of our mind consistently believes in good (light) and evil (dark), then we are continually feeding beliefs to our soul consciousness of responsibility (Eve) to the effect where we will experience these beliefs in the physical, either in this lifetime or in future lifetimes. Thus know, the Apocalypse is not about Yeshua or the end of the world. It is revealing the truth to whom we are at our core consciousness, and this is why we are the only one worthy to open the seven seals.

And this is why our adrenal area (solar plexus) is the connecting link between our Christ consciousness, our positive-masculine, feminine-negative side of the mind, and our ego-personalities of many lifetimes. Therefore, we are incapable of penetrating the emotional bridge that controls the lower nature of our physical body and our belief in polarity, because we see it as good and evil, right and wrong, light and dark (sin). This is also why most of humanity, about ninety-seven percent, are not yet ready to open the seals in this lifetime.

We all have forgotten long ago that we agreed to cut ourselves off from the qualities of our Christ consciousness in favor of our mind-soul and ego consciousness as to whom we are in setting our energy signature frequency (DNA). Hence, it was us, souls who set the stage to become weak-willed, quickly led, susceptible, indecisive, confused, and ignorant, lacking clear knowledge and understanding of what the *"wine of duality"* would bring into our life of discovery. This uncertainty and susceptibility became our fall from a higher consciousness, and not that some God kicked us out of higher consciousness (Garden).

The covenant we believe we made with this God of the Bible was with our own higher self, promising ourselves that we eventually will purify our mind/soul through sowing and reaping. And then, we will integrate all that we are as "one consciousness" again. We have forgotten the vows we took in past lifetimes to a God outside of us, and now those vows have inhibited us from becoming awakened by our Christ consciousness and the natural flow of our divine energy.

We have taken vows of poverty, suffering, servitude, and such, trying to justify what we feel are our sinful ways. Thus, the time has come to get over any guilt that we believe we have and move beyond that deeply embedded shame within our soul by letting go of those vows. Our Christ consciousness has kept its promise not to interfere with our mental and opposing creations since we left higher consciousness. And now, the time has come when we can release our "I AM" from that promise because we have experienced a full range of choices, good and bad.

And, once the promise is released, we come to where we can choose to take off the veil of our emotions and let those old vows, promises, and rituals go. And, like Yeshua, take yourself off the cross and reinstate (resurrect) yourself as a Christ again.

We learn through Revelation 5:5, *"one of the elders"* speaking to John is symbolic of our consciousness of courage, as we learn that our solar plexus (adrenal gland) is where we find the "two-edged sword of Justice" for soul growth. And that is where we become balanced in energy and in consciousness. And, if this is maintained, then the life-giving forces freely cross the solar plexus each time we pass from higher to lower consciousness. Know that it is the solar plexus (the Church of Pergamum) that is the center that separates our lower from our higher consciousness because of the two-edged sword of justice.

It is from this center that we can fall short in giving birth to higher thoughts about us being more than just a human. Thoughts of anger, impulsive reactions, such as judgment, evil urges, and just believing in polarity as being real, keep us locked into the solar plexus level. Therefore, the adrenal area of the physical body becomes our weakest point. And, if we do not commit to some study to our belief in polarity, then by way of those same beliefs, we will create and throw stumbling blocks into our own path until we become aware.

If we will open our eyes, heart, and mind to other possibilities, our Christ consciousness promises us that we can eat from the hidden manna (divine truths) and receive a new name, "I AM That I AM," or a Christ also. And, if we do not learn to listen to our gut feelings, then those feelings automatically transfer the energy coming into the mind to our intellect as "something to reason with" as our truths. Thus, we produce a powerful, irresponsible outcome that can slow down when the day we can open up to the memory of the seals and the reason they are closed off to us.

If we allow ourselves to listen to our gut feelings more than the intellect of the mind, we will awaken to the powerful forces of grace, forgiveness, and compassion that triggers the opening of our memory of the seven seals. We all hold the power that exercises either the sword of destruction or fruitful creations. The mastering of our belief in opposing energies through our heart center will help us improve our chances for spiritual awakening in this lifetime. Thus, we can open the seven seals to all memory.

Yeshua was the first to signify the sacrifice of the self, and since we all have done the same, we can take ourselves down off the cross of karma as he did and now move past the solar plexus emotional level. Thus, we come face to face with our Christ consciousness. When we, through our thoughts and actions, do not adulterate the pure energy of light coming into our mind, the energy within us rises directly from our gonads to our pineal without stopping at our adrenal level. Thus, allowing us, from the mind (intellect), to make choices that come more from the light of truth to reach our pituitary level of responsibility.

John 5:19, *"the son (mind) can do nothing for himself, but what he seeth the Father do."* Only the self can face our memories of good and evil and release the blocked-up memories that relate to the seven seals, because we humans are the *"lamp standing in the midst of the throne,* along with *"the four living creatures and the elders,"* Revelation 5:6. Since it was we who made the sacrifice, the one that chose to journey through many lifetimes, physical and nonphysical, to explore the unknown principle of polarity, then some of us have come to a place in consciousness where we can receive our inheritance.

Know that some of us are a breath away from changing our consciousness from the old way of understanding karma to a new way of understanding karma and self. Our DNA frequency coding of good and evil experiences can be washed away just by recognizing ourselves as a Christ, forgiving ourselves because we are worthy to open the seven seals.

The *"four living creatures, the Lion, Calf, Man, and Eagle"* are all associated with the four elements of life, (i) fire, (ii) earth, (iii) water, and (iv) air. We are living today out of the belief more in line with the Eagle in flight, symbolic of our ability to create a mental perception of our journey through time and space. The Eagle in flight represents air, which means we are living our life, making choices, and creating our experiences from a belief associated with our intellect, reasoning, and perception, signified by the Church of Thyatira. Even the Bible supports this perception.

"He had seven horns and seven eyes," Revelation 5:6, refers to us humans. All of us who are beginning to awaken, to recognize ourselves as the sacrificial lamb, are the ones sent out into the world to explore the unknown principle of polarity. Therefore, these *"seven stars,"* in Revelation 1:16 and the *"seven seals,"* in Revelation 6:1-17 and 8:1 are opened as:

Channeling of the Ascended Masters on the Apocalypse

Seven Spirits/Stars	Seven Major Expressions	Seven Seals	Seven Churches
1. Physical Body	Desires	Belief in Separation	Ephesus
2. Etheric Body	Choices	Belief in Sanity	Smyrna
3. Emotional Body	Memory	Belief in Satan/Duality	Pergamum
4. Mental/Soul Body	Growth	Belief in Sin & Guilt	Thyatira
5. Intuitive Body	Free Will	Belief in Suffering	Sardis
6. Mind-Body	Relationships	Belief in Salvation	Philadelphia
7. Spirit Body	Responsibility	Knowing one in Christ	Laodicea

The *"seven eyes"* has the same meaning as Revelation 1:14 and later in Revelation 19:16. The "I" (eyes) is symbolic of us souls journeying through many ego lifetimes expressing our manifestations to our Christ consciousness, and the sowing and reaping are required to become balanced. It is the many you's (I's) in other lifetimes that are connected to each layer of expressions and what they carry for influences about how you will carry those many "I's" (egos) in memory.

How passionate are we in responding and reacting to these seven expressions and or influences on an emotional and mental level, and how they relate to each level of our total consciousness (seven spirits) given above? Please refer to these *"seven major expressions/influences,"* as they are arranged according to each level shown above.

Seven Major Expressions/Influences

1. Desires: propagation, form, feeding of the mind, creations, calf, earth
2. Choices: sustenance, being, time, temptation, man, water
3. Memory: justice, courage, karma, madness, preservation, idea, lion, fire
4. Growth: duality, ego, incarnation, gratification, love, eagle, mental, air
5. Free Will: morals, ethics, philosophy, ideology, ideals, purpose, psychic
6. Relationship: name, space, confusion, chaos, mind
7. Responsibility: heaven, higher understanding, silence, strength, patience

These are the *"seven eyes"* or the "seven expressions and influences" that we work with every day of our existence throughout eternity. That is why we must take full responsibility for those expressions, influences, and what we create, or we will journey through many more lifetimes experiencing the dualistic forces of positive and negative, even though they are not real.

The *"seven horns"* can symbolize many things, such as noise-making devices or projections of horns on animals, such as cattle or sheep or even from birds, reptiles, or insects. But, the most well-known horns are those of the devil's head. Therefore, Yeshua and the Ascended Masters refer to these *"seven horns"* as the seven deadliest sins known to man, even though there is no such thing as sin. And they are (i) Sadness, (ii) Anger, (iii) Lust for Power, (iv) Envy, (v) Pride, (vi) Greed, and (vii) Laziness.

The story of Adam and Eve, among others, brings to consciousness a belief in blaming someone or something rather than taking full responsibility for one's own choices and actions. Hence, the symbolism of Adam and Eve's acts puts forward the concept that we created an image (mental picture) within us called our ego-personality that carried a beastly nature (Satan) to blame. However, this mental picture is our own creation, and not that there is a Satan character outside of us.

Matthew 16:21–23, we read about Yeshua telling his disciples he would be killed if he went back to Jerusalem, and that is when Simon Peter took Yeshua aside and said that nothing like this must happen. And, Yeshua's reply to Peter was, *"out of my way, Satan! You stand in my path."* Now, Yeshua was not saying that Satan possessed Peter or that Peter was Satan. He was referring to the outward reaction to Peter's ego. Thus, Satan is not a real person but is a symbol of our ego-personality consciousness, moving into a stubborn and blaming mode.

Remember, Matthew 16:24–25, *"If anyone wants to follow in my footsteps, he must give up all rights to himself, take up his cross and follow me. For the man who wants to save his life will lose it, but the man who loses his life for my sake will find it."* The following in Yeshua's footsteps is to take the path of evolution, for we have temporarily given up our Christ identity *(right to himself)* and have agreed to lower our consciousness to an ego physical personality consciousness. And, at the same time, we have decided to play with polarity. However, whatever we experienced, good or bad, we would have to take full responsibility for the choice, or we would have to sow and reap *(take up our cross)*.

Therefore, the Soul who wants to *"save his life"* is a souled being who is not willing to descend into a physical personality body for learning wisdom and taking responsibility for one's own acts. This soul then becomes dead to any potential for learning wisdom gained by experiencing polarity. From a soul not willing to incarnate into a physical body, that soul becomes very limited. But, a soul who *"loses his life"* (forgetting that one is a Christ for a while), for the sake of learning the wisdom of polarity by taking responsibility, is a soul who takes on multiple lifetimes to gain a wealth of wisdom, understanding, and then returning home to a much higher consciousness than before that soul left the first creations.

Religions proclaim we are a sinner! However, in the eyes of Yeshua and the Ascended Masters, we are not and never have been a sinner. But we are a soul that must take full responsibility for our creations. And, since our ego-personality consciousness has no authority, for that belongs to our mind-soul, it is the part of us that must incarnate into the physical body rather than our Christ and mind-soul consciousness. We are a three-dimensional consciousness, but it is our ego personality consciousness that must ride the rails of lifetimes sowing and reaping.

Thus, the symbolic meaning of this ego-personality consciousness is taken up as our Satan (beast) consciousness. And, this defiant consciousness fights hard to maintain its power over Christ and the mind-soul consciousness. Satan, or the Beast, or whatever we wish to call this personality consciousness, is what descended into the belief in power and opposing energy.

In other words, we confront the "beast" within us every second of the day. No wonder we are so afraid of Satan (the beast), and it is because we are filled with so much fear. We all fight hard against our own Christ consciousness, as did Disciple Peter, which blocks out any learning about our "I AM," all because of our fear of letting go of our deep-seated beliefs. Instead, we allow our unawakened mind, the Anti-Christ, to support the beast (ego) in its effort to maintain its control and power over our total consciousness. And it is our consciousness that brings life into manifestation for us to experience.

It takes the evolution of our ego-personality consciousness moving through the lower energies for what the *"seven horns"* symbolize in initiating many ego-personality incarnations to help us become awakened to this understanding. And, once we come and *"receive the scroll"* (soul memories) in Revelation 5:7, that is when we awaken and realize that we are the sacrificial lamb. Thus, activating the remembrance of our soul's activities, and in the way, we played them out in each lifetime.

Therefore, the time has come for some of us to acknowledge to ourselves, "I have met Christ, and he is me in the flesh." Thus, are you among many that are beginning to awaken to the truth that you volunteered long ago to be here on earth for a while to evolve into a Christ and into a knowing that "you are not of this world?" When this is understood, then this is when the *"four living creatures and the twenty-four elders,"* Revelation 5:8, will bow down to you as their master.

We all can overcome the forces of (i) earth, (ii) fire, (iii) water, and (iv) air, and the twenty-four activities of the left and right hemispheres of the mind by getting to understand how these activities have been part of the "twelve endocrine systems senses" and the "twelve major systems of the physical body" for us to feel and experience the forces of opposing energy. The mind and its left and right brain activities have become the head angels in our yielding to choices, beliefs, and actions that belong to this opposing energy.

However, it has helped us move our ego physical personality consciousness to an awareness of being a Christ also. We get to understand that matter is just slowed-down vibrational energy that plays opposite roles and, therefore, it is nothing more than an illusion. We all are playing a game as we would play upon a theater stage, and somehow, we have forgotten that our good and bad experiences have nothing to do with right or wrong. It is just us playing with energy. Thus, this is confirmed by the *"harp and gold bowls filled with incense"* in Revelation 5:8

The *"harp"* is you, from the mind level, moving from a knowing that energy is "one," to a belief in a force that created vibrational energy as "two." And now, a new expansional energy of four has entered the earth, giving off various impulses where your left and right brain activities are responding to the spirit of acceptance by your ego-personality (the beast) while in the flesh.

To help become balanced and neutral again, this new expansion energy of four surrounds us now, waiting for us to transform this vibrational energy of two, positive and negative, to a New Expansional Energy of "Four," where our human consciousness reaches out multi-dimensionally. And, this New Expansional Energy of four is:

1. Positive
2. Negative
3. The Consciousness of no force (Neutrality)
4. The Gnost-Solution Consciousness! (The consciousness that can answer any question no matter what it is)

The *"golden bowl,"* Revelation 5:8, is symbolic of the wisdom we hold deep within our super subconsciousness and subconsciousness. It is such a high frequency that if we take a moment to rethink *(repent)* about its vibrational tone of duality, and what we are receiving in our mind as being real, we would feel the illusion of it. Then, take note, because it could be the tone of New Expansional Energy of Four coming into our life. And with this New Expansional Energy of Four, we will see ourselves more multi-dimensional than just a three-dimensional human. Thus, we are the Son of God, the Lord of Lords, washing away our memories of the past, good, and evil (sin) using our mind and ego.

The *"incense"* is the finer essences of our physical body transmuting to what is termed the fourth and fifth dimensions. That is where we inherit the kingdom of God. At this firm foundation, we set the stage to move past the three-dimensional stronghold of polarity to the New Expansional Energy of Four. This process takes place whenever our "I AM" Christ consciousness makes its union with the physical human personality. Perhaps the *"four living creatures"* are our lower animal nature (beast) going through a refinement, so we, from a mental level, are ready for a change in consciousness.

Once we transform our physical personality consciousness to an awareness of knowing we are a Christ also, we shift our consciousness in the twinkling of an eye to this New Expansional Energy of Four. Once we choose this from the heart center, we do sing a new reality (new hymn- Revelation 5:9), because we do evolve to a new level of understanding for knowing Christ. Once we move our focus from the energy of two when making choices to focusing on the energy of four, we transform our beastly ego-personality to a whole new unconditional reality.

Thus, we begin to realize that the *"twenty-four elders"* have carried the memories and lessons of our many lifetimes to a conscious physical level where we can tap into the wisdom of those experiences. Thus, we change our life experiences. Once we focus on this New Expansion Energy of Four, tapping into our total memories, we move into a position where we can have total recall.

Therefore, only you, not Yeshua, can tap into your memories *(scroll)* and *"break open the seals,"* because it is only you who has paid the price by experiencing polarity. The ramification of this *"new hymn"* is you, while in the flesh, raising your energy frequency where you become a living Christ in your own right. Thus, you create a whole new reality for you to play and experience. Your worthiness to receive the scroll and break the seven seals refers to you coming into full awareness as a Christ. And, when you accept this revelation, you will enter into your authority (power).

It is through our authority as a Christ, that we in the flesh, can now invite in our "I AM" Christ, symbolized by Yeshua, and then meet within our own mind *(in the air)* and ego and become one body of consciousness as we were in the first creation but with a twist, you become a sovereign being. This is symbolized by the eagle and the thymus level.

When we accept that we are a living God-Goddess and a Christ also, we get to understand our redemption comes from the managing *(purchase)* of our energy *(blood)*, our held belief systems, the many stories we played out in each lifetime, and the way we managed our thoughts and memories *("from every tribe and tongue, people and nation"* (Revelation 5:9).

The word "cities" symbolizes a fixed state of consciousness of the collective mass-energy and how the group beliefs and viewpoints are fixed within the nerve centers of our physical body. Hence, the major controlling factor of our beliefs, as they pertain to the meaning of a city, is found in the purpose of its name. Combine this with being part of a tribe (our angelic family), the language we speak, and our ability to express our thoughts and actions *(tongue)* to the people and nations, as people represent our personality aspects and nations represent our memories.

To simplify! It is all from our outer, extended, mental level of consciousness where the movement sprang forth within our subconscious (mind) that activated our belief patterns that formed into manifested memories (nations) of a psychological concept of inflexibility to anything other than the makeup of the four lower elements of life (air, fire, water, and earth). When we come into physical form to experience the forces of (i) fire (memories/justice), (ii) earth (desires/form), (iii) water (choices/beingness), and (iv) air (growth/incarnations), we forget about our past belief systems, even the family heritage and religion we once supported.

And now, we may hold some of those beliefs so deeply within our being (Smyrna) that they have become part of our total memory (Pergamum). And, because of this, we have become very limited in a three-dimensional physical body (Ephesus) and how we play out our karmic conditions (Thyatira). Therefore, according to which soul family group that we belong to, we will experience the beliefs generated from the memories (nations) of that group. Thus, this is why we all have different belief systems and religious ties because everything is related to when and where we were born in this lifetime.

Each soul group *(clan)* comprises of multiple families, claiming a common ancestry with each other, and this is why we follow the same hereditary line as our parents. From these soul family groups (symbolized by cities, nations, individual states, and religions), each individual genetically transmits to the self, through reincarnation, the issues the self has not yet overcome.

For example, we gain and release many belief systems through our family, town, state, and nation where we live and travel. Because we are often our ancestors, we can come into this world often to experience a disease or a talent that is passed down through family lines; usually, we are handing it down to ourselves. This is how memories are turned into *"a kingdom of priest for your 'I AM' and how they will reign on earth,"* Revelation 5:10.

Luke 17:20–21: *"The coming of the kingdom of God cannot be observed, and no one will announce, 'Look, here it is,' or 'There it is.' For behold, the kingdom of God is among you."* To find the Kingdom of God (I AM Christ), we must first overcome our belief in polarity (the Tree of Knowledge of Good and Evil), and then become conscious of our divinity and its realm of divine concepts.

And this answers the question of why Adam and Eve were in the Garden of the Tree of Life before moving into the Garden of the Tree of Knowledge of Good and Evil. Adam (our mind) and Eve (our soul consciousness of responsibility) descended to a lower level of understanding to move consciousness to a dualistic belief.

When Yeshua compared the kingdom to a seed in Matthew 13:31-32, the seed is likened to a belief system, because a belief contains built-up mental capacities about how we all look at truth and our beliefs. Therefore, the seed needs planting in the soil of our subconsciousness that is best suited for soul growth. And, when we study Revelation 5:11-12, the angels that surround the throne are not the angels of heaven; they are the numerous memories of our many past personality aspects of light and dark creations where we have journeyed through the four lower elemental forces of (i) fire, (ii) earth, (iii) water and (iv) air.

Always remember, we have created many ego-personality aspects of ourselves (angels) that have not as of yet been part of the physical realm. These non-physical aspects of us search out for new ways to experience life other than physical. However, according to Revelation 5:11-12, we have had many light and dark ego-personality aspects (lifetimes) that have worked in the flesh and have done their job, bringing us to a new awareness that we are more than a human.

We all have had many lifetimes where we *"cried out in a loud voice,"* praying to some God, because of what we have experienced in the past or are experiencing now. The *"crying out,"* even though it is not coming from the human level, is us, from deep within, trying to reach the history *(record)* of everything that we have done since the beginning of our awakening back in the first creation. We all have countless memories (angels), and these memories can be referred to in the Bible as carrying the words of *"ten thousand times ten thousand, and thousands of thousands,"* referred to in Revelation 9:16 as twelve hundred million. This number may be declared differently in other Bible versions, but the meaning is the same.

However, no matter what version we use, the definition of numbers remain the same, as the numbers reduce to their lowest value of 1 and 10. The number 10 is associated with us coming into our completeness while in the flesh and becoming one again with our "I AM" Christ consciousness.

From the *"ten thousand times ten thousand,"* we have the number 10,000 X 10,000 = 100,000,000. *"Thousands of thousands"* is linked to what is given in Revelation 9:16 as *"twelve hundred million,"* which is symbolic of us humans having billions of opportunities and potentials to explore and experience, through memory, if we so choose. This means a great majority of us have already experienced this circle of polarity energy.

And, if some of us are ready, we can now expand into this New Expansional Energy of Four. However, before we choose to do this, then know that our memories are filled with the wisdom of those experiences we played out using this dual opposing energy. Therefore, we, the self, are *"the lamb that was slain,"* and now we can *"receive power and riches, wisdom and strength, honor and glory and blessings"* for what we have accomplished. This is why, in Revelation 5:14, the four elements of the earth bow down to us as their master.

Chapter 18

THE OPENING OF THE SEALS

The opening of the "seven seals" has nothing to do with religions and historian's interpretations as "plagues" coming to earth. It is more in line with the plagues we create and cause within ourselves because of being asleep to whom we indeed are in the scheme of things. What we reflect within also reflects without as a reminder of what we are creating. This is why we have storms, earthquakes, and many other happenings around the world. Even our politicians we elect reflects outward what we, as a group consciousness, reflect within ourselves.

From the interpretations given by Yeshua and the Ascended Masters, the "seven seals" are the opening of our soul memories where we quickly learn the wisdom behind the "whys of our suffering." When we learn how to open up to our soul memories, we will soon understand that light and dark, good and bad, right and wrong, come from the same energy we call the God of light. Even though we feel the duality within our creations, the fact remains that it is nothing more than an illusion so we can play and learn about how consciousness and energy work.

When we learn that God is neither good nor bad, light or dark, we open up to the wisdom behind the "omnipresent universal mind field of pure neutralized god energy of light" as the only energy that is real. Therefore, by ignoring or rejecting our darkness, we deny our Christ consciousness because the darkness is an integral part of our total consciousness. When religions speak of good and evil as being real, they overlook the importance of our imbalanced energy and how it causes us suffering here on earth.

When we understand the "seven seals" as relating to our many belief patterns of light and dark creations instead of comparing them to some

God's plagues, that is when we will take a leap in frequency and meet up with our Christ and Solution consciousness. The plagues of God are symbolic of us souls sending down to ourselves only what we do not understand about consciousness, energy, ourselves, love, and how it relates to our light and dark creations.

And, as most religions believe, the energy (power) of Christ belongs to one man, keeping us all into a fear-based consciousness where the only thing that is real is sin, judgment, and punishment. It is to know that the real Christ is not with one man, nor any particular sect or religious denomination. The real identity of Christ, and its mystery, is a universal code symbolizing our divinity.

We all have forgotten that "light" needs the "dark" and vice versa so we can feel our experiences, just as a car battery needs positive and negative to start the car. If everything was only of "light" (right), then the quality of us experiencing our choices could never be measured. And, if everything were "dark" (wrong), it would all seem without purpose and trivial; thus, feeling unimportant. That is why both "light" and "dark" work together to bring balance, and not that we should favor one over the other by shouting down the dark or light.

When we deny our dark creations as part of our soul memories (Akashic Record), we suffocate any spiritual growth and understanding. Thus, bringing to us more imbalanced, stuck energy to work out in the physical as plagues (sins). How can we heal, bring in riches, or have great relationships if we continuously see ourselves only as good and light? Without understanding the dark side of ourselves as being part of our total consciousness, we run from ourselves and the Christ we are, thus losing the opportunity to become balanced.

For instance, my sister-in-law died of cancer in 2010, and to the end, even on her death bed, she said she would heal herself. How could my sister-in-law have cured herself of cancer when she continued to look at the "light" as all there is about her? She forgot, the more she fought the "dark," the more the game of cancer continued. My sister-in-law and I had many talks on the subject of healing. And she always indicated that she understood what it takes to heal herself. So, why did her cancer persist? It persisted because of her past lifetime beliefs in good and evil and how she was not aware of them in her present lifetime.

What was forgotten by my sister-in-law was that cancer came from her past lifetime aspects, where, as she did in her present lifetime, agreed "light" was beautiful, but the "dark" was terrible. She had forgotten that "light" needed "dark" and visa vera to make her present consciousness complete. In other words, her past personality lifetime aspects, along with her current character as Linda in this lifetime, only sought out "light" and ignored the "dark" as if it did not exist. Thus, in her current life as Linda, she attracted cancer or the "dark" side of her previous personality aspects instead of balancing them.

However, after my sister-in-law passed away, she found that "light" was no higher than "dark," nor "dark" lower than "light," for both were just energy seeking to become balanced. She found it was all about integrating the "light" and "dark" into one body of consciousness, allowing them to come together as one; into a completion where the term "light" and "dark" no longer applied. Therefore, when my sister-in-law passed beyond the physical veil, she remembered why she chose cancer in this lifetime.

Therefore, I do urge everyone not to forget that it is not the "dark" that is evil. It is our perception and judgment that makes the dark look evil. When our beliefs about good and evil get wrapped up into our real essence (divinity) as memories, and then held there until we are ready to open our heart and minds to the concept of "darkness" being as much part of the "light" as "light" is of the "dark," we suffer. When our strong beliefs about light and dark are always projected out there as two differing energies, it brings into our life imbalanced energy.

We all have forgotten that the light and dark come from the same energy we all call God. They are merely different expressions of God's energy. Therefore, take a moment and feel into your light and dark creations, because they speak the same language. Thus, the dark is not what it appears to be. And, the more you fight the dark and seek the light, the more you bring up barriers of both in helping you integrate them as one.

By releasing yourself from the belief that light is good and dark is bad, you release old stuck energy that has become part of each of your lifetimes. And, when you awaken to your Christ and Gnost consciousness, you, like Yeshua, become free to ascend to the next cycle/circle (zero), leaving behind the plagues (sins) of what dark and light brings you to experience. When we begin to recognize our soul memories, both light and dark, as a place for our awakening, we become a student, teacher, and a witness for the unfolding of those memories.

The portrayal of Christ, presented in Apocalypse, is not about Yeshua and what he passed down to his servant John. It is about us humans as a Christ, passing down to our ego-personality of today, for what John's name represents, and to follow in the footsteps of Yeshua. Therefore, the opening of the *"seven seals"* is the opening of our divine memories (Akashic Records), giving us the ability to understand light and dark, and how it has worked on our behalf, moving us toward our redemption and as a sovereign being.

1 Corinthians 12:13, *"it was one spirit that all of us, whether Jew or Greek, slave or free, were baptized into one body."* We souled being are the Spirit of One, the Goddess, and we are part of the "Christ consciousness," for we, together, are "one body of consciousness." Therefore, whether we go to a church or not that carries the name "Christ," or we belong to a religious sect that claims to know Christ firsthand, or we believe in Yeshua as the only Christ, or we are good or bad, it all makes no difference, for all souls are from the same Spirit of One.

If we believe we are not a Christ, then we become dead by intellectualizing what Yeshua taught and established when he walked the earth over two thousand years ago. If our mind-soul is not used in its proper eminence, then it becomes dead to our Christ consciousness and to the life-giving forces within it. Therefore, it is that we are the Lamb in Revelation 6:1-17 and in Revelation 8:1, who broke open the *"seven seals."*

It is you who has the authority to open your soul memories to the "seven most powerful belief patterns" ever devised because you are the one that has chosen to hide from your Christ consciousness. Remember, the *"four living creatures"* that *"cried out"* the loudest in Revelation 6:1, is about the light and the dark creations of justice. Yeshua and the Ascended Masters call this the "fire of justice." And, you, like all souls, accepted this conflicting dual energy of justice by having the courage of a lion to deal with your light and dark memories in taking responsibility for them.

Because of our many trials and tribulations journeying through the fire of justice (dual-energy) lifetime after lifetime, our memories have come to serve us well in learning the wisdom found within our Christ consciousness, symbolized by the *"white horse"* in Revelation 6:1-2. And, the *"rider with the bow"* is also us humans having the courage to reshape and expand our consciousness beyond the mental and physical belief in separation, symbolized by the *"first seal"* in Revelation 6:1.

Therefore, the *"first seal"* revealed in Apocalypse is not about Yeshua riding in on a white horse or cloud, but it is about us humans taking on the belief long ago about being "separated" from our Christ consciousness. The feeling came from moving outside of our "oneness of consciousness" and into a mental and ego-personality consciousness that gave us the perception that we were "separate" from our Christ consciousness. This separation felt so real! So, we all finally came to accept it as truth. It is very important to understand this! Yeshua, when he walked the earth, set the example on how to open this "separation" belief (seal), but we were too busy working out of the mind and ego, and we forgot our place in consciousness.

The *"white horse"* represents our strength and authority as a Christ. Thus, we as a "rider" (lamb), earn the *"crown"* of wisdom by journeying through many lifetimes playing with fire, dual-polarity energy. And now, if we allow our awakening, we can be more *"victorious"* in our creations than ever before since the time we left our higher consciousness (Garden).

The *"second seal,"* Revelation 6:3-4, can sound more frightening than the opening of all the seals itself. But Yeshua and the Ascended Masters assured me that no angel from heaven is coming to earth to take away peace and harmony from humankind. When religions, scholars, and Bible historians misinterpret the Apocalypse, they become the *"rider in red,"* because their teachings take away our power. Thus, the *"second seal"* is linked to "self-awareness," and the idea to open up to the real truth, as you are a Christ also.

The feeling of being separate and independent from our Christ consciousness eons ago produced a new passion within us that asked these questions; Who am I? Why am I here on earth? Why am I no longer feeling my higher consciousness (home-heaven) as before? And, why has my Christ consciousness rejected me? Because of these feelings and questions, we were experiencing and projecting outward, in consciousness, a belief of a higher supreme being created us. Thus, giving us the feeling, we were kicked out of heaven. Remember, "heaven" is symbolic of us humans working out of a higher awareness of consciousness.

As Yeshua and the Ascended Masters channeled, it was through "self-awareness" that gave us the desire of self-discovery to answer those questions. Therefore, we have been on a journey of self-discovery for a long time, trying to discover our relationship with our own Christ consciousness. When we realize that we are the "lamb" having the authority to open up our soul memories or Akashic Record, we come to a place in consciousness where we learn that we have been *"crying out to be heard"* in many lifetimes. And now, we have come to a place in consciousness where our Christ consciousness has heard our prayer.

However, are we listening? If we continue to believe in "separation," we will continue to produce many more like images of ourselves to experience more lifetimes, presented by the second creature, the calf, in Revelation 6:3-4. Because of the stubbornness of our religious views and rituals, we reproduce more lifetimes in the appearance of polarity energy beliefs because of the emotional ties to them. Therefore, the *"horse and its rider"* in Revelation 6:3-4 become conditions and experiences through what we give way to old truths, beliefs, logic, reason, and our intellectualization of a God who created us, is above us and is outside of us.

This *"red rider"* is an aspect of us choosing between good and evil, right and wrong, dual-energy, in taking action. Therefore, it is our mind, the *red rider*, that misleads us to the point of losing our self-awareness of being a Christ also. However, this is okay and not that we have sinned, because we allowed ourselves to move into many physical bodies using the *"sword of justice"* (sowing and reaping) as the means to balance our consciousness and energy.

Therefore, when Yeshua and the Ascended Masters speak of the *"third seal"* in Revelation 6:5-6, it not only relates to polarity energy, it also correlates to the belief in a *"Satan character."* Satan is simply energy (power) created and formed by the mass human consciousness in the belief that Satan is real. However, the belief in Satan makes him real, as evidenced in what we all experience every day.

Therefore, the *"third living creature crying out"* is us all in a three-dimensional physical body creating conditions for ourselves that bring thoughts of judgment, conditional love, and the belief that Satan is real. And this is confirmed by religions teaching us to choose between God and Satan. However, Apocalypse reveals that God and Satan come from the same oneness of energy.

There are no two differing energies in the Kingdom of Oneness. There is only one creative energy that is infinite, pure, unprocessed, and neutralized, having no form to it but light until we, as creators, bring it into our consciousness to serve us. It is when we bring to light this universal neutralized energy into our awareness and add our beliefs to it, that we give sustenance (life) to what we believe as our truths. Therefore, there is no God and Satan above or below us! There is only the choice of what we believe God and Satan represent to us.

The concept of Satan has become embedded within us because of many lifetimes feeling the division of our energy into good (light) and evil (dark), male and female. This feeling of division has created fear-based energy of blame to where we all project God and Satan as two entities and energies. It is the same with Christ and the Antichrist. The Antichrist simply characterizes a person's mind in a hypnotic sleep state, while the Christ characterizes a person in an awakening state.

Therefore, the *"black horse"* and *"its rider,"* in Revelation 6:5-6, are symbolic of our "stubborn ego-personality," the part of us in consciousness that holds the *"scales of justice"* (sowing and reaping) in our own hand. Thus, the voice coming from the *"four living creatures"* is the voice of the human in us all continuing to express light and dark as something real, even though it is all an illusion.

The *"ration of wheat for a day's pay"* in Revelation 6:6 is speaking of the vibrational polarity energy of light and dark, as this dual energy is limited to a three-dimensional consciousness when nurtured and cultivated by what we feed the mind and ego all day long. The same goes for *"barley,"* as it represents the understanding of our spirit, mind-soul, ego, Christ, and our solution Gnost consciousness becoming part of the physical consciousness. It is each layer of consciousness within us all that carries its ingredients, beliefs, and choices, as they all become part of the food we eat here on earth.

This is confirmed with the *"third seal,"* in Revelation, as it represents our disobedient ego-personality here on earth, symbolized by Satan and the Beast. And the "rider in black" is our ego riding the rails of earthly lifetimes repeatedly, sowing and reaping all because of repeating the same beliefs repeatedly in different lifetimes. And, this will go on until we let go of the belief in light and dark (opposing energy) that holds us as a slave to our mind, ego, and other beliefs.

However, the *"do not damage the olive oil or the wine"* in Revelation 6:6 symbolizes the Christ within us, serves us with "unconditional love" because our spirit is Divine. Thus, giving our creations, of light and dark, life no matter how good or bad we think we are. The *"wine"* represents our vitality that forms the connecting link between our soul memories and our physical ego consciousness body. And, the *"olive oil"* symbolizes the relationship of our (holy) spirit and physical body, as it represents the belief that we are an everlasting Christ and not the creator of anything disharmonious.

However, if we hold the belief in light and dark (opposing energy) as being real, we will carry the guilt of sin without end, or until we learn to let it go. As long as we continue to blaspheme our Christ identity by believing we are a sinner, we will continue to suffer under the personality of our disobedient Ego (Satan) because we closed ourselves off from the inflow of our divine energy of healing, peace, and harmony. Therefore, how can we forgive ourselves and let go of the belief in sin if we continue to use our polarized mind (the Anti-Christ) as the powerhouse behind the throne? Our spirit, mind-soul, and ego must learn to work as one unit.

When we, as the Lamb (an ego aspect) of our "I AM," broke open the "fourth seal," we took on the "belief in sin" about what we have created in the realm of polarity energy, both physical and non-physical. And, since we left our higher consciousness (Garden), we have been carrying a lot of shame and guilt for what we have created using polarity energy, and therefore we took on a firm belief in "sin." Because of it, we carry a lot of shame and guilt built within our soul as memories. And, it was because of the way we were taught about sin from our leaders we all fell to a God of judgment.

The opening of the *"fourth seal"* is about us humans, realizing that there was never a reason to feel guilty because there is no such thing as "sin." There is only experiencing, playing, and learning what polarity energy (light and dark) is and how it works. Therefore, it is us humans that are *"crying out"* in Revelation 6:6-7, to our many ego-personalities of past lifetimes to wake up, move forward, and free themselves from the old dogmatic belief in "sin."

The voice we hear coming from the *"fourth living creature"* in Revelation 6:6-7 is our "mind" and how we are questioning sin as if it is real. The *"come forward"* is our mind asking the self to reconsider the belief in sin, for it is not the correct word to use in describing our good and bad creations. The word or concept to use is "experiencing" to learn wisdom because there is no such thing as good and bad. The *"pale green horse"* confirms this by using opposing energy for our growth patterns in what we have learned about ourselves in experiencing light and dark. Just as the color green symbolizes vegetation, *"sickly green"* is tied to outgrowth, or us souls, the mass, becoming judgmental, full of jealousy, and fear.

Also, what confirms the word meaning of truth, is the *"rider was named Death, and Hades accompanied him,"* Revelation 6:6-7. The "rider" is us, humans, in this lifetime, because of our strong belief in sin and hell *(*symbolized by *Hades)*, and how it has accompanied us through our trials and tribulations. Hades is a Greek word, and the Hebrew word for "Hades" as "Sheol." In the English version of the Bible (King James), in the New Testament, it is translated as "hell."

In the Old Testament, Sheol is interpreted as the grave or pit (Genesis 37:35; 42:38; 1 Samuel 2:6; Job 14:13). In the American Standard Version, the word "Sheol" is used in the texts as "Hell." Also, Hades refers to the outer darkness, the realm of sense in contrast to the inner spirit. When we play with the energies of polarity (love and hate, good and bad), it is necessary to live in a physical body where Hades (Hell) is considered the realm of discarnate souls that play in the darkest realms.

This is a place where we die in the physical realm while still believing in sin, hell, and Satan. Therefore, in one's consciousness, it is comparable to the dark conditions of one's erroneous thinking and refusal to believe that one has created appalling things. Thus, we withdraw from owning our dark creations. Therefore, the word Hades represents how we bury deep within our soul; these dreadful things we did and how they are buried deep within our soul memories where they are out of sight and out of mind.

And, since most of us deny these appalling actions, or that we even played them out in a lifetime, we then take on a belief in sin and punishment. However, we do have the authority as a Christ to override these four lower elements of life. And all we have to do is learn of their effects on us while in human form.

The human body represents *"quarter of the earth,"* mentioned in Revelation 6:6-7. Also, using the formula of numerology, one fourth, as in $1/4^{th}$, signifies the oneness (1) of the self is infinite and a master of one's external circumstance. The four (4) is where we humans, here on earth, are focusing out of a consciousness that gave us a foundation that uses the four elements as our reality instead of seeing them as just a creation to experience our choices.

These four elements again are:

<u>Physical Force</u>	<u>Creatures</u>	<u>Nature</u>	<u>Physical Mind</u>	<u>Spirit</u>
1. Fire	Lion	Courage	Justice	Memory
2. Earth	Calf	Reproduction	Form	Desire
3. Water	Man	Sustenance	Being	Choices
4. Air	Eagle	Gratification	Incarnation	Growth

The element of "fire" represents the passionate aspect of our energy; while the water represents our lifeblood (spirit) of creation; air fills the spaces between the energies of our soul (fire) and our spirit (water), and earth represents thoughts, belief patterns, concepts, desires, and form (many physical bodies) until we let go of the belief in "sin."

When we look into the *"fifth seal"* in Revelation 6:9-11, the masters are speaking of "letting go of our suffering." We all have the capability and the means to transform our stubborn ego-personality consciousness and become a witness to all our underlying lifetime personalities, signified by *"underneath the altar,"* where we have played with the forces of the light and dark, polarity energies). Remember, it is all because of our strong belief in "sin," where we have manifested and lived many lifetimes of suffering.

The *"souls of those who had been slaughtered because of the witness they bore"* in Revelation 6:9-11 is referring to our many past lifetimes and how we acted upon a great desire to create certain beliefs that set up the framework for many false realities to experience. Thus, our many ego-personalities of past lifetimes become great witnesses to what we have expressed as our realities. With each of our previous lifetimes, we have expressed and gave life to whatever we desired to experience as our reality.

Religions talk about the scriptures as the *"word of God,"* but their lack of understanding of scriptures comes from the way they taught us long ago, which was from an intellectual and scientific approach. Thus, by looking into the *"word of God"* with a rational view, because of dual-energy, we become a slave to the forces of sin, judgment, and suffering. And this is why religions teach us that sin and suffering are real, and yet, it is a false reality. The words in the Bible were written in code to hide the deeper wisdom behind the written words, or at least until the time was right for new understanding.

Now, the time has come for some of us to move beyond the human senses and witness the real *"word of God"* by creating a new reality for us to experience. This new reality is where our Christ consciousness shines through as being who we are, and once this is understood, our suffering becomes nonexistent forever. Once responsibility is learned and taken seriously, then our many past lifetimes *(inhabitants)*, where they (you in other lifetimes) played out their karmic affairs on earth, become purified *(avenged)*. That is when our energy *(blood)* becomes balanced to where we can move beyond thoughts of sin, duality, and judgment.

By lifting our thoughts to a higher frequency, these ego-personality aspects of many, and our beliefs beyond dual-energy and sin *(judgment)*, become one again with our Christ consciousness. By moving beyond the belief in polarity energy, sin, and judgment, we manifest a new concept, a new belief, and a new beginning here on *earth*, where we, and all our ego-personality aspects of many, earn the *white robe* of a Master.

The *"white robe"* can also be symbolic of our consciousness and energy rising in frequency. So, release your suffering, because you have been patient long enough. When Yeshua and the Ascended Masters speak of the "sixth seal" in Revelation 6:12-13, it is the belief that we need rescuing and, therefore, given salvation. It will not be Yeshua/Jesus or his army of angels, and not even a spaceship, that will come to save us from the Beast (our defiant ego). Only we can rescue ourselves from our "ego-personalities" of many, for salvation is within us already.

Salvation comes as soon as we see through our dogmatic beliefs, and the truth about polarity energy, good and bad, are just illusions that our mind-soul created to experience the opposite of whom we are at our core consciousness. We are God, the Son, Christ, and Satan (beast) all rolled up into one consciousness. An earthquake, the sun turning black, and the moon becoming like blood is nothing more than our mind-soul and ego consciousness following the path of dualistic truths as being real.

Religions teach us there is only salvation through Yeshua. However, the Apocalypse teaches that no one person holds the title of the Christ, because that title is held by those of us who have journeyed through the earth realm, lifetime after lifetime, clearing up the belief in sin, judgment, and punishment. We need not worship Yeshua to get to heaven, because we are already in heaven, because "heaven" is symbolic for higher consciousness. We have always been in heaven because it is part of our total consciousness. But, because we believe in dual-energy, sin, punishment, and that we have to worship someone outside of us that claims created us, the vibrational frequency signature (DNA) of our ego-consciousness remains stuck. That is the illusion of it all.

Yeshua was the real example that showed us how to step into our Christhood; therefore, heaven (higher consciousness) comes to us automatically just by raising our consciousness and energy frequency to where we, as a souled being, become one body of consciousness. Yeshua does not want us to worship him; he wants us to follow his example and become Christ-like.

The *"great earthquake"* is illustrative of how we long ago took aggressive and hostile approaches with our creative abilities that resulted in concepts of turmoil, confusion, and upheavals. This activity transformed our intelligence *(sun)* to a belief in a force of two opposing energies, light and dark, as real. Thus, one chooses either darkness and ignorance *(black as dark sackcloth)* or light and understanding.

The *"moon becoming red like blood"* represents how we humans intellectually rationalized a supreme being outside of us that is going to come and be our savior and our salvation. However, like the "moon" and how it represents the mind! And, like our mind, the light comes from our spirit like the sun reflects its light onto the moon. Therefore, if it weren't for the sun (symbolized by our spirit), the moon (our mind) would have no light.

"Red like blood" is that of our mind, the mental, using the life force (blood), and acting as the creator in giving life to polarity energy for us to play in an illusion.

The *"stars falling to earth and the sky dividing like a scroll"* symbolizes how our spirit, mind-soul, intuition, emotions, and the etheric body fell into an earthly physical body *(stars)*. And, that is where we separated *(divided)* our divine intelligence from our mental, intellectual intelligence. And, once we separated and hid our higher intelligence from our lower intellectual intelligence of the mind, our memories of polarity took on the appearance of our creations as being real.

Therefore, no matter what we have done in life, good, bad, or evil, our salvation is already guaranteed. We just are not understanding our soul as of yet! The confirmation comes from Revelation 6:14, where the *"sky being divided like a torn scroll curling up,"* as it represents where we, eons ago, divided or separated our higher intelligence by focusing out from a mind of polarity. Thus, we became very intellectual with our intelligence when it came to learning about spirit. For this reason, our mind and ego know nothing of spirit and the Christ consciousness within. Therefore, the *"mountains"* and the *"islands"* are symbolic of our higher spirit intelligence that were uprooted from out of our mind long ago, having us feel separate and divided from our own Christ consciousness.

The *"kings of the earth"* in Revelation 6:15-16 represents our many past lifetimes and what we (they) believed to be our (their) truths during each lifetime. These many ego-personality aspects from our past, and what they (you) hold in memory as beliefs, are our ruling behavior patterns today. Therefore, the kings of the earth are not so much our ruling adversaries, for they fall under our ego and the human mass consciousness. It is the mass human consciousness that dictates how our leaders *(nobles, the military officers, the rich, the powerful)* will rule over us. Without realizing it, we have become a slave to them and the mass, and an adversary to the ruling behavior patterns of our past lifetime ego-personality aspects.

Whatever we are experiencing today, ninety-seven percent comes from our beliefs from our past lifetime ego-personality aspects, and what we call nobles, the rich, and the powerful, by us staying true to the belief in polarity energy. This sets up judgment, what we hold as a position in life, and that some God created us. As the words "slave" and "free" signify how we have always had "free will" in choosing what we desired to experience in each lifetime. And yet, we still somehow blame others and conditions for our suffering. We have forgotten that we have allowed ourselves to be controlled by others and our memories of the past.

Because of our guilt feelings and belief in sin and punishment, we, and all the lifetimes we have played out, are now hiding from the *"face of the*

One who sits on the throne and from the wrath of the Lamb" in Revelation 6:16. Simply put, it means you, since it is you who sits on the throne, that fears your Christ consciousness. And, the reason you are afraid, believe it or not, is because your Christ consciousness holds in memory all your dark creations.

There are many people today who will not admit that they have had other lifetimes where they have played with the forces of evil. Therefore, they, on a subconscious level, reject those lifetimes and any idea that they have ever played with evil creations. These people would rather hide by saying there is no such thing as past lifetimes or from any suggestion that they have committed such heinous acts. However, these people have also forgotten that they have paid the price. And now, they are ready to let it all go. The only thing holding them back is their strong belief in dual opposing energy, and that they are a sinner.

By letting go of the belief in dual-energy and accepting responsibility for all lifetimes you have played out here on earth, then *"the great day of the wrath"* in Revelation 6:17 becomes fulfilled. Thus, allowing yourself to rise in frequency where your consciousness can meet up with your Christ consciousness among the ignorance (clouds) of your mind and ego personalities.

According to Yeshua and the Ascended Masters, the *"sixth seal"* is where ninety-seven percent of the population is today, as they refuse to let go of their belief in dual-energy (light and dark). Because of the mass's strong belief in dual-energy, the "sixth seal" will remain closed to them until they realize that they are a Christ also, for whom they are waiting. Therefore, how many lifetimes will it take for you to look into your emotions when it comes to the belief in dual-energy?

Know that the wisdom found here in Revelation 6:17 is that the vengeance has come and gone for those who are ready to move forward in accepting their salivation. That is why, in this verse, *"Who can stand it?"* means who has the courage to let go of their suffering and their long, tired beliefs in good and evil, and move beyond the fear of separation, Satan, and Sin.

Religion and many people misunderstand the second coming of Christ by believing there is a literal appearance of Yeshua coming down out of the clouds with his army of angels. But, let it be known what Yeshua said in Matthew 24:4, 11:23-24. *"See that no one deceives you. For many will come in my name, saying, 'I am the Messiah,' and they will deceive many. Many false prophets will arise and deceive many. If anyone says to you then, 'look, here is the Messiah!' or 'there he is!' do not believe it. False Messiahs and false prophets will arise, and they will perform signs and wonders so great as to deceive, if that were possible, even the elect."*

Consider, *"they will perform signs and wonders,"* because it relates to Matthew 24:25-27: *"Behold, I have told it to you beforehand. So, if they say to you, 'He (Christ) is in the desert,' do not go out there; if they say, 'He is in the inner rooms,' do not believe it. For just as the lightning comes from the east and is seen as far as the west, so will the coming of the Son of Man."*

When Yeshua and the Ascended Masters speak of the word *"east,"* they are referring to "within the self," and the word *"west"* refers to the "outer ego-self" in expression. Therefore, as we awaken to our Christ consciousness within (from the east), we will understand how our consciousness can expand (and is seen) beyond our outer ego-based consciousness in the flesh (as far as the west). Thus, because of this expansion of consciousness, our ego-personality of today will inform us that we are the Son/Daughter of Man, the Christ, and the Messiah for whom we have been waiting *("so will the coming of the Son of Man be").*

Why would you follow someone who claims to be the only Christ? Why would you wait for someone to ride in on a cloud to save you? Understand that clouds signify nothing more than one being ignorant of the self, is Christ. A false prophet will always tell you that you are not God, not Christ, not the Messiah, and not the Son. A false prophet will also tell you it is a sin if you do not follow Yeshua when in truth, they want you to follow them (religions). Therefore, if they say to you, *"Look, he is in the desert, don't go out, or if they say, He is in the inner rooms, don't believe it."* Why? Because you are Christ! So, follow your own "I AM," the Christ you are.

The second coming of Christ is a very personal experience for those who are ready to move beyond believing in Satan, sin, suffering, separation, and salvation coming from someone outside of you. The second coming of Christ happens within you, not outside of you because everything outside of you is an illusion. The second coming is you, while still in the flesh, learning and reuniting with all that you are and ever have been.

In 2 Peter 3:10, *"the day of the Lord will come like a thief in the night, and then the heavens will pass away with a mighty roar, and the elements will be dissolved by fire, and the earth and everything done on it will be found out."*

Suddenly, perhaps at the most unexpected time, like today (like a thief in the night), something may awaken you from the darkness of your ignorance, bringing you into a New Expansional Energy (new earth) where you come to know that you are Christ. Then, as portrayed in the rest of the verse, all the foundations of your truths built on dual-energy (sin) will crumble, allowing you to come alive in a new awareness of consciousness and into an energy frequency of being free and a sovereign Christ in your own right.

Chapter 19

THE SEALING OF THE THOUSANDS

The amazing thing about this Chapter is "how it relates to when we souled beings moved into a physical body." Genesis 1:2; *"the earth was a formless wasteland, and the darkness covered the depth, while a mighty wind swept over the waters."* My friends, before earth could become a planet, it first had to be a thought, a desire, a concept, a belief, and an idea coming from the creator. And, if we have been paying attention so far in the study of this book, we would know that according to Apocalypse, we souled beings are the creator of the earth.

When we souled beings first moved outside of higher consciousness (Garden), we were only consciousness and light in the beginning, and that is when we entered a formless void of nothingness, referred to in Genesis as the "abyss." Thus, *"formless"* in the Book of Genesis is referring to a lack of developmental thought patterns coming from us souled beings when we first entered into this "formless" nothingness. And, this nothingness was the absence of any life, light, and form, because we, the mass consciousness, were at first inactive and unaware of our own "I AM" Christ consciousness.

Therefore, the *"darkness"* in Genesis is symbolic of nothingness (void) and was the underlying beginning until we souled beings filled that nothingness with somethingness. In the beginning, before earth and flesh, we souls had no idea how to create because we had no wisdom! However, once we became conscious and aware of the desire to create, we then filled this nothingness (darkness) with all kinds of somethingness.

For example, Adam and Eve were not real people! So, their wandering through the Garden (or higher consciousness) symbolizes our mind and soul consciousness of responsibility in the beginning stages of our creations lacking wisdom. And, before physical earth and our bodies were created, we souls were at a loss for understanding our existence and life. However, once our ego-personality (serpent) took over the creative process from our mind and soul (Adam and Eve), that was when our mind and soul filled the nothingness (darkness) with many diverse astral and physical dimensional realms, using polarity energy to create opposites.

When Yeshua referred to these multidimensional realms in John 14:2, as *"in my father's house are many dwelling places,"* Yeshua's channeled answer was "in my father's house" is symbolized by what is called an "omnipresent universal mind force of pure neutralized god energy of light" that our mind (Adam), soul consciousness of responsibility (Eve), and our ego (Serpent) used to manifest polarity energy where we could learn to oppose self and each other. That is when we souled beings felt our separation from the "whole of creation" and our own "oneness of the Christ consciousness." And this "separation" is symbolized by the *"first seal"* in Revelation 6:1-2.

It was from polarity energy where we souls played and fought hard with each other, creating and destroying, using this "universal omnipresent, pure god energy of light" in every possible way, or until in our self-induced chaos, our consciousness, and energy, came to a standstill. Let us not forget that we are a God/Goddesses in the making. In the beginning, our creations happened faster than the speed of thought. And because of it, we could not experience the pain, joy, or any real consequence of what we were creating.

It was like having a mind of an eight-year-old child and being a Goddess. We did not know what we were doing, so we kept on playing with this opposing energy, and because of it, our energy became dimmer and more solid until we all became stuck. Throughout this process, we absentminded souls separated into different soul groups, just like eight-year-olds would do when they first attend school.

We all flocked with those who harbored the same beliefs and ideals as our own. Ultimately, according to Yeshua and the Ascended Masters, we divided into 144,000 soul groups, all looking for the road that would lead us back to higher compassionate consciousness (Garden). Therefore, the Oneness of Home (Heaven) is not the same as it was when we souls first left higher consciousness eons ago. However, because of those beliefs, we souled beings split up into 144,000 soul groups, having the maturity level of an eight-year-old, trying to figure out what happened to our higher consciousness (Heaven-Garden). And this was all before material Earth even became a thought or as the third planet from the sun.

Because of our confusion about what was happening to us, as far as energy and consciousness slowing down almost to a standstill, we souls eventually called a group meeting and laid aside our differences for a while to come up with a common goal to find our way out of this confusion. We souls eventually found the answer by gathering this polarity energy that surrounded us and created a material world and a physical universe. And, in doing so, we would learn to release our God-given pure neutral energy and enter into many physical bodies to liberate ourselves from this stuck and very slow energy.

In this state of physical consciousness, we would repeat what we had done in the astral/etheric realms, but at a much slower vibrational energy than before so we could experience our choices in a more solid realm to feel pain, sorrow, and happiness in what we created. Doing this, we would then learn responsibility for our actions and gain the wisdom from the choices made. Note: Since we souled beings are made up as a three-dimensional consciousness, using dual-energy, we may now understand why we live on a three-dimensional planet called Earth.

At the beginning of us souled beings playing with this opposing energy, we could barely imagine what it felt like to do something when we were in our real, pure state. However, if we could deliver ourselves in the physical state, we could experience pain, joy, and the consequences of our choices. In this way, we would learn responsibility and the wisdom of the choice.

Therefore, those of us who incarnated into physical form was not fallen angels as religion teaches. Instead, we were the pioneers going through incredible challenges and difficulties in learning about the unknown principles of polarity energy. There were multitudes of souls that did not have the courage to move into a physical body as we humans did; therefore, consider yourself a unique angel and not one who has sinned against some God above you.

As we souls agreed to move into the flesh, we also agreed to what we learned about the flesh we would pass it on to those angels that did not have the courage to enter the flesh. And we did it by working with energy at a slower vibration than what we experienced in higher consciousness (first creation). By regressing our consciousness to using time and space, we moved in and out of our physical bodies to recap what we chose to experience in the flesh. And, by learning to feel our choices, our existence, and our experiences using polarity, positive and negative, it became a vehicle for us to let go of this dual opposing energy belief later when awakened.

We chose a material existence to reintegrate the parts and pieces of ourselves that were shattered upon entering the crystal, cosmic, and earth energy when we first left our higher consciousness (Garden). The idea was to reverse what we had done in spirit but at a much slower rate of vibration. This way, we would gain an ocean of knowledge, understanding, and wisdom. Thus, finding our way back to higher consciousness (Home-Heaven-Garden). Not only would we find higher consciousness again, but we would also become a sovereign Goddess in our own right.

Before coming into physical form, we, along with all souls, had to create the physical universe. And, within this creation, we produced reminders to help us one day return to a knowing of our true identity. For example, the mass soul group created a star called the sun to show us how, as the Earth rotates on its axis, the light turns to dark and then becomes light again. This feature would help remind us that we too journey from light to dark, and now we are working our way back to the light.

We called upon the patterned energies of the 144,000 angelic soul-families. And, from these families, we chose one angelic member to represent the prescribed order that was created to help us find a solution for our energy gridlock that we were in. Then we called in the Spirit of Gaia to help breathe life into this rock and fill its surface with air, water, fire, vegetation, birds, fish, and the entire animal kingdom (Earth). In our early stages on Earth, we were the template for developing our human body as Gaia breathed in the crystalline energies to help with the crystal, cosmic, and earth energies in developing our physical body.

This birthing energy of the crystalline was used as a type of balance between the physical and non-physical realms. And, from my understanding with Yeshua and the Ascended Masters, Gaia placed crystalline energy at the center of the earth to maintain the very delicate balance of the energies of positive and negative. Gaia also agreed to stay closely associated with the living essence of the earth until we humans took responsibility for our physical home.

Fire, the first living creature in Apocalypse (symbolic of the lion), became characteristic of the energy used in our creations. Earth, the second living creature in the book of Apocalypse (symbolic of the calf), became the holding place of our energy while we are in physical form. Water, the third living creature in the book of Apocalypse (symbolic of the man), became our lifeblood. And, air, the fourth living creature found in Apocalypse (symbolic of the eagle), became the space between our "I

AM" Christ consciousness and our physical consciousness, which is our mental consciousness.

From the 144,000 soul-groups, only a relative few from each group volunteered to take the plunge into a physical body. We felt this was the only way for our "I AM" spirit to find rest from the energy gridlock and chaos we were experiencing from the mental level. Through the understanding and wisdom gained from this experience, we, who volunteered to come first, would each become a unique angel, for we would become teachers to those who never took the route of the flesh. And this is where Noah and the ark came into the picture. Noah's ark symbolizes our three-dimensional consciousness, as in our spirit, mind-soul, and ego-personality.

This story symbolizes our entry into a physical body and a material world. The ark portrayed in Genesis is not only a boat, but it is also the title we gave to the 144,000 archangels that formed into a great assembly of patterned energies to protect us as we made the plunge into the flesh. The ark of Noah is a portrayal of us in physical form, where the ark consists of the three attributes or levels of our consciousness and reality. They are:

1. We are spirit first (first deck).
2. We have a mind that consists of positive and negative (second deck or two of every kind).
3. Our ego has manifested many personality aspects of light and dark lifetimes that portray us working with dual opposing energy in a physical body (third deck).

Our Christ-spirit (the first deck) comprises of absoluteness, unconditional and divine love, trustworthiness, and compassion, without judgment, fear, or guilt. It is the first circle of creation and the Oneness of Consciousness from which we all came.

The mind (the second deck) is the realm of thought-forms or images where our belief patterns are manifested as the light and dark or two of every kind.

The ego-consciousness (the third deck) is the realm where we play out our manifested denser animalistic forms and realities in the flesh. The second (mind) and third (ego-animalistic) layers are where everything has been created since we souls left higher consciousness (home).

Revelation 7:1, the *"four angels, four corners of the earth, and the four winds"* are referring to the foundation of our existence here in the flesh, as they are:

1. Dei Un Gnost-Solution Consciousness (south)
2. Ego/Physical Body (west)

3. Spirit/Christ Consciousness (east)
4. Mind-soul/Adam and Eve (north)

The "four winds" of the Earth represent:

1. South (fire, energy, justice, gnost)
2. West (earth, form, desires)
3. East (water, spirit, negative, Christ Identity, and choices and temptations. And this is the breath of life with which our spirit gives life to our creations. It is also our true identity and the fingerprint of our beingness)
4. North (air, mental, positive, and growth, evil, and love)

Our Christ consciousness is at rest within our heart center (east), waiting for the time when our outer (west) ego-personality aspects of many physical bodies (land) have filled our total subconsciousness (sea) with a knowing that we have the creative solutions (south) for all levels of our beingness. We had lost or put away our "Dei Un Gnost Solution" consciousness long ago when we (our angelic family and all 144,000 soul families) branched out from the higher consciousness (Garden) to experience choices and responsibility.

This branching out is not only related to our many stubborn ego-personality aspects of many lifetimes spread throughout the multidimensional realms; it also refers to us souls following the lineage of our own angelic family *(tree)* through those lifetimes. We can become our ancestors, as we may be our great-great-grandfather or grandmother today.

When we look into Revelation 7:2, the angel from the *"east, holding the seal of the living God"* represents all 144,000 soul group families, as you are a member of one of them. As the "seal" represents the Christ consciousness within *(east)* all souled beings, no one is left out, not even the worst of the worst of us; the "seal" (our divinity, the Christ within) is answering a question we souled beings asked a long ago, "Who am I?" It deals with those souls in physical consciousness coming into awareness and the wisdom of knowing one is the Christ.

For those of us among the 144,000 soul families that incarnated on Earth a long time ago, the question about who we are need not be asked any longer, because some of us are awakening to the Christ within. By learning of the Christ within ourselves, we will leave behind everything that concerns human reasoning, logic, and a solitary white male God who judges. It is about integrating our "I AM" Christ-spirit, mind-soul, ego personality, and our solution consciousness. This includes our many past light and dark personality aspects with our physical consciousness of today. Thus, we will become "one body of consciousness."

The *"crying out at the top of your voice"* to the "four angels" represents our "I AM" Christ consciousness sitting at a frequency higher than the aspect self:

1. De Un Gnost/Solution Consciousness (south)
2. Mind-Soul (north)
3. Spirit/Oversoul (east)
4. Ego-physical consciousness (west)

These *"four angels"* in Revelation 7:2, were given the authority *(power)* to create life or havoc *(ravage)* over our limited physical forms *(land)* to bring us better understanding and wisdom to our total consciousness *(sea)*. For, the chaos and disorder come by way of polarity energy (the tree of knowledge of good and evil). However, in Revelation 7:3, no one is to *"damage the land or the sea or the trees until we put the seal on the foreheads of the servants of our God."*

In short! This means no harm can come to us in the physical, to our Oversoul, to our mind-soul consciousness *(sea)*, to our soul family *(tree)*, and all our past light and dark ego personality aspects, even to the worst of the worst lifetimes we have created to be our *"servants."* Also, though we entered into a physical body of consciousness of a limited nature *(land)*, there is nothing we can do to harm, or even anger, our Christ consciousness. For better wording, it is impossible to destroy our "I AM" Christ consciousness because it is always in forgiveness and compassion no matter what we do or have done.

We souls have established and imprinted within our heart center a knowing that we are part of the Christ consciousness *(seal)*. And, everything we have created since the time we left higher consciousness (Garden) is now part of our outer physical consciousness, symbolized by the imprint on the *(forehead)*. Even how we played our many lifetimes out to benefit all 144,000 family groups is part of our physicalness. Therefore, our physical body is the place of worship and not a church building, for the temple of the living God (our divinity-the seal) is within the physical body.

There is nothing like the human body as the vehicle for our "I AM" Christ-spirit in learning about polarity energy and how it works with the forces of positive and negative. Can we see how amazing it has been and challenging for us to be in a human body, allowing ourselves to go so deep into experiencing opposing energy, good and bad, light and dark, and that we lost trust in ourselves as a Christ?

Channeling of the Ascended Masters on the Apocalypse

When we left the first creation (our higher understanding), this trust in the self as a Christ also was lost, and it is one of the most devastating things we have ever experienced. This loss of confidence with our Christ consciousness became the remoteness and vastness in consciousness *(symbolized by space and the stars that appear in the sky)* between our many false ego personalities and our "I AM" Christ consciousness.

To confirm what is being said by Yeshua and the Ascended Masters, they refer you to Revelation 7:4, the sealing of the *"one hundred and forty-four thousand marked from every tribe of Israelites."* As most religions recognize this number associated with the 144,000 martyrs described in Revelation 7:4 and the first to be sealed and protected from what is coming soon, it is all 144,000 thousand soul families. Even today, Yeshua and the Ascended Masters tell me, since the beginning, we are still with 144,000 soul families.

As this number is associated with the twelve tribes of Israel and how each tribe comprises 12,000, then the "sealing of the 144,000" is symbolic in describing the number of the many angelic soul families that left higher consciousness long ago. Therefore, the number has nothing to do with the 144,000 martyred Jews mentioned in the Bible. The number is associated with every souled being that left higher consciousness long ago. Thus, every soul family, all 144,000, is representative of a Jew. And this also means no one is left behind, because every soul, whether good or evil, belongs to the 144,000 angelic soul families.

Religions proclaim that having the seal of God makes us humans his spiritual child. However, Paul explains that God has *"set his seal of ownership on us"* already (2 Corinthians 1:22), meaning no exceptions. Religions have overlooked the meaning of the state of "Israel" and why it is used for the 144,000 martyred Jews when as the Masters say, it is a representation for all 144,000 soul families that left higher consciousness long ago.

Perhaps you have read the story of how Jacob's name was changed to Israel after he had wrestled with a "man" all night. Because of his success, Jacob obtained a blessing from God (Genesis 32:25–33). And this story became a metaphor about why the state of Israel became known as the Prince of God. Since all humankind is noted in Genesis as the Children of God, whereas, in truth, we are extensions of the Spirit of One, then you, through the faculties of your mind, for which Jacob represents, are part of the 144,000 talked about in Revelation.

And since Esau was Jacob's brother, he represents the outer physical nature of humankind, for Esau was a hairy man. Thus, he represents man's external animal nature. Therefore, the name Israel is the name for all of humanity and all souls, rather than just the Jews. As your ego physical consciousness signifies the birth of your rebellious personality (like it was for Jacob), then you, in the physical today, can join in rulership with "all that was" and "is," your total consciousness.

Your struggle to find your way home is like Jacob's struggle to get back to his birthplace (back to higher consciousness). The Prince of God (symbolized as your mind) and your ego nature (symbolized by Esau) eventually prevail, and your "I AM" Christ consciousness (signified by the word God) gives you, and every souled being born on earth, as being an Israelite." The human race is an Israelite.

Thus, the symbolization of the Israelites is the key to finding your way back home to the Promised Land (higher consciousness). (Read Genesis 26–33 for full details on Jacob and his brother Esau.) Therefore, know that your stubborn and rebellious ego-personality aspect of today can be the name you hold in this lifetime as the super aspect to call in your "I AM" Christ consciousness into your life. Thus, you can change your reality just by learning you are Christ.

With this understanding, then know every souled being, not only the Jews, but is a Christ also, because "God" is simply another name for all 144,000 soul families at a higher consciousness. Therefore, whether you are a Jew, Arab, Hindu, American, or any sect, it makes no difference, because you, and the human race, are the Prince of God and the Goddess.

Even though the number of souled beings that left higher consciousness (first creation) is too great to count, it is without question; we humans belong to one of the 144,000 angelic families. The country of Israel represents every man, woman, child, race, and religion on earth; no one is left out because everyone is a Christ also.

Chapter 20

THE TWELVE TRIBES OF ISRAEL AND HOW THEY RELATE TO THE PHYSICAL BODY (12,000 X 12,000 = 144,000)

The *"twelve thousand marked from the tribe of Judah, twelve thousand from the tribe of Reuben, and the twelve thousand from the tribe of Gad,"* in Revelation 7:5, comes from the twelve sons of Jacob, and how they relate to the sealing of the twelve thousand, in combination with the physical body as a three-dimensional consciousness. The physical universe is made up of sacred geometry because of polarity energy; thus, translating it to what we call numerology where the primary value of numbers, like the twelve thousand (12,000), is reduced to its lowest value of three (3).

For example, the numbers 1 + 2 + 0 + 0 + 0 = 3, indicating that we humans are of a three-dimensional being journeying through three cycles (zeros) of activities as a sovereign God-Goddess. The one (1) represents our higher neutralized consciousness in the beginning stages of our activities in creation was that we were of spirit only.

The two (2) represent us souls splitting our "oneness of consciousness" into two opposing consciousnesses where we souls created what we call polarity energy that opposed each other, positive and negative, male and female, mind and soul. This allowed us, souls, to create activities of good and evil and yet, still be part of the spirit of one.

The first zero (0) represents us souls in the Garden per se (the first cycle) where we souls worked together as an "oneness of consciousness." The second zero is tied to the astral/mental and physical consciousness where we souls created materialism to learn wisdom. The third zero is where we humans finish our work here on Earth playing with polarity energy and then move into a new cycle where we become a sovereign God-Goddess in our own right.

Once we souls have completed our two cycles (zeros) of activities, we move on to the next cycle or third zero as a Christ in our own right, while in the flesh. The third cycle (zero) is a consciousness where we use our magic (authority) because that is when we learn about how consciousness and energy work together. It is also the cycle where we become an Ascended Masters in our own right, where we, as a God-Goddess, can go out and create a whole new life and world using Crystalline Energy instead of just Crystal, Cosmic, and Earth energy for our creations to experience. Of course, we can use these energies by understanding that there is only neutral energy.

The number 12,000 becomes significant when we recognize ourselves as the Creator instead of looking for a creator. When we move our focus into a consciousness understanding about who we are as a Christ, the third cycle (zero) becomes our salvation, where we bring into our life a New Expansional Energy that allows us to explore the magic (authority) we hold as a God-Goddess.

To elaborate on these three cycles (zeros) as a three-dimensional being, the first cycle (zero) is about us working out of a higher consciousness of oneness where we did not express ourselves in a dualistic opposing way. Our Christ-spirit simply resided in consciousness as the Goddess we seek. We souls at the time never contemplated a desire to know more about ourselves until our "I AM" Christ-spirit asked the question, "Who am I?" And, that is when we souls created an expression where our higher consciousness activated an "omnipresent universal mind force of pure neutralized god energy of light," that gave us the ability to create for ourselves a mind-soul region of responsibility and an ego-personality to see ourselves in action.

The second cycle (zero) is everything created outside of the first zero since we left higher consciousness (Garden). We never left; we just placed all our focus on the mental image that we created as our mind. Therefore, out of the nothingness (the abyss), we souled being created the astral nonphysical and physical realms where we have been playing with vibrational energy, positive and negative, light and dark, for a very long time learning the wisdom of our choices.

Channeling of the Ascended Masters on the Apocalypse

When our "I AM" Christ Consciousness awakened as an individualized souled being and as an extension of the Spirit of One, and after creating our mind-soul consciousness, while in our higher consciousness, our "I AM" gave us no rules to follow, not even having to honor our divine self. We all were given the freedom to express, love, experience, and do as we please, even to turn our own back on our "I AM." We were given the essence, purity, depth, and light of the Spirit of One, for it was her way of sharing everything she had with us.

We souls always have had the same creative ability and authority (power) as the Spirit of One, the Mother Goddess. So, why are we, as humans, giving our authority away to others? When we move our ego personality-consciousness beyond good and evil, right and wrong, judgment, and away from the belief in sin and punishment, we expand our consciousness into new and safe energy where we never have to worry about healing, money, happiness, or true love.

Once we understand the significance of the $1 + 4 + 4 + 0 + 0 + 0 = 9$, we come into our completion as an Ascended Master. And, this is when we move into the third cycle (zero) as a true creator God-Goddess in our own right, filled with overwhelming wisdom, which is reflected by the wisdom and significance of the 12,000 from each tribe.

The Hebrew meaning of the name *Judah* is "praise Yahweh," and not Jehovah, for Jehovah is a false God because of its association with judgment and duality. In other words, believing that the "you shall commandments," sin, punishment, and playing with polarity energy as being something real. Therefore, Judah symbolizes the spiritual intelligence center within us that corresponds to what we have accumulated as memories within our mental soul and Oversoul. And, from these polarity memories, we can speed up the mind in stimulating the forces that need to be played out here on earth to help awaken us from our sleep.

Once we are reconnected to our spiritual intelligence center, we communicate the intelligence of our divine mind outwardly, while in the flesh. This spiritual intelligence center is our super-sub-consciousness (spirit), and it is above the various layers of our mind-soul but not separate from it. All excellent ideas, or what best serves us in our evolution, comes from this center. It is where we receive the inspiration for those ideals that are true and real for us.

When we pray, we usually look up as if God is somewhere in the sky. Instead, what needs to happen is for us to look deep within ourselves for answers because we are the living God and Goddess in the sky. The spiritual intelligence center is at the top of the head (pineal gland, the holiest center in the human body). And, once the center is activated, our attention is naturally drawn to it. As the Hebrew meaning of Judah is "praise Yahweh, not Jehovah," we express *(praise)* our trust in ourselves as a God, Goddess, Christ, and Son/Daughter, and then honor those thoughts, ideas, and memories of light and dark that we played out here on earth.

From honoring and accepting our past lifetimes playing in dual-energy, we come in touch with universal truths that cause us to rise to a higher life and consciousness. When we express only dualistic thoughts, ideas, and beliefs about sin, a God that created us, and a God of judgment, we attract the forces of cause and effect. Thus, we repeat many lifetimes until we are awakened to the process. All of it leads to false ideas that find outer expression in poverty, illness, sadness, so-called accidents, chaos, and incidents we experience in life.

Also, since the tribe of Judah means praise to Yahweh, the "I AM" within the self, this tribe is used to designate the wholeness of the mass consciousness and the memories associated with all souls that left higher consciousness (the garden) long ago and how they represent the Jewish nation. Also, "Judah" and "praise to Yahweh" describe the non-dualistic nature within all the souls when acting with honor and compassion for each other's truths and beliefs. This compassion then activates our authority within us as an Ascended Master, which then opens the inner portals of the soul and all that is within our memories. My fellow gods, this is where our increase in life activities begin.

The *"twelve thousand marked from the tribe of Reuben"* in Revelation 7:5, symbolizes "sight" or our ability to see, understand, and trust in ourselves as the Son of God, for our mind is the designated (chosen) "Son of Goddess."

Reuben was the eldest son of Jacob by wife Leah (Genesis 29:32). And, the twelve sons of Jacob not only represent the twelve tribes of Israel, but they also represent the twelve foundation faculties of the mind (twelve left-brain activities given in Revelation 4:4). The name of each son of Jacob represents the development and office of spirit, mind, and body. When the sons of Jacob were born, their mothers revealed the personality faculty associated with each son. In the case of Reuben, his mother emphasized the words "looked," "a son seen," and "behold a son" (Genesis 29–30).

When we read these chapters, it becomes clear that "Reuben" refers to the bringing forth of "sight," which means "understanding." Also, the twelve sons of Jacob represents the left-brain activities of the mind (the natural soul), bringing forth our mental power of reasoning or the intellect.

And this will eventually become the right-brain activity of our mind as a higher expression, which is symbolized by the twelve disciples of Yeshua.

The *"twelve thousand from the tribe of Gad,"* Revelation 7:5, the name *Gad* symbolizes power, good fortune, and abundance. Moses' blessing on the tribe of Gad was, *"Blessed be he who has made Gad so vast! He lies there like a lion that has seized the arm and head of the prey. He saw that the best should be his when the princely portion was assigned, while the heads of the people were gathered. He carried out the justice of the Lord and his decrees respecting Israel."* (Deut. 33:20–21).

Jacob's blessing to his son Gad found in Genesis 49:19, means that we humans may have power and fortune in this world, but only if it comes to us through the forces of duality, not from non-duality spiritual expressions. Therefore, our power and fortune are only of this three-dimensional world. Once we move onto the next dimension after physical death, our wealth, or everything we own is left behind.

The *"twelve thousand from the tribe of Asher,"* Revelation 7:6, symbolizes the bringing forth of spiritual ideas, happiness, or our spirit's understanding beyond physical ideas and viewpoints. Asher was Jacob's second son by Zilpah, Leah's handmaid. When Leah called out the child's name, she said, *"Happy am I, for the daughters will call me happy"* (Genesis 30:12–13). In his blessing, Jacob said, *"Out of Asher his bread shall be fat, and he shall yield royal dainties"* (Genesis 49:20). Moses' blessing in Deuteronomy 33:24 was, *"Blessed be Asher with children (above sons), let him be acceptable unto his brethren and let him dip his foot in oil."*

The symbolism of the name "Asher" and the blessings given to him point both to our understanding of the spirit and to our physical reality, which we can touch and feel when we express the practical value of pure ideas, pure spiritual food, and universal truth. Both Jacob and Moses, in their blessings, announced the time would come when we will learn that our abilities and power come from within ourselves and not from material and flesh.

"Blessed be Asher above sons" in Deut. 33:24 refers to our bringing forth non-duality thoughts, ideas, expressions, and actions while we are still part of the material world as a divine-human. It is okay to have dual thoughts and ideas as long as we bring them in from a balanced energy.

The words *"let him be acceptable unto his brethren and let him dip his foot in oil,"* refers to our "I AM" Christ, which should be considered when we work with polarity energy. It is not just that we understand Christ as someone outside of us or from a religious viewpoint. It is about becoming aware of our "I AM" identity and our understanding that "Christ" is more than just one man. Maybe we have had some deep feelings about Christ being more than one man, but we ignore those feelings because of our upbringing.

When Leah said at the birth of Asher in Gen. 30:13, *"The daughters will call me happy,"* this indicates the significance of establishing within us the true spiritual food that is now part of our soul memory. In Proverbs 3:13–18, we are told of the happiness that comes to those who gain wisdom and understanding and the priceless value of having these qualities.

The *"twelve thousand from the tribe of Naphtali,"* the sixth son of Jacob and the second son of Bilhah, Rachel's handmaid, as she said, *"with mighty wrestling's of God have I wrestled with my sister and have prevailed."* She called him "Naphtali" (Genesis 30:7–8). Jacob's blessing upon this son was: *"Naphtali is a hind let loose; he giveth goodly words"* (Genesis 49:21). Moses' blessing upon the tribe of Naphtali was: "*O Naphtali, satisfied with favor, and full with the blessing of Jehovah, possess thou the west and the south*" (Deut. 33:23).

The symbolism here is about us having the strength and the understanding to maintain a harmonious way of thinking about being God and a Christ too. The left-brain hemisphere that "Naphtali" signifies is in the back area of the body, which controls the function of the kidneys. And, as known, the kidneys direct the elimination of certain watery elements from the blood. This area of left-brain activity is called "strength" because it keeps our energy (blood) circulating to benefit keeping us healthy in the flesh.

When we worship a God of duality, good and evil (Jehovah), as the real God, and fill our minds with only thoughts, ideas, and belief systems about our physical condition, it reduces the quality and the strength of our soul. When we claim that our strength and power are coming from the mind, then the parts that most affect our physical body are the kidneys. When our thoughts are all about materialistic living or from a God of judgment and or duality principles, then we weaken our understanding when it comes to knowing Christ. Thus, it affects the strength center in the back area of our body.

By allowing thoughts of compassion, unconditional love, and the release of dual opposing beliefs, we open ourselves up to the power (authority) and strength of a new Christ light (understanding). Through this new understanding of Christ, our power (authority) and strength increase day by day. That is when our mind-soul and ego personality integrate with our "I AM" Christ consciousness. That is when our whole being is purified and significantly increased in strength.

Channeling of the Ascended Masters on the Apocalypse

The *"twelve thousand from the tribe of Manasseh"* comes from the son of Joseph and not Jacob (Genesis 41:51). His descendants became one of the tribes of Israel (Numbers 2:20). The symbology of Manasseh is *"one who creates conditions to forget."* Manasseh also represents one's understanding of the divine plan (will). Manasseh had a brother named Ephraim, whose name meant "twice as creative and successful" and "free will." When these two memory faculties of divine will and free will come into harmony as one, then divine order is established within us. Free will (Ephraim) and understanding (Manasseh) of our divine nature have their centers of activity in the head or front of the brain.

When we understand that the physical, mental mind rules over us all without the balancing forces of our free will (divine will), then we are led to worship false gods. Why? Because of the belief we have about power coming from the mind. And, it can become so strong and entrenched within our memories that it regulates our life only as polarity thinking. We give our power away to the mass, to those we feel are above us, to luck, politicians, religions, family, friends, businesses, societies, and others, without even realizing we are doing it.

We also give our faith not to God but to everything and anything outside of ourselves, including the God we believe created us. Thus, we are worshipping false gods. We, as humans, have been snowballed for centuries by our governments, our religions, big businesses, families, and our minds. We place all faith in a power outside of our "I AM" dominion. And this is where our "forgetfulness" (Manasseh) has kept our power outside of the self and place it with others.

Because we have forgotten that we are a God-Goddess and that power is only an illusion, our real understanding of God is put in chains, and we become a slave to the dual-energy beliefs that sin and punishment are real. By putting Christ and Satan above, or below us, or as two individuals, then we follow a false god. Israel is the prime example of this today. Remember, the Jews do not believe in Yeshua being the Christ; therefore, they do not accept that Christ has returned yet. This means that we, and the mass consciousness (world), do not believe Christ has returned, even though most of us say we believe he will come again.

Yeshua was the first person to introduce the Christ consciousness on earth over two thousand years ago, and now there are many of us coming into a knowing that we humans are the second coming of Christ. However, many of us have a hard time believing it. Hence, all religions around the world are following a false God and an idea that someone is coming to save them and their followers from some Anti-Christ.

When we open our mind and free will (divine will) to our "I AM" Christ consciousness and declare for ourselves the power of Christ that is within and not outside us, then our understanding of the real Christ is recognized. Thus, the name "Manasseh" represents the idea of us understanding the mind's reasoning negative aspect is just that, "negative." This meaning did confuse me a little because Manasseh was the son of Joseph and not of Jacob, and yet, according to Revelation 7:6, he became one of the twelve tribes of Israel.

Why is that? If you look in Genesis 30:6, Dan was the fifth son of Jacob; his mother was Bilhah, Rachel's handmaid, and when Dan was born, Rachel said, *"God has vindicated me; indeed, he has heeded my plea and given me a son."* Therefore, she named him Dan. In blessing Dan, Jacob said, *"Dan shall achieve justice for his kindred like any other tribe of Israel. Let Dan be a serpent by the roadside, a horned viper by the path that bites the horse's heel so that the rider tumbles backward. (I long for your deliverance, O Lord!)"* (Genesis 49:16–18).

As you can see, Dan also became one of the twelve tribes of Israel, as did Manasseh (Josh. 19:47–48). In blessing the tribe of Dan, Moses said, *"Dan is a lion's whelp that springs forth from Bashan!"* (Deut. 33:22). Therefore, this symbolizes the strength, dominant power, and productivity (lion and Bashan) that lie back of good judgment rightly expressed. The metaphysical meaning of "Dan" carries a sense of good judgment, even though we are still mental in our expressions. However, some of us are very close to lifting those judgments to a new spiritual plane.

Most of us have to learn that our sense of judgment, when expressed from a dual nature, often makes us critical; therefore, our words have a backbiting quality to them. Thus, we need to learn to be non-judgmental through the process of compassion and unconditional love.

When looking at the *"twelve thousand from the tribe of Simeon,"* he represents those of us who hear and follow the guidance coming from our "I AM" Christ identity. Simeon was the second son of Jacob by Leah. After she bore this child, she said, *"The Lord heard that I was unloved, and therefore he has given me this one also,"* and she named him Simeon (Genesis 29:33). Jacob's blessing to this son was, *"Simeon and Levi, brothers indeed, weapons of violence are their knives. Let not my soul enter their council, or my spirit be joined with their company; for in their fury, they slew men, in their willfulness, they maimed oxen. Cursed be their fury so fierce, and their rage so cruel! I will scatter them in Jacob, disperse them throughout Israel."* (Genesis 49:5–7).

In Moses' blessing of the tribes of Israel, Simeon is not mentioned. In the Promised Land, *"their inheritance was in the midst of the inheritance of the children of Judah."* In Joshua 19:1, *"The second lot fell to Simeon. The heritage of the clans of the tribe of Simeonites lay within that of the Judahites."* Simeon, whose name means "the bringing forth of hearing," did not, according to history, fulfill what the name implies.

You see, "hearing," in its higher aspect, refers to the state of mind of those who devotedly believe they are a Christ and who looks for and expects spiritual guidance and instruction directly from the "I AM," and not from a single-minded God. It may be summed up with words like "receptiveness," "openness of mind," and "willingness to accept new ideas."

Luke 2:25, *"Now there was a man in Jerusalem whose name was Simeon. This man was righteous and devout, awaiting the consolation of Israel, and the Holy Spirit was upon him,"* Luke 2:29, *"Now, Master, you may let your servant go in peace, according to your word,"* which means we have found a new consciousness of indwelling, everlasting life that replaces hope, expectancy, and obedience (Simeon).

The *"twelve thousand from the tribe of Levi,"* Revelation 7:7, represents the third son of Jacob by Leah. *"Again, she conceived and bore a son, and she said, 'Now, at last, my husband will become attached to me, since I have now borne him three sons;' that is why she named him Levi"* (Genesis 29:34). Jacob's blessing of his son Levi was given jointly to his son Simeon (Genesis 49:5–7), which can be read above under the name of Simeon.

Moses' blessing on the tribe of Levi was this: *"To Levi belong your Thummim, to the man of your favor your Urim; for you put him to the test at Massah and you contended with him at the waters of Meribah. He said of his father, 'I regard him not;' his brothers he would not acknowledge, and his own children he refused to recognize. Thus, the Levites keep your words, and your covenant they uphold. They broadcast your decisions to Jacob and your law to Israel. They bring the smoke of sacrifice to your nostrils and burnt offerings to your altar. Bless, O Lord, his possessions and accept the ministry of his hands. Break the backs of his adversaries and of his foes, that they may not rise."* (Deut. 33:8–11).

Levi, then, symbolizes the power of love and service that we have within us. Love is the uniting, joining of our divinity in action. When Leah (representative of the human soul) brought forth Levi, she said, *"Now this time will my husband* [your mind of reasoning] *be joined unto me."* This means we attach the forces of polarity (positive/light and negative/dark) to whatever we focus our love on, whether it be religion, family, God, or other things. If we love our intellect and we proclaim our religious beliefs as our truths, then what we believe becomes part of our experiences. That is when we lose the ability to enter into the dominion of our "I AM" Christ consciousness.

God told Moses not to make any graven images of him because graven images become fixed in the mind as the only prevailing quality of something that is not real. When we place our thoughts of a judgmental God into a place called heaven (graven image) or on a cross, it produces such a mental image where we become brainwashed into worshipping that imaginary being instead of the true Goddess. When we look at Jacob's blessing to Levi, it seems more like a curse than a blessing. Why? It reveals how strong we get emotional when we place our full attention on our minds as understanding God.

It is our emotions and feelings that play a big part in the decisions we make in life; therefore, we act in adverse and destructive ways giving no thought to where it is coming from. And, this is not what true unconditional love is about. When love is expressed through an emotional mind, and we interpret it as feelings, then violence and bad decisions can result instead of compassion and unconditional love. Moses' blessings on the tribe of Levi reveal the need to uplift our mental perception of love to a new consciousness of compassion and unconditional love without using the forces of dual opposing energy or judgment tied to it.

As we can see today, most people in this stage of their lives are still interpreting love from the intellectual viewpoint, although they have attained some degree of perception about its perfection.

The *"twelve thousand from the tribe of Issachar,"* Revelation 7:7. A son of Jacob and Leah. *"And God heard her prayer; she conceived and bore a fifth son to Jacob." Leah then said, 'God has given me my reward for having my husband have my maidservant'; so, she named him Issachar"* (Genesis 30:17–18). Jacob's blessing upon Issachar was, *"Issachar is a rawboned ass, crouching between the saddlebags. When he saw how good a settled life was, and how pleasant the country, he bent his shoulder to the burden and became a toiling serf"* (Genesis 49:14–15).

Moses' blessing upon the tribe of Issachar was connected to the blessing he gave to Zebulun: *"Rejoice, O Zebulun, in your pursuits, and you, Issachar, in your tents! You who invite the tribes to the mountains where feasts are duly held because you suck up the abundance of the seas and the hidden treasures of the sand"* (Deuteronomy 33:18–19).

The symbolism here is that "Issachar" possesses the hidden treasures of the sand, meaning we all possess the *"hidden treasures"* of the Father/Mother God-Goddess, and they are within the memories of our Oversoul (*treasures of the sand*). These memories are from the time we were part of higher consciousness (Garden), through the time we left higher consciousness (Garden), to where we fell to the bottom in consciousness, right up to the present moment. So, rejoice while we are still in our physical body *(tent)* because it is full of zeal and can be touched and felt by our spirit.

When we realize that all life given within the foundation of unconditional love, compassion, and without a trace of force, judgment, guilt, or fear, then truth makes all things possible for us to experience. As we learn to elevate our beliefs beyond polarity energy, and those that love power, and finally let go of the belief in the Tree of Knowledge of Good (light) and Evil (dark), we will receive grace and wisdom and be fulfilled, guided, and directed toward even more perfect knowledge of our place in the universe.

It comes to understanding, without experiencing the illusions of our choices, our "I AM" Christ consciousness would have no knowledge or understanding of life (good and bad). Therefore, our "I AM" learns what life is all about through our many ego-personality aspects of the past and present when experiencing life in human form. Without experiencing the "tree of knowledge of good and evil (dual opposing energy), life would not have been known. Without experiencing light and dark, the spirit would have no understanding of life and the wisdom that comes with it. This is why our "I AM" Christ consciousness is always blessing our creations, no matter if it is good or bad.

The *"twelve thousand from the tribe of Zebulun,"* Revelation 7:8, *Zebulun* was Jacob's tenth son and the sixth son by Leah. *"Leah conceived again and bore a sixth son to Jacob, and she said, 'God has brought me a precious gift. This time my husband will offer me presents, now that I have borne him six sons'; so, she named him Zebulun"* (Genesis 30:19–20). Jacob's blessing on his son Zebulun, *"Zebulun shall dwell by the seashore [meaning a shore for ships], and his flank shall be based on Sidon"* (Genesis 49:13). This means the blessings of Moses on the tribe of Zebulun are given in conjunction with that of Issachar above (Deut. 33:18–19).

"Zebulun" symbolizes the abundance we hold within our total consciousness, as the includes universal intelligence and that part of the universal God's mind and Goddess consciousness. We can tap into this universal God energy of light and the Goddess consciousness when we are ready to open up to its existence and the belief that we all are a Goddess. This requires us to move past the idea of light and dark as two different forces and see self as "all that is, is neutrality and unconditional love."

"Zebulun" has also been known as the intelligence center in the stomach area that directs the digestion and presides over the chemistry of our physical body. And this area of the digestive system separates and distributes the energy (food) to each part of the body and makes sure every part has its share. Also, this means "Zebulun" is related to the area of our abdomen or navel area.

The "twelve thousand from the tribe of Joseph, Revelation 7:8, as Joseph was the elder of the two sons born to Jacob by Rachel. *"She conceived and bore a son, and she said, 'God has removed my disgrace.' So, she named him Joseph, meaning, 'May the Lord add another son to this one for me!'* (Genesis 30:23–24).

Jacob's blessing for Joseph, *"Joseph is a wild colt, a wild colt by a spring, a wild ass on a hillside. Harrying and attacking, the archers opposed him; but each one's bow remained stiff, as their arms were unsteady, By the power of the Mighty One of Jacob, because of the Shepherd, the Rock of Israel, the God of your father, who helps you, God Almighty, who blesses you, with the blessings of the heavens above, the blessings of the abyss that crouches below, the blessings of breasts and womb, the blessings of fresh grain and blossoms, the blessings of the everlasting mountains, the delights of the eternal hills. May they rest on the head of Joseph, on the brow of the prince among his brothers"* (Genesis 49:22—26).

Moses blessed the tribe of Joseph through Joseph's two sons: *"Of Joseph he said: 'Blessed by the Lord is his land with the best of the skies above and of the abyss crouching beneath; With the best of the produce of the year, and the choicest sheaves of the months; With the finest gifts of the age-old mountains and the best from the timeless hills; With the best of the earth and its fullness, and the favor of him who dwells in the bush. These shall come upon the head of Joseph and upon the brow of the prince among his brothers, the majestic bull, his father's first-born, whose horns are those of the wild ox with which to gore the nations, even those at the ends of the earth [These are the myriads of Ephraim and the thousands of Manasseh.]"* (Deut. 33:13–17).

From the name "Joseph" comes a state of consciousness in which we increase our imagination and authority to express and form every idea that we can conceive or believe. Joseph was clothed with a coat of many colors; he was a dreamer and an interpreter of dreams. He had a remarkable ability to perceive spirit rather than using the mind as the focal point of his actions.

Joseph, at first, was a slave in Egypt until he interpreted a dream for Pharaoh (Gen. 41:25–31). Hence, this represents our mind being a slave to our outer, obscured physical ego-consciousness, and to the intelligence center of our mind. And, since Joseph used his ability to interpret dreams more from a spiritual point than from the intellectual mind, he could also represent our highest perception of truths for dealing with our physical body and material environment and how we bring it into a more orderly state.

"Joseph" symbolizes our higher, imaginative excellence when defining truth, which comes down into our Egyptian state of mind or consciousness (obscurity, darkness, and ignorance). Under the law of cause-and-effect (being a slave to the idea of polarity energy (Gen. 39:1)), we finally raise our consciousness into a new truth, where we realize that good (light), evil (dark), and all that is of dual opposing ideas are just illusions created to understand our choices, who we are, and life purposes.

If you have read the Bible like most people say they do, then you should know the story of Joseph and how his brothers plotted to kill him (Gen. 37:17–28); however, Joseph was sold into Egypt as a slave (Gen. 39:1). Then he was thrown in jail by his master because the master's wife accused Joseph of attacking her (Gen. 39:20). After Joseph spent a few years in prison, he met up with two of Pharaoh's courtiers that Pharaoh had put in the same jail cell as Joseph (Gen. 40:1–3).

After Joseph interpreted a dream for one of the couriers, the courtier was released from jail and returned to his post in the Pharaoh's court. That is when the Pharaoh learned about Joseph's ability to interpret dreams. So, the Pharaoh sent for Joseph to interpret his dreams, which nobody else could interpret (Gen. 41:25–31). Joseph interpreted the Pharaoh's dreams as representing seven years of abundance, followed by seven years of famine (Gen. 41:29–31). Then Pharaoh decided to put Joseph in charge of all of Egypt (Gen. 41:44).

Once the famine began throughout the land of Egypt and Canaan, Jacob (Israel) sent his sons to Egypt to buy grain (Gen. 42:1–3). When Jacob learned that his son Joseph had become the overseer of all of Egypt, he gathered all his belongings, his family, the families of his sons and their descendants and flocks and went down into Egypt to meet Joseph and live out their remaining lives in a new land (Gen. 46:5–30).

This story of Jacob (Israel) and his family, the families of his sons, their descendants, and flocks moving down into Egypt is a depiction of the mass (all souls) moving into a whole new land of obscurity, ignorance, and darkness. Egypt, during the times of the Pharaohs, represents the realm of material life in the depths of ignorance and obscurity in a physical body. And, to the stubborn and unyielding mental consciousness, it is in the land of darkness and mystery, as it represents the physical body of consciousness.

We all associate the family of Israel (all souls, not just the Jews) with the hidden, non-dual opposing forces within our physical body and with our ego-personality consciousness. The symbolism of the story depicts the unification of the "I AM" within the self (Jacob/Israel) with all the faculties of the life forces (left/right brain activities, the endocrine system, and the twelve major systems of the physical body. It also becomes one with the essence of the whole self (all aspects of you, light and dark), our descendants (spirit family), and our Son's family (all that was created by the mind, including thoughts, ideas, potentials, and many other things (flocks)).

Remember, Jacob (Israel) and his family (all soul-groups) dwelt in the land of Goshen (Gen. 47:1), which means unification between the "I AM" Spirit Jacob/Israel) and all of our faculties of the mind. The children of Israel multiplying in the land of Egypt despite their oppression, their eventual threat or concern to the Egyptians, and performing hard services with mortar and brick to make other people's lives better (Ex. 1:12–13) all have symbolic meaning. It is related to you and the movement of mass consciousness into materialism and a physical body that has become obscured by materialistic living *(mortar and brick)*.

And now, because we believe in polarity energy (light and dark), we remain a slave to our Egyptian state of mind (darkness and ignorance). And, we will remain there until we recognize the deliverer is the "I AM" Christ within the self, symbolized by Moses. Because of our ignorance, we remain under the law of sowing and reaping (an eye for an eye), until we finally raise our consciousness to a new truth where we realize that we are God, Goddess, and a Christ too.

Moses was born a Jew but was adopted by the Egyptians and lived as one for many years. After he was grown, he was introduced to his true heritage. So, think of yourself as Moses in a strange family. In your infant stage of life, you fall into darkness and obscurity (Egyptians) for a while. And now, you are finally grown up and are being introduced to your true heritage, for which you are, "I AM" Christ, "I AM" God, and "I AM" the Goddess. Therefore, look at your "I AM" consciousness as the burning bush.

The story of the Jews and how they are known as the Children of God is significant because their very existence signifies every human on earth is an extension of the Spirit of One (Goddess). Therefore, the Jewish people and the country of Israel symbolize all souls who left home (the first creation) long ago to go out on a journey of discovery. Therefore, every soul on earth and beyond is an Israelite in the true sense of the word. And, we have played with different aspects of that belief for many lifetimes now.

Because of living so many lifetimes in darkness and obscurity (Egypt), we have become ignorant and forgetful of our true "I AM" identity (Jacob/Israel). Yet this darkness and obscurity (Egypt) have become the essential part of bringing our understanding and wisdom to light. You could even say we have never made a mistake. How can a mistake happen if we always learn wisdom from the mistake made?

When we reach a deeper understanding of God as pure neutralized energy and not as an individual outside of us, as Moses did in his time, we take on a new belief while releasing and destroying the validity of old beliefs. Thus, freedom comes to us in a manner beyond our understanding! However, at this point, duality may kick in, and then those old views and opinions begin to destroy our new thoughts, beliefs, and choices (represented by the Jews who did not believe in the God of Moses) that are intended to move us beyond the fear of being less than God (represented by the Jews who did believe in the God of Moses) (Ex. 32:1–35).

When we are willing to raise our consciousness and move into new beliefs and understanding about all things, then the evolutionary law that is part of our soul begins to release our old beliefs that have limited our expressions and experiences until now. That is when our healing, abundance, and joy begin to well up from our "I AM" Christ-spirit as an eternal spring of life-giving water. It is through our interpretations of God's laws that we observe and experience the effects of polarity energy (light and dark) and our belief in sin. What we perceive as mistakes or sin has brought us through our lessons of sowing and reaping. However, now it is time to graduate and move past the belief in sin and dual-energy.

The *"twelve thousand were marked from the tribe of Benjamin,"* Revelation 7:8. Benjamin was the younger of the two sons of Rachel and Jacob. *"With her last breath, for she was at the point of death, she called him Ben-oni; his father, however, named him Benjamin. Thus, Rachel died, and she was buried on the road to Ephrath (that is, Bethlehem)"* (Gen. 35:18–19). Jacob's blessing upon Benjamin *"is a ravenous wolf; mornings he devours the prey, and evenings he distributes the spoils"* (Gen. 49:27). Moses' blessing: *"Benjamin is the beloved of the Lord, who shelters him all day, while he abides securely at his breast"* (Deut. 33:12).

"Benjamin" symbolizes active trust in yourself as God-Goddess, and not one looking for God. By seeing ourselves as a Christ also, one praises (Judah) and establishes the trust (Benjamin) as for strength in conquering our thoughts of polarity energy (sin) as something real. Notice the division of the twelve tribes into four different verses in Revelation, with each verse mentioning the three groups of tribes. It may add some credibility to the 3 X 4 mentioned in section 7:4 above.

The number three relates to our three-dimensional consciousness: spirit/super-subconsciousness, the mind-soul subconsciousness, and the outer ego/physical consciousness evolving through the four lower elements of materialism. These three groups or tribes could also be associated with our evolution on a personal note. And this can be determined only by reading this book. The confirmation of this may come from the next chapter.

Chapter 21

THE RETURN TO HIGHER CONSCIOUSNESS

By looking into Revelation 7:9, the *"huge crowd"* represents all 144,000 soul group families that left higher consciousness (Garden) eons ago and moved forward into the "wall of fire," as this represents polarity, or dual opposing energy, at work in a three-dimensional world.

All humans, from every race and nation, including all galaxies, universes, and dimensions, non-physical and physical, are all part of the 144,000 angelic soul families. The *"count from every nation and race, people and tongue"* in Revelation 7:9 represents the soul count in each spiritual family group. The count can contain hundreds, thousands, millions, and perhaps billions of souls within each family group.

"Standing before the throne," Revelation 7:9 represents the seat of our "I AM" Divine Christ consciousness, and there sits our mind-soul consciousness of responsibility (*"sacrificial lamb"*) maintaining the memories of everything we do and have learned in wisdom because of our chosen experiences in many lifetimes. We become purified through the branches of many lifetimes, sowing and reaping (trial by fire), and now, some of us are on the verge of becoming a Master and the Lord of Lords *(white robes)* over our many, many ego-personality consciousnesses.

Some of us have triumphed *(palm branches)* and have become victorious in our labor *(hand)* over many lifetimes to become now a Christ in the flesh in this lifetime. All that is left for us to do is awaken to it and allow it to come into our consciousness as something real. When we keep in mind what John saw (symbolized by our ego-personality aspect of today) as his creations while learning to become a Christ in his lifetime, we can see that some of us here today are beginning to understand our own departure from higher consciousness (Garden) eons ago.

When studying Revelation, Chapter 7:9-17, the verses represent us, humans, from the mind-soul and ego-personality consciousness, moving through our period of trials and tribulations, and learning the responsibilities of our choices. And this comes down to how we place the results of our memory response patterns into every cell of our physical body through the metaphoric meaning of what the twelve tribes of Israel represent.

By allowing the forces of opposing polarity energy to create our experiences, we have allowed our "I AM" to be preserved *(sealed)* through the process of soul memory. Hence, we create our own *"white robe,"* and now the "white robe" is worn by every ego-personality aspect (lifetime) that we have created so we can experience many potentials, including the dark creations that have come back to us for integration.

The *"holding of the palm branches in their hands"* in Revelation 7:9 refers to your success in integrating some of your ego-personality aspects of light and dark (lifetimes). And, with this acceptance of a new consciousness that works with your spirit-Christ consciousness, you gain a new understanding and a new redeemed state of mind (Jerusalem), and you enter into a knowing that you are Christ. The only way to redeem your mind-soul is to look upon light and dark, as one. And then, integrate them in expressing perfection through your mental faculties (twelve disciples) and their division under the dominion of your "I AM" Christ consciousness.

Jerusalem is the City of David, and it symbolizes the nerve center that is in the back of the heart. From this point, our "I AM" Christ consciousness sends its measure of radiant New Expansional Energy to all parts of our spirit, mind, and ego-personality forms (aspects) just as the heart sends blood to all the cells in our physical body.

Yeshua's journey to Jerusalem (Matthew 20:17) represents that some of us are now taking our last steps with this belief in polarity energy (light and dark). Thus, we are preparing our way to take the final step with our ego-personality of today to learn that it has been crucified because of old belief systems. And now, it is time to take ourselves off the cross, and then release our old way of thinking about sin, punishment, and Christ. And, when our thoughts of light and dark, sin and earth are crossed out (or let go, as in trust), then spiritual truth about opposing energy and its manifestations in the body takes form within our consciousness, and we realize they are only illusions.

Channeling of the Ascended Masters on the Apocalypse

When looking into Revelation 7:10, *"the crying out in a loud voice, Salvation is from God who is seated on the throne,"* represents that we can bring salvation to ourselves in this lifetime if we so choose and allow. No one can offer you salvation, but you alone because you are the Christ *"seated on the throne."* Thus, *"all the angels who were standing around the throne and the elders and the four living creatures falling down before the throne to worship God"* signifies the 144,000 angelic soul families (you and me) that left higher consciousness (Garden) eons ago to journey out into the abyss (unknown opposing energy). And then, they filled the abyss with multiple dimensions, including a physical universe.

The *"elders"* that stood around the throne represent the wholeness of the self, including your left and right brain hemispheres, your physical makeup of the twelve endocrine systems senses, and the twelve major systems of the physical body (Reference Revelation 4:4).

Throughout this book, it has been determined that we are a three-dimensional being when in the flesh. Therefore, if we calculate the "twenty-four others" and the "twenty-four elders" as part of each dimensional realm, along with the "six divine attributes of spirit" found in Revelation 4:4 in this book, we come up with the sacred geometric number of fifty-four (54).

When broken down to its lowest value, 5 + 4 = 9, the number "9" applies to our three-dimensional consciousness (Spirit, Mind-soul, and Ego). Thus, creating a geometric value of 999. Each value nine "9" represents our completeness in (i) spirit, (ii) mind-soul, and (iii) ego-personality forms (physical bodies). And since the number nine (9) is the highest value, then the only thing that comes after nine is one again, completeness, or as follows: 999 + 1 = 1000.

When first awakened in spirit, we were an "oneness of consciousness" until we split our neutralized, pure "consciousness" into a dual mental mind and soul consciousness of responsibility. And this action transmitted opposing energy of polarity that was used for our creations as if being real. After completing our non-positive and non-negative creations in the first cycle, symbolized by the number nine (9), we moved into the second cycle of nine (9), where our mental consciousness was tied to a belief in polarity energy (positive and negative) that lead to the third nine (9), symbolized by our consciousness and physical body.

After playing in the second cycle of opposing energy, creating multiple non-physical and physical realms to experience our choices, some of us were ready to complete this second cycle of nine (9) and move to the third cycle where the third nine (9) becomes significant for our (i) completion. And (ii), the only thing that comes after 9 is 10, which means we come back to our oneness of consciousness again but this time with a twist of wisdom. Because of our many lifetimes playing with this opposing energy, we became filled with great wisdom and understanding.

When we have journeyed through the cycles of what the numbers "999" represent, we then move into the third cycle or circle referred to in the number of 144,000. And, once we journey through the elements of (i) fire, (ii) earth, (iii) water, and (iv) air and see how each element relates to memory, desires, choices, and growth (four living creatures) of our consciousness, then we become like Yeshua, a Christ in our own right. These "four living creatures" become our footstool as they did for Yeshua.

Therefore, you created yourself, and you are the only one who can forgive yourself, save yourself, and let go of the old thinking that sin is real. No man needs to worship anyone other than the self because you are Christ, God and the Goddess, the Father, and the Mother. It is you to whom you give *"praise, glory, thanksgiving, honor, and power forever and ever"* and no one else, because salvation comes from within you and not from Yeshua. Yeshua just showed us how to get there.

Using the number 144,000, the masters will show us how to move into the fifth dimension or fourth density. Take $1 + 4 + 4 + 0 + 0 + 0 = 9$, and then look at our journey through the first two cycles (zeros) where we followed neutrality, and then followed opposing energy. We come up with $9 + 9 = 18$, and when we break down $1 + 8$ to equal nine (9) again, we come back to our oneness – because what comes after 9 but 1 again ($1 + 0 = 1$). Once we complete these two cycles of 9's, we enter into a whole new cycle (the third zero), where we are the one sovereign God and Goddess in our own right. Later in the book, we will learn how this also applies to the number of 1000 years of peace ($999 + 1 = 1000$).

By clinging onto the belief in polarity energy, light, and dark, the mind can only decipher things intellectually or with reason and judgment. Therefore, the mind only understands itself as having opposing energy (good versus evil) as its source because of the three-dimensional behavior patterns that seem real, and yet it is not real. Those who learn how to move beyond polarity energy and into the fourth and fifth dimension of physicality where positive and negative become balanced within oneself, then they become very multidimensional.

Who is the *"elder who spoke up"* in Revelation 7:13-14? It is our adrenal gland and represents the Church of Pergamum. Remember the *"seven angels"* (seven churches) in Revelation 5:2 who proclaimed the loudest? It is our adrenal gland that proclaims the loudest and is the angel, guardian, and protector between our outer and inner consciousness. And this is indicated by the division between the right and left-brain hemispheres. In our sleep-state, there is no direct communication between the two, other than through our memory and emotions.

In Revelation 5:2, it mentioned that no man (male or female) is worthy to open the seals of his/her memory (Book of Life) until he/she becomes a Son of Man (or our mind becoming awakened) in the flesh. Therefore, the Son of Man appears when our ego-personality (the name on our birth certificate) finally overcomes the emotional belief in a solitary single-male God who created us and the myth that Yeshua comes and saves us. Because of our focus on good and evil for centuries and centuries, lifetime after lifetime, our emotional body (adrenal gland) keeps us from communicating intuitively with our "I AM" Christ.

It is because of our strong belief in a God who created us and is outside of us, our mind-soul finds it impossible to communicate with our "I AM" identity. After all, we do not believe we are Christ, God, and the Goddess, or do you? If we still believe that we are only human, how can we communicate with our "I AM" if we do not believe we are Christ? Yeshua could speak to his "I AM" because he was awakened to whom he was. But, once we humans move past our three-dimensional understanding of God (light) and Satan (dark) as two different entities, we, like Yeshua, can also begin our third cycle using New Expansional Energy that is of the fourth and fifth dimension (even though we are in the flesh).

The fourth and fifth dimension is about you, while in the flesh, merging your outer physical consciousness with your mental subconsciousness and becoming one again (or the right and left-brain hemispheres and all that you are moving into one body of consciousness). Once you enter the fourth and fifth dimension, you begin to recognize everything around you as an illusion and not as real *("My lord, you are the one who knows")*, Revelation 7:13-14.

After recognizing the Christ, God, and the Goddess as yourself, and the many images of yourself that you have created throughout time and space as personality aspects of light and dark (lifetimes), you learn wisdom. That is when you begin to understand why you are your own servant and the *"one who has survived the time of great distress"* mentioned in Revelation 7:14. Once awakened, our many light and dark ego-personality aspects have come out of their great tribulations (sowing and reaping) and are now part of our memories. That means we can now tap into the wisdom of all those experiences at will.

Remember, for a long time, these light and dark personality aspects have withstood the test of polarity energy, and they have held us to our original purpose for soul growth *("washed their robes and made them white in the blood of the Lamb")* Revelation 7:14. And now, because of our courageous decision to learn responsibility and the wisdom behind polarity energy, these many ego-personality aspects of light and dark (lifetimes) to which we are connected, have experienced many great hardships, afflictions, and suffering. And now, these ego-personality aspects from our past are ready for recognition, love, and support by coming home to their creator, the self.

However, once we recognize that the Son of Man (the mind) has taken charge of our outer consciousness, then the many ego-personality aspects from our past lifetimes become free, saved by the *"blood of the Lamb"* (Revelation 7:14), or us in this lifetime.

Since the "lamb" is you, here in the flesh in this lifetime, then you (by way of energy and consciousness) are in the middle of your many ego-personality aspects that are spread throughout the many physical and non-physical dimensions. And, this is why you have the understanding to *shepherd* in "all that you are in memory," back to your heavenly state of consciousness (Revelation 7:17). Thereby, freeing both them and yourself from any more suffering if you so choose.

It is you, the Christ you are, with the authority and the capability to *"lead them* (all light and dark ego-personality aspects of you) *to springs of life-giving water,"* or back to neutralized pure energy again, Revelation 7:17.

Chapter 22

TOTAL RECALL

Chapter 22 is also an exciting and revealing chapter because of the *"seventh seal,"* Revelation 8:1. The opening of the *"seventh seal"* grants the seven angels to sound off in unison, allowing us humans to come into self-governing rulership as opposed to others ruling us through religion, government, separation of race, opposing views, that Satan is real, sin, suffering, and a need of a savior. The *"seventh seal"* is not only the unfolding of the mystery of the Apocalypse, but it also uncovers the mystery behind Christ's return to earth.

From the works of Geoffrey Hoppe, Crimson Circle, I read a Shoud where Tobias mentions, and I quote, "the seventh seal is the butterfly (us humans) leaving the effectiveness of the cocoon (three-dimensional consciousness), which has hidden our true identity for eons of time." My friends, we all have forgotten the *"seventh seal"* has been part of our consciousness since we left the first creation (or higher consciousness). And now, because of our many lifetimes sowing and reaping (bearing our own cross), we have the potential to move through the fourth to the fifth dimension if we so choose.

(A Shoud is a monthly gathering of the Ascended Masters from the other side of the veil, channeled through Geoffrey Hoppe, Crimson Circle, Colorado, helping humanity awaken).

When looking into the fourth dimension, it is considered a formless realm, much like the second dimension (our mental state), and how it is part of our three-dimensional physical body and three-dimensional world. The difference between the two dimensional and the fourth dimension, even though they are both mental states, is the fourth dimension has no makeup beliefs of any sin and judgment based on vibrational polarity energy, or good and evil. It is through the fourth dimension, where we enter the fifth-dimensional world of physicality. Also, the fifth dimension is the gateway for tapping into New Expansional Energy (New Earth).

The fifth-dimensional physical consciousness is more expanded than the old traditional three-dimensional physical consciousness. It is also with the energy we use for our creations. A fifth-dimensional consciousness holds no judgment against anyone or belief in any separateness from one's "I AM" Christ-identity. Right now, many are teetering between the two.

Our two-dimensional consciousness (mind-soul) is of non-form, and that is where our mental perception of polarity energy feels real to us, as we play it out in a three-dimensional physical form as something right and wrong, good and bad. The belief in separation (opposing energy, Satan, sin, judgment, punishment, and the need to be saved) dominates our two and three-dimensional consciousness as if all that we are is human. The opening of the *"seventh seal"* in Revelation 8:1 is to bring remembrance to the idea that we no longer need to play in a two and three-dimensional consciousness and energy.

When we allow for ascension (rapture), we move from a two and three-dimensional consciousness to a four and five-dimensional consciousness where a "knowing" comes in through our heart center (intuitive body), instead of through the "human intellect" (mind-body) as we have been taught. Thus, we open up to a New Expansional Energy to whom the church calls New Earth! It is through the fourth-dimensional mental realm of non-form that becomes the tool to help us rid ourselves of polarity energy, conditional love, sin, and judgment.

If we desire to know where we stand with three-dimensional consciousness versus five-dimensional living, we only have to consider what we are thinking at this very moment. If we have thoughts of judgment, drama, being a sinner, atheism, or believing that God and Satan are separate from us, then we are living the life of a three-dimensional person that only understands ourselves as only human, and that when we die, that is it. Only thoughts or beliefs of non-opposing energy, unconditional love, and compassion for others and ourselves can survive in the fourth-dimension. Anything of opposing energy beliefs and that control and power are real cannot survive in the fourth and the fifth dimension.

When we learn to move our consciousness to a non-judgmental attitude and trust ourselves as a Christ, God, and the Goddess, our consciousness moves to a fifth-dimensional living; thus, inconceivable magic occurs around us that a three-dimensional being would never see. We choose what to experience in the flesh as a Christ instead of following others that believe they are less than Christ. When our thoughts are of

Channeling of the Ascended Masters on the Apocalypse

non-opposing beliefs, we set ourselves up to live in a whole New Earth where we become free of disease, poverty, and bad relationships. Be it wealth, happiness, good health, or writing a book. We can experience our heart desires when we come into a knowing of being Christ.

Belief systems are like strong radar signals that call out through the many realms of opposing energy to have us believe that positive begets positive and negative begets negative. Thus, we create from this stuck energy, and that causes us to follow the destiny of karma. When we make a conscious choice to let go of the belief in judgment, Satan, good and evil, we set ourselves up to move into a whole New World (consciousness) where we understand that no one can create our reality but self. Thus, karma becomes non-existent.

Do you remember being taught by your religious leaders that you will be lifted in the air to be with Yeshua in the clouds? By being raised in the air, it is symbolic of you moving beyond the ignorance of being less than a Christ. Thus, the lifting up in the air is that of your mental state moving into a frequency higher than what it was vibrating at in the three-dimensional world. Thus, this is known as the rapture in what religions teach their followers and how they will be lifted in the air to meet Jesus in the clouds.

My friends, it is not as religions proclaim! It is nothing more than you raising your energy and consciousness vibrations from a two and three-dimensional frequency to a four and five-dimensional frequency while still part of the physical realm. Yeshua could move from a two and three-dimensional consciousness to a four and five, right on up to seven to nine at will, which is why people worship him instead of seeing him as an example of becoming a Christ.

Most of the Ascended Masters come from the sixth and seventh dimensions. And, when Yeshua was on earth over two thousand years ago, he could move to the ninth dimension at will, allowing himself to transport himself from any place on earth. This accounts for Yeshua being seen in places that cannot be explained otherwise.

According to Yeshua and the Ascended Masters, September 2007 marked the beginning of the vibrational energy frequency of two and three-dimensional (Old Earth) to a New Expansional Energy of Four and Five-dimensional consciousness (New Earth) where you can expand inward, outward, and multi-dimensionally all at once. Those who will not accept the concept of New Expansional Energy (New Earth), and that you are a Christ also will continue to suffer the consequences of living with polarity energy and what it brings into their lives.

Terry L. Newbegin

When looking into the *"opening of the seventh seal where there was silence in heaven for about half-hour,"* Revelation 8:1, it has to do with the "silencing of the mind" when making choices to be manifested to experience. Let's say from the time we left higher consciousness (Garden), all that we have chosen to experience was polarity energy. Now the opportunity has presented itself where we can open the "seventh seal," symbolized by the "silencing of our mind" before any "consciousness act." This act is with our pituitary gland, for which the Church of Laodicea symbolizes.

The *"silence in heaven for about half an hour"* is representative where we transformed our "oneness of consciousness" to a consciousness of a two and a three-dimensional consciousness (1/2 = 30 minutes). Thus, we all have a left and right brain hemisphere that play with the concept of polarity energy as something being real. And, as in Genesis, Chapter Two, where God rested on the "seventh day," has nothing to do with any day of the week or us attending church. It is about us, before making a choice, needing to silence (quiet) the mind and contemplate on the choice that we are seeking to express to this opposing energy to experience.

Before choosing, it becomes imperative to feel into the vibrations of what you are choosing to experience. Otherwise, it could lead to a catastrophic outcome. Know that the "seventh day" is the link between your higher (heaven) and lower physical consciousness (hell) where choices could lead to pain and suffering. And, to reach an integrated state of higher consciousness, you need to condition the mind to be silent to allow the forces of polarity energy to flow through you before choosing and manifesting what you desire to experience as your reality. And the best method I know for silencing the mind is through deep breathing for at least thirty minutes before making any major decision.

From here, Yeshua and the Ascended Masters mentioned Revelation 8:2, about the *"seven angels"* and the *"seven trumpets"* and how they were previously addressed with interpreting Revelation 1:20 and 5:6, in this book.

The *"seven angels"* represent our "seven subtle bodies" and how they relate to the "seven inner and outer expressions of our total consciousness," symbolized as the *"seven trumpets."* Also, as part of our "seven subtle bodies," along with the *"seven seals"* and *"seven churches,"* I have listed them again below for better understanding. I, therefore, have listed the position of the *"seven seals"* in order from the lowest to the highest consciousness because that is how we all chose to evolve.

Channeling of the Ascended Masters on the Apocalypse

Seven Stars/ Angels	Seven Inner Expressions	Seven Outer (trumpets/seals) Seven Expressions	Churches
1. Physical Body	Desires	Belief in Separation	Ephesus
2. Etheric Body	Choices	Becoming Self-Aware	Smyrna
3. Emotional Body	Memory	Belief in Satan/Duality	Pergamum
4. Mental/Soul Body	Growth	Belief in Sin/Guilt	Thyatira
5. Intuitive Body	Free Will	Belief in Suffering	Sardis
6. Mind-Body	Relationships	Belief in Salvation	Philadelphia
7. Spirit Body	Responsibility	Knowing One is Christ	Laodicea

Our own "I AM" Christ spirit invited us to participate in something that became such a challenge that we forgot our supremacy as a Christ, God, and a Goddess. Our mental and physical consciousness became a fantastic place for us to hide and play with limited vibrational energy to learn in ways that we could not have done on any other level but a three-dimensional one.

When we all came to earth, we agreed to lower our energy and consciousness, which felt like a fall, and we became susceptible to the influences and the forces of this polarity energy. And this is what brought in the attributes of the "seven most deadly sins." In reality, these are no sins. It is only our perception of their existence that says they are sins:

1. Anger
2. Lust for power
3. Envy
4. Greed
5. Pride
6. Sadness
7. Laziness

When these "seven attributes of a deadly nature" were introduced into our reality a long time ago, we became the exact opposite of our "I AM" Christ consciousness. You could say that we became an "Anti-Christ because of our belief that we are not Christ," but we did it on purpose, and not that we were kicked out of heaven. It was us souled beings who created this polarity energy and a philosophy of concepts that put forth a set of beliefs that became devoted to guiding us to practice basic principles to play with to understand the full extent of us not being Christ.

We souls are the eternal Godhead pretending to be subject to energies of opposing nature, pretending that we cannot perceive nonphysical beings, and allowing a deep belief that Satan can overwhelm and render us helpless. But it is all an illusion, including our actions, choices, physical body, the universe, and all that we understand as being our philosophies and truths. All of it is just a dimension that was created by all souls to play in, and yet we believe that we are only human.

It is our beliefs and philosophies that keep us stuck in a mental whirlwind of suffering because we have allowed our human sensory perceptions to determine our actions and beliefs as being real. Thus, building our reality into something that feels real, and yet it is not real. The strong belief we have held about a God who is white, male, punishing, judgmental, and even jealous and all-knowing, has kept us in a sleep state, rather than opening us up to a full awareness of what we have genuinely created to experience to learn wisdom.

Most all of us have taken on the belief that nothing is real unless it is materialistic and tangible, and even our portrayal of God conveys a character that is materialistic and human-like. We discount anything that cannot be understood with the mind and to accept whatever the mind, our friends, and our religious teachers perceive as our reality. Yeshua gave his life trying to tell us that the kingdom of heaven (home) is within and not outside of us. However, his teachings have been distorted, and we have been trained to look outside of ourselves for the answers as to why we suffer. And maybe this is why we have been going through the seven outer expressions (beliefs) represented by the seven seals.

When looking into the *"other angel"* in Revelation 8:3, Yeshua and the Ascended Masters are speaking of our "I AM" Christ spirit and how it works through our pituitary center (Church of Laodicea). It has always been our "I AM" Christ spirit that gave us the means to explore the results of polarity energy and its effect. And right now, our "I AM" Christ spirit stands before our mind-soul and ego-personality consciousness (representing the *"altar"* in Revelation 8:3), as it holds the agreement *(gold censer)* we made with our "I AM" long ago to create a three-dimensional place where we learn and understand responsibility, real love, and how to become a sovereign God/Goddess in our own right.

You have forgotten that we have been playing from out of our mind-soul and ego forms for eons of time, and our mind has become custom to interpreting and analyzing everything we experience and feel as real. Because of playing in two and three-dimensional illusions for so long, we have come to believe the mind is the headmaster of all that we are, a mere human. Because of this belief, we have lost sight of our true identity, and every time we have a small feeling that there might be more to life than what we have been taught, our mind rushes in to defend the illusion we are experiencing and the beliefs created as being real.

You are the angel who stands before the image of yourself projecting your desires, choices, and the beliefs from your brothers, sisters, and your many ego-personality aspects that are spread throughout the multidimensional realms. The smoke of the incense hides the real you, and it takes fire to burn away (sowing and reaping) the many images of the false you (devil or rebellious ego). The agreement you hold *(censer)* in your heart and the smokescreen that has kept you hidden and separate from your "I AM" needs releasing before your left and right brain hemispheres to come together as one.

Because of lifetimes sowing and reaping, some of us are now ready to move into a fourth and fifth-dimensional consciousness, where the *"golden censer,"* Revelation 8:3, represents the wisdom found within our "I AM," helping us to release all outdated agreements of poverty, suffering, sin, and anything else that portrays us as only human. Our "I AM" has recognized the multiple ego-personality aspects of us, as they are the *holy ones* who have carried their crosses. And now, in this lifetime, we can open our eyes, heart, and mind and welcome in the Christ we are. When we reach this level of understanding, our "I AM" then reveals to us the mystery behind what happened to us since the time we left higher consciousness (garden) long ago.

Revelation 8:4 is about you hiding behind your material existence and belief systems, not realizing you are the *"holy one"* that is ready to integrate all of your ego-personalities from many lifetimes. It is you who stands before your "I AM" Christ spirit, and all you have to do is extend your hand in welcoming your "I AM" into your life. Thus, authorizing you to allow your five divine senses to integrate with your five physical senses.

To help with the clarification of your five divine senses, I have listed them as follows.

1. Awareness – Knowing you are Christ, God, and the Goddess
2. Imagination – Which brings your thoughts to life
3. Compassion – The capacity to trust, forgive, allow, accept, and honor who you are by accepting every choice and experience you have chosen to play out, good and bad.
4. Consciousness – A type of power that gives you the ability to blend your pure god energy, your imagination, and compassion into a focus that brings your creations to life in a new expansional reality.
5. Expression – The true state of a creator Christ, God, and a Goddess (you) in human form.

Know that it was the *"burning coals from the altar"* in Revelation 8:5, presented as the fire of justice (karma) manifested as the condition that allowed us to play in opposing vibrational energy to learn wisdom and to answer the question, "Who am I?" It took our "I AM" Christ spirit to *"hurl us (you) down to earth"* giving us a chance to create a concept to lower our pure, neutral god energy of light to vibrational energy that opposed each other. Thus, allowing the influences of light and dark, duality, to manifest into a solid form called our physical body so we could play a game of make-believe to understand choice, responsibility, and wisdom.

The *"peals of thunder, rumblings, flashes of lightning,"* Revelation 8:5, all pertain to the outburst and sudden expansion of our consciousness eons ago to a mind-soul consciousness that produced multitudes of ego-personality aspects" of light and dark (lifetimes) creations to experience a mirror image of ourselves to learn the wisdom behind our choices. And, because of this sudden expansion of long ago, we patterned our desires, thoughts, and beliefs into a make-believe energy source of positive and negative that felt real to us. This then sealed in the actions of a strong upward movement toward uncontrollable thought patterns of light and dark creations.

This led to some of our many ego-personality aspects to take on a cruel and destructive nature that created outbreaks of epidemic proportions *(earthquakes)* at the subconscious level without any warning. And with this subconscious *"underground eruptions"* and how they shaped our thoughts, ideas, beliefs, and personality aspects into energetic conflicts, it caused us to become lost and afraid for many lifetimes. In seeking to discover who we were and are, we offered ourselves before the highest authority within ourselves, or the "I AM." And that is where we aired our desire outwardly to an imaginary opposing force that created positive and negative as our reality to experience.

Channeling of the Ascended Masters on the Apocalypse

The example can be found in Genesis by our higher consciousness (God's) rejection of our rebellious ego-personality as the controlling factor in our life, symbolized by Cain's offering. Again, we, in our higher consciousness, are pure, and we can use this neutral energy for our creations, but we adulterated this pure, neutralized god energy of light by taking on ideas and desires that acted through the gonad level where we claim we are a three-dimensional being.

It was this "act in consciousness" where our awareness of being "I AM" Christ was blocked from our mind-soul and our many ego-personalities. This is symbolized by Cain (our rebellious ego) killing Abel, symbolized by our higher awareness of being a Christ. And this is why we feel separated from Christ, God, and the Goddess within. Therefore, the *"seven angels,"* as representative of our "seven subtle bodies" in Revelation 8:6, prepared themselves to take on whatever was the will of their master, which is our mind and ego.

It was you and the mass consciousness working from a mental level, manifesting a rebellious ego part of you and the physical body to play the game of make-believe, even to the point of inviting in your many beastly ego personalities to do horrible actions, like corruption, devastation, lies, and deceitful acts. We can all see this today with all that is happening in the United States with the destroying of life and property and then disguising it as protesting.

Just know that in a lifetime past, any one of us could have been yellow, brown, red, white, and have been a black slave, but in this lifetime, the black slave is white to encounter the opposite. But in this lifetime, many are looking at the race card as something to use against someone. Know that it is not wrong to be white, black, brown, yellow, red, male, or female in this lifetime. Why? Because we all have been part of many races and genders, and now, we are on our way back to higher consciousness. Thus, forgive them who act this way and then forgive yourself and move on.

However, in the end, after completing the second cycle (zero), these horrid actions will, at some point, turn into contentment, compassion, and joy because of the wisdom we have learned from the actions taken. And it works through our "seven subtle bodies" and how they influence us through the impulses of the endocrine system, through our expressions, and through our belief systems. In a unique way, they are all helping us believe that we are indeed separate from our "I AM" consciousness. Thus, it is through these many good and bad ego-personality aspects of us that we come to understand the answer to the questions of "Who am I?" and "What is my purpose?"

Therefore, without you realizing it, your ego-personality aspects of many can influence the way you act in this lifetime. And because of the attribute of memory, you can learn to reveal to yourself all those ego-personalities that need integrating and balancing. If you are experiencing pain and suffering right now, then what aspects of you, past or present, are you not accepting about yourself? And, you can learn about these ego-personality aspects (lifetimes) just by looking in the eyes of your family, friends, those you work with, and what you believe are your truths.

The people you meet and interact with, your biased opinions, and your accidents reflect the ego-personality aspects that you try to hide deep within your soul. And when you move beyond the belief of polarity energy and begin to understand everything through the eyes of your Christ consciousness, you will know that everything you have created since the time you left higher consciousness was appropriate for your soul growth. Again, forgive yourself, forgive others, and then move on with your life.

Knowing this helps you finally release your dark stuck creations from your Christ-spirit. And that will be the time when your "I AM" will come in to empower you in a whole new way. This empowerment is an awakening where you become aware of your hypnotic sleep state and find that you use the energy of light (God) for your creations and that you are Christ and Satan embodied within one consciousness while you are still in the flesh.

Once we awaken and realize that we are a Christ also in the flesh and that our dark creations are part of us, then our sowing and reaping (karma) can be over in the twinkling of an eye. This awakening is signified by the thymus (Thyatira, the fourth church). An example of this awakening is found in Revelation 8:7, as the *"third of the land was burned up, along with a third of the trees and all green grass;"* as life is not about worship, rules of religious principles, or something is written down for us to follow. It is about the passion of our "I AM" Christ consciousness to learn, grow, expand, sense, and have experienced. Thus, the fulfilling and unfolding of our beliefs using polarity energy in finding the wisdom behind our choices.

Understand and know what we choose to do or have already done is not about sin and punishment. It is us humans continually changing and bringing fulfillment and wisdom to our "I AM" so that we can become a sovereign God and Goddess in our own right. From the phrase *"a third of the land was burned up,"* for example, is not about land or the earth. It is about us living in a three-dimensional physical form where our outer physical consciousness *(land)* is limited when it comes to reproducing like images of ourselves that can heal us. We instead produce more of the same images of ourselves in the flesh over and over again until we learn to awaken to the process.

The ones that carry addiction, pain, and suffering seem to be the ones that spread themselves throughout the omniverse (multi-dimensions) as they are the favorites for creating drama and living life to the fullest.

"The hail and fire mixed with blood" in Revelation 8:7 is the result of us souls crystallizing our pure life energy *(blood)* into physical form, which resulted in physical patterns that became very destructive while working out of our gonad level (Church of Ephesus). Thus, this caused us to believe in "separation" from our "I AM" Christ consciousness (symbolized by the first seal). By airing our beliefs in dualistic terms and expressing them outwardly using polarity energy, we gave life to many characters and personalities of ourselves, where we became lost in our good and bad creations. And, these many ego personalities of good and evil are the total makeup of us today, even though they are just an image of us.

We, without realizing it, automatically place within each of those lifetimes a life force that will repeat itself over and over, until our belief systems are changed. When we try to justify our belief patterns using polarity energy, we cast those beliefs out before the throne (or our "I AM" Christ consciousness) for purification *(trial by fire)*, which is why we repeat lifetimes over and overdoing the same thing. If we have a strong belief in the Catholic religion in this lifetime, we will probably set ourselves up to have a strong belief in being a Protestant, etc., in the next.

The burning desire to move forward in the beginning stages of our soul growth came through the medium of our two and three-dimensional mental and physical consciousness. And, it was from these two beginning outward dimensions where the building blocks formed our mind, spirit, and many ego personalities, physical and non-physical, the beliefs that guided us through our trials and tribulations, lifetime after lifetime to acquire the balancing of our energy.

The symbolization of the *"third of the trees and all green grass"* in Revelation 8:7, again expresses us, humans, in our three-dimensional state and has nothing to do with the earth's trees or green grass. The *"trees"* represent our connection to all components of the self, or all aspects of our past and future lifetimes that are being played out. And, the *"green grass"* represents our soul's growth while we play in the consciousness of opposing energy, for it is the reality we created to feel our creations as real. Just as trees are interconnected by an extensive root system, so is our total consciousness. We planted many layers and levels of belief systems that connect to every ego-personality aspect that has ever existed.

Now, these ego-personality aspects of many are hidden from us because we buried them deep within our subconscious memories, as this is how polarity energy works. We tend to bury bad, dark, and negative aspects of ourselves deep within our consciousness, and then pretend that they do not exist. This is why we are afraid to dig deep within our consciousness for answers or listen to those that may be in the know. We choose to ignore who we are and what we created because of feeling the shame deep within how we used energy. Thus, this causes us to open up to taking on more and more of the belief systems of others and religions every time we decide to incarnate.

We can say that fear our divinity (God), and we identify that fear as "fearing the devil" because it feels dark to us. It feels dark because those dark aspects of ourselves are held by our Christ consciousness until we are ready to face those choices we made. Thus, we designate those feelings as the "devil" working hard to deceive us. Thus, the angel that is working from the gonad level is sounding the trumpet, declaring *(make known)* the time has come for some of us to awaken from our hypnotic sleep state and stop denying these dark aspects of us. And, when we do, this angel will bring us back to the memory of why we used polarity energy to experience earth (three-dimensional physical level). So, now you know these verses are about you having a total recall.

Chapter 23

THE REALIZATION OF OUR DARK CREATIONS

Many of us, especially those that attend church believing they abide by God's laws, have a hard time accepting that we had anything to do with creating evil things because of thinking we done nothing wrong. However, Revelation 8:8-9, *"when the second angel blew his trumpet, something like a large burning mountain was hurled into the sea. A third of the sea turned to blood, a third of the creatures in the sea died, and a third of the ships were wrecked."*

Overdramatic as these two verses sound, the *"second angel"* represents our own Etheric Body and how it knows our history and where we all took notice of our awareness that eventually led to a belief in "separation" from our own "I AM" Christ consciousness. Hence, before we moved into a three-dimensional body, we all made it known to our "I AM" that we agreed with the 144,000 soul families to hide our dark creations from our "I AM" when in an incarnation. This is represented by the *"large burning mountain!"*

We all hid our dark creations from previous lifetimes deep within our subconsciousness so that we would forget about what we did in order to live in our present lifetime without shame or guilt, which is represented by the *"sea."* And, *"a third of the sea turned to blood,"* is not only speaking of our past lifetimes, but all 144,000 soul group families, moving from an Etheric Body to a three-dimensional Body where our pure, balanced, neutral life energy *(blood)* became defined in a more dense form than when it was in a two-dimensional mental consciousness.

However, once we transformed our Etheric Mental Body to a Physical Body, we became part of a belief system where we created many good and evil ego-personalities to learn wisdom, physical and non-physical. And, once we souls created this, that is when we lost sight (died) of our many ego-personalities that carries our dark and evil creations. And today, in this lifetime, we feel those aspects and creations as something sinful. And that is when shame, guilt, and dishonor became part of our total consciousness. Thus, we ignored those dark lifetimes as something we would never do.

The example of this is with the *"third of the ships wrecked."* The *"ships"* represent our many dark lifetimes on earth living in a physical body where we all carry a cargo of dark creations that reflects our belief in sin and punishment today. We do not realize that those dark creations were to help us experience potentials in such a way that they bring us great wisdom and clarity. The "third" of those created lifetimes we played out on earth is tied to where our indulgence in the forces of evil came more apparent to learn wisdom. And, because of these dark self-indulgences, we have buried many dark ego-personalities so deep within our total consciousness *(sea)*, we do not want to take ownership or take responsibility for them. Instead, we deny them by not believing in reincarnation.

To us in our present-day or incarnation, those dark and evil lifetimes *(ships)* we created do not exist because we buried them deep within our subconsciousness, and this comes hard for us to understand and accept that we at one time did terrible things. If you are here on earth at this time, then know, at one time or another, you did things like stealing, raping, killing, and all kinds of evil and malicious acts, and yet you will not own up to them in this lifetime. You can feel this to be so within your heart, yet you deny it all by saying there is no such thing as reincarnation.

But be assured, you have incarnated, and some of you have born your cross of karma. So, why do you hold onto the guilt and shame associated with these acts? This is the main reason why you suffer. We all have forgotten that earth was created to resolve our issues using polarity energies that had become stuck within us. And, once the issues are resolved, we then let them go; otherwise, we will come back to earth repeatedly until we do.

This *"second angel"* in Revelation 8:8 is associated with the Church of Smyrna and is represented by the root chakra of the physical body related to the Lyden center (navel or lower abdomen area of the body). It is also known as the seat of the soul! This area is where we build up choices and then give them substance (life) to experience them in the physical, either now or in the future. This is another reason why the second seal represents "self-awareness."

Channeling of the Ascended Masters on the Apocalypse

It took "self-awareness" for us to choose the appropriate actions, bringing in karma, creativity, and the creative use of the life forces for us to become balanced again. We have suffered many hardships, poverty, and the idea that we are less than a Goddess all because we have forgotten that some God of the Bible does not preordain our experiences in life. It is not that we are evolving through many lifetimes to prove ourselves worthy of a false god. We all are evolving to become a sovereign God-Goddess in our own right.

We are creating every moment of our life, and therefore we are responsible for ourselves and not Yeshua, nor any religious sect or government. We are a spiritual artist who creates a pathway that can lead us to our freedom. And, all that we have to do is wakeup to those forces around us that only loves power and control. We are being brainwashed every day without realizing it, all because of not wanting to take responsibility for our beliefs.

I remember viewing a television program where scholars of the Bible were giving their interpretation about the Apocalypse, Revelation 8:10-11, and how it related to the ending of humankind and Earth. These scholars were even using science to support their points of view about the end times. While watching this program, I noticed how these scholars used special effects to illustrate the way God's wrath will come upon Earth and us. The graphics they used were so frightening that I am surprised people could not see through the deceptive and misleading views that were presented. It is all about mind control and power.

Revelation 8:10-11 has nothing to do with the destruction of man, Earth, or any stars falling from the sky. The *"third angel"* is talking about us from our emotional level, where, in the beginning stages of us creating many ego-personalities (physical and nonphysical), we felt enthusiastic, passionate, committed, and eager to move forward with our ideas of both good and evil. We could even call it our internal flame helping to propel us forward to become a wise and complete Christ, God, and Goddess in our own right. Thus, speeding up what is taking place within our consciousness today.

The *"large star burning like a torch"* is not an asteroid, spaceship, or planet coming at Earth. It is about our revelations of truth, both good and evil, hidden deep within our subconsciousness. In other words, exposure time has come upon us humans that love power and manipulation. The human mind cannot conceive of the wonders of our higher consciousness, where we are equal to Goddess. Thus, it disregards anything resembling personal divinity. It is just plain hard for the human mind and ego to accept the idea that we are equal to Christ, God, and the Goddess, which is why Yeshua was crucified. When Yeshua said that he was equal to God, humankind could not accept it, so the mass killed him.

We all have forgotten our commitment to move forward in learning the wisdom behind polarity energy. And, because of it, we created a belief in a Satan character that does not even exist. Thus, we tear down the inner conviction of our divineness in favor of a *"falling star,"* or us, from the mind (the Son of Goddess), moving our consciousness from a higher awareness of being Christ and the Goddess to a lower consciousness where we perceive ourselves as less than a Christ and Goddess. Thus, we need saving!

The star that pointed the way for the wise men to find Yeshua was in the east, and therefore, symbolically speaking of this star of light is within ourselves and not outside of ourselves. It symbolizes the conviction of our divine mind (Sonship) and that we are equal to Christ because we are the Goddess. This inner conviction of being a divine-human is our ability to accomplish whatever we undertake because it brings out the very best in us, which helps us succeed where others may fail.

The accumulated memories of wisdom and the experiences of our many ego-personalities *(wise men from the East)* will always rejoice when we learn to trust in ourselves by following in the footsteps of Yeshua, symbolized by our "I AM" Christ. If we allow and honor this, that is when our "I AM" Christ consciousness rises within *(east)* our consciousness, and all the riches of our experiences *(great wealth of information)* are bestowed on the new self, or the those of "us" that know we are a Christ also.

The star falling *"on a third of the rivers and the springs of water,"* is about our three-dimensional state of mind. As the *"water"* represents our potential in the race of our polarity thoughts, emotions, and choices that we have formed from deep within our subconsciousness *(the sea)* and how they speak of how we must trust in ourselves as a Christ also; and not allow our emotions or mind to control our thoughts before we can evolve *(walk)* safely above them. In other words, we do not have to suffer or walk on water to follow Yeshua.

The walking on water and his crucifixion are just lessons in allowing our mind of reason to overcome the faith we have in a God outside of us, and instead learn to trust ourselves as a Christ. Once we become a Christ in human form, as Yeshua did, we too will be resurrected (bring back to life) from our dogmatic beliefs in a God of sin and judgment.

The *"river"* is the flow of influences that come from our "I AM" Christ consciousness, signifying that we have access to infinite intelligence and pure, neutral, expansional energy if we so choose to open up to it. And, we can use that intelligence and expansional energy in giving life to any form of reality we choose. Because a *"river"* continuously flows, it means our consciousness is endless, as are the four branches in Genesis 2:10 that pertains to our ability to understand our "I AM" Christ-spirit and what we feel with our emotions. This understanding also takes on growth, wisdom, and having a consciousness of choice.

For example, the river *"Pishon"* means "outpouring, full-flowing, real existence," and it indicates that something is carried to its highest degree of understanding when one has an open mind. It is descriptive of our "I AM" Christ-spirit at work within our subconsciousness, spreading intelligence, wisdom, and the understanding of our many dark ego-personality consciousnesses.

The second river *"Gihon"* pertains to our thought patterns, desires, beliefs, dreams, and our reality, and it represents the divine breath of our "I AM" Christ-spirit and how this divine breath (inspiration and growth) will flow through our darkest thoughts and aspects. This also means our "I AM" Christ-spirit is in the middle of every created act and aspect of self, whether good or evil, and whether we know it or not. It comes down to having the ability and the wisdom to understand that nothing can exist outside of the Spirit of One (consciousness of the Goddess), and this makes us a Christ, God, and a Goddess also.

The third river *"Tigris"* pertains to our sealed-up memories, symbolized by the seven seals, such as our subtle body forms and the many physical lifetimes that we have had on earth. This river will flow east, within our consciousness (sub), and there sets the spiritual treasures (wisdom) of our "I AM" Christ spirit and all that we have learned throughout our journey.

The fourth river, *"Euphrates,"* pertains to choice. The act of choosing sets in motion changes that can be affected by various influences from the awakening of each member as individualized consciousness. Remember, we extensions of the Spirit of One have the same authority as the Father-Mother God-Goddess in choosing what expressions to bring to life to experience. Our physical consciousness can breathe life into any form, illusion, or belief we desire. Thus, we are the creator of our reality, even our dark creations. Therefore, fate does not take us places we do not want to go.

If we (whether as an individual, nation, or world) believe in good and evil, light and dark, and in the existence of Satan and polarity energy, then that is what we, the mass, will experience because we, as the collective group, are choosing it (breathing life into it). It's that simple! However, if we (as an individual, nation, or world) decide to have compassion for those who are still playing their games with polarity energy, good and evil, then we move beyond this belief in opposing energy and create a very different experience for ourselves, like the example of Yeshua walking on water.

We all can be part of the flow of the river (divine spirit), or we can be separate from it, creating what we desire to experience instead of someone else creating it for us via hypnotism, mind control. "Water" can also represent material cleansing, while "fire" can represent spiritual cleansing. When John, the Baptist, baptized with water, he was washing away the symbol of sin as an external composition to our makeup today.

We did not enter into the subconsciousness of our memory patterns with evil incarnations because it takes something more powerful than water to purify the inner workings of memories that were created by us. It takes "fire," the burning away of our memories through sowing and reaping lifetime after lifetime (incarnations), which is indeed the hell we claim we will never see if we are a churchgoer. Remember, it has nothing to do with religion or going to church to escape hell. We are already playing in hell to become balanced. Heaven is becoming awaken to this process.

The word *"wormwood"* in *"the star was called wormwood,"* means "a bitter-tasting plant." This angel comes from our emotional level, which is the level that proclaims the influences of our memories and how they affect the flow of what we give life to in a three-dimensional physical body, which is *"bitter-tasting."* This angel also relates to the Church of Pergamum and our adrenal area, which symbolizes our intellectual center where we foolishly try to guard against any idea that no God or Satan is fighting for our soul.

Our adrenal center is the birthplace of anger, impulsive reactions, and evil urges. And, because of our emotional ties to these behavior patterns, we strongly believe in polarity energy, as they become our weakest link. The influences of our memories affect the flow of what we give life to in a three-dimensional world, which can be very *"bitter."* But, once we moved outside of our higher consciousness long ago, we removed our focus from this limited two-dimensional mental level to a three-dimensional physical reality so we could play with opposing energy.

That act alone caused us to believe in vibrational energy, which then led to a belief in Satan and a God character outside of us, causing us to take on some *"sweet ideas"* that God and Satan are outside of us. Still, when we digested these ideas, they became *"bitter in our belly,"* which is signified by the adrenal area of the physical body and is the reason why *"a third of all the water turned to wormwood"* (bitter-tasting) when we experienced them in a lifetime.

When we try to define God through rules, rituals, and old dogmatic ways of thinking, our "I AM" Christ spirit, and many other ego-personality aspects of us, especially our dark creations, cannot come through to be integrated with the self in this lifetime because we cannot feel them as being us. Oh, we may say that we can feel something around us that seems at odds with what we should be doing. However, as we experience our choices from an emotional and opposing level, instead of learning to integrate them as our creations, we move rapidly in the opposite direction, denying their very existence; therefore, denying our "I AM" Christ consciousness.

Our mind, on an emotional level, has been recording every thought, deed, belief, and choice we have ever made since the time we left higher consciousness (Garden). And, through this process of record-keeping, we were given a blueprint that enabled us to fulfill our desire to become unlimited. But, before we reach the oneness of higher understanding again, we first must pass through the adrenal area of the body in the way we intellectualize things to blend and integrate everything we have created and learned about polarity energy (old earth).

Remember, what we may not realize is that we do eventually move toward the source of life (our "I AM") when we are ready. If you feel stuck right now, it is due to the way you intellectualize and look at things like God, sin, and Satan on an emotional level. Because of this, you could lose an opportunity to return home or back to higher consciousness. Your emotional consciousness has been at work for a long time as you journeyed through multiple lifetimes experiencing multiple potentials, good, bad, right, wrong, positive, and negative, as your structured belief system.

Remember, in the end. It makes no difference to our "I AM" what we created, good or evil, because the experience of those potentials can make our task successful because it gives us forward motion in completing our cycle of lifetimes. This is why in God's eyes, we have done nothing wrong because we have never sinned. It is only through human perception and judgment that we believe we've sinned.

The *"fourth angel"* in Revelation 8:12 is the activity of the thymus gland, representative of the Church of Thyatira, and it is also the seal that is associated with the belief in sin and guilt. The "fourth angel" is also related to the activity of love and ego, and how it is associated with the mental level and the growth of the soul. When we talk about "a third" of anything, it is more than likely associated with a three-dimensional physical lifetime on earth.

The *"third of the sun"* in Revelation 8:12 represents our spiritual intelligence, as this intelligence is not associated with our two and three-dimensional consciousnesses, but with our "I AM" Christ consciousness. Therefore, what blocks the "sun" (our I AM) out is our mind-soul and ego-personality consciousness, and its perception of it being "all that we are is just a human." The "light" of the sun is a symbol of intelligence, and the "sun" itself is symbolic of us all being the supreme source for this light. Therefore, it represents the highest form of intelligence, and we are part of this universal intelligence. Still, we fail to see this intelligence as being universal because we only see what our mind and ego perceives as being intelligent.

The *"moon"* characterizes the mind of the intellect without realizing it receives all of its light (intelligence) from universal intelligence (the sun). Therefore, the real source for this high level of intelligence comes from our "I AM" Christ consciousness and not from the mind or ego. Of course, our mind accelerates or speeds up its growth when we become more receptive to the inflow of our Christ spirit. Therefore, the first step in becoming aware of our true identity is having an open mind and heart. Be aware of that until your awakening!

We are simply hypnotized and asleep because of our strong belief in a God of opposing viewpoints. And because we are so focused on our mental consciousness, our mind of the intellect (reasoning level, *the moon)* becomes our revelation of truth, which is why we, and all religions, interpret the Apocalypse in literal terms. We overlook the human mind and how it cannot conceive the wonders of us being Christ. That is why the *"star"* (us in our higher consciousness) was affected by a temporary lapse of memory (stuck).

This "act in consciousness" projected us from a higher understanding *(day)* to a level of ignorance and forgetfulness *(night)*. *"The day lost its light for a third of the time, as did the night"* in Revelation 8:12, means we were part of the "oneness of consciousness," before the split of our consciousness into a mental and physical level, and where we concealed this higher, universal, intelligence center from our three-dimensional physical level. This is why we view, feel, and believe our intelligence only comes from the mind.

Once we became a three-dimensional being, we lost our relationship and our connection to this higher, universal intelligence center, and that is when we took on a mental perception that our intelligence comes from the mind, which is only one-third of our total consciousness.

"Day and night" in Revelation 7:14, 14:11, has the same meaning as in Genesis 1:5. In the *"daytime,"* we can distinguish things in detail while at *"nighttime,"* we cannot see as clearly. Therefore, the word *"day"* in the Bible denotes intelligence, understanding, and awareness, and a knowing that we can, at any time, manifest an everlasting force of potentiality, universal intelligence, higher understanding, and overwhelming wisdom to an active expression.

"Night" has the meaning of ignorance, limitation, or that we are dead or unaware (asleep) of us being the source and the Goddess we seek. *"Night"* also represents the conditions of unconscious three-dimensional living, while *"day"* represents our love of the self as a God-Goddess and a divine-human that is equal to God, Goddess, and Yeshua.

Nearly everyone always has a stream of both light and dark thoughts continually flowing from the mind to the outer ego-personality, and this stream is symbolized by the river Jordan. The metaphysical meaning of the Jordan Plain is "the descending one, the south-flowing one, the dispenser from above or flowing of judgments." Because of our ignorance, we consigned ourselves to a life of eternal punishment (unredeemed state of mind) because the mind became very confused with our intellectual concepts of spirit wisdom and duality living.

Our thought stream, because of the belief in sin, right and wrong, has been explored and transformed as we journey from one lifetime to another. We, like the children of Israel of long ago, can cross into the promised land (new expansional energy) when we are ready to let go of the belief in sin, punishment, right and wrong. When we moved our pure energy in the opposite direction of our divine nature, we lost trust in our infinite self as a Christ; thus, we created the opposite of faith, which was doubt, as Lot represents this in Genesis.

The stream of dualistic thoughts (light and dark) that continuously flow from our mind eventually cut us off from knowing that we are part of divine expression. By us cutting ourselves off from our "I AM," we blocked up the free flow of pure, neutral energies *(waters)* within our mind and many ego-personalities, thus creating a subconsciousness *(sea)* of fear and doubt (Lot-Jordan Plain). These doubts and fears that we hold within our memories today are what keep us from being aware that our energy is stuck within our physical body. And, this stuck energy will remain until we learn to release the belief in sin, which represents the opening of the fourth seal.

Know that our stubborn ego-personalities of today (the Beast) are waiting for the mind (Anti-Christ) to release them from the burden of cause and effect (sin). Thus, allowing our energy to flow freely again without it being blocked by erroneous beliefs about good and evil, light and dark. When these thoughts about light (the understanding that we are Christ) and dark (we are ignorant of being Christ) are removed from our consciousness, we will fully express the flow of our divine nature. Our "I AM" Christ spirit is predestined to perceive and accept divine order and balance throughout all time and space because it is the absolute authority of our true nature.

Therefore, the Christ within us (the greater light) is all that we are, and this is where all wisdom, awareness, and understanding are found, which we can tap into at any time. The physicalness we are experiencing right now is only an illusion made to feel real because of our strong belief in it. And, as long as we believe and perceive good, evil, light, dark, and sin as who we are, we will always experience life using polarity energy as our source. We will experience *"seedtime and harvest, time and space, cold and heat, summer and winter, day and night,"* and sowing and reaping until we learn to release the belief in all sin.

As we understand Revelation 8:1-13, the first four angels sounding off are associated with the centers dealing with the elements of (i) earth, (ii) fire, (iii) air, and (iv) water. These four elements created the temperaments of our many ego-personality aspects of light and dark, of which we purposely spread throughout the astral/physical dimensions (physical and nonphysical). And, as mentioned, these *"four angels"* are called our lower nature, while the *"eagle flying high overhead crying out"* represents our mental state (air) expressing our truths, perceptions, and beliefs on a conscious level, but we ignore them.

It is from these truths, perceptions, and beliefs that we continue to focus on life gratification, incarnations, love, good and bad, light and dark, and, most of all, our soul growth. The three *"woes"* in Revelation 8:13 may relate to the influences that are not directly under our control by the ego but are essential to our development in a three-dimensional world. These influences relate to our:

1. Spirit of responsibility (knowing one is Christ)
2. The outer mind and its relationships to our ego-personality aspects of light and dark, including other souls (inhabitants of the earth), and our belief in a savior
3. The intuitive consciousness and how it relates to our divine plan in bringing forth our perception about having to suffer

Channeling of the Ascended Masters on the Apocalypse

These are the "three angels" that are about to blast their horns, or more appropriately, the vibrations within each level that will carry the dualistic forces of memory, desire, choice, and growth, including their natures bound in the images we create.

Chapter 24

MOVING FROM ONE INCARNATION TO THE NEXT

When studying Revelation 9:1-21, it mostly pertains to where we play in many physical bodies journeying through time, space, and incarnations. Therefore, this chapter brings out our purpose being on earth and why we incarnate. First, our purpose is to evolve, grow, learn responsibility, and discover that we are a living Christ in our own right. Second, we work under the divine rules that we set for ourselves eons ago, known as our own divine plan. We are not here to increase our control over others or gain power because all that brings is just more karma.

By learning to trust in the self as a living Christ, we do eventually reach a vibrational frequency where we become invisible to those who are still vibrating at the lower awareness. We even become inconspicuous to our family members, even though they may be standing right next to us, literally or figuratively. They just stay unconscious and unaware of our words and actions.

When we begin to expand our consciousness beyond the belief in light and dark, good and evil, our energy and consciousness begin to rise in frequency waves where those around us who choose to remain governed by control and power are simply not part of our world. When we trust the process of letting go of our controls, fears, beliefs in good and evil, power, and the idea that we die because of sin, we will find our world becoming happier, healthier, and much more abundant than those still playing the game of good versus evil.

Channeling of the Ascended Masters on the Apocalypse

When this happens, it indicates that we are crossing the barrier from a lower vibrational energy frequency (Old Earth) to a higher expansional energy frequency (New Earth) where we can transcend our mind, ego, and physical body to a healthier and joyful life. And, the conscious crossing of this barrier was the path shown by Yeshua over two thousand years ago.

For example, remember the "two persons working in a field and one taken up in the air" (Luke 17:36)? The person taken in the air is symbolic of one who has raised their mental mind consciousness frequency to a "New Expansional Multidimensional Consciousness" where one lives a life far removed from those on earth who are still playing the game of drama, judgment, and a life based on good and evil. When we move beyond the belief in (i) separation, (ii) duality (polarity energy), (iii) Satan, (iv) suffering, (v) Sin, and (vi) needing a savior, which is the opening of the six seals, we break free from the polarized pull of a three-dimensional world of sin, punishment, and karma.

Thus, we cease to exist to those who are playing so hard in a life of opposing energy as they play out their karmic contracts and those who awaken move on to unlimited potentials, expressions, and being Christ-like. Unawakened people forget that the mind-soul only represents one-third of their total consciousness and is the seat of their memories. They also only see their answers to their questions about the spirit being too complex to understand. The reason is that they will always take the position of their intellect (intelligence), their emotions, and the way they were brought up to believe.

I am not saying there is something wrong with using our intellect! However, just know if we do any research about Christ or Spirit, we will find that nearly all teachings of faith come from the reasoning side of man's mind, which the church admits. Religions warn that the faithful are to hold fast to the traditions passed down to them either by word of mouth or by religious teachings. And then, they must fight in defense of that faith.

It is teachings like this that bring war, fear, judgment, lack of awareness, guilt, and the worship of false gods. And this is why Yeshua, the Ascended Masters, and I ask these questions! Do you believe that God wants you to fight and force your will on others to uphold a belief in something that was passed down by religious traditions, even if it meant killing someone to uphold that belief? Is it your faith in your religion or faith in God or his prophets that keep you strong with your beliefs?

And, if you answer "all three questions as having faith in all or just having faith in God," then don't you think, even while using your intellect, that God would update his teachings sometimes as you evolve in consciousness? You are not the same human as your ancestors! You have always overlooked the high possibility of you coming to earth in a new physical body and environment to evolve in wisdom and consciousness.

As we learn to trust in the unseen forces and move beyond the mind of reason, divine guidance will simply become part of our conscious awareness. We will not need to make any special effort to be obedient to some God or prophet, or any religious group. The trust I am speaking of has nothing to do with believing in God or Yeshua as Christ. But it has everything to do with establishing within ourselves the awareness that consists of evolution, shifting belief systems, modifying our truths, expanding our consciousness, and the wisdom gained through many lifetimes.

The Bible repeatedly speaks of Abraham's faith. Abraham believed God, and his faith was dependent on God for righteousness (Genesis 15:6). But when we look at the early stages of Abraham's life, we will notice that God first called him Abram. Why Abram? Because Abram characterizes the early establishment of the trust (faith) we had in the early stages of our divided consciousness. This is why Abram is a metaphor for trusting in ourselves as a Christ (Goddess).

Because of how Abram lived his life, he became the symbol for us, humans, to move through many different levels of consciousnesses using our intellect as the basis for our faith, and this is represented by the fourth angel in Rev. 8:12–13. To understand the lessons of Abraham's life, we must have a certain familiarity with each layer of our consciousness. It is also important to understand that we need not change our physical body (residence) to enter a new lifetime (country).

In Genesis 12, *"the land that I will show you,"* represents a new concept in our thinking that should not be overlooked when it comes to Christ (Goddess) because there is nothing that exists without a purpose. And, our purpose in life is to discover our existence and how it relates to understanding Christ without seeing God and the Goddess as a mystery. When we look into Genesis or Revelation through the eyes of spirit, we do begin to understand the divine plan that each of us devised to become a much wiser Goddess than we were before leaving our higher consciousness (the first creation).

When we learn to understand and let go of our attachment to fear, control, power, right and wrong, sin and punishment, we finally affirm our unity with our "I AM" Christ spirit. And that is when we will enter a whole New Expanded Consciousness and a new reality. Religion has failed to understand and comprehend the importance of Abraham's choice in lying down with his wife's slave-girl, Hagar. And as we know, Hagar became the mother of Abraham's son, Ishmael (Genesis 16:2–4).

Not only did Abraham have intercourse with his wife's maid, but he also told Pharaoh that his wife was his sister to feel safe (Genesis 12:18). We all can see that Abraham lacked true faith (trust) in God. First, when God said that he would have a son through Sarai (his wife) and, second, when he lacked faith that God would protect him as he journeyed through Egypt. Therefore, Abraham lied not only to God but to himself.

In both cases, Abraham demonstrated that his intellect and the reasoning of the mind were something that he could trust more than God himself. And, as we can see, Abraham's reasoning moved to a level of thinking that God needed help. And, because of Abraham's reasoning of the situation, caused by fear, man and religion still follow Abraham's example today. We humans a long time ago, moved from a consciousness of knowing we are Christ to using only "one third" of our consciousness. And, that "one third" is where the perception of intellectualizing things to comprehend what we think God wants for (or from) us.

Genesis 12:1, the Lord tells Abram! *"Go forth from the land of your kinsfolk and from your father's house to a land that I will show you,"* as this is an ideal example why the operations of materialism, time, space, and incarnations have become the means to learn who we are, why we are here on earth and, who God is. Ever since we left the first creation, our focus and our journey have been outward instead of inward, because we cannot remember being in the first creation. We only understand the first creation as a place where our ancestors once lived.

However, we have forgotten that we were there! The memories of our higher consciousness (Garden) and who we are remain, and we can remember if we so choose to. Once we, like Abraham, moved our focus to a mental consciousness, we gave all control over to the reasoning side of our mind. And, in doing so, we created the ability to manifest unlimited potentials and ego-personality aspects that deal with experiences of doubt and trust from a mental reasoning side. However, eventually, we all moved toward doubt, for which "Lot," Abraham's brother, represents. In other words, we say we trust God, and at the same time, we doubt his existence.

We also established within our Oversoul the intuitive knowing that we are in direct communication with our source of existence, our Christ-spirit, the Goddess. We just have forgotten because of having faith in our mind of reason. Abram was a real person who once lived on the earth, and his name, and other names in the Bible, carry a spiritual significance that helps us evolve to a higher understanding when we are ready. It is like our parents and teachers using metaphoric characters to help us understand something as a child, but now as an adult, we know the deeper meanings of life and no longer need the literalization of these characters or, for that matter, the Bible itself.

When we reawaken to the fact that we are Christ, God, and the Goddess, we transform our energy of two (the Old Energy of duality (Old Earth)) into a New Energy of Four. Thus, we become complete and expansional! In other words, instead of having the resistance of positive and negative like before, we begin working with a New Energy of:

1. Positive
2. Negative
3. Neutrality
4. Crystalline Energy

Once we learn to work with Crystalline Energy, we become connected to our gnost solution consciousness, where all problems can be solved by ourselves. Our struggles, pain, and sadness transform our energy so we can feel our sovereignty and dominion over our old and new creations. When we allow this to happen, our ego-personality aspect in this lifetime (our personality of today) can merge with our divine nature, and that is when we become the Father/Mother-Christ Goddess while we are still part of the flesh. To get what I am trying to convey here, I would love to share an experience I had a few years ago. I have also mentioned this experience is some of my other books.

I found myself standing on the shoreline of a large body of water. And, as I looked up at the sun, it seemed at least a thousand times larger than the Earth's sun. The sky was blue, with no clouds in sight. And as I looked up at the vastness of this sun, I felt the warmth of the energy coming from it, feeding me with overwhelming power, yet it was not burning or blinding like the sun's rays we have here on Earth.

After looking at this enormous large sun, I suddenly noticed that the air that I was breathing had a consciousness. So, I took in big deep breaths of air. And, as I breathed it in, I could feel the consciousness of the air flowing through my entire body. Then I noticed there were about five other people with me, and they were doing the same thing I was doing. I had the feeling this was their first time experiencing it, as it was for me.

Then we all moved toward this large body of water. As I walked on the rocks and ground, and with every step I took, I could feel their consciousness run up from my feet, to my legs, and then through my entire body. It was a fantastic feeling! I could feel everything around me

Channeling of the Ascended Masters on the Apocalypse

as if all were alive. The air, the ground, and the rocks, everything was alive just like I was alive having a consciousness.

As all five of us walked together toward this vast body of water, I decided to step into it, but the rest of the people stood on the shore and look on at me. As I entered the water, it did not take long before the water was up to my neck. That was when I noticed my whole body seemed to become one with the water, and yet I still felt individualized. One more thing, I cannot describe how the water felt because I do not know what to compare it with. All that I know, it looked like water, and at the same time, it didn't feel like water. In fact, I would describe it as not being water, but I would describe it as something life-giving.

However, as I submerged my body into the water except for my head, I felt as if my body was part of the water, so I had a thought to raise my arm out of the water just to see if my arm still existed. And, when I did, my arm was completely dry and intact. I even came up with the courage to dip my head into the water, and when I lifted it out, again, my head and hair were completely dry and intact. This water, if it was water, not only surrounded me as if we were one, but it also hugged me as if to protect me.

I felt the strength, peace, harmony, and unconditional love coming from it, as my whole body was cleansed as if I was being prepared for something. And, when I became conscious again, I felt spiritually high for days. I even felt my worries lifted from me. And even today, I do not feel the weight on my shoulders as I did before this experience. I also have difficulty describing the experience because it is hard to find the human words to describe what I felt. However, I will do my best to explain the experience and what it meant spiritually.

According to Yeshua and the Ascended Masters, I understand it as a baptism, the beginning of my awakening in consciousness as a sovereign souled being. I believe this to be so because there was one major thing that I noticed having this experience; there were no leaders, Gods, or guides to show me around or tell me what to do. I was utterly free to make any choice I desired to experience. When I walked on the shoreline of the vast ocean, I could feel the equalness to all that were standing with me.

Therefore, I took the experience as a message where, before coming to earth and before entering the abyss of nothingness, I was experiencing the first creation of what most of us call the Garden of Eden. In other words, the total "oneness of consciousness" with the Spirit of One (the Goddess). The large sun represents the Father-God, as I could feel the pure, neutralized energy coming from it, allowing me and the others standing there to use it at will, as it felt like power, and yet there was no power to it because it seemed equally distributed among all that was there including the rocks, the air, the sand beneath my feet, and all that I seen and experienced.

The vast body of water, if you want to call it that, represents the Spirit of One, or the Christ consciousness, and the wholeness of the Mother-Goddess. And when I was in the water, I felt how I was such an essential part of her consciousness, and simultaneously knowing my individualization, or knowing I was not separate from the Mother-Goddess. I could feel my individualization as if I had no rules to follow, but only the rules and limitations that I put onto myself. That is when I understood that I chose to leave the first creation and move into the creation of polarity energy to feel my experiences first hand.

And, when that choice was made, I did not hear or see a God with a white beard kicking me out of that beautiful place I experienced. I left voluntarily because the vision showed that there were no leaders or any one person in charge telling me what to do or that I had to leave. There was not even a serpent trying to trick me. Why? Because the clear, blue sky indicated that all knowledge, wisdom, and understanding come directly from my Oversoul and not from my mind, from other people, or from some God separate from me, including Yeshua.

If I need information, wisdom, understanding, healing, or a question answered, I have only to expand my consciousness by stepping into the water (spirit), and I will find it all at my fingertips. Why? Because I know that I am an essential part of the water (Mother-Goddess). And, once I learned to expand my consciousness beyond my mind of opposing energy to a knowing I am the source and creator of my reality, that is when I understood I could command this New Energy just with thought and belief.

My friends, we humans are an extension of the Mother-Goddess or Christ consciousness, and this includes air, water, rocks, insects, animals, plants, the universe, planets, and stars, all exist as part of the Mother-Goddess consciousness because nothing can exist outside of her consciousness. All of us, in our true core nature, including Yeshua, are on the same level as the Mother Goddess, which makes no one any better than anyone else. Even what we call power is evenly distributed to all souled beings, leaving no soul having more power than another.

The evil that we see is simply ignorance of the fact that one is Christ, and that one is part of the wholeness of the water (Mother-Goddess). And, once realized, then all evil and imbalance will simply disappear from the earth. More examples are found in Revelation 9:1, where the *"fifth angel blew his trumpet and saw a star fallen from the sky to earth, as it was given the key for the passage to the abyss."*

From the interpretations, the "fifth angel" represents our intuitive body and how it relates to expressing our divine plan, as some may understand it as our divine will, to lower our energy frequency to a level where we could create a physical body that contains an ego-personality that would become rebellious and judgmental. Thus, symbolizing the taking the bite of the apple.

This decision of lowering our consciousness frequency and losing our intuitive consciousness to memory is where our divine plan becomes a servant to our "I AM" Christ consciousness to learn wisdom. And, because of feeling this loss, our rebellious ego nature, represented by the serpent in the garden, came up with an alternate "will" to follow called "free will." And, this "free will" is tied to all that is mental! However, this was our "divine plan" right along because we needed our mind-soul and ego-personality consciousness to feel and know we all have a "free will."

It was through our mind-soul and ego-personality beliefs of having a "free will" that moved our focus from our higher divine plan to a mental consciousness where "free will" gave us the feeling of individuality. We created "free will" that way not just to feel our individuality, but because it gave us the feeling of having power even though it was an illusion. It also gave us the feeling that we fell from something more supreme than ourselves.

The *"stars"* in conjunction with human consciousness represent the guiding influences that come from the intelligence center of our higher consciousness *(sky)* where higher understanding (heaven) is already part of our Oversoul. The "stars" can also represent our revelations of truth that we have not yet fully developed and are, therefore, not clearly understood by our human consciousness. Our mind cannot comprehend the wonders of divine intelligence and supernatural forces and why we must learn to move beyond the intellect. Otherwise, we will never get to know how great a Goddess (Christ) we are.

For example, a servant works for another person for a wage and is regarded as an asset to the owner. So, it is the same with our "free will" and "intuitive body," for they are servants of our "I AM" Christ consciousness. Therefore, if it weren't for our "free will" and "intuitive body," even though "free will" today is an illusion, it gives us the feeling of strength and power. Otherwise, our "I AM" Christ consciousness would not have learned the wisdom we gained in each lifetime by believing we have "free will."

The perception of power and having "free will," even though all of what we choose comes from a rational nature, gives us the capability to define our expressions, experiences, beliefs, and conditions as good (light) and bad (dark), not forgetting those immoral and destructive forces that cause us great harm, misfortune, and unpleasant events throughout our many lifetimes. And, as we consider the story of Abraham, Sarai, and her Egyptian maidservant girl Hagar, who became the mother of Ishmael, fathered by Abraham (Genesis 16:2), Hagar represents our mind-soul consciousness, the mental, and Ishmael represents "free will" coming from our mind level of consciousness.

When Abraham moved his faith from his higher self (Goddess), he opened up a consciousness supporting an intellectual and mental nature where he believed that free will is intellectually there to serve him. Hence, Abraham moved away from the true trust in his "I AM" God-Goddess, symbolized by his Oversoul for which Sarai represents, and focused his trust from an intellectual supporting free will and mental (soul) consciousness, represented by Hagar and Ishmael.

Therefore, after that occurrence, our "I AM" Christ spirit consciousness had no way to know itself except through our mental soul consciousness (symbolized by Hagar) and a "free will" tied to reason and perceptive understanding (symbolized by Ishmael). Therefore, the only way we could know and understand ourselves as a Christ was through form, our mind-soul, intellectual reasoning, and our Etheric and Physical bodies.

Our "I AM" Oversoul (represented by Sarai) is divine. Therefore, we cannot unite with conditions of make-believe, such as polarity energy, mental conditions, and intellectual thinking like sin, fear, and judgment. Thus, it took an "artificial" self or a mirror image of self where we have a mental soul (a servant girl like Hagar replaced Eve) to form an emotional feeling within to assist us in feeling our freedom or separateness from our "I AM" Christ consciousness. Thus, giving us the feeling of being separate from our true essence. And yet, all of it is just a game and an illusion brought on by our "I AM" Christ consciousness or our Oversoul to learn wisdom.

When Abraham heeded Sarai's request, it reflected our mental soul consciousness (Hagar) as a servant to our "I AM" Oversoul (Sarai) where this created us the opportunity to bring about the seed (Ishmael-free will) for multitudes of potentials, ideas, experiences, and ego personalities to play in the physical form feeling it has the "free will" to choose any experiences using polarity energy as its source. Thus, the illusion we manifested was a false belief in a rational God who created us and the environment in which we live.

Therefore, it was the intuitive and free will mental consciousness that opened the doorway for our "I AM" Christ consciousness (Oversoul) to express our dominance as an individual creator. It was from feeling our individuality that moved our consciousness of no form into *"the passage of the abyss,"* Revelation 9:2, which is symbolized by the endless space of rational potentials for us to choose and play using opposing energy, positive and negative, as our source of power.

Once we moved our consciousness of no form outside of our "I AM," our energy took on a vaporous substance of a hypothetical, electromagnetic medium (or an Etheric Body), implied by the word *"smoke"* in Revelation 9:2. From this Etheric Body, and from the very first time we felt our energy being ripped into billions and billions of coherent pieces, we tried to regain our balance. But, the more we tried, the more shattered our energy and consciousness became.

It was during that time when chaos, terror, and feeling shame and guilt for losing sight of our "I AM" is when we saw something that scared us even more. Because, for the very first time, we saw an image of ourselves that seemed to take on a darkened shape that instantly connected with us. And, that was our own divinity, the Christ that we are. And, once we felt this connection to our divinity, we knew exactly why it took on a darkened look, for, in reality, it was just a shadow look that we souls interpreted as a "darkened look."

As Yeshua and the Ascended Masters mentioned, this was the very first time where we felt fear, guilt, and shame all at once, and it made us feel uncomfortable, embarrassed, and concerned. And this is why we tried to hide from this darkened image of the self, called our Christ consciousness. What we did not know was that we were trying to hide from our divinity, the Christ we are at our core. We ran from this darkened image because we believed that it was what caused us the terror and pain that we felt while moving through this "opposing energy" that felt like fire. And, at the time, the more we tried to hide from our divinity, the closer this darkened image came to us. Meanwhile, the rest of our consciousness and energy was torn into more and more coherent pieces.

Throughout this experience moving into this opposing energy, this wall of fire, we also experienced and felt every potential lifetime that we might have, including every thought and desire that we would ever experience. These pieces of energy that were torn away from us all while we were moving through this opposing energy (abyss) represent every well-argued potential we felt, lifetimes we lived, thoughts and desires we had, and every souled being we have met.

These billions and billions of potentials that we already experienced in the Etheric body while moving into this opposing energy of fire are all the paths in the physical that we might take, for they are only potentials. Also, according to Yeshua and the Ascended Masters, the experience we had moving into the fire of the opposing energy seemed to tear down all hope of us ever returning back to higher consciousness (Garden), because it was ripping away all the memories of us ever having a higher consciousness or that we were ever Christ. It was even destroying beyond recognition everything that we felt and saw back when we lived out of higher consciousness.

Also, when we tried to bring the focus back to our higher awareness of being Christ, another vibrational wave hit and shattered our energy and consciousness even more, and that is when we all finally gave up. Therefore, we stopped trying to remember who we were because when we did, it was too painful. Once we souled beings became focused again, we saw these energies of potentials, good and evil, that we created, long before coming to earth to experience as a means to return to higher consciousness (home-heaven), as a failure. The only way we could return to higher consciousness again was to play out some of those good and bad potentials, as it expanded our consciousness to where memory would occur.

Because of these billions of potentials of good and evil seemed unfamiliar to us at the time, we did not want to experience them. So, many of us pulled back and did not want to participate in them. However, these many coherent potentials of good and bad pulled at us with tremendous force, and that is when some of us chose them to play out in the flesh. And this is why we are here on Earth today.

Because of the tremendous force of the opposing energy of two that we could not fight anymore, we just did not have the strength to continue, so we gave in, and that is when we allowed ourselves to fall completely into the endless space (abyss) to play out as many potentials as we could. And the more we played, everything began to quiet down, and that is when we felt isolation and darkness for the first time. It was so dark we thought we would not exist because we were empty of desires with nothing left to choose. Thus, a feeling of non-existence came over us. However, hope came alive, as something happened to us in our darkest moment that caused us to feel renewed to where we lost that feeling of going out of existence.

Remember that shadowy, dark image I mentioned? Well, it appeared and caused us to realize, even though we were in complete nothingness (abyss), we were still alive. We felt alive because we could hear ourselves thinking. It was in that moment of hearing our thoughts and feeling alive that we said to ourselves, "I do exist." And, if "I exist," then that is when we realized why we did not know why we existed. Thus, the questions came to, "Who am I?" and "Where did I come from?" That is how our "divine plan" came to awareness to answer the questions. Thus, all that we did know was that we were there in consciousness. And, if we were there, then "I AM That I AM" is "all that I am."

The abyss mentioned in the Bible is a metaphor to help us understand the beginning stages of our consciousness and how it produced every potential, thought, and experience that we would ever express and experience. Therefore, the abyss and the explosion were not the beginning of Earth as science proclaims. They were the beginning of our souls moving away from higher consciousness. Thus, "all that was at the beginning," known as our higher consciousness (heaven), no longer exists, for we souls created a New Expansional Consciousness (New Heaven-Earth) without realizing we have been fulfilling our divine plan (will) to become a sovereign Christ, God and a Goddess in our own right.

What we are experiencing right now is one or many of those potentials that we created when we shattered our energy and consciousness by moving into polarity, the opposing energy of duality. Because of our ego *(serpent)* taking control of our evolution from the mind, it condensed our pure, neutral Crystalline energy into a more solid form now called our physical body. Thus, we went from only a spirit, consciousness, and light (no form) to having an etheric body; then, over time and space, we moved into a physical form that caused us to forget where we came from originally.

Today, we create our illusions and realities by working with the mass human consciousness to form all of what we see and experience here on earth. It was group consciousness (all souls) that created a belief system that took us all to the highest understanding of being Christ and a Goddess just as it was that took us to forget we are Christ. And, when we left higher consciousness (Garden) and went through the wall of fire (that of opposing energy), that is when we felt like we went through a *huge furnace,* creating positive and negative energy to manipulate. That is when we found ourselves in a position of great power and skill, and yet, all is an illusion.

The Bible story where God scattered man throughout the earth and caused him to speak many separate languages (Genesis 11:8) is actually about us souled beings going through the fire of opposing energy and leaving a higher consciousness frequency (Garden) to a lower vibrational frequency. And then, we manifested countless dimensional non-physical and physical realms to play in, including earth. When Yeshua said: *"In my Father's house there are many dwelling places. Otherwise, how could I have told you that I was going to prepare a place for you?"* (John 14:2). This is referencing the separation of languages in Genesis 11:8, as we souls are part of many dimensions.

The separate dwelling places are what we do from our "I AM" Christ consciousness because of the way we think and act from a mental level. Thus, causing us to create multiple light and dark personality aspects of ourselves to play the game of being a human. And, because of the veil of forgetfulness, we ended up asking a few fundamental questions: "Who am I?" "Where did I come from?" and "Why am I here?" From all these belief systems that we created, it became evident that we did not understand each other or our "I AM" Godhood. Even today, those of us here on earth are still experiencing many different dimensions though we are in the flesh simultaneously experiencing life.

It was at this point where we began to battle each other over who was right and wrong. The confusion escalated as we fought, which in the end caused our energy to slow down to a standstill. This standstill of energy caused our many ego bodies to become denser and denser. That is when we souled beings, working together, created the earth as a place to sort everything out. To live out some of those multiple potentials and to gain some understanding of what was slowing our energy down. However, for us souls to succeed, we had to take on the veil of forgetfulness. And this is what Revelation 9:1-21 is all about.

The *"locusts"* in Revelation 9:3 is a grasshopper that migrates, swarms, and devours crops and vegetation, and therefore, represents our transitory deceptive ego nature moving (migrating) us souls in and out of many physical lifetimes. This allowed us to *"swarm"* together as a group of souls and create multitudes of potentials and dimensional realms where we could incarnate in a physical body and become limited with our creations *(onto land)*. And not only did we fill the abyss with numerous creations of positive and negative potentials to play things out, but we also produced a harvest (crops) of light and dark ego-personality aspects of ourselves to experience.

The *"scorpions on the earth"* in Revelation 9:3 is the beginning where karma began, or sowing and reaping, on earth. The "scorpion" has a stinger that can be lethal, thus referring to where we use opposing energy and how our belief in it can create for us many incarnations of sorrows and woes. The many ego-personality aspects of us, symbolized by the locusts, are *"not to hurt the grass or trees"* in Revelation 9:4, because of our natural growth patterns in taking full responsibility for our creations, good and bad.

The only manifestations that will be tormented, but not killed, are our temperaments and our intellect incarnations. These ego-personalities do not have the seal of God on their forehead, but all our other ego-personalities do. When our Oversoul calls out to an ego-personality aspect of us, while in physical form, it is not about being killed, it is only to torment us for a while because of the belief patterns we carry in memory from each of our ego-personality aspects. The torment comes from karma that we created for ourselves using the five physical senses (smell, touch, taste, sight, and hear), for which the *"five months"* represent in Revelation 9:5.

The *"five months"* represent the operations of our five physical senses as we journey through time and space, reincarnating learning the wisdom of our choices. The *"infliction of the scorpion and its sting"* in Revelation 9:5 represents our strong belief in sin and punishment, karma, which is why we experience it. Therefore, we move through many lifetimes sowing and reaping until we learn to release those beliefs tied to opposing energy. It is our belief in fear and opposing energy that prevents us from connecting with our Christ consciousness and our many ego-personality aspects of light and dark.

The *"people who seek death"* in Revelation 9:6 represent our many dark ego-personality aspects that have not yet become balanced. How can we escape death if we continue to believe in sin and punishment? This shows how much we torment ourselves because of the belief in separation, opposing energy, Satin, sin, and suffering to receive salvation. Our strong belief in the idea of God and Satan as two individuals become our afflictions and can cause our anguish when our "I AM" Christ consciousness rejects them as truth.

The *"locusts ready for battle like the horses,"* Revelation 9:7, represents the opposing energy forces (horses) and how they relate to our ego-personality aspects of many (locusts) that are spread throughout the multiple realms trying to find their balance with us in this lifetime. The *"locusts have crowns on their heads and their faces like human faces,"* because the *"gold crowns"* represents our many lifetimes having the deceptive appearance of being real and separate from us. When, in fact, we do not realize how many faces of consciousness we have spread throughout many dimensions, all seeking us out in this lifetime, asking for our forgiveness.

But we keep on looking at them as nonexistent, saying they are not our creations. Thus, justifying to ourselves, there is no such thing as reincarnation. When we deny and judge others around us because of their differences and our belief in good and evil, we deny ourselves as a Christ. The *"inflection of the scorpion and its sting,"* Revelation 9:5, is symbolized by our belief in sin and punishment, karma.

Genesis 3:15, *"he will strike at your head while you strike at his heel,"* has a meaning where our soul region of responsibility (Eve) will always give the breath of life (consciousness) to what our mind (Adam) desires to experience. Thereby, we alone are the creator of our many ego-personality versions of the self, all tied to opposing energy. The *"head"* is the mind where we believe our intelligence and understanding of God is understood, and yet our ego pays more attention to what we interpret as good and evil. Thus, we become deceived in our ability to discern the real truth about Christ.

We deny Christ, even though we say we honor Christ as our savior, which is why we ignore the dark and negative lifetimes we have had on earth. Instead of accepting them as our creations, we deny, suppress, and ignore them because of refusing to take responsibility for them.

The name *"Abaddon"* in the Hebrew language and *"Apollyon"* in the Greek language is a King who governs over the great army of locusts that came out of the abyss to destroy (Revelation 9:11). The name *"Abaddon"* supports the view of erroneous beliefs, thoughts, and how we relate to the importance of opposing energy, good and evil, as being real. Remember, our "I AM" Christ consciousness, the real you, cannot be destroyed. It is only the outer illusionary version of us that can be destroyed.

When we keep a strong belief in opposing energy, the abyss (the illusion) becomes our King. Thus, all aspects of us become a slave to the King. Therefore, as long as we believe in physicality, a God, and Satan separate from us, that we are all different, we will always experience destruction and suffering. Thus, suffering becomes necessary until we learn to move past the belief, we are only human. Remember, there is only one power and one presence in the universe, and that is you working from your "I AM" Christ consciousness.

The *"sixth angel,"* Revelation 9:13-14, is symbolic of our mind-body and how it interacts with our "I AM" Christ consciousness, our memories, our multiple ego-personalities, the pineal area, and the relationships we have with ourselves and others. When reading into the mind, Revelation 9:13-14, it pertains to where our mind is trying to proclaim its rightful place in consciousness. Through our creations, as part of our consciousness and our mind-body, we developed a relationship so special with our "I AM" Christ spirit that it gave us the means to discover who we are at our core essence.

Channeling of the Ascended Masters on the Apocalypse

Once our mind proclaimed (heard a voice) itself as the authoritative power behind the throne, we released the idea of what the *"four horns"* signify, which is, (i) justice, (ii) physical form, (iii) individuality, and (iv) incarnations. It may seem that these "four horns" would have four different vibrational sound waves. However, the essence of these "four horns" carries the same message (energy frequency). Therefore, since the "four horns" and the "four angels" carry the same energy frequency (message) and influences (opposing energy), then they carry the four forces of nature, (i) fire, (ii) earth, (iii) water, and (iv) air.

This is why our mind-soul and ego personalities become purified through sowing and reaping. When *"releasing the four angels who are bound at the banks of the great river Euphrates,* Revelation 9:14. Yeshua and the Ascended Masters are speaking of releasing specific human belief systems:

1. The belief our "I AM" Christ-spirit, mind-soul, and ego personalities of many are separated from us instead of seeing ourselves as "one body of consciousness, the Goddess.
2. The second is the justice we receive by our choices;
3. We are only human; and,
4. The releasing of our incarnations that we have bound in chains because of our strong belief they do not exist.

The river "Euphrates" pertains to our choices and how we set in motion the various influences that the "four angels" represented by fire, earth, water, and air. And, as we use the essence of the four elements and what they represent journeying through many lifetimes, we eventually awaken to a need to develop a "New Expansional Consciousness" and belief system to realize that we need no savior because our salvation is already assured, for one is Christ.

When Isaiah talks about the things of long ago in 41:22, *"that we may reflect on them and know their outcome,"* he is referring to the understanding that we cannot see the future unless we look at our personal history. Isaiah is not talking about a specific nation or about what will happen to earth and humankind because that will all take care of itself when we souls look at our history as an individualized soul. When we evolve enough in consciousness to an understanding that we have had many lifetimes to get where we are now, then we need to take the time to reflect on our history.

Why does Yeshua and the Ascended Masters say this? First, they do not want anyone to live in the past, but to study the past. It is the past that brings us wisdom. Ninety-seven percent of the population's future has always been based on the beliefs of their past lifetimes. As an individual or as a group consciousness, we choose our beliefs according to the emotions of our many past lifetime ego aspects without realizing we are doing it, and we live them out in our present lifetime as if to correct our history instead of looking at our history as something special.

By studying and accepting our past lifetimes, no matter what we have done, we learn not to worry about our unbalanced dark creations because they have served us in one way or another. And now, all ego-aspects of us can work together in being one consciousness. Therefore, no one knows the future, not even Goddess herself, because it cannot happen until we, the creator, put our energy signature on it. If religions and evangelists are using the Bible for their predictions and for interpreting the rapture, then what makes them think the Bible is correct, especially if God himself does not even know the future?

When speaking, *"who were prepared for this hour, day, month, and year?"* Revelation 9:15, the word *"hour"* represents time and space. *"Day"* refers to our understanding and the wisdom gained through our journey of many lifetimes. *"Month"* (30) refers to our three-dimensional body and how we comprise a spirit, mind-soul, and ego consciousness that created multiple light and dark personality aspects to journey in lifetime cycles. The *"years"* refer to patience, persistence, and the endurance we must overcome as we move from one lifetime to the next, forgetting that we have lived other lifetimes *(to kill a third of the human race)*.

Since religious scholars may get tied up with interpreting Revelation 9:16, *"the number of the cavalry troops was two hundred million,"* Yeshua and the Ascended Masters gave its meaning for their benefit. Cavalry troops are mobile units where soldiers train to fight on horseback. In today's world, vehicles have engines, and they carry a certain horsepower. Therefore, the troops that make up the army of two hundred million are not as much as soldiers but indicate an almost unlimited number of potentials and memories that have become part of our soul's makeup because of those many lifetimes.

Everything, no matter what that is, will always reflect on the outside what we believe is the truth from the inside. Can you even imagine the unlimited potentials (good, bad, and new energy) we have at our disposal to be played out in the physical? We all have memory patterns deep within where we have the answers and solutions to every potential that we have ever expressed and created since the time we left higher consciousness (Garden).

Therefore, symbolically speaking, the number two (2) of the "two hundred million" signifies us souls splitting our consciousness into positive and negative, (opposing energy) long ago; and, in the end, this has helped us shape our consciousness into multitudes of non-physical and physical ego-personality aspects, along with many potentials, answers, and solutions to every situation we find ourselves in. Thus, we have created for ourselves billions upon billions of possibilities for us to experience. And most of us have already experienced over "two hundred million."

The *"third killed,"* Revelation 9:18, is not about death. It is about ridding ourselves of the old beliefs and memories that were our truths in many past lifetimes. Suffering comes from our many ego-personality aspects, representing the one-third part of our consciousness, and what rides the rails of incarnations to rid ourselves of the emotional beliefs in separation, Satan, sin, and punishment. It takes sowing and reaping *(fire of justice)* and the illusion of light and dark to conceal *(smoke)* polarity energy to help us understand who we are at our core. It also takes *"sulfur"* as the transforming force to help us undergo a total change in the way we think and believe when it comes to choosing, suffering, and learning wisdom.

The *"power of the horses,"* Revelation 9:19, represents the power that seems to escape us to acknowledge the real truth about being a sovereign Goddess in our own right, equal to Goddess. Instead, we give away our authority (power) to others because of the emotional ties to our many past lifetime beliefs. Every time we support and defend our religious beliefs, our political party, our opinions based on opposing energy, or that a person who is right and wrong must prevail, we give our Christ power away to those that love to control us.

The *"tails that are like snakes,"* Revelation 9:19, is symbolic of our many, past, dark, and gray ego-personality aspects where we played out lifetimes having an appetite of a devouring nature. The *"heads that inflict harm"* are symbolic of how those dark ego-personality aspects from the past still inflict harm on us because of not willing to let go of duality thinking. Because of what we did in some past lifetime, where we acted like a snake, betraying and deceiving others (even though we have paid our debt and born our cross), we still hold guilt for acting that way.

It can be hard for us to bring in one of our dark creations from the past and look at it because the dark can be very intimidating. However, according to Yeshua and the Ascended Masters, "The dark is not what it is made out to be, and neither is light, for they are both just belief systems measured by the perception of our judgment upon them."

Reincarnation presupposes that karmic laws guarantee us we will sow what we reap. Scripture tells us that *"those who live by the sword will sooner or later be destroyed by the sword,"* Matthew 26:52. If this is not so, then why does an innocent child contract a fatal disease? Or, why are we all not born with wealth, health, beauty, and education without discrimination?

Paul's first letter to the Corinthians, *"God gives a body to it as he pleases, to each seed its own fruition"* and *"There are heavenly bodies, and there are earthy bodies. The splendor of the heavenly bodies is one thing, that of the earthly another,"* 1 Cor. 15:38, 40. Well, what are seeds, and what are bodies? Our beliefs, perceptions, and actions are the seeds for our physical experiences, and it can sometimes take many lifetimes of bearing bitter fruit before we finally let our old beliefs fall away. Eventually, we will realize that it takes many cycles of learning to work out all the "effects" of the "causes" we have set in motion.

Paul wrote another letter to the Hebrews: *"Just as it is appointed that men die once, and after death be judged, so Christ was offered up once to take away the sins of many; he will appear a second time and not to take away sin but to bring salvation to those who eagerly await him,"* Heb. 9:27–28. It is not that we die one time and then be judged by some God above us. The symbolism here!

When we made a decision eons ago to move our consciousness into the abyss using opposing energy, and that is when we began a journey of forgetting (die) that we are the creator. Thus, our first death is losing the awareness of us being Christ, God, and the Goddess. So, after our first death, we, from the mind and the physical ego level, became the accepted authority and liaison (judge) for our creations, which of course, exposed us to sowing and reaping (sin).

Even though we have had many incarnations, we only died once, which was when we forgot that we are Christ, God, and the Goddess. Thus, our Christ-identity was *"offered up"* as the means to hold our creations, good and evil, within its memory until we eventually allowed our Christ-identity to wash away *(take away)* our sins (belief in duality). This cleansing occurs through our mind-soul when our many ego-physical bodies incarnate, sowing and reaping, which also correlates with what Paul wrote in 1 Corinthians 15:38: *"God gives it a body as he chooses."*

In other words, we are the Goddess that gives ourselves a body as we choose. Thus, our salvation comes when we allow our "I AM" Christ within to awaken us from our first death. And, once we allow this, we will *"appear a second time,"* when we finally realized, while still in the flesh, that we are finished with sowing and reaping (sin), and that we are the Christ and the Goddess we seek.

Therefore, we do not need to bow down or give worship to anyone, not even Yeshua, but only to our divinity. Show respect and love for all creation, including those who trespass against us. It is okay to "bow down" to a fellow Goddess like Yeshua, the Ascended Masters, and to our fellow Goddess to show respect, but not because they are our savior, king, or God. We (or the self) are the God and the Goddess!

Chapter 25

HOW CRYSTAL, COSMIC AND EARTH ENERGIES WORK WITH OUR DIVINE PLAN

When looking into Revelation 10:1, *"Then I saw another mighty angel come down from heaven wrapped in a cloud, with a halo around his head, his face like the sun and feet were like pillars of fire."* We must not forget that John was a servant to his own "I AM" Christ consciousness. Thus, John represents all of us in the flesh as a servant to our own "I AM" Christ consciousness. Therefore, it is the ego and the mind-soul self, or you wrapped up in obscurity and ignorance, who is *"coming down from heaven wrapped in a cloud"* to meet up with your "I AM" Christ consciousness and not Yeshua.

Because of the question we souls asked eons ago, "Who am I?", way before Earth was ever created, we souls burst forth into manifesting an aspect of ourselves that is now identified as our mind and soul consciousness of responsibility. And, from our mind and soul, we all gave life to an ego-personality that made us feel individualized and separated from our "I AM" Christ consciousness. And, from this sparked mental consciousness, we souls generated multitudes of light and dark ego-personality aspects of ourselves to experience as many potentials as possible, physical and non-physical.

And, once we souled beings (the creators) justified our creations to our own "I AM" Christ consciousness, we then used this "universal omnipresent mind field of pure neutral, unbiased god energy of light." We came up with a new layered energy called Crystalline Energy. As mentioned, when we souls evolved in consciousness, we then split our "oneness of consciousness" to where we created another layer of our consciousness called our mind and soul. And, in doing so, we transformed this Crystalline energy into "four different energies" and not just as the two opposing energies we first thought.

As mentioned before, we souls at first were just consciousness, having no form to us but light, as the Crystalline energy appeared to us as "light." And then, we developed a great desire to feel our creations and to see ourselves, like in a mirror. Therefore, we souled beings created what is called today, "Crystal Energy." This energy is a little different than Crystalline Energy, as it is mostly pure and neutral like Crystalline Energy, but it has a twist of duality to it. It was from this Crystal Energy where we souls created the full fledge polarity energy that consisted of a mental nature called "Cosmic Energy" that we souls could use for imaging our desires to experience. In fact, the universe is made up of Cosmic Energy.

However, these three energies, (i) Crystalline energy, (ii) Crystal energy, and (iii) Cosmic energy, were not enough for us souls to feel, taste, smell, see, and hear our creations on an emotional and physical level. Therefore, since Crystal energy has a duality to it and Cosmic energy displays the extensiveness of positive and negative, we were able to feel the emotional and intellectual response of transparency that became very solid when we used it in an unbalanced directive. Thus, (iv) Earth Energy was organized enough to create materialism, like the planets, stars, and physical bodies. And it is for this reason, the Crystalline Energy is different than it was before we all left higher consciousness (Garden).

As Revelation 10:1 pronounces, *"his feet were like pillars of fire,"* as this represents our mental soul moving into very dense Earth, Energy where positive and negative became the means to feel our creations. Therefore, the *"feet were like pillars of fire"* represents us, souls, in human form, sowing and reaping due to playing with the Earth Energy of polarity. When we start letting go of the belief in Crystal, Cosmic, and Earth energies, then the feet of Christ represent our recognizing the self as a Christ. Thus, our ego-personality becomes the *"pillar of fire"* because of our many lifetimes sowing and reaping and baring our cross, as Yeshua did.

It was from the Crystal, Cosmic, and Earth energies that we souls accepted a belief system of mental imaging, combined with positive and negative, or polarity, we forgot our true identity as a Christ. We also forgot that we are the intelligent center *(sun)* for our mind-soul and ego. And this forgetting (first death) was reinforced by the use of Cosmic and Earth energies, where these energies allowed us to play with the illusion of what we were experiencing be real.

Therefore, the higher consciousness (heaven) we souls once knew a long time ago exists no longer because we cannot uncreate the wisdom of what we have learned journeying through these illusional energies. It was through Crystalline Energy and the illusional energies of Crystal, Cosmic, and Earth that gave us the avenue to hear, feel, touch, smell, and see our creations.

We all know the rainbow is caused by light passing through the raindrops, and therefore, rain is caused by vapor condensed from the atmosphere turning it into water. Thus, it describes the *"halo around his head."* When we come to a place in consciousness where we understand the rainbow is a complete circle with only a half-circle showing in the physical realm and the other half in the spiritual realms, then symbolically, our physical eyes are seeing an illusion. Therefore, the rainbow we are seeing is just a reflection of the real, just as our Etheric body and physical body see the completed self as an "I AM" Christ. It is just that we cannot see the other side of ourselves, or the Christ side *(halo)* like we cannot see the other side of the moon.

We all may say we do see the rainbow, but as we move about or walk toward it, it is not there in reality. It is the same as the physical realm. We may see and feel the physical realm, but it is only an illusion. It feels real because of how we condensed Earth Energy, even though Earth Energy is transparent. The physical realm, like the seven colors of the rainbow (red, orange, yellow, green, blue, indigo, and violet), are just reflections of the real self projecting itself outward using Comic (mental) and Earth (solid) energy.

This is a beautiful metaphor, as the rainbow shows how Crystalline energy became condensed from moving through the "seven most popular expressions." This, in turn, created Crystal, Cosmic, and Earth energies as being real, even though these energies are only illusions, as they are just a reflection of the Crystalline Energy.

When looking into Revelation 10:2-3, most know Yeshua will not place one foot on the sea and the other on land, as described in scripture. It is figuratively a universal memory coming from our subconsciousness *(sea)* where we are hidden from the physical consciousness *(land)* entering into a knowing we are a Christ. The *"small scroll opened"* is defined as us souls giving the command, as a Christ, to open our soul memories to "all the parts and pieces of our creations." And this allows the flow of memories to come in and be engaged while in physical form.

Channeling of the Ascended Masters on the Apocalypse

When we allow the opening of the *"seven seals,"* we will have at our disposal "all that we have ever thought, believed, and done ever since we left higher consciousness long ago." The *"right foot upon the sea"* is signified by an awakened ego-personality consciousness in this lifetime, and how it has been part of our "I AM" Christ consciousness (super subconsciousness) ever since we left the first creation. And now, for the very first time, while in the flesh *(land)*, we can reconnect to our super-subconsciousness if we so choose.

The one *"crying out in a loud voice like a lion,"* Revelation 10:2-3, is and was us, souls, when we first left higher consciousness-awareness (Garden) long ago. We had the courage like a lion and the instinct to separate ourselves from higher consciousness to answer the questions, "Who am I?" Why do you think Adam and Eve were naked in the garden? Maybe they did not know the difference? Adam did not know who he was, male or female, and neither did Eve. How could they have known if we humans comprise both male and female?

We are just choosing one over the other when we come to earth using Earth's energy to experience life. Also, Adam and Eve were not real people! They symbolize the male and female aspects within us all, which is why we had no idea who we were in the beginning stages of our opening up to consciousness and energy. The nakedness comes from the mind and soul (Adam-Eve), exposing ourselves to polarity energy that is made-up of Crystal, Cosmic, and Earth energies to feel our creations. However, in the end, only to find once again, our Crystalline energy is what makes up all energy.

It took courage on our part to split our "oneness of consciousness" into a limited inner (Eve-*sea*) and outer (Adam-*land*) consciousness where we created an ego-personality consciousness *(foot)* to answer the question, "Who am I?" And, as explained before, do not lose sight of our "one body of consciousness" is the makeup of all separate parts and pieces of us. This feeling of separateness from our higher consciousness was created just to allow us, without interference coming from our "I AM" Christ self, to experience opposites, male or female, good or bad, right or wrong.

By experiencing polarity energy, it gave us the method to become aware of those influences that seemed to motivate us in distinguishing who we were, who we are now, and what our purpose is. Our mental consciousness has an intelligent center (intellect), and it has the power to perceive, create an idea pattern, and shape our belief systems into what we desire to experience. And that can be many things, like a physical or non-physical body.

We have an intuitive consciousness where we can learn of the ability to follow through with our desires and choices where we could experience many potentials, good and bad. And we have an emotional consciousness that affects every belief we have ever put away in memory. Therefore, our emotional consciousness can inspire or govern over reasoning and free will.

The *"seventh angel blowing his trumpet,"* in Revelation 10:7, represents our "I AM" Christ consciousness (spirit-body) giving life to a "divine plan" for our evolution, and can be described as a *"mysterious plan,"* in Revelation 10:7. And, this "divine plan" for soul growth (development and evolution) must be *fulfilled* to the letter once we began our journey eons ago. It was you who promised your multiple light and dark ego-personality aspects (servants or prophets) to interpret the "divine plan" and not some church or others outside of you.

We set the tone for our "divine plan," our "revelation," and "the way we would experience life," and not Yeshua or anyone else. Thus, you and only you can bring in your salvation! Revelation 10:7 is what sets the tone for introducing us to physical life and our choice to reincarnate before we can experience the full meaning behind all four energies, our total memories, and the activities of our right and left brain.

Under the influences of the mind, our etheric, and physical body, we have no choice but to take responsibility for everything that happens in our life. Why? Because we are the only ones that created every bit of what we are experiencing. As cited above in the *"mysterious plan"* where it must be fulfilled before the "seventh angel" blows his trumpet, it is calling to our attention the beliefs that have caused us to forget we are Christ. And, once we know we are Christ, then the mystery behind our "divine plan" can be revealed to us through our "revelations."

The voice that speaks to our ego-personality of today is our "I AM" Christ spirit (the Oversoul) urging us, while in the flesh, to tap into our total memories *(scroll)* by using our super-subconsciousness, our subconsciousness *(sea)*, and our physical consciousness *(land)*. And then, accept all levels of you as the means for you to move toward your evolution.

By John asking for the *"small scroll"* in Revelation 10:9-10, he is referring to our "I AM" Christ (the Oversoul) in offering ourselves, from the mental and physical level, to reveal to us those locked up memories of everything we have done since the time we left the "oneness of our own consciousness." And, once those memories are known, we will learn that the sufferings we are experiencing today are coming from the behavior patterns and beliefs of our many past lifetimes.

Channeling of the Ascended Masters on the Apocalypse

The *"scroll"* symbolically implies that all of our memories have been recorded by our many lifetime activities and how we have acted them out on earth since the time we left the oneness of our consciousness. And now, these memories are available to us where we can enjoy our "divine plan" as a sovereign Goddess. When we allow ourselves to awaken to the Christ within the self, the memories of suffering will fall under the control of our Oversoul (Christ) because we are the ones that stand upon the sea of our super and subconsciousness, overlooking our earthly physical consciousness.

Thus, it is up to you to forgive yourself for any sin you think and believe you may have committed. Yeshua himself was trying to convey this message to us, but we keep on missing the point because of our strong belief in Yeshua is the only Christ. Thus, our only savior! John taking the scroll, swallowing it, tasting sweetness, and then experiencing sourness (Revelation 10:9-10) is to show us, by using our divine plan, how it was our Oversoul that helped create multiple physical and non-physical bodies for us to experience the polarity energy, as it took all four layers of energy to learn the wisdom of our choices.

By comparing our many light and dark ego-personality aspects to countless cells in our physical body, and if those cells are not on the same wavelength as our "divine plan, then chaos, confusion, and suffering follow because we are working with Earth and Cosmic energy, (both of polarity) to manifest our creations. Thus, we are guaranteed we will experience polarity. However, education and wisdom come when trying to become balanced again.

We, from a higher consciousness, set up our divine plan eons ago in choosing a method of creating multitudes of ego polarized personalities to learn the wisdom behind every choice we have made while playing with Crystal, Comic, and Earth energies. And, even though we are asleep to our "divine plan" to become a wise and sovereign Goddess in our own right, we have an inner passion for doing so. But, to our human physical consciousness, our suffering is a consequence of coming into some sin, which then creates a consciousness belief of unworthiness and fear.

Because of this belief and fear of unworthiness, many of our light and dark ego-personalities (lifetimes) are still trapped in a mindset that causes us to create more unwanted experiences in this lifetime. Working with reincarnation and how Crystal, Cosmic, and Earth energies work, we learn to integrate all the parts and pieces of us that we consider good, but still refuse any incarnations that we believe is bad. Thus, because of our "divine plan" to express life and help us become free of polarity energy, reincarnation is the tool for us to work out those hidden, dark lifetimes where we played with a belief in evil.

By allowing ourselves to play the victim and the aggressor in different lifetimes, it helps us to release those deep wounds that are stuck within our total memory. Know and understand that we are the creator, and by taking full responsibility for our creations, good and evil, we remain and have always been, a Christ, God, and a Goddess. Therefore, understand that we have done no wrong, nor have we sinned because all of it has been for soul growth and wisdom.

From my study into the spirit, every past life, whether physical or nonphysical, is a personality aspect of us that wants to come home to its creator, the self. We have created countless sub-aspects or sub-ego personalities of us, and now they want to come home to the self. Though many of these light aspects of us are helpful, others can be very dark and troublesome; therefore, on the road to ascension, these aspects (personalities) must return home to their creator, us souled beings.

It is just up to you to accept them as your creations. Without realizing it, consciously or unconsciously, you did ask your Oversoul, the Christ within, to help you integrate these many personality aspects. Yeshua did it, and now the time has come for us humans to do the same.

When we speak of the Lord's prey! *"Lead me not into temptation, but deliver me from evil!"* This is when we are asking our divinity (Oversoul) to guide and lead us out of this ignorance for believing in polarity energy as something real. Thus our "I AM" Christ consciousness will set us free from all illusions containing the belief in sin. Because, in the end, we have never sinned. And, Revelation 10:11 spells that out for us.

To *"prophesy"* is to apply, allow, and be relevant in our quest to answer the questions, "Who am I?" and "What is my purpose for being on earth in physical form?" And we do this through physical application and accepting responsibility for both our total memories and the revelations we have experienced on earth. This allows us to eventually realize what Yeshua meant about bringing to remembrance all things, even from the foundations of the world.

The *"many peoples,"* Revelation 10:11, is about our many light, clear, gray, and dark ego-personality aspects that we all have created to experience life. The word *"peoples"* is associated with the phrase descendants, for both represent distinct, false faces of our total consciousness, including our belief systems, lies, and the realities that we, as individuals and as a group consciousness, experience by reincarnating here on earth many times. And, from these many false faces (reincarnations), we have activated many belief patterns that are held in memories *(nations)* to be manifested and experienced to become free and sovereign.

As for the *"kings"* of the earth! They are not so much as kings, governments, and dictators as one would think, they symbolize the many ruling ego-personalities from past lifetimes that keep us as a slave in this lifetime without realizing it. These ruling ego-personality aspects of our past lifetimes speak many different languages *(tongues)* because of their many different belief systems, lifetimes, and the lies that we hold in memory as to whom we are. When we come to earth in a new lifetime, we forget about our many different belief systems *(tongues)* mentioned in those past lifetimes. And, the only way we can free ourselves from these many beliefs is to follow our "divine plan" to become awakened to the illusion of it all.

Without even realizing it, we genetically transmit and pass down to ourselves, through reincarnation, what we have not yet overcome with belief systems. Paul, 1 Corinthians 3:16–17: *"Do you not know that you are the temple of God and that the Spirit of God dwells in you? If anyone destroys God's temple, God will destroy that person; for the temple of God, which you are, is holy."* Paul, 1 Corinthians 12:13: *"For in one Spirit we were all baptized into one body, whether Jews or Greeks, slaves or free persons, and we were all given to drink of the one Spirit."* And, in verse 27, the same chapter, Paul states: *"You are Christ's body and individually parts of it."*

From Paul's words, we are indeed all Gods and Goddesses, and we together are what make up the total consciousness of the Spirit of One. And yet, the whole is more than the sum of its parts! We have no beginning, nor will we ever experience an end, because we are the Spirit of One, the Christ, God, and a Goddess always creating experiences to learn wisdom. We souls have triggered this universal omnipresent Crystalline Energy Mind Field of Neutrality, and now we are the telepathic grid of continually expanding our consciousness where we created all that is today and all that we will create tomorrow.

Know and understand that some of us have awakened to our individuality from the Spirit of One and have been given time, intuitive understanding, intelligence, and eternal power to form our desires to experience them in the flesh. There was a time when we, like a small frightened child who needs firm boundaries, wanted the literal interpretations of the Bible. And this is reflected in the way some people cling to the Bible as the only source of truth. But the Bible tells another story, because embedded deep within it, is the unmistakable stories where there are plenty of reminders that we can embrace the wisdom of whom we are as a Christ, God, and a Goddess.

By becoming sovereign and free from all "three opposing energies" and belief systems, including the perception of materialism, we can experience all that we are as a Goddess. Thus, we become unlimited in what we can create to experience. Why? Because our memories retain the wisdom and intelligence of all our experiences, good and bad. Not only that but also our higher consciousness. And that is how wisdom becomes more valuable than any treasures built upon earth. It is our wisdom that serves as a constant driving force to move us forward in our quest to become free of limitations, including those restrictive and dogmatic religious beliefs that have kept us as a slave for many lifetimes.

Because of this constant drive to become free, we move forward with our "divine plan" to grow in consciousness through the actions and choices we make based upon our belief systems to become awakened in the flesh. But now, the time has come to understand that the "divine plan" is that of the "divine will" of the Goddess to following and honoring the Christ within us, for we are who we seek. Thus, the power of the resurrection is the Christ-consciousness within us, all trying to make itself known to us in this lifetime.

John 11:25: *"I am the resurrection and the life,"* as this resurrection is not in the future, it is *"now made manifest through the appearance of (y)our own savior Christ (you), who destroyed death and brought life and immortality to light"* (2 Tim 1:10). Look at the resurrection as lifting your total made up consciousness of all ego personalities into becoming one with your own Christ-consciousness. Thus, we all are to become a completed Christ, God, and a Goddess in our own right.

When we awaken to the divine plan that each of us set up eons ago where we took on a mind-soul and ego-personality that believed in polarity energy and a body of physicality as being real, then the resurrection is about us humans integrating all the facets of our consciousness into one body of consciousness (light, clear, gray, and dark personality aspects of the self). When we allow this, we conform to the absolute truth that we are a sovereign divine being.

This renewal or rebirth of consciousness brings about a transformation of our physical body so that every cell becomes incorruptible and immortal, while we are still part of the flesh. The resurrection is a natural occurrence that takes place daily in all who are learning to conform to their being divine humans, equal in deity to the one we call God.

Those who raise into higher understanding and frequency to this truth will eventually let go of all that is illusionary and egocentric personalities in their relationships to all things. They will come into total compassion for

Channeling of the Ascended Masters on the Apocalypse

self and others, and with universal love, which brings healing, abundance, joy, and unconditional love into their lives because the old, limiting beliefs and personal relationships of polarity energy cannot continue in this resurrection.

Chapter 26

MOVING FROM A THREE-DENSITY TO A FOUR-DENSITY CONSCIOUSNESS

When we first left higher consciousness (Garden) long ago, we made an oath and a commitment to set apart our "I AM" Christ consciousness from something that we are not today, a human looking for a savior. And, by taking this oath, we and our many mental and ego physical bodies became the *"true temple of God"* for our own universal God energy of light that we use for our creations (1 Corinthians 3:16–17). From this oath, we sacrificed our "I AM" Christ consciousness and forfeited the best part of us in favor of experiencing the flesh to learn wisdom. It was the forfeiting of our "I AM" Christ consciousness and our divine magic that allowed us to enter into a physical body to expand our three-dimensional consciousness from a three-density consciousness to a four-density consciousness.

Please make a note: I will explain the difference between dimensions and density consciousness later in this chapter. For now, this method allowed us to perform spiritual service to ourselves, to our angelic family, and to the whole of creation. Therefore, fulfilling this oath first took place in the temple of worship, represented by our many etheric mental and physical bodies of consciousnesses that we lived out at one time or another upon the earth.

These many physical bodies are now part of our total consciousness, as they are spread throughout the astral and etheric realms as our many ego-personality aspects. And, the fascinating thing about them, is that they are still playing out their stories and beliefs in ways we are not even aware of. And, when Yeshua and the Ascended Masters speak about "worshiping," it has nothing to do with worshiping in a church or worshiping a God outside of us or in a building because the *"temple of God"* resides within our "physical body" as "pure universal energy of light" that is mentioned throughout this book.

If you desire to worship, then go no further than yourself treating, honoring, and respecting the self as a Christ also. And, at the same time, honor and respect all of your human bodies that you once lived upon the earth. When processing who you are from the aspect of your ego-personality, then know that all your many lifetime ego personality aspects are the "altar" and the "temple" for your "I AM" Christ consciousness when playing them out in the flesh.

When we learn to recognize that heaven is a state of consciousness rather than a place where we go after death, then heaven on earth rings true when we accept full responsibility for all that we have chosen, done, and experienced since we have left higher consciousness eons ago. Also, it is not so much that we left higher consciousness eons ago; it is that higher consciousness defines us as we were always an ascended master working out of higher consciousness. We are just learning how we got there when we are on earth. Therefore, an ascended master is a condition that we always were not that it is a title or something we work toward.

Know that you and no one else, not even God, created your many physical bodies as a temple to hold your pure god energy of light and for you to use for your creations. Not that you have to steal energy from others to get what you desire in life because all the energy you need is right there at your deposal. How often have you heard about the transformation of Earthmoving into rapture from your religious leaders? And yet, on an individual scale, it cannot happen unless you allow some dramatic changes to come into your life. Changes that will help you let go of your old, dogmatic beliefs that keep you tied to a consciousness that believes you are weak and a sinner.

The *"measuring of the temple"* in Revelation 11:1 is about how we view and understand our mental, physical, and ego consciousness (representing the *altar*) in recognizing this "pure god energy of light" to serve us and our physical body (*the temple*) in what we desire to experience. Therefore, the *"measuring of the temple"* is not about some God above us, a building, or a platform for someone to stand upon for us to worship. By believing in a life force that resides in a church building as all that is of God, we then miss the whole point of Christ's return.

By holding onto beliefs and thoughts of a God that needs you to worship him, the chance of shifting to a fourth-density consciousness becomes much harder for you to complete. Thus, you stay in the second cycle (zero) where choices are tied to right and wrong, good and bad, duality.

For example: to *"exclude the outer court of the temple,"* Revelation 11:2, represents how you, in this lifetime, need to be careful not to exclude your many other physical bodies that were used in other lifetimes because they, too, still hold the energy of the "temple of God." Remember, you have created many physical bodies using this "universal pure energy of light (God)," and those lifetimes helped you become the sacrificial Lamb in this lifetime. Remember, there is always a unity between the mental and the physical by which they both render a unified service for you while in the physical form.

Being *"handed over to the Gentiles,"* Revelation 11:2, represents us souls moving outside of our "I AM" Christ consciousness and into a mental and physical body to play within a three-density consciousness where all choices are based upon good and bad, right and wrong, sin and punishment, along with polarity. And, once we moved outside of our "I AM" consciousness, that is when we committed to a mental and physical ego consciousness that set us apart from our Christ consciousness. Thus, freeing us to experience opposing energy, positive and negative, right and wrong, with no interference coming from our higher self (Oversoul).

The *"Gentiles"* denotes our many unreformed beliefs and acts as our "sinful ways" that we took up playing in many ego-personality physical bodies (*holy city*), sowing and reaping. The *"forty-two months"* in Revelation 11:2 has the same meaning as Genesis 7:4, where *"forty days and forty nights"* represents completion, as in four-square, and this describes us in the flesh completing our cycles of lifetimes by shifting from a three-density consciousness to a four-density consciousness. For example, the number four (4) means:

1. Length (quality): Symbolic of measuring how many lifetime physical bodies it will take sowing and reaping before we remember we are Christ.
2. Width (breath): Symbolic of air, the mental consciousness, which allows us to imagine life as being real, and then manifest the image to experience.

3. Height (depth): Symbolizes the remoteness that we will journey through the darkness of forgetting (bottom), and then returning to light (top) again; bringing with us patience, unconditional love, and understanding, for which the fourth-density consciousness represents.
4. Time and Space: Symbolic saying that we are unlimited when it comes to bringing in as many potentials and lifetimes as possible to experience. Each time we choose a physical body to experience life, that is when we will measure them with passion and purpose about how we will play them out, shifting from one density consciousness to higher ones.

The number two (2) represents our split consciousness again, as we have taken on a mind-soul body (mental) that believes and consists of positive and negative as being real. The word *"months"* implies thirty-days (30) and not thirty-one, as the average months in a year is 30.42 days. The three (3) symbolizes our evolution from a two-dimensional split consciousness into a three-dimensional physical consciousness laboring with the four elements of this planet (air, fire, water, earth) journeying through a cycle (representing the zero) of many lifetimes playing with this dual (2) or polarity energy. It is here, in this cycle, where we play out as many potentials and lifetimes as possible to answer the question, "Who am I?"

It will also come from this cycle (zero) where we, in a two-dimensional and three-dimensional physical consciousness, become the *"measuring rod"* for what we perceive as right and wrong, good and bad, as we journey through many lifetimes playing with a three-density consciousness. It is from this "measuring" (judgment), the "law of destiny" will interpret what we will experience as to what density consciousness we will play in.

Note! I use the phrase "dimension(s)" and "density" to explain our multi-dimensional consciousness. But, in reality, there is only "sense consciousness," as "dimension(s)" and "density" have the meaning of "consciousness frequency." Thus, giving us souls many different ways to experience truth and reality.

This is why when the Ascended Masters speak about "higher consciousness," we souls have never left the higher consciousness. It seems that way because all that we are doing is experiencing different frequency senses that place us in an induced truth and reality that fits that frequency or belief pattern - this is why "truth" expands as our consciousness expands. However, the Ascended Masters prefer me to keep it simple by speaking of "sense consciousness" as dimensions or density.

Remember, higher consciousness just defines us as always being divine and a master. We are just learning how we got to be a master. It is like we have never left higher consciousness. And that is the beauty of having the wisdom of every lifetime experience. Therefore, enlightenment is a natural thing that happens to us anyway as we explore these many different frequencies. Not that we have to work toward enlightenment, any truth, or needing to find heaven. All that we have to do is allow enlightenment and truth to expand within us as we live out each lifetime.

Hence, the sacrificial Lamb is comprised of many light, clear, gray, and dark ego-personality aspects of us that are now spread throughout the multi-dimensional realms, physical and non-physical, for us to bring into balance. It is also us humans, Revelation 11:3, that *"(I) will commission my two witnesses to prophesy for twelve hundred and sixty days (1260), wearing sackcloth."*

The "I" represents our "I AM" Christ consciousness creating *(commissioning)* the avenue for our mind-soul and our many ego-personalities (lifetimes) to be the *"two witnesses"* for our journey through the three-density consciousness using the polarity energy of two as our reality. However, together, our two-dimensional mind-soul and three-dimensional physical consciousness will work as one, as they share the same memories at each density (sense) consciousness, including our "I AM" consciousness.

Most people cannot comprehend the idea of having a subconsciousness, let alone a super-subconsciousness, that holds all memories of their past lifetimes and the secrets of life. Most people do not understand that they work mostly out of their subconsciousness and their outer physical consciousness, and this is why they experience a three-density (sense) consciousness that deals with the belief in good and evil, right and wrong, sin and punishment as their truth. How can they, or anyone, know God, Goddess, Yeshua, Satan, and themselves if they continue with their beliefs/truths that polarity energy is real? They can't!

Therefore, the only way out of this dilemma is by having many incarnations and using memory to record everything that you have ever done in whatever density (sense) consciousness you played them out (physical or nonphysical). Thus, time and space became the avenue for us souls to measure our choices to help bring balance to our belief systems.

Therefore, these *"two witnesses"* represent our mind-soul and our outer ego physical consciousness, as they both are part of our Oversoul. But we are not aware of it because we are too busy focusing out of a small part of our total sense consciousness. Because of our understanding that everything is logical, reasonable, good, and evil and that God and Satan are real, then we have forgotten the purpose behind what we have chosen and experienced in other lifetimes.

Therefore, the spirit in which we did an act (past or present) then becomes a memory and part of our soul record to be played out in a three-density consciousness as either positive or negative. These memories need to be played out for us to understand and feel the purpose behind the choice and the act created. Thus, we usually taste the bitterness of what we eat (or what we think about all day long as being our truths) and what we place in our belly (or emotions) instead of our head (higher self).

It can get very confusing to think about having numerous light, gray, and dark ego-personality aspects operating within and outside of us, especially when it seems as if we only exist in a physical body that is the self today. Why do we not know about these other ego-personality aspects of us? The answer can be quite simple! Most of our attention is focused on fixed beliefs and dogmatic truths more than on seeing truths change as we evolve in consciousness. The truth of something one thousand years ago is not the same truth today. Instead, we hang onto old beliefs and truths because, for example, the belief in one lifetime that seems so real to us. Another example, let's look further into Revelation 11:3, *"to prophesy for twelve hundred and sixty days* (1260), *wearing sackcloth."*

The number one (1) represents the oneness of consciousness that we were in the beginning before we split our consciousness into an opposing consciousness of two (2) (the mind (positive) - soul (negative)). The six (6) represents the "six divine attributes" of the Christ consciousness found in Revelation 4:4, and the "six days of creation" in Genesis 1:1-31. However, all of it represents us souls as a Christ, first and foremost.

We are an infinite, everlasting, Christ, and the Goddess that uses pure, neutral energy of light (God) that occupies all space, dimensions, and time. Our "I AM" Christ consciousness is the essence of life within everything that exists, including our many gray, clear, light, and dark ego-personality aspects as us that embraces the total god energy within our physical body *(the temple of God)*. We souls are surrounded, when in the flesh and when not in the flesh, with:

1. An infinite consciousness that is forever active
2. Intelligence that is of a universal nature
3. A consciousness that supports growth and expansion
4. A divine plan (will) that was set in the beginning to journey outside of our "I AM" Christ consciousness to learn who we are as a Goddess

5. A spiritual essence about us that gives life to many thoughts, beliefs, ideas, and personality aspects of us
6. A spirit about us that is of a divine love state that is unchangeable and unconditional

The zero (0) again represents the cycle in which we incarnated into using many physical bodies playing with a three-density consciousness that deals with polarity energy as something real to learn love for self and others, and the wisdom of our choices.

Back in the days of the Bible, *"sackcloth"* was made of black goat's hair. It was coarse, rough, and thick, and was used for sacks. Thus, it represents us souls taking on a coarse, rough, and more uncomfortable consciousness, like our physical body. And, when we break down the number of 1260 to $1 + 2 + 6 + 0 =$ it adds up to the number nine (9). This means after we complete our cycles of lifetimes playing within a three-density consciousness, we, and our physical body, shift into a fourth-density consciousness where the belief in good and bad, sin and punishment, and conditional love shifts to balance and unconditional love.

When speaking of a two-dimensional and three-dimensional consciousness, it differs from two-density consciousness or three-density consciousness, even though they are all "sense consciousness" because of frequency input. A dimensional consciousness is a consciousness that becomes layered with many potentials, beliefs, and an energy that vibrates at different frequencies. A density consciousness is where a person is working with the elements of a particular planet that he/she resides, such as Earth.

The first-density consciousness is that of electrons, protons, molecules, solids, liquids, gases, and archetypical elements such as fire, water, air, and earth. The second-density consciousness composes vegetable, animal, the beginning of single-cell, even bacteria. Also, the second-density consciousness usually works with group consciousness, like the plant and animal kingdom.

However, for example, once a dog or cat shows some signs of originality, like individualism, usually their next lifetime is taken up as a human. Now, do you see how unique you and animals are, even if you did bad things. Remember, we Goddesses desire to "know all that there is to know."

The third-density consciousness deals with humans and their choices based on duality or opposing energy, like the belief in good and evil, right and wrong, sin and punishment, God and Satan, conditional love, even the belief we left higher consciousness, etc. This density consciousness also deals with karma, a cycle of many lifetimes before moving to the fourth-density consciousness.

The fourth-density consciousness deals with the individual and as a collective group consciousness. This level also deals with the necessity to not cause harm to ourselves and others. And, on some level, we have some realization of being connected to the source more than in the third-density as we feel love, compassion, and harmony. Also, at this level, we begin to recognize our emotions as something we need to be careful of, as they are powerful enough to keep us disconnected from knowing our Christ consciousness.

The fifth-density consciousness deals with pure wisdom where we begin to understand our uniqueness, individuality, and yet, one with all that there is. It is a level where we do not compromise our identity and integrity. At this level, we have gained enough wisdom to know how to work with energy. Also, at this level, we may explore the physical senses and how our senses to all consciousnesses expand beyond just the physical senses.

The sixth-density consciousness deals with having the ability and awareness to perceive all sides to any circumstances beyond duality beliefs. It is also the level where we confront all that remains of negativity and separation. This is where we can create experiences that hold no karma to our acts because of understanding energy and what needs to be balanced.

The seventh-density consciousness deals with pure consciousness with no boundaries, as we are fully connected to the "I AM." At this level, we void anything to do with bringing in creations that are distorted. We keep our creations pure and simple. Now, there are more densities, but at this time, there is no need to move further than the seventh-density. This density or sense consciousness also deals with the opening of the third eye, as one connects to the Pinal Gland in the physical body. In other words, one knows who one is with no doubt coming from the emotional level.

When speaking of the *"two olive trees"* and the *"two lampstands"* standing before the *"Lord of the Earth,"* Revelation 11:4, they correlate with what was just said in the above paragraphs. For example, the *"two olive trees"* relates to our "I AM" Christ consciousness (the super-subconsciousness) and the mind-soul (or subconsciousness). However, it is our outer physical ego consciousness that rides the rails of incarnations, sowing, and reaping, to where it ascends to higher density consciousness along with our mind.

It is with our outer ego physical consciousness where we build up memories based upon our choices and actions taken in life. And then, our mind-soul (two-dimensional subconsciousness), along with our "I AM" super subconsciousness, holds those memories, good and evil, until we are ready to face them in the physical realm to be played out. How we experience them is according to the density or sense consciousness we are working through. It is because of this action that we receive the impulses of these clear, gray, light, and dark memories from our mind-soul and physical consciousness (*the two witnesses*) rather than acquiring them by our experiences.

It is the memories of our past lifetimes and the ones we build-up in this lifetime that become fruit-bearing because they stand before the *"two lampstands,"* represented by unconditional love and wisdom. Also, the *"olive trees"* can signify the "spirit of love" because olive oil is symbolic of the "holy spirit," or us souls in our divine state.

Remember the dove returning to Noah in the ark with an olive leaf? And, in Psalm 52:8, David said, *"I am like a green olive-tree in the house of God: I trust in the loving-kindness of God forever and ever."* The *"house of God"* is our physical body, the *"green olive tree"* is our "I AM" Christ spirit, protected from the false ego while we are in the physical body. Remember, it was foretold that we would *"subdue"* the earth (Genesis 1:28). In other words, our world of misbeliefs comes from us, the mass, because we believe in polarity energy.

Even Revelation 11:5 agrees with what I said in the above paragraph because the verse is speaking of karma, sowing, and reaping. If any man, woman, or child harms another, including the hurting of oneself, then the fire of justice (karma) will prevail. Why? It is all tied to the belief in polarity energy. However, by accepting who you are as a Christ also, without doubt, and then take full responsibility for all of your creations; even those lifetimes that you cannot remember, you can uncreate your karmic conditions to where you can begin to rebalance your energy to harmonizing your physical body.

By trying to force our healing through the belief that someone can cure us, we acknowledge that we are less than "I AM" Christ. By thinking of the self as less than Christ, we bring in this opposing energy to serve us. And we wonder why we still suffer. If we do not take up the study of being equal to God and Christ and rethink (repent) about our beliefs, we will be consumed *(devour)* by the law of justice *(fire)* over and over until we learn to let go of any idea that God is our creator and is someone that rules and controls us.

If we do not allow ourselves the time to rethink our position about dogmatic polarity beliefs, then we, in effect, distort or kill the inner workings of the mind and our ego-physical personalities (two witnesses). Thus, we create a return path back to earth again and again, until we finally let go of this belief that we are only human. For example, Revelation 11:6, *"they (two witnesses) have the power to close up the sky so no rain can fall during the time of prophesying."*

Since we live our lives based on polarity energy beliefs, then who do you think has the power to *"close up"* our "I AM" Christ consciousness and the deep wisdom it holds? It is the self, from a two-dimensional and three-dimensional physical consciousness *(the two witnesses)*, playing out of a three-density consciousness. Also, the *"turning water into blood,"* Revelation 11:6, is about us humans utilizing our "I AM" Christ-spirit *(water)* and allowing it to give life (blood) to our mind-soul to create some type of physical body for us to use here on earth.

Because of our many opposing belief systems held in memory, the energy we bring into our mind carries a specific vibrational signature where blood clots can manifest within our physical body. And, it all depends on what we feed our mind as truths. Water (spirit) will flow freely if we, as humans, do not dam it up by the energy used for our creations. The same with the blood flows through our human body. If we do not dam it up with dogmatic beliefs, then the blood (spirit) flows with no obstruction.

It is the same if we look at family, government, religious ties, and loyalties that take priority over other ideas and relationships that deal with the spirit. Whether we believe in reincarnation is up to us, because it makes no difference to our spirit. All that matters to our spirit is that she will expand and experience her creations. And, she does it by having many lifetimes played out in a physical body.

It is not that Yeshua, the Ascended Masters, and I are trying to convince you of reincarnation or that you are Christ and the Anti-Christ simultaneously. We are here to reveal how you can be hypnotized by what you perceive to be the truth because of your training and sense of consciousness. For me, it is not about "believing in Christ or God." It is about trusting, knowing, and allowing your "I AM" Christ to be known to you, and that you are the creator of all that is for you!

It was because of our many past lifetime beastly ego-personalities *"waging war against"* our mind and the ego-personality of today *(the two-witness)*, Revelation 11:7, where we have forgotten our mind is the Lord of Lords and the creator of our experiences. However, when looking into Revelation 11:8, *"Sodom"* was one of the cities of the plain where Abraham's nephew Lot lived for a time and was later destroyed by fire because of its wickedness.

Therefore, *"Sodom"* represents our many hidden, egotistical, deceitful, dark ego-personality aspects that are concealed and obscured from us in this lifetime because of our belief that reincarnation is not real. The concealment is symbolized by "Egypt," where it represents us, from the mental-mind level of consciousness, and us becoming the Anti-Christ that believes in a God of polarity. And now, these dark ego aspects of us are held hostage within our own memories as radical belief systems. We can see these radical beliefs being played out here on earth today to remind us all to open up to our own radical beliefs deep within to recognize them, and then let them go with forgiveness, love, and peace.

Since Sodom represents our radical hidden dark ego-personality aspects from past lifetimes, and Gomorrah represents a state of mind that opposes our "I AM" Christ spirit, then know we are the Anti-Christ fighting against our own Christ consciousness. These two wicked cities (memories), and what they symbolize, must first consent to the purification of those radical ego-personalities. And the only way this can happen is through physical reincarnation, sowing, and reaping, represented by the sins of Sodom and Gomorrah (beliefs of a dogmatic nature).

It was because of our split consciousness where we produced a consciousness of doubt, symbolized by Abraham's nephew "Lot." And, it was our doubting consciousness (Lot) that became a stand-in for our trusting consciousness that led to a reasoning consciousness, symbolized by Abraham.

Thus, it was through our reasoning consciousness (where religious philosophies are today) that we produced a fear consciousness that finally led us to create multiple light, clear, gray, and dark ego-personalities that became full of wickedness and destruction. Thus, our mind of doubt became symbolized by the Anti-Christ, and our ego-personality of destruction became the Beast working together to gain power and control.

It is because of us humans, working from the mind and ego levels, and taking on the title of the Anti-Christ and the Beast, where most of us are today. On a conscious level, we keep denying this process because of our strong belief in polarity energy, that race exists, and that we have only one lifetime. Therefore, I hope this book, channeled by Yeshua and the Ascended Masters, can help reconnect you to this trust that we are Christ, and we, as the human race, are as one.

By accepting and acknowledging all of our beastly ego-personality aspects, including those tied to wickedness and destruction, we will, from the mind and ego level (third-density), gain enough freedom to ascend to the fourth, fifth, sixth, or seventh density consciousness. And, once the mind recognizes this, our ego will gain a full new understanding of Christ. And that is when we will fill our life with healing, abundance, and joy because of moving into New Expansional Energy (New Earth) while still part of the flesh.

By accepting these many radical beastly past lifetime ego-personality aspects as our creations, we set up a consciousness to heal them and then release them with only forgiveness and unconditional love. Thus, we heal all parts and pieces of our consciousness. And, when done, while in the flesh, we transform our old energy of polarity (old earth) to a New Expansional Energy of safety, health, and abundance (new earth). Allow yourself to stop worrying about your sins and then forgive yourself because you have never sinned. Just know that your Christ-consciousness has already forgiven you eons ago.

The reference given in Revelation 11:9, from *"every people, tribe, tongue, and nation,"* applies to the makeup of a city, nation, community, ethnic group, or the human race, and even the countless multitudes of souls that left higher consciousness eons ago (first creation). These are the souls who went through the wall of polarity energy (fire) and into the second creation creating multiple nonphysical and physical dimensions to play with this opposing energy, and you are one of them.

Every human on earth, from every nation, color, and race, is part of the 144,000 soul-groups mentioned in Revelation. And, each soul-group or family tends to join together to form a type of bond, whether based on geography, race, religion, or some other factor, like certain beliefs. Therefore, no matter what gender, *"nation, race, people, or tongue"* you speak or believe in, we humans are one and a Christ in expression. And, from this Christ expression, we belong to one of those 144,000 multiple families claiming a common ancestry that follows one inherited belief that feels this opposing energy is real.

We genetically transmit to ourselves, through reincarnation, the issues and beliefs that we have not yet overcome and have forgotten since we have chosen reincarnation as the vehicle to learn wisdom, and to become one with love. These memories and lifetimes have become dead to us in this lifetime because we refuse to release our belief in a God that created polarity energy and our dogmatic views to it.

For example, we gain and release many belief systems *(tongues)* through our family tree and group consciousness *(tribe)* while in the flesh. And, because we are often our own ancestors, we can come into this world many times to experience a disease or a talent that can be passed down through family lines. We can even take on karma from an ancestral line that we never created in some past lifetime. We volunteer to take it on to help the family tree. And, this is why when we become awakened, we must let go of the family tree and become a sovereign Christ in our own right.

The phrase *"three and a half days"* is a metaphor symbolizing a leap in consciousness where we move from a three-density consciousness to a four-density expansional consciousness. The three (3) represents our spirit, mind-soul, and physical ego forms in a three-dimensional body playing in a three-density consciousness that only understands good and bad as something real. The one half (½) symbolizes the integration of many of our ego-personalities with the oneness (1) of the self, and the (2) under the one represents the split of our consciousness (positive and negative) coming together and joining a consciousness of New Expansional Energy of Four. It is there where we can use this New Expansional Energy of Four for our creations instead of the vibrational polarity energy of positive and negative.

It was our willingness to move from the oneness of consciousness (first creation) to a three-density consciousness and reality (second creation) that allowed our mind-soul and outer physical consciousness *(two witnesses)* to be obscured *(hidden)* by creating multiple ego-personality aspects of self to play with potentials. This made it possible for us in this lifetime not to *"allow their corpses to be buried"* (our many ego-personalities) too deep within our consciousness where we would be lost to them for a long time. However, after many lifetimes playing with the forces of polarity energy, we can overcome this obscurity by releasing our dogmatic beliefs in opposing energy. You can see this in Revelation 11:10, where we first came to earth in a three-dimensional physical body long ago as a resident of earth.

At first, we were very excited about expressing multitudes of self-satisfying experiences, and we gloated about them because, in the end, it resulted in personal wisdom. We gloated because we created many potentials and ego personalities, good and evil (signified by the *"tormented the inhabitants of the earth"*) to choose from and experience. And, they have served us well in answering our questions about our purpose here on earth. However, we all have forgotten that out of those billions upon billions of potentials that we created in the Etheric realms, some of them are virtually energy neutral, waiting for us, their creators, to activate them from a conscious physical level.

It is because of the way we were taught about polarity energy that keeps us stuck into studying anything that goes beyond our religious beliefs. And, because of our strong belief in polarity, we created not only dark and many wicked ego-personalities, we also created drama, conflicts, and many other issues that torment us today. And, then, we ask ourselves, "Why do we suffer?" and "What did we do to deserve this?"

It is because of this process; we became dead to whom we indeed are, creating for ourselves sadness, illnesses, and many other human conditions to feel alive and separate from our "I AM" Christ spirit. And, it is through religion, family, friends, politics, and many other situations that keep us from learning the real truth. Why? Because it is hard to let go of our matter-of-fact family beliefs. Also, what creates our suffering is that our many ego-personalities of past lifetimes do not realize that we today are not just another ego-personality, for we are the superego aspect for our Oversoul to call in all aspects of us into "one body of consciousness."

Our Oversoul has chosen the current "you" in this lifetime to welcome back home these wicked and conventional ego-personalities. This is all in an effort to integrate them with you as "one body of consciousness," living under the rule of your "I AM" Christ consciousness. This lifetime is the exceptional one if you so choose it to be because your Oversoul has chosen you to integrate "all that you are and have been" into "one body of consciousness."

The example is with Revelation 11:11-12, *"after the three and a half days, a breath of life from God entered them."* Again, the *"three and a half days"* is a metaphor when we leaped in consciousness where we split our consciousness of oneness to work with the vibrational polarity energy of two (mind-soul). But, once our "I AM" Christ consciousness (Goddess) entered the two-dimensional consciousness, we became a three-dimensional consciousness where we allowed ourselves to focus on a frequency that led to an ego physical consciousness of dissent that became the testing portion of our total consciousness.

Revelation 11:11-12, *"the loud voice from heaven saying to them, 'come up here,'"* is symbolic, while in the flesh, of our mind and ego personalities of today that are beginning to vibrate loudly enough where we can now reconnect to a higher density consciousness. The *"after the three and a half days,"* Revelation 11-11-12, is a metaphor where we can take a leap in consciousness to meet up with our many light, clear, gray, and dark ego-personalities to have them fall under the influence of our "I AM" Christ consciousness. Remember, you are the "I AM!"

And now, in our current lifetime, these many light, clear, gray, and dark ego-personalities that were spread throughout multi-dimensional realms are part of our higher consciousness because they currently know they were obstructed by their belief in polarity energy *(went up to heaven in a cloud)* Revelation 11:11-12. So, take a deep breath and allow yourself to radiate, expand, and feel your "I AM" Christ consciousness, your mind-soul, and your many ego-personality aspects within become unified as "one body of consciousness."

And, *"as their enemies looked on,"* Revelation 11:11-12, this is symbolic of still having some dimensional ego-personalities that refuse to come home to you. And as such, they see you and those other ego-personalities as their enemies. Why? Because these ego-personality aspects still believe strongly in polarity energy as being real because they love power and control. This is why it takes many lifetimes working our way to a seven-density consciousness.

However, some of us have integrated enough of our ego-personalities, where we can take a leap in consciousness and become aware that we are the ones creating our day-to-day belief patterns and experiences. This changes our course of action because now we can move faster into higher consciousness with full awareness of what we are doing.

According to Yeshua and the Ascended Masters, there are invisible layers of our previous incarnations within our cells, and in the DNA of our physical body. And, all that we have to do is bring the memory of those incarnations forward to our physical consciousness. These layers of our many ego-personality aspects are stored or held in other dimensional realms waiting for us to reconnect them with our Oversoul because these ego-personality aspects (lifetimes) are part of our spiritual heritage and identity of today.

The Ascended Masters that work with me have said, and I paraphrase here, "You can call upon strengths from a previous incarnation to help compensate for a present weakness. At the cellular and DNA levels, your physical body not only carries memories of your present lifetime but memories of other incarnations as well. The foundation of your individuality (as a witness) is interconnected with all of your existence and all your lifetimes. From this, you can draw, consciously or unconsciously, the wisdom of previous personality insights, activities, and characteristics (the other witness)."

From this place of ignorance, without realizing it, we have been following those who accumulate power because we have mistakenly interpreted power as intelligence, position in life, control, and having money, which unfortunately still happens today. And, because of many incarnations playing with power, we began to feel comfortable with those in power and deciding for us. So, we became hypnotized, limited, and controlled by all those who claimed to know firsthand the secret of life or God. However, by way of reincarnation, our "I AM" Christ-spirit began to peel away those layers of false consciousnesses because it was not meant for us to live in ignorance forever.

Matthew 24:39–41 says: *"In those days before the flood people were eating, drinking, marrying and given in marriage until the very day that Noah went into the ark, and knew nothing about the flood until it came and destroyed them all. So, will it be at the coming of the Son of Man? Two men will be in the field, one taken, and one is left behind. Two women will be grinding at the handmill; one taken and one is left behind."*

The "two men" in a field represent those of us who are ready to move beyond the belief in polarity energy, while others are unwilling to leave behind their dogmatic beliefs. The one left in the field remains very mental and intellectual in consciousness about life, like God and Satan as two different individuals. They are sticking firmly to their dogmatic beliefs, and therefore, they are the ones who do not yet want to ascend to higher consciousness. They prefer to stick to the old belief patterns of good versus evil, Democrat versus Republican, gender versus gender, race versus race, no matter what.

When we decide to move beyond the intellect and in thinking about all these things of duality, using only the mind and our beastly nature to discern who God is and who we are, we become part of the New Expansional Energy of Four (New Earth) that stands at the threshold of a higher density consciousness. This New Expansional Energy of Four, and us living in a higher density consciousness, will learn not to take any part in the belief of good (light) versus evil (dark) or who is right or wrong, for it is the energy of expansion. And, it encompasses all that is happening on earth in total honor and compassion.

By moving beyond the belief in good (light) and evil (dark), right and wrong, and power and control, we disappear to those who persist in duality. The word "disappear" can mean many different things – death, breaking free, or losing sight of something. It also could mean that once we reach a consciousness of a higher density, we break free from the polarized pull of the negative and positive energy of the mass consciousness. We are not a Republican or a Democrat, a conservative or a liberal anymore. We are just a Goddess that has compassion and unconditional love for those who are still playing the game of being a Republican or a Democrat, a conservative or a liberal.

A person who believes only in polarity energy will experience viruses versus health, good versus evil, right versus wrong, fear versus assurance as to their reality. On the other hand, a person who expands their consciousness beyond the belief in good (light) and evil (dark) will experience their reality with joy, happiness, healing, abundance, and all manner of grace and blessings. When we step out of mass consciousness, we become nearly invisible to those who do not understand where we are in the evolution of our soul.

Evolving from a lower to a higher consciousness is what the Ascended Masters call "ascension" and what religions call the "rapture." It is something that we have to choose to do for ourselves. It is not about Yeshua coming to save us or being lifted into the air by some magical force as religions teach today. Everything in the Bible is metaphorical, like air representing the mental-mind rising to higher consciousness, and the clouds representing obscurity to new truths.

Once we move past the belief in polarity energy and a three-dimensional reality, we begin to free the mind of its dualistic duties. This act alone sends trembling, shaking, and shock to the left activity of the mind, where it is associated with dualistic belief systems.

The *"tenth of the city fell in ruins,"* Revelation 11:13, relates to our memories connected to the same side of the mind. Therefore, what *"fell into ruins"* are our many dark ego-personality aspects (lifetimes) that still live in the shadows of our memory. However, if we decide to choose a better understanding of how polarity energy works in a three-dimensional world, then we can begin to take full responsibility for them. The demonstration is with the *"tenth of the city,"* as the number one (1) is associated with some of us completing our cycle of lifetimes, for which the zero (0) represents, because of the memory and believing in polarity energy as being real.

The *"seven thousand people (7,000),"* Revelation 11:13, killed during the earthquake, has nothing to do with people killed, even though an earthquake could occur with that many people dying. However, these people associated with the verse are linked to the *"seven horns"* mentioned in Revelation 5:6, as it represents the liberation of the *"seven deadly sins"* we all use in a polarity world. The expression is symbolic of our journey through the earth and three cycles of activities, for what the zeros symbolize.

For example, the number 7 represents the seven oldest belief systems, as in the "seven deadliest sins," that we have accepted and carried within memory since the time we left higher consciousness long ago. The first of the three zeros (0)00) represents us in our higher consciousness of oneness (Garden), before Adam and Eve took the metaphorical bite of the apple, where we were pure, neutral, and knew nothing about polarity energy.

The second zero (0(0)0) is associated with leaving our higher consciousness of oneness (Garden) and moving into a cycle where we accepted polarity energy as being real. Thus, we found ourselves playing in a cycle of many lifetimes using polarity energy to understand who we are and what is our purpose. Also, the second zero is about our journey through this cycle, creating many nonphysical and physical bodies that had been going on for thousands or perhaps millions of years.

The third zero (00(0)) is about us humans awakening from our hypnotic sleep state and move past theses "seven deadliest belief patterns" and into a "knowing" that we all are Christ. Thus, we, if we so choose, can move into the third cycle of expansional energy, where our energy frequency and consciousness are lifted into a higher density consciousness reality, creating to our heart's content, knowing that we are Christ, God, and the Goddess. And, in this consciousness, we would not experience pain and suffering.

It was from the seven deadliest sins that caused us to forget (died) who we were. But, once we allow the opening of the seven seals in Revelation 6:1-17 and 8:1 to occur, we can move into a new understanding about who we are, who God is, who Satan is, and what our purpose is on earth. We genetically transmitted, through reincarnation, the issues we have not yet overcome and have forgotten because the memories and lifetimes have become dead to us.

However, in this lifetime, some of us have gained enough understanding and awareness to release those "seven deadliest belief patterns *(tongues),"* if we dare to allow. Once we learn to let go of sin, family, friends, religions, businesses, and the group human consciousness who still believe in polarity energy, then we can integrate those lingering dark ego-personalities that are *"terrified"* of us because they have to give *"glory"* to this new higher understanding of Christ that we all are *(God of heaven)*.

When speaking of the second "woe" in Revelation 11:14, it represents we, in this lifetime, coming into a new expansional consciousness and understanding about why we were playing in endless space (dimensional realms) and time, measuring (reviewing) our growth in consciousness and comprehending taking full responsibility for our choices. This was necessary because the *"third woe coming soon"* represents us having patience in what we create.

The *"seventh angel,"* Revelation 11:15, has to do with our spirit-Christ body that we are living in a human body. This angel is associated with our pituitary gland or third eye, and it refers to understanding the necessity for giving strength, compassion, unconditional love, and taking responsibility for the energy that we use in our creations. The calling of the *"blowing his trumpet"* refers to the vibrational polarity energy coming into play to reveal the necessity to take full responsibility for our creations before we can be in full awareness that we are Christ.

Therefore, are you ready to take complete responsibility for what you are experiencing right now, or do you still see yourself as a victim and a sinner? If you see yourself as a victim and a sinner, or you cannot let go of the concept of right and wrong, then you are still working with polarity energy and a three-dimensional world. When Yeshua and the Ascended Masters mention the *"loud voices in heaven saying, 'The Kingdom of the world now belongs to our Lord and his Anointed,'"* Revelation 11:15, they are speaking of our mind and our ego-personalities, for they are the "Anointed One" in this lifetime that can integrate the "Christ-Messiah" to become part of our human life.

John, the Apostle, represents our ego-personality of today that is beginning to express *(hearing great voices)* unconditional love, compassion, forgiveness, and divine love *(heaven)* for self and others as the key to integrating the Christ within us. Therefore, are you ready to feel and allow these powerful forces deep within your consciousness to be heard? Are you prepared to accept "all that you are," what you have done throughout your many lifetimes, and are you ready to let it all go without shame or guilt?

The good news: Enough memories have been revealed where we can now choose to become a Christ, and the savior of our own personal world, and reign forever, or we can choose to stay in our victimhood of right and wrong. The choice is ours! Remember, *"the kingdom of the world now belongs to our Lord,"* meaning our mind, *"and his Anointed One,"* is our ego-personality of today can *"reign forever and ever."* However, that is if we have the courage to allow ourselves to become Christ in the flesh.

As we come to understand the mind transforming itself from seeing itself as the Anti-Christ to seeing itself as the "Lord of Lords," it becomes clear the "Messiah" is referring to us humans while we are operating out of the ego-physical level. This can be our awakening to a higher consciousness frequency if we are ready to allow it to come into our life. Therefore, the Messiah is a person who has learned to rebalance his/her total beingness (spirit, mind, ego forms, and gnost) as one body of consciousness.

Remember, Yeshua said, "Follow me," not worship him! It was the religions of the world that taught us to worship and follow them. As Yeshua and the Ascended Masters proclaim, the opposing energy forces do work through the twenty-four activities of the mind (left and right brain hemispheres), the physical makeup of the twelve endocrine system senses, and the twelve major systems of the physical body (Revelation 4:4). And, as this occurs, our acceptance and rejections of our light and dark creations were the first of the Earth's energy to form our memories, and now they are the first to recognize us as a Christ also (Revelation 11:17-17).

Therefore, these twenty-four left and right brain activities of the mind, the twelve endocrine system senses, and the twelve major systems of the physical body, or us in our human form, have fulfilled our promise established in Revelation 5:9. Thus, *"worthy are you to receive the scroll and to break open its seals, for you were slain and with your blood."* We have paid the price to know Christ is that of the self, and all that we have to do now is accept and allow the Christ within us to illuminate.

The "twenty-four elders" became the forces of the dark, light, and our nature in many earthly lifetimes; therefore, they became the faces of our many ego-personality aspects for many lifetimes. Now, they stretch *(prostrated)* out to us in other non-physical realms, like a priest giving himself to Christ, knowing we have the courage to bring them all home to the self, the Christ within.

Because all energy comes from one central authority, our "I AM" Christ spirit body (like the central sun of the universe), then we have to learn to take complete responsibility for our creations, nothing can be left out, or our "third eye" will not open for our ego-personality consciousness to be heard. (See Revelation 4:4 for details.)

Revelation 11:18 speaks of the *"nations raging, and your wrath has come, and the time for the dead to be judged."* This sounds scary! But, Yeshua and the Ascended Masters are speaking of our fixed physical state of consciousness and the collectiveness of light and dark ego-personality aspects of our Oversoul, and how they are tied to the various centers of our memory cells throughout the physical body. These light and dark ego-personality aspects of us became the natural way for our Oversoul to find wisdom through the experiences of the human form in different lifetimes. The good and bad, king and slave, rich and poor, male and female, and all parts of many religions, and what they taught, have become part of our Oversoul's desire to express and experience.

Therefore, we are the divine being who recognized the potential of conscious choice long ago, and we used choice to manifest many light and dark personality aspects (lifetimes) to go beyond all that was unknown by our "I AM" Christ consciousness, such as polarity energy. And now, every one of those ego-personality aspects, where we believe we played out as good and evil, king and slave, rich and poor, male and female, have served a sacred purpose for our Oversoul. And now, know that every aspect of us, no matter how we judge them, has served us well.

Whether we created an aspect to be temporary or to linger in nonphysical realms for millions of years, each one of them provided our Oversoul with great experiences and overwhelming wisdom. Thus, every aspect we created must return home to the self! When those ego-personality aspects do return home to the integrating super-aspect that some of us are in this lifetime, they will dissolve back into the oneness of our consciousness of today. And this will bring us the wisdom, joy, and the celebration of life as we come into a realization of the "I AM That I AM," a Christ also. This realization also helps us leave behind all judgment, wounds, and imbalances, and therefore, the only thing left is the wisdom learned.

Your Oversoul has chosen you to be the super ego-aspect in this lifetime, if you allow, to integrate all other aspects of you. And it has to be done while you are in human consciousness.

The *"holy ones"* in Revelation 11:18 are those ego-personality aspects that you may have created just to test a theory, and then integrate instantly. Of course, the ones *"that fear your name"* are those dark ego-personality aspects that do not like you or respect you because they look upon you as a weak person. The masters say weak because those dark ego-personality aspects of our past are very much confused and angry with us because we keep on pushing them away by keeping on lying and denying their existence.

You have forgotten that you created lifetimes of committing rape, being cruel and evil, and betraying others. And now, you do not want to own up to what you have created. And because of it, many of these dark ego-personality aspects have become fragmented because you gave up the responsibility for them. This is the definition of not taking full responsibility for them and yourself. Instead, you decided to pass these ego-personalities over to a false God or to some church, preacher, or government who would take the responsibility.

How can those dark ego-personality aspects of you come back home to your Oversoul if you are not home (aware) to accept them? How can you be whole again if you keep on refusing to take complete responsibility for them? Maybe you can feel these aspects around you, and therefore, you fear the thought of reincarnation. Those dark ego-personality aspects that generate fear throughout your body are what frustrates you to no end. You become confused because you think you are under the umbrella of some God or church, and therefore, you cannot be harmed.

However, to our surprise, we find ourselves dealing with cancer, accidents, poverty, bad luck, and many other unexplained happenings that we do not like. We even write off these unexplained happenings by believing that it is God's will about why we are suffering. It is time to open our eyes, heart, and mind, to have compassion and show unconditional love for them, evil or not because, in the end, none of them sinned. And that is when we will *"recompense our servants,"* Revelation 11:18, rewarding them by allowing them to come home to self.

When we feel their presence and their darkness around us, do not close the door of the mind and heart; just allow them in. Even though some may still be angry, they still have the spark of the radiance of their creator, you. Allow them to come in and stop fighting them because you feel fear. Do not fear them! Even if you have strange dreams at night, all that they are doing is testing your love and sincerity. They just want to know if it is safe to return home to you.

Know in Revelation 11:18, the *"wrath has come, and the time for the dead to be judged,"* represents you have already paid the price for those lifetimes where you played in the dark. You paid the price by moving on to other lifetimes where you reaped with profound sowing and reaping, and the only thing left to do now is to let go of your fear, your shame, and your guilt associated with them, for you are not them or that lifetime anymore. It is through fear, guilt, and shame that keeps you punishing them *(the wrath)* and yourself by not acknowledging them as being part of your Oversoul. You judge them as not being part of you instead of looking at them as choices made a long time ago to experience life.

However, remember, this is about compassion and unconditional love without judgment, and not trying to force or change them: no persuading, no bargaining, and no praying for them. By praying, you are saying that you are not Christ or the super aspect to bring them home, back to higher understanding. Just let these wounded ego-personality aspects of your past know that you are breathing deeply, that you are living, and that you will stay here in the present moment and welcome them home to your Oversoul when they are ready. If you feel someone talking in your head, wanting to ask questions, then simply reply: "'I AM That I AM' a Christ also, and welcome home!"

Know that the *"flashes of lightning, rumblings, and peals of thunder, an earthquake, and a violent hailstorm,"* Revelation 11:19, refers to our "I AM" Christ consciousness showing us who we are in the scheme of things. And, like a *"flash of lightning,"* our "I AM" Christ emits a repetitive frequency feeling within our heart where we can feel our completeness coming together as "one body of consciousness." Know that *"God's temple in heaven was opened"* refers to our physical consciousness of today opening up to our higher "I AM" Christ consciousness in asking us if we are ready to receive our inheritance.

Know that the *"rumblings and peals of thunder"* are those ego-personality aspects of long ago that are confused and tormented, waiting for us to forgive them and accept them as our creations. And when we have the first indication of our acceptance, our energy frequency will rise to a new expanded level, and we can get excited about opening up to this New Expansional Energy of Four.

Therefore, what you choose today is yours! You do not have to be smart, poor, or rich. All you need is to allow your "I AM That I AM" to be recognized as you.

Chapter 27

YOU ARE A DIVINE BEING

What is a Divine Being? A Divine Being is all gazillions upon gazillions of us souled beings that burst forth from the "oneness of consciousness" and into an individualized awakening consciousness that had no idea of our beginning or who we were. We souls were always there in consciousness, but we were unaware of our consciousness being the creator of our desire to answer the question, "Who am I?" The question arose because we souls did not even have any form to us, not even light in the beginning stages of consciousness. It wasn't until we souls created a "universal omnipresent mind field of pure unbiased energy" that became part of our consciousness and appeared as "light" before we seemed to become complete as a divine being.

That is when our spirit illuminated as the "absolute" supreme Mother Goddess of unquestionable and unchangeable deity that created energy (God) to use for our creations to answer the question, "Who am I?" It was us souled beings that created God and not that God created us. When we souled beings learned of our consciousness creating this God energy of light (Father), with having no beginning or end (limitless energy), and that is when we souls awoke to the individualized "I AM" Christ consciousness as to "who we are in consciousness."

The confirmation to this is found in Revelation 12:1, as *"a great sign appeared in the sky, a woman clothed with the sun, and the moon under her feet, and on her head a crown of twelve stars."* The *"sign appearing in the sky"* represents the overwhelming high level of intelligence that is found within our own "I AM" Christ Consciousness (Goddess). Because of our

"I AM" it caused all that we see today as energy, stars, planets, universes, galaxies, moons, vegetation, animals, fish of the seas, birds, and let us not forget our mind of a mental nature, the positive (male) and negative (female) and ego, as it makes us the total Goddess of the highest.

Let us remember that males and females are not of two different energies. It just seems that way because of the spiral of the energy going to the right and the other going left. And yet, it is just pure energy. Our mind of a mental nature gives it a twist to give us the illusion that it is two different energies. And since we souls are the collectiveness of the Godhead, then divine intelligence is not limited or devoted to one super-entity sitting on a throne.

It comes down to understanding that divine intelligence is clothed with a "universal omnipresent mind field of pure unconditional energy of light" that we souls can tap into at any time to create or manifest our desires. As this is the meaning behind *"woman clothed with the sun."* The woman is our "I AM" Christ consciousness and how it is surrounded by very high intelligence. And, since all creations come from the "I AM" within all souls, then all that is created has a consciousness to it, either animated and active in spirit or inanimate and non-active, where there is consciousness but no spirit to activate it to give it life.

For example, a rock, tree, house, car, table, etc., all have consciousness, but that is all that they know they are, a rock, tree, house, car, or table, for none of these have individuality to make choices. It is only souled beings that have the divine spark that can give life to these things, including energy. Therefore, all that is consciousness represents women or females.

"The moon under her feet" represents our mind-soul (moon) and ego (feet) and how they get their energy of light from the "I AM" Christ consciousness (sun). And since our mind-soul and ego get all of their energy (light) from our "I AM" (the sun), then our mind-soul and ego are the very foundation that we build all our creations upon, both positive and negative. It is also with our mind-soul and ego, where we learn the results of our choices and consciousness acts that transform into wisdom.

However, because our mind looks upon this source as dual-energy and a matter of principle of law, it then reflects our intelligence as being intellectual. Thus, power seems real but is not. And because of this reflection of our higher intelligence is being misinterpreted, our ego response to it by allowing it to think it has power. And this is why *"on her head a crown of twelve stars"* correlates with the "twelve signs of the Zodiac," where it represents the "twelve senses in the physical body."

Channeling of the Ascended Masters on the Apocalypse

Let me explain the five physical senses and the seven endocrine system senses and how they associate with the "seven planetary influences." The "twelve senses" are not only associated with the magic number of twelve itself, but they are also the basis for the twelve tribes of Israel and the forces behind the choosing of the twelve disciples of Yeshua, as they are both part of the mind (left and right Hemisphere activities). The twelve stars can also mean that our "I AM" at its core:

1. Is in the form of consciousness
2. Is part of universal intelligence
3. Is expansional
4. Is divine
5. Is the source of life
6. Is unchangeable, unconditional and multidimensional
7. Is quiet and patient
8. Is or has an imagination
9. Is very compassionate
10. Is very expressive
11. Has the same authoritative power as Goddess; thus, we are all equal in power/authority
12. Is very aware of its purity/neutrality (without sin)

And with all of these wonderful attributes of the Goddess, we gave life to versions of ourselves to feel life, record thoughts, and to experience our choices. Thus, we must also take full responsibility for the actions and creations we manifest to experience. If we consistently believe in good and evil as being real, then we will continually feed our mind and soul region of responsibility (Eve), a belief system passed on to our "I AM" to give those beliefs life to be played out either in this lifetime or the next.

Remember, whatever we think, express, and manifest in life has to be stored somewhere. It cannot be stored within our masculine side, because that is the part of us that makes choices and experiences life. Therefore, it is held or stored by our feminine side, the soul. The example of this is found in Revelation 12:2, where *"she was with child and wailed in pain as she gave birth."*

This represents our divine souled being (the "I AM" consciousness) giving birth to a son-daughter (our mind-soul consciousness of responsibility), and when the gazillion of spirits (souls) came into an awakening in consciousness, we souls, as a group consciousness, generated thought patterns that combined our "I AM," our mind-soul, and our ego that caused a huge flash of light that symbolized the big bang theory.

Therefore, in an instant, like the twinkling of an eye, our spirit gave life to a mind and energy that ended up as representing time and space.

And, as mentioned in the beginning stages of our awareness, time and space had not existed or even a thought as of yet. But once the mind-soul and ego became part of our "I AM" spirit, transforming us into a three-dimensional being, we then contemplated the many questions about:

"Who am I?"
"What is my purpose?"
"What can I create?"
"What more is there other than consciousness and light?"

That is when our "I AM" spirit said to itself, "I AM" That I AM," a Goddess in my own right, and therefore what consciousness does, I find myself as the "I AM?" And, with that thought being generated by the gazillions upon gazillions of us souls, time and space instantaneously appeared as darkness (nothingness). That is when we souls turned this nothingness into everything that we see today, including every potential that could be thought or dreamed up, no matter if it was good or bad.

From these multitudes of potentials, good and bad, which were brought forth through expression, we souled beings, symbolized by the feminine side of self because of consciousness, then acted as one body of consciousness and gave birth to every form of a potential, idea, and reality, physical and nonphysical. In effect, when our "I AM" spirit gave life to the mind-soul and ego, we forgot (died) about being God, Goddess, Christ, and the Lord of Lords, as this symbolizes our first death.

This gave us souls a chance to come to a physical world and be born again and again until we were resurrected from this first death. Being "born again" was referred to by Yeshua when he spoke to Nicodemus, *"Except a man be born again, he cannot see the kingdom of God"* (John 3:3). Yeshua also said, *"that which is born of the flesh is flesh, and that which is born of the Spirit is spirit"* (John 3:6). Thus, the birth of a child is that of our mind-soul, and we came to earth to play out some of those billions upon billions of potentials to experience as our reality.

Yeshua, *"that which is born of the flesh is flesh"* signifies "that which is born of energy is energy" and *"that which is born of the spirit is spirit,"* which signifies "that which is born of consciousness is consciousness." Thus, the *"wailing aloud in pain"* in Revelation 12:2 is our "I AM" spirit giving life to our mind-soul (Adam-Eve) and our ego personality (serpent) to play upon Mother Earth, giving birth to multitudes of ego-personalities (physical and nonphysical) to experience life. Therefore, the pangs of this birth in consciousness created many different realities where we now experience our choices, trials, and tribulations that come from the applications of our belief systems.

Free will become the basis of our choices here on earth, and it will continue until we reach an awakening that we are more than human. We were not given free will as something separate from our divine will because the very essence of our soul is working from a divine plan that we created for us to follow to remember again. Recall, our mind was created in the image and likeness of our "I AM" Christ consciousness, other than it being of a mental nature. Thus, once our mind and ego were created, then our mind-soul could not uncreate our "divine plan" just as our "free will" cannot be taken away.

However, "free will" can be stolen from us by other souls where our "divine plan" cannot. Since our "free will" was a manifestation of our mind-soul, we feel that our "I AM's" divine plan is something outside of us and, therefore, the reason why we interpreted it as losing something. This is why it comes hard for some people to give up their "free will" to follow their own "divine plan." It is all about learning to trust in integrating our mind-soul, free will, and our many distinctive ego personalities, with our "I AM" divine plan.

It is just that we, from the mind and ego levels, do not feel this "divine plan" is part of our total consciousness. We feel instead, on an emotional level, that we are giving up our free will, so we rebel against our "I AM's" divine plan. Thus, we keep our consciousness focused on following the rules of power, control, and polarity energy that is very much opposing. We have forgotten our divine plan in favor of following "free will" as something real, and yet, it can be lost just by believing in duality.

Because of forgetting who we are, we continue to create a kingdom of our own in the name of "free will" to learn our true "divine plan." The real battle is not about God and Satan, or good and evil, or who is right or wrong. It is between what we all believe is our "free will" and our "divine plan," and the thought of having to give something up, not realizing our "free will" is just an extension of our "divine plan" to become awakened to our divinity. And, this battle within is manifested through the division of our mind found in Revelation 4:4, the right and left-brain hemispheres.

This battle of wills is what is known as the battle of Armageddon, found in Revelation 16:16, which I will discuss later. In the first creation (garden), we discovered that it was going to take more than just playing with positive (light) and negative (dark) if we wanted to feel and experience all possibilities of life. We needed something that would help us forget about being God, Goddess, and Christ. So, our spirit came up with the idea of creating an ego-consciousness that would manifest a lower version of itself called personality aspects to defy our true nature, thus interrupting the energy flow coming from our "I AM" Christ consciousness as something dark and unknown, which is why we fear the dark and the unknown.

With the understanding that we had in the beginning, it was the only thing that could be done for us to experience all possibilities of life. Therefore, it was our rebellious ego-personality nature (symbolized by the serpent in the garden) that became the solution for discovering the self. It was, and is, the three-dimensional consciousness that helped us forget who we are as a Christ by having the ego part of us create such a revolutionary personality of defiance *(serpent)* that we blamed both sides of self, the positive-masculine (Adam) side and our inner, negative-feminine (Eve) side. That is, in fact, where the first battle in higher consciousness (heaven) began, as it was with our mind-soul and our ego.

After many creations using the energy of polarity, we souls finally moved to a place in consciousness where we decided and believed we were separate for God, Goddess, and Christ. However, it was in mind only! That was the time when we souls decided if we did not like what we created, we could just blame it on this rebellious ego-personality part of ourselves that we all call Satan or the Devil. This gave us souls the opportunity to make it easier on ourselves not to take the blame for creations that looked to us as wrong or bad.

Therefore, it was us souled beings that have brought Satan to life by misinterpreting our consciousness acts, the energy that surrounds us, our beliefs, and our experiences. We souls, eons ago, have created an attitude based on external (illusionary) psychological or emotional factors that had us believing we were separate from our choices. This influenced our belief systems and our divine plan so that now what we interpret as our free will to choose has cost us the loss of our memory to whom we indeed are at the divine level.

From the study of our ego-personality, the *"red dragon"* in Revelation 12:3, represents us, humans, from the mind and ego level, denying any creations that we believe are contrary to perceiving ourselves as someone of a dependable nature and, therefore, as something that is not our fault. And since the *"red dragon"* is allied with our mind and ego-personality, then the "seven heads" are associated with the "seven most deadly repetitive vibratory forces" that keep us locked into a belief of sin and punishment.

And the "seven heads" of the dragon are the "seven repetitive" sins that influence us through the endocrine system of the physical body that we repeat over and over in different lifetimes. And these "seven heads" are:

1. Sadness
2. Anger
3. Lust for Power
4. Envy
5. Pride
6. Greed
7. Laziness

The *"ten horns"* are again associated with our mind and ego-personality (Satan) working out of a mental nature where we are journeying through the vibrational energy of polarity in the physical world over and over, lifetime after lifetime, until we awaken or return to our oneness again. The number "ten" (10) relates to the vibrational energy of sin and punishment coming in from our five physical senses ((i) taste, (ii) smell, (iii) touch, (iv) sight, and (v) hear, and how they relate to what we receive from the five lower kings ((i) gonad, (ii) Lyden, (iii) adrenal, (iv) thymus and (v) thyroid)).

We all carry within us these "five physical senses" and the "five lower kings" as we journey through the cycle of the mental-astral and physical earth plane until we return to our oneness as a sovereign being. By the numbers 1 through 9 and back to one (1 or 10) again, it is about us humans completing our cycle of lifetimes through the astral-mental and physical realms over and over, again and again, until we learn that we are indeed the creator of our experiences, good and evil, thus our reality. And therefore, we must take full responsibility for what we are choosing and experiencing without any exceptions.

It is not so much as going back to oneness as it was before leaving higher consciousness (heaven) because that is impossible because of the creation of the mind-soul and ego. And, it is not going back to the Garden as religions interpret as Heaven, for that is what we have been trying to do for eons of time. We are not children who are lost in some forest trying to find our way back home. It is about going back into our own oneness, as in our spirit, mind-soul, and ego, as a divine being and a Goddess in our own right. Therefore, the *"red dragon"* is there to help us complete our cycle of sowing and reaping in such a way we move forward to this awakening of being Christ, God, and the Goddess.

The *"seven diadems"* represent what we have achieved as our "devilish crowns." And we did it by lowering our consciousness frequency to an opposing, fighting, and a devouring consciousness that created a personality perception of free will (represented by Ishmael) to become our teacher of discovery and responsibility. And, it was through "free will" that gave us the means to choose or reject those dualistic influences that arouse the physical body at the gonad level that effects what the *"ten horns"* represent.

These *"seven devilish crowns"* are also known as the "seven seals" in Revelation 6:1-17 & 8:1) that we sealed up within us, for they are again:

1. Belief in separation
2. Being self-aware
3. Belief in Satan/duality
4. Belief in sin/guilt
5. Belief in suffering
6. Belief in a savior
7. Knowing we are a Christ also

Because of the "I AM's" deep desire to find the meaning of life, it gave life to a personality consciousness and free will that would pull us toward a belief in separation and survival. From this level, we created a vibrational wave of energy that brought in these "seven belief systems" that, in the end, caused our first death (the forgetting of our true identity).

From Job 1:12, *"the Lord said to Satan, 'Behold, all that he has is in your power; only do not lay a hand upon his person.' So, Satan went forth from the presence of the Lord."* Job 2:6, *"and the Lord said to Satan, 'he is in your power; only spare his life.'"* These are the two charges to Satan about his tormenting of Job. And, from the context of these two verses, we can see that Satan is a servant to God.

In other words, from the beginning, we desired to learn more about ourselves as a Goddess, about life, and polarity energy. Therefore, it was us, souls, from the "I AM" level, who passed down all authority to our mind and our defiant ego-personality (Satan-Beast) for them to become a servant to our "I AM," the Goddess. This is reflected in the story of humankind upon the earth as it shows the high-minded nature of our own "I AM" Christ, as recorded by John 3:16. *"For God so loved the world that he gave his only Son so that everyone who believes in him might not perish but might have eternal life."*

The story of Adam and Eve brings to life a belief system of blaming someone or something that is not real rather than taking full responsibility for their own actions. Hence, out of themselves, Adam and Eve (representative of man's mind and soul) created an image of Satan to blame, but the image was totally their own creation. And, that creation was an ego-personality that became very contrary and revolutionary (symbolized by Cain) where all memory was lost to their connection to the "I AM."

After we left the first creation (higher consciousness (garden)), our contrary and revolutionary ego-personality became not only the principal holder of our god energy of light but also the point of focus for our individuality. Therefore, our ego-personality in the flesh became an illusionary character called Satan (Beast), and this Satan (ego) filled our consciousness with such fear that we developed a belief that we are not worthy of God's forgiveness or his presence. This fear and this Satan character (this ego-self) can be released once we, from the human mind and ego level, begin to take full responsibility for everything in our life.

It was because of the need to place blame, the mythical story of Adam and Eve's bite of the apple, that characterizes a distinctive ego-personality within us all that developed into a very abusive, stubborn, and controlling factor in forming our thought patterns filled with falsehoods that eventually became our truths. However, since Satan (Beast) is symbolic of our ego-personality consciousness in the flesh at any given lifetime, then surely this same ego-personality deep within has a belief that someday it, too, would be saved from itself, just as we in our mental state would be saved.

Job 1:1 says, *"In the land of Uz there was a blameless and upright man named Job, who feared God and avoided evil."* The *"land of Uz"* is mentioned in Jeremiah 25:20, and it represents that we have a mind-soul and an ego-personality consciousness of such an imagination, concentration, growth, and purpose that advises and makes firm what we believe to be our truths. Therefore, the process of our thoughts and beliefs through which we finally arrive at a conclusion (free will) is then established within our ego-personality consciousness as being either true or false. Thus, the meaning of the *"land of Uz"* fits perfectly with the lessons Job's experience teaches us.

When Job had an argument with his three friends and then finally arrived at the truth, it produced a great change in his life. Therefore, this argument depicts the inner workings of our "I AM" spirit, our mental mind-soul, and our outer controlling ego-personality consciousness (representative of the three friends) as coming into a spiritual awakening about how we experience various phases of our physical ego-personality before we arrive at the real truth about Christ, God, Satan, and the Goddess.

The dragon's *"tail sweeping away a third of the stars in the sky and [hurling] them down to the earth,"* Revelation 12:4, is not about a country or government firing off atomic missiles or asteroids visiting earth. It does, however, represent our three-dimensional consciousness eons ago entering the physical earth to work out our false beliefs about "who we are," using the dragon's fire of sowing and reaping to become balanced. The earth is our hell! And the "dragon" is the fire we all experience, sowing and reaping.

What we brought with us in this three-dimensional phase of our consciousness was satanic like opposing vibrational energy where the belief in evil became part of our emotional body, etheric body, and physical body *(third of the stars)*. This was when we moved our consciousness from having highly intelligent ideas *(sky)* to having very low, evil *(dark)* ideas while incarnating here on earth.

These satanic vibrations of very aggressive and evil ideas then became composed of our positive and negative energy in order to leave our higher consciousness (heaven) and to experience life in a dualistic way. This was to experience our choices (free will) and what it feels like to be operating in much slower energy. Thus, the "fall of consciousness" is symbolic of our mind-soul, our ego, and our many defiant ego personalities (Satan and his army) being kicked out of higher consciousness (Heaven) so our false beliefs could be played out. And yet, all of it is an illusion!

"The dragon standing before the woman about to give birth," Revelation 12:4, portrays how we, as a Goddess, along with all of our false beliefs about Satan being part of our ego-personality in the flesh, brought in the idea of evil and darkness as something outside of us. Thus, Mother Earth became clothed with our energy of polarity (duality) for the challenging of our false ideas of being less than Goddess in the flesh. And, because of these false beliefs, we owe a debt to the flesh and also to Mother Earth that we all have been paying off lifetime after lifetime.

"To devour her child when she gave birth," Revelation 12:4, represents our "I AM" Christ consciousness and Mother Earth giving birth to a physical body where we souls were born into polarity energy that will *"devour"* us if we are not careful with our beliefs when it comes to the blame game. We have forgotten that the energy we brought with us on earth is ours, each of us, and our individualized consciousness is what ignites this energy.

It is our consciousness that puts our energy to work for us. And, if we carry many false beliefs about what is good and evil, and then blame our suffering on someone else, then we risk being devoured by this same energy as it brings us through many, many lifetimes learning to take full responsibility for the energy we use for our creations. Remember, we cannot experience pain or suffering unless we have created it somewhere during our many lifetimes believing that our suffering is not our fault.

Channeling of the Ascended Masters on the Apocalypse

This is all confirmed with Revelation 12:5, "*She gave birth to a son, a male child, destined to rule all the nations with an iron rod. Her child was caught up to God and his throne.*" When looking at this verse, we assume the male child is Jesus (Yeshua), and yet, it represents the mind becoming Christ-like. For example, *"this one shall be called Woman, for out of 'her man' this one has been taken"* Genesis 2:23. Mother Mary and the birth of Yeshua explains the meaning of Genesis 2:23 and the male child and how he is to *"rule all nations with an iron rod,"* Revelation 12:5.

First, let's look at Mother Mary (she) and how she represents our "I AM" Christ consciousness giving birth to a Son, symbolized by our mind, the positive/masculine side of the self without the help of a physical man (our ego). Remember, it is only our ego that rides the rails of incarnations, and our mind is always there in the flesh but transparent.

The Bible states that Mother Mary was seeded by God and not from physical man, which correlates with Genesis 2:23, for out of this "universal omnipresent mind field of pure virgin God energy of light," our "I AM" Christ consciousness (symbolized by Mother Mary) conceived an idea and produced a son, a likeness of self, called our mind of a masculine nature. This is symbolized by the birth of Yeshua. And, the reason Yeshua took on the appearance of a white male in the physical sense and depicting himself as the Son of God, was to represent that our mind is pure and is part of the divine consciousness.

Mother Mary not only represents our "I AM" Christ essence, but she also represents the feminine part of us that split our consciousness into a dualistic consciousness that birthed a masculine side of us. It was for the purpose of experiencing a mental part that has the authority to create images of the self using energy that shows up as opposites (good and bad). This again is confirmed by Mother Mary giving life to a Son that illustrates how we souls became part of an outer mental mind that carries a masculine-positive energy that creates belief systems while our feminine-negative soul consciousness of responsibility holds those beliefs until the masculine side of us chooses what beliefs to manifest for us to experience.

The reason Mary conceived Yeshua (her Son) without the help of a physical man is because our physical form was conceived (imagined) by our controlled ego-personality nature (Satan) and not from our "I AM" Christ consciousness, even though our "I AM" Christ consciousness gave it life energy. It was our outer positive-masculine aspect that chose to give life to another portion or personality of us called the ego and represents the Satan principle.

Our outer mental version (her child, the Son) mimicked our "I AM" Christ consciousness and used that same pure virgin God energy of light to manifest an opposing ego personality that allowed us to enter earth in a physical body. But what happened? Our newly formed, opposing ego-personality made us feel even more independent than we did when we were working from a higher consciousness of oneness (Garden). This is why our controlled ego-personality consciousness is now the aspect of us that partakes in the physical world. This is the answer to the mystery behind Mother Mary conceiving Yeshua without the help of a man because physicality here on earth is always derived from the ego principle of disobedience (Satan).

Remember, Satan (our ego-personality) and our mind (the Anti-Christ) were kicked out of higher consciousness (Garden). How could we experience life and learn about polarity energy if we knew we are Christ, God, and the Goddess that holds an everlasting divine consciousness? It took the masculine side of our mind having all authority to create and manifest the billions and billions of good and bad potentials to learn wisdom. And, it took our inner feminine soul consciousness of responsibility to hold those beliefs of good and evil over many lifetimes or until our mind was ready to manifest them to experience.

However, this is what we have been doing now for many, many lifetimes. And now, we have come to that place in consciousness where our ego-personality here on earth can inherit its place upon the throne (divinity). But when our outer mind is ready to become the Christ man-child who is *"destined to rule all the nations (our memories) with an iron rod,"* Revelation 12:5.

This verse in revelation is the first sign of a new beginning for our ego-personality becoming the super aspect that has come to earth to awaken us to our own divinity, and that we are the Christ coming down out of the clouds of ignorance to learn the real truth that we are a divine being. Thus, take hold of yourself and learn to govern your memories *(nations)* with the authority of a Christ, for you are a sovereign God-Goddess in your own right.

Use this study of Revelation like an "iron rod" in this lifetime and take our power back like an ascended master and integrate all of the many light and dark ego-personality aspects of ourselves that we have given life. This includes our mind and all the facets of our stubborn ego nature (Satan). And, once we have integrated all that we are, then the *"iron rod"* becomes the symbol for our ego-personality of today becoming awakened, and that is when we realize that we have been under the control of others.

And, in Revelation 12:5, *"her child was caught up to God and his throne,"* it is not that we will be taken up in the sky to meet up with Yeshua, but we will meet up with our own "I AM" Christ consciousness, as we learn that we are a divine being. We will also learn that we are the savior who is to come like a flash of lightning to claim all our many light and dark ego-personality aspects and integrate them as "one body of consciousness." And, this was ordained even from the beginning, because we are the one called the "first Son of God."

When we come to this realization, we will understand the wisdom of the words written in the Bible and how it has led us to a knowing that we have followed our divine plan right along, for we are the one that wrote our own story to follow becoming a sovereign Goddess in our own right.

Out of our own "I AM" Christ consciousness, we split our consciousness, as one side of us is of a positive (male), and the other side is of a negative (female) consciousness. In other words, "bone of my bone" in Genesis represents "energy comes from energy," and "flesh of my flesh" represents "consciousness comes from consciousness." And, we thought we were using "free will" without realizing we have been following our divine plan

Chapter 28

THE CONFLICT AMONG CONSCIOUSNESS, OUR MIND, AND EGO-PERSONALITIES

Revelation 12:7-8 mentions, *"war broke out in heaven; Michael and his angels battled the dragon,"* and when the *"dragon and its angels fought back, they did not prevail and there was no longer a place for them."* This war in heaven was not so much a place; it was the war we had within ourselves between our consciousness, our mind, and our ego-personality of defiance that ended up where all souled beings fell from a higher frequency consciousness (heaven) to a much lower state of consciousness that carried a very low energy frequency (earth).

When this happened, instead of being connected to higher consciousness, we looked upon our mind-soul and ego as the source of our intelligence, and that caused us to create a physical universe and a physical world to play upon using polarity energy *(dragon)* as something real. The name *"Michael"* represents our divine inspiration and a realization of the all-conquering authority of the "I AM" Christ consciousness (the Goddess) with its truth guiding us while we fell into consciousness and energy that set the table for us to learn about polarity energy, consciousness, our mind-soul, and our many ego-personalities.

Therefore, it was us souled beings working together as one that called forth the forces of an external expression apart from the source of life, the "I AM," to feel and experience our mind-soul, ego, and our beliefs in very dense energy. The battle we encountered within ourselves, on a three-dimensional level, is when we gave in to polarity energy *(dragon)* that was so strong that our thoughts of divine inspirations and truth *(Michael)* lost its ground within our higher consciousness (heaven).

Because of the many strong beliefs we had about polarity energy being real, these beliefs then had no stronghold within our higher consciousness and therefore had to remain as part of our mind-soul and ego levels of consciousness. We set up the cross-currents within our higher consciousness to experience life from the perspective of polarity energy instead of using pure neutral energy and consciousness for our creations.

Therefore, the battle seemed like a divine, internal visitation for us souls to release the natural forces of positive and negative in the flesh. This dual opposing energy *(dragon)* became the universal conflict illustrated by the war between the Lord (our mind of the divine) and the Lord of Darkness (our defiant ego-personality-Satan) and the testing of polarity energy that light and dark bring to us here on earth.

It was because of our opposing and stubborn ego nature (the beast) that our higher divine state of consciousness *(heaven)* had to place these belief patterns of good and evil into a holding mental mind-soul consciousness of responsibility for expressing, learning, and experiencing, until such a time when the wisdom and the memories of those choices can be integrated with the "I AM" Christ consciousness.

Helped by our divine mind (the Son) and the inspiration of truth being universal as we grow in consciousness *(Michael)*, we cast those belief patterns in light and dark out into an outer ego-personality consciousness that eventually has become part of a physical world. This is why our ego-personality aspects seem to serve the dark, but they are serving the light as well because the light and the dark together make the difference in bringing us clarity and transparency when all is said about them. (*"huge dragon, the ancient serpent, who deceived the whole world was thrown down to earth and its angels with it,"* Revelation 12:9).

Revelation 12:9 represents not only the Devil or Satan; it is also about your opposing stubborn ego-personality perceiving power and consciousness as having the ability to control and influence others to bow down to your ideas as if your ideas are better than anyone else's ideas. When we express ideas that are of a false perception about consciousness, power, and energy, then we set up the forces of sowing and reaping within us that generates only ego-personality aspects of us that create thoughts of good and evil to be played out here on earth. And, from this perspective, this becomes like a poison in our physical body that creates the suffering we experience today. Therefore, all our suffering is confined to the physical earth and the many lower astral non-physical realms.

The *"angels were thrown down with it,"* Revelation 12:9, represents your many ego-personality lifetimes, light and dark, that you have created to serve you in your quest to learn about consciousness, energy, choices, wisdom, and responsibility. Thus, you have had many ego-personality lifetime aspects that have played in the dark and have played in the light. And now, some of these dark ego-personality aspects are desiring to integrate with you, the self, in this lifetime.

By learning we can create different ego-personality aspects of ourselves to hide from us because of what they created; this allows us to understand how we are indeed a highly creative divine being that had to set up an avenue to take responsibility. And, once we understood the principle of our consciousness and how energy works, we found that we could no longer blame others or things for what we created. When we realize that we are the ones who created what we are experiencing today, then know we have created it all, even if what we are experiencing right now is not our fault.

When we awaken to consciousness and understand that we are the creator of what happens to us, that is when we will learn that there is no such thing as mistakes or accidents. And, to help us understand our ego-personality aspects, all we have to do is feel them as part of our energy and consciousness. And, once we dive into that deep feeling, don't fear them. Just allow yourself to experience this fear, and that is when we will feel their purpose. Once we feel their purpose and then accept them without judgment, that is when they will integrate with us.

It is about having total acceptance and compassion and welcoming them back home without judgment. After all, you paid the price for what you (they) did in that lifetime; therefore, allow yourself to let go of the guilt and shame that you feel deep within. When you learn to let go of old, dogmatic beliefs, you create a safe space for the other parts of you to integrate with you, thus bringing your energy and consciousness back into total balance.

The *"loud voice in heaven,"* Revelation 12:10, is our "I AM" Christ consciousness vibrating at a high level, so our many light and dark ego-personality aspects (Satan's assembly) will carry the influences of our darkest aspects to the surface so we can allow for their salvation. However, it is up to us if we wish to hear (allow) them or not in this lifetime.

The *"Kingdom of God and the authority of his Anointed"* in Revelation 12:10 is us, humans, in the flesh, from the mind level *(the anointed)*, awakening to a conscious understanding that the *"Kingdom of Goddess"* is within us as our "I AM" Christ consciousness. And, since our many ego-personality lifetime aspects *(brothers)* have been working in other dimensions without our knowledge, then *"who accuses them before (our) God day and night?"* It is the self! Before we can find the "Kingdom of Goddess" within our mind-soul and ego-personality today, we first must become aware of "consciousness."

Once we learn of "consciousness is everything," then it is up to us to adjust our mental perception about these ego-personalities of light *(day)* and those of ignorance *(night)*, and how they have been working with thoughts and belief systems that have kept them and ourselves as a slave to our personality and this polarity energy, we take as God. Thereby, we deny both these ego-personalities and ourselves the opportunity to become one again with the "I AM" Christ consciousness.

Earth has always been a place of vibrational opposing energy, and we use this vibrational energy as our playground to experience power, control, sowing and reaping, and life. But there does come a time when we say to ourselves, "I have had enough of this game of make-believe. I have learned all that I can, using polarity energy, and now the time has come for me to expand my consciousness beyond what is seen as only this lifetime."

But once we experienced many physical lifetimes, then those ego-personalities had to be played out in a physical body to feel our chosen beliefs. And, this is why our mind (*the Lamb* and the firstborn), through time and space, lifetime after lifetime, battled and conquered our many light and dark ego-personalities where they now can give *"their testimony of love for life"* and yet, *"it did not deter them from death* (because of forgetfulness)," Revelation 12:11.

As we can see, this verse shows the results of the battle between our ego-personality of a stubborn and defiant nature (Satan) and how we played them out in the Etheric realms before the earth was even created. And, if the battle of the angels (or we souled beings) had not happened first in the etheric/astral realms, as the battle in heaven is described, then the earth or physical realm would not have ever happened. Therefore, the earth as we know it is merely the unfolding of everything we souls had ever done (good and bad) in the etheric/astral realms before the earth was ever created so that we souls could work them out in the flesh.

Earth became the stage for us to work out our differences with each other and with our mind-soul and our stubborn, defiant nature (the beast part of us) until we had enough of this battling and playing in a consciousness that is asleep to energy and how it works. *"Therefore, rejoice you in heaven, and who dwell in them,"* Revelation 12:12, as this represents you and all those ego-personality aspects that are ready to reconnect to your higher "I AM" Christ consciousness.

This means nothing outside of your consciousness is real even though it feels and seems real. Therefore, power, physicality, polarity energy, and any philosophy regarding God, Satan, and sin are just illusions. Know that in the beginning, the Consciousness of Oneness (Kingdom), we souls were limited because we could not understand who we were or our relationship to other souled beings. Thus, we lacked true fulfillment and the understanding of our consciousness, life, and the purpose of our existence. So, we created a mind-soul and an ego-personality to acquire information about our existence as a divine being, and how energy works with creation.

And once we all created this polarity energy and our defiant ego-personality, we eventually learned how to fabricate the framework in which we could inflate our sense of feeling power and superior over others. This framework became known as our physicality, and it allowed us souls to go out and discover a sense of whom we are and to find our purpose for being here on earth in the flesh. Our "I AM" Christ consciousness gave us the tools needed to meet our divine plan in finding the answer to whom we are, why we are on earth, and what it felt like playing in energy that was so dense we forgot about our "I AM" Christ consciousness as being "all that is" about us.

It was through the use of polarity energy, positive and negative (symbolic of the Tree of Knowledge of Good and Evil), and our physical body, our mind-soul, and the defiant ego-personality that gave us the feeling of being masculine or feminine. This then allowed us to magnify and feel our separateness first hand so we could experience both sides of ourselves. However, the time has come for us to look at the many layers of our multiple lifetimes and stories and understand that they are the old ways of processing information, especially when desiring to learn about Consciousness, Christ, Spirit, and God as just pure energy.

It is time now for our stubborn and defiant ego-personality to give way to our divine intelligence, where we can now understand and become aware of our "consciousness" and to let go of our mental perception of ourselves, and how consciousness and energy works.

"But woe to you, earth and sea, for the Devil has come down to you in great fury, for he knows he has but a short time," Revelation 12:12. The *"woe"* factor correlates to what is being mentioned here, as it relates to our manifesting and creating an outer consciousness eons ago that became very mental

that resulted in creating a consciousness that was completely lost to physical sensations.

Because we all have a subconsciousness of an etheric level (representing the *"sea"*) that became filled with doubt and unrest, it caused us to experience multitudes of thoughts, beliefs, and ideas of power are real, and that is when we all became lost within our own consciousness. Through our subconsciousness (representative of the "sea"), our deep memories are filled with unexpressed and unformed thoughts and ideas that contain the all-potentiality of experiencing polarity energy.

However, because of our defiant ego-personality consciousness (Satan) being confined to the lower astral and physical realms, we can now only be influenced by our mind of reason, logic, and our many ego-personality aspects that are spread throughout the omniverse when we come to earth. As understood in Genesis, the need to blame something or someone became part of everyone's inherent character. From this character of our defiant ego nature, we developed a personality aspect of ourselves that became the interpreter and controlling factor in forming our opinions, beliefs, and thought patterns in which we then formed into the truths we perceive as being real today.

Therefore, Satan is kept alive because we give "him" our consciousness and energy through the belief in him, whether as a group or as an individual. Yet, this Satan character is only an illusion we all created in service to ourselves! Our experiences in the flesh are all about us (on an ego level), deceiving ourselves into believing that we are someone we are not and that someone will come and save us. And, we are doing it through a consciousness of reason, perception, and logic. It was with our defiant ego-personality from the beginning that became the central factor in blaming others, even imaginary characters like Satan and power for our problems.

Hasn't anyone ever wondered why humanity is still "lost in sin" because of something that Adam and Eve did long ago? Have we even questioned why "God" still blames Adam and Eve and their ancestors for the bite of the apple? After all, Adam and Eve's ancestors did not choose to bite the apple, so how long does humanity have to pay for Adam and Eve's sin? In fact, why would God punish Adam and Eve for just trying to understand themselves? To me, and the Ascended Masters, it is not about disobedience or that Adam and Eve have done something wrong. It is about learning the wisdom of our consciousness acts!

If God did not want Adam and Eve to experience the Tree of Knowledge of Good and Evil, then why was it in the garden? Was it there just to test our obedience to him, or was it for us to learn about consciousness and energy? It is not some God in heaven who planted this "tree of knowledge of good and bad" to test our obedience. It is about us souled beings learning that "consciousness is everything." It begins with consciousness, and then everything else follows, like our mind-soul, ego, energy, and all that comes from it. And if consciousness is everything, then it begins with "I Exist."

Consciousness is not something we mentally repeat over and over. It is something we feel and are aware of that "I Exist." Consciousness is not about our religious philosophies, our thoughts, or beliefs, or our spiritual truths, or how we even got here on earth. It is about "I Exist" independent of anything else. It is not even that we souls exist together or as one body of consciousness, though we come from the Spirit of One. It is "I Exist" as a sovereign being.

I say this because thoughts and beliefs are mental, predictable, and linear, as they follow a time sequence. Consciousness is beyond time and space, and that consciousness is not made of energy as it only activates energy. And, since there is no energy in consciousness, then confusion sets in between the two. Consciousness does not need energy or power, and therefore power is an illusion because there is no power in the non-physical realms. It is just that we humans here on earth buy into power because of status, money, and position.

Once we can understand, there is no such thing as power or energy within consciousness, that is when we will learn to set ourselves free. However, know that energy is attracted to consciousness in a very physical and mental way. We get exactly the amount of energy put into our physical creations based on our consciousness beliefs. So, be careful about what you believe in! If you believe strongly in polarity energy, good and bad, then that is the energy your consciousness will bring into your life for you to experience. It is that simple!

If you have a belief that you are the Christ, then only the energy of the Crystalline comes into your consciousness to serve you. But remember, Crystalline energy is pure and neutral. So, if you try to use it in a negative way, then you are not bringing in Crystalline energy; you brought in earth energy. The best thing you can do if you desire to experience more joy, abundance, and health is to be more conscious of your thoughts and beliefs, and how energy works around you.

If you are experiencing suffering and lack of money, then you should check your consciousness and how it activates your beliefs and thoughts that are coming from your mental consciousness. Remember, "all that you are" is your "I AM" consciousness. Everything else created is an illusion. Therefore, all that you have read and studied about money, power, the Bible, and all of its contents, are just an illusion, including what was written in the Book of Genesis and the Book of Revelation. All that is written in them is just to awaken you from your mental sleep state.

You have been on a journey to become enlightened about who you are. Because of it, you have created (by way of your mental and ego-consciousness, and through the distraction of others, including the belief in power) many parts and pieces of yourself. And now, you seek total integration of every part and piece of you to come together as one body of consciousness. And the only way you can do that is through your soul consciousness of responsibility.

There is no way you can find or understand enlightenment because all that you know about spirit and God comes from your human mind, where all your thoughts and beliefs generate from. Thus, how can you ever know the "I AM" Christ consciousness, as to all that you are, if you keep operating out from your mind of reason that believes enlightenment is something you study and search. It is not about your mind and ego anymore. It is about you coming into a newly expanded truth, so you can move forward in consciousness to meet the adult version of yourself in becoming a sovereign Christ, God, and Goddess in your own right.

Again, for the sake of clarification, you exist in consciousness only and not in your physical bodies or on earth, because both your physical body and earth are only illusions. Think of it this way. In a spiritual sense, the earth is symbolic of thought-forms, which means the earth is a world of dreams and illusions where you can look at something but not see what is there. That is how you often look at one another, unable to see what and who one really is! We judge others and ourselves by our dogmatic belief systems rather than as a Christ and Goddess who is experimenting with our own god energy of light.

Remember, divine love and neutralized energy are unconditional, totally free of all limiting perceptions of whom we are and what we have done. And, if you choose, you have the compassion within you to accept everyone exactly as they are without fault. If we can see the Christ in our worst enemy, then this God of the garden should have seen the Christ in Adam, thus forgiving him the second he disobeyed him, which is why everything in the Bible has to be taken as symbolic and not as being real.

It is to evolve to a consciousness of knowing that your Oversoul is filled with memories of everything that you have ever done. Therefore, you in your higher divine state, or you from a four-density consciousness, cannot be influenced by your many ego-personalities that work from a mind of reason. This is where most of the population is today when it comes to understanding God, Christ, and Satan. And what confirms the above is the consistency of Revelation 12:13, *"the dragon saw that it had been thrown down to earth, and it pursued the woman who had given birth to the male child."*

The *"dragon"* again refers to our biased ego-personality consciousness and how it associates itself with the polarity energy, good and evil. And since our stubborn and defiant ego-personality consciousness is the lowest of our three-dimensional consciousness, it strives hard to achieve acceptance with our mind, our soul consciousness of responsibility, and our "I AM" Christ consciousness, symbolized by the *"woman"* in the verse. Remember that the *"woman"* in Revelation 12:13 is not about an individual. She represents our soul region of responsibility and our "I AM" that brings forth what is in accord with the oneness of a neutralized consciousness that is sovereign.

It is all about accepting ourselves with no conditions, judgments, or beliefs that one is limited. Therefore, the dragon (our rebellious ego nature playing in opposing energy) does not persecute us, but it does single out the influential forces of what opposing energy is all about. Thus, this keeps us from becoming unified with our "I AM" Christ consciousness. Because of our strong belief in a Satan character that seems to be always chasing after our soul, and that some God created us, we unknowingly follow the dualistic principles of good and evil. And this is why we seem to play out our state of affairs over and over.

We suffer the wrath of what we believe to be true because it feels so real. However, since we are being exposed to Yeshua and the Ascended Masters and their message, it may be the time to regain our authority as a Christ also. And we can make this happen if we open up our mind, heart, and ego to reincarnation. Thus, giving us the avenue to integrate our spirit, mind-soul, and all our ego-personality aspects.

And, in Revelation 12:14, *"the woman was given two wings of the great eagle so that she could fly to her place in the desert."* The "woman" represents our "I AM" and soul region of responsibility, as we were given the opportunity to withdraw from the influences of polarity energy. However, as long as we, from the mind (representative of the Eagle in flight and how it stands for air/mental) keeps on believing in gratification, fear, and good and evil, and not in soul growth and reincarnation, then the influence of polarity energy loses its place with understanding consciousness and how it works with energy.

Channeling of the Ascended Masters on the Apocalypse

The *"desert"* represents our consciousness, and it is the place where "all that we understand about consciousness" comes from the mental version of self, for which the *"eagle"* represents. Our "I AM" and soul consciousness of responsibility knows where we stand in consciousness today because of our many lifetimes on earth sowing and reaping. This is why, while in the physical realm, our super consciousness and subconsciousness *(desert)* seem *"far away"* from our stubborn and defiant ego-personality consciousness *(Serpent)*, but in reality, they are only a breath away (Revelation 12:14).

"Begin taken care of," in Revelation 12:14, represents our "I AM" and our soul consciousness of responsibility that have accepted the responsibility of being the guiding influences while we play in the physical realm, and with polarity energy. And, when we move away from these higher influences, our soul consciousness of responsibility will school us in taking full responsibility for our creations as we journey through time and space, believing in polarity energy.

The *"year, two years, and a half year"* in Revelation 12:14 has the same meaning as Dan 12:7, *"for a time, and times, and half time,"* because in the end, it all equates to whether we are ready to move forward from a three-density consciousness to a four-density consciousness or not. A year has twelve months (12) and is associated with the time element. However, since there is no such thing as time, then the number 12 when broken down to its lowest value, 1 + 2 = 3. This three (3) represents how we were once part of the physical realm and how we measured our three-dimensional consciousness when it came to spiritual growth, the understanding of consciousness, and the wisdom gathered as we journeyed through time and space in many physical bodies.

The *"two years"* has 24 months and is associated with the time element. However, again since there is no such thing as time, we must add in the first year (12) to the second two years (24) since it says a *"year, two years, and a half."* In other words, 12 + 24 = 36, and when broken down to its lowest value of 3 + 6 = 9. And, what does the number "nine" (9) mean in spirit? It means completion, as nothing is higher than nine. Therefore, the nine (9) represents us souls who have been around in the flesh for many lifetimes that are now ready to move forward into a new density consciousness.

The half-year or six months (6) denotes this transformation by adding 12 + 24 + 6 = 42, then broken down to its lowest value, 4 + 2 = 6, we have the number six (6). However, this six (6), since it represents a half year (½), it represents the one over the two, meaning some of us here on earth are about to take a leap in consciousness from a three-density to a four-density consciousness while we are still part of the flesh. The number one over the two (½) represents our oneness of consciousness, and when added to the number nine (9), it adds up to number ten (10).

This means some of us have completed our time on earth using the measurement of a three-density consciousness. And, since the number two below the one half (½) represents polarity energy, it means some of us will move forward to a four-density consciousness and yet, still be part of a three-dimensional world. It is (was) because of our beliefs in polarity energy that it gave us the perception that power is real, and therefore having us feel separate from our "I AM" Christ consciousness.

How we learn to reconnect to our "I AM" is what the half ½ year is all about. It represents our leap into a new consciousness about how energy works and how we interact with it while still in the flesh. Because of our capacity to persist, endure, and give life to multiple potentials and physical lifetimes, we do eventually come to a place in consciousness where we finish our work playing in a three-density consciousness. We do come to a place in consciousness where karmic conditions no longer bound us. When we realize that good and evil, light and dark, right and wrong, do not exist, then our karmic obligations will stop immediately.

Genesis 24:22, *"When the camels had finished drinking, the man took out a gold ring weighing half a shekel, which he fastened on her nose, and two gold bracelets weighing ten shekels, which he put on her wrists."* The phrase in Genesis 24:22, *"The man took out a gold ring weighing half a shekel,"* represents this: Once you, from the mental level, have recorded enough lifetimes to understand that your wisdom *(gold)* has come from many light and dark lifetimes that you have played out on earth, then you do come to where you become free of your karmic conditions.

A *"shekel,"* Genesis 24:22, represents energy, which is limited because of its value, and how we spend or consume it, journeying through many cycles of lifetimes learning responsibility. The *"half-shekel"* represents us consuming *half* of our energy moving through experiences in the etheric/astral realms, and the other half is the physical realm. And, when considering, Genesis 24:22, *"which he fastened on her nose,"* and since "nose" is part of the face and the organ of smell, then it represents our ability to recognize things about our many lifetimes intuitively, and our time in the astral realms just by opening our awareness to them.

First, we feel the desire to know who we are. Then we must let go of all the old, dogmatic beliefs that would block that knowing. And then finally, we must let go of our fear of a God who created us and the idea that we are a sinner. Stop worrying about health, money, happiness, or being punished. Just realize that we only have been playing with energy in an opposing way to understand the principle of playing opposite to whom we indeed are as a Christ and Goddess.

This is seen with the *"bracelets"* in Genesis 24:22, as they represent an act in consciousness that caused a chain reaction that helped us align our minds, this polarity energy (wrists), and all of our ego-personality aspects of the past. This all resulted in all parts and pieces of us working together to achieve a common goal (divine plan), the desire to become an unlimited sovereign Goddess in our own right.

The *"two gold bracelets"* represents the splitting of our consciousness into contrasting forces of opposing energy, positive and negative, that work in circular movements, opposite each other, like one hand of the clock moving clockwise and the other counterclockwise. The chain symbolized by the bracelets also signifies how we are linked with every ego-personality name and story that we have ever portrayed in any given lifetime.

Chapter 29

THE BEAST AND THE ANTI-CHRIST REVEALED

Maybe this is the chapter that everyone has been waiting for, as this chapter reveals the number of the Beast and its master, the Anti-Christ. Revelation 13:1, *"Then I saw the beast come out of the sea with ten horns and seven heads; on its horns were ten diadems and on its heads blasphemous names."* It was from our mind and soul consciousness of responsibility (subconsciousness), symbolized by *"out of the sea,"* is where our defiant ego-personality *(the serpent)* became the ruling consciousness in persuading us to explore all facets of our mind and the energy of polarity, positive and negative.

It was from this ruling consciousness where we souled beings fell from higher consciousness (Garden) to a lower consciousness that became our world of sin, consequences, and torment. And, once we souled beings transformed our neutral energy into polarity energy, that is when our mind fell under a hypnotic state where our ego-personality of a defiant nature rejected all that was not of polarity, good and evil, light and dark, right and wrong.

In reference to the *"ten horns,"* Revelation 13:1, scholars and religions believe the "ten horns" are related to the ten empires of earth, and that could be, but in the spirit, they represent our "many ego-personality consciousnesses" journeying through a mental/physical cycle of many lifetimes playing with polarity energy. This cycle of a mental nature is where we souled beings participated in discovering our consciousness, our energy, our belief systems, and our choices. Then we realized that all that we were doing was rearranging our energy and consciousness into a cycle of many images of self that were not the real self.

Channeling of the Ascended Masters on the Apocalypse

An example of this can be found in the number of one (1), as in our "oneness of consciousness" is filled with many-layered images of consciousnesses of self to learn the wisdom of our choices. The zero (0) confirms how we all journey through a cycle of many ego-personality lifetimes playing with the influences and energy of polarity until we all return to our oneness of pure consciousness again. The *"horn"* represents our many ego-personalities that believe polarity energy is real.

Remember, consciousness has nothing to do with thoughts because thoughts belong to the mental and that of linear. And, since we journey in a cycle of having many ego-personalities, then we, from this mental consciousness cycle, are living our past, present, and future lifetimes simultaneously. Things we did five, ten, twenty, or thirty years ago are still being acted out in many-dimensional realms, but within the same mental cycle. Therefore, there is no past or future because everything is occurring in the present. This is also why we do not die!

However, as long as we continue down the same road of belief systems that are tied to polarity energy, and that it is real, the more we divide our consciousness and energy into more layered ego-personalities to life on earth. Allow me to repeat this; "consciousness is everything, as it all starts with consciousness, then everything else follows (created). Thus, consciousness is being aware that we exist as an "I AM," the Master, and a Christ also."

Keep in mind that "horns" are usually associated with the Devil when it comes to the Apocalypse. Therefore, the *"horns"* represent our many ego-personalities that work and believe in polarity as being real. Thus, the *"seven heads"* relate to our many ego-personalities (beast), while they are in the flesh, and are associated with the seven-endocrine systems of the physical body. And, this is where the impulses from our "I AM" are transposed into flesh impulses. Also, these seven endocrine systems of the physical body are associated with the seven churches mentioned in the Book of Revelation.

Endocrine Systems	Seven Churches
1. Gonads	1. Ephesus
2. Leydig	2. Smyrna
3. Adrenals	3. Pergamum
4. Thymus	4. Thyatira
5. Thyroid	5. Sardis
6. Pineal	6. Philadelphia
7. Pituitary	7. Laodicea

These are the seven ways that we can be influenced through the physical body, which is the endocrine system. This is how the earth and mental forces work within us while here in the physical realm.

"And on its horns were ten diadems," Revelation 13:1. These *"ten diadems"* refer to the "ten crowning influences" that come from polarity energy and how they affect our mind and ego-personalities as we move from the astral to the physical, recycling.

As the Ascended Masters have mentioned, a lifetime on earth is like wearing a shirt (physical body). And, once we are finished with that shirt, we take it off and put on another one. However, allow me to list these "ten diadems," as they are:

Mind/Mental Realm	Seven Churches
1. Perception	1. Smell
2. Gratification of appetites	2. Taste
3. Understanding	3. Sight
4. Feelings/emotions	4. Touch
5. Vibrations of duality	5. Hearing

It is our mental and ego-personalities of the astral and physical realm that exploit these "ten crowning influences" tied to polarity energy by expressing the symbolic meaning behind, *"and on its heads blasphemous names,"* Revelation 13:1, as the "seven deadliest acts in consciousness."

Let us remember verse 13:1 is speaking of the "seven heads" and not the "ten horns." Therefore, the depiction *"on its heads blasphemous names"* represent the "seven deadliest acts in consciousness" that we should overcome when making choices. And, they are presented as the "seven deadliest sins" because these acts can disrespect and reject our "I AM" Christ consciousness with a vengeance.

1. Sadness
2. Anger
3. Lust for power
4. Envy
5. Pride
6. Greed
7. Laziness

Therefore, the Anti-Christ and the Beast that is feared by the religious world is the self in expressing ourselves from the mind and our ego-personality that refuses to conform and integrate with our "I AM" Christ consciousness. And, a mind that refuses to see itself as part of the

"I AM" Christ consciousness then becomes the Anti-Christ. And, any ego-personality that refuses to change one's thoughts and beliefs about polarity energy is then the Beast in Revelation. We all fear our "I AM" Christ consciousness, and we will fight it until we learn that we are Christ.

This also means that we can release our fear once we integrate our "I AM" essence and take full responsibility for everything in our lives, including our accidents, diseases, bad relationships, and lack of money. And now, what we are hearing from deep within our subconsciousness are the voices of our many ego-personality aspects wanting to be heard. However, remember what we may not understand about these ego-personalities from our past and future at this time, as they are really not us in the present. But how often have we felt fear running down our spine and then learned later that we had nothing to fear?

This feeling is caused by those dark ego-personality aspects that are sometimes all around us. Remember, all that we are in consciousness are the ego personalities that we have created, playing in the same circle as we are now in the present. And, they are very confused and in pain because of what they chose during that particular lifetime. And, it is because of these ego-aspects of our past per se is where we have become stuck, on a mental and physical level, in this lifetime. And this is why our physical body breaks down.

Revelation 13:2 confirms that the *"beast was like a leopard,"* as this represents our defiant ego-personality in the flesh, still refusing to accept that we are a Christ in the flesh. And, like a leopard, our ego-personality will not change its spots until we learn to unify all layers of consciousnesses as "one body of consciousness."

It was from the mixtures of all our belief systems, from the mind and ego level, that created the mark behind polarity energy, and the idea of the power that took up two distinctive influences that says, we are Christ, and we are also the Anti-Christ.

The *"feet like a bear,"* Revelation 13:2, relates to our ego-personality of a defiant nature and how we look at Christ and the Anti-Christ as something outside and separate from us. A bear can stand on its two feet. And, it can be gentle or very overbearing. A bear can also devour us, rapidly and completely. Our ego-personality can get very animalistic and become very destructive, obsessed, and overpowering. Thus, leading us to believe that Christ and the Anti-Christ are two different individuals.

"And its mouth was like the mouth of a lion," Revelation 13:2 refers to us having a devouring personality that relates to the adrenal activity (memory and the solar plexus area) shown in Revelation, Chapter 4, which also

relates to karma (sowing and reaping) and our emotional ties to a belief system of there being a Christ and an Anti-Christ outside of us. And, now we know where the phrase "the devil made me do it" comes from!

From reading Apocalypse, most of us here on earth came to believe in the dark as Satan (Beast), the mind as the Anti-Christ, and the light as Christ. And because of this, two different entities emerged as something real, and yet, they are both the self. Because of our split consciousness and energy, in the beginning, light became something that was known because we had experienced it before splitting our consciousness, and dark became unknown until we experience it. Therefore, how could we know they were of the same consciousness until we have experienced them both?

And, since we work from a mental and physical cycle, what is said in Revelation 13:2, *"to it the dragon gave its own power and throne, along with great authority,* is referring to our free will, our emotional choices, and our many ego-personalities that inherited the power of the dragon (polarity energy) to work out our karma to become balanced with our choices. This is why our ego-personality (the beast) tends to deceive us more while in physical form than while we are in our etheric form. And, this is why the Ascended Masters say we grow more in the physical realm than in the etheric realm.

It is through our physical senses where we get to experience our free will and the choices we make using the influences of polarity energy (symbolized by the dragon), and how they affect us in physical (animal) form. The seven heads involved in Revelation 13:1, is where *"one of its heads,"* in Revelation 13:3, that is associated with the seven endocrine systems in the physical body, is the part of us that seems to have been *"mortally wounded."* And, that is, our mental body or the thymus area of the physical body.

As we learned, the mind comes in two parts, one being the inner soul consciousness of responsibility and the other our outer mind that makes choices. It was our outer mind (Adam) that chose to split in consciousness to where our inner mind (Eve) gave life to a defiant consciousness (Cain) that became the means to learn about polarity energy. And is why we (humanity) suffer? This is illustrated by Cain in Genesis 4:16, where *"Cain left the Lord's presence and settled in the land of Nod, east of Eden."*

This means that after any positive action of the mind within *("east of Eden"),* there will always be a negative reaction outside of ourselves *("in the land of Nod").* And, the "land of Nod," as we know it today, is the condition of sleep. "Nod," according to the Metaphysical Bible Dictionary by Charles Fillmore (1931), means "disturbed or troubled journey (flight)." This wandering with uncertainty suggests the unguided and unstable activity of our subconscious mind during periods of sleep (or us unaware of being Christ) and our outer, negative physical reactions to this sleep state. Therefore, the fundamental idea of "Nod" is bewilderment and uncertainty of the mind.

This means that our ego gave way to a personality of forgetfulness that is now part of our physical reality, which is why we are asleep and unaware of being the Christ we seek. The story of Cain and Abel, Genesis 4:1-26, is the perfect example of what reflects our outward sleep and unawareness to whom we truly are. As the story goes, Cain was the firstborn and the tiller of the soil. Thus, Cain reflects an ego-personality of us that took the action of forgetting because of his horrendous act in killing his brother Abel.

Therefore, our Cain personality refers directly to that part of us that lowered our energy and consciousness frequency into a defiant ego-personality frequency that strives to acquire and possess all power (energy) for self-expression using polarity energy. This distinguishes us as being part of a materialistic base, while Cain's brother Abel symbolizes a personality within us that had an awareness of being a Christ in the flesh at one time, but we killed that higher awareness with our self-absorbed beliefs that only comes from an ego-consciousness of defiance.

Since our defiant and stubborn ego-personality (Satan) assumes various personalities, illustrated by Cain, to obscure our higher ego-personality awareness, illustrated by Abel, we then lose sight of being Christ. Cain, having killed Abel, represents our defiant ego-personality demanding possession of all the resources of our mind (Adam) and soul (Eve), thereby obscuring our awareness of being Christ to only an ego-based personality of defiance that obscures (kills) the real truth to whom we indeed are at our core essence.

Because of this obscurity, Cain, our conflicting ego, joined with a personality that became so intertwined that we solidified our pure, neutralized god energy of light into a material body of being unaware of being a Christ. Therefore, Cain and Satan both derive from the same energy as our stubborn and defiant ego-personality, and this is why Cain is allied more toward the physical (tiller of soil) than to spirit.

The statement of *"mortally wounded,"* in Revelation 13:3, reflects us having an ego-personality (represented by Abel) that, at first, before the fall, we very much knew being a Christ also. But, once we took on the belief in opposing energy as something real, "the tree of knowledge of good and evil," we killed off that higher awareness in favor of living out of emotional consciousness. But the good news is that the *"mortal wound was healed,"* Revelation 13:3.

However, the healing cannot occur until we have finished our cycle of many lifetimes, and then let go of any beliefs connected to polarity energy as being real. Everything that we have been doing since we lost the higher awareness of being Christ has been reflected through our many defiant ego-personalities that have been *"following the beast"* instead of us following what is Christ, you.

And, once you, in this lifetime, integrate all that is defiant in knowing you are Christ, then healing of the wound on the head (mental level) gains the ability to overcome the emotional block of polarity energy as being real. Yeshua is the example of this by the crucifixion of his physical ego-personality, symbolized by the "son of man," to where he recognized himself as the Christ (Son of Goddess).

When Yeshua spoke of the *"Holy Spirit bring all things to your remembrance, even from the foundations of the world,"* John 14:26, this is Yeshua telling us here on earth, either through this book or other means, that we are a Christ also just as much as he is. To confirm this, Revelation 13:5 would be an excellent example for understanding. *"The beast was given a mouth uttering proud boasts and blasphemies, and it was given authority to act for forty-two months."*

As mentioned before, a month is equivalent to thirty-days (30), and therefore represent us having a three-dimensional consciousness (spirit, mind-soul, and ego personality) that journeys through a mental cycle (zero) consisting of opposing energies over and over until we learn that we are the Christ creating it all by way of our beliefs and consciousness acts. The *"beast"* is our many ego-personalities of defiance that we played out in each lifetime, and our mind (Anti-Christ) was what gives them the *authority* and power over this polarity energy to use at will. And, no matter whether we voiced *(uttered)* it as being real, or vented as our truths *(boasts)*, or offended with those truths *(blasphemies)*, it made no difference to us.

It was all about the belief in polarity energy is where we became obsessed with structuring those beliefs into material form to play the game of make-believe. However, this obsession is what shaped our many ego-personality lifetimes into something disrespectful and mischievous. And now, after we have played out many lifetimes here on earth, using the four (4) destructive elements of our physical nature, and with using polarity energy (2), they want to come home to their creator. But we keep on denying them as not being our creations. These four elements again are (i) air, (ii) fire, (iii) water, and (iv) earth.

And this is the meaning of the number 42 months or 42 X 30 Days = 1,260 days. As the number one (1) represents that we are of "one consciousness." The number two (2) represents the energy of opposing influences, positive and negative. The number six (6) represents the last number behind the beast's name. And, the zero represents how we have been journeying through a mental cycle over and over. And, we will until we become awakened to the mental images that we believe are our name, occupation, that power is real, and that we are less than God, Goddess, and Christ.

Before getting into the number of the beast (666) in Revelation 13:18, let's discover the wisdom behind Revelation 13:11-12. *"Then I saw another beast come up out of earth, it had two horns like a lamb's but spoke like a dragon."* The *"first beast"* is that of our opposing ego-personalities that come from out of our subconsciousness and how they became part of the physical realm. And, with this *"first beast,"* every physical lifetime we have had on earth took on a defiant personality nature that gave birth to multitudes of unexpressed and unformed light and dark potentials to be played out here on earth.

Therefore, the *"beast coming out of the earth"* that had *"two horns like a lamb"* represents our defiant ego-personality, physically and non-physically, uses this polarity energy *(two horns)* like it is our mind *(lamb)* for us to experience our choices (creations). The illusion is found both with our ego and mind, but our ego acts as if it was our mind *(lamb)* giving the orders. Yet, all orders were coming from the behavior patterns and beliefs of our many ego-personalities.

The *"first beast"* gives us the feeling that we are separate and independent from our "I AM" Christ consciousness, and that our many ego-personality lifetime aspects, that are spread throughout the astral/physical realms, are separate from us in this lifetime. The *"second beast"* coming up from the earth represents us taking on a mental consciousness (mind) that believes polarity energy (the tree of good and evil) is real. Thus, the mind's virtue is that it can use reason and logic to solve any problem or situation, including defining Christ, God, Goddess, and Satan. And this is why we feel that our subconsciousness and our outer masculine consciousness are as one (the mind).

However, the *"second beast"* has two minds to use to help us feel, think, have power and to control the polarity energy influences coming in from all other parts and pieces of us that are spread throughout other dimensions. But the big surprise is those thoughts of power and control are not really thoughts coming from our minds. They are coming from the *"first beast,"* our many ego-personality aspects.

In other words, our defiant ego-personality (the first beast) is deceiving us into believing that our mind (the second beast) is in control of all our thoughts, the belief in opposing energy, our intelligence, and all that our mind considers as power and control. But, reality, these thoughts and beliefs of power and control are coming from our many defiant ego-personalities (first beast).

This is why our mind looks at whatever is good comes from God and whatever is bad comes from the devil. But, in truth, our mind (the Anti-Christ) is controlled by our many ego-personality aspects (the Beast). We just do not know how much we are deceived by our ego-personality aspects while in the flesh (the beast). And of course, the *"two horns"* represent the influences of duality that comes from using it as our source of energy (positive and negative), as our ego-personality keeps on deceiving us to believe our mind of reason is in charge of our choices (free will) and yet, we are following the beast (our ego) every time.

This is why, once we become awakened to this process, our defiant ego-personality will be healed by its mortal wound first before our mind. Once we contact our many ego-personalities of the past and future and then integrate them as part of our creations, that is when we will awaken to the mind as being the Anti-Christ. Thus, we become wise to our many ego-personalities where they hand us back to our "I AM" Christ consciousness.

To confirm what was just interpreted by Yeshua and the Ascended Masters, allow me to present to you Revelation 13:18. The *"wisdom is needed here; one who understands can calculate the number of the beast, for it is a number that stands for a person. His number is six hundred and sixty-six* (666)." Most of us could guess as to whom the beast is and how the name is calculated to "666?"

From the study into the Book of Revelation, the wisdom of the "Beast" and its calculated number "666" is not about one particular person, or devil, or a highly educated politician, nor a religious person. The wisdom of the "Beast" and its calculated number is found with all of humanity, male and female. The wisdom comes from knowing who you are and how numbers play a big part in translating physical matter using sacred geometry.

The whole universe has been created through what is called sacred geometry (mathematics) as the method and the road map of our physical existence here on earth. And, by understanding how our "I AM" Christ-spirit, mind-soul, and ego-personalities are translated into geometric principles of geometry, this helps us understand how numbers deal with mathematics. The measuring effects such things as lines, angles, squares, circles, and surfaces where the outcome can be for the manifestation into physical reality.

Channeling of the Ascended Masters on the Apocalypse

As was discussed in Revelation 4:4, Chapter 16 of this book, numerology is the study of the influences of numbers and what they mean, because everything in life, earth, and all things physical are affected by numbers. And, by understanding how our "I AM" Christ-spirit, our mind-soul, and our ego-personality is translated into numbers, we can come into an understanding about how physicality is manifested.

From the Ascended Masters interpretation of Revelation 4:4, Chapter 16 of my book, when we look at the beginning of time and space, we can see how our "I AM" Christ consciousness transformed "nothingness" into an "unidentified unknown thing" that came to be an energy of an opposing nature called positive and negative. The Bible calls it *"the tree of knowledge of good and bad"* (Genesis 2:9). And, as we know, the Bible is full of numbers, and they represent the geometric pattern of turning "nothingness" into "somethingness."

As mentioned in Chapter 16 of my book, Revelation 4:4, without mathematics or sacred geometry, there would be no universe, stars, planets, earth, physical body, rocks, trees, animals, or anything else that has form. Know that the building blocks of space, time, earth, and all physical manifestation, including our physical body, do come from the geometric configurations of our "I AM" Christ consciousness (spirit).

The Bible says to serve the Lord and be careful of the Beast, and yet, we humans have always pondered over this number "666," and "Who the beast is?" The question can be easily answered once we move into an awareness that we, as a human group, are the Lord of Lords and the creator of our world. And, when this awareness lights up within us, we will understand that we need to learn to serve ourselves as the "almighty" and the cause of all our creations.

When we recognize that through consciousness and the law of mind action, we become what we hold as our belief systems. And, if we see only fear, then fear becomes the law we manifest to experience here on earth because we are the Christ, God, and the Goddess bringing it into existence. An example of this is with the Coronavirus. We are born with all known and unknown viruses, and when a virus is detected or announced by our scientists and the media as it being something we need to fear, then, by all means, people that fear it will catch the virus because of that fear. Therefore, the "wisdom" behind the number "666," and its meaning, has to do with sacred geometry.

As mentioned in my study, we all are a multidimensional being, and everything outside of consciousness is not real, including fear and this so-called coronavirus. Do you recall my words saying that "consciousness is all that we are!" It begins with "consciousness," and everything else that follows, no matter what that is, our mind, ego, physical form, and beliefs come from "consciousness." This means, which is very important to understand, the "beast and its number '666'" is not someone outside of us, as a person or devil; it is the ego in fear of losing its power.

Therefore, the "beast and its calculated number '666,'" is part of our "I AM" Christ consciousness, our mind-soul, and our ego personality, and with all of what our ego-consciousness took up in many lifetimes, good and bad. This means, we are the Beast, we are also the Antichrist, and the Christ simultaneously. Where else could our "I AM" Christ consciousness hide the wisdom of the "Beast" but within our own consciousness? We humans are not only the Beast and Anti-Christ, but we are also the true creator in manifestation!

Thus, we are the creator of all our viruses and diseases, including cancer and this coronavirus. If we all allowed ourselves to let go of fear, then our ego-consciousness would be vibrating at a frequency that would not allow these illnesses to be part of our lives. Know that we all had a great desire to experience this unknown principle of polarity energy (light and dark), and part of that desire was to experience it and fear in the flesh without any interference coming from our "I AM" to learn the wisdom of our choices.

In Chapter 16 of my book? It was mentioned that the *"four living creatures and how each of them had six wings that were covered with eyes inside and out"* (Revelation 4:8). These *"six wings"* represent the influences that we put on each level of our three-dimensional consciousness *(inside and out)*; right from our super subconsciousness (the "I AM"), to our subconsciousness (the mind-soul), and onto our outer ego physical consciousness that is filled with fear. This also includes the consciousnesses of our multidimensional ego-personalities that are still alive in other dimensional realms waiting for us, their creator, to accept them as part of our consciousness today.

In other words, within each of these past, present, and future lifetimes, since we are living them out simultaneously, we have a name and a story being played out as if it was our only lifetime. Therefore, our super-subconsciousness (the "I AM"), our subconsciousness (the mental-mind), and our outer defiant ego-physical consciousness all carry these *"six wings"* of influences within each consciousness part of our three-dimensional consciousness.

The *"six wings"* of our "I AM" Christ consciousness represent the first "six days of creation" given in Genesis 1:1–31, and are described as the "perfection of the six divine attributes of our "I AM" spirit, and can be seen in Revelation 4:4. It is through these "six divine attributes" of our "I AM" Christ consciousness (represented by the six wings of our "I AM-spirit) that make us humans a true creator God-Goddess in our own right.

It is these "six divine attributes" or wings that make us an infinite creator of perfection, even though we may not think so. We humans, at our core essence, are perfect and unchangeable and without sin. It is only through our mental-mind and the ego-personality that we are portraying right now, judging what we choose to experience as being a sin. And yet, sin only comes from the personality traits of who we believe we are and not from our core essence.

In other words, our "I AM" Christ consciousness does not see sin or that we are doing something wrong. It only sees us playing with fear and polarity energy that consists of positive and negative to experience life. Therefore, these six divine attributes of our "I AM" spirit (wings) denotes the first number of the Beast ((6)66) found in Revelation 13:18. And, since the wisdom of the Beast is so important in this presentation, I will list these "six divine attributes" of our "I AM" Christ consciousness once again.

These "six divine attributes" are also associated with the "seven spirits before the throne" that can be found in Revelation 4:4, Chapter 16 of my book. These "six divine attributes" (wings) are what makes us all a living Christ, God, and Goddess, and represents the first six (6) found in Revelation 13:18; they are as follows: Also, remember, for our completion in consciousness these "six divine attributes" will also be part of our mental and physical consciousness.

1. We all have an infinite consciousness that is forever active.
2. We have a high level of intelligence that is divine, and this intelligence comes from us being multidimensional.
3. We have a consciousness that always seeks growth and expansion.
4. We all have a divine plan (will) that needs to be integrated with our free will of a mental nature.
5. We all have a spiritual essence about us that gives life to our thoughts, beliefs, and ideas, including our many light and dark ego-personality aspects that play in other dimensions, including earth.
6. We have a consciousness that is only of a divine love state in nature. It is unconditional and unchangeable and was set in place before the beginning of time, space, and physicality.

As each of these six identifying divine attributes can perfectly express the spirit, idea, and purpose behind the essence of whatever we, the true creators, desires to manifest. As both Revelation 2:1 and Genesis, 1:1–31 refers to our mind-soul consciousness and the fact that it, too, consists of the perfection of the "six divine attributes" given above. This is also true for the "seventh divine attribute," known as "silence," signified by the "seventh day" in Genesis 1:1–31 as well.

When we add this "Day of Silence" to the "six divine attributes" (wings) as the "seventh divine attribute," along with the duality factor of one (1), we come up with the number 15, broken down to 1 + 5 = the second six (6) of the beast calculated number. Allow me to explain!

Take the first six (6) divine attributes found above that make up our "I AM" Christ consciousness and add them to the "seventh divine attribute" of silence (6 + 1 = 7, symbolized by the "seventh day in Genesis." This is also why the "first six wings" are associated with the "seven spirits before the throne."

In my book, Chapter 6, the Ascended Masters and I gave the meaning behind the wisdom of Revelation 1:16 and to Revelation 1:20, Chapter 7, as the "seven subtle bodies of our mind-body," and also known as the "seven stars." And, when we add these "seven (7) subtle bodies (seven stars)" to the first "seven divine attributes" (the six (6) divine attributes, plus the "Day of Silence" (1), along with the opposing energy of positive and negative as one (1). We would have 7 + 7 + 1 = 15. Then, break down the number fifteen (15) to its primary value of 1 + 5 = 6. This is the second six in the number of the Beast (6(6)6) given in Revelation 13:18.

Not to confuse you! Since our "I AM," Christ consciousness begins with the "six divine attributes, it represents the first six (6) of the beast number. And, since it has been established that our second level of a mental consciousness also consists of these "six divine attributes," plus the "Day of Silence (1)," along with opposing energy as one (1), and our "seven (7) subtle bodies," then our mind-soul mental consciousness make up is of 6 + 1 + 1 + 7 = 15. Then 1 + 5 = 6, the mind-soul, and is the second (6) found in Revelation 13:18.

When we move onto the third level of physical consciousness, as we are a three-dimensional consciousness, we begin with the "six (6) divine attributes," the "Day of Silence (1)," along with opposing energy as one (1), and our "seven (7) subtle bodies." But, since we are working from a physical consciousness, as they add up again to: 6 + 1 + 1 + 7 = 15. However, we have to add the "seven (7) deadly acts" of our physical nature to this calculated number 15, as they are (i) sadness, (ii) anger, (iii) lust for power, (iv) envy, (v) pride, (vi) greed, and (vii) laziness) that was given in Chapter 6 as the wisdom found behind Revelation 1:16, to the number 15 + 7 = 22.

From here, we have to add the four (4) elements of the physical realm, (i) fire, (ii) water, (iii) air, and (iv) earth, along with the five (5) physical senses of (i) sight, (ii) taste (iii) smell, (iv) touch, and (v) hear; and to top it all off, let's not forget about the god masculine energy of light as (1) and our Oversoul of a feminine nature as (1). In other words, we have a calculation of 15 + 7 + 4 + 5 + 2 = 33, broken down to 3 + 3 = 6, the third calculated six (6) behind the number of 66(6). Or, if we like, 6 + 1 +1 + 7 + 7 + 4 + 5 + 2 = 33, broken down to 3 + 3 = 6, the third number found as the beast number.

The last six (6) calculated as the "beast" number may seem very complicated because it represents not only our ego-personality in the flesh but the wholeness of our three-dimensional consciousness complete as a man in the flesh. Therefore, the "Beast" is nothing more than man on the earth very much unaware *(dead)* that he/she is Satan, Christ, God, and a Goddess. Thus, the wisdom of the "beast" and his/her name is revealed as the number of "mankind" upon this earth.

This means that Satan is not a person with horns but a metaphorical figure telling us that the "beast" represents humanity in the flesh as a Goddess journey through many lifetimes being very much unaware of playing with polarity energy doing everything we can to oppose our own "I AM" Christ consciousness. Thus, as we journey through time and space, incarnating again and again in physical bodies, our "I AM" Christ consciousness, our mind-soul body of responsibility consciousness, and our many opposing ego-personalities become part of what the number "666" represents.

If we take the number of the "Beast" and break it down to its primary value, we come up with the number nine (6 + 6 + 6 = 18, then 1 + 8 = 9), which is very significant because:

It is the number for our completion, and

The only thing that comes after 9 is 10, or our awakening to whom we indeed are.

This means again that we humans are the Alpha and the Omega, the first and the last, for we are the one true Christ, God, and Goddess. Therefore, put no other gods before you, not even Yeshua. In other words, after our journey through the mental cycle of activities in a three-density existence, we do come to the number ten (10) where we are awakened as a sovereign Goddess in our own right (1 + 0 = 1). So, please let go of your fear, and that is when all illnesses will disappear.

When we awaken to the Beast character in the Bible being the self in the flesh, we will have come full circle as a human, for its number represents man in the flesh as the Beast (666), whose primary value is nine (9) and the number of completion. Then we expand into a whole new circle of creation, a creation that brings in the New Expansional Energy of Four. Thus, a set of whole new potentials for us to play with that has no illnesses tied to it.

The Apocalypse is not about the ending of earth or humanity. It is about us humans moving from a three-density consciousness to a four-density consciousness, thereby completing our separation of consciousnesses and our journey through the astral/physical realms and the two cycles (zeros) of activities of the left and right brain hemispheres. This makes us ready to enter the third cycle (zero) where we learn of being a full creator God-Goddess, and a Christ in our own right. It is through this higher awareness that we are introduced to our Christ-Gnost consciousness, where the calendar of physical life and its prophecies are fulfilled.

It was from the Tobias materials, as channeled by Geoffrey Hoppe, Crimson Circle, that Tobias talked about the missing piece, the lack of which has caused us, humans, to wonder why things are so difficult in our lives. Tobias called this missing piece "De Un Gnost." This means that we come into a new consciousness of expansion once we reach our completion of the number nine (9) in each cycle.

Therefore, the third zero associated with the number 144,000 represents completeness, which is where we move into a consciousness of "knowing" and of "solutions," validating that we are indeed Christ, God, Goddess, and the true creator. Therefore, destiny or karma has no role in our life because some of us are beginning to move into a place of consciousness that chooses what we want the outcome to be instead of fearing the outcome.

We all have forgotten that Yeshua said that his kingdom was not of earth, so why are we preaching that he will come out of the clouds with his army of angels and slay all those that have gone against him? Yeshua did not overthrow any governments of the earth back in his day, and he is not going to do so in our time. Yeshua died on the cross to illustrate to us that the kingdom of heaven (God) is not of the physical earth but with our "I AM" Christ consciousness within. This is why the earth and our physical body are not real. They are only shadows of what is real, and so is the Anti-Christ.

If you would take the time to look at the prefix "Anti," you would learn that it is about man in his ego-state, expressing and holding views that oppose the true state of his own being. Therefore, the Anti-Christ is you in a sleep state where you have lost your awareness of being Christ. We just don't realize that the end of the world is just symbolic of the end of a state of consciousness where the old beliefs (old earth) that hold to a God who is white, male, sits on a throne, has a long white beard, and passes judgment against us, is finished. This includes all those that love power, for power is an illusion.

A new truth is beginning to unlock human consciousness, and this new truth is about a New Expansional Energy of Four (new earth) that has nothing to do with duality, positive and negative, good and bad, right and wrong, light and dark, or having authority (power) over others. Therefore, the Son of Man (our ego-personality awakened) has already made his return upon the earth, and most of the human race is not keeping a watchful eye according to what was predicted by Yeshua himself in Mark 13:32–36:

"But of that day or hour, no one knows, neither the angels in heaven, nor the Son, but only the Father. Be watchful! Be alert! You do not know when the time will come. It is like a man traveling abroad. He leaves home and places his servants in charge, each with his work, and orders the gatekeeper to be on the watch. Watch, therefore; you do not know when the lord of the house is coming, whether in the evening, or at midnight, or at cockcrow, or in the morning. May he not come suddenly and find you sleeping."

Chapter 30

OVERCOMING THE SEPARATION OF OUR MIND

From Revelation 14:2-3, *"I heard a sound from heaven like rushing water or loud thunder."* This is a measured intuitive message coming from our higher consciousness struggling to convey to our mind the meaning behind why we are here on Earth in a physical body. Once we come into a realization that we are Christ in the flesh, this will echo throughout every cell in our body as if a *"loud thunder,"* reminding us energetically to balance our mind-soul and physical consciousness. Otherwise, we cannot tap into the memories of our Oversoul, where all wisdom of being Christ can be found.

By paying attention to our beliefs about sin, punishment, power, and polarity energy, our mind-soul and our many ego-personalities will move into balance. Thus, exposing those unexpressed beliefs, potentials, and possibilities that embodies certain weaknesses, negativity, and mental potentiality where we can now cleanse them of any dual thinking. Water in its different aspects can represent weakness, negativity, cleansing, and mental potentiality, and sometimes, if we are not balanced, our "I AM" can give life to those expressions.

And, when *"sounding of the harpist playing the harps and the singing of a new hymn before the throne, the four living creatures, and the elders,"* Revelation 14:2-3, represents our original purpose for coming into the flesh and working with our many ego-personality aspects was to learn wisdom and to know who we are. Thus, we become awakened to the truth that we are the Christ coming to save ourselves. Therefore, our many ego-personality aspects are the first to be redeemed, then our mind, and not some tribe of Israel.

If we learn to quiet our mind, we can feel these many ego-personality aspects around us desiring to reconnect with us by the thin "silver cords of the *harp*" that links them with our Lyden Center (you becoming aware) and our pineal area of the body (you being the savior). This happens by way of the stringed vibrational waves of the "*harp*" used between our many ego-personality aspects that are awakened to a "knowing" that we are the Christ bringing in this new energy frequency (*new hymn*) to serve us, and while we are still part of the flesh.

It is with this new energy frequency (*new hymn*) that reconnects us to the remembrance of our "divine plan" for coming to earth, and how our four lower regions of consciousness; (i) desires, (ii) choices, (iii) memories, and (iv) the growth of our soul (*four living creatures*, known as our gonads, Leyden, adrend, and thymus) played a big part in our awakening today. And now, our eyes should be wide open about who we are and who Christ is. Thus, the *"new hymn before the throne"* are those of us that are awakened and begin a new "energy frequency" of a "four-density consciousness" to experience life here on earth in a whole new way.

As we observe the happenings of the old opposing energy being played out on earth by the mass in a most dramatic way, politics, families, businesses, religions, and other ways that keep them tied to a three-density consciousness of choosing things, they are missing out of moving forward because of it. Yeshua validated this when he walked the earth when he learned to master the four elements of earth (i) fire (memory), (ii) earth (form), (iii) water (spirit source), and (iv) air (mental growth), which explains the miracles.

These four elements came to obey and serve Yeshua, as it will for those who dare to move forward without doubt about who they are. This awakening is to a new energy frequency where neutrality is more customary with our creations than opposing energy. For example, *"then I looked, and there was a Lamb standing on Mount Zion, and with him a hundred and forty-four thousand who had his name and his Father's name written on their foreheads,"* Revelation 14:1.

Mount Zion was a fortified hill that David took from the Jebusites. David built his palace there (2 Samuel 5:7), and it was called the City of David. The tent of the meeting and the Ark of the Covenant was on Mount Zion during David's reign (1 Kings 8:1). This is why it was called the "holy mountain" (Psalms 2:6). Later, Mount Zion became part of the City of Jerusalem. In the Bible, Mount Zion refers to the whole City of

Jerusalem (Isaiah 33:20) and is sometimes used as a metaphor for the New Jerusalem or New Earth (Hebrew 12:22).

Therefore, Mount Zion represents our divine love state, coming into a phase where we humans are beginning to feel and know the real truth about Christ and who he is rather than believing what is presented as intellectual evidence. All philosophies tied to polarity energy only exist in the mind of perception, where we judge them to be our truths. However, it is time to intuitively feel the real truth that we are the Messiah instead of us looking for the Messiah. And, as these new feelings abide within our heart center (symbolized by the New Jerusalem), that is when the Son of God(dess) returns as the Messiah.

Since *"Mount Zion"* represents the New Jerusalem, it also represents the New Expansional Energy of Four (New Earth) that replaces the old Jerusalem or old opposing energy (Old Earth). Remember, the Jews do not believe that Jesus is the Messiah! Therefore, the symbolism of the Jews represents one's ego-personality in defiance of one being Christ. And this is why the New Jerusalem (New Earth or New Expansional Energy) becomes known as the *"holy hill,"* which is why the *"Lamb"* of God is our mind overturning its Anti-Christ concept in favor of being Christ.

The *"holy hill"* is about some of us in this lifetime coming into an understanding that the Son of Man represents our ego-personality in the flesh. The *"Lamb"* (Son of Man) is you reaching spiritual attainment where you can allow your "I AM" Christ-spirit (Oversoul) to come into your mind and flesh body and integrate all that you are and ever have been. This achievement comes when we, while in the flesh, submit to our intuitive consciousness and allow ourselves to let go of the belief in sin, suffering, perception, and polarity energy as the foundation of our Beingness. When we do, that is when we manifest the wisdom of God's words in plain language.

In Revelation 14:1, *"with him a hundred and forty-four thousand."* This number was previously shown to mean more than just the 144,000 Jews. From the Bible, we can see why this number is associated with the twelve tribes of Israel because they represent the 144,000 different soul-groups that left the first creation (higher consciousness) long ago. All humans are Jews incarnated.

Since Mount Zion is a mountain that we can climb to a higher place, at least from a religious viewpoint, then the number 144,000 is associated with the operations of our spirit-body more than our mind-body, our physical bodies, the twelve tribes of Israel, and the 144,000 different soul-groups. When we consider the Son of Man representing our ego-personality in the flesh and evolving to where we come in contact with our "I AM" Christ-spirit-body, then we have become complete in the eyes of our "I AM."

We can see this in the numerical statement $1 + 4 + 4 + 0 + 0 + 0 = 9$). This number nine (9) again has the same mathematical geometry mentioned previously. And that is because:

1. It is the number for completion.
2. The only thing that comes after 9 is 10. This means we all come back to our oneness again, but this time we come home (back to higher consciousness) with our eyes wide opened instead of being closed to who Christ is.

To clarify this 144,000 again, please go back to Chapters 19 and 20, where we referenced the meaning of Revelation 7:4.

Once we complete our karmic conditions in this second circle (cycle) using polarity energy, we enter a third circle (cycle) where we return to our oneness ($1 + 0 = 1$) in knowing we are Christ, but this time with our eyes wide open. And, we bring with us the wisdom of everything that we have learned using neutral energy in the first circle (cycle), and what we have learned using polarity energy journeying through the second circle (cycle). This includes the wholeness of the mass (all souls) and what they created.

It was from our discussion in Chapter 16, interpreting Revelation 4:4, that we reach the understanding of these cycles that we have become a true creator God-Goddess in our own right who has found the way home (higher understanding) by home finding us. Therefore, the third zero (cycle) represents the New Jerusalem (New Expansional Energy) coming to earth to replace the old Jerusalem (old vibrational energy) where duality, suffering, perception, and separation are not part of our consciousness anymore. Therefore, the angels of expressions listed in the next several verses represent a higher divine consciousness than the angels that are associated with our lower mind or ego-body. This becomes apparent when we are fully aware of what we had to do to fulfill our destiny.

In Revelation. 14:1, *"Who had his name and his Father's name written on their foreheads,"* is why the *"Father's name written on their forehead"* is you, and those who are ready to ascend in this lifetime to a whole new understanding of God, Goddess, Satan, and a Christ. And, as stated in Chapters 19 and 20, interpreting Revelation 7:4, we recognize this number being associated with the 144,000 martyrs and the first to be sealed and protected from what is coming soon.

However, what is being overlooked here by our religious scholars is that this 144,000 is associated with the foundation of our existence, because we are all Jews, God, Goddesses, and a Christs, and the makeup of our existence today is that we are playing in a three-dimensional world where we experience our choices using polarity energy. However, that can change when we are ready to make the change from old to new.

Again, the number one (1) is associated with us humans coming from "all that was and existed" in the beginning was our "consciousness of oneness," symbolized by the Garden and the "first circle (cycle). And, when we souled beings asked ourselves, "Who am I?" This manifested what the first four (4) means in the number 144,000, as we created a:

1. "Dei Un Gnost" Christ consciousness
2. Spirit that became aware of itself
3. Mind-soul that produced an image of the self that could split our consciousness and energy into two opposing parts.
4. Ego-personality manifested many physical bodies to explore individuality and the meaning of life.

In exploring our individuality, we then took up what the second four (4) means from the 144,000 and moved our existence into what has become known as:

1. Fire (energy, memory, courage, and justice or sowing and reaping)
2. Earth (desires, form, and reproducing)
3. Water (to sustain our choices and beingness and to give us the means to create through belief systems)
4. Air (to help us give life to many light and dark ego-personality aspects of ourselves, thus expanding ((growth)) our consciousness through our mental state in a positive and negative way)

And, as mentioned earlier in the discussion of Chapter 19 and 20 in interpreting Revelation 7:4. The *"forehead"* is the sanctuary for our light and dark ego-personality aspects of an etheric nature entering a physical body to become a servant for our "I AM" spirit-consciousness (Goddess). Therefore, we are the shepherds because the *"name and his Father's name written on the forehead"* is our physical body that is layered with many consciousnesses, faces, and names while on earth. Thus, our physical body is a place of worship (temple of the living God) because it is the place where we express and experience the potentials that we have already chosen in the astral realms before coming to earth.

Therefore, there is nothing like the human body as a vehicle for us to learn about differing energies, forms, choices, and how opposing energy works. I remember in a channeling session with Ascended Master Melchezidek. He called me "Adam." At first, I was puzzled when he called me Adam because I was not sure what he meant by it. However, after further talks with him, I realized that the name "Adam" represents the human race in a flesh body.

Therefore, Adam represents us humans working out of a mental and physical body of consciousness. Eve represents that part of us that gives life to whatever thought we would like to experience (positive or negative) under the conditions of feeling our choices and then taking full responsibility for them. When we, while in the flesh, male or female, are ready to choose, the seed of that choice comes from the masculine side of the mind and then given over to our feminine soul side of that same mind to give that choice life.

This is symbolic of Eve taking the first bite of the apple. But, symbolically speaking, Adam took the first bite because it is always the masculine side of the mind that chooses what to express and experience. The feminine-soul side of that same mind only holds the seed until the masculine side is ready to have it manifested to experience. This also means that Adam and Eve were not two people, or even real people, as they together represent our split mind. When we souls first came to earth in the physical, we were all called Adam, no matter if male or female.

It is because of us souled beings moving into a void of nothingness, that we, as a group consciousness, created polarity energy, and then fragmented it into billions upon billions of pieces. Each piece represented a potential for us to experience. Whether positive or negative potentials made no difference to our soul side of responsibility. However, to play out those billions upon billions of potentials and possibilities, we created multitudes of ego-personality aspects to help us play them out in the physical and non-physical realms.

This means we all have many ego-personality aspects that have never experienced physical lifetimes or earth. Hence, there are billions of virgin memories of potentials that have not yet yielded to the submission of the flesh. This also means that we all still have many ego-personality aspects that hold to their original purpose, never participated in the fall of consciousness. Therefore, they are without fault or sinned *("on their lips no deceit has been found; they are unblemished")*, Revelation 14:4-5.

These ego-personality aspects of the self do not know what separation feels like because they have never experienced the flesh. Therefore, they are not *"defiled or tainted"* by the self. Thus, there is no having to take responsibility for something they (you) did not do as of yet because you only have created them to help guide you back to the realization that you are Christ, God, and the Goddess. And, since these ego-personality aspects of you have never defiled polarity energy, they are the first to be intergraded with your "I AM" Christ consciousness at your first awakening of spirit.

This is true because deep within, we can feel some reverence of us being greater than our humanness here on earth. However, because of our many ego-personalities that did ride the rails of incarnations playing with polarity energy *(those that defiled the woman, your Oversoul)*, we feel only human. We have forgotten that we have many ego aspects of ourselves still part of our consciousness. And, they are waiting for us, the one in the flesh, to integrate them along with the others into our human form of today.

You contain an incredible level of built-in intelligence deep within because you helped design and create the entire universe, this incredible physical lifetime you are experiencing now, and you have created the reason for desiring flesh over an etheric body in which to play with energy. Also, this intelligence is of such a high degree that when you look at it from the human viewpoint, you see it as something far beyond anything you can achieve. However, this infinite intelligence is already part of your soul memory, and you can tap into it when you feel ready.

Do you remember the narrative of Moses fleeing to the wilderness, Exodus 2:14–15? Moses represents the discipline and patience that we have undergone in the search for answering the questions "Who am I?" and "Why am I here?"

Exodus 3:1–2 talks about Moses coming to Horeb, which is the mountain of God. In this place, an angel of the Lord appeared to Moses in a flaming bush. Therefore, Horeb means solitude of the "I AM;" that is, we have to be willing to be alone and go within to tap into our "I AM" before we can find our divine plan, or what is the angel of the Lord. This is done through deep breathing and meditation. Therefore, Moses, on the mound that day, was hearing his own "I AM That I AM," speaking with Moses' ego-personality of his day.

To be alone and go within ourselves, we don't have to leave our home or join a monastery or some religious group to find God. All we have to do is sit in a nice, quiet room and take deep breaths, not by just filling the lungs but the stomach too. And, when we do this, then the mind and these ego-personality aspects of us that *"never defiled the woman"* in Revelation 14:4 (or lived by the human system) will lead us and all our other ego-personality aspects *(flocks) (that did experience the flesh)* out of the wilderness (ignorance/darkness of consciousness) and into freedom as they come home to us, their creator, for integration.

It was through our many other ego-personality aspects where we were in training for forty years, as this represents our Christ-spirit, mind-soul, ego, and all of our ego-personality aspects coming into completion. And, that is when we arrive at a balanced state of mind (four-sided) where we can overcome the separated mind of old. They hold ground in Exodus 3:5 is the substance upon which our physical life is built because it is the resting place for our "I AM," waiting for us to "come up here" (home) and reconnect to it.

When we approach the realization of our completeness and accept "all that we are and all that we have been," right and wrong, we begin to shed all concepts and experiences of limitations. This is when our inner wisdom proclaims that we are the "I AM," the "Father-Mother," "the Son-daughter," and a "Christ." We may have other ego-personality aspects that have never experienced earth (male or female), or one race or another, health or illness, intelligence or stupidity, love, or hate in a way that no angel can ever love or hate. However, it was those ego aspect experiences that helped us find the realization (home) that we are Christ.

When we look at Genesis 6:4, the *"heroes of old, the men of renown,"* it is not only talking about us and our many ego-personality aspects but about other souls that have never experienced life or flesh. And, as we have learned in this study, once we moved outside of "I AM," our ego-personality took control of our mind and energy. And, as we all have struggled, learned, grown, and evolved, we have become a teacher for those souls who did not journey the path of the earth.

Through our many lifetimes here on earth, we have become an idol and a *"hero"* to those souls that have taken no type of physical form, such as becoming a Master and a teacher *(renown)* to those souls who did not choose to journey through the materialistic world of the flesh. We are a Master in our own right, and we don't even know it. And, when we consider what we have learned reading this book, then maybe we can see our "divine plan" governing it all.

Therefore, in the eyes of our "I AM" Christ consciousness, and the rest of all that is, we are a blessed and unique angel. In fact, in the eyes of those angels who never took the journey in the flesh, we are men and women of honor and importance. And that is why we are here on earth, creating our experiences! And, when we read about the *"new hymn"* in Revelation 14:3, it reveals how the "rapture" is to come about.

It comes through us humans ascending from a three-density being to a four-density being. Therefore, Yeshua is not coming to earth for our salvation. It is you, by way of your mind-soul and ego-personalities, moving into a New Expansional Energy of Four. You attract energy into your spirit body, your mind-soul body, and your physical body based on your own consciousness beliefs. And, if you desire healing, abundance, or good relationships, then be more conscious of your choices. Just trust that there is more energy around you then there is in a whole country of America. So, think about that!

When John had seen the *"angel flying high"* in Revelation 14:6, it represents us, humans, in physical form, growing and integrating our mind-soul with having a consciousness to overcome our mind's belief in salvation, and that polarity energy is real. It is when we become conscious of our beliefs that brings *"everlasting good news."* Why? It is because some of us have moved from a lower quality mind to a higher divine mind where our eyes are now wide open to every memory *(nation)*, family tree *(tribe)*, belief system *(tongue)*, and reality and story (people) that opposes us in becoming a sovereign Christ in the flesh.

It is sovereignty that brings to us "freedom." Not freedom from government, or from our past lifetimes, because our past isn't what we think it is anyway. It is through understanding our consciousness is "all that we are." Our mind and physical body are not who we are, and this knowing prevents us from trying to steal energy from others by putting them down or for us to try to interfere with the way they choose to live their life. Just know and be conscious that energy is all right there, ready to serve us, bringing us freedom from limitations.

And, according to Revelation 14:7, it is not our mind or our ego-personality that brings us enlightenment. *"He said in a loud voice, 'fear God' and give him glory, for his time has come to sit in judgment. Worship him who made heaven and earth, the sea, and springs of water."* It is our Oversoul, the "I AM" essence within because it has already integrated many of our ego-personalities of our past. Our mind and our human ego-personality know nothing of our wisdom, our "I AM" Christ consciousness, and how energy works, because the mind will always default to only what it knows in any present lifetime. Remember, it takes the collective wisdom of all our ego-personality lifetimes to become a Master in the flesh.

The mind only operates through its intelligence, false beliefs, judgments, and what it knows about God on an emotional level. The *"loud voice"* and *"fear God and give him glory"* comes from feeling guilty and ashamed of how we have used this pure unbiased God energy of light in an unfitting way. However, all is not lost, because there are many of us that have now paid the price through sowing and reaping. We have paid the price by following and worshipping the forces of polarity energy (dragon) for many lifetimes, and this manifested this *"fear of God."* The experiences of illnesses, being broke, having bad relationships, or other unfortunate happenings have always seemed beyond our understanding. Yet, we must give credit to whatever we are experiencing.

We all give glory and praise to the belief in polarity energy without even being conscious of the act coming from our mind of an emotional level. Therefore, we have replaced the "I AM" Christ consciousness (the real (God)dess) in favor of a God (mind) of judgment, jealousy, sin, punishment, right and wrong, good and evil, and that polarity energy is something real. However, *"for his time has come to sit in judgment,"* is the self, from the mind level, the one that replaced Goddess with a God of judgment and duality, is beginning to pass judgment upon the self.

This judgment comes from our emotions, where we perceived good, bad, sin, and punishment as being truth. And, this causes our many past ego-personalities from coming home to us, the creator, to integrate. It is our mind of an emotional nature trying to understand enlightenment of the spirit that comes from the intellectual side of our mind, which is why we continue to *"worship"* our mind (false God), the one *"who made heaven and earth"* as a place of falseness and lies, instead of allowing the *"springs of water,"* (the source of life) come from our "I AM" Christ spirit.

And, this will continue until we reach a lifetime where we come across something that will open our eyes and awaken us to the "I AM" essence of being (God)dess. Thus, awakening us to the memories of lies buried deep within our subconsciousness *(the sea)* where we all were locked into a mind that could not distinguish between enlightenment or the perception of enlightenment.

Without realizing it, we are being influenced by our mind, and all of our many ego-personalities of the past because reason, logic, and perception have become the God of intelligence in our life. However, do not concern yourself because our mind is not responsible for our enlightenment. It is our Oversoul! Our Oversoul (Christ consciousness) is doing a great job because it takes every experience we have chosen and extracts the lesson learned into wisdom. It strips away all details, the judgments, the hatreds, and it takes away all the emotions and brings it down to just wisdom.

Therefore, allow your Oversoul (Christ) to come to you. It is not that you have to look for your Oversoul (Christ); it comes to you at the perfect moment in your life. Especially when you say "I AM Ready," and then "Allow." However, remember, it is not going to be what you always thought it would be or what you have studied. Do not be surprised that it could tear your human identity to shreds, which is why Revelation 14:8, the *"second angel followed, saying, 'fallen is Babylon the great, that made all the nations drink the wine of her licentious passion.'"*

This *"second angel,"* is our mind (Son of God) finally comes to the point in fulfilling our divine plan. If we studied our thoughts, we would find where we are going and where we have been because they will clearly point to the nature of our physical beliefs and what we will manifest next to experience. Our feelings, thoughts, and beliefs, whether consciously or unconsciously, alter and form our physical body to what we desire to experience, and the world in which we desire to live them out. Our body does not just happen to be thin, fat, tall, short, healthy, or ill. These characteristics are created in the mind first and then thrust outward as an image of the self. Our characteristics at birth were there for a reason because we chose and created them from the inner levels of our beliefs first.

Remember, we did not arrive on earth as a baby without a history. Our personality was always hidden away within our soul memories, and our history of beliefs has created all that we are in this lifetime. Therefore, the *"fallen, fallen is Babylon the great"* represents our mental confusion about "who we are" is becoming clear because we have played out many lifetimes sowing and reaping because of a system that accepts good and evil as truth. And, because of this, we can create a better life for ourselves. As the City of Babylon signifies the mixture of many belief systems of mass consciousness, it can also signify our many, made-up belief systems.

"Babylon the great," Revelation 14:8, is not so much about the Middle East, even though we humans put outside of ourselves a physical counterpart to remind us who we are within. It refers to you and group consciousness in creating (using our mind) multitudes of social standards of conduct based on good and evil, right and wrong, God and Satan, and then spreading those collective society standards throughout multiple dimensions as being real and true. For example, Religion tells us what to do by way of a controlling God instead of teaching us to go within ourselves to find God.

The word *"fallen"* itself is for us to pay attention to our creative abilities and how we, and the collective group consciousness, can form a whole new city of belief systems where we can set in motion a world of occurrences that are not real but feel real. Thus, we could experience them. But once we open our eyes and awaken to these beliefs of group consciousness and the system created outside of ourselves (Babylon the great), then the complexity of the system as we know it becomes less troublesome for us to experience.

And, what we see in, *"that made all the nations drink the wine of her licentious passion,"* Revelation 14:8, represents you and the human group-consciousness first becoming part of the physical world and using polarity energy of positive and negative, and that of a belief in a system of a God that created us as our banner and yardstick to follow. We, as a group consciousness, became overwhelmed by the forces of duality and judgment that caused us to become impaired by the intensity of a system of lies *(the wine)*. And, because of our intense intellectual belief in a system to know God as real, we became unaware of being part of something much greater than our human existence.

When we look into the wisdom behind Revelation 14:9-10, *"A third angel followed them and said in a loud voice, 'Anyone who worships the beast or its image, or accepts its mark on forehead or hand, will also drink the wine of God's fury, poured full strength into the cup of his wrath, and will be tormented in burning sulfur before the holy angels and before the Lamb."* This seems to be a "wow factor" because it all sounds terrifying for those that will worship the beast. However, let us see how much of a "wow factor" it really is!

The *"third angel"* is our intuition consciousness, and the *"loud voice"* is the vibrational frequency that is coming from our remaining past ego-personality aspects that have accepted the mark and have worshipped their egos (beast), but as of yet, they have not intergraded with us in this lifetime. It is these remaining ego-personality aspects of us that have the *"mark on the forehead or hand,"* and they fear coming home to us in this lifetime because guilt and shame are what holds them to the system. However, all of them have (you) submitted to the law of balance or cause-and-effect. So, do not despair! It is because of the belief in the law of cause and effect (the system) that they show fear, guilt, and shame, which is why we too feel this within our consciousness.

It is time to realize that some of us are finished with our karma. And now, we have given them the avenue to return home to us in this lifetime. In retrospect, they have done nothing wrong anyway. It is just a strong belief in the system that we have planted deep within that we have done something wrong. It is them and us in this lifetime that became a slave to our own memories, our Oversoul, and our mind of a system that says it is real. And this is why these memories of old are pouring down *(fury pours)* on us today, and they will continue until we are ready to accept them as our creations.

Remember, they are part of us as much as we are part of them. To our many ego-personalities of the past, the beast and its image are our physical mind and form, which means more to them than their own intuitive nature. It was and is because of our past lifetimes forgetting who they are, and then refusing to take responsibility for their actions, they had to drink the wine of duality. And now, we feel that we are experiencing the wrath of our own "I AM" Christ spirit *(God's fury)*, even though our "I AM" Christ spirit does not judge, condemn, or sends down any type of wrath on us. In effect, we condemn ourselves because of our mental perception that the mind is the master of our ship (body).

Therefore, it is you who judges yourself and condemns yourself to this wrath (truth). And, those of our ego aspects which still hold to their dogmatic beliefs about the system, such as good and evil, fire, brimstone, and hell, where they will suffer the justice of the law of karma until they are ready to come home to you in this lifetime. This torment is manifested through the *"holy angels"* or the seven churches and your mind *(Lamb)* found in Chapters 8–14, Revelation 2 and 3:

1. Gonads/Ephesus/physical body
2. Leyden/Smyrna/etheric/astral body
3. Adrend/Pergamum/emotional body
4. Thymus/Thyatira/mental body
5. Thyroid/Sardis/intuitive body
6. Pineal/Philadelphia/mind-body
7. Pituitary/Laodicea/spirit body

It will be through these *"seven holy angels"* that will eventually lead our many ego-personality aspects back toward the light of understanding that we are the Christ and the forgiver of their so-called sins. However, they continue to experience hell because they still believe in a God who is more powerful than them, a belief that Yeshua is their salvation, and a belief in sin. Therefore, through time and space, our mind in this lifetime, and our ego-personalities of the past will eventually learn obedience through the things they suffer.

And this is why our many ego-personalities that have followed the *"mark of the beast"* will eventually come home to the self, their creator, sometimes in this lifetime if we allow it. As this is seen in Revelation 14:11, *"The smoke of the fire that torments them will rise forever and ever, and there will be no relief day or night for those who worship the beast or its image or accept the mark of its name."* Smoke is usually caused by fire, and its ashes rise in the air, and then finally dissipates and becomes part of the sky.

Therefore, smoke represents how confused we are about vibrational polarity energy (positive and negative) and how our many ego-personality aspects of the past became blindsided (unaware) by the ashes of this confusion. It came to be that they cultivated (raised) a mental belief about understanding their acts of consciousness was always right, and therefore never wrong. Because of these ego-personality aspects from our past and present, we come to worship our defiant ego (Beast) and whatever we have created as our truths in this lifetime. Therefore, we suffer the consequences (torment) as an individual and as a group consciousness.

And, as long as we continue to believe in an Antichrist or Beast, a God separate from us, a God superior to us, a God who judges, and the concept of right and wrong, we will have no relief from our sins day or night. We will experience no relief until we learn hell is nothing more than us meeting ourselves through reincarnation, and that we are equal to Goddess, God, and the Christ. By believing in Satan and the idea of good and evil, we are accepting his *"mark"* upon our *"forehead"* (outer consciousness) without even realizing it.

By continuing to give credit to our defiant ego-personality (Beast), we, through karma, will continue to identify ourselves with our creations of sadness and suffering. However, if we *"sustain the holy ones who keep God's commandments and their faith in Jesus,"* Revelation 14:12, then it is through our patience, persistence, and endurance in keeping the endocrine system *(holy ones)* senses of the physical body and the mind clear to focus on our "divine plan" (commandments) and our faith in "I AM" Christ (Jesus); thus, it will show us the way to freedom. By taking responsibility for everything that is happening in our lives, even if it's cancer, and then letting go of the system, we bring about grace in such a way that we may not have to endure the full effects of what we are reaping.

Patience, persistence, and endurance are the measures of understanding our purpose in following our divine plan. Thus, we learn "why such things happen in our life." By taking full responsibility for our consciousness acts, our creations, and why we may be experiencing what we are experiencing in our life today actually help us to heal our past works where we did not take responsibility. And, once we understand our tormenting experiences are no longer necessary to keep confronting what is happening to us today, grace will always follow. The realization to whom we indeed are as a Goddess is when we allow no more battling within the self.

By accepting yourself as being equal to Christ, God, and the Goddess, and truly trust in yourself as Christ, and then taking responsibility for your creations, you heal your past. Thus, your sowing and reaping (karma) can end, including even your cancer or anything else that is happening in your life. Healing also comes when you understand how your consciousness and energy work with each other.

There are many dimensions (life stories) that we have created. Although they are all illusionary and false, as hell does not exist either, and those who believe in them are deeply tormented. And, the purpose of the torment is to train ourselves to create consciously and take responsibility for what is and has been created. In the most basic sense, as I repeat this, the purpose of life is to help us understand consciousness, how energy works, and knowing who you indeed are at our core. This is very important to understand!

As long as the belief in good and evil is continuously being formed within our memories of the past, then those memories *(nations)* will surface as expressions, and then manifestation. And you, as both individual and group, will experience the extremes of their consequences. Always remember what we believe produces our thoughts; our thoughts produce our feelings (passion); our feelings (intuitive consciousness) produce our life actions, and our actions determine our picture of reality. The universe is all-serving. It observes what we classify as our reality and gradually rearranges itself to support our beliefs. Hence, it is our duty to take full responsibility for everything that happens in our life.

Chapter 31

OUR MIND (ANTI-CHRIST) BECOMES THE SAVIOR

The *"voice from heaven,"* Revelation 14:13, is an expression *(voice)* coming from our own "I AM" Christ consciousness (Oversoul) revealing to us our "divine plan," via through the awakening of our intuitive consciousness instead of seeing our mental level (the fourth angel) as the means for finding Christ. How can we complete our "divine plan" if we continuously work out of our old mind values and believes in free will and polarity as real?

"Free-will" and "polarity" are products that come from our mind-soul mental consciousness (the church of Sardis) where self-expression, creative ideas, and our successes in the material world come from the belief in power, and that all intelligence comes from the mind. And yet, the mystical and magical successes of life come from our "divine plan" that we created to follow from the beginning until we reawaken to whom we truly are at our core essence. Why? It is because our "divine plan" has come from the "I AM" Christ within, and not from our mind (the Anti-Christ).

Christ's request that John *"write this,"* Revelation 14:13, represents the Christ within us all gives blessings to our ego-personality aspect of today by opening us up to memory and all that we have ever been since the time we left home (first creation or Higher Consciousness). In return, once we are awakened, our 'I AM" Christ consciousness (Oversoul) will release all that it has recorded to memory *(write down)* and how we have played those memories out as our divine plan to become awakened to the sowing and reaping that we have been doing in each lifetime.

Terry L. Newbegin

"Blessed are the dead who die in the Lord from now on," Revelation 14:13. From my understanding of the Ascended Masters, I interpret the "Lord" as the part of our mind (right side) that represents Jesus, the Son of God, and the *"dead"* are all those ego-personality aspects of us that are not awakened to the self, being the Christ and their savior. But, once we, in this lifetime, become awakened to our own "divine plan," the left side of our mind becomes one with the right side of our mind. Thus, our mind-soul (symbolized by the Son of God) then becomes the savior for all of our ego-personalities.

Our mind, the Anti-Christ, becomes the Christ and savior in the flesh for all ego-personalities by the left and right side of our mind becoming one with our total consciousness. Since we create many physical bodies using time and space as the vehicle to understand life, then physical death is nothing more than us humans committing to memory all the fixed ideas, beliefs, and concepts of what we have chosen and experienced in each lifetime. This is why it is necessary for us to return to earth again and again in a new body.

And, once awakened to whom we are, we learn to call in those ego-personality aspects from other lifetimes to integrate them, for they are no longer *"dead"* to the truth. By choosing and experiencing many physical and non-physical lifetimes, we eventually release all of our dogmatic beliefs of a system that is of duality based, thereby bringing to celebration our Lordship as a savior. For we are the Son of God coming into an awareness that we are also the Christ-savior for all that we are and ever have been.

Jesus became Christ in his day, and people called him the savior because of the shedding of his blood to save us from sin. However, Jesus (Yeshua) was the example, as we too have shed our blood (energy) and bared our cross (sowing and reaping). And now, it is time for us to follow in his footsteps and become the savor of self. It is that we cannot save anyone else but ourselves because everyone has their own "divine plan" to follow. It is about our divine mind, the higher quality mind, that becomes one again with our outer mental, limited mind so that our many ego-personality aspects may now come home to rest from their labors (suffering).

As Revelation 14:13, *"for their works accompany them,"* refers to the works of our old dogmatic beliefs that followed us in each lifetime. Thus, it is you who bears witness to the ideas and beliefs of vibrational energy that exists nowhere other than within your own mind that believes in sin, power, and polarity energy as to whom you are. And, of course, what you do intellectually (and mentally) becomes the essence of your soul in action. Everything that was constructed outside of you comes from polarity energy and how it reflects what you are today, and nothing is or was excluded.

The only way to understand that you are God, Goddess, Christ, and Satan is through a mind (the Son) that is awakened to the illusion of you being less than God, both inner and outer. You do not just show up here on earth for no apparent reason, go through some random sequence of events and experiences, and then disappear. You are part of continuous, creative experience and, as a soul-being, you are part of the foundation of the wholeness of a "Universal God of pure energy and light (neutrality) that man has envisioned to be a solitary white person sitting on a throne waiting to judge you for your sins.

This is called a mind that works hard to control all aspects of itself through power, judgment, and punishment. Thus, the Anti-Christ at work! Remember, as John 14:6, *"Jesus said to him, I am the way, the truth, and the life. No one comes to the Father except through me."* The "Father God" is of an "omnipresent universal mind field of pure unbiased God energy of light. The Son is that of the Mind that is fully awakened and aware that it is part of the "I AM" Christ consciousness, and the ego is the Son of Man becoming awakened to it all. Therefore, a fully awakened mind (the Lord Prince) is the only way to get you back home to your "I AM" Christ consciousness.

After journeying through many physical lifetimes, choosing and experiencing the seven deadly acts; (i) sadness, (ii) anger, (iii) lust for power, (iv) envy, (v) greed, (vi) pride, and (vii) laziness, we do finally awaken as a divine-human in the flesh. A divine-human is someone that has learned to balance their spirit, mind, and ego as "one body of consciousness." However, the question is, do we want to make it happen in this lifetime, the next one, or the one after that? It is all up to you!

When we look at Revelation 14:14, the *"white cloud,"* it represents us, humans, learning to purify ourselves through the Crystalline Energy (blood) of our own "I AM" Christ consciousness. When we learn to let go of vibrational energy (polarity) and take full responsibility for our life, we finally let go of the belief in the existence of the "Tree of Knowledge of Good and Evil." We learn of our own authority as a true Goddess, and how we can overcome our old thoughts, beliefs, actions, and experiences tied to positive and negative. And one way we can do it is by seeing ourselves as equal to God/Goddess, and not less than.

Once we learn to let go and awaken to whom we are, the Son of Man and the Son of God, we can heal our past by remembering sin, punishment, and power was all about learning wisdom. This process is reflected in the meaning of the *"golden crown"* on Son's head, or I should say our head.

For example, the *"sharp sickle,"* Revelation 14:14, is associated with us experiencing both sides of the sword (positive and negative) to learn the meaning of the "Tree of Knowledge of Good and Evil." We are a creator God/Goddess, and our true name and identity go far beyond our human name and identity because, in truth, our real name is "I AM That I AM," and no one can change that, not even the self.

The other *"angel coming out of the temple, crying out in a loud voice to the one sitting on the cloud,"* Revelation 14:15, represents our emotional body of consciousness (the sixth angel) working out of our physical body *(temple)* reaping *(crying out)* what we have sown over many lifetimes. And now, the influences of our emotional body is looking upon our left and right mind activities to convey a new feeling, thought, and idea about this vibrational opposing energy and how it differs from this New Expansional Energy of Four.

Again, the *"one sitting on the cloud,"* Revelation 14:15, is us, souls, in human form, working through our left (outer) and right (inner) mind as the ultimate Ruler of ourselves. It has always been the left side of our mind (outer) that has seen itself as the true intellect in manifesting our desires as either good and evil. As earth's elements (i) fire, (ii) water, (iii) air, and (iv) form (earth and physical body) became the servants for our mind, they also became the servants under our influences about sin and power being real.

It was our emotional consciousness of the physical that cried out for us to *"use our sickle and reap the harvest, for the time to reap has come,"* Revelation 14:15, as this represents us using sowing and reaping as the means to balance our energy and our consciousnesses. And because *"the harvest is fully ripe,"* Revelation 14:15, it indicates what we have been doing for many millions of years in working to balance our energy and consciousnesses. It was with this method of incarnations and the belief in opposing energy, the actions we have chosen to experience in this lifetime are now an embodiment of the way we understand what we have learned as a Christ also.

It is because of these many past lifetimes upon the earth sowing and reaping, we have today reached an awareness where we have been tried by fire, purified, and purged to where some of us are now ready to take full responsibility for all things we chose to experience. However, know that the emotional consciousness is the hardest to overcome all because of family, friends, politics, guilt, shame, and our religious ties. Therefore, the time has come for us to gather all of what we have learned (the crops) from the beginning of our evolution and get on with our work in letting go of the belief in a system that believes in opposing energy, such as sin and punishment.

Since you are the *"one sitting on the throne on the cloud swinging your sickle,"* Revelation 14:16, then the "harvesting" of your many ego-personalities are ready to come home to their creator, you, with a mind and ego, fully awakened to the Christ you are. However, only if you so choose! By journeying through time and space, sowing and reaping, the Son of Man (our ego-personalities) have cleansed us of all the desires of good and evil, and all the memories tied to them. And now, this action prepared you and your physical body to be the one to integrate with your mind-soul, all of your many ego-personalities, and your "I AM" Christ consciousness. Again, only if you so choose!

Therefore, *"one like the Son of Man"* (our ego-personality of today), Revelation 14:14, is the "beast" redeemed. And, *"how long, oh Lord,"* Psalm 13, represents our outer mind, the masculine, transforming from an Anti-Christ and redeemed to be Christ. It is addressing how long will arrogance be, and the belief in Yeshua coming to save you (egotism), and govern the meek (the humbleness of a redeem mind and ego). This is like our "I AM" Christ consciousness answering by saying that everything has a season (lifetimes) to grow (evolve), and then yield the full fruit by keeping the agreement (Noah's flood) made with our "I AM" long ago.

You reap what you sow because a long time ago, you agreed with your "I AM" not to interfere with your beliefs and creations. And, it was because of this agreement, you entered earth a long time ago to clean up those beliefs and creations, and now the time has come to let go of those old beliefs. As you have been learning throughout the book, you do come to a point in life, this one or the next, when you will say along with Yeshua (Jesus); *"you know neither me nor my Father. If you knew me, you would know my Father also"* (John 8:19).

And this is why *"the Father and I are one"* (John 10:30).

As this, all represents, how can you know the "Father" (this universal God energy of light) if you do not even know that you are Christ? And this is why the Christ you are, is the one with this "universal God energy of light." However, *"the harvest is abundant but the workers are few"* (Luke 10:2). Why? Because there are so few of us who realize that it is time to take themselves down off the cross by using opposing energy behind their beliefs, thoughts and that suffering is the means to reach heaven. Suffering gets you nowhere but more suffering!

People are still asleep because they *"keep looking back"* (Luke 9:62) to what has already been plowed, looking back to the past and to the old energy of duality for their answers. Yeshua's suffering on the cross represents our journey through many lifetimes sowing and reaping. However, because of our mind and ego-personalities, many of us find ourselves still working with Revelation 14:7, *"Then another angel came out of the temple in heaven who also had a sharp sickle."* And, this angel is associated with our Astral Body.

When we come to that place in the flesh where our physical body (temple) dies, our Astral Body also carries the "sharp sickle" of sowing and reaping because death in the physical is not the end of us. We take with us all of our belief systems, lies, and illusions about God and who we think we are as a sinner. The *"sharp sickle"* of karma will pick up again when we come back to earth in another physical body all because of the belief in karma. Therefore, suffering never ends until we realize that we came to earth eons ago to play out our "divine plan" in order to become a wise sovereign God, Goddess, and Christ in our own right. Remember, it takes a "master" to bring about the realization of being a "master" like Yeshua.

Because of our many lifetimes, our "free will" of the mind affects our ability to wake from our sleep state of being a Christ also. The mind, and its free will, is very skilled and knowledgeable about its environment (astral/physical), and it knows how to persuade, hide, and influence us with our choices since everything we know is tied to duality beliefs. We believe in our heart of hearts that "free will," rather than our connection to our "divine plan," is the great searcher and discoverer of God. And, maybe this is why in *"Paran was a wilderness between Sinai and Canaan, and the scene of much of the Israelites wandering on their way to the Promised Land"* Genesis 21:21, as this represents us souled beings wandering around in ignorance.

We all have many confused and undisciplined ego-personalities spread throughout many astral realms right now, and they are earnestly searching after the truth, which is why in this lifetime people are so confused when it comes to religion, family, and governments. It is a feeling deep within each of these ego-aspects that it is the only way to find their way to the Promised Land (higher consciousness).

The *"angel coming out of the altar"* is our physical body. And, the angel in Revelation 14:17 is our astral body, and it is given direction by the angel of our physical body in Revelation 14:18. The coming out of the astral realm is the physical body is a creation that comes forth from our inner mental consciousness, and therefore becomes the sacrificial consciousness (altar) for offering the self up to learn responsibility.

Remember, you, in the physical world, and from the mind level, are the Master and the Lord of Lords in *"charge of the fire,"* Revelation 14:18, as this represents you as the Master planner in what you will experience in the flesh when you come back to earth for more sowing and reaping. Responsibility of your choices are planned in the astral and carried out through the fire of justice in the flesh. When karma *(sharp sickle)* is used to *"cut the clusters from the earth's vines,"* Revelation 14:18, the forces of positive and negative, good and bad, sin and punishment, you, the Master creator, eventually change the directions of all your light and dark ego-personality aspects that have served you well in many lifetimes.

The *"vines"* represents your energy being tied to every ego-personality aspect that you have created since the time you left the first creation (higher consciousness) eons ago. *"For its grapes are ripe,"* Revelation 14:18, has the same meaning as "wine." In the process, the juices of the wine represent your experiences resulting from your own dual beliefs, and how they cloud and impair you from being aware of being Christ.

In other words, it became very difficult for us to understand our situations in life, let alone to understand that we are the creator of them. The meaning here is that our ego-personality of the flesh did not understand or view our beliefs of good and evil, right and wrong as illusions, as they see them as truth. Therefore, we ignore our "I AM" Christ consciousness in preference to our mental and ego perception of being a sinner. This gave us a way out of not taking responsibility for our own creations.

As the Catholics use in prayer, "thy will be done," just implies that God's will is separate from our own divine plan. Thus, having us feel separate from our creations and from our "I AM" Christ consciousness. It is all just a perception on the mind's end because there is no separation between our "free will" and our "divine plan" other than perception.

For example, *"the Father himself {does not} judge no one, but has assigned all judgment to the Son, so that all men may honor the Son just as they honor the Father,"* John 5:22-23. No wonder we are confused about God and life's choices because the "Son" is you working from out of your mind of reason, judgment, and the belief in a God outside of you, which is why all judgments come from your mind and not some God above you. This is why man honors their mind as to whom they truly are more so than their own Spirit.

This is also why religions say to lie down or give away your most valuable possessions or give them money because they view God as the

God of right and wrong, sin and punishment, and a God of salvation. However, this God of duality is placed outside of you as representing your mind, and if religions say this God is part of you, then they are right because this God of the Bible is in the image of your mind of arrogance, for this God wants all power for himself.

Learn to feel your "I AM" Christ-spirit within your heart rather than trying to figure God out through your mind and ego. Do not allow your trust (faith) to be a slave to the mind (the Son) or to be held back by the limitations of believing you are only human, and therefore need to suffer to gain God's favor. If you place your faith in only what the mind comprehends, then your understanding of good and evil (sin) remains active, causing disharmony and pain to occur over and over. This is seen in Revelation 14:19, as the *"angel swung his sickle over the earth and cut the earth's vintage."*

The *"swinging off his sickle over the earth"* is about the law of karma as the means to balance our energy because of the belief in good and evil. And, if we ignore the route of karma as part of a three-density world, that is when we cut ourselves off from our many ego-personality aspects that are still playing in other dimensions. This is hiding from yourself!

"I do nothing of myself; but as my Father hath taught me?" John 8:28. This is the unbiased god energy of light, teaching us that we are in command of the energy around us and how it works under the physical umbrella. And, if we use it in an unclean way, then that same energy comes back to us as a lesson. This may explain why humanity is unaware that his ego-personality in the flesh can take on a beastly nature, and his mind is what judges everything that travels through it.

As established earlier in the book, a "city" represents a fixed state of consciousness of a collective group, like humanity, and how the group's views and beliefs affect the various nerve centers of the group's physical body. If we have a small city that is filled with hate and very unbalanced energy, then karma belongs to the whole group, which is why a bad storm can devastate a city.

In Revelation 14:20, *"blood poured out of the winepress to the height of a horse's bridle,"* represents that our life-giving energy *(blood)* was given over to cause and effect to learn responsibility, as an individual and as a group consciousness, like a city, state, country, and as a world. And, when the memories of each are cleansed by living in a three-density world and consciousness, that is when we, all groups, develop and raise our ego-personality consciousness to new *"heights."* It is here where we awaken to exercise control over our beliefs, thoughts, and judgments, as the *"horse's bridle"* symbolizes that control when awakened.

This reminds me of the horses in Revelation 6:2, the "white horse" (I AM) helps to open our awareness of being Christ in the flesh. The "red horse," Revelation 6:4, helps us to understand that our mind (the Anti-Christ) and polarity energy are just an illusion. The "black horse," Revelation 6:8, helps us recognize that the belief in sin and punishment is about us using energy in such a way that it brings us karma to learn responsibility. And, the *"pale green horse,"* Revelation 6:8, helps us understand that our suffering in a three-density consciousness is only temporary.

Remember that the earth realm can affect us from many different levels of consciousness, spirit, mind-soul, and from our many ego-personalities that are spread throughout other dimensions, whether we know it or not. Therefore, the *"blood being poured out of the winepress,"* Revelation 14:20, is about us removing from our memories all the energy (blood) we used in giving animation to our many lifetimes. Memories such as the belief in polarity energy, sin, punishment, that we are not Christ or anything that we solidified in our hearts as our truths, are actually lies. And, only by taking responsibility for those memories of old beliefs can we remember who we are, a Christ in our own right.

Since duality or opposing energy is part of the earth's forces working through our three-dimensional flesh body to help us meet ourselves through time and space, then our energy *(blood)*, even *"to the height of a horse's bridle,"* shows that our evolution or rein (exercising our power) on earth has come from working outside of ourselves instead of making decisions using the consciousness of knowing that we can be misled by our mind of a mental nature. This statement helps us absorb Yeshua's words when he was on the earth but not of the earth.

The *"two hundred miles,"* Revelation 14:20, represents the splitting of our mind, as we all have a mind-soul type consciousness. Thus, we all have a right (feminine-negative-inner) and a left (masculine-positive-outer) consciousness where we can experience both sides of self. The "two zeros" are associated with our beginning stages of evolution, as the "first zero" is associated with us experiencing nothing but oneness in the First Creation under the umbrella of the "I AM" Christ (Garden).

The "second zero" is associated with the split mind-soul becoming in charge or control of all energy used for what we desire to experience. It is the "second zero," where we misunderstood polarity energy and became stuck in multiple astral realms and a physical realm using the mind as if it was God. This is also where we came to believe in power. And, what comes with power? Control. However, in the end, it takes the Anti-Christ (the lost mind) to introduce us to our "I AM" Christ consciousness, thus our savior.

Chapter 32

TAPPING INTO OUR MEMORIES

This chapter reveals the deep secrets of our buried egotistical memories that we may not want to believe exist because they belong to other lifetimes that we take as being our natural instincts of today. In reading this chapter, I hope to explore as to why we play certain games in our life that lead to all those annoying and frustrating occurrences that we like blaming others. This chapter may answer questions like, "Why do bad things happen to me? "Why was I born poor and ill, while others born rich and healthy?" "Why does God take a loved one that is so good and leave behind those of questionable character?" There are many more questions like this we could ask God.

How about you? Can you answer these questions with all honesty? Why is it that God can be so cruel sometimes and yet be so loving and gentle? The answer, of course, God is not responsible for what we experience in life. We are the ones responsible for the way we look, being born poor, ill, rich, or healthy. Is it hard to understand that we, as an individual or group, are indeed responsible for whatever we are experiencing in life? All that our "I AM" Christ consciousness did was set the stage for us to "act in consciousness." And, when we did, we all chose energy that allowed us to experience both sides of a coin.

Thus, we souled beings, and not God, are the ones who set the stage for the *"wrath of God."* And yet, this wrath has nothing to do with being punished or the experiencing of karma, but it is about how we used this God energy of light, and now it comes back to us in the same way we used it. Memory became the tool for us souled beings to set up our own "divine plan" to learn the wisdom behind our "consciousness acts" without the interference of our "I AM." And, in this act, we fully became responsible for our choices and how we used energy (God). We can say that our mind, the designated Son of Goddess, or the Adam principle, set the way for us to learn a long time ago who we are and how we used energy (God) for our creations.

When going over Revelation 15:1, *"I saw in heaven another sign, great, and awe-inspiring: Seven angels with the seven plagues,"* as this helps us realize just how hard we have made it for ourselves to get what we wanted in life, good or bad made no difference to us. Believe it or not, we made the choices going back before the universe was ever created, and now, we are plagued with the results of how we used our energy. So, why complain? This was a good thing because how else were we to learn to be a co-creator (mind and ego levels) with our "I AM?"

Through our own choices and refusal to take responsibility for what we created, we brought down the wrath upon ourselves. And, to help with this understanding, allow Yeshua and the Ascended Masters to consider Genesis 3:4, where the serpent said to Eve, *"You certainly will not die."* And, in truth, the serpent was not lying. However, the serpent could have added, "all that we have to do is take full responsibility for all our creations and how we used our energy."

Note here! Realization is knowing what you use for your creations is an energy that comes directly from you, as you are the creator Goddess bringing about that energy, and therefore it belongs to no one else but you. Thus, you are responsible for whatever you are experiencing, even if you claim it is not your fault. And, as most know, the story of Adam and Eve blamed what they did on something outside of themselves instead of taking full responsibility for their own choice. It was from this act in consciousness coming from the mind-soul level that we supposedly got kicked out of the Garden for disobeying Goddess.

The whole story of Adam, Eve, and the Serpent is a metaphor to help us all to understand our beginning as a three-dimensional being and how, at first, we were not part of any physical consciousness or world at the time. However, before coming to earth eons ago, we all were layered as three different consciousnesses (spirit, mind-soul, and ego) while we were still aware of being the "I AM" Christ. But, once we, from the mind-soul level, made a choice to split our consciousness into a left (masculine-positive) and right (feminine-negative) brain hemisphere, our ego (the serpent) became the power behind the throne, which is why our ego said and knew we could not die.

How could we die if the perfection of us being a Christ of an everlasting Spirit of One has already been established within our mind-soul and ego levels of consciousness? This is what our ego already knew and why our ego fooled our mind and soul to take over the creation process. It was supposed to have been our mind (the masculine) to take on the creative process while our soul consciousness of responsibility (the feminine) was to keep us reminded of what we were choosing.

However, our mind lost control of our ego, and that is when we manipulated our own created energy in a matter to control it as if it was power. This illusion of power coming from our ego is where we all manifested experiences according to ego preferences tied to playing opposites. But, because of our ego-personality had no power, it learned how to manipulate our mind and soul by giving up its authority (power) to create. Thus, our ego seized that power and controlled away from our mind and soul consciousness of responsibility without telling us that we are the only ones who can cast ourselves out of our own perfection.

And it is done by allowing our emotional side of the mind (Eve) to wrap itself up with many false beliefs coming from our mind (Adam) of perception. Thus, all those false beliefs recorded by our soul were coming from our many ego-personalities. It was our ego that had us feel separate from our "I AM" Christ consciousness, and from the energy (God) that surrounded us, and made it look like it was coming from our mind and a God outside of us. It was at this point that we began to lose sight of being God and the Goddess. Thus, we forgot that we are Christ, and this led to us losing our memory of ever being Christ *(surely die)*.

And, in Genesis 3:5, *"God knows well that the moment you eat of it, your eyes will open and you will be like gods who know what is good and what is bad."* From this verse alone, it tells us outright that the process we chose as souls a long time ago to move outside of our "I AM" Christ consciousness was required on our part to explore the process of polarity energy to learn the wisdom behind what is good and evil, and what is right and wrong. Thus, we become like Gods, but Gods that are filled with wisdom. When our defiant ego nature (serpent-Beast) failed to tell us to read between the lines, we learned the consequences of our choices the hard way.

The moment we went through the wall of fire (polarity energy), which is depicted as kicked out of the garden, we immediately became aware *(your eyes will be opened)* of the dualistic forces of positive and negative energy. And that is when we began learning to take responsibility for whatever we created *(be like gods)*. It was the only way we could find the answer to the questions, "Who am I?" "What is my purpose?" and "Why do I believe I have power?"

We all became lost within an ego-personality (serpent) that thought it was God, and then blamed others for what it had done. And all we have to do is look around us for the truth because everything motivated comes from the ego, as we all are ego-driven, instead of spirit driven. So, we can say, *"We surely died,"* because we felt isolated from our own "I AM" Christ spirit. It was in our perceived isolation and despair, we all felt a growing resentment and anger toward our own "I AM" Christ-spirit, thinking it had created us to fail. This sentiment eventually turned into the belief that God is punishing us for our choices. And that was the beginning of the blame game.

It has been a long time since we fell into a reality built on belief systems about who we are. Because of it, we took on a lot of guilt for leaving the garden (our oneness) and how we played and used the energy of duality for self-gratification. Even today, we hold this guilt within us. By living many lifetimes exploring and creating, this guilt has spread throughout our consciousness to the point of blotting out the awareness of why we left home (our perfection) in the first place. And, once we took on a belief in sin, it has become part of our personality ever since. Sin is fortified and fixed within our mind every day by religion, government, the media, family members, and businesses. The result of all this guilt and belief in sin, is fear.

Once we left the first creation (the garden) and entered into the void, we had to choose how we would experience the energy of duality for self-expression. We all had the choice to move toward the light (known) or toward darkness (unknown). Of course, light and dark are only a perception. They are not real, and in the end, the light became part of what is known, while darkness became an energy that was not known to us at the time. Therefore, we called the dark evil.

Therefore, the divine plan was to deny any awareness of our spirit, and that of our pure energy of light (God), so we could move beyond what was known as our "I AM" Christ and learn about the unknown principles of polarity energy and duality experiences. We souls, who religions describe as "fallen" and "sinful," made this choice freely and, therefore, never were we kicked out of any Garden. It is just that we souled beings called this energy of duality the "abyss," which is why we believe space is infinitely deep and unknown. And yet, space is known to us. It feels unknown because we keep looking outside of ourselves to explore it instead of looking deep within the self, for all that we want to know about space would be revealed.

In order to feel we were not God or a Goddess, confusion and chaos had to play a big part in our creations. So, our mind-soul and ego sparked that confusion and chaos by having us believe in sin and the concept that we were created by some God outside of us. In this process, we forgot that we were everything, God and Goddess, including our darkness and duality. We have forgotten that our "I AM" Christ spirit lives in everything that exists, even if it is what we call evil or bad. This is how our spirit (you) feels and experiences all possibilities of life and gains the wisdom (throne) to be a mature and liable Goddess.

Therefore, we all come to earth from many different dimensional realms, planets, and universes (God's kingdom), bringing with us many different issues to be played out. We are using the energy space of materialism to experience good and evil, right and wrong, light and dark. And, by incarnating on earth, we are learning how to make choices, how to use our free will, how to use our imagination, and in the end, how to become a much wiser Goddess *("desirable for gaining wisdom,)"* as stated in Genesis 3:6*)*.

It was our "I AM" Christ spirit that allowed us to generate a belief that nothing can be engineered or understood unless it comes from the intellectual side of our mind (the Adam principle). And, because of this belief, our "I AM" Christ spirit and our soul consciousness of responsibility (Eve) eventually became a shadow to our outer sense of responsibility. Using the energy of duality as our true reality, our divinity began to form a cloudy or etheric presence over our true identity. And, since our ego gave us a true feeling of being individualized, it gave us a personality that manifested a form like consciousness *("and made loincloths for themselves),"* Genesis 3:7, as this was our physical body.

As we clothed our energetic astral body with belief systems, it transformed our energy into a more solid form than before. And, that is when we began to forget who we were. Through eons of time playing in the abyss (endless space using dual-energy), we eventually transformed our consciousness and energy into multiple layers of dimensional realms, as the material realm is one of them. And, in doing this, our defiant ego nature continued shaping and structuring our energy into ultimately creating a denser consciousness and physical body as seen today.

The dense physical form was chosen because it could hold our energy in such a way that it would isolate us from our perfection (the heavens) and other dimensions and seeing planets and universes as if they were outside of us. This isolation allowed us to grow, learn, and evolve through many different lifetimes and experiences of good and evil without interference from our own "I AM" Christ spirit. This is what is meant by *"made loincloths for themselves"* in Genesis 3:7. A loincloth is a type of clothing, and this clothing is what *"inspired the seven angels with the seven last plagues, for through them God's fury is accomplished" Revelation 15:1)*

It was because of working with the illusionary energy of positive and negative, light and dark, for eons of time, we became lost to our creations. Thus, we lost our identity. Therefore, our "I AM" Christ spirit had to take over, or we would have been lost forever, and forever is a very long time. We are slow learners, which is why our "I AM" Christ spirit created the "seven angels" to help us become aware of what comprises our true reality and who we indeed are.

Of course, we believe these "seven angels" to be plagues, but in reality, we created them to learn responsibility and to learn who we are. As our defiant ego nature (beast) held our energy in isolation, it caused us to cloth our formless energetic body with seven subtle bodies that make up our consciousness today. These seven subtle bodies are the seven angels or seven stars found in Revelation 1:20 and in 15:1, as I have listed them again for better understanding.

It is through our seven subtle bodies where our "I AM" Christ spirit carries the plagues of our energy's (God's) fury. Thus, the mercy of our energy (God) works through these "seven angels," which is what we experience today. Again, these seven angels are:

1. Spirit   Laodicea/pituitary   Responsibility
2. Mind   Philadelphia/pineal   Relationships
3. Intuition   Sardis/thyroid   Control/power/free will
4. Mental   Thyatira/thymus   Growth/expansion
5. Emotion   Pergamum/adrenals   Memory/intellect
6. Etheric/Astral Smyrna/Lyden   Substance
7. Physical   Ephesus/gonad   Desires

Embedded within each layer of our consciousness, there are many belief patterns and memories behind what has been happening in our lives. The memories of why inexplicable things happen to us personally are hidden from us because we have not yet opened our eyes to the reality of memory, consciousness, energy, and past lifetimes.

As in Revelation, Chapter Two and Chapter Three, we may have thought that the angels of the churches were a blessing. And, in this verse, these angels seem like they are filled with the plagues of God's wrath. From the Bible itself, we accept that God is a vengeful and jealous God. But perhaps the Bible has either been misinterpreted or has been rewritten by those in power to keep us in fear of this vengeful and jealous God.

According to Yeshua and the Ascended Masters, this vengeful and jealous God of the Bible are the attributes of man's ego and not from energy of light (God) and of the "I AM" Christ of unconditional love. Therefore, all teachings that we accept as God's wrath only come from our own memories and what we justify and believe as some power over us that created us to control us as being his people. Exodus 6:7, *"If you will be my people, I will be your God."* That Bible verse tells us that the Bible has been rewritten to serve those in power, as they, the Church, will be our God, and we will be their sheep (people).

Maybe we may have misunderstood the meaning of the *"wrath of God"* because of not looking behind the real wisdom of the message. If we could remember all of our past lifetimes and what we did in each of those lifetimes (good and bad), would we say God's wrath means "truth," "energy," and "unconditional love?" Can we know the truth behind the mysteries of what we are experiencing today, but not be able to explain the sin (unbalanced energy) that caused it?

What if you came down with cancer or something else that seems to be a curse? Can you explain what is happening to you, or are you asking why it is happening? Can you explain the loss of a job, losing a loved one, or the inability to get ahead? At times like these, do you ask yourself, "Why me God?" or "Why does God allow this?" From all of what you have been reading in this book, then maybe you can understand that these "plagues" could be interpreted as "truths," "energy," and "unconditional love" being revealed to you through the love of spirit.

A true and loving God-Goddess has no anger toward you, is never jealous or judges what you do in life, and a true God-Goddess never punishes you for sinning. What we do as humans, we analyze sin from a mental and emotional level as something we did wrong. And yet, we bring the plagues on ourselves to understand energy, positive and negative, light and dark.

Therefore, our "I AM" Christ spirit (Goddess) kicked no one out of the Garden for sinning. Instead, our "I AM" God spirit allowed us, from the mental and emotional level, to accept responsibility for choosing to purposely leave the garden to understand our choices and how energy works. *"Learning to become like gods"* means learning the mysteries behind what is happening to us and the reason we cannot explain it, other than to say that God is punishing us for our sins.

Since this chapter is about plagues given by God, then how you remember them seems to become important. The sequence in which you remember these plagues indicates that your last memory would be the first memory you created, and your first memory would be the last. Therefore, in memory, the last incarnation you had on earth is the easiest to recall and integrate, while the first incarnation you had on earth a long time ago would be the hardest to remember and integrate because it is stored so deep within your soul memories.

We have certain abilities and instincts that we think cannot be explained. And yet, these abilities and instincts are just memories of our last incarnation more than our first, which is why sometimes we cannot seem to move beyond what we are experiencing today. A person could be experiencing a simple thing like back pain, where another person is experiencing cancer. But both could remedy their situations just by awakening to their first incarnations and seeing what is held within their Oversoul that needs to be released and integrated.

The mysteries behind the sudden illness, loss of job or home, and many other happenings are caused by misunderstanding energy (God) and what we should do about our situations in life. Once we understand the concept of whom we are, how consciousness and energy works, we can understand the symbols behind the Apocalypse. This can help in relieving us from what we are experiencing today. It is through the realization of you being Christ that you know all lifetime aspects desire to come back home to you.

It is in your best interest to consider the literal writings of the Bible, especially Genesis and Revelation, as not being real. Let's disregard the whole Bible. Why do I say this? Revelation 15:2-3, *"Then I saw something like a sea of glass mingled with fire."* Obviously, this has a meaning different from what John saw. For me, saying *"sea of glass"* is like saying, "water will mix with fire." And, we all know that water does not mix with fire, but fire can produce "glass" from the sand.

Therefore, the Ascended Masters and I interpret John's *"on the sea of glass were standing those who had won the victory over the beast and its image, and the number that signified its name,"* refers to you, the one reading this book right now, coming to an understanding and an awareness that you transported your pure neutral energy, long ago, into opposing polarity energy, and that of many physical bodies (lifetimes). And now, these many lifetimes of your past can be easily seen through the protective cover of your inner and outer consciousness *(the sea of glass)*.

Considering how memories work and how some are related to our past incarnations, our light and dark ego-personality aspects nearest us are the first memories that will come to mind to remember and wanting to integrate with us. Through karma, most of us are working out the plagues (truths) originating from our past lifetimes in this lifetime, and most of us have integrated those ego-personalities and their beliefs of old, dogmatic views with our consciousness of today.

Channeling of the Ascended Masters on the Apocalypse

Some of your ego-personality aspects from the past have now overcome their erroneous thinking and misunderstanding of energy (God). They are now part of your wisdom today. All you have to do is integrate them, and the wisdom learned in that lifetime as being one with you. Through this action of moving through many incarnations, you have crystallized your spirit in all things you chose to experience, and now you have many ego-personality aspects that, by their own testimonies, stand purified and ready to be received by you, their creator.

Through karma and incarnations, we have invented a way to balance our energy. Karma is a perception of right and wrong, good and evil, and a lie that keeps us stuck to a contract that we made long ago with our "I AM" Christ spirit to work out our choices and truths *(plagues)* in a physical body that plays with dual-energy. It is time to get off the karmic cycle of incarnations and let go of the idea that we have sinned against some God of the Bible that loves power and control. The belief in sowing and reaping came from the teachings of the Bible, which is nothing more than the old energy waiting to be transformed into new energy.

And, because of these ego-personality aspects of us coming forth in memory, we can take our belief in karma and place it into the flame of New Expansional Energy. In this way, we transform and change our energy, thus setting ourselves free of the agreements we made with ourselves to add wisdom to our Oversoul. It was us who set ourselves up for the fall, and now, because of "trial by fire," we can choose what we desire to experience.

We have gone out and searched for the answers to our questions, and now these answers are within our memory. All we have to do to find those answers is to move past our ego and our mind of the intellect and allow ourselves to tap into the memories of our Oversoul. Consider the question in Revelation 15:4, *"Who will not fear you, Lord, or glorify your name?"* How can you fear yourself? For *"you alone are the holy one,"* and your memories *"(nations) will come and worship before you for your righteous acts have been revealed"* to you because of knowing who you are.

However, many people do fear their own "holiness." They prefer to use titles and people such as the pope or some saint who has devoted their life to this God of the Bible. And, in return, they are assigned to be God's shepherds in taking responsibility for our soul. You see this with priests, pastors, ministers, and anyone else who proclaims himself to be a shepherd of God. We pay them money, build them a church to preach from, and provide them with comfort and security for their service to save our soul. And, in the end, it will not work!

Is it hard for you to say that you are a being of such holiness that you are equal to God? The Bible tells you that you were created in the image of God, and yet God's image was not human. God's image is of pure neutral energy of light, and the holiness of your "I AM" Christ spirit is proclaimed as equal to whom people call God. Even Yeshua proclaimed himself equal to God, and he taught that truth when he walked the earth over two thousand years ago. Yeshua was put to death by the religions of his day for proclaiming such truth. Today, we would not be put to death, but people will look at you with disgustness and shock.

You are the Lord of Lords, and when you have the courage to accept yourself as a Christ, you will, like Yeshua, begin to feel all aspects of yourself, including your defiant beastly nature wanting to come home to you, their creator. You, from the mind level, are the Lord of Lords sitting on the throne, and once you allow your memories to open up to you, all parts and pieces of your consciousness and energy will come home to their creator, you. Therefore, you are the one who needs to "glorify" yourself, as your name in this lifetime is the "holy" name. So, who then will you fear?

All memories *(nations)* and ego-aspects of you can now recall their oneness with you, for you are their creator (God-Goddess) from which they came. It was in your nature as a Christ to learn more about the unknown principles of duality, and you did it by hiding your true essence behind other aspects of yourself, and yet your true essence ("I AM" Christ) was part of each of them. Therefore, your righteous act of creating many light and dark personality aspects has now revealed that the real Christ is you! That is why these aspects and your memories (nations) come in and worship you, their creator.

Revelation 11:19, the temple of God, was opened. This referred to the physical body and the mind being the starting place for all influences of polarity energy, positive and negative. It was about our Oversoul and mind giving the assurance that we will, one day, come to realize and remember that we are Christ, the Son of Goddess, the Son of Man, and the King and Queen. We are Christ, God, and the Goddess.

Revelation 15:5, the *"heavenly tent"* and the *"temple"* is a place in consciousness where our rational mind and physical body are not in play when we move to a knowing *(testimony)* that all life experiences have been placed in the Akashic Records (the Oversoul), also known as the Book of Life. It becomes important to recognize that our physical body and our mind of an emotional level are part of our "I AM" Christ consciousness *(the heavenly temple)*. Therefore, we are connected to all of our life's records through memory and not that there is a hall of records somewhere in heaven.

Because of these seven subtle bodies (seven angels/churches) carrying love, wisdom, and truths (plagues) to our "I AM" Christ consciousness, we have been following our divine plan through time and space all along in fulfilling of the law of karma. And now, if we choose to awaken, we are in completion of this old earth of duality beliefs. It shows this in Revelation 15:6, *"they were dressed in clean white linen, with a gold sash around their chests,"* refers to the exploration of the energy of duality that took place within our makeup:

1. Spirit body
2. Etheric/astral body
3. Emotional body
4. Mental/soul body
5. Intuitive body
6. Mind body
7. Physical body

These were the angels dressed in *"clean white linen,"* a phrase that signifies our essence living life in a materialistic world under a three-density consciousness. It is about us performing a service to ourselves or "I AM" Christ spirit, and about how we used energy (God) to perform in the material, earning us a *"gold sash around your chests,"* symbolic of a mirror-image of our wisdom.

This *"gold sash around your chest"* is there to remind you that you no longer have to experience karma (sowing and reaping) because you are now nourished by the memories of your many lifetimes of the past and the wisdom they hold. This nourishment comes in through the seven subtle bodies and the seven endocrine systems, also known as the seven churches. Thus, you hold a chest full of wisdom. All that is left for you to do is to tap into this wisdom.

Since we all chose the flesh to be our companion in working out responsibility as karma, then the activities of our choices must be revealed to us through memory. This is why the adrenal area is part of our memory and the storehouse for our karma. As Revelation 15:7 mentions, *"one of the four living creatures"* that gave the *"seven angels the seven-gold bowls filled with fury,"* is the "Lion." In the beginning stages of our journey outside of our "I AM" Christ consciousness, our defiant ego-personality (the Beast) clarified that it would be the aggressor and not our mind in helping us meet our "divine plan" to learn our truths (wrath) by delivering it to us from the lower seat of our intuition and emotional body.

Also, the *"fury of God,"* Revelation 15:7, has nothing to do with God punishing us, but it has everything to do with our "I AM" Christ spirit having great compassion and unconditional love for everything that we have created using energy, whether good or bad. Therefore, this *"fury"* being generated through our subtle bodies *(seven angels)* can be seen as an excellent service to us, because in the end, it helps us become one with our "I AM" Christ consciousness. And, this is not something to fear!

It comes hard for us sometimes to know what is real and what is not real. If we are a multi-dimensional being, then why can't we open up to the other parts and pieces of us that operate within those dimensional realms? The answer lies with us creating a mental block because we have accepted what others have told us about this reality. And, because of it, we focus on just being human. I guess most of us believe it is easier to stay focused right here in this reality, where we can confront the devil as to whom we believe he is.

We all have forgotten about the other realms and the magic contained within them because all of what we played in other lifetimes are right there for us to meet ourselves, see our past, and our potential futures. That is when we get to realize and understand how energy (God) works with matter, which is very important if we desire to know who we indeed are as a grand creator. It is about opening up with no resistance coming from the mind and ego, as they will be the first to jump in and tell us, "this is a bunch of nonsense" because the mind and ego are focused on this physical realm only.

We have forgotten the other realms don't have density and the definition as the Earth realm. Thus, we don't perceive these other realms the same way as we do here on earth. From the earth realm, we see with our eyes, and because of it, we tie our eyes with this reality of thoughts, like "if I cannot see it, then it doesn't exist." We also use hearing, touching, smelling, and tasting as a measure to what we believe is true. Because of being so focused on physical matter, we seem to forget that our five physical senses work differently in these other realms. Because of what we see and feel in those other realms, it is not clearly defined as if we were seeing and feeling it from the physical realm.

For example: Something I read from Ascended Master Adamus, "From other realms, you can run into a tree at top speed, and the tree is like soft cotton. It cushions you; it holds you; it cuddles you, and then it releases you. Try doing that here in just the physical realms – it hurts." When we allow ourselves to open up to other remembrances (realities), it may also bring in some of the pain and suffering we did in some past lifetime. The good news is, it may also open us to the reasons that we shut ourselves down.

Look at it this way! Our mind might remember a few things when we were one, two, three, or four years old, but not much. However, we were very active in consciousness during those years. We simply left in consciousness to visit these other realms of the land of fairies, magic, and great possibilities. However, as we grew in age, we also grew in consciousness, where we were always told to stay focused on this three-density world.

We were told by our parents to stay focused on what we want to do when we grow up. Thus, we committed our consciousness to make things work out by understanding our minds and our environment. And that is when the walls, the barriers, and shields were put in place so we could just focus on this reality. Oh, I know you cannot pretend that they are not there, because they feel very real to you. But we can take a deep breath and expand our consciousness, and that will cause us to flow right through the many dimensions that are all around us.

From this explanation, you can now understand that any *"wrath of God"* heading your way is nothing more than you, in your true essence *(who lives forever and ever)*, sending love and truth to yourself. The phrase *"forever and ever"* merely shows that your unspoken words are of unconditional love that eventually leads to new truths *(fury of God)*. Thus, this is the divine plan that helps free you from the old vibrational energy of the Tree of Knowledge of Good and Evil.

If we do not accept responsibility for our creations and let go of old, dogmatic belief systems, such as sin and punishment, then the energy of our illusions in past lifetimes stays stuck. Thus we suffer until we learn to open up to other possibilities than just this physical realm. When we learn to accept who we are at our core and let go of our old beliefs about duality and sin, then the stuck energy can release itself from whatever judgment we put around it during that lifetime we lived it out here on earth. Thus, our suffering ends.

This book is for those that are ready to free themselves from their past without carrying shame and guilt. You do it by inviting all ego-personality aspects of your past, present, and future, including your "I AM, to integrate with you in this now moment. Once this is done, you release the judgments they carried within them. This then sets you free of what religion calls the "unpardonable sin." The Ascended Masters understand that this can be a big challenge for you, especially when they say, "I am equal to God because I am God." After all, it is a quantum leap in consciousness, don't you think?

When we first came into the abyss or this endless nothingness/space, we chose the vibrational energy of duality as the method by which our physical body would feel the results of the fire of justice (karma/God's fury), thus purifying our memories and burning away our false beliefs about being only human.

And, as we can see in Revelation 15:8, no one was able to enter the temple (a physical body) until our seven subtle bodies were filled with the love and truth of our "I AM" (seven plagues). This, of course, is associated with the seven seals found in Revelation 6. Once our seven subtle bodies were filled with false ideas and beliefs, symbolized by the seven seals as given:

1. Separated from our "I AM" Christ spirit
2. Lost our awareness of being Christ, God, and the Goddess
3. We believed in Satan/duality
4. We believed in sin/guilt
5. We believed in suffering
6. We believed we needed salvation
7. And, we lost all memory of ever being Christ

Once these seven plagues (beliefs/truths) were rooted within the memory of our first physical body (temple), and within each subtle body of our layered consciousness, then our defiant ego-personality (the Beast) took on its first lifetime upon the earth. And now, after many lifetimes playing with the energy forces of positive and negative, some of us have reaped what we sowed in a physical body, and we are about ready to make a quantum leap in consciousness.

Our physical body, our mind, and ego have shown us what we have done and what we have put to memory to be played out. Thus, our "I AM" Christ spirit reveals to us these seven plagues that we have been playing with through time and space (incarnations). They may seem like the wrath of God, but they are the means for learning responsibility for what we have created. And, once we learn to meet ourselves through our memories and the lifetimes in which we played them out, we then discover a whole new magic in consciousness where we move into a realization that we are Christ.

When we accept responsibility for whatever is happening in our life today, no matter if we believe we caused it or not, we heal our past and, therefore, our present. And, by accepting responsibility for everything we are experiencing in our life, we change the course of our future. Because of how consciousness and energy work, we do not realize that our past has determined our future. The journey we took in our past lifetimes became our course of action today, which then sets the course for our future tomorrows.

When we become enlightened about who we are as Christ, we can heal what comes before us today. Therefore, accept what you are experiencing, love it, and embrace the wisdom from the experience. After all, you put it there to experience! But what comes from this knowing is the fact we can do something about it now.

Our memory holds the understanding of our divine plan and how it can never be changed, damaged, or destroyed. In fact, our "I AM" Christ spirit never judges us for what we do or have done, for it is part of us, loving us unconditional, taking everything we experience in our journey, and transmuting it into wisdom that is eternal. Therefore, none of what we have experienced in our many past lifetimes supports a lesson from some God because we have sinned. The lessons we learned through sowing and reaping (karma) come from us and only us as humans.

The harshest thing we all did was leaving higher consciousness (the first creation-Garden) because it caused us the loss of trust in oneself is a Christ. That was perhaps the most painful thing we have ever experienced, and it has put a distance between our dark creations that we curse and run from. And, every time we run and hide from our dark creations, we are hiding from our "I AM" Christ consciousness. Remember, our dark side is not of the Beast, devil, or Satan that is talked about in this book. It is our "I AM" Christ spirit calling us to accept these dark creations and integrate them since we are their creator. However, we push them away as sinning because it reminds us of how we used energy (God).

We have forgotten that our "I AM" Christ spirit loves us so much that it said to us a long ago to "go out and experience life without any judgment coming from me." Freely experience anything you want, because someday you will learn that you are me." Therefore, our mind was the perfect place to hide because it helped to blind us from loving ourselves unconditionally. Thus, the trust in ourselves became clouded within our hearts because we took on a judgmental role.

When you realize that your mind saw and understood everything with facts, figures, and details spelled out in an intellectual and reasoning way, that was the sign for you to forget about trusting in yourself as a Christ also. And because of it, you build up your falseness of the mind by pretending that you are smart or that you know everything, but the fact remains that you are still running and hiding, and you know it.

The "harvest" mentioned in the Bible occurs the moment you learn to surrender to trusting that you are a Christ also without shame, guilt, or reservation. As the words are, "I AM that I AM" Christ in my own right, and "I love everything about me." When you choose to surrender to whom you actually are – not the aspect you created while pretending to be someone else – then you will feel your ascension.

Chapter 33

HELL CONVERTS TO HEAVEN

If you have a deep desire to know Christ, then you must know both sides of your face because there are an ignorant dark side and a realization light side that you must come to terms with. To recognize Christ is to come into the realization that your memories of past lifetimes essentially become the gateway to understanding who you indeed are and who Christ is. And, to discover this realization, you have to uncover your truths, deceptions, and lies that you have denied journeying through many lifetimes.

However, before realization can take hold in consciousness, these lifetimes of lies and deceptions have to be accepted by you in this physical lifetime. Also, you have to have the courage to dig deep into your consciousness to discover the collective wisdom of all your lifetimes. And, this discovery may take you through hell before you find heaven. To help you begin your search, the study of Revelation 16:1-21 will uncover the biggest lie and deception known today, and that is, you are not the creator of your experiences when, in truth, you are. You will also learn in your study of Revelation 16:1-21 is that your "I AM" Christ consciousness (Oversoul) took on the role of hiding your dark creations until you were ready to face them with courage.

Because we could not bear to look at our past lifetimes filled with deceit, lies, and the destruction that we caused in past lifetimes, our "I AM" Christ consciousness (Oversoul) allowed itself to withdraw itself from our consciousness as far as awareness is concerned. And, in this process, we became tormented and confused with our "I AM" Christ-

Oversoul because we felt as if it was our darkness without realizing it was our "heavenly Christ consciousness" taking on our horrific creations (sins). All because we could not stand the idea of creating such things as evil.

It has been the dark creations we did not want to take responsibility for or anything we thought was contrary to us being Christ, that has caused us to go through the fires of "hell." However, once we accept "all that we created as our creations," no matter if good and evil, and without judgment, then we would finally let go of the old and open up to a "heavenly consciousness of wisdom." Even today, we continue to battle the light and dark deep within our consciousness by trying to deny and destroy everything that reminds us of our horrific creations, not realizing that these dark creations are part of our "I AM" Christ consciousness, as in, Christ taking on the sins of the world, our world.

Our "I AM" Christ consciousness (spirit-Oversoul) loves us so much that it allowed us to dump all that we did not like about ourselves and our creations (dark and light) into our "I AM" Christ consciousness. And, Revelation 16:1-21 brings out that darkness by showing that our dark creations are not what we think they are. Everything we fear, reject, and deny about ourselves today comes from our many lifetimes past where we dumped all that we did not like about what we created into our "I AM" Christ consciousness. And now, we have come to a place in consciousness where our Christ/Oversoul can help us understand that God's fury is nothing more than us coming into the realization of our divine plan to learn wisdom and after, become balanced again.

The balance comes to us through our light and dark creations that we rejected and stored within our "I AM" Christ consciousness (Oversoul), and to be presented to us later when we were ready to accept them as to what we have created, good and bad, to be played out in the flesh. Thus, we are, in effect, sending love and truth to ourselves from a much higher understanding. And, by fighting the light and the dark within and without, we create a wall that prevents us from integrating all that we are, including our "I AM" Christ-identity (Oversoul).

This fight portrays how our energy of light (God) will always seek resolution because in the beginning stages of us leaving higher consciousness (Garden), our "I AM" Christ spirit loved us so much that it took on all of our burdens and the creations we rejected to free ourselves in creating whatever we desired to experience, good and bad. But now our "I AM" Christ consciousness desires to come back into our lives, for it has been hidden within our consciousness ever since we left the first creation. Our "I AM" Christ spirit seeks to be released from being the demon, and the hated one, all because of it being the dumping ground for our destructive creations during many lifetimes.

How often have we prayed for our "I AM" "Christ" spirit to come into our lives to help us with healing and to set us free from our burdens? And now, some of us are learning that our "I AM" Christ spirit has been there waiting for the human self to come into the realization in accepting our many creations, good and evil (sins), no matter if we believe we did not create them because of not remembering. We just have had hundreds or perhaps thousands of lifetimes, and therefore our conscious memories of them become hard to remember.

From the study of this chapter, you will learn that your "I AM" Christ spirit (Oversoul) has always been the "shadow" that you have feared because of it feeling dark to you. And, with all that was happening, you were just feeling the refusal of taking responsibility for your actions. And now, it is time to acknowledge your dark creations and stop fighting your own "I AM" Christ spirit as if it is a demon.

If you are still judging and battling your neighbors, friends, family, and hate what the mass consciousness is doing today, then you are refusing to enter into the realization of certain lifetime aspects, which still feel the pain of you not accepting them as your own creations. Thus, you feel their wrath in this lifetime because of karma. How else are you to learn the justice involved in taking full responsibility for your choices and actions?

Now, I may not be clear enough to give you a full understanding of what this chapter is all about. However, there is one thing I feel is very clear! The acceptance of responsibility seems part of every verse in Revelation 16, and how it is about what karma can do to you and your body when you are ignorant of the effects of your thoughts, beliefs, choices, and memories of past lifetimes. Therefore, the plagues (truths) coming from your memories and how they are being poured out onto your many astral and physical bodies depend upon your acceptance of them today. Remember, you accepted the law of responsibility (karma, that comes as plagues) a very long time ago to help with the remembering of who you truly are, a Christ in your own right.

As we all know, there are all kinds of unrecognized conflicts and diseases, like Covid-19, Cancer, etc., to help remind us of our many lifetime creations and how we could manifest them on earth. And now, some of us are infected with these diseases to set up our plagues to meet our karma, which simultaneously awakens us to whom we are as a Christ. Therefore, no God is punishing us by plagues or neglecting us, only the human mass consciousness playing out its role by bringing upon themselves all that we neglect to take responsibility for within ourselves here on earth.

The *"loud voice"* in Revelation 16:1 is our soul's record, and the recorder is our Oversoul (the I AM) giving the authority, through memory, to guide us through the law of karma that we created while journeying through many lifetimes. This record of memories is called the Akashic Records (voice) that come from deep within our spirit (Oversoul), mental (soul), and physical consciousness *(the temple)*, and how it relates to us humans believing, playing, and worshiping polarity energy (God) to manifest and give form to our light and dark creations. And, we use many incarnations to work them out in the physical.

I understand that some of us think of the Akashic Records as a library in heaven or some higher dimension than earth. We also know that basically every thought, idea, and action taken from the past, present, and future is stored in these records. And, if this is so, then time is irrelevant when it comes to the memory of all those creations. What we did or thought a billion years ago, or one million years ago, or 2,000 years ago, or today, is still accessible to us.

Therefore, our memory contains every act, expression, feeling, thought, and intent that has ever occurred in the history of our consciousness awakening. Thus, our memory records are interactive with every personality aspect, and they have a tremendous influence on our everyday choices, relationships, belief systems, what we contract as a disease, and the potential realities we draw toward ourselves.

The Akashic Records (memory) are part of every souled being, and that they are not out there in some library in the sky. This is what Revelation 16:1 is all about. So, empower yourself and wake up to the wisdom, guidance, and the energetic support that surrounds you today. Through these memories, you can now understand the meaning of Christ taking on the sins of the world. Because those sins, and the world, is what you, yourself, created to experience throughout many lifetimes acting on behalf of your "I AM" Christ spirit to learn wisdom and soul growth.

Therefore, our "I AM" Christ spirit (Oversoul) never left that part of our higher consciousness, and that is why we feel our "I AM" Christ consciousness as a shadow that gives us the impression of it being dark. It feels dark because our "I AM" Christ spirit is holding in memory all those dark creations that we claim we never created. And, we do it by denying reincarnation!

Because of free will, we have the choice to move in any opposing direction from what our "I AM" Christ spirit has already set up (divine plan) for us to experience. And therefore, the direction we take depends wholly upon the thoughts and beliefs we hold in memory. And, because of the "divine plan" that we set up eons ago, our "I AM" Christ spirit gifted us the permission to worship that part of our mind that speaks of "free will" as the means to choose from good and evil with no interference coming from our "I AM" Christ spirit.

The only way to awaken to our true identity as a Christ also, our memories (Akashic Records) had to work from behind the scenes by having us meet ourselves in a physical body so we could play out in the flesh what we worship as our beliefs. This gives us a chance to see one of the *"seven angels,"* given in Revelation 16:2, calling for the earthly forces to pour out the love and the potential for us to let go of those old dualistic beliefs. This may seem like the wrath of God, but it all comes down to the will of our mind in a more defiant way, which is the Anti-Christ, as we each battle against our own divine plan as hard as we can.

The *"first angel"* represents the first church (Ephesus) and our gonad level in the physical body, and this has nothing to do with a literal angel pouring down God's vengeance upon us or earth. Remember, from the earlier chapters that John wrote, it was not only about seeing a message for humanity but a message for each spiritual center within his own human body. And, within each section of the seven endocrine glands (seven churches/angels) is a description of how each angel (gland) plays a role in the physical body, thus molding the forces of positive and negative within us.

The molding process hurts and causes all kinds of "festering feelings," which then arouses the mind to produce many light and dark personality aspects (lifetimes) that will fall under the influence of our defiant ego nature (mark of the Beast) to learn the wisdom of polarity and responsibility. It is from these lifetimes of our past that we chose to worship images *(lies)* of our beastly nature, where we created great hostility and pain upon ourselves and others. This resulted in many lifetimes of experiencing painful injuries, infections, and a great deal of suffering *(ugly sores)*.

And, because we chose earth as the means to learn the wisdom of polarity and responsibility, the elements of the earth became how we feel pain and suffering in what we create, which is, by the way, produced by the gonad activity. This is why the *"first angel"* (gonad level) is that molding force within us that gets to the heart of where we create forms and images (lifetimes) of our desires to experience.

When you turn to Revelation 16:3, *"the second angel pouring out his bowl on the sea,"* this presents the second church (Smyrna) and how it is related to our subconsciousness *(sea)* and how our physical body is associated with the "Lyden Center, Navel, or Lower Abdomen area. This area is also known as the "seat of the soul," which is connected to our Etheric-Astral Body.

"*The sea turning to blood like that from a corpse and every creature living in the sea died,*" Revelation 16:3. This refers to us, at the subconscious level *(sea),* where our Etheric-Astral Body exists, forming our energy *(blood)* into taking up many physical and nonphysical bodies and then spreading those ego-personality aspects throughout multidimensional realms in order to play out as many potentials as possible. It is from our etheric-astral body, we build up our choices within our subconsciousness, via soul memory, and then now or later, we can present them to the opposing forces of polarity energy (God) and manifest a physical form so we can carry out our choices. This is why God (our pure energy) is in the middle of every experience.

And, as you can see, from Revelation 16:3, how could every creature in the sea die? Think about it! Why would Goddess be so mad that she would kill every man, woman, and child, let alone every creature in the sea and on land? My friends, this is a false God because the real God doesn't get mad or kills, not even the worst of the worst of us because the real God is of a "universal mind field of pure neutral energy of light" that we souls use for our creations. Therefore, this false God of the Bible replaced the real God a long time ago by order of man to gain power and control over himself and his environment.

We all have forgotten that our many ego-personality aspects from past lifetimes have devoted their energy (blood) to creating horrendous acts against humanity, and then died in that lifetime. These ego-personalities from our past still carry within them our energy (blood), and now these aspects of us are dead to us because we keep on ignoring them repeatedly for what they did. And, when we ignore them, we are failing to take responsibility for them. And, as given, we are their creator, and we are responsible for them. Why? Because they are an extension of our Oversoul when we created that past lifetime story to serve us and our divine plan.

Therefore, what we create must sooner or later return home to us. But they will not return home unless we accept that part of us that feels angry and sad. Our personality aspects reflect the love that the Spirit of One (Goddess) had for us when, in the beginning, it said, "Go forth. I give you freedom, a mind-soul, an ego-personality, and a divine plan to follow. And then, go beyond all that is unknown to you and create to make it known." This is what our "I AM" Christ spirit said to our mind-soul and ego-personality a very long time ago. And, that is when we went forth as a souled being fulfilling a quest to learn about the wisdom of our choices, and then to become a sovereign Christ, God-Goddess of unconditional love in our own right.

Know that you have an Oversoul that is Christ-like, you have a mind-soul of a mental nature, and an ego-personality that operates in the physical and non-physical realms, and you are blessed with a divine plan to go forth and experience what is unknown as polarity energy. And, the first thing your mind-soul consciousness did was to mimic your "I AM" Christ spirit by creating multiple ego-personality aspects, and then spreading them throughout the astral realms to learn the wisdom of your choices. These ego-personality aspects came in as either male or female, and ever since then, your mind-soul has continued to create them, lifetime after lifetime.

Every aspect that our mind-soul created has served a purpose in expressing and experiencing what we, the true creator, did not know about the opposing forces of polarity (the God of the Bible) and how it affected us spiritually. Thus, we have created ego-personality aspects that have played with the forces of evil and with the light. And, in the end, all aspects of us must return home to the self, their creator. And, the sooner we accept them as our creations, the sooner our realization and ascension come to us.

Some people or religions may consider this the loss of our soul. However, no soul can be lost or destroyed because our Oversoul always remains pure and neutral, waiting for the time when we bring home all of what we created, good and bad. And now, some of our ego-personality aspects have already integrated back to our Oversoul, and some are lingering in other dimensions where they have been for millions of years, waiting for us to accept them as our creations. Remember, millions of years compared to eternity is like a blink of an eye to the "I AM."

And, when these ego-personality aspects return home to us, they dissolve back into the oneness of our Oversoul. And they bring with them all of what they expressed, positive and negative, and all of what they experienced while journeying through time and space, sowing and reaping. In fact, they leave behind all judgment, wounds, and imbalances. The only thing that comes back to our Oversoul is the wisdom of the experience, as it needs no details of the experience. Therefore, no matter how imbalanced we think we are, no matter how unresolved or undecided our ego-personality aspects might become, our Oversoul remains pure, for it is filled with wisdom.

Your physical existence of today is the personality-aspect that has been chosen to integrate the other aspects of you. It has to be done in the physical because you cannot call back your other aspects in many non-physical realms. You have to do it here in a physical body. If you could stop your mind for a moment, you would hear those deep voices telling you to either love or hate, to battle those who offer enlightenment or welcome that enlightenment in, to argue with yourself from a subconscious and conscious level.

You actually have aspects of yourself that feel the changes you made in your belief systems, and they rejoice, but you also have many aspects that are confused and very angry at you. Why do you think you have chosen this book to read? It is because the aspect of you in this lifetime has awakened to where it feels the need to integrate all your ego-personality aspects on behalf of your Oversoul. This is why things sometimes make no sense to you. Of course, your mind tries to wrap around this thought to figure it out. And that is why everything may seem clear just before, and then out of the blue, another wave of dead memories *(corpse)* comes through to cause more chaos and uncertainty in your life.

Not that you are trying to bring these things into your life consciously; it is that you have aspects of you that are out there in many different layers of your consciousness. You have personality aspects with distinct human attributes, some from the angelic realm, and some from the past and future, and that is why you have these happenings around you. It is what Yeshua mentioned a long time ago, and something we all misunderstood. "It is not that Jesus is the chalice. You are the chalice for receiving all your aspects."

It is you, the one reading this book, who is the savior and the Messiah for all of your ego-personality aspects. It is you who can take away the sins of all your world and other lifetime personality aspects. The rapture is not about you meeting Yeshua (Jesus) in the sky. It is allowing all of your other personality aspects to meet up with you, the Christ, in the midst of the mass confusion of doubt and ignorance (cloud) that is being displayed on earth right now on a mental level (air). So, are you ready to be the Messiah for all your ego-personalities and forgive them of their sins? Remember, when you do, you forgive yourself.

Are you ready to take full responsibility for your creations? Know that you gave this responsibility away to other lifetimes, to religions, governments, family, friends, and businesses. And because of it, how can you expect those personality aspects, still fragmented and lost, to come home when you are not even ready to receive them for what (they) you created in those past lifetimes? However, if you are ready to take responsibility for them, then these personality aspects might ask you, "Do you really mean it? Do you want to integrate, to be whole, and to take responsibility?" It comes down to you being ready to be a sovereign Goddess and a Christ in your own right.

In Matthew 8:22, *"Jesus answered him, 'Follow me, and let the dead bury their dead.'"* How can a dead person literally bury a dead person? What Yeshua meant is that we can give our lives to forms or aspects (lifetimes) that we have created in our past that are dead to us in this lifetime. And, we give them our power to act in our stead, for they are our habits, our beliefs, and our truths in this lifetime. And, because of this, these aspects of ours rule our present life, our thoughts, our belief systems, and then make our choices for us.

Thus, we live and experience our life of today using "dead" images, leaving us with no life of our own in the present because we have given our energy away to a physical body where we act as "a corpse" (dead to the real truth). We are dead to our Oversoul (the Christ), dead to our subconsciousness of a mental nature (the sea), and we are dead to our many ego-personality aspects that are spread throughout many dimensions. And yet, we call ourselves the living.

We are even dead (asleep) to the *"third angel"* in Revelation 16:4-7, *pouring out his bowl on the rivers and spring water,"* as this is our mind filled with emotional judgments and how we feel unworthy of being more than just human. This feeling of unworthiness traps our energy *(turned to blood)* in the lower chakras, thus preventing us from reaching creative expressions and the full use of our mental and spiritual abilities. This stuck energy (blood) can become very destructive, which brings problems to the adrenal activities of our physical body.

The emotional and the adrenal area of the body bring forward karmic conditions for us to experience because of our doubts and memories of our past, which are "true and just," for we are the creator creating it. This area of the physical body is also associated with the church of Pergamum, which is symbolic of the bridge between our upper and lower areas of the physical body. It relates to the intestines, pancreas, liver, and kidneys, also known as the solar plexus area. It is within our solar plexus area, and we may still have experiences that need to be tapped in memory because of our past lifetimes.

However, since we are dead to our past lifetimes, the patterns of our memories come forth to meet us by experiencing karmic conditions. Whether we consciously know it or not makes no difference to our

Oversoul. The impulse to meet our karma comes from the memory cells of our physical body, as indicated by the *"rivers and spring of waters."* This represents our Christ spirit becoming the sacrifice for the energy *(blood)* spilled *(wasted)* by reacting toward our beliefs in polarity energy and then placing judgment on ourselves and others because of what we believe as our truths.

Even though the emotional body *(the third angel)* recognizes that we are the righteous Godhead, regardless of our karmic memories of other lifetimes, we follow the will of our dead ego-personality aspects of the past more than our current lifetime. And, because of our judgments, we place on ourselves the existence of positive and negative, light and dark, and how we continue to worship those ego aspects of our past and a God of duality they created. Thus, we choose and live under what they dictate to be our experiences today.

Revelation 16:4-7, *"You are the "Holy One, who are and who were, in passing this sentence"* upon yourself because you move your energy *(blood)* in many different directions, taking on many layers of identities (ego personality aspects) that are not you in this lifetime. We all have many clear, gray, and dark aspects of ourselves that span throughout our total consciousness, and we are not even aware of them, which is why we *"pass this sentence"* on them, and then self.

Our many ego-personality aspects of past lifetimes *"have shed our blood (energy)"* because *"we have given them our blood (energy) to drink"* in excessive amounts to create according to our beliefs, which is why our ego-personality aspects of the past *(they)* deserved what judgments, on a subconscious level, we placed upon them, for it was *"true and just."*

By finding understanding and learning of the law of karma, we enhance our outer consciousness beyond the realm of us just being human in this lifetime. By understanding our other personality aspects as light and dark, we, in this lifetime, become *"the victor"* in bringing in our "I AM" Christ-spirit and the *"hidden manna."* We, from our "I AM" Christ consciousness, will also give ourselves *"a white stone upon which is inscribed a new name, to be known only by him* (I AM That I AM) *who receives it"* (Revelation 2:17). Your real name is "I AM THAT I AM."

The *"fourth angel,"* Revelation 16:8-9, represents our mental body and is also known as the thymus center in the physical body, and the Church of Thyatira. The thymus center is connected to our heart, lungs, shoulders, and back. It is also the chakra of love, both for the self and others, and our ability to give and receive. A healthy heart pumps the vital life force to every cell in our physical body through the blood. And, trusting in self as Christ and accepting others as they are, radiate outward, and reflect back to us just who we are in our evolution. When we criticize and judge ourselves and others because of what they do or believe, we block the vital pathways of our blood (energy) to our physical body, thus creating illnesses and many other ailments.

You create suffering for yourself, which is why it is you who brings the wrath of God (dual-energy) upon yourself. The *"pouring out his bowl on the sun,"* Revelation 16:8, represents your ego-aspect or physical nature, giving way to an intelligence center of a mental nature. This means that many of us have great intelligence that belongs to book-learning and following other's opinions, which opens us up to giving away our God's energy and power to other aspects of ourselves and to others around us. And, in the end, we pay the price by using the fire of justice (sowing and reaping) as our means to become balanced.

The *"people being scorched,"* Revelation 16:9, by the heat of the sun represent those dark emotional aspects of you that insult *(blaspheme)* you, the real creator, and the *"God who has the power over their fears, hatreds, confusions, and their afflictions (plagues)."* How often have you sworn at yourself or called yourself names, saying that you're stupid, you have no talent, you're not smart enough to make money, you can't do anything right, etc. Well! These are the dark aspects of you that are *"being scorched"* by the karmic conditions that they (you) have set up for them and you to experience. And now, you are beginning to hear deep within your consciousness their pleas to let them come home and integrate with you, their creator, for karma to stop.

Remember, our dark aspects believe in their own power, and they also believe that we are not smart enough to be their creator. This is why we question ourselves all the time about our worth. They cause us to get out of our hearts (feelings) and move us toward our minds for answers. This causes us to look upon ourselves as not being intelligent or spiritual enough even to create them in the first place. This causes us to wonder about ourselves, especially if we have not had higher education in the subject. We desire to manifest for ourselves to experience, which is why we may feel weak and worthless.

Most of these dark aspects (dark lifetimes) are those personality aspects that raped, killed, stole, committed suicide, and were killed by others. Now, these ego-personality aspects show their anger and contempt toward you in this lifetime because you run away from them because of your old dogmatic beliefs. You have forgotten that you created them. These dark personality aspects will *"not repent or give him (you) glory"* (Revelation 16:9) because you, the creator, keep pushing them away by saying you could not have created them because you never lived before.

Because you push them away, they curse, threaten, and promise you things, but in the end, they just show their anger and contempt toward you. These dark aspects try to develop a partnership with you to steal your energy and your soul. You can even feel this deep within, but you deny those feelings because you don't want to believe that you could do something horrendous and ugly. Now, don't feel bad or upset about this because, for every evil energy you created along your path of evolution and growth, there is a spark of love within them, and they want to come back home to you, their creator.

Again, the reason most of us cannot integrate these dark aspects of ourselves is that we do not believe that we even created them. We just deny the idea of having other lifetimes. How can these dark aspects spark that energy of love toward us if we, the creator, will not own up to creating them? These dark aspects cannot repent for evil deeds when the orders came from the self.

Remember, you are the soul aspect in this lifetime, bringing all aspects of yourself home, back to realization. These dark aspects get very frustrated because you do not open the door of your consciousness and allow them to return home to their creator. Take a moment and feel all your aspects, even your dark ones that still are attached to you. You do not have to understand them or try to reason with them; just acknowledge them and allow them to come home to you.

We can integrate all of our aspects (clear, gray, light, and dark) by making a conscious choice to do so, even the most difficult ones. The process allows itself to come to fulfillment. You will know that you have succeeded by not feeling any more resistance, tension, or anxiety in your life. Actually, you begin to feel clear and complete. The tiredness of your body and mind will go away as you begin to feel a constant circulation of your blood (energy), causing you to feel renewed.

The *"fifth angel,"* Revelation 16:10-11, is our intuitive body and how it relates to our free will and our thyroid gland. This angel also relates to the Church of Sardis and how it deals with suffering. The angel, our intuitive body, free will, thyroid gland, and our suffering are all connected to the "sixth seal" in Revelation 6:12. Since our thyroid gland is associated with how we express our ideas, thoughts, and belief systems through our vocal chords, this sets the tone for the battle of wills between our defiant ego-personality (Beast), our mind, and our divine plan (the "I AM"). It is our belief in the power of free will that seems to close off our mind to other possible truths, whereas our divine plan sets us into a place of our "I AM That I AM," the Goddess coming alive within.

It is our "I AM" Christ spirit (Oversoul) that gives us the authority that we only need to learn who we indeed are, and it is done by using our divine plan. Consider prayer as to how to voice our belief in healing, and I am not saying that prayer is wrong, but prayer assumes that things in our life are not in balance. However, as we learn that we are Christ and the Goddess, we will come to understand the power of healing comes from our "I AM" Christ consciousness. By knowing we are the creator, we no longer need to pray to an outside force (God of the Bible) that beliefs in good and bad for help.

Our imprint or signature in life is in the energy that comes through our spoken words (*tongue*). All energy, either of opposing (good and bad) or expansional and unconditional, will always come in through our thoughts, feelings, or the spirit that we put behind every choice we make in life. We have the choice to do what we please because we all went from being a Christ to be a free-will agent, but it was all mental. And, because of this, we created many exciting things that caused us to suffer at the hands of our own defiant ego nature (Beast).

This suffering caused us to forget who we are and that our divine plan is not owned by some God outside of us but is contained within us. We have always had free will (even though it is an illusion) since the time we left the garden. It has served us well in creating many personality aspects of ourselves (light, gray, clear, dark, and in groups) to go out and discover the meaning of polarity energy (duality), or this God of the Bible that is an illusion. Free will allows us to see our light and dark creations, our ups and downs, and how they have helped us to understand our limitations because of group consciousness.

Our strong belief in God's gift of free will becomes very personal to us and is, therefore, a great challenge for us to move into our divine plan as the will of our "I AM" Christ spirit. We have a hard time defining the attributes of our divine plan because we live solely in an outer dualistic consciousness of a physical nature. Therefore, we are not willing to rethink (repent) our position on the subject, because it makes us feel wrong and separate from God. We cannot know who God is, or even who we are unless we allow ourselves to step out of our free will and into our divine plan (will) first.

Oh, I know, it makes us feel that we are giving up free will, but don't forget that those feelings are coming from our mental level and not from our "I AM" divine level. We all have been playing and living out of our free will for so many lifetimes that it becomes tough for us to let go of this wonderful opposing energy of duality, known as the God of the Bible.

Yes, duality and free will (false God) go hand in hand, and we have experienced this energy as all that we are and know. However, we are more than just a spirit, mind-soul, and an ego-personality that lives under the rules of a false God that works to undercut our true nature. We all are Christ, God, Goddess, and our divine plan is grander than any free will because our divine plan is the real self that is setting the true self free from the false self.

When we learn, we are a sovereign being in our own right, we connect to all parts and pieces of ourselves, including our light, clear, gray, dark, and group aspects of self. And, it takes our divine plan to complete the circle of all our ego-personality aspects and the experiences they have created for us since the time we left the first creation (Garden). Your free will, the false you, cannot do this because your free will only understand things as right and wrong, good and bad, God and Satan. Therefore, when we awaken to our divine plan, we move into a whole new consciousness, understanding, and an awakening about the way expansional energy works.

Because we believe in someone creating us, we all fell into a cloud of darkness (ignorance) that brought us only pain and suffering. And now, because of this pain and suffering, we *"blaspheme"* our own "I AM" Christ spirit by saying we are sinners. And, if we remember Revelation 6:5–6, it revealed that this would continue without end until we choose to let go of our belief that we are less than a God.

The *"sixth angel,"* Revelation 16:12, relates to the pineal gland within the physical body, also known as the crown chakra. As we move toward our pineal gland, we become more dedicated to expressing only unconditional love and compassion for ourselves, our ego-personality aspects of the past, and in the way we make choices. Do you remember the "key of David" mentioned in Revelation 1:10–11 and 3:7? It represents the key that connects us to our own "I AM" Christ-self. (See Rev. 3:7–13 for more information on the pineal gland and how it relates to the key of David).

This angel is also connected to the Church of Philadelphia. From what was written about the pineal gland earlier in this book and how it is considered one of the holiest centers in the physical body, we can understand why Edgar Cayce referred to it as "the mount of God."

Once we let go of our belief in duality thoughts, we make clear to our "I AM" Christ spirit that we are ready for change because we know now that this God of the Bible was placed there to help us run the course of playing with dual-energy. And, this change in our thinking is where our mind now understands that we are the Messiah and the Savior and not the man Yeshua (Jesus) coming to save us. The change is about us being ready for a new relationship with our "I AM" and all those other ego-personality aspects that we have created since the time we left the first creation.

In Genesis 2:10–14, the *"river rising in Eden"* is speaking of the flow of influences that come from our own "I AM" Christ spirit. Therefore, the *"great river"* signifies that we have access to our "I AM" Christ spirit at all times. And, because of it, we give life to any belief, truth, or form (body) we choose. And, since a "river" continuously flows, it means that our total consciousness is endless, for it has no boundaries or limitations. It is only the operating from the mind that gives us limitations. Learn to work from your own "I AM" Christ spirit, for you are a sovereign being, having no limitations or restrictions in what you can express and create for you to experience. This is why deep within, we all retain the memory and the truth of our real name, nature, and our purpose in life.

In Genesis 2:14, the river Euphrates and how, in the metaphysical, it pertains to us humans making choices and how it affects the bloodstream in the physical body. Our endocrine (circulatory) system receives and distributes the nutrients contained in the food we eat. Thus, the bloodstream becomes the vehicle to these food nutrients to our bones, muscles, brain, and every part of our body to keep the physical body alive. Our choices in life affect the energy that we distribute throughout our bodies when it comes to what we are feeding our minds.

It would also be the same when we make choices that set in motion the changes that affect the various influences that come to us from each of what we have manifested through time and space, including all ego-personality aspects (clear, gray, light, or dark). The *"drying up of the river"* in Revelation 16:12 signifies a change in our outer, defiant ego consciousness (the beast) where we bypass the regular flow of dualistic influences coming from our gray, clear, light, and dark aspects, in the way, we respond to them.

This would be "a drying up" of our involvement with these ego-personality aspects, where we bypass the endocrine system and move our responses directly to the pineal level. Because we all left behind many physical bodies where we played upon the earth, we do come into a lifetime (maybe this one) where we decide to be still in whatever we are experiencing to bring about a change within. This allows us to bypass the flow of influences that come into our mind from our ego personality aspects of the past.

This means we can now choose not to create any more ego aspects. By being still with our judgments, we dry up our involvement with all our ego-personality aspects, thus giving us an avenue to bypass our endocrine system activities and bring about better awareness and understanding of polarity energy, duality. By allowing this, we prepare the way for great changes in our life, such as bringing in New Expansional Energy to explore a whole new consciousness and a new life.

As we comprehend absolute unconditional divine love and compassion for everything we have created, the dark, gray, clear, and our light personality aspects become integrated; thus, we come into balance. And, once the balance is established, all karmic conditions (sowing and reaping) are not needed anymore. It is that simple!

The third river, "Tigris," pertains to the memories of our subtle forms, such as our (i) physical bodies (lifetimes) and (ii) our etheric, (iii) emotional, (iv) mental/soul, (v) intuitive, (vi) mind, and (vii) our spirit body. This "river will flow east" (or into our subconsciousness), thereby bringing us all the spiritual treasures (wisdom) of our "I AM" Christ spirit. All that is left is to bring up for expression and execution what the fourth river "Euphrates" symbolizes, thus "setting in motion the changes for which we have been searching."

To *"prepare the way for the kings of the East"* in Revelation 16:12 means we arrive at a new beginning, a new awareness, and a new understanding that we humans no longer need a savior other than the self. Being prepared means coming into a knowing that a new consciousness and a new expansional energy have found us because we allowed ourselves to explore the ground rules of polarity energy (God of duality) journeying through time and space (incarnating).

In Revelation 12:13, we read about the "dragon" and how it is associated with polarity energy and our defiant ego-personality (Beast). Therefore, the *"three unclean spirits like frogs,"* Revelation 16:13, are associated with evil per se, or one's distorted intellect, and the appalling things one does. These *"three unclean spirits"* represents (i) vibrational opposing energy (God of the Bible), (ii) the concept of the flesh, and (iii) the purpose behind it that comes from the same source as one's defiant ego-personality (Beast). Collectively, however, they all work together to benefit one's own revelations.

The *"coming from out of the mouth of the dragon, the beast, and the false prophet,"* Revelation 16:13, is the influences of polarity energy and how we, from the ego-personality consciousness, expressed this vibrational force (positive and negative) as the only source for our creations, activities, and what we believe to be our truths. Therefore, the major symbolism of the *"dragon"* refers to polarity energy, like positive and negative, good and bad, the devil, Satan, or the like, through which we assert within our ego-personality consciousness that has become part of our physicality. This opposing consciousness is the place where we call forth these forces of external expressions to justify our beliefs and truths. And, if these truths are not justified, then sowing and reaping occur at a more severe scale.

Our defiant ego-personality (the Beast) inherited the power of the dragon, which is the opposing energy forces of polarity through the mind of a false God that we all created to deceive ourselves (the Son/Adam/mind of the real God) and our acceptance principle of responsibility (Eve/soul) while in the first creation. And we also did the same while in a physical body (the second creation).

Through our physical senses, we get to experience our free will and the choices we make using the influences of a mind filled with polarity energy (dragon) and how they affect us in the physical nature. Once we entered the void (endless space) and into the physical body long ago, we did only worship the dragon (the concept of a mind that believes in polarity as real), freely giving our authority and power to a belief system that our defiant ego-personality (Beast) is to fulfill our purpose, and to answer the questions, "Who am I?" and "Why am I here?" This is why we follow and believe in this God of the Bible, for this God is a false God brought about our own ego since it is all about good and evil, right and wrong, light and dark.

And, as we move on to the symbolism of the "false prophet," Revelation 16:13, I do believe that this is the first time I have seen any reference to a false prophet in Revelation. There have been often in this book where you have read about the outer conscious mind and how it formed an alliance between your "I AM" Christ spirit (the real Goddess-Oversoul) and your ego-personality in the flesh. And, since your mind of the masculine is the go-between, you see how your outer false mind can identify itself as being all that there is about you.

It sees itself as being the intelligence center for your survival, your ability to make money, the measure of your intellect, and many other things, like how you continue to follow a God of sin and judgment. And, it leaves you, because of ego, with the feeling that your "I AM" is only human, which is why you do not believe you are a Goddess and a Christ also.

While growing up, I often encountered individuals under the influence of alcohol roaming the streets, and they were labeled lazy, pathetic, and unskilled. And, most of us look upon these people as being a nuisance because we only see them as drunken fools and sinners. We have forgotten that every soul has their own way to grow in consciousness according to their own divine plan. And, the "I AM" allows every soul to discover its own unique way by giving them the experiences they need to discover their divine plan and the realization to whom they truly are.

How do we know that this drunken fool isn't a very advanced soul giving himself/herself the experience of losing everything in life to understand the experience? When we look at it in this light, the *"false prophet"* is not some person out there who is very intelligent, educated, and grandiose with the ability to sway you and the elite. The "false prophet" is part of everyone's consciousness, and it is the part that believes in a "false idea" that there are two different forces, God and Satan, and therefore we judge what it sees. This belief causes us all to judge ourselves and others as a means to measure our own progress.

The magnificence of the belief in duality, polarity energy, creates within our consciousness a delusion so strong that it can sway both the elite and the uneducated. Therefore, the "false prophet" is not about one overbearing person, like an Anti-Christ, who has taken over the world0; it is one's outer, conscious masculine side of the mind meeting up with one's very opposing and defiant ego-personality (the Beast) to cause chaos and disorder because of the belief that they are right in what they believe. It is always the false you (our mind and ego-personality) that sees right, wrong, and one's beliefs as the foundation of God's kingdom and never realizes that it's all an illusion and false.

It is because of the "false prophet" within everyone that has built up in memory many lifetimes of erroneous thinking when it comes to Christ, God, and Satan. And, because of this, the lie of us being Christ is that part of our creatorship that distorts our true feelings, our inner nature, and the truth of us being Christ, a God, and Goddess in training. The deception itself is not a bad thing because it brings us the ability to claim ourselves as the king and the ruler of our many layers of consciousness.

Some people here on earth have already moved forward in their thinking and have allowed themselves to feel their own "I AM" Christ spirit awaken within. But most of humanity refuses to allow the awakening of their divinity to come forth into their outer conscious mind. They cannot give up their beliefs, their rituals, and their inflexible teachings when it comes to polarity energy. Thus, they continue to follow the *"false prophet" (the Anti-Christ)*, the mind that holds true of a God that is judgmental, jealous, and condemns us for creating sin.

I have been a scholar and a "man of the cloth" throughout many of my past lifetimes. And, in this lifetime, I am a high school graduate who was never trained or educated in the art of business or religious academics, and yet here I am today a very successful businessman, and I am a "priest under the order of Melchezidek." Therefore, where does this training come from? It does not come from this lifetime. It comes from my history of choices that I have made throughout many lifetimes of the past, and now I can tap into the memories (Akashic Records) to learn "all that I am today."

There is a code found in the Bible, including Revelation, that is not tied to any literal interpretation or intellectual idea. And, it has nothing to do with the general principles of how man should behave or how nature, reality, or events are perceived. Rather, this code is tied to the wisdom of our own "I AM" Christ spirit and its memory of "all that we have ever done," and not only as a divine being but also as part of the Antichrist (false prophet) that everyone fears.

There have been many scholars throughout the ages, myself included, who have been studying the scriptures, looking for a secret code because we can sense that there is more than what meets the eye when it comes to God and the Bible. I would even go so far to say that we know it is there because we helped to write it on a subconscious level! And today, we have some scholars who are claiming they have this code figured out. The problem is, when they use their codes, they only reveal events that have already happened. Why is that? They cannot reveal any future events because the future has not yet been created or written by human group-consciousness.

Now, why do these scholars have to wait until the present day before they can use their code to reveal their findings? It is because mass consciousness (everyone is God-Goddess) has not written the future yet and has no agenda but to experience life in the "now moment." The catastrophic prophecies that scholars extract from the Bible were not caused by God punishing humanity for their sins or taking revenge for their behavior. These disasters were chosen, caused, and manifested by humanity alone because of their belief in a "false prophet" and a God that hates sin. Know the real Goddess does not hate sin, for she welcomes it because it brings in wisdom.

Man does not work from his Christ-spirit. He works from his reasoning mind, his emotions, and his intellect. Even the predictions of Nostradamus and Edgar Cayce about a magnetic pole shift in the year 2012, or something we might imagine as Armageddon, are simply strong potentials if we continue on the same path we have been following for over two thousand years. God is not going to condemn man or destroy the earth because of our sins. There are no sins and no God to condemn us, other than the mass consciousness that produces the belief in a God that will place his revenge on us for doing bad things.

Because we believe in duality, choices, ideas, purpose, and the actions we perform, we (the mass) choose to bring in the disasters we experience. Now, here we are today, waiting for Armageddon to come, just to see if the "false prophet" will appear before us, not realizing we humans are the "false prophet." If we, the collective Godhead, continue down the path of fear and belief in duality, then those potentials seen by Edgar Cayce and Nostradamus could indeed come about. But, as always, there is some good news!

Humanity has already chosen to move beyond the potential for the total destruction of the earth. Why? Because, according to Yeshua and the Ascended Masters, a quantum leap in consciousness have already taken place back on September 18, 2007. This means that the prophecies of Nostradamus and Edgar Cayce and the disasters prophesied in the Bible, including Revelation, will not come about, except for a possible shift in the magnetic pole, which may cause some changes to weather patterns.

Now, this does not make Cayce, Nostradamus, the Bible prophets, or those who say they have the code figured out wrong. It is that everything is based on potentials, and these potentials are based on where we are with spirit as a human group-consciousness. It is important to study but not live in our past because ninety-five percent of our future has always been based on our past.

This solves the mystery of why people have accidents, illnesses, and other bad or good things happen to them out of the blue. These things occur because of how we lived in those many past lifetimes and how they perceived good and evil as their truths. And now, in this lifetime, we carry the memory cells of those beliefs throughout our physical body, which makes past memories part of our conscious mind in making decisions today.

Because of our conscious mind and what we hold as our past memories, our belief today is that we need a savior, and we will gladly sacrifice our money and life to others to meet up with the savior because, in our mind, we envision the savior as someone other than the self. As individuals and as a group consciousness, we choose our belief systems according to the emotions of our past lifetimes, our free will, and how we interpret them in our lifetime of today.

There are many who, because of family belief systems, religions, and political affiliation, feel unworthy to be a divine-human. Therefore, they continue to listen to the experts in defining themselves. And because of this, most of the human population follows a false image of an Anti-Christ without even knowing they are doing it. Why is it that most need to experience a major earthquake, an accident, a virus or bad illness, or losing a loved one, or losing possessions before they ask, "Why?"

By celebrating our past instead of destroying it, including all shame and guilt, we rise into a new level of consciousness where we become proud of who we are today. Thus, we begin the process of bringing home all those dark and gray personality aspects of us to integrate. And this integration brings to us energy balance where prosperity, health, and wealth come to us automatically.

If you are reading this book right now, then know that you may have chosen to be on earth right now while choosing to become fully aware of who you are and what you are doing here. And, by honoring your past lifetimes, no matter what you (they) did, is the beginning of taking full responsibility for your life. It is a time where you come to understand that all those accidents, illnesses, poverty, rejections, and "sins" you believed you created were all part of the cause and effect you created for yourself to understand responsibility, who you are, and your purpose for living in physical form.

And, by studying and accepting your own past lifetimes, you learn not to worry anymore about your unbalanced energy or your dark creations. They have all served you well in one way or another, and now they can all work together as one with you, the creator. When you acknowledge your past lifetimes and release everything that you have ever done with love, compassion, honor, and no judgment, then you can move completely into the new expanded energy without guilt, shame, or worry. It is the same with all that is going on today with those that are working hard to destroy our past.

All that is happening is that they are afraid to learn about their own past where they were the abusers and the victimizers, and here they are today trying hard to destroy the past that they created. They feel deep within by destroying the past; it will relieve them of their so-called sin. When we allow ourselves to follow our "I AM" Christ spirit and let go of the concept of destroying our past, we set ourselves up for self-forgiveness. This, we create our future by eliminating all the emotion-based limitations of our past. This is when we awaken to the treasure of self-forgiveness and the wisdom of our past.

When we look into Revelation 16:14, *"These were demonic spirits who performed signs,"* it correlates and works with the sixth angel, our mind-soul body, and the relationship we have with the pineal gland in expressing our new desire to awaken to our "I AM" Christ spirit. Because of how we process our outer senses (smell, touch, hearing, taste, and sight) to acquire information about our surroundings and situations, we long ago created a false belief that the mind (the false prophet) is the intelligence center for what we need to survive in the physical world, including our spiritual training.

It is from these five physical senses that our belief in duality (sin and punishment) is part of why we manifested the seven deadly acts of (i) sadness, (ii) anger, (iii) lust for power, (iv) envy, (v) pride, (vi) greed, and (vii) laziness (demonic spirits). And, from these acts of defiance, we developed a belief so deep within us that we somehow needed a savior to come and rescue us. Therefore, Revelation 16:14 is about an echo coming from our defiant ego-personality, by which we repeatedly repeat (through karma) what we believe to be our truths. And yet, these truths are all based on polarity energy, and what we believe is fair.

We continue this process lifetime after lifetime until we come to an awakening that it is all nothing more than our demonic nature expressing and performing our ideas of duality as something we need to correct or else we will burn forever in a hell of torture. And, because of memory and our act of hiding our dark creations (dark ego-personality aspects of self and what we (they) did in those lifetimes), we caused an echo of reoccurring demonic influences that give life to more and more parts and pieces of us that work from a strong belief in polarity energy, and that power is real.

These parts make up the seven endocrine systems of the physical body, and every time we come back to earth in physical form, these demonic influences revisit these seven endocrine systems until the energy stuck within each level is released. Here they are, listed again, starting from the lowest to the highest.

1. Gonad, where desires are first conceived
2. Lyden, where choices are made
3. Adrenal, where all of our choices move to memory
4. Thymus, where growth and expansion come forth because of our desires, choices, and what we put to memory
5. Thyroid, where we first learn to control and take power over what we create
6. Pineal, where we express our relationship with all of what we created
7. Pituitary, where we must learn to take responsibility for everything, we have created

Channeling of the Ascended Masters on the Apocalypse

The *"kings of the whole world,"* Revelation 16:14, differ from *"the kings of the east,"* Revelation 16:12 because the "kings of the east" represent those of us setting a new beginning and a whole new understanding that we no longer need a savior but ourselves.

Our super-subconsciousness ("I AM" Christ spirit) has found us because we have allowed ourselves to explore the foundations of polarity energy, including how we explored the *"kings of the world,"* symbolized by how we allowed our outer mind (false prophet), our defiant ego-personality (Beast), our belief in duality (dragon), our free will, and our dark and gray creations to influence us into believing that we need a savior.

This sets up within us a battle of wills between our divine plan (our "I AM" Christ spirit or "God almighty") and our belief that an outside God created us with free will. This battle between free will and our divine plan begins with failing to believe that we are Christ, God, the Goddess, and the Messiah. And, with Revelation 16:15, *"behold, I am coming like a thief. Blessed is the one who watches and keeps his clothes ready so that he may not go naked and people see him exposed,"* is without doubt, that we all are the Christ we have been seeking and waiting. And, as one can see today, there are a lot of people that belong to the system being exposed, for their nakedness (vulnerability) is without a doubt of their intentions.

In 2 Peter 3:10, it says, *"The day of the Lord will come like a thief in the night, and then the heavens will pass away with a mighty roar, and the elements will be dissolved by fire, and the earth and everything done on it will be found out."* This means that suddenly – perhaps at the most unexpected time (a thief in the night), maybe even today – something awakens you from the darkness of your ignorance and vulnerability and brings you into an awakening where you now know that you are a Christ also. Thus, the rest of the verse portrays the crumbling foundations of your truths that were once your lies because they were built upon polarity energy and a false God.

The crumbling of the old opposing energy of polarity has made room for a New Energy to be used as the foundation of our manifestations. This New Energy is what the Bible recognizes as the "New Earth." It is taken up as New Expansional Energy because it differs greatly from the old energy of polarity (the old God of the Bible). First, it does not vibrate like the old energy (old earth). Rather, it expands beyond the mind and into all of creation where we can choose which reality we desire to experience. We simply allow it to happen and watch and *"keep (y)our clothes"* (new beliefs) ready to take a quantum leap (rapture) into our multi-dimensional consciousness, where all treasures of the heart and lifetimes can be found.

By not trusting in self as being a Christ and the Messiah, some of us will expose our dual way of thinking to our many ego-personality aspects, demonstrating to them that some of us are not ready to be the King of Kings, the Lord of Lords, and the ruler of the self. Therefore, those of you, from the mind and ego level, that are not ready to be lifted in the air as the true creator in meeting with your own "I AM" Christ spirit (Oversoul), may have to recycle through another twenty-five thousand-year cycle playing with this polarity energy again until you awaken.

Why? It is because you are not acknowledging your outer mind as being the false prophet (Anti-Christ) and your ego-personality as the beast to be integrated with your "I AM" Christ-spirit (Oversoul). If you continue with your belief in good and evil, and that one owes the world because of past deeds, then those same beliefs will betray you by what you create to experience. The judgments you put on yourself and others, because of what they do, what they believe, the way they look, or the way you see them act and suffer, will betray you in the end!

The falsehoods associated with your righteousness, saying you follow the Bible, this God of judgment as to your creator, and others philosophies, become your nakedness in the end. Thus, exposing the lies you follow, and you also show your shame when you ask the rest of us to admit that we are sinners. When awakened, you will see the Bible and Revelation as a road map and guide for your journey in becoming a Christ and a Goddess in your own right. Do not give your life to an illusionary God and a devil that lives only in a book and in your mind just to excuse yourself for not taking responsibility for your actions.

The question is: How do you know this God of the Bible is an illusionary God? It is easy; this God seems to keep all power to himself and demands to be worshipped, wants your money, and, if necessary, your very life. And, in return, this God of the Bible (the false prophet) will give you joy, wealth, and peace, but you will only receive it after death. But, to your surprise after death, you will learn that it was all false. This means you will never receive it. Instead, you will receive more suffering.

In Deuteronomy 6:1–2, 4, 14–15, it says: *"These then are the commandments, the statutes, and decrees which the Lord, your God, has ordered that you be taught to observe in the land into which you are crossing for conquest, so that you and your son and your grandson may fear the Lord, your God, and keep, throughout the days of your lives, all his statutes and commandments which I enjoin on you, and thus have long life.... O Israel! The Lord is our God, the Lord alone! Therefore, you shall love the Lord, your God, with all your heart, and with all your soul, and with all your strength....You shall not follow other gods, such as those of the surrounding nations, lest the wrath of the Lord, your God, flare up against you, and he destroys you from the face of the land; for the Lord, your God, who is in your midst, is a jealous God."*

There are hundreds of other passages in the Bible about God's anger and the revenge he takes on those who do not believe in him. In Psalm 60:3-5, we read: *"O God, you have rejected us and broken our defenses; you have been angry; rally us! You have rocked the country and split it open; repair the cracks in it, for it is tottering. You have made your people feel hardships; you have given us stupefying wine."* Chapter after chapter, verse after verse, the Bible is filled with judgment, curses, revenge, and anger against all who defy this God of the Bible. And, if you read the Bible with a pure heart, you would see with your own eyes that this God lacks compassion and unconditional love for his children (creation).

Thus, according to Yeshua and the Ascended Masters, this love that comes from this God sounds more like a closed-minded, vindictive human, and not some God of absolute unconditional love! Still today, man fails to see the division of God as a method for control and power. And this division of God comes in many beliefs and religions of the world.

How is it that we cannot see this God of the Bible is not absolute in his love for his people, for this God has only contempt in his heart. Look how this God declares a duality principle of saints versus sinners, or "my people" "versus the devil's people," those "heathens" who don't believe in any righteous God, all of it has nothing to do with unconditional love and the God-Goddess. The real God-Goddess has no agenda for humanity! She doesn't need to be worshipped and praised like an insecure ruler.

It is you and the mass consciousness that are the rulers of the world. All that we did was adopt this God of the Bible in our image, using our mind-soul and ego-personality, and then we gave this God of the Bible our power to control our lives for us not to take responsibility for our creations. We humans, are in charge of what we experience as far as viruses or plagues, and not some God outside of us.

Take Covid-19, for example; once we humans decide we do not need it any longer, the virus will disappear as fast as it came. Another example is the "harvest" everyone talks about. Not that the hour is near when man and earth will be destroyed. It just signifies our awakening to the wisdom we possess as a Christ. There are people in this world that are very concerned about us learning of us being a sovereign God/Christ in our own right. Why? It is because it means the end of their world of power and control over us.

Terry L. Newbegin

If we look at our surroundings, like our religious leaders, politicians, and those of the elite, we can see how everything is under male-dominated control. And this correlates with our conscious mind (the false prophet-Anti-Christ) and our ego (the beast) being in charge. Every conflict and battle today are, at its core, about the struggle between our "I AM" Christ consciousness (represented by Yeshua-Jesus), our conscious mind (represented by the false prophet), and our ego (the beast).

Yes, the conflicts may appear to be about land, race, inequity, global warming, money, power, religion, or resources, but in truth, they are simply the energies of the old, dualistic, and polarity beliefs trying to hang on to their power and control over us. According to Yeshua and the Ascended Masters, it is time to mark the end of an era and the beginning of a new one.

To ascend in the physical body, while having a total realization of you being a Christ, you become free of polarity energy battling you. So, why are we so afraid of ascension? Our religious teachers speak every day of a Rapture, and yet, we are so distracted when it comes to consciousness because we worry too much about our immortality, our family, our jobs, and our spiritual footprint. Many of us congregate in spiritual gathers to get a bit of understanding about God. Then we get our pep talk! And then, we go back to our routine, waiting until next week to get the same pep talk.

The Ascended Masters speak of how it breaks their hearts, seeing us so hypnotized into the same routines, the same limitations, and the same lectures about how much God loves us. The Ascended Masters have told me that ninety-percent (90%) of our biology and our thoughts are not even our thoughts, as they belong to our ancestors, our past lifetimes, the mass consciousness, and to being hypnotized to the fact we are not a Christ.

As the Ascended Masters spoke about the New Age consciousness, it began over two thousand years ago when Yeshua (Jesus) came to earth planting the seed of the Christ consciousness. That was the birth of New Age humans. And, this Christ seed led to religions about Yeshua, which was good for its time. However, religions have gone astray, as they present to us today a God of vengeance, a God of hate, a God of jealously, a God of punishment, a God of love but only with conditions, and a God that needs worshipping. Therefore, according to the Ascended Masters, this era of New Age has now come to an end.

It is time for New Age to evolve, as in *"thy will be done as it is in heaven,"* Matthew 6:9-13. Meaning, our "divine plan" is complete and balanced if we so choose; therefore, we have transformed our humanness into a divine-human while still part of the earth. And this is why the Ascended Masters say, "there are so few who will choose ascension over New Age." Why? It is because too many New Age Light Workers have too much invested in what they do, and rightfully so because they have worked very hard trying to bring the message of Christ to the mass.

The ego of these hard workers will not allow them to let go, and that is where controversy sets in, and many will overlook what is happening right around them. They overlook that consciousness evolves just like it did before Yeshua came to earth over two thousand years ago. The New Agers preach about Yeshua' (Jesus) return without realizing Yeshaus' return is not about himself, but the Christ seed of the Age of Consciousness and Crystalline Energy.

This Age of Consciousness is not about thought or our mind and ego; it is about experiencing pure consciousness, and then feel into "I Exist." That is when we will understand the difference between thought, energy, and consciousness. The miracle is that "I Exist" as an independent Christlike being, a sovereign being who is not owned or controlled by anyone outside of my "I Exist." It is a "knowingness" and an "awareness" that finds the real God-Goddess as the "I" in "I AM That I AM, and "I Exist" as a Christ in my own right.

We humans have been trained not to look within themselves for answers because we are told that it is selfish. We all have been hypnotized into believing that it is selfish to take care of ourselves, to know ourselves, love ourselves, and care for ourselves first before others. And yet, according to Yeshua and the Ascended Masters, that is the least selfish thing we could do for ourselves and this earth we live on. Religions tell us to take care of everybody else, to be in service to everybody, but ourselves. That is not being in service. That is being a servant to them. It is time to honor ourselves as Christ also. It is okay to help others, but not to the point that we lose who we are as a Christ. It is now time to be human and divine at the same time.

Most of us have heard the prophecies about Armageddon as the final battle between good and evil, and it will be played out in the Middle East. And, according to Christian interpretations, the Messiah, the Lord Jesus, will return to earth and defeat the Anti-Christ along with the beast. However, Revelation 16:16, the *"assembling of the kings in the place named Armageddon in Hebrew,"* comes from Hebrew har Megiddo, meaning "mountain of Megiddo."

Megiddo was the location of many decisive battles in ancient times. The town is approximately twety-fives miles (forty kilometers) west of the southern tip of the Sea of Galilee (or Lake Tiberias to the Romans) in the Kishon River area. Therefore, according to my research, Apostle John, the writer of the Book of Revelation, Armageddon is a Hebrew word, yet it seems to appear nowhere in Hebrew literature; therefore, there is some doubt as to its proper spelling in Greek.

Aside from the highly symbolic language of Revelation 16:16, there is no other frame of reference or explanation available other than 16:16. The conservative voice of Christian scholars says the words mean an end to the world or the definitive battle between God and Satan. Actually, the word Armageddon can be used metaphorically to indicate a final, personal battle within the self, or it can mean the ultimate result of a great battle between the armies of the earth, thus eliminating all of what we see as evil in the world.

Because of these two different views, the spirit of the Book of Revelation calls upon us not to be taken literally but as a historical text in which the words, phrases, and passages are more symbolic than literal. Rejection of the idea that Armageddon is a literal battle played out on the earth is the first step in becoming awakened to the symbology of it all. This leads to our defiant ego-based consciousness (the Beast), our conscious mind (the false prophet/Antichrist), and our "I AM" Christ consciousness to be part of our conflicts in dealing with the opposing forces taking place within ourselves. In fact, our mind battles with our defiant ego beastly nature while our "I AM" Christ struggles to release our old, dogmatic belief systems tied to polarity energy and a God that loves power and control.

In a very real way, it is the end of the world as we know it if we learn to let go of the belief in polarity energy and then see ourselves as a Christ. When this is done in physical form, we enter into the higher dimensions (heavens) of true freedom, higher understanding, no limitations, and a treasure of wisdom to tap into. Therefore, Armageddon is not about the battle of good and evil; it is about the battle we have within our own mind about the belief in polarity (good versus evil) that we have always believed to be real. Therefore, this is not a literal battle, but a battle fought within each person.

The sixth angel (pineal gland in the physical body) had the job of watching over the operations of our mind for us to understand the workings of polarity energy (God of the Bible). In the pouring-out of the plagues given in Revelation, we can see the symbology of the great battle taking place within all aspects of our own consciousness. Hence, this is the battle of "the wills," and the free will to choose polarity energy (God of the Bible) as being our framework versus our sovereignty as a God, Goddess, and Christ in disguise.

The battle between our lower and higher being is our own battle, just as Jesus (Yeshua) fought his own battle within himself when he walked in the desert. By overcoming our lower ego-self, we become a pillar of strength in the temple of our physical body (Revelation 3:12). We do not have to wait to die to recall the memory of whom we are, who we were, or why we are here on earth. Our memories have become a permanent state of consciousness (pillar) that identifies us in this lifetime as being the head, the king, and the Lord of Lords ("the temple of God"). We just all have forgotten!

In our silent and solitary communications with the burning bush of our own "I AM," the battle between the higher and lower self becomes clear to us, and the true way of release is indicated by the pouring out of the plagues, which means, our truths (Lies) of old. This is when we see the true meaning behind the Jews and the Promised Land. So, we can now rethink (repent) what we understand as our truths. Moses was very meek, and this caused him to say, "Who am I that I should go to Pharaoh and lead the Israelites out of Egypt?" (Exodus 3:11).

When this doubt comes into our thinking, we have the assurance of our own "I AM" Christ spirit informing us: "I will be with you; and this shall be your proof that it is I who have sent you: when you bring my people (other ego-personality aspects of yourself) out of Egypt (darkness, obscurity, and ignorance), you will revere your own "I AM" Christ consciousness on this very mountain (the pineal area of the physical body)" (Exodus 3:12). So, think about that!

Moses said to God, *"When I go to the Israelites and say to them, 'The God of your fathers has sent me to you,' if they ask me, 'What is his name?' what am I to tell them?" God replied, "I am who I am,"* meaning *"I AM That I AM." Then he added, "This is what you shall tell the Israelites: I AM sent me to you"* (Exodus 3:13–14). By recognizing the power and presence of our own "I AM" Christ spirit, we humans are confirming to ourselves that our strengths, wisdom, and abilities become available to all our ego-personality aspects when we allow ourselves to rethink (repent) what we believe about dual opposing energy.

And, when looking into the *"seventh angel,"* Revelation 16:17, it represents our "I AM" Christ spirit and how it relates to our pituitary gland in the physical body. This angel is also associated with the seventh church (Laodicea) and that of responsibility. Once we recognize and accept full responsibility for the things we created to feel and experience life, the masculine side of our mind (false prophet) and our ego-personality nature (the Beast) acknowledge the self as a Christ. This is when we transcend our old polarity energy of a vibrational nature into a New Expansional Energy, known as New Earth (Rev. 3:14–22).

Because of the plagues (truths) being poured out on the gonads, Lyden, adrenal, thymus, thyroid, pineal, and pituitary center, and because of sowing and reaping, karma, some of us may, in this lifetime, become either cold or hot when it comes to the real truth about Christ and his mysterious ways. We should be approaching some understanding and self-awareness that we are not separate from our "I AM" Christ-identity. We should understand by now that good and evil (duality) is an illusion and a perception of the mind; thus, the idea of sin, guilt, and suffering should be released and let go.

And, the *"loud voice coming out of the temple from the throne,"* Revelation 16:17, refers to our awakened state of consciousness while still in physical form, knowing that we all are the Christ and the Father/Mother God-Goddess. And, by saying, "it is done," we are confirming to our "I AM" Christ spirit, to our mind-soul, our ego, and all our ego-personality aspects (clear, gray, and dark) that we have accomplished what we set out to do; to answer the questions, "Who am I?" and "Why am I here?"

From reading this verse, we would think that we are in for more suffering, but that is not true. Even though this verse seems to talk about very harsh and unforgiving earthquakes never felt by humanity before, the verse is telling us the position of our outer conscious mind (the false prophet) and how it is now taking on a new belief pattern, leaving behind the old dogmatic patterns that were once held in memory as our truths (plagues).

The *"lightning flashes,"* as previously described in Revelation 4:5, is now seen as the repetitive, vibrational feelings of duality coming from our super-subconsciousness (Christ-self). They are informing our outer self (mind and ego) that everything we have experienced since the time we left the garden long ago has now turned to wisdom. And, this wisdom is now stored up in memory, our Oversoul. Because of the cleansing forces of water, air, earth, and form, our memory cells are now cleansed of any opposing energy beliefs. They have been brought forth to our consciousness with such violent ego-personalities (great earthquakes) that it has led us into experiencing things that we have never experienced before.

With the help of our many light, gray, and dark ego-personality aspects, our defiant ego (beast) took on a strong, upward movement that led us into expressing very destructive behavior patterns, which then led us into creating great eruptions at the conscious level with no warning.

Because of all that we have experienced through time and space, sowing and reaping, we do come to a place in consciousness, sooner or later, where our mind and the personality traits of our past ego aspects accept the rising of our energy vibrations (rumblings, and peals of thunder) to a higher energy frequency.

The *"violent earthquake that has never been seen since the human race began,"* Revelation 16:18, is about how we humans have never experienced such upheavals in consciousness like the one that we have experienced journeying through so many lifetimes. Remember, we, in the beginning, idealized two realms of consciousness (Genesis 1:1, *"the heavens and the earth)."* Heaven became the realm of pure ideals, such as learning more about who we are and what our purpose is on earth. And the other, finding the answers to these questions by us leaning more toward manifesting an outer false self, and then giving it compassion without judgment or rules.

The creative process, since the time we went through the Order of the Ark and entered into the void of endless space, has been an ongoing event. We have created great masses of thoughts and belief patterns, good and bad, that have never been seen by any man before, which correlates with Revelation 16:18, *"violent earthquakes like never seen before by no man."*

The *"great city"* in Revelation 16:19, taken literally, is about Babylon. Religious scholars look at Babylon as man's established system, symbolic of the self or our memory *(city)* of long ago, splitting our Consciousness into three parts, our spirit, mind-soul, and ego forms.

The *"gentile cities that fell,"* Revelation 16:19, are our many physical bodies where we externalized our unreformed beliefs and acts (sinful ways) through the functioning of our mind (false prophet) and our opposing defiant ego-personality (Beast); as this ego-personality became the base for our many other lifetimes that came from fear-based beliefs (symbolized by nations or gentiles).

"God remembering great Babylon," Revelation 16:19, represents our "I AM" Christ spirit remembering our split in consciousness. And now, our "I AM" is awakening us, from the mind-soul and ego level, if we allow it.

Therefore, here you are in this now moment, having the opportunity to remember your divine plan that you created long ago. It was because of this plan that you and the mass had to drink from the *"cup of your own fury and wrath,"* Revelation 16:19, because you believed and played out your unreformed acts as your truths. We cursed ourselves by accepting the idea of God and Satan as two different energies. However, because we drank from the cup of sowing and reaping, the great wrath of God has ended, if we all choose it to be!

By this presentation, the belief in polarity, or duality (good and bad), became the main ingredient of man's consciousness and his limited world to play. Therefore, every aspect of you became an *"island"* of its own, Revelation 16:20, separate from others and from its creator, you. All because of the accepted belief in a force of polarity energy (God of the Bible) as being real. And, in each lifetime where we created unethical and immoral acts, our dark aspects ran and hid from us, feeling guilty and ashamed by the way our energy was used for destructive purposes.

Each of our many ego aspects felt separate from us and from each other because of our limited, distorted perception of our total consciousness. This reflects back to the concept that we are less fortunate than those with more education, power, money, or refined Bible teachings. This gives us the feeling that we needed a God to rescue us from our sinful ways.

Remember, our outer mind (false prophet) is limited, and we cannot use it to get out of our illusions of polarity, duality. Our "I AM" Christ spirit, on the other hand, is unlimited and free to soar to the highest of mountains (highest of dimensions) and to the lowest valleys (lowest of dimensions), which then removes the idea that we have to give honor and favor to some God outside of us. When we, the true creators, remove those mountains of untruths, we begin to recognize our own divine nature, moving to its highest point within our consciousness.

As we know, islands and mountains are very much a fixed state. Therefore, they symbolize the consciousness that we have held as our absolute truth for many lifetimes, regardless of the consequences we have paid by retaining that truth (lie). We became an "island" of false ideas, beliefs, and images that formed our reality and hide our true identity from the self today. We ignore the real truth about ourselves because we pretended that we were someone with a human name and only one life story to live. But now, if we so choose, we can arrive at a new place in consciousness where we know who we really are, just by understanding that we purposely deceived ourselves until we became totally lost.

The time has come now for us to stop serving false gods (those that believe in duality as all that there is) and live as the true creator of our life. When we choose to be a true creator in our own right, we will look closely at the reality we have built up around us and realize that it is all an illusion built on lies. If you are feeling the energy of these words within your heart, then perhaps you have outgrown the Bible as you understand it and are ready to move ahead, beyond the old energy of the Bible and what it represents.

Channeling of the Ascended Masters on the Apocalypse

The *"large hailstones like huge weights,"* Revelation 16:21, in a literal sense, are ice pellets, hardened snowballs that fall like rain from the sky. "Hailstones" can come in various "weights," which are determined by gravity acting on their mass. Therefore, "hailstones" represent our fixed truths, ideas, and talents formed by our ego-personality aspects while playing out a story to serve us, the creators. Now those ego aspects of our past seem to be a heavy mental burden in this lifetime if we allow it. Why? Because these light and dark personality aspects from our past lifetimes carry within them such a heavy influence of persuasion that they cause us to become stuck in a belief that denies our position as a creator.

Because of this heavy burden on our outer consciousness, these fixed truths, ideas, and talents gained from past lifetimes will fall from their place of thinking that they are a higher intelligence *(sky)* than ourselves. We have paid the price for those lifetimes where we created unscrupulous acts, killing, raping, and stealing. And, we have purged those dark acts from our soul by choosing lifetimes where we suffered dearly for them. And now, those dark aspects still linger around us in this lifetime because we do not want to take responsibility for creating them.

By ignoring the fact that we have created other lifetimes where we played in the dark, those ego aspects look upon us as a great insult to our Christhood. Because we deny creating such acts of long ago, our dark aspects look upon us, the true Christ, as a joke. Even though we paid the price for the acts in other lifetimes, we still deny them by not allowing them to come home to their creator. We humans keep on saying to ourselves, "Why am I responsible for them? After all, this is the only lifetime I have ever lived."

"The plagues of hail" in Revelation 16:21 are severe when we suffer for what we do, but we still try to hide from these dark ego aspects of us. And, some of us have chosen this lifetime to integrate all our aspects. Others of us, when we feel the energy of our dark aspects, fear any idea that we are their creator. Instead, we revert back to the idea of this lifetime being the only lifetime that we have ever lived.

By persistently denying their existence, we don't realize how angry, hurt, and traumatized these dark aspects have become. This causes them not to want to come home to us. This would be like God saying that you are too evil to go to heaven, and you paying for your sins did not matter because you are destined to hell forever and ever anyway. Can you imagine God telling you that you cannot come to heaven forever and ever because you are not good enough? You would get mad too, and in the end, you would hate God with a passion because he didn't want to forgive you.

Well! You are that God and the creator of those dark ego aspects of you! So, have compassion for them and yourself and welcome them home as part of your total consciousness.

Allow your ignorance (hell) to transform into a consciousness of "I Exist," regardless of anything that comes from out of the mind when it comes to its philosophies and spiritual concepts about Christ and its higher understanding (heaven).

Chapter 34

HOW WE BECAME A SLAVE TO OUR EGO, THE MIND, AND THE SYSTEM

Are you ready to meet face to face with your own falseness and what you have believed as being real but is really not? What you believe is real around you, including the human self, is, in truth, the "harlot" you have indulged in throughout your many lifetimes while playing in polarity energy. In Revelation 2:20–21, we discussed the "harlot" and how she represents the blending of your pure spirit, the feminine part of you, with an outer ego-personality that is masculine in nature (no matter if you are male or female), which took on a belief system of polarity energy as the root of your total consciousness.

However, if you remember, we found that the word "harlot" appeared to be an expression of criticism for a woman of bad character. It also referred to a jester of either gender, but by the close of the seventeenth century, its usage about males disappeared completely. Today most of us look at the word "harlot" as referring to females and to a system in which a political unit is governed. Thus, the word "harlot" becomes representative of one's false outer ego-personality. The name on your birth certificate and the word "harlotry" represents the whole human race following a system that is not real but feels real.

The word "harlotry" can also signify the many other ego-personality aspects (lifetimes) that we have created. Therefore, all adulterating energies come from us while we humans play in many physical lifetimes, and not from our neutralized Oversoul, the Christ. Because of our many lifetimes on earth, we have forgotten that our own mental soul (Eve) uses our perception of dual opposing energy to cleanse the outer false ego-personalities that we have created to become balanced through time.

Everything that we have created in our many lifetimes has become the steps for our evolution through a series of events, good and bad, that helped us become the person we are today. Our unique and total makeup of today (all that we are), and the capability of our false ego-personality, contains and employs all truths because of how it is being transmitted from our mental soul and Oversoul to the false ego-personality of today (our physical name).

By taking many steps or lifetimes to evolve from our sleep state of being God-Goddess and Christ rather than trying to evolve all at once, our Oversoul reveals to us our outer false ego-personality of today the need to re-examine our old belief systems. Because of people being on different levels of understanding and awareness (by their own free choice), a person will generally perceive only those elements of divine truths that correspond to his or her currently held spiritual state and belief patterns.

The deeper we choose to go in the evolution of our spirit, the deeper and more comprehension can be revealed. This is why truth is universal and multidimensional and not tied to any specific belief pattern that controls ideas about heaven and earth or God and Satan. Luke 17:20–21, Jesus was asked by the Pharisees, *"When is the kingdom of God coming?"* Jesus replied, *"The kingdom of God never comes by watching for it. Man cannot say, 'Look, here it is,' or 'there it is,' for the Kingdom of God is inside you."*

To research this, even more, let us look at Revelation 17:1, *"One of the seven angels who were holding the seven bowls came and said, 'Come here. I will show you the judgment on the great harlot who lives near the many waters.'"* The angel holding the "seven bowls" is not identified by the "I AM" Christ-consciousness, according to our ego-personality (the false you), but rather by the intuitive center in the physical body. Why is that? Once we move through this book, it might become apparent to some of us that it is all about taking full responsibility for our acts and how we processed them through time and space, playing with karma (sowing and reaping).

Also, since it is the intuitive center holding the seven bowls (plagues), the time has come in our evolution, where we might need additional time to consider our truths. We may need extra hours, days, weeks, months, years, or perhaps additional lifetimes to work out our understanding of this false God of the Bible, known as polarity energy. The question remains, are some of you ready to make the quantum leap into a knowing that you are God, Goddess, and the Christ, and then take full responsibility for your life?

Because of free will, we all chose long ago to believe in suffering, or karma, as the means to come home to our own higher divine understanding (heaven). And, because of this belief in "what goes around comes around," as a fundamental principle of God's judgments and punishments, some of us may need extra time, maybe lifetimes, before we come to the awareness that we are God, Goddess, and a Christ, and therefore we can stop this judgment upon ourselves. If, after reading this book, some of us still have doubts about who we really are, then maybe we need extra time.

The idea of being God-Goddess and Christ, and that we are equal to God-Goddess, and a Christ, cannot be taught. Why can't it be taught? The outer mind and our false ego-personality will always generate its thoughts, ideas, and perception of life from old memories of dogmatic beliefs, which in turn feed our doubt of its validity. Our realization of the truth about who we are must come from a collection of all our memories in all lifetimes, including this one, before we get to understand that we are the one true God-Goddess and the Christ. It takes one to be a Master to come into the realization that one is Christ.

Since we have to use the unfolding of our memories of all lifetimes before understanding who we are, I would like to paraphrase from J. Everett Irion's book, "Interpreting the Revelation" with Edgar Cayce."

From Everett's book, he mentions the unfolding of the memories "allows us to remember our way back to whom we truly are, meeting along the way all that we have done, how we have treated ourselves and others. In us, just as in Jesus (Yeshua), the facts as we remember them are not at all necessary; it is the essences behind or in the use of the Creative Forces in life that are the real and necessary remembrances. Regardless of whatever is remembered, we should first recognize that we are using memory as a tool for comprehension."

"We must consider memory as a normal fact of life. Generally, we relate all memory to the activity of the brain and its use of the brain cells which appear to be involved. The confining of memory to the activity of the brain and brain cells is much too narrow a concept. We should instead consider that every cell in the body is a storehouse of memory, and, potentially, at least, the brain can receive impulses from each of them."

According to Edgar Cayce: "Each cell has its own mind and is, in its own way, a model of the entire universe. If this is true, then communication between the cells and us would be by way of vibrations, which seemingly travel along with the nervous systems in the body. Since there are billions of cells in the body, each cell could well be compared to a storage place of at least one 'byte' of computer language memory; however, each cell could also be capable of storing many 'byte' similar to the computer's "bubble" memory storage capacity."

"The above might be enough for recording and playback of memories stored while awake, but we must also consider the subconscious ones, as well as our instincts, which appear to be outside the range of memory. Let us consider these unconscious memories, the basis of our inborn characteristics and elusive urges, which are very much like our natural instincts. This, however, requires recognition of the psychological processes involved in the operation of physiological responses to the body arising from or through the endocrine system…"

"The endocrine system as points of physical contact for the transformation of psychological impulses and reactions, as well as being relative to inherent and inherited body/mind urges. These impulses are of a vibratory nature and are similar to an electrical impulse in our computer, to or from memory, and from whatever source."

"The opening up of our memories allows us to remember our way back to a knowledge of being the Father/Mother God-Goddess, meeting along the way all that we have done in each lifetime. By considering that each cell has its own "mind," we can recall these memories via vibrational wavelengths, and because of new energy, we can now call them "expansional wavelengths."

Therefore, my friends, our return to oneness and neutrality is a journey of acceptance and responsibility. It is a reintroduction and reintegration of all our many light and dark ego-personality aspects (different lifetimes), which have been forgotten or denied by us for a long time. Our oneness and neutrality are not a destination that we strive toward, even though we often speak about our impending return to it. Oneness and neutrality are an active means of balancing our belief in opposing energy so that we can become free of any specific reality format.

We all can play with words, but remember that this "play in words" we engage in are serious because of our evolution in consciousness is serious. Hidden within the words we use every day are the doorways that can connect us, not only to multidimensional realms but also to other density beings. Therefore, it would be wise to listen and pay attention to what we say and think because everything is tied to polarity in this three-density world. If our words lead us to create a negative consciousness than our experiences will lead us to more suffering in the end because of recycling in a three-density consciousness.

If our words lead us to create a positive consciousness than our experiences can lead us to experience a higher evolutional frequency where we could become more in tune with the love of others and ourselves working toward balancing our energy. Thus, healing, joy, and abundance become our norm. However, if our words are more in a neutral unconditional love state with our creations, then we can experience a consciousness frequency where we move into a fourth-density consciousness where unconditional love becomes our standard for making choices.

Remember, ninety-seven percent (97%) of all thoughts and ideas in a three-density world comes from the perception of polarity, God versus Satan, right versus wrong, good versus evil, because of our many incarnations. All of these thoughts and ideas do separate us from choices of neutrality and unconditional love. Thus, leading us to work toward a negative or positive consciousness that ensures us to reexperience cycles of more lifetimes until we awaken to this perception of polarity.

The first step in reconnecting to our higher awareness or higher "I AM" Christ self is a willingness to change our beliefs and the perception of polarity. This also means that we have to let go of this God of the Bible, because everything about this God of a three-density world is of polarity. Everything that we could possibly need to answer our questions about who we are and why we are on earth is in front of us because of this book. Therefore, know that the energy and consciousness of Yeshua (Jesus) coming to earth is really about us coming to a new frequency where we can reconnect to our own "I AM" Christ-identity.

The *"angel that is holding the seven bowls"* in Revelation 17:1 is our intuitive consciousness. And, what was said about Revelation 6:10–11, our thyroid gland is associated with how we express our thoughts, ideas, and belief systems through our vocal cords. This sets the tone for the battle of wills between our rebellious ego-personality of today and our divine nature. Thus, the illusion of free will can close off our minds to other possibilities of truths, while our divine will set us into a place of moving forward as a complete Christ in our own right.

Our intuitive consciousness (one of the seven angels) is telling the false self or our ego-personality of today (signified by John) to awaken and understand that our outer mind of polarity (the false prophet) has the capability and opportunity to integrate with our "I AM" Christ spirit (the neutralized self). The *"coming here"* speaks of us, from a conscious and ego level, rising to an awareness and understanding that we are no longer required to live more lifetimes in a polarity consciousness or world to recognize that our journey has been about the evolution of our consciousness. And, polarity is just one part of our total consciousness.

This chapter is about the influences of fear and how we are afraid to let go of polarity because it feels so real to us. However, can we be daring and bold enough to let go of this relationship that we have with our rebellious nature? Just think it has been our false perception of a God sold to us in the nature of us having to worship him, and if not, we are destined to hell. This is easy to see that this God of the Bible, sold to us by the Church, loves this control over our choices.

The time has come for us, the year 2020, to bring in a new relationship and a new beginning with whom we indeed are as an "I AM" Christ also. It is time to take that leap and walk through the door of our subconsciousness and find the total self as being more than just a human. When we feel difficulties springing up around us when we know intuitively that there is a challenge coming up into our reality, and we are trying to deny it or pretend it is not there, then transform that fear into wisdom, into awareness, and move it into our awakened consciousness for solutions.

The *"I will show you the judgment on the great harlot"* in Revelation 17:1, is again our intuitive consciousness presenting to the false self a whole new concept about being God. Had we listened to our gut feelings long ago, instead of our intellect, we would have seen the reason for our suffering throughout many lifetimes, including this one. Our suffering, whether we believe it or not, actually comes from us and what we believe to be our truths, not from God or even Satan.

Because of the persuasive power of governments, religions, businesses, family, the Media, and friends (the great harlot), they influence everything we feel, all that we perceive through the five physical senses and our choices in what to believe. Everything we see, smell, taste, touch, and hearing, physical and nonphysical, are joined together and influenced by one another. Everything and everyone – our spirit, mind, ego, other aspects of ourselves, other humans, water, air, trees, animals, insects, etc. – are all joined together with human consciousness in a belief system (hypnotic state) that defines our reality only from an outer, intellectual level where every thought we have is related to a mental and emotional process.

These are the "kings of the earth" mentioned in the next verse that we follow even to our death. The phrase *"who lives near the many waters"* in Revelation 17:1 refers to the flow of our life force and how it works together with the forces of polarity in becoming the overseer for our physical body and all that is physical. This includes any spiritual acts that we may deem holy but cause judgment on ourselves or others.

The air we breathe, what we see, hear, taste, smell, touch, and even the idea of gravity, set the hypnotic tone that we are only human. This sets the perception that what we are experiencing today is real, even though it is all just an illusion. Every act, idea, or thought we do or have or that has been suggested by another soul is a hypnotic submission that goes into what we believe as our reality. This helps to maintain the illusion we have about ourselves and about a God who created us.

When we look into Revelation 17:2, *"The kings of the earth had intercourse with her, and the inhabitants of the earth became drunk on the wine of her harlotry."* This is the ruling ego-personality tendencies from our past lifetimes that are now part of our memories today and how they influence every choice we make in this lifetime according to their beliefs. Therefore, this speaks of the judgment or rebalancing of our belief systems and all the conditions placed on us, and this is symbolized by the "beast" (our ego) that must be accomplished by each of us alone.

"Having intercourse with her" is about our false ego personalities of many, along with the whole of the human race taking on a mutual agreement where we, as humans, express a common belief in plurality. The word "intercourse" is not just sexual acts; it also relates to mutual dealings between people and nations that commit to a governed state in plurality to establish a general rule of law living upon this earth or realm. In some Bibles, the word "fornication" is used instead of "intercourse," thus "fornication" can be said to mean "the practice of adultery" (Jeremiah 3:1–2; Ezekiel 16:1–3, 16:14–15).

In Jeremiah, Ezekiel, and Isaiah 1:21, Jerusalem is mentioned as a harlot, which means that the word "her" represents a system by which religions and governments are governed or ruled. Therefore, the *"great whore or harlot"* is not about a woman. It refers to the political system of governments, the concept of religion, and the mass human consciousness as a whole, all living under the rule of polarity and emotions as its foundation for truth.

"The inhabitants of the earth" in Revelation 17:2 are the many ego-personality aspects (forms) of our past, the human group-consciousness, and our many belief systems, ideals, ideas, thoughts, governments, religions, the media, family, businesses, friends, etc. coming together as being our foundation for the truth upon this three-density planet.

The meaning of *"became drunk on the wine of her harlotry"* is related to a person or group (like human consciousness, governments, religions, the media, family, friends, and businesses) becoming drunk or unaware of losing their sense of what they are doing. Therefore, this relates to when we first became part of the physical world and how we became overwhelmed and judgmentally impaired (drunk) by the intensity of polarity (positive and negative, the tree of knowledge of good and evil).

Because of our intense beliefs in polarity, we and the entire human race and the other holy ego aspects of our past became unaware of being part of something much greater than our human existence in each lifetime. When we took on physicalness, the juices of the wine (the experiences resulting from our polarity beliefs) impaired our awareness of being more than just humans. It became very difficult for us, and for the human group-consciousness, to understand our situations, let alone the idea that we created them.

Most people do not realize what they are doing with their supporting role in group-consciousness. The part we play in mass consciousness can go as far as helping to create crime, viruses, disasters, and war, and creating things such as love, trust, and a sense of community even though we say we are not participating in it. If people understood that their consciousness creates events all over the world without physically being there, then they would realize that it is just as easy to create everything their heart desires.

If the people of the world would move their beliefs beyond polarity and take full responsibility for themselves, they could immediately create total harmony among themselves and the whole world without lifting a finger. This would dismantle racial hatred, crime, political disappointments, war, and suffering of all kinds. This could be accomplished simply by moving our consciousness beyond the belief in duality and a God that judges things through sin, emotions, and punishment.

In Revelation 17:3, when John was *"carried away in spirit to a deserted place where he saw a woman seated on a scarlet beast that was covered with blasphemous names, with seven heads and ten horns,"* this allowed John to view and understand the confusion that his many ego-personalities of the past were causing on earth, as he lived them out. Therefore, if we choose today and are ready to be open-minded, our intuitive body (the fifth angel) can create a channel or route for us to witness and understand our own confusion that we are experiencing today since we have been serving the "kings of the earth" (endocrine system).

We all have expressed many doubts, fears, and excessive appetites and desires that have caused us to undergo many unpleasant lifetimes. And, because of this, we are very confused and undisciplined with our thoughts and desires. Thus, we, as a group consciousness, continue to manifest uncultivated *(deserted place)* belief patterns to experience as plagues. This is seen with John's vision of the *"woman seated on a scarlet beast that was covered with blasphemous names,"* as this is symbolic where some of us are now coming into an understanding that the *"woman seated"* is the principle of acceptance where some of us have been taking full responsibility for our choices, acts, and creations.

This is shown with the meaning of *"blasphemous names with seven heads and ten horns,"* that was given back on Revelation 12:3, 13:1, 3, as a representation of the devil's head or our ego-personality nature in action. Therefore, the "seven heads" are associated with the "seven endocrine systems" of the physical body and the way the impulses from our soul memories are shaped and formed. This happens through the interchanging lifetimes and situations in each of these seven layers for us to develop and grow in consciousness.

The *"blasphemous names"* we have chosen to work through the "seven centers of the physical body" are those of the "seven deadliest sins" than can be found in what we interpreted for Revelation 13:1. The *"ten horns"* are again associated with the influences of our rebellious ego-personality nature, bringing our mind of falseness beliefs through cycles of the astral/physical realms, lifetime after lifetime, or until this falseness, we carry in memory returns to its oneness of consciousness (Revelation 12:3).

We have been living with polarity influences contributed with the numbers of 1 through 9 and back to the number 1 again, or 10, for a long time, which is the completed cycle of us moving through the astral and physical realms. And, when we are willing to move into new truths and understandings about all things, then the evolutionary law that is part of our soul record today releases the old truths that have limited our expressions and experiences until now. That is when our healing, abundance, and joy begin to well up or expand from our "I AM" Christ-spirit as an everlasting spring of life-giving water.

Through our interpretations of polarity, we observed and experienced the effects of our belief in sin and a God of duality. And now, what we have perceived as mistakes, good and bad, or sin have brought us through our lessons of sowing and reaping. Therefore, it is time for some of us to graduate from this polarity influences and return to no more karma.

The holy ground (Exodus 3:5) is the substance upon which our physical life is built, for it is the resting place of our divinity. And, when we approach the realization of our completeness and accept all that we are and all that we have been, we shed all concepts and experiences of duality and limitations. This is when our inner wisdom proclaims that we are the Father, Mother, God, Goddess, and the Son, therefore the Christ.

In our silent and solitary communication with the burning bush of our divinity, the bondage of the higher to the lower becomes clear, and the true way of release is indicated. This is when we see the true meaning of the Jews and the Promised Land. Thus, we raise our understanding of truth. Through this recognition of the power and presence of our own "I AM," we are saying to ourselves that our strength, wisdom, and abilities become available to us when we allow ourselves to rethink (repent) what we believe when we say, "I AM That I AM."

The *"woman"* in Revelation 17 and 17:4 is the consciousness of our acceptance principle of responsibility or our soul, and this consciousness is clothed with a great deal of history, such as the experiences and wisdom we have accumulated until now. Since our soul consciousness of responsibility, symbolized by Eve, is "wearing purple," then this consciousness is of imperial rank. This means we all have a consciousness within that has the full authority (power) to produce many, many stories or lifetimes where we can generate belief systems that we are only human.

However, our acceptance principle (soul) has carried a fabrication, an animated image of us being someone we are not. And this promoted this lie that we are the opposite of being a Christ, God, Goddess, and the "I AM." Just in the word "scarlet", it means bright red, and therefore is symbolic of our emotional level, where we all can get angry over the memories of our dual acts and creations that became the root of our many false expressions that led to all manners of choices.

However, by owning up to what we have accumulated in memory, good and evil, and recognize the lies, these memories can quickly pass. When we work from only the intellect and our emotions (the mind), the five physical senses reflect only judgment. We will only judge according to appearances and our limited concepts about our truths that we hold as treasures. The mind of polarity, the false self, and its intellect will always form beliefs and truths only from observation and the study of relative conditions. Therefore, we will always distinguish truths only through what we understand of the environment that surrounds us.

When understanding comes to us through teachers, books, or anything outside of us, then the wisdom of the heart center (intuitive center) is completely lost to a lie and an illusion. However, when we learn to trust in ourselves as the God-Goddess and the Christ and look for understanding within, then confidence in the soul develops into a knowing that we are

Christ. This trust awakens our pituitary gland to responsibility, allowing us to enter into a "knowing" with no doubt of being a Christ.

This is what the *"gold"* in Revelation 17:4 is all about! Our outer, masculine, conscious mind, or the mental part of us that is the false prophet-Antichrist, and our rebellious ego-personality (the Beast) coming into an intuitive knowing that we are Christ and the Son of Man in the flesh.

The *"precious stones"* in Revelation 17:4 is symbolic of the eternal, everlasting, indestructible self, for it is impossible to destroy our soul, no matter how far our false self falls into the pit of hell. We have always been told to think and rationalize God, but thinking and rationalizing God has gotten us humans only suffering. The time has come for some of us to stop our thinking, praying to some false god, and the rationalization of a God and how he will save us.

"She held in her hand a gold cup that was filled with the abominable and sordid deeds of her harlotry," Revelation 17:4, as the woman, our mental soul or acceptance principle of responsibility, now holds within memory all the actions that our emotional mind took in measuring and judging what we consumed from the wine of polarity. Therefore, we have within our memories everything that we have played out in our many life stories. We all carry many stories within our soul memories, where we played with the dark and light, and the religious industry calls it sin because we labeled the dark as sin.

Most of us come to believe that we are a certain type of individual, even an individual that may fall into hell forever and ever. Or we may see ourselves as a person who once committed outrageous acts early in life but later became well-respected for our religious beliefs, and is now assured heaven. We even labeled some religions as the devil's den, but their truths are just as strong as the truths of those who claim to believe the true religion of God. All that we can say about this is that it all has been a great lie, because all we are doing is living out a story that, in reality, is not who we truly are; it's all an illusion.

One of the primary premises of the lie – powerful and seductive and accepted as truth – is fear of a mysterious God that holds all power to himself. Because we have a strongly implanted belief that we are unworthy of God, the reverse energy of polarity, believe it or not, is always working on our behalf. Know that our "I AM" Christ-spirit has no agenda other than desiring to experience itself. Therefore, we, as humans, are nothing more than the desire we choose to experience. So, be careful about your thoughts and desires.

From Revelation 17:5, *"on her forehead was written a name,"* as this is just like the "mark of the beast" in Revelation 13:16. The only difference is that the "mark" refers to those of us who dared to move beyond the original oneness of the Spirit of One and entered into the second creation where we are now playing with polarity and the ignorance to whom we indeed are as a Christ. The *"name"* on the forehead in 17:5 refers to the self in this lifetime (you), taking full acceptance and responsibility for everything in your life, including what you believe you did not create.

The *"mystery"* in Revelation 17:5 belongs to the great *"Babylon, the mother of harlots,"* which is nothing more than the outer, mental phase of our mind. It is our mind that is in a state of confusion and chaotic conditions all because we believe in polarity, sin, and punishment as the root of our existence. This *"mystery"* of the *"mother of harlots"* symbolizes our thinking that we can understand and communicate with our "I AM" Christ state on a mental level or through the mind.

By attempting to use the mind or our intellect to understand God or Christ, we will always become confused and lost. It is only through the silencing of the mind that we can contact our perfection and the real Christ that we are. Looking outside of ourselves or above in some sky, for God or Christ, will only bring us a confused state of mind. Why? Because our falseness to whom we indeed are can only see that it belongs to a world of duality – good people and bad people.

The word *"harlots"* refers to the mixed and confused states of mind in each of our many false ego-personality aspects (lifetimes) of the past. It also symbolizes the mass consciousness playing in a physical realm of polarity where we all are involved with moving beyond the idea of only being human. Because of a lack of understanding about life and God, human perception *(Babylonian city)* has brought about great confusion through the belief in the existence of such things as hate, jealousy, greed, good, bad, evil, God, and Satan.

In Revelation 17:6, *"I saw the woman was drunk on the blood of the hold ones,"* is referring to our mental soul where it became inundated and very judgmentally impaired by our ego-personality believing in polarity, good and evil, to the point we became blind, confused and susceptible to group consciousness. And, in the end, we caused a strong belief in sin and suffering. This belief in polarity caused us to become weak and narrow-minded, thus causing our energy (blood) to become stuck in a perception where we have no power to rise above our confused conditions.

Because of time and space, we have had many incarnations where we indulged our energy in seeking power and recognition, causing us intense fear in ourselves and others, and then refusing to accept responsibility for those acts. These acts of transgression that we displayed as our truths killed those desires and instinctive ideas (the holy ones) within ourselves that would lead us back to the light of understanding, overwhelming intelligence, and to an awareness of knowing that we are God, Goddess, and the Christ.

The name "Jesus," in Revelation 17:6, symbolizes the three in one – the Son of God (pure energy), the Son of Man (our ego-personality in the flesh coming into a knowing that "all is one"), and the "I AM" Christ consciousness that has helped us greatly to accelerate our soul growth as we moved through lifetimes sowing and reaping.

And, *"when I saw her, I was greatly amazed,"* Revelation 17:6 relates to once we conclude that we set the precedence for accepting responsibility for our acts. There is nothing left but to be amazed about how simple it is to take responsibility for our acts. Because of the complexity of plurality and fear, we generated and launched the foundation for the takeover of our mind by our ego and that of other's beliefs. The time has come for some of us to understand the real truth about the harvest, as it is about our ascension to a new level of consciousness and understanding where our eyes become completely opened to the falseness of it all, including sin.

The verse in Revelation 17:7 is quite profound when it comes to an understanding of the *"angels' statement"* about *"why are we amazed"* about *"the mystery of the woman and of the beast that carries her, having the seven heads and the ten horns?"* As this is referring to our intuitive consciousness (the angel) and where we can feel in our gut that what we are reading here has some merit to it. When we come into the realization that we are God, Goddess, Christ, the Son/Daughter, the False Prophet, and the Beast all rolled up into "one body of consciousness," that is when we ascend to a consciousness of a four density, a consciousness of love, forgiveness, and accepting who we truly are in the scheme of things.

And, once we learn of who we indeed are, that is when we become aware of all ego-personality aspects (incarnations) of us through the threads of energy (good and bad) that we have put into each lifetime. It would be like each light bulb being aware of the electricity flowing through them, thereby causing their light to either shine or become dark. Thus, the *"mystery of the women"* is about our many ego-personality aspects of the past follows a consciousness where they are dishonest with themselves in accepting responsibility for their life. Why? Because we misunderstand *"the beast"* as being someone separate from us. Thus, we continue to worship the belief of a false narrative that polarity, good and evil, is real.

Back in Revelation 12:3, we, as a group consciousness, gave life to a defiant ego-personality that caused us to misinterpret our experiences as good and evil, right and wrong, all because of the belief in external emotional factors that affected our choices. And this created the belief in the "seven deadly sins," represented by the *"seven heads,"* and as the *"ten horns"* representing the dual opposing influences associated with the defiant ego-personalities that cause us to move through cycles of astral and physical realms until we return to our oneness of consciousness again.

The *"horns"* are connected to our many ego-personality incarnations working with the belief in polarity, and the number ten (10) is that we need to complete this polarity cycle before we can awaken to our oneness of consciousness. Also, know the only way these "seven heads" (sadness, anger, lust for power, envy, pride, greed, and laziness) can influence us is through the endocrine system of the physical body. Remember, it is the zero (0) in the number ten (10) that associates our past defiant ego-personalities with the influences of polarity and how they carry us through cycles of nonphysical and physical lifetimes until we return to the oneness of knowing we are the Christ.

Revelation 17:8 kind of says it all because *"the beast that is seen existed once but now exists no longer,"* are our ego-personalities bringing us to our limits and as low into materialism as we desired, all because of reincarnation. It is our focus on choices of separation, duality, sin, and suffering that awakens us to our false creations and beliefs, and how we played them out on earth. The mental images we see about ourselves and others around us have no life of their own and do not exist in reality. They only exist in the mind as real because of our strong belief that they are real.

However, we do eventually come to that completion in Revelation 17:7, as we awaken to the "beast" (our defiant ego), where all aspects of self will integrate with us. Thus, their existence will *"no longer exists"* because, in the beginning, when we created them to grow in consciousness to gain wisdom, they were already *"headed for destruction"* (Revelation 17:8) because of the illusion of it all.

We all gave ourselves the illusion of having free will and the freedom to express whatever we chose to experience in the flesh. It did not matter where we journeyed, what we chose (good or evil) to experience, or what we did to understand who we are. We just knew that we would one day become sovereign. And now, suddenly, believe it or not, our journey of many lifetimes for some of us is coming to an end. We have gone as far as we have ever gone before, and now we no longer have to play in polarity. This means some of us are on the very edge of discovering why we are here on earth, and it is all amazing to us because we thought we might be heading for destruction.

This feeling is coming from the results of our journey of many lifetimes of forgetting that we have paid the price for everything we have done. The only thing left for us to do is open our eyes and let go of the shame, guilt, and the idea that we are a sinner.

The *"inhabitants of the earth,"* Revelation 17:8, represents the many false light and dark ego aspects of us from when we played upon the earth, and we worked them out with human group consciousness. And, the phrase *"whose names have not been written in the book of life"* signifies that our Anti-Christ mind and ego (beast) will no longer be part of the Book of Life, signified by our Oversoul, for they have died (integrated with our Oversoul as one body of consciousness).

Those who hang onto the belief in polarity will not move beyond group-consciousness (the harlot/Babylonians, the system). Instead, they will, even after the death of their physical body, be controlled by their lower animal nature or false mind. This means that once those people come to earth again, their idea of polarity will remain, and therefore their false self *"will come again"* for *"a short while"* (Revelation 17:10) to haunt them until they learn to let their polarity beliefs go.

When we look at our total consciousness as the entire book, then we will get to understand that our Oversoul is the "Book of Life" where the higher self has recorded everything that is false about us, even though it all feels real. Where do you think true wisdom comes from? It was what enables me to write this book because I have allowed my old world (defiant ego and the falseness of my mind (Anti-Christ) to die and integrate with my "I AM" Christ spirit. And now, I have a new Christ-like mind and an awakening ego personality that has no belief that I am a sinner.

The greatest thing that will hold you back from tapping into the wisdom of any chapter in your own Book of Life (soul memories) is the belief that you are outside of the book and that you are not its author. Awaken to the Book of Life is nothing more than your own Oversoul revealing to you who you really are and what your purpose has been here on earth. The entire universe, including humanity, is instilled with balanced energy of positive and negative, and by reaching your predestined state of completion in this lifetime, you can cause a readjustment and healing to set in, thus bringing balance and resolution to every transgression of the law of polarity that you may be experiencing right now.

The *"clue for the one who has wisdom"* in Revelation 17:9 will recognize the *"seven heads,"* the *"seven hills,"* and the *"seven kings,"* as they are all associated with the endocrine system centers of activity in the physical body. They are the impulses coming from our "I AM" Christ (Oversoul) being transported to each ruling level of the body, via Gonads, Leydig, Adrenals, Thymus, Thyroid, Pineal, and Pituitary.

Since the *"seven heads"* are associated with the "seven deadly sins," the "hills" mentioned in most Bibles are associated with "mountains," and therefore symbolizes those of us who have cleansed the memories of our five lower centers through the process of sowing and reaping in the flesh. These individuals are now ready to move beyond those five lower centers of their body (the *"five that have already fallen"*), for they have worked them out in becoming balanced.

The two remaining centers are the pineal and pituitary areas. These higher levels of consciousness *(mountains)* will come to those of us who are ready to accept the falseness of our outer self and the polarity that we have worshipped for so long. The *"one still remains"* is the pineal gland.

Revelation 1:10–11 talked about the pineal gland as one of the holiest centers in the physical body, and according to Edgar Cayce, it is the place of "the mount of God." By devoting our thoughts and feelings to friends, family, and our relationships with others, unconditionally and with compassion, then our "I AM" Christ-spirit will draw our lower earthly centers up to a higher understanding *(hill)* and unite our five lower centers (*those that have already fallen*) with our own "I AM" Christ-spirit (crown chakra).

When looking at the population of the earth, we do find the majority of people of earth are still working out of their five lower levels, and the grandest ruler (first king) is the gonad level because it causes us to believe in separation. The belief in being separate from God and that we are a creation of a supreme being sets the stage for us to fall into a consciousness of "survival at all cost." Most people still misunderstand their real existence, all because they have misunderstood the Tree of Knowledge of Good and Evil, and why we moved into it.

It comes down to understanding that energy itself is actually an illusion because, at its core, energy does not have a positive or negative charge to it. Remember, energy in its truest form or non-form is pure, neutral, and universal. Our true freedom will come when we allow ourselves to know without a doubt that what seems and feels real to us is nothing more than an illusion created by us Goddesses, the true creators.

Every human carries within them the temple of God; therefore, we are our church, and our spirit is the body of Christ. Remember, the Law of One is about all things and creations being equal in importance to the one collectiveness of pure, neutral god energy of light. Therefore, we as Goddesses, measure our progress and wisdom by which we use this "universal mind field of pure neutralized god energy of light," as we each have our different abilities, talents, and beingness.

Contrary to popular belief, we are not inherently superior or inferior to trees, rocks, birds, insects, or any other part of creation, because we are made from the same absolute, pure, neutral god energy of light and consciousness (Father-Mother God-Goddess) as everything else in creation. All things are composed of perfection, without errors, flaws, faults, or laws. Our body is simply the vehicle used for expanding and experiencing the joys or pains of consciousness. Therefore, there is no separation between God, Goddess, Christ, the self, and the whole of creation, including the lowest form of life; all come from the one great source, and eventually, we will all return to our own source.

Do you remember the self-righteous Pharisees who refused to be baptized by John the Baptist? Why were they afraid of John's baptism? It is because they felt comfortable with their beliefs and did not feel that they needed the repentance (re-thinking) that John demanded of them. They thought they were already good enough to take high places in the kingdom of God because of their popularly accepted religious supremacy. This is not a reason to judge them, because they were not wrong in what they thought. The path of their soul's evolution simply had not yet brought them to where they were ready to step out of their old dogmatic polarity beliefs.

Many people today have the same belief the Pharisees had back then. And, we can see it in our priests, ministers, evangelists, religious leaders, and their followers. Intellectually, they believe they are already in favor with God because of the rituals they practice, the beliefs they profess, the time they spend in church, and the money they give and collect in the name of God. However, they are still subject to the appetites and passions of the physical, and they will continue to be so until they accept a new way of thinking.

Many of us have completed our journey learning about the Tree of Knowledge of Good and Evil, and now it is time to move beyond polarity. It is time to trust the self enough and have the courage to step forward into this New Energy of Four, for this is the true meaning of the harvest (rapture). From our past until now, we have built our identity with polarity belief patterns, and now the time has come for some of us to release this old energy of polarity and move into completion – to a "New Energy of Four," which are:

Terry L. Newbegin

1. Positive consciousness
2. Negative consciousness
3. Consciousness of "no force" as it moves back and forth to light and dark
4. Christ-consciousness (also called our gnost solution)

And, the conclusion of Revelation 17:10, *"and the last has not yet come, and when he comes, he must remain only a short while,"* refers to the realization consciousness that we are, without doubt, God, the Goddess, and the Christ. And, when we come to this realization, we will retain this wisdom in our fleshly body for a short time, or until we allow our old stories to die (integrate with our Oversoul).

Once we reach a level of understanding of our true identity at the pituitary level, we will understand that we must let our old body "die," and along with it, all of our old beliefs in polarity. From this higher understanding, the Son of Man (the name people call us today) learns to integrate the outer, false consciousness with the "I AM" Christ-consciousness. And, in doing so, we create a whole new physical body.

In Revelation 17:11, the verse helps us to understand Revelation 17:9-10 even more, by telling us that our defiant ego-personality of polarity, the name in which we were born within this lifetime, exist as the "seventh king," because of our pituitary gland being tied to polarity, which is still old energy. However, after we have reached this level of realization from this pituitary level, we can move our belief in polarity to being the "eighth king," which in effect is still part of the "seventh king" (pituitary).

Once our ego-personality of today (Son of Man) becomes one with the falseness that we have been displaying for many lifetimes, we then have the choice to bring in this "eight king," or our connection to our "I AM" Christ divinity, while we, from the pituitary level (the seventh king), are still part of the flesh. By integrating our false identity with our real self (divinity), this changes our beastly and Anti-Christ nature to a consciousness that exists no longer, because we, on a physical ego level, have now reached a knowing and a realization that we are a Christ in the flesh.

This knowing becomes obvious to us because we are reaching the level of our third eye (pituitary), which is still part of the "seventh king." Again, I site Luke 17:20–21; the Pharisees asked Jesus when the kingdom of God was coming. His reply was, *"The kingdom of God never comes by watching for it. Men cannot say, 'Look, here it is,' or 'there it is,' for the kingdom of God is inside you."*

In Revelation 17:12-13, the *"ten horns that you saw represent ten kings who have not yet been crowned,"* as this again associates us working outside of ourselves, journeying through the vibrational energy of polarity, over and over, lifetime after lifetime, or until we return to our oneness of consciousness. The number "ten" (10) again relates to the vibrational energy of sin coming from our five physical senses of the body (taste, smell, touch, sight, and hear) and how they relate to what we received from the five lower endocrine glands (gonad, Lyden, adrenal, thymus, and thyroid).

Each of the *"ten kings"* interpreted the vibrations of sin they received as real, and it was their crowning moment when they received their authority along with our defiant ego-personality. The *"one hour"* is symbolic of time and space, where we use the illusion of time and space and incarnations to measure our choices and experiences to understand responsibility.

"They are of one mind" in Revelation 17:13 is how the deceiving phase of our mind is fixed on our being only human. This mind (false prophet) and the "ten kings," the five physical senses, and our five lower systems of the endocrine, will be under the influence of our defiant ego-personality for as long as it takes on various forms of lifetimes believing in polarity.

Revelation 17:14, *"they will fight with the Lamb, but the Lamb will conquer them, for he is Lord of Lords, and those with him are called, chosen and faithful."* Who is the "Lamb?" It is a lifetime where you open your eyes and come into an awakened state to realize that you are, from an awakening mind, the Lamb, thus the Lord of Lords and the King of Kings. It is you who reaches a lifetime where you overcome your defiant ego-personalities of many and restore them where you overcome their defiant nature and breathe in purity and balance.

It is you, while in the flesh, that determines to move beyond *(fight)* the belief in polarity, and all that it implies as positive and negative. The phrase *"those that are with him called the chosen and faithful,"* refers to those unwavering belief systems, thoughts, expressions, false ego aspects of self, and those dreams coming in line with trusting yourself as being Christ in committing to yourself to being Christ in the flesh.

"Then he said to me," Revelation 17:15, refers to our intuitive center, and the *"waters"* that are seen are those life-giving forces tied to group consciousness (such as family, businesses, humans, and governments) that speak the same language. The *"large number of peoples, nations, and tongues"* are not only our many light and dark false personality aspects of past lifetimes and the memories *(nations)* associated with them; they are also the consciousness of the human race and how we follow their many different belief systems *(tongues)*, which we accepted as our truths and reality (where the harlot lives).

Through our ignorance, we follow the beliefs, images, habits, and thought patterns of group-consciousness without realizing that we are giving life to them as being our reality. We become the person we judge to differ from us. Because of what we see, taste, smell, touch, and hear, we experience what we judge through the energetic network of the five senses and the five lower centers of the physical body represented by "the ten horns."

Because free will (which is illusionary) is associated with our intuitive center, it is within this center (thyroid) that we suffer the most because it is the center that deals with power, control, and the ruling tendencies of our past lifetimes, including this one. It is our "word" (truths) that gives testimony to what we believe is our reality. Thus, we give life to every bit of that reality we have ever experienced, good and bad.

A belief system is a potent energy that calls out to other like energies (peoples) to support and confirm it. It is like a magnet (positive and negative) that draws in the support energy needed to bring that belief system into reality. Therefore, it is like we are living in a huge matrix system, and this system (harlot) brings hundreds, thousands, and millions of belief systems into our life to support our truths (lies) as we understand them.

As we have learned, the *"ten horns that we saw,"* Revelation 17:16, refers to what we taste, smell, touch, hear, and sight as we play them out through the five lower centers of the physical body. These sensations are real because we experience the pain and suffering associated with them through these five lower endocrine centers.

We all have belief systems that say we are a spiritual being, and yet we also have multitudes of belief systems that say we are only human and, therefore, weak, limited, and victimized. This creates a struggle within us that manifests our choices as our destiny. Thus, our choices are all based on beliefs that create a force that predetermines what we will experience as our reality each time we incarnate. This struggle within creates a tendency to search for answers, trying to discover what is wrong with us and why there is so much suffering.

What we do not realize is that this force comes from human mass-consciousness, and the system they have accepted as their truths or lies is the "harlot." How many of us are fed up with government, religions, family, the media, and friends who judge us because we think differently from them? How often have we seen businesses, religion, friends, and family take advantage of us?   As we stress over what is going on in the world, we feel alone and deserted, which then causes a deeper, intuitive feeling within us to search for something new. The search becomes long and painful, until one day, we finally come to a point where an awakening occurs and causes us to rethink (repent) about what we have always defended as our truths.

In our search, we find that those truths were false truths because they came from the system of the matrix (harlot). I use the word "matrix" because it is tied to a particular movie that seems to correlate with what I am trying to explain here. This causes us to *"leave her (the system) desolate and naked,"* Revelation 17:16.

"They will eat her flesh and consume her with fire," Revelation 17:16, as the energy of balancing (karma) do finally reach a point where we become awakened to the real self, the matrix or system (harlot), and how it has lost us as its source of power. We have *"eaten her flesh"* by journeying through many lifetimes, giving her (the system) our power. And now, because we are awakened to her lies and deceit, she (the system) has been *"consumed with the fire"* of justice (karma), thus losing her power and control over us.

In Revelation 17:17, this verse is not about a one God concept that many beliefs carry out some purpose for our salvation. It is the fulfillment of the five physical senses and the five lower systems of the endocrine coming in to follow the divine plan of our own "I AM" Christ consciousness (Oversoul). And it also refers to all ego-aspects of us, all parts of our physical body, and all the memories of our past, remembering their purpose.

And remember, in Revelation 17:18, a city represents the collective beliefs of our many past ego-personalities and the beliefs of group consciousness. The *"great city"* signifies that the collective group consciousness (the matrix-system) holds a belief in chaotic conditions, which has caused confusion to be manifested. And this allowed the *"kings of the earth"* (the seven major endocrine centers of the physical body) to become slaves to the system.

Thus, the *"great city"* of Babylon, which represents confusion or generally chaotic conditions, is found when we find ourselves in confusion about how we pay more attention to the beliefs of the group, such as government, religion, family, the media, friends, and businesses. Because of our attention to them is so strong and powerful, the system has us in complete slavery. And this is symbolized by the captivity in Babylon.

Chapter 35

WHY DO WE FEEL WE FELL FROM GRACE?

This chapter is about memories being the cause of our feeling that we fell from grace. When these memories are removed through sowing and reaping, the outer mind of polarity awakens to its ego-personality of playing good versus evil. And that is "all that we are" open up to a mind and an ego-personality of realization, unconditional love, and corporation. The removal of our past memories is imperative to our Oversoul, the "I AM" spirit consciousness, so as for us to move forward to other potentials of creations. Once these memories of our past are removed, then our new mind and ego-personality become free to tap into the fullness of our wisdom.

Therefore, the "fall in grace" is simply the removal of our old memories of polarity and their effect on our endocrine system of the body and our spirit. Actually, we have been paying more attention to our past memories as the basis for making our decisions than to our mind and ego of today and how everything flows through the endocrine system. The result is that we have soiled our pure god energy of light with desires of an unclean nature (positive and negative). And, from these desires of polarity, we formed the basis for most of our memories that caused a false self to emerge in place of the real self.

The removal of our memories became the greatest challenge to our Oversoul and that of our mental soul. This set the stage for us to free our true identity from the unnatural state we found ourselves in (physical form and the belief in polarity) because we followed the beliefs of group-consciousness and the world of polarity. We became part of a system (the harlot) where we journeyed through the earth forces, often experiencing karma.

We could not understand and learn about playing opposites (positive and negative) unless we became part of the group-consciousness and a system of beliefs tied to a God and Satan that seemed to have their power base, separate from ours. However, through many incarnations, sowing, and reaping, we learn to become obedient to the divine plan (will) of our "I AM" instead of an illusionary mind and many ego-personalities that believe polarity is real.

Revelation 18:1 is written in such a way that the *"angel coming down from heaven having great authority"* has been interpreted by religions as being Jesus coming to earth in his glory to become our Savior. However, the real angel coming down from heaven is not Jesus, but you in your Christ-like consciousness coming to earth in your own glory because the polarity is now passing straight through the pineal area of the mind in expressing the truth of you being the savior of yourself.

It is you that has the *"great authority"* to illuminate your mind and ego-personality of polarity to understand the truth about who you truly are at this very moment. When you realize that the endocrine glands are being bypassed by the light of your wisdom because of your many experiences, your human self begins to recognize a new you. And, it is this new you that awakens the old you in serving a new day and a new understanding that you, not Jesus, is the savior coming to save yourself from any more suffering.

In Revelation 18:2, *"He who cried out in a mighty voice: 'Fallen, fallen is Babylon the great,'"* is about you, in this lifetime, coming into a new realization of consciousness where you awaken to the "I AM" Christ you are, and how this "I AM" of you can now speak directly (intuitively) to your mind and ego of polarity in such a way that it will cause the "fall of your old beliefs" in everything tied to dualistic attitudes. This also includes the lies of mass consciousness.

When we become awakened to the self as a Christ also, then we can claim our greatness and let go of the idea that someone outside of us needs to save us, including our family, friends, religions, governments, our politicians, and all that belongs to the system of polarity (Babylon the great). Hence, that is when we say, *"Babylon the great has fallen."*

We spoke of the system of polarity (Harlot) and human consciousness *(Babylon the great)* becoming the very means for enslaving our spirit, mind, ego, and every personality aspect (lifetime) that we have created in working out our karma. The rituals of worshipping others and the rules of the system that control all the influences *(unclean birds)*, good and bad, to take away our freedom, we now have a choice. Be free or stay within the system (matrix).

The symbolism *"for all the nations,* Revelation 18:3, is the sum total of all our memories from the time we were part of the "oneness of spirit consciousness (garden) up to our present day, these memories are still part of the cells in our physical body. From the way we *"drank the wine"* of polarity long ago and became part of a physical life, we fell under the influence of a mind and ego that caused us to pursue acts that were appalling, and yet in a sense, they are not really sins, it was those appalling acts that brought to us treasures of wisdom.

The *"kings of the earth,"* Revelation 18:3, refers to the seven endocrine systems of the body, and to our many light and dark ego-personality aspects (lifetimes) that we used to communicate *("had intercourse with her,"* the system) with the surrounding, external influences that set the conditions in which we, and group consciousness, created many belief patterns and ego-personalities *(merchants)* that participated in the expansion of our consciousness and growth in wisdom, via pleasurable and self-indulgent activities.

Within the very cells of our physical body, we all hold these lifetime memories and every act that we have worked out through time and space, experiencing the *"wine of her licentious* (immoral) *passion"* (group-consciousness behavior patterns in the belief that polarity is real). Once our defiant ego-personality (the Beast) evaluated itself as being real and not an illusion, we tried to grow in richness by aggressively working to achieve power, which is why we and the group consciousness indulged in the things that help bring in that power.

It was from the wine of polarity, where we all became drunk and lost a sense of what is real and what is not. We all became weighed down and judgmentally impaired by the intensity of the system of dualistic forces (the harlot). Thus, we became lost in a world of make-believe. Some scientists call it a hologram.

When *"Noah became drunk with wine and laid naked inside of his tent"* Genesis 9:21, it refers to when we became overwhelmed by the experiences of our physical reality and the polarity we were experiencing long ago, for we exposed ourselves (naked) to all kinds of belief systems. We lost our garment of higher divine understanding because we mixed our lost and misguided defiant ego-personality and our outer mental consciousness with the new wine of polarity and physical life, which is why we lost our memory of being God, Goddess, and the Christ.

Metaphorically speaking, as we souls managed throughout higher consciousness (the garden) possessing a mental mind and ego in exploring the very edges of our new found consciousnesses of three, we became curious about what it would be like to explore beyond the edges of our Oneness, and this new double framed energy of polarity we were feeling. We knew that our higher consciousness (garden) was absolute oneness, where we possessed unlimited power, but we also realized that we had no direct objective for measuring that power. So, the decision to leave higher consciousness (garden) was quite simple.

At the time, we did not understand the physics of this pure neutralized god energy of light, or the motion of this doubled framed energy of polarity we were feeling, or how it worked with matter, especially the way it produced a force that went in two different directions. Perhaps we knew nothing about being physical or how this newfound polarized energy reacted toward our spirit, mind-soul, and our ego, or how it would affect our intelligence and feelings. Therefore, we all decided to enter the physical world to learn the behavior patterns of this polarized energy.

However, when we souls left higher consciousness (garden), we did not realize that we brought home our higher consciousness, right along with us! Therefore, heaven is not a place far out in some distant space or some dimension. Heaven (home) is within us all, and the only way we can get there is to remember who we are and then evolve (walk) through time and space, reincarnating in a physical body to experience our choices, and then take responsibility for them. That is when we will become one again with our heavenly consciousness.

Heaven (higher consciousness) comes to us all (or enters our awareness) when we are ready to receive it within our heart center. We need not wait to get to heaven someday or worry whether we have been good enough to get there. It is that we will find ourselves in heaven when our deceptive and misleading ego-consciousness evolves enough to accept us as being the God, Goddess, and the Christ we seek. We need only to release our old, dogmatic beliefs in a God of judgment, sin, and punishment, and that good versus evil is real.

The confirmation in leaving our higher consciousness to work out of a multi-dimensional consciousness is found in Revelation 18:4-5, in John's words, *"depart from her, my people, so as not to take part in her sins and receive a share in her plagues,"* This verse refers to us souls in the flesh today working out of an ego-personality that now recognizes the need to open our eyes and awake from our sleep state. *"My people"* refers to the many defiant ego-personalities from other lifetimes where we did partake in what we call sins.

However, what refers to, *"so as not take part in her sins,"* is to those many ego-personalities of past lifetimes that are now beginning to integrate with our Oversoul while we are still part of the flesh. And with this new awareness, some of us are allowing our memories of good and evil to become one again with our Oversoul. And, once these many defiant ego-personalities of the past are integrated, they and you will never again have to experience the unpleasantness of polarity or karma that stems from them, and from group consciousness and their beliefs (harlot).

Some of us have purified our memories from our bodies by journeying through many lifetimes, sowing, and reaping. And now, we no longer need to express suffering, judgment, being separate, or the feeling that we have somehow fallen from grace. The sins we imposed on ourselves through time and space were all based on the confusion and misunderstanding polarity. Those group consciousness beliefs built up within our memories to where they finally reached our "I AM" Christ consciousness *(piled up to the sky)*. And, that is when we began to remember the falseness of polarity and all that it contains *(her crimes)*.

Our journey took us through many new places, far beyond where we had ever gone before, and we were making a memory of what we created. We wandered throughout multiple dimensions, totally surprised at what we were creating (light and dark), perceiving, and absorbing. We brought all this into the deepest parts of our soul, little knowing that we were planting the seeds for wisdom and remembering.

Because of the way we tested the forces of polarity, we chose the law of cause-and-effect to meet ourselves in what we had done, good and bad. The phrase *"pay her back double for her deeds,"* Revelation 18:6, comes from the results of our outer, defiant, beastly nature and human group-consciousness working together to form belief systems of polarity to be worked out in the flesh. In other words, *"double pay"* represents our karmic conditions that we have created, good and bad, through both our belief systems and that of human group-consciousness. Thus, double payment!

Because our divine nature was unlimited, we not only moved the self outside of our original Oneness; we also gave the self an outer, false mind that would birth what we desired to experience using ego personalities. Genesis 4:25, Adam and Eve gave birth to a new son named Seth. Thus, the meaning of Adam is that of our mental mind; the meaning of Eve is that of our soul consciousness of responsibility, and the meaning of Seth became an ego-personality within us that believes in destiny.

Thus, this Seth consciousness within us took over the consciousness of us being aware of being Christ, which is symbolized by Abel. The Abel consciousness within us at the time was very much aware of being Christ. But, this awareness consciousness (Abel) was killed away by us souls falling into a consciousness that became very defiant and self-absorbed (symbolized by Cain).

Seth, according to the Metaphysical Bible Dictionary, was a settler who founded, established, and disposed of things in his days. Thus, the Seth consciousness within us represents the root energy that encloses and defines our physical existence, establishes it, and eventually disposes of it. Therefore, the Seth consciousness became symbolic of the root energy that defines our transgressions and then resolves them when we journey through many lifetimes setting up our surroundings. Thus, bringing in potentials of good and bad for us to experience, and then disposing of our transgressions through karma.

This Seth consciousness, which we all still possess, actually became the first principle of life that placed the law of destiny (known as karma) within our human consciousness for resolution and balancing our energy. It is this law of sowing and reaping that determines, compensates, settles, establishes, and disposes of the polarity energies in our life. It appoints within our physical level the elements of time and space (incarnations) to assist us in knowing once again that we are God, Goddess, and the Christ.

Abel, the second son of Adam and Eve, originally represented the keeper or the balancer for our energy, spirit, mind, and the many offshoots of our ego-personality aspects. However, they have all been forgotten (killed) because of our defiant ego-personality (Cain) that had slain our awareness of being God, Goddess, and the Christ (symbolized by Abel). And because of it, our "I AM" consciousness planted a new seed within our consciousness called the law of cause-and-effect, which is represented by the name Seth, the third son of Adam and Eve.

In Genesis 3:18, we read about the *"thorns and thistles"* that God said man would experience, as he *"eats of the plants of the field."* We all know that a "thorn" is a sharp, woody growth projecting from the stem of a shrub, and a "thistle" is a smaller, sharp, prickly weed. Therefore, the metaphoric meaning is when we took on the belief of sowing and reaping *(plants)* within our consciousness *(field),* and then grew in wisdom and used evolution to become part of our journey to awakening to whom we indeed are. Thus, there is no escape, because we cannot escape from the self!

Since the word *"her"* in Revelation 18:7 is symbolic of Babylon the great, the *"measuring of her boasting and wantonness"* refers to you and the human group-consciousness journeying through time and space, lifetime after lifetime, sowing and reaping because of the illusion that you, as an individual and as a group-consciousness, believe sin to be real, when in fact it is just experiencing. This verse shows the reasons why we keep on meeting ourselves over and over, again and again.

The woman, *the harlot*, symbolizes the system, such as religion, family, friends, the media, government, and businesses. She has no husband other than you and group consciousness, and the people who will not follow after her *"will never know grief,"* because "grief" is passed down to those individuals who believe in her (the system). Having no husband other than you and the human group-consciousness signifies that she (the system) carries no energy unless the system steals it from you and from the group consciousness. And, if the system as no energy, it has no power. Think about that!

Therefore, what keeps us asleep and dead to the real truth is not only our belief in polarity but also the system of the matrix (religions, family, friends, media, government, and businesses), which has been claiming to be the ruler over our lives. It has always been our spirit, the source of life, which has given our mental mind of polarity (false prophet) and our defiant ego-personality (the Beast) the authority, influence, and power in bringing forth our creations, good and bad, to experience.

Because of this, we give our power and energy to the system of the matrix, thus bringing into manifestation the beliefs of the system. If the system believes in fear, anger, hate, poverty, deadly diseases, destruction, a God who judges us and sends us to hell, or a Satan who causes us to suffer, then that is where storms, earthquakes, many disasters, and good things come from. These things do not come from God. They come from the system where we, as humans, give away our power to them.

Because of the way we accept control over us, the mind then blends in with mass group consciousness, which causes us to follow the systems of governments, religions, family, friends, the media, and businesses, and to see their truths as the only truths. Therefore, we believe that we are only human and that we need the system to survive, where in fact, the systems need us to survive. But deep within this massive belief system that we all designed and built together, we can find that we are only pure consciousness.

This means we chose to allow these experiences of control, deception, and false realities to come in and be part of our life. Therefore, only we, and not Jesus, can take responsibility for the choices we have made. We have become experts at lying, being two-faced, false, and dishonest. And, it will take us alone to turn that around.

Channeling of the Ascended Masters on the Apocalypse

When we stopped trusting in the self as being God, Goddess, and the Christ, we lost the connection with our own "I AM" Oversoul in favor of trusting the intellect (signified by Abraham) and the beliefs of group consciousness. And, with each lifetime, this caused us to go deeper and deeper into the game of lies and deception that caused us to engage in a *"wantonness"* that brought every one of us great harm (Revelation 18:9). That is when we learned that we had helped to create the system (matrix) we are in today.

However, because some of us are starting to awaken to the real truth due to operating from our pituitary level, we have been receiving impulses from our Oversoul that are beginning to burn away the falseness around us. When we begin to open our eyes and understand that the cure involves us producing enough internal fire to consume ourselves into our awakening, we will enter into a new lifetime. This lifetime may be the one where we can discover what was behind the smokescreen of lies that caused us to be *"her pyre"* (the system) for centuries (Revelation 18:9).

When we stopped eons ago acting like God, Goddess, and the Christ, we made choices based on what was happening around us. This caused us to shape our lives and reality without choosing them, except just enough to survive. Therefore, the outside elements of the physical world (earth, fire, water, and air) and the belief systems of the group-consciousness, along with polarity energy, we became the *"kings of the earth who we had intercourse with her,"* the system (Revelation 18:9).

Thus, *"the kings of the earth"* became our religions, governments, friends, businesses, and human consciousness, along with our many ego-personalities of light and dark that are not ready to release their grip on you as far as polarity. Therefore, these ego-personalities of our past *"keep their distance for fear of the torment"* that may be imposed on them because of our complex ideas, beliefs, and the way group consciousness evaluates (measures) their (our) acts according to group opinion *(inflicted on her)*.

The *"one hour"* (Revelation 18:9) is symbolic of time and space, as we humans measure and experience our choices to grow in consciousness. One hour is that of 60 minutes; thus, we humans, including our six divine attributes, journey through a cycle (zero) of many lifetimes, collecting many thoughts, ideas, and aspects of self that form a state of mind within each person on earth as part of the ruling armies of the world (great City of Babylon).

It is not so much that of governments, religions, family, friends, the media, and businesses in and of themselves that is the "great city of Babylon (harlot)." Instead, the false ego-aspects of the people follow these groups and give them their power to do as they please. Know that the great harlot is the mental phase of our consciousness feeding these groups by supporting the system of polarity and materialism as if they are real. This is why Babylon is such a mighty city; it represents the combination of people, their memories of many lifetimes, our ego-aspects, and the way the people set the parameters (physical networks) that establish what is real and what is not.

By journeying through time and space, we do learn to uplift our consciousness and change our beliefs about good and evil. This helps us change our beliefs about a God who is filled with hatred, judgment, jealousy, revenge, and punishment. And, if you find yourself experiencing some kind of hell right now, then understand that you put yourself there. It was not God judging you or testing your character, and it was not Satan having his way with you. It is all because of you, reaping something that you have sown in this lifetime or a past lifetime.

The thing to remember here is that you are not doomed, and you can get out of hell anytime! It is only a perception created by what you believe about yourself and the world around you. Life does not just happen accidentally; neither is it controlled by external forces of good and evil. It happens the way it does because, at a subconscious level, it is what you desire to experience, either as an individual or as a group.

Do you remember the story of the blind beggar in John 9:1–41? In this story, the blind beggar represents a person who has no awareness of his/her ability to rise above his/her conditions and suffering. Therefore, according to Yeshua, the sin of the beggar's blindness is greater than the sin of his begging for money.

When we look into Revelation 18:11-13, *"the merchants of the earth will weep and mourn for her, because there will be no more markets for their cargo."* This relates to the self, us humans, and our memories trading spiritual furnishings and gifts for materialistic furnishing and gifts without even realizing these things are of temporary substance. The gifts mentioned in the verses represent the things we all value the most, and we package these gifts to mask the real truth about our creations. These gifts show how deeply we are all caught up in the web of group-consciousness (matrix), and how we all have become slaves to the system of vibrational energy, polarity.

These external things are merely illusions and shadows of ourselves, and how we meet ourselves by cleansing the memories from our soul. The *"gold,"* Revelation 18:11-13, being one of the most precious substances in the world, represents our ability to choose wisely because we are rich already. *"Frankincense"* is one of the richest of all perfumes. It represents the sense of smell that is allied closely with our perception of the mental and how rational we get about the awareness that we are God, Goddess, and Christ; therefore, converting our mental impressions of polarity to wisdom.

When the Christ within us works in the body *(tabernacle)*, it has to meet many obstacles of our ego-personality; thus, a constant refining process becomes necessary.

"Myrrh" represents the power of love. God told Moses to take myrrh and certain other oils to anoint all the instruments used for worship in the tabernacle (physical body). Since the tabernacle is the physical body, we anoint every part of our body with the love of knowing we are God, Goddess, and the Christ (myrrh) through the wisdom of the mind.

"Silver" is a shiny, metallic element that represents high quality and our ability to transmit electrical currents (power and communication) among ourselves, to all of our ego-personality aspects, and group-consciousness. Since our energy took on a mathematical value of being a three-density being, we have been journeying through the first two cycles of activities, and now some of us are ready to enter the third cycle.

"Bronze and stones" are symbolic of the mental and materialistic flesh parts of us. The *"expensive wood"* (which comes from trees) is symbolic of everything about us that is interconnected, like our masculine-feminine consciousness, spirit, mind, and body (nonphysical and physical realm), and our connection to the system or group-consciousness (matrix).

"Wood" also concerns the management of forestlands for maximum yield *(cultivation)*. Therefore, the *"wood"* can also represent the harvesting (quantity and quality) of our many light and dark ego-personality aspects *(pearls)* that are spread throughout multiple dimensions, for they do vary according to our development and growth.

The *"wine"* represents all our lifetimes of being intoxicated with the vital belief in polarity energy. We formed a connecting link between our soul, our Christ consciousness, our mind-soul, our ego, and our physical body where, in the end, we successfully become "one sovereign body of consciousness" that is everlasting and indestructible. The temporal body is where we worship God in a tent, which means our physical body is the temporary, perishable body. Yet, our physical body was chosen by group consciousness to be the great temple that was built by Moses in Exodus 40:2.

The outer structure was of *"fine linen"* (or the flesh), *"purple silk"* (the power of choices), and *"scarlet cloth"* (our emotions). The altar (our total consciousness), laver or the tabernacle and temple worship of the Jews, (through our heart center), *candlestick* (our intelligence), the ark of the covenant (our agreement between our outer, masculine and inner, feminine self), and all the inner *utensils* (the remanding parts that make up the physical body) were of *gold* (our ability to choose, free will), *silver* (polarity, the energy of two different expressions, positive and negative), and *precious stones*, Exodus 40:2, (everlasting and indestructible).

The central functions of the physical body are enduring; it is the flesh covering that is perishable, not the real you. When you, the ruler of self (Lord), built your temporary tabernacle long ago, there was the promise of a permanent one. Therefore, the *"tabernacle of the tent of meeting"* was where you established yourself in a physical body as a temporary dwelling place until you (the ruler of self) remembered God's promise, which is sacred and unique (Exodus 40:2).

No human hand, other than you, was allowed to touch the Ark of the Covenant (the agreement you made with yourself) because you, and only you, had stored there the indescribable spark that links you to your "I AM" Christ consciousness. But before you can enter into the consciousness of an everlasting, eternal body, while in the flesh, you must breathe life into those clusters of beliefs that are so closely packed together with group-consciousness and allow them to enter every part of your temporary body for cleansing and processing.

The incense-burning is the offering of our mental mind and many ego forms to go forth and establish a permanent resolution: to purify our energy through an agreement (covenant) between our defiant nature and our own "I AM" Christ consciousness using the law of cause-and-effect to become balanced.

"Cinnamon," Revelation 18:11-13, is a reddish-brown spice that represents us taking on a physical form and coming to earth to grow in wisdom. Cinnamon comes from a tropical evergreen tree that is native to Asia. Therefore, "Asia" refers to a state of mind saturated with old, decayed, worn-out, materialistic ideas that should have been left behind long ago by anyone desiring spiritual progress. (See Rev. 1:4 for more details on the meaning of Asia.) Through our Asian mind of mentality (dogmatic beliefs,) we became crystallized and hardened like a rock *(marble)*.

Because of our strong belief in polarity, we transformed our etheric body into a very dense and solid form. This created a harsh personality within us, which is so strong that most people are unyielding and determined *(iron)* not to fall for any sign of movement beyond what they already believe as their truths. They cover themselves up with beliefs that are generated by the system (governments, religions, teachers, families, friends, media, and businesses), and they become firmly locked under their control.

The symbol of *"olive oil"* can also be read about in Revelation 6:5–6; 11:4. It symbolizes the spirit of unconditional love because our spirit is the "holy spirit" that gives life to our creations, good and bad. To believe otherwise, we create conflict within ourselves that form the idea that we are a sinner. We have gone through many difficult lifetimes and gained much compassion and wisdom along the way. Therefore, a new understanding of spirit is dawning, allowing us to see ourselves and our ego-personality aspects (lifetimes/sheep) in a whole new light and realization. Maybe this is why you are reading this book.

The *"sheep"* or ram refers to the quality of strength, might, nobility, and power of the physical consciousness and how our many ego-personality aspects are at work, like a sheep, sacrificing themselves to the matrix (the system). Always remember, we are a grandmaster, and some of us are on the verge of overcoming the difficulties and challenges created by placing our consciousness into a physical body, thereby limiting ourselves to a three-density reality. However, because of this, we can now integrate all parts of us just by allowing.

Those lifetimes are where we sacrificed ourselves *(sheep/ram)* and fell into a deep sleep for our true identity to learn the wisdom behind the forces of polarity and all that we chose to experience. But now, the time has come where New Energy is upon the earth, and if we are ready, our own "I AM" Christ consciousness is ready to awaken us from our sleep.

"Horses and chariots" in Revelation 18:13 signify the strong, fixed energy that lays hold of the vital forces of our ego-personality aspects and uses them for *"keeping up"* a consciousness with a ruling intellect. This causes strength and the centralization of forced physical energy rather than the inner spiritual nature, and we are therefore carried to the point of inflexible body activities *(chariots)*.

"Wheat" is grain in temperate regions, harvested once a year from a widely cultivated area for making flour, bread, pasta, and other foods. It is also native to southwestern Asia. This means that *wheat* is tied to the understanding that polarity energy is limited when cultivation comes from what we feed the mind all day long.

The mind is not really the true creator. And therefore, "Asia" actually refers to a state of mind saturated with old, decayed, worn-out, materialistic ideas that should have been left behind long ago by those who would desire to progress spiritually. (See Rev. 1:4 for more details on the meaning of Asia.)

Revelation 18:14 is a good verse because it is asking us to choose to let go of our old dogmatic belief systems about the mystery of God, Satan, and Christ.

If you have come this far in the book, then maybe you have come far enough in consciousness to let go of the beliefs you have worshipped and followed for so long. Why does the Ascended Masters say this? It is with the *"fruit you craved"* in Revelation 18:14 that are the fruits that produced polarity belief systems, and through that same duality, positive and negative, we all have blossomed from an immature Goddess to a very mature God, Goddess, and Christ in our own right.

The Ascended Masters agree that there are some of us of the current system (harlot) that are now ready to leave the system, by knowing who they are, why they came to earth, and why they were locked into a hypnotic state. Some of us are entering a consciousness right now, where we are questioning the old belief patterns of polarity. And yet, there are ego-personality aspects of us that are still hanging on to the old beliefs, which keeps us suffering. These ego aspects are still having a hard time seeing the illusion of it all. But the main thing to do is not to worry, for in time, they will integrate with us, their creator.

The religions of the world have laid out this energy of fearing God, Christ, and Satan for many lifetimes, and it has been part of our reality in this lifetime. Instead of understanding the concept of God as the wholeness of one's total consciousness, the collective human group-consciousness held onto religious beliefs as the means to understand the divine seed. And, ever since Abraham, especially in the last two thousand years, we have created branches and branches of churches to understand the coming of the Christ consciousness to earth.

Because we are so easily affected and influenced by fear, it becomes tough for us to maintain the divine seed in a hostile world. It was easier to build physical churches and say they were holy and sacred, that they could house the Christ-energy until it was time to spread it throughout the world. But the energy of Christ has become distorted and abused by those who desire to hold power and control for themselves. And now, there are a few of us with different ideas about what Christ represents.

Remember, real love has no connection to feeling fondness for someone or showing great kindness. Real love lets you be who you are and express who you are with no judgment from another person, not even family, because of your beliefs, social class, or ethnicity. True unconditional love is accepting the full embodiment of yourself and others as to whom they feel they are without question. It is accepting that you have been creating and projecting your stories of drama, hate, blame, and fears onto others without condemnation of the self. Real love is when you stop fighting and defending yourself from your family, friends, religions, and all those who condemn you for your views about spirit, God, Goddess, Christ, and people as a whole.

Once we become awakened from our hypnotic sleep state and recognize the truth that *"all our luxury and splendor,"* Revelation 18:17, has been about the comfort of polarity living and how the force of opposites has helped us cleanse our memories, then all that is left is to gather the wisdom from all the experiences and let the rest go.

Speaking for myself, I would rather create my own life and reality than give my authority away to some group, religion, or individual to decide for me. Many of us, however, are so hypnotized by someone else's version of life that we freely give away our power to them just to keep the peace. We only need to watch the television for a few minutes or read one page of a newspaper to see that the general population is governed by fear. Just look into the mask most wear on their faces because of the virus, as it represents the self hiding behind their fear.

I hope by now, you have some understanding that beliefs do create your reality. Note, a fundamental truth: No one can do anything to you if you do not agree to it on some level. Whether it appears to be good or evil, or whether you are conscious of an agreement or not, it does not matter. The authority to create your own life lies solely in your own hands, whether you believe it or not. No one can have power over you, not even a virus, unless you give it to them because everyone has the gift of free will and the ability to choose what to do with it, even if you follow what someone else says is truth.

We assume that what the media and our politicians are telling us is true without question. Most do not understand that no sickness or virus can touch you, even if one with a virus breathes in your face, when your consciousness is vibrating at a frequency higher than the sickens or virus. As we can see, the mind has become very vulnerable and susceptible to outside suggestions that come from superficial individuals. These individuals claim to know everything because of their status and authority, and our mind becomes programmed to accept information outside of itself as being reality. Yet, it is all false and a lie. Thus, we feel that we fell from grace, and yet, we never left higher consciousness.

The two verses in Revelation 18:15-16 repeat the things I have already mentioned here in the previous verses because the split mind (left and right) needs to be cleansed by evolving beyond the belief in polarity. These verses again are all about self meeting self through reincarnation and through group belief systems (matrix) so as for us to become awakened to being God, Goddess, and Christ. And, when you know you are Christ, without doubt, no sickness can touch you. We are not who we think we are, for we are more. Even the belief systems we would kill and die for are not real. They are all just illusions.

Chapter 36

COMING INTO OUR AWAKENING

When we look into Revelation 18:17-18, and up to Revelation 18:24, everything is guided toward the "coming into our awakening." From Revelation 18:17-18, the *"one hour"* again (60 minutes) represents time and space as the means for us to incarnate into many physical bodies playing out a cycle of many experiences using polarity, good and bad, to measure our choices. And, from these measured choices, we then reflect a total cleansing of our soul from what seemed real but was found to be a way to gain wisdom. And now, this *"great wealth"* of potentials and experiences that we acted on has come to a state of completion *(been ruined)*, where some of us are ready to let go and awaken to our true identity.

"Every captain of a ship," Revelation 18:17-18, refers to our many light and dark ego-personality aspects that are the *"traveler at sea,"* as this is symbolic of each lifetime was about exploring every unexpressed and undeveloped potentiality so that we could learn wisdom. The "sailors" are symbolic of the mass human consciousness journeying through time and space, lifetime after lifetime, learning responsibility.

The *"seafaring merchant,"* in Revelation 18:17-18, represents our belief patterns and the way we have built them up in memories, which then determines what we choose to participate in while expanding our consciousness through potentials of good and evil. As our many ego-personalities *"stood at a distance and cried out when they saw the smoke of her pyre,"* this refers to those of us coming into some awakening and understanding about how memories work within the system of the matrix.

And, once these memories of old dogmatic beliefs are exposed, we can burn them away through karma. Once burned away, our feeling of being separate from the real wisdom behind the smokescreen of lies that caused us to be "*her pyre*" begins to fade away from the system of the matrix (or human group consciousness).

"*What city could compare with the great city?*" Revelation 18:17-18, as this "city" is about the collective memories in the various cells of our physical body where our fixed state of a mental consciousness could be compared with that of the human group consciousness *(the great city)* in believing that polarity is real. Therefore, the cleansing process would be like a holocaust of sowing and reaping when we revisit a city of memories and ego-personalities associated with each lifetime.

The words *"threw dust on their head,"* Revelation 18:19, describes our many lifetimes on earth and the way we used physical matter as a place to work out our karma *(crying out and mourning*, Revelation 18:19). When we place our physical body into its grave after death in each lifetime, some say that it is reduced to only dust. And yet, Mother Earth holds the energy of that lifetime until we are ready to claim it as our own.

So, when we are ready to leave Mother Earth instead of putting our physical body in the ground to decay and turn into dust, why not take our energy and all of its components with us when we leave earth? Does this sound impossible? We can read about it in the Bible because with this new energy (New Earth), everything is possible! What do you think the rapture is all about? We can have our body cremated, as when a body is cremated, all energy of that dead body returns to its creator, you.

If you can believe that the Christian interpretation of the rapture applies to the second coming of Jesus and where you will meet him in the sky, then why can't you believe it's possible to take every component of your physical body with you when you die? This includes all the energy and wisdom in your body, your memories of past lifetimes, all aspects of your past personalities, your bones, and the total makeup of your flesh body.

Remember, the physical body is just energy, even though it looks solid, which means you can bring it with you when you are ready to leave earth. When you choose this from a divine level, without a doubt of being a Christ also, you set in motion the characterization that you are indeed a sovereign Goddess in your own right. You set yourself free from the forces of polarity and the belief systems of the mass consciousness (the system) that hold onto your energy. This is the true meaning of *"her being ruined"* in Revelation 18:19.

Channeling of the Ascended Masters on the Apocalypse

Time and space (incarnations) measure our reactions to our collection of memories, thoughts, ideas, and the belief systems of group-consciousness, thereby creating a very special illusion that we are solid. And yet, our physical body is nothing more than energy, including our bones and internal organs. Because of our many lifetimes on earth, we have accumulated a great deal of wisdom (wealth) when it comes to choosing ascension rather than having our body buried in the ground.

By placing our bodies in the ground, it becomes a sure thing that we will be back to earth for another incarnation. Most Christian religions teach that when Jesus comes back to earth, he will raise from the graves all those who have died, to be taken up to heaven with him. When we, while still in the flesh, have released all of our belief systems in a God of sin and judgment, then our karma has been fulfilled, and the idea of sin is let go.

When we finally realize and accept who we really are, we are no longer bound to or limited by our past, including all those lifetimes in the physical where we have been buried in the ground. By letting go of the illusion of polarity and that we are solid, then our many past false personality aspects that died and were buried will be released by Mother Earth. The energy we left behind in those dead bodies can now leave earth (the grave) and move back to its true creator, the self.

Our many past personality aspects have been waiting for the day when we come into the wisdom of knowing that we are the Christ coming from out behind our ignorance (cloud), which will then allow our energy to return to us in this lifetime to ascend with all parts and pieces of us. This "knowing" allows each aspect from the past, no matter where they (we) have lived upon the earth, the freedom to be released from their earthly bond (grave).

Every time we lived and died, the body we occupied was usually buried in the earth, and therefore much of our energy has remained trapped within the earth. This is especially true of the lifetimes where we identified ourselves solely with our physical form and our dramatized polarity beliefs. Therefore, much of our past energy has been held by Mother Earth until our resurrection (realization) when we and all aspects of ourselves are reconnected to our own "I AM" Christ neutral energy. This is the real meaning of Christ raising the dead from the grave.

Yes, all humans are the Christ, and those that are ready can raise their trapped energy of many lifetimes and integrating them with their total self of today when they are ready to let go and allow themselves to be Christ in the flesh. When your ego-aspect in this lifetime realizes that you are the Son of Man, the Son of God, and the Christ, you will be ready to release all the energetic ties to your other ego aspects, thus allowing you to integrate all that you are, including all of your energy.

This allows you to go back within yourself, knowing that all that you are is there and waiting for you to be the Master. Therefore, trust yourself as being God, the Goddess, and Christ! Take ownership of your life and be the captain of your ship. Know that there is no destiny here as you might think, for that ends when you come into your realization to your real name, "I AM THAT I AM," Christ. Now is the time to choose what you want to experience. Be the creator and use your imagination and your real name, telling the rest of your parts and pieces to support your choices.

You only need to use your heart and intuitive feelings. You don't really need your mind to deal with this reality, because the mind was developed to help you stay here in the flesh and make the best of polarity while you are here. Now is the time to go beyond the mind and that of polarity belief systems and expand your consciousness multidimensionally. That is where new energy is created.

This phrase *"rejoice over her,"* Revelation 18:20, refers to you coming into your awakened state and recognizing that the system (governments, religions, the media, family, friends, and businesses) have led you down the road of slavery and suffering. Thus, *"heaven,"* Revelation 18:20, is a new beginning where higher consciousness is about to be launched for those who have come far enough in consciousness to move beyond belief in polarity, sin, punishment, and judgment.

You are the *"holy ones, apostles, and prophets,"* and you, in your God-Goddess-Christ state, have *"judged"* your journey of many lifetimes and stories *(case), Revelation 18:20*. And now, after all these lifetimes, you realize that you and only you caused your suffering. The *"rejoicing"* is about you coming into your awakened state and disconnecting yourself from the system (matrix) because the former you are now purged and gone, and the new you have emerged.

The *"mighty angel,"* Revelation 18:21, refers to those who are beginning to awaken and take responsibility for everything they have created, good and bad, since time and space began. On the surface, it seems that people are not willing to take full responsibility for their actions, but behind the scenes, every one of us has created many lifetimes and stories that call out to our own souls to explore polarity and learn responsibility. And, the *"millstone,"* Revelation 18:21, is about that same responsibility we have placed upon ourselves by creating many stories (lifetimes) and battles that we have fought to understand the inner workings of our subconsciousness, represented by *"the sea,"* Revelation 18:21.

Channeling of the Ascended Masters on the Apocalypse

Our journey through many lifetimes experiencing karma has been all about us humans misunderstanding energy, who we are, and how we have been following the path (beliefs) of group-consciousness for a very long time without realizing it (*Babylon, the great city*, Revelation 18:21). But once we awaken to the real self, a choice has to be made. Either we stay within the system of the matrix and what it produces for us to experience, or we leave it behind and become a sovereign Christ in our own right. Remember, we are the Creator, and our radiance is the extension of our creations.

Through our memories, all our energy is tied up in our stories and beliefs of the past our belief systems of today. When we learn to take leadership and responsibility for our mind and our reality, we will radiate our true selves in such a way that a whole new flame will flow out from us, and everything will open up to us as if magic. We can choose to let go of the controls, because our divinity is all around us right now, waiting for our decision. Letting go of the system of polarity beliefs allows our "I AM" to come in and meld with our human self.

From the unbalanced energy of polarity, we created the energy of fear, and from this fear, we filled our mind, heart, and soul with memories of only good and evil (sin). And, because of this belief in fear, we then replaced our "knowing and trusting" in being God-Goddess to an intellectual thinker who opposed our "I AM" Christ self, which is why God changed Abram's name to Abraham. Once we became an intellectual thinker, we doubted ourselves as a true creator, thus creating a mind and an ego that forgot that we are indeed a Christ also.

We gave up our trust in being God-Goddess and replaced it with faith in what our outer mind could comprehend and control by its intelligence. Once we placed our trust in our intellect, we lost our trust in the self as Christ. Once we questioned the trust coming from our "I AM" (Oversoul), we obstructed our communications between our mind, ego, and our "I AM."

By questioning and unseating our "I AM" as our true consciousness, our power of communications, and our feeling of being Christ weakened. This meant that our mind began to express the same belief patterns as our ego and what group-consciousness believed to be the truth. This was the first time that our trust in being Christ, God-Goddess, moved to a faith consciousness, and this is why Abram's name changed to Abraham (Gen. 17:5).

When Abram told his wife Sarai to tell the Egyptians that she was his sister instead of his wife (Gen. 12:13), he lost his trust in God and moved his faith to the intellectual and rational reasoning level because of fear. This is when our thought patterns of polarity (good and bad) became more attractive to us than what we felt before leaving higher consciousness (the garden-first creation). Once we moved outside of ourselves, our soul consciousness of responsibility (women) gave way to intellectual belief patterns that gave life to a bunch of lies that we called truths.

This was the beginning of understanding the differences between our many ego consciousnesses, our outer mind, and our inner soul consciousness in what we would express and manifest as real. From the mind and ego points of view, we felt individualized or separated from the wholeness of being Christ, God, and the Goddess. Once we had gone to the depths of our rebellious ego nature (Beast), the only way back to knowing that we are Christ, God, and the Goddess again was through the rational mind (false prophet), which then moved through to the Christ consciousness once awakened, and this is represented by Jesus walking on earth.

Genesis 12:14–15 says, *"When Abram came to Egypt, the Egyptians saw how beautiful the woman was; and when Pharaoh's courtiers saw her, they praised her to Pharaoh. So, she was taken into Pharaoh's palace."* The Pharaoh represents the sun god, and being a king, which symbolizes the intelligence center of the mind, is the controlling factor of our life today. The mind became a place where we all spent a lot of time admiring *(praising)* our intelligence to such a degree that we gave in to the forces of limited perception and opinionated truths that, in reality, are lies.

With all of what we did in creating many lies, we turned around. We gave thanks and approval to the intelligence center of our outer mind (Pharaoh), and the many light and dark ego personalities of our past lifetimes (represented by the Egyptians) for our achievements, instead of thanking our own "I AM" Christ self for not interfering. When our intelligence center of the mind became something to reckon with, it caused us, humans, to give thanks to a God that is completely intellectual, judgmental, and a God that wants to be worshipped.

Thus, worshipping our mind, symbolized by the God of the Bible, caused an obstruction between our "I AM" Christ spirit and the wholeness of our total consciousness and universal intelligence. This is when we humans expressed belief patterns tied to a deceitful consciousness, which brought about self-absorption that turned into self-importance, pride, and egotism. These new qualities then produced unlimited light and dark ego-personality aspects to play out in the physical world.

In the Garden (higher consciousness), we were all equal in knowledge, intelligence, and ability, for we were all God-Goddesses. However, we were God-Goddesses that lacked wisdom! So, that is when a lot of souled beings volunteered to descend to a mental and physical level to exercise their newfound power and place that power in our creations. Because we are all a God-Goddess, we have, deep within us, the memory of our divine plan (will) to know and understand the difference between thoughts of good and evil, and the illusion of their existence.

Therefore, we can gain the wisdom of our experiences that comes from working with polarity and then eventually ascend to where we move beyond the illusion of power and how the intelligence of the mind is nothing compared to divine intelligence. If we souled beings did not create positive and negative eons ago, we humans would have no wisdom for understanding power and intelligence. Therefore, power, control, and intelligence, like sin, are not real, because from the "I AM" consciousness, we are all equal in authority for creating our desires to experience.

Have you noticed that people, religions, and governments all over the world seem to be in a never-ending struggle for power? This is because we have all been measuring our power and intelligence by how much we can control our environment and the people who surround us. We think that intelligence and power equal control (being a king), but in reality, intelligence and power are simply energy, just like our physical body. However, the illusion that intelligence and power are of the mind enables us to expand our consciousness to learn how energy works. And, in the end, this brings us great wisdom.

Once we humans feel the energy and truth of our "I AM" Christ-consciousness speaking to us from the human level, we will readily understand that our outer mind can only be part of the intellect and not of our "I AM" consciousness. Thus, our mind alone cannot accomplish anything without the support of our "I AM." As a result, our work will be done only through the power of our divine "I AM" spirit and the knowledge that we are Christ, God, and the Goddess in the flesh.

The "musicians" in Revelation 18:22 symbolizes that some of us are coming to the end of our journey in this lifetime, and we no longer will be having to create more ego-personality aspects of ourselves to do our bidding. This is great news because now we can do it from the "I AM" level. This verse 18:22 is interesting, for it proclaims the end of the person we perceive ourselves to be. It talks about the old, polarity thinking of you and gives evidence that you are more than just a human living in a material world.

As Jesus lived, died, and was not of this world, so it is with you. Jesus, according to the New Testament, was considered not to have been of this world. During Jesus's stay on earth, he learned how to gain direct access to the Christ consciousness and the neutralized God's energy of light. Thus, creating things that looked like miracles. Therefore, if you so choose, today can be the day where you come into the realization that you are the Christ and always have been.

There is no separation between you, your "I AM" Christ-Spirit, your Mind, your ego personalities, and your angelic roots (heaven). There is no judgment upon you or that you have to suffer. Suffering comes from you choosing it from an unawakening level. It is just a choice to be made by you getting off the path of polarity, sin, punishment, the path of an emotional mind, your past lifetimes, and the memories tied to them. That is when you move into your now moment as a sovereign Christ, God, and Goddess in your own right.

When we choose no longer express the vibrational energy of polarity within our physical body on a linear pattern and from group consciousness (system) that identify themselves only with the concept of fear, power, and control, this is what is meant by *"no melodies of harpist,"* Revelation 18:22, for the vibrational tone of polarity can be transformed into expansional energy. All that we have to do is accept all that we have been, forgive ourselves and others, and then release any idea or belief of having to resolve some unspecified issues (sin) that may have happened in the past.

The *"trumpeters,"* Revelation 18:22, symbolizes you, if you so choose, coming into your completion here on earth and proclaiming the waves of harmonious energy of neutrality, which now works through every part of your Oversoul, mind-soul, ego, and the body. When your heart is filled with gratitude and unconditional love, and you express yourself in thanksgiving to your "I AM," you skillfully use the material world as a place to become an expert creator *(craftsman)*. And, all that is left is the ascension process (or what is called the rapture) as the final step in your realization.

In your realization state, you do attain an enormous consciousness of a universal nature that becomes one with the Father/Mother God-Goddess within yourself. That is when your physicality loses its limitations, and you take on the substance of being a Christ in the flesh. That is when you transcend your limitations of time, space, and polarity energy and take full control and responsibility for your "I AM" spirit, mind-soul, ego personalities, and the material world. My friends, that is when you accept your inheritance as a Christ also.

Channeling of the Ascended Masters on the Apocalypse

After this, you will never again be burdened by your creations of old, dualistic patterns because now you know what is real and not real, which symbolizes in Revelation 18:22 as *"no sound of the millstone will ever be heard in you again."* When we realize spirit, the earthly forces and the tones of polarity in the body no longer operate as they have in the past. This is because polarity now bypasses the endocrine system altogether (seven churches).

The forces of the earth and the tones of polarity to become silent, having no vibrational energy (sound) arising to your awareness. Thus, your "I AM" Christ, is the savior of you, transforming the earthly forces and the tone of polarity into their spiritual components of New Energy (New Earth):

1. Positive
2. Negative
3. Neutrality
4. The "I AM" Christ gnost consciousness at work

And, in Revelation 18:23, *"no light from a lamp"* refers to the lampstands found in Revelation 1:12 where they symbolize the angels of the seven churches (endocrine system) are no longer feeding the mind and ego of separation, the belief in Satan, sin, suffering, and the need for a savor.

The influential forces of the earth and the vibrational tone of polarity enter from the gonad level, then to the pineal are now silent, for it was through these areas of the physical body that deceit led to inflexible beliefs. Therefore, these lampstands (endocrine system) within the body will no longer give you direction, because everything, all ego-personality aspects of you have been transformed and integrated with your "I AM," thus now you know you are Christ.

The phrase *"no voices of bride and groom will ever be heard in you again,"* Revelation 18:23, symbolizes your "I AM" Christ spirit, and your mental soul (bride), the feminine part of you, that is no longer expressing or seeking understanding in the mind (groom) and flesh (ego), because your mental soul (bride) now understands the Tree of Knowledge of Good and Evil, and associates it with wisdom and realization.

Therefore, my friends, the Book of Revelation is a message about you coming into an awakening and a realization, after multitudes of lifetimes, where you release yourself from old, dogmatic beliefs and the illusion of being only human. Thus, removing yourself from the system of polarity beliefs (matrix). The message is to help you open your eyes to the fullness of your "I AM" Christ spirit, knowing that there is no judgment upon you for your past. And, most of all, you know that you need never experience another challenge here on earth unless you choose it from a realization consciousness to whom you indeed are.

Know that once "realization" sets in, you can no longer return to what the churches call heaven because heaven has changed. Heaven is nowhere in this now moment, waiting for you to awaken to it. Everything has changed because your mental soul (bride) and outer mind (groom) fell deeply in love with each other and ultimately gave life to multitudes of ego personality aspects (children/lifetimes) and billions of potentials for you to experience. This was the perfect expression, for their passion created in them a great desire for learning.

When your outer mind (groom/Adam) expressed the ability to adapt to the environment of nothingness (endless space) and later a material world, your mental soul (bride/Eve) gave birth to multiple ego-personality aspects (lifetimes) without rules or laws for them to follow. Thus, the growth of your "I AM" spirit consciousness became evident. Your "I AM" spirit and your mind-soul did not tell your many ego-personality aspects what to do or who to worship, because you, on a spiritual level, giving all of your ego-personality aspects the free will to act on your (I AM's) behalf.

As you journeyed through many lifetimes, absolutely amazed at what you were created to experience, little did you know that one day you would awaken from the deceptive appearance that you are only human? And, because of your ability to create many aspects of self, you worked kindly toward experiencing every choice, thought, and belief tied to polarity energy, and now those experiences are contained within your Oversoul as wisdom. Thus, heaven comes to you when the realization of who you are becomes known to all parts and pieces of you.

You are complete right now; there is no longer any need to look upon yourself as a sinner because everything that you are is complete already. When you awaken to your sovereignty as a Christ also, you will know that you have always been free, have always been the creator God-Goddess, and contained within you, is a real divine essence that nobody can take from you.

No religions, family, governments, the media, friends, or businesses can take away your soul! Oh, you can play games with them by giving them your support and loyalty for a while. But in reality, some of you have already achieved your Christ sovereignty. You have become aware of your polarity games because of your many ego personalities, as they were the great ones that brought you wisdom (*"your merchants were the great ones of the world"*) Revelation 18:23.

Yes, you played in consciousness of multiple potentials, for how could you ever come to know yourself as a Christ also if you stayed within the first circle of Oneness? Therefore, there are no wrongs or rights, no such thing as bad or good, no positive or negative, no God or Satan but you, and there is no shame coming from your "I AM" spirit placed on you in this lifetime. It was just a grand journey and a perfect divine plan in discovering yourself as being a Christ, God, and Goddess too.

You did it by allowing your memories (nations) to be *"led astray by the magic portion"* of forgetfulness (Revelation 18:23). You purposely created many lifetimes, unacceptable behavior, and a lot of different paths to get there, but you did get there. However, it did not matter how you got there. It is that you did, eventually, get there. All your worries about money, relationships, disease, and all the little dramas of family members over belief systems, all of it doesn't matter, because, in the end, you get to heaven because heaven comes to you. You are already there! It just comes down to how you choose to experience your Christ sovereignty.

Your many external expressions and manifestations were simply experiencing and have nothing to do with sin. The mind (groom) and soul (bride) understood those experiences to be the wisdom needed to help you understand the meaning of "I AM That I AM," a Christ also. All the pain and wounds you experienced through time and space were not felt by your "I AM" because she received these experiences through the mind (groom) in the form of wisdom. Again, there is no sin, only experiences!

According to Yeshua and the Ascended Masters, everyone has their journey and carries within them the memories of their own beliefs. Each person grows at their own pace and according to their own choices and the desires of their own "I AM" spirit. No one is above, ahead, or behind anyone else. This is as it should be because every individual will eventually find its sovereign place as a Christ. The answer will not come from the Bible or from some intellectual who claims to know God personally; the answer will come from you – for how can you follow someone who claims to be the Christ when, in fact, you are Christ?

Know that *"the blood of the prophets and the holy ones,"* Revelation 18:24, is speaking about you, for you are the holy ones, and all of your many light and dark ego personality aspects were the *"prophets"* that were *"slain"* playing in a physical body giving into the beliefs generated by group consciousness (the system), and without realizing it, you (they) chose to do it on a deeper level to gain wisdom. Because of your "I AM's" desire to learn about life, the marriage between your outer mind, and inner soul created many ego-personalities in fulfilling the divine plan to become a sovereign Christ in your own right. Thus they (you) became the sacrificial lamb upon the earth.

Chapter 37

THE COMING OF CHRIST

According to Yeshua and the Ascended Masters, we now have come to one of the most fascinating chapters in Revelation. Traditionally, the meaning of this chapter refers to Yeshua (Jesus) coming to earth for the salvation of good and religious people. However, I hate to disappoint, but up to this point in history, any meaning outside of the traditional one would be beyond the reach of human understanding. And yet, in today's world, this chapter presents itself as meaning something more than Yeshua coming to earth.

Yeshua has been here on earth in the last few years, working with channelers of new expanded consciousness that are receptive to him and the Masters to bring about an awakening to those that are ready to hear it. Therefore, this book and especially this chapter, is for those of us that are ready to ascend and come into a realization that one is Christ and the savior of self. It is about human integrating with the "I AM."

As outlined in Revelation 17 and 18, our destruction over many lifetimes has been identified, via our memory, as believing and seeing ourselves as merely a human in need of a savior. We humans, without realizing it, have been for many lifetimes controlled by a system of beliefs brought about by the self and that of group consciousness. The Masters prefer not to look at this destruction as a negative thing where one must die physically to obtain a Mastership, but rather as a transformation from a hypnotic sleep state to an awakened state where we have the freedom to reach our highest potential in human form as a Christ also. It is where we know on a conscious level that we bow only to our own "I AM," divinity, and not to any God that proclaims himself as our creator.

Channeling of the Ascended Masters on the Apocalypse

Because of karma, the human group-consciousness, the self-included, set our destiny a long time ago using memory, belief systems, polarity energy, and group hypnosis to explore the question of "Who am I?" And, once the question was asked, it had to be answered from the viewpoint of our "I AM" Christ within. That is when our divine plan for each of us came to life, thus, from a mental level. With great misunderstanding, we spirits set up the law of destiny and worshipping a system of beliefs tied to good and evil and a God of hate, conditional love, jealousy, and punishment.

From the divine level, we have always possessed these two greatest gifts, "choice and feeling," but we have forgotten them because of the "system" we all play out here on earth as something real. When appropriately integrated, "choice and feeling" will allow us as a co-creator to energize the consciousness of new energy in launching our ascension (rapture) to where our "divine plan" becomes the ruling authority in making our choices from an awakening state of being a Christ instead of it coming from the system that beliefs we are not worthy of Christ.

The system of polarity, the deep state, and our favorite religion have obscured our real purpose on earth for a long time by keeping us in a hypnotic sleep state by having us fight each other over race, religion, politics, and manmade viruses. Religions used the icon of a solitary male God and proclaimed him to be a mystery until a future time when the Savior himself would come to earth and become king of the world. They did this despite knowing that Yeshua's second coming would never happen the way they told the story.

Therefore, to learn the real truth, we must use our capacity to feel intuitively regarding religious teachings about Yeshua's return. As Yeshua himself says, if he came to earth as a king, then every man, woman, and child would have to live under rulership of an individual, thus taking away our own sovereign identity as a Christ also to make our own choices. From Yeshua's perspective, this is just giving up one ruler (the system) for another.

Remember, Yeshua said that he was not of this world. Grant, you, Yeshua's rule may be more peaceful than the old rulers of the system. However, the bottom line is that we humans still would not have been saved or freed. Trading one ruler for another is not the answer, as per Yeshua and the Ascended Masters. All religions claim that they understand the truth about the Messiah and Yeshua's second coming, which is why they teach us that they are guardians of truth, privy to God and what he wants for us. And yet, these religious groups cannot even agree among themselves about what day to worship God, let alone determine his wishes for humanity.

Some religions even declare that people have allied with the devil just by disagreeing with the standard philosophy of Jesus as a Savior. And, if a person has a different opinion about Yeshua, or any other divine character, being the only Messiah, the dissenting one is somehow following the devil. If we took the time to study the Bible and the deep state which claims they know better than we do, using feeling instead of rationalization, we would find that most religious groups, all of which claim to know God and his ways, deem it necessary for us to be rehabilitated, convinced, or forced to believe that Yeshua (Jesus), or another divine character, is the savior of humanity.

Religious groups fundamentally believe that they can get people to turn to Yeshua or some other Messiah without force; but for some radical believers, force is the only way, because they see themselves as God's enforcers. However, if we use our intuitive feelings instead of our mind to read the Bible, then we can see that Yeshua does not work like that. Yeshua, God, or the Goddess is rather clear about this: *"No one can come to me unless the Father who sent me draws him, and I will raise him on the last day"* (John 6:44). John states that "no man can go through Yeshua (Jesus) unless God himself," the one who sent Yeshua, first calls one to Yeshua.

Religions of the world, no matter what church or denomination they belong to, can certainly misinterpret the written words in the Bible. As John was declaring that no one, not even through deeds, religious sects, or preaching, can come to Yeshua, unless God himself personally calls (draws) upon them to do so. Religions fail to understand this message. Instead, they claim that the framework of God's plan is based on a very simple truth, that all humanity must worship Yeshua and devote themselves to him as their God and Savior.

Yeshua's death on the cross was not because of our evil deeds (sins) or because of religious teachings. It occurred because God-Goddess him-herself called (drew) upon Yeshua to raise himself from the cross on the last day. Religion did not call upon Yeshua to raise himself from the cross; religion (symbolized by the system) caused the Christ to be crucified and buried, as ninety-seven percent of the world population today still love to do.

Because of the system (governments, religions, friends, the media, family, and businesses), Yeshua was put to death for speaking the truth about common folks being God, the Goddess, and a Christ also, and equal to the "I AM" God-Goddess. John 10:34 states, *"Is it not written in your law? 'I said, "You are gods."'"* As we can see here, Yeshua understood his intimate connection to the Godhead as a Christ, and yet he also knew that he was an individualized member of the Spirit of One.

Channeling of the Ascended Masters on the Apocalypse

Therefore, *"drawing the Christ upon the last days"* is not about drawing up Yeshua, the man, but is drawing up the Christ consciousness within himself to be shown in physical form. When we allow our sovereign "I AM" Christ-spirit to rise within the falseness of our outer mind, ego, and human form, we move our consciousness beyond the strange and confusing dogmas that religion has adopted as the most sacred code of beliefs ever written. It is these sacred, dogmatic belief systems that form the thought patterns of the mass, keeping us dead on the cross of suffering. Why do you think religions keep promoting Yeshua on the cross as their idol? It is to keep us focused on fear and sin!

From an energy standpoint, the ascension process (raising us from the dead) begins when the energy frequency within us rises through the pathway of our consciousness and the seven chakras (churches) in the physical body. As this higher energy frequency enters the brain chakra of the pituitary, the body becomes energized enough for us to enter another phase of consciousness (allowing for new truths) where we change our three-density, dualistic consciousness into a four-density expanded consciousness (new earth).

Religions promote the worship of God on the Sabbath, Sunday for most Christians, Saturday for most Jews, and Friday for most Arabs. And, according to religion, if we are not willing to accept the basic truth of a particular Sabbath day (seventh day), then God will deny us in the last days because we are not willing to receive him (Yeshua) in a church setting. Remember, it is not about any church building. It is about your physical body rising in frequency to allow new energy and new consciousness to become part of the earth. Anyway, after coming this far in the book, what day of the week is the true Sabbath?

Before one can answer the question, consider that most people maintain their religious beliefs according to what they have been taught by their ancestors. Catholics will always produce Catholics, Baptists produce Baptists, and Muslims produce Muslims, and so on. So, the bottom line is about the perplexing seventh day (or Sabbath) that has nothing to do with any day of the week but has everything to do with the "seven churches" as symbolizing the Endocrine System.

By paying tribute and gratitude to our higher brain center (pituitary gland), the energy frequency coming into the mind becomes activated within us so that our intuition (feeling) and our sovereign divine plan will open up to us on a physical conscious level. Then we can make choices from an awareness that we are God, Goddess, and Christ also. When we reach this point in our evolution, we do become a Master of what we desire to experience instead of living life on other's beliefs.

We could say that when we pass through the first stumbling block of polarity, the "valley of death," we will no longer show fear of any system. For example: Yeshua rose from the dead! And we can too! After all, what is death? When Yeshua said that he would rise in the last days, he was not talking about coming to earth for those who faithfully attended a church building. Yeshua was talking about the Christ-identity within himself, rising to an awareness where his lower chakra centers will transform the impulses of polarity to a consciousness that holds a light body of the ascension. This is what will happen to us once we allow our lower chakra center to transform the impulses of polarity.

Therefore, before we can be lifted off the cross of suffering, we must transcend our fears of God, Satan, governments, religion, the media, businesses, family, friends, and all that feels unknown to us, like a virus, to a newly awakened consciousness. Why do you think Yeshua said, *"Father, have you forsaken me?"* (Mark 15:34, Matthew 27:46, Psalm 22:1). Before Yeshua died on the cross, he was in the final stages of releasing all his fears, including his fear of death. Are you ready to release all your fears, including the fear of death?

This is very important to understand! Before we can move into our new, expanded consciousness (new earth), the element of fear must be overcome because the system (the harlot-the deep state) works hard to control our destiny by telling us we are not good enough to be God-Goddess or Christ. Why? Because the system does not profit from us being free. And as you know, the system is a master at projecting fear because of its overwhelming resources to keep us asleep.

Its biggest control is the media because it is easy to convince the masses that we must fear the unknown. By overcoming our fear of the unknown, God, Satan, government, family, friends, the media, businesses, and especially dying, we ultimately attain a higher awareness where we are completely free from any rules (beliefs) other than what we place on ourselves as a human. Remember, fear draws only limitations that would define us as merely a human in need.

We all must let go of who we *think* we are and move into a higher divine truth where we *know* who we are placing no doubt. Letting go of doubt triggers the process of refining our physical body and how we did use many lifetimes of sowing and reaping. And now, some of us today, from an ego level (represented by John), can feel *(hear)* the vibrations *(loud voice)* coming through to our new expanded consciousness *(heaven)*, Revelation 19:1-2. These vibrations allow all of our ego personalities of the past to integrate with our human self.

Channeling of the Ascended Masters on the Apocalypse

This *"voice of a great multitude,"* Revelation 19:1-2, comes from our memories of many lifetimes and is not directly associated with us in the flesh today. These memories of our past lifetimes may be at a very deep level, but they can be recalled in this lifetime because some of us have become the Son of Man (an awakened ego) and the Son of God (a mind that is awakened to the Christ) while still in human form. This is why we can say, *"Alleluia," for "salvation, glory, and honor,"* belong to our God, now known as our own "I AM" sovereign Christ-self, and not to some solitary God outside of us or to any system.

It is you, and it has always been you, who is the true and just God, Goddess, and Christ. It took your experiences and your judgments of them to open your consciousness to a whole new expanded consciousness (new world). You have been operating from a very complex system, having multitudes of ego personality aspects and many different levels of truths (lies) that made you confused about who you are and what part of you is the Master. Because of all this confusion, your "I AM" sovereign essence (the Christ) has stayed out of your human life until you were ready to accept yourself as a Christ.

"They" in Revelation 19:3, is all that we are in consciousness, all of our ego personality aspects coming together in this lifetime and wanting to integrate with our "I AM," The shouting of *"alleluia"* for the *"second time,"* comes from an intuitive urge to remember the justice we received by journeying through many lifetimes sowing and reaping. Thus, some of us, in this lifetime, can integrate "all that we are" and become a sovereign God-Goddess and Christ in our own right *"forever and ever,"* Revelation 19:3, just as Yeshua did in his day.

The phrase *"smoke will rise from her forever and ever,"* Revelation 19:3, is about our memories of the past that have been cleansed by the fire of justice (sowing and reaping). These memories now help us recognize that the *"great harlot"* has been all of us humans, our beliefs, and our dualistic thinking. And now, we will not "ever" allow ourselves to be absorbed, controlled, and obscured by the traps of the system (her) riddled with dualistic thoughts and dogmatic beliefs that hide the real truth from us again.

Most of us have closed off our "I AM" Christ identity because of our difficulties and our emotional ties to the system, thus denying that we are divine. So, take a deep breath and allow the "I AM" to integrate with the human self. And, when fear is eliminated, we will witness great miracles, like the healing of our relationships, money problems, and, most of all, our body!

In Revelation 19:4, we find the same body influences we first mentioned in Revelation 4:4, because this verse still refers to the cleansing process of our memories and physical body. The *"twenty-four elders"* now bow down to us, the self, as the true creator and the Christ who is on the throne of wisdom. And now, these *"elders"* and the *"four living creatures"* (gonad, Lyden, adrenals, and thymus) worship us, their true creator. (Please see more details about the meaning of the four living creatures in Revelation 4:7.)

When we learn to integrate all that we are, including our "I AM" Christ-spirit, we come to where we barely need a doctor because all parts of our body are fully integrated with the essence of being the Lord of Lords. Therefore, the body learns to take care of itself. Our body comes to understand what it needs to live in physical reality all because the body awakens to its consciousness of staying healthy. It will take in any foods we feed it, process the food accordingly, and dispose of anything that's not needed, and use the energy that is needed. The body itself will do this because of being conscious of its duty to stay healthy.

When our "I AM" identity is fully integrated with our mind, ego, and physical body, we understand our imbalances of energy very quickly. Thus, healing becomes apparent because we understand the cleansing process of our body and how unbalanced energy will always seek to become balanced. When we fully integrate our "I AM" identity with our human self, our mind need not try to figure things out or protect us against group-consciousness anymore (the system), because the newly awakened mind has no fear of tomorrow.

The newly awakened mind works in cooperation with our "I AM" spirit, and the answer to our problems, situations, and questions in life become solved as if magic. Our minds chatter ego thoughts and the controlling personalities will dissolve back into the "I AM" before our very eyes. The newly awakened mind becomes very sharp and efficient as it is freed of its clutter. We even find that we have a tremendous amount of energy that we haven't had before. We may find that our "stress" headaches disappear altogether.

The phrase *"let us rejoice and give Him glory,"* Revelation 19:7, refers to those that are ready to awaken. All of Revelation is about those of us who are ready to become Christ in the flesh, as the written words open up to us to see if we are ready to function as "one consciousness" again. The difference this time is that we will have the awareness and the understanding of our experiences throughout time and space.

Channeling of the Ascended Masters on the Apocalypse

The symbolism of this verse is about the outer, masculine side of our mind (husband/Adam), and if it is ready to merge with all parts and pieces of us, including our "I AM" Christ consciousness (Oversoul) and the feminine soul part (wife/Eve) of us that is mental. It refers to the two hemispheres of the mind coming together with the "I AM" and becoming one body of consciousness again that has a spirit, a mind, and an ego that work together as one. This is what is meant by the "Oneness of God."

The phrase *"wedding day of the Lamb has come,"* Revelation 19:7, is again about our outer human self (known as the masculine part) giving honor, birth, and recognition to the soul-feminine part. And, as known, our masculine and feminine parts (min-soul) have been apart for a long time, along with our ego, and now they are all ready to become one again with your "I AM" spirit.

The word *"his"* refers to the Son of Man or our ego in the flesh today, giving allegiance to our "I AM" Christ-spirit, believing that all parts of the self are equal because now they work as "one consciousness." Thus, our "I AM" Christ-spirit (Oversoul), the bride, *"has made herself ready,"* Revelation 19:7, to become "one consciousness" with the Son of Man and the Son of God (our mind-soul and ego), to be a sovereign ruler of the self and one's creations. The story of the prodigal son fits here, as our Mind and Ego become awakened to the self being Christ.

Feel your sovereignty knocking on the door of your outer consciousness. Feel this new expanded energy filling your body, mind, and consciousness, welcoming you back home (garden), the home where your Christ-spirit has opened (exposed) to your outer, masculine Adam side without shame or guilt. So, take a deep breath and receive your Christ-spirit, for she (your new bride) has been waiting for you for a long time.

Because of the system, many of us thought that home (heaven) was somewhere up there in the sky, and we thought this because our human self became lost in the belief system of the mass and the lower chakras of the body. Take a deep breath and feel this message, feel your sovereign spirit crying out to you right now, and feel the essence of the real you that wants to come back home to you, the Master. Know that the mystery of God and the second coming of Christ is this: both of them are you. You are a unique angel with the opportunity to make a choice in this very now moment and allow the Christ-you to enter your consciousness while you are still part of the flesh.

And, if you have a question about: "What would happen to me if my Christ-spirit sees some of the things I have done is appalling?" This uneasy feeling is what makes you afraid of your own "I AM" spirit. This uneasiness also makes you feel that you are unworthy of being Christ. Therefore, you follow and stay with what you have always feared as Satan and a solitary God outside of you.

Dear friends, this is anxiety over what your "I AM" Christ-spirit might think of your creations. Know that everything that you have created, believed, and acted on has been a great lie, and that has been the mystery! This is why you are worried about inviting in your "I AM" Christ-spirit into your life. You are afraid that you might turn this event into a lie as well. So deep down, you don't want to take that chance, and by doing so, you resist your ascension into a higher frequency of energy.

Well, before you make up your mind and not allow your "I AM" into your life because of the fear of exposing yourself, here is something to think about. Neither your "I AM" Christ-spirit nor Yeshua will come to you in judgment. Only your outer awakened mind judges what you don't understand. Your "I AM" Christ-spirit does not see your life as a lie or that you did something appalling. Why? Because your sovereign Christ-spirit understands that you have been working and operating from the limited energy of polarity and physicalness to benefit the "I AM." Your "I AM" Christ-spirit wonders how you ever endured.

Know that your "I AM" Christ spirit only looks upon you as a unique angel that dared to take up residency in the flesh without knowing you were part of something bigger than you being just human. My friends, according to Yeshua and the Ascended Masters, your "I AM" Christ spirit honors you, applauds your outer mind of the intellect and your defiant ego personalities for what they (you) have done, even if they (you) chose only evil acts.

Your "I AM" Christ spirit honors and pays tribute to you, because, if it wasn't for your human identity, and what you have done through many lifetimes, your "I AM" Christ spirit would never have reached the wisdom it has now. So, no matter how much you read the Bible, attend religious schools, or listen to your families and friends about God or Jesus, they cannot integrate your "I AM" Christ-spirit back into you. Yeshua or your religion cannot do it for you. The analyzing, praying, and searching cannot bring your "I AM" Christ-spirit in. Only *you* can do that!

So, take a deep breath and, and if you have the courage, invite in your "I AM" into your human self. Never forget that the essence of your "I AM" Christ-spirit and your soul is you, along with all your other ego aspects and experiences. Note in Revelation 19:8, where *"she was allowed to wear a bright, clean linen garment,"* as the linen represents the righteous deeds of the holy ones in Revelation 18:24. This verse spells everything out for us, as our soul is now cleansed of all memories of what our human mind (masculine self) has done, good and bad, throughout time and space.

The masculine side of our mind gave seed to multitudes of lifetimes that have played in darkness and light, and because of karma, the human self and our soul have cleansed themselves from all ignorance of spirit, including what we call sin. When we, while in human form, let go of our erroneous beliefs tied to polarity and the thought of being a sinner, our soul (Eve) may *"wear bright, clean linen,"* as it means our human body is now pure in its reactions toward the forces of polarity, all because we hold the wisdom learned from our experiences from the beginning until our present now moment.

When again speaking of *"the righteous deeds of the holy ones,"* Revelation 18:24, they are speaking of all the ego parts of us that have lived on earth, taking unpleasant and appalling actions during various lifetimes, and all in the name of the "I AM." And now, because of these ego-personality aspects having paid their debt to you and group-consciousness, they now have become the *"righteous and the holy ones"* to be lifted to a new awareness (heaven). And, this my friends, shows that the Masters are not speaking of church going people. They are speaking to those that are ready to let go of fear and become one with your "I AM."

The *"angel,"* in Revelation 19:9, is your "I AM" Christ spirit expressing to your human ego and mind that the "Son of Man" relates to you in your everyday living experiences in the flesh. Therefore, there is no mystery about the end days, because the Apocalypse is not about some far place or time; nor is it about Yeshua returning to earth. It is about your daily life experiences continuing until you learn to let go of your belief in sin and polarity, and the system that keeps you a slave to it.

The phrase *"writing down,"* Revelation 19:9, is about the many false faces (ego personalities), symbolized by John, recording and placing all choices, thoughts, judgments, and experiences to memory. And, when the time is right, our soul releases those memories of good and evil right back to us to work out in the physical realm. And, in the end, we learn how to be a much wiser God-Goddess, and a Christ than when we all first left higher consciousness (Garden).

And, when we read in Revelation 19:9, *"blessed are those who have been called to the wedding feast of the Lamb,"* it symbolizes all of our many ego-personality aspects that have been working lifetime after lifetime, sowing and reaping to learn wisdom on behalf of the "I AM," (Oversoul). And now, because of us being the "Sacrificial Lamb," we are invited to the *"wedding feast."* And, since most wedding feasts are held at night, it indicates that our ignorance of who Christ is, is coming to an end for some of us here on earth.

We know *"these words to be true, because they come from God (the Goddess),"* Revelation 19:9, as this means that it was us humans that created the first expression in desiring to experience polarity. As thought is our mode of manifestation, then our only way to accomplish our manifestations is to think the thoughts that we know correspond with our own words of truth or lies. And, as we all know, thoughts can be controlled and regulated by the words we speak. Therefore, when we come to understand this, we acknowledge that our words create our beliefs, and our beliefs create our reality.

Every word we speak outwardly is backed by the power of our spirit, mind, and ego personalities. Thus, we create our world (disease, poverty, viruses, happiness, abundance, or health) through our thoughts, beliefs, and expressions (words) we speak. When we take the words of the mass and integrate them as our own words, then we live by the two primary attitudes of the mind, positive and negative, right and wrong, good and evil as being real. This belief then builds within us the world we wish to experience.

The people invited to the wedding feast are those with the courage to let go of the idea of polarity and a God that created them. Yeshua overcame his physical identity and polarity thinking by integrating his "I AM" Christ spirit with his human self. Thus, the Father-Mother God-Goddess (Spirit of One) of the "I AM" could express itself through him while he was still part of the flesh more clearly than through any beliefs united solely by polarity issues. When Yeshua overcame polarity, he allowed himself to become multi-dimensional, and it can be the same with us when we learn to let go.

The *"I,"* in Revelation 19:10, may say it all when it comes to *"falling at his feet to worship him,"* as this is you today, the super ego-personality, that came into this lifetime to call in your many lifetimes to become integrated with the "I AM." Therefore, you are not to worship your mind-soul or ego, because they were your "servants" and fellow aspects of you *"who is to bear witness"* to your "I AM" Christ spirit, symbolized by Yeshua (Jesus), that you are ready to ascend.

Therefore, the words you speak in this lifetime, as the super-aspect, like John, is to call in all your other ego aspects *(brothers)* who will *"bear witness to"* you deserving to attend the wedding of your "I AM" Christ spirit to all that you are and have become. The words, *"witness to Jesus is the spirit of prophecy,"* Revelation 19:10, as it represents our journey through many lifetimes sowing and reaping. And now, the testimony was given by our "I AM" Christ spirit (symbolized by Jesus) about asking us a long time ago to give life and form to a personality aspect that could live in ignorance to learn the wisdom of our choices while playing in polarity, which is in the form of prophesying.

When we lowered our consciousness frequency, we fell into a consciousness of polarity, where we indeed became the prophesier of our experiences. My friends, some of us are at a wonderful point in our life right now, where a few are brave enough to take the first step in developing a relationship with our own "I AM" Christ-spirit on a conscious level. And, the key is to start right now to develop some kind of relationship with our "I AM," because that is the part of us that has been guiding us to this point because of our divine plan.

So, the Ascended Masters and I ask, why not hold the hand of your "I AM" Christ-spirit and take the first step toward letting go of your belief in polarity, sin, and fear? In your truest, "I AM" nature, you are pure and uncorrupted by the system. Know that the one who sees the *"heavens open,"* in Revelation 19:11, is you because you can witness the opening of a multi-dimensional consciousness where you can expand in consciousness to learn all about your total self and what you have been up to for eons of time.

By you choosing in this lifetime to be the super aspect to integrate all that you are, your defiant ego (the beast) is now ready to redeem itself and become the Son of Man while you are still in the flesh. This is the symbol of you coming to some awareness of what needs to be done to fulfill your union with your "I AM who sits upon the *"white horse."* And, if you so choose, you can be the *"rider" called "faithful and true"* who can overcome the old system of polarity of two and bring in the new expansional energy of four that will provide a connection between your "I AM," and all that you are and ever have been.

You are the groom, male or female, to be married with your "I AM" Goddess consciousness (your Oversoul). And once you are married, all situations in your life have no obstacles, for the *"rider"* and the *"white horse"* signify you in the flesh, coming full circle, uniting your many ego personalities, your mind-soul, and all that you feel you did right and wrong back into the oneness of consciousness of being free as a Christ also.

And, once you open up to this new expanded consciousness, while in the flesh, your mind and ego become very *"faithful and true"* to the "I AM" because of the evidence (testimony) given on your behalf. Because you allowed yourself to enter earth a long time ago, the baptism of that choice is now calling out to you, saying, *"This is my beloved Son, with whom I am well pleased"* (Matt. 3:17).

This awakening to being a Christ is the *"fulfillment of all righteousness"* given in Matthew 3:15, where your outer, redeemed, false self shows your outer, beastly nature, the experiences your soul has revealed to you because your "I AM" Christ-spirit had already accepted the need to redeem the outer you from your entanglements with the flesh.

From this understanding, we can now see why the phrase *"he judges and wages war in righteousness"* thus, symbolizes the *"rider"* as the human self becoming awakened to becoming a Christ also while still part of the flesh. And, if you allow it, the outer, masculine self, the mind, will ride (journey) with the influential forces of expansional energy of "four" (new earth) without adulterating it with the forces of polarity thinking (old earth

Chapter 38

SALVATION COMES TO THOSE WHO SEEK IT

From reading Revelation 19:12-13, *"his eyes were (like) a fiery flame, and on his head were many diadems,"* we can understand that the human self is the groom clothed with the ability to see and understand the illusion of what we are doing here on earth. The "eyes" symbolize our authority as a creator to express our choices and bring about judgment upon ourselves, evidenced by our journey through many lifetimes sowing and reaping. It was our passionate nature that inflamed *(fiery flame)* our consciousness to grow in wisdom and understanding, which then finally brought us to a knowing that we are God, Goddess, and the Christ. (Also see Revelation 1:14).

The many *"diadems"* on our head is symbolic of us being a sovereign and divine being first and foremost, which demonstrates how we can overcome all the earth forces, the trials of testing the forces of polarity, and the way these forces of opposites appealed to us and persuaded us to participate with them.

The *"name inscribed that no one knows except himself,"* Revelation 19:12-13, is the name of our outer, false, human self that is becoming the Son of Man, and who is now ready to become the Christ here on earth if one so chooses. Some of us here on earth have won all the battles with the self, and now we can become a new being, thus earning a new name for ourselves: "I AM That I AM"; for there is none other who can bring this Christ-position to us except the self.

In the phrase "*he wore a cloak that had been dipped in blood,"* Revelation 19:12-13, the "cloak" is our human body in this lifetime. And, as we look into these verses and assign them to Yeshua dying on the cross, we can see the connection to ourselves. As Yeshua was nailed to the cross, his blood (energy) and water (spirit) poured from his side (flesh), as he had to shed his fear and beliefs of polarity for Yeshua to become a free spirit. Thus, all ties to the flesh had to be severed.

It was necessary for the cord to be cut from his fleshly body, breaking away any relationship that might tie him ever again to the flesh. Therefore, my friends, it is the same for us or those in this lifetime that are ready to sever the old energy beliefs in polarity to a new expansional energy of four. This means that Yeshua is not coming to earth a second time to be our savior. It is you, the Christ within, coming to earth to be a savior to "all that you are in consciousness."

Yeshua, our brother, became the Lamb and the sacrificial example of what we have done throughout many lifetimes. What we are doing here on earth is following the example of what Yeshua has already done. Yeshua freed himself from the flesh over two thousand years ago, and now some of us here on earth can free ourselves from the earthly forces of polarity and become a real "I AM" Christ in our own right, just like Yeshua. By shedding all our ties to the earth forces of duality, we return to our divinity as an "I AM" Christ and become the King of Kings over all parts and pieces of ourselves, and at the same time, over earth and what it contains.

It is like the human ego returning the free will back to our mind, and our mind integrating it with our "I AM" Christ self. It is us humans that are the "prodigal son," Luke 15:11-32, that is returning what was freely given to us by our own "I AM" Christ-spirit, and now our human ego-self is freely giving it back to the "I AM, the true creator. That is how we, in human ego form, become "his name" and the "Word of God," for each of us is the God, Goddess, and the Christ. When we are back in our sacred and revered consciousness, even if we are in the flesh, we become the "I AM" in the flesh, as Yeshua did.

This is when we learn to, as Yeshua did, go beyond the games and the fears that people display all day long. We go beyond the dogmatic beliefs, the analyzing, and the studying of religions. We even go beyond wanting to go home to spirit (Goddess) because we are the spirit (Goddess), and we are already home. How many right now desires to become awakened, but when confronted with a new concept of God, we freeze in our tracks because of fear. Oh, we say that we want to know God, but we fear anything that takes us away from our comfort zone so elegantly demonstrated by religion.

People have a hard time giving up their free will of the intellect for the divine will because they fear losing their human identity that they have so lovingly created. The free will of the human self creates its barriers, its confusion, and its self-doubt. The mystery of God no longer needs to be a mystery, and our "I AM" Christ spirit no longer needs to be hidden. Our Christ-spirit no longer has to be kept away from us because of our fear of God.

It is time for the Book of Revelation to become known to us in all ways, not literally or as a single reality. It is time for us to know who we are and to become one again with our own "I AM" Christ-spirit, to come back to occupy our consciousness with a knowing of who we are at our core. Perhaps the time has come for the mind and ego to let go and allow our "I AM" Christ-spirit to come in and be one with all that we are in consciousness.

Even when looking into Revelation 19:14, the "armies of heaven followed him" refers to the armies of memories and actions that we, as a creator, experienced throughout time and space here on the earth. The manifested words of God, like thoughts and actions, came from us because we alone give our words life. Therefore, the *"armies of heaven"* (or memories) and the many ego-personality aspects that we all have manifested are the ones that bear witness to the message coming from our own "I AM" Christ-spirit. These armies of memories and the many ego aspects of ourselves have followed us wherever we went, just as we follow Yeshua as Christ.

This army of memories, ego aspects of our past, and all those spiritualized cells in the human body that are now pure of spirit, and they *"wear the clean white linen,"* thus uniting with us in this lifetime to fulfill our mission here on earth to integrate with the "I AM." We have always felt cut off from God, but we have simply forgotten that we are God, Goddess, and Christ, and we left on our journey by choice. However, once we fell into a consciousness of destiny (karma), we felt like we had no more choices, not realizing we still have many choices to make.

The many armies of Christ have always symbolized our spiritual memories, which have been carried through our journey of lifetimes. And today, our human self and our "I AM" Christ-spirit call out to us in the flesh, and to our many ego aspects, to awaken themselves in glory, for we have the means to overcome any obstacles that our unawakened mind (Antichrist), our rebellious ego nature (the Beast), and all those "unspiritualized" memories that can be thrown at us.

We all have had multitudes of experiences in the flesh and non-flesh, and we all have had ego aspects of ourselves that have experienced the darkest of the dark and the lightest of light. We have had ego aspects that played the game of drama and trauma. This was just part of the journey we took, partly by our own choice, partly by following destiny, and ultimately, we got closer to our "I AM" Christ spirit.

We all have chosen many paths to get where we are today; nevertheless, we got here, and we are well-known to our own "I AM" Christ-spirit, and all those ego soul memories of ours. So have faith and trust yourself as a God, Goddess, and a Christ. Trust in yourself as Christ and leave behind everything and anything that tells you to blame, judge, fear, and condemn another. Once this is done, then *"out of your mouth,"* Revelation 19:15, you will speak the name of your own "I AM" Christ, for you are the true creator of all your experiences, including your suffering, joy, and abundance.

The *"sharp sword"* of justice (karma), Revelation 19:15, has divided your memories (nations) into two groups, and in the last days of coming into your own "I AM" Christ spirit, the light, and the dark will desire to come together and come home to you.

My friends, one group of memories *(nations and ego personalities)* has heard the words of your "I AM" Christ spirit and has been spiritualized (cleansed of duality) by accepting the full range of responsibility, while other memories (nations and ego personalities) within you are looking to be released from their burdens of old, dogmatic beliefs by you forgiving them and asking them to come home to you, their creator.

The *"iron rod,"* Revelation 19:15, is symbolic of your spiritual authority as a Christ, which can deliver energy so powerful that it will overcome *(striking)* all those memories (ego-personalities-armies/nations) of old and have them brought home to you in this lifetime. Know that the rapture talked about in the Bible is your final step toward adjusting your thinking about Christ to being you here on earth. You are the Christ coming down out of the clouds of your ignorance and drawing in those old memories of your many ego aspects to become integrated with you in this lifetime.

"He himself," Revelation 19:15, is our new consciousness of expansion, evolving *(tread out)* toward a new path that leads us to a realization that one is Christ in the flesh. It follows where our human self and consciousness see no limitations and takes on the substance of what God, Goddess, and Christ represent. It is about our human self becoming one with your Christ-spirit, transcending time and space, and taking full control over our physical body, its functions, and all that is in our world (earth).

It is where our Christ-spirit says to our ego and mind, *"Lo I am with you always"* (Matt. 28:20), which in truth is real because of our ascension to a level of oneness and understanding is very real. The *"wind press of the fury and wrath of God the Almighty,"* Revelation 19:15, symbolizes our divine plan that has "pressed forward" into action those memories (ego-personalities and memories (nations)) that have felt the love and truth *(wrath)* of our "I AM" Christ-spirit. And, these memories are now cleansed and ready to serve us, the Master, to bring about a healthy body, a happy life, and the abundance we desire.

The *"wine of the fury"* can also symbolize the vitality and durability of our physical body and its connecting link to our "I AM" Christ-spirit. This wine of life frees our energy up. It then presents itself in large quantities to blend our thoughts, memories of our ego personalities, and our life here on earth in becoming successful with all situations in life.

In the days of Abraham, placing one's hand under another's thigh would be similar to placing one's hand on a Bible today, binding you by your word. The thigh of an individual back in those days was recognized as the seat of one's procreative power. Therefore, the *"name written on his cloak,"* Revelation 19:16, represents our physical body. And, the "name" linked to this physical body is our real name, the "I AM That I AM," for "I AM" God, Goddess, and the Christ. Let know one tell you any differently!

Thus, you are the King of Kings and the Lord of Lords in manifesting all your creations. Therefore, all the other kings, your many ego-personality aspects from other lifetimes, fall under the Master, *you* in this lifetime, for you are the super-aspect to bring your consciousness back to the oneness that it is. And, once you come into your realization of who you indeed are as a Christ also, the other kings, like fire, water, air, and form. Likewise, with your seven endocrine systems (churches), and *"the angel standing on the sun"* (Revelation 19:17), bow down to you, their master.

The *"angel standing on the sun"* is you in the flesh today connecting to your multidimensional intelligence, *"crying out,"* Revelation 19:17, to your human ego self to receive the highest of influences that hold great authority (power), wisdom, understanding, and the overwhelming qualities that make you a sovereign being in your own right. These attributes you carry within radiate a much higher frequency and are now at your fingertips to behold as to your success in answering the question you asked eons ago about "Who am I?"

This is confirmed by Revelation 19:17-18 with the statement, *"come here, gather for God's great feast."* Most know by reading this book that "eating" would be a symbol that you have been appropriating your spirit and pure God energy of light into all of your manifestations, good and bad, as it makes no difference. Therefore, when we enter into this higher divine intelligence of being a Christ also, the outer symbols are no longer necessary, as the Bible and its contents become the example.

When looking over the rest of Revelation 19:17-18, *"to eat the flesh of kings, the military officers, the warriors, the horses and their riders, and the flesh of all, free and slave, small and great,"* refers to your journey through many lifetimes unconsciously consuming all kinds of physical bodies and using them as an officer over people, being a warrior. A ruling king that thought you were free, and yet, you were a slave to it all. You were nothing more than the *"horses and their riders"* taken up as many ego-personalities aspects of light and dark riding the rails of incarnations sowing and reaping all because of your choices tied to the belief in sin and polarity.

Yes, most of us have done it all using many physical bodies, memories, belief systems, what was supposed to be good and bad for us, being a victim and a victimizer, and losing our memory of who we are at our core essence. Yes, we all were great, small, a slave, a king, a peasant, and everything in-between. However, the time has come now for some of us to release and let go of it all and shed all the effects that caused us to suffer because of feasting on the influential beliefs of others.

Even with *"the birds flying high overhead,"* Revelation 19:17-18, indicates how much we were stuck within our mind of reason and intellectual thinking, which created even more karmic debts to the flesh. And, this is why, in Revelation 19:19, the *"beast"* (our ego in defiance) and the *"kings of the earth and their armies gathered to fight against the one riding the horse,"* (our many ego-personality lifetimes of light and dark). The *"one riding the horse"* is the self or you in this lifetime becoming awakened to the Christ within you.

Because of some of us in this lifetime awakening to the Christ we are, we have gathered these lost ego aspects of ourselves and have learned to integrate them as being "one consciousness." Therefore, we have been cleansed and purified through the fires of sowing and reaping. And now, we have reached a consciousness awareness as a Master who sits upon the white horse using our authority (power) as a messenger and savior to all those other ego aspects of ourselves to come and integrate with us while we are still in the flesh.

And, this is how the *"beast"* (our defiant ego-personality) *"was caught along with the false prophet who had performed the signs by which led us astray by accepting the mark of the beast to worship,"* Revelation 19:20. It was from our unawakened mind (the Anti-Christ) that allowed our many ego-personality aspects throughout many lifetimes that ruled our beliefs, choices, and manifestations to where our thoughts were based on only fear, confusion, and that we were weak as a lamb to be slaughtered by those that love power and controls.

Now, because of our awakening to whom we indeed are as a Christ, most of us here on earth have *"thrown our beastly ego nature and our unawakening mind into the fiery pool burning with sulfur,"* Revelation 19:20. This means that our cycle of many lifetimes here on earth has ended because the elements of the earth's forces have transformed us into a newly awakened angel that now understands consciousness and energy.

When we pray and cry out for help to this God of the Bible, an external God, we do not realize that we are praying to a God that is not real but feels real because we believe in him. We pray to this God for truth and to bring us to heaven, but there is no such God. We all have become involved in a consciousness built on our submission, which we freely accept in giving our authority (power) away to this God of the Bible. Even now, there are parts of us (ego aspects) that are still trying to define their (our) reality from within that same belief in a God of sin and punishment.

Some people may say that the battle between Satan and Christ is real, but I say to these people that the confrontation between Satan and Christ, along with their armies, is an image that they worship as real, and yet it is just an illusion built upon one's belief in it.

My friends, if everything influences everything, then everything around us right now is influencing our reality in the way we perceive and understand it to be. Thus, reality builds upon itself and applies itself to our own internal and external world. Our thoughts, ideas, beliefs, and the suggestions of yesterday become what we worship as our truth today.

Once we accept this new awareness and understanding, we begin to look down on a new road that is not filled with struggles, obstacles, sorrow, cruelty, and punishment. When we accept our own "I AM" Christ-spirit as being the self, our past is healed, which means our body then feels the grace and forgiveness of our "I AM" Christ-spirit healing us from our illnesses, poverty, and bad relationships. Thus, we journey down a road that is different from what we just experienced.

Once you open your eyes and become awakened to accepting the truth that you are a Christ also coming to save your human self, and all that you have created as defiant ego-personality aspects of the past that were following and worshipping an unawakened mind (Antichrist), you immediately transform their energy and integrate it with you in this lifetime.

This is seen in Revelation 19:21, *"the rest were killed by the sword that comes out of the mouth of the one riding the horse."* This refers to you in your glorified awakened state of consciousness, giving the spoken word to all that is left in memory and still needs to integrate with you. It signifies you in a new awareness, welcoming your "I AM" Christ-spirit into your human reality that you have allowed coming in. And, once this is allowed, your "I AM" Christ-spirit shapes your life with new energy, expansional energy where you can tap into all parts of you, including those ego aspects that followed the false you.

Because of those influential forces of polarity *"gorging,"* Revelation 19:21, on your consciousnesses of the past, these ego aspects of you now understand that the creator and the Christ are *you*. Your past ego aspects that were stubborn and inflexible about their belief in the system are now ready to be integrated with you, their creator. And now, because you allowed the "I AM" to come into your life, these ego aspects of you see a glorious vessel (your physical body) to come home to.

Chapter 39

OUR JOURNEY THROUGH TIME AND SPACE

This chapter is also an exciting one as well because of the clarity of us souled beings, *"angels coming down from heaven,"* Revelation 20:1, as this refers to our great desire to discover ourselves to answer the question, "Who am I and why do I exist?" What we all have learned coming from Yeshua and the Ascended Masters in this book is that we are the ones who *"hold in our hand the key to the abyss"* Revelation 20:1. We hold the key because we souled beings are the ones that created the abyss and filled it with boundless possibilities and potentials to feel and experience our creations.

The abyss is also a symbol of how deep we all sank, entrapping ourselves into a physical form and realm where the earth's influential force of polarity became our norm. The abyss is nothing more than us souls, allowing our unwise mind and ego personality to fall into a hell of suffering where it confined our ignorance of consciousness and energy to its highest mark in creation. In fact, there is no other planet in the cosmos that is so dense as Earth, and this caused us to forget our own "I AM" Christ spirit.

It is us souled beings here on earth that carry the *"heavy chain,"* Revelation 20:1, of events that we all have created together to experience a journey of lifetimes for millions of years to understand our choices and manifestations. We have played out our beliefs here on earth in a restricted movement that feels like it was sequential to learn the wisdom behind our choices, and yet, it was all done simultaneously. And, when we begin to see the big picture of it all, we can observe that every human, each in our way, sooner or later, will come to know and understand that we, as a group consciousness, are the creator of the universe and all that it contains, including earth.

By stepping out of our mind for a bit and allowing our hearts to be heard, we will draw those forces to us that will give us a whole new understanding about ourselves and the God and Satan we thought we knew. We will also realize that we are and always have been the Christ we seek. Even the *"seized dragon, which is the Devil or Satan being tied up for a thousand years,"* Revelation 20-2, symbolizes that part of our mind that became stuck in a belief where our defiant ego *(the ancient serpent)* became the vehicle that resulted in us souled beings embracing the opportunity to move our consciousness outside of the self and cling to a mind of a mental nature that believed in polarity (dragon) as real.

It took this mental mind and our defiant ego nature to create many light and dark personality aspects (lifetimes) to gain the wisdom necessary to answer the question: "Who am I?" Thus, we all restricted our mental mind of reasoning (Anti-Christ) to an appalling ego-personality (the beast) where our many ego-personality aspects would be tied up with polarity for *"one thousand years,"* Revelation 20:2.

The number of "one" (1) became known as our beginning was with the "oneness of consciousness" being only of an unconditional love state of neutrality that also created a universal god energy of neutrality that appeared to us as light. And yet, the two together became the Father/Mother God/Goddess within each of us as being our sovereignty as a God, Goddess, and a Christ in our own right. Therefore, the essence of life, including all that exists, the collectiveness of the mass, life in every dimension and every form, the total energy of "all that was," including the self, which is part of "all that is today," for we gave it life.

The first zero (0) behind the "one thousand years" represents the first cycle where we souled being existed in a limited oneness of consciousness (the garden) that we and religions call heaven. Our beginning of consciousness was the oneness of what the first cycle represents, our spirit only knowing what was known as being absolute, everlasting, and having a consciousness of no wisdom.

The second zero (0) represents our movement into the abyss (or endless space), which is sometimes called the void or complete darkness. In this "void of darkness," we souled beings played with a force called polarity, filling that "endless darken space" with multitudes of nonphysical dimensions to experience, which then helped to create the physical body, universe, and earth.

Even though every soul participated in creating everything visible or invisible, not every soul has experienced the earth's physical realm. There are many, many souls from the 144,000 different soul-groups waiting to see how we volunteers do, waiting for us to show them the way. Even now, since our awakening as a souled being, eons ago, we all are still part of the "second zero," or cycle because this second cycle is all about polarity.

Believe it or not, we humans on earth are the bravest of all the angels, for we agreed to forget who we were in the quest to bring wisdom and compassion to "all that is" now. This is why we are a unique and valuable angel, no matter what we think we have done or what station we feel we hold in life. Feel this fact within the heart and know how unique we are, for we are the Christ taking on the sins of what we all created in our world to show other souls what not to do.

The third zero (0) represents that some of us today are awakening to a new expansional consciousness and energy (New Earth) where we learn of the Christ being the self while still part of the second cycle. Because of the *"dragon"* (our mental mind) and the *"ancient serpent,"* our defiant ego, played in polarity throughout the second cycle, reincarnating, sowing, and reaping, most of us are no longer in need karma as a way of life.

Why? Because now we know who we are, a Christ in our own right. This awakening comes after we have journeyed through the first and second cycles, gaining incredible wisdom from our choices, experiences, and learning responsibility for what we create. At this point, we move beyond the forces of polarity, finally remembering our true identity as God, Goddess, and Christ. After completing the first two cycles in not knowing who we are, we do come to where we learn about the stuck energy of polarity, symbolized by the one thousand years being tied up in a belief that we are less than Christ. To enter into this third cycle (0), we must become a complete and sovereign God/Goddess and a Christ in our own right.

By allowing ourselves to journey outside of the first cycle (0) taking on belief patterns of good, evil, and ignorance of not knowing who we are at our core, we set the course for many lifetime incarnations playing in trapped energy of polarity (Tree of Knowledge of Good and Evil) to complete the second cycle to gain wisdom. Once the second cycle is completed, those of us that made it, our consciousness will rise through a spiritual awakening (ascension-rapture) where we understand enough to complete this cycle to move us into a four-density consciousness.

This ascended consciousness is where we can begin a new cycle (0) and completely understand ourselves as a Christ also.

Now, that is true peace! Everything you create will be in harmony from this point on with all aspects of yourself. The rapture signifies us coming full circle, which means we can now release all karma (sin) and ascend into a New Heaven and a New Earth that carries:

1. Magical energy of healing, abundance, and joy
2. A knowing that we are part of the Christ-consciousness
3. A balanced masculine/feminine energy where everything is in harmony with your thoughts, beliefs, and creations
4. An access to the divine solution energy of the Gnost

My friends, by the time you get to Revelation 20:3, *"and threw it into the abyss, which locked over it and sealed, so it could no longer lead the nations astray until the thousand years are completed,"* you should be coming into a realization where the "dragon" has cleared away your old beliefs that led your memories *(nations)* on a course experiencing the unknown principles of polarity (the Tree of Knowledge of Good and Evil) until you reached the completion (over) of your first and second cycles. And now, all that is left for you to do is to tap into your memory and reap the wisdom of those experiences. That is when you will enter into the third cycle to become an actual creator in your own right.

And, I quote, *"to be released for a short time,"* Revelation 20:3 means, once we move out of polarity and into the new expansional energy of four, it will take a little time to adjust and fully realize that we no longer need to have our mind and our ego to control the workings of our consciousness acts. In other words, it will take some time for us to adjust to being free from the system of old beliefs tied to polarity. We have spent thousands of lifetimes fearing the system that brought nothing to us but lies and suffering.

My friends, everything is changing, and now the time has come for you to decide to live without fear and learn the real truth about who you indeed are. We all know the story of Adam and Eve to avoid eating the fruit of the tree of knowledge of good and evil, for they would surely die. This is evident that this story is merely your own "I AM" Christ spirit speaking to your divided mind, represented by Adam and Eve, and your ego-personality, represented by the serpent, to be careful if you choose to participate in the fruits of polarity. Because, if you did, you could lose sight (forget) of its effect on you.

If you believe, from an intellectual level, that your ego-personality in this lifetime (the name on your birth certificate) is all that you are, then you cut yourself off from the source of life ("I AM" Christ spirit). This causes you to revolve (cycles of lifetimes) in a mental whirlpool where your dominant beliefs recognize polarity, good and evil, birth, and death as being real.

When you came to earth, you gave yourself a boundary to measure your choices, belief systems, responsibility, and wisdom. And, once you recognize that this boundary is the belief in polarity, your "I AM" Christ spirit then moves to awaken you from your sleep. My friends, is this the day for you to awake from your sleep and realize that you are still in the garden (heaven)?

Most memories of what we did from the time we souled beings left the first creation (first cycle-zero) until today have been cleansed, via many lifetimes sowing and reaping. And now, these memories have been judged worthy to witness the resurrected Christ within you. And, as Revelation 20:4 is all about those redeemed memories of potentials and personality aspects, we are still filled with many more memories of potentials to experience beyond polarity where we can create future aspects of self to play them out.

Know that the "first resurrection," Revelation 20:5, is where we awaken to be the Christ, the Lord of Lords, in the flesh coming to save "all that we are in creation!" This is where we raise our human consciousness out of ignorance (death) and into a knowing and realization that we are the Christ in human form. And, *"blessed one who shares in the first resurrection,"* Revelation 20:6, is referring to those of us who are ready to transform from our old way of thinking (karma) to a whole new way of thinking (no karma).

Once this is understood, we move into the third cycle (0), where we enter into our sovereignty and *reign* as a living God, Goddess, and Christ while still part of the physical body. Note: Because a person can awaken by taking steps to be more than human, one may not take the first step toward an integration because one still sees the self not wanting to take full responsibility for their life. By refusing to let go of all that is tied to old dogmatic beliefs, including forgiveness of others and self, one can remain stuck in the old energy. Thus, one will not ascend!

There are many people in this world today who study God and their place as humans. Because of this, many reach a certain level of understanding where they can take themselves "off the cross of karma." But because of overwhelming attachments to materialistic living and religious nurturing, they have great difficulty letting go of their old ways of looking at God and the angels.

And, many believe in life after death, that we are our creator, that we have other lifetimes, karma, and many other things that bring us to a certain awareness that we are more than just human. But deep within, there may be some self-seeking memories that conflict *(warring)* with any part of us that believes we could be a Christ. These deep-rooted beliefs keep us continually battling the forces of polarity, thus creating much turmoil in our life. This is the meaning of "Gog and Magog" in Revelation 20:8.

When a person keeps pushing and pulling on the forces of polarity as their basic belief system, even though they call themselves awakened and among the first to ascend, the only result is a conflict with the mind. When a person only sees himself as a being of flesh, with an educated mind to answer all questions to achieve success, understanding, and healing, then one will suffer a second death until they rise above the intellectual mind and understand that there is no such thing as light and dark. For those people who have moved beyond belief in karma, sin, light and dark, and the intellectual mind is all that one is, a second death has no power over them.

When Yeshua walked the earth, he moved in and out of dimensions, which is why he was seen in various parts of the world. Therefore, those of us who learn to let go and move past the idea of polarity "will be the priests of God and Christ," because they have transformed the forces of polarity and their many ego-personalities of the past to a whole new energy of "four":

1. Positive
2. Negative
3. Neutrality
4. A Gnost Consciousness of solutions

A *"priests of God"* are those individuals who have made their journey through the first two cycles and are now ready to enter into their third cycle of sovereignty, symbolized by the thousand years. And, to those who claim to be priests of God, but teach that the physical church is the place to find God, are clinging to thought and belief patterns coming from their memories of non-integrated personalities. These memories pertain to lifetimes where they devoted themselves to religious vows and ideas, and now these vows of commitments (commandments) are their ruling tendencies in this lifetime, keeping them hypnotized and preventing them from meeting the "I AM" Christ within the self.

This is why in Revelation 20:7, *"when the thousand years are completed, Satan will be released from his prison,"* as this can seem quite confusing because it indicates the possibility of our defiant ego-personality (Satan) may still act out in a dualistic manner, even though we have completed our cycles of lifetimes and finished our karmic debt to ourselves and others. The understanding of Revelation 20:7 is related to some of us that may still have some deep memories that belong to past vows and commitments, and to some religious rules that have been buried deep within our consciousness.

Revelation 20:7 is not about being tempted again by our current ego-personality to do evil things. It is about holding deep memories within our soul consciousness that pertain to our vows and commitments to old, dogmatic beliefs. For example: someone can have an overwhelming sense of being a spirit first before being human, but down deep within their soul, some individuals may still believe that churches need to represent us before God.

Speaking for myself, I have had many close connections and lifetimes dealing with the church because of having many lifetime experiences as a priest, monk, prophet, a Sheik, and as a rabbi many times. Perhaps I have helped build the original core energy of what religions are today. However, I did have a lifetime as a disciple of Yeshua when he walked the earth. And, in that lifetime as a disciple and many more after, I moved my search for God being in a church building to seeking Yeshua as being my God.

In that lifetime as a disciple, I asked two questions to Yeshua. Am I from the light, or am I from the dark? And Am I good, or am I bad? After all, I had left my beliefs as a Jew, not believing in a Christ. Then, in this lifetime, the first thing I did was resist the churches and their ways of worship. I came into this lifetime without someone trying to set me up with following a bunch of given rules by which to live. It was that I discovered my spiritual path, and all that comes with it. Perhaps I never allowed a church to dictate what I should eat, say, or wear.

Therefore, to my surprise, in learning how to free myself from this God of sin and punishment and the Church building that goes with it, I answered my questions about the light and the dark. And, after some time channeling Yeshua and the Ascended Masters, I have learned that I was both light and dark. Thus, the light and dark within me are balanced.

I came to understand that light could not exist without dark, and dark could not exist without the light. And, when I accepted this truth, these two energies of light and dark within me integrated back together as one within me. And now, I am no longer dark or light, good or bad; I am my sovereign oneness. Look at the moon and how it has one side that is completely dark while the other side is light, and yet, they are both as one. Thus, neither side is good or bad. It is just there as one.

Once I allowed in my "I AM" Christ spirit (symbolized by me channeling Yeshua, the man who walked the earth over two-thousand years ago) became one with me in this lifetime, I then realized that the dark could never destroy the light or the light destroy the dark. Meaning, I had these two equal energies of positive and negative, light and dark, free will (mental mind) and divine will (I AM Christ-spirit) existing within me since I left higher consciousness, battling for superiority and control over my total consciousness. And this was going on for many lifetimes without my realizing it. However, it all ended when I realized that there is no such thing as light and dark, for everything is of an absolute neutralized consciousness.

This is happening to human consciousness today. People are asleep and dead to their divine plan (will) that was put in place by their own "I AM" Christ-spirit, eons ago, came in conflict with their Mind of the intellect, and how they have misinterpreted it as the "free will" to make choices. And yet, they are *the same* and not *two*. Since I have embraced the belief that "free will" and my "divine plan" (will) is the same, I no longer see the light and dark as real, for it is not part of my consciousness today. Therefore, I do not need to improve or reform the dark within me or outside of me, because I no longer have a shadow of darkness around me, causing me fear.

I learned from Yeshua and the Ascended Masters that the darkness was where my "I AM" Christ-spirit was waiting for me to accept everything about myself, including all of my past creations, good and bad. And, as per Yeshua, darkness is just the lack of accepting yourself as the creator of your experiences, including your illnesses, sorrows, what you look like, and what you are experiencing.

Without the help of religion in this lifetime, I have found that the light, or what we consider God and heaven, was just a destination that everyone seemed to strive for but never reaches. No matter how hard we work to be totally in the light, we just cannot be all light. Our "I AM" Christ-spirit is neither light nor dark because the real self is only our spirit and consciousness. Yes, we can continue searching for the light (God), but we will never find it without the dark (Satan) staring us in the face. Why? Because there is neither! There is no light or dark because everything we are at our core is *one*. We are neither light nor dark, and yet we are both.

Most of us keep studying the old literal text of the Bible without seeing the underlying messages waiting there for us to find. Yes, the text has been changed often over the centuries by our government leaders and religion, but the dark forces have forgotten about the divine wisdom behind their changed text. We struggle to learn, we keep on going to church for answers, but in the end, we are delaying the inevitable. However, some of us already know, down deep within our soul, that the old sacred ways are gone forever because we have lived lifetimes in the past where we have gotten to understand that hidden wisdom behind the text.

The only thing to do for those that are in the "know" and have allowed this wisdom to come through is to integrate our "I AM" Christ-spirit with our human self. Thus, allowing this God of polarity (light and dark) in the Bible to be part of our past. And, if we are too busy mapping our life using polarity as our guide for truth, then how will we be lifted to the heavens? It is not that we have to do this because our "I AM" Christ-spirit is so compassionate with our creations that she will wait until another time, which is why Revelation 20:6 calls for a second death.

When Yeshua mentioned in John 18:36 that he was not of this world, he means that the "I AM" Christ within you is not of this human world because your "I AM" Christ spirit is your true state of consciousness. Yeshua took the challenges of the flesh as we are doing now, and he overcame the physical and the polarity energy of light and dark. Thus, Yeshua moved beyond any belief in karma, sin, and power. When we humans too integrate with our own "I AM" Christ spirit, hopefully in this lifetime, how can we experience a second death (going back into our sleep state because of fearing to move beyond polarity and the church rituals)?

From Revelation 20:8, "to deceive the nations" is a descriptive expression about our memories of old, dogmatic beliefs and how they are part of our physicalness, our spirit, our mind-soul body, and our ego, which represent the *"four corners of the earth"* in Revelation 20:8. In Ezekiel 38:2-3, *"son of man"* (our ego) *turned toward Gog (the land of Magog), the chief prince of Meshech and Tubal, and prophesy against him: Thus, says the Lord God: See! I am coming at you, God, chief prince of Meshech and Tubal."*

What this means, or the wisdom behind it, is that for some of us, our ego, the name we hold in this lifetime, are awakening to being more than just humans that still relies on the perception of our outer five physical senses in making choices. Thus, coming from a higher place within us (I AM Christ spirit), is asking about our consciousness, since we feel an awakening coming, to turn toward the mind (north), our outer ego of today, (west), our inner soul (east), and to our "I AM" Christ spirit (south) to learn the real wisdom about who we indeed are.

When we feel the "I AM" Christ spirit within expressing this message to us, she is asking us to turn toward Gog (the land of Magog) where we have been self-absorbed by thoughts, ideas, and beliefs that keep warring (battling) against the real self, the "I AM" Christ spirit. We all have been so absorbed with thoughts, ideas, and beliefs about our religion, governments, family, friends, the media, and big businesses, that we have overlooked about how much they control our lives and our world, keeping us in bondage so they can feed off our energy.

However, "to gather them for battle," Revelation 20:8, refers to us and how we all have been battling those beliefs and memories (nations) for a long time. And, because of it, some of us have reached a level of wisdom where we, if we so choose, can ascend to a new understanding about polarity and those that battle to keep us as sheep. This is why there are so many of us who can sense a deep feeling that there is more to our human life than what we are seeing out there but cannot seem to put our finger on it. This "not putting our finger on it" is caused by the question we asked the self, "What else could there be other than what is good and bad?"

Just by understanding Revelation 20:8, *"sands of the sea,"* it can bring us some comfort because of its meaning, and it is nothing other than our memories of old, dogmatic beliefs that are connected more to our subconsciousness (the sea) than our outer physical consciousness (land). These memories of old are coming from our many ego-personalities of past lifetimes. Therefore, we need to bring forth these dogmatic beliefs to be brought forward to be faced directly with our human consciousness. By facing these dogmatic beliefs head-on, while in the flesh body, we take the last step toward moving into our "I AM" Christ spirit as Yeshua did over two thousand years ago.

The name Meshech is mentioned in Genesis 10:2 and 1 Chronicles 1:17. Mash, the son of Aram, is called Meshech. Meshech is also mentioned in Ezekiel 27:13, along with Tubal and Javan, two other sons of Japheth. In Ezekiel, the names no doubt refer to countries or tribes of people descended from these men. Therefore, the wisdom behind the name "Meshech" is that of perception through the five senses, judgment according to exterior manifestations, the work of the mind in concluding, and the conception of false, illusionary ideas or beliefs.

The name *Tubal* derives from the son of Japheth and the grandson of Noah (Genesis 10:2); Gomer, Magog, Madai, Javan, and Tiras descended from him. Metaphysically speaking, Noah's three sons: Shem, Ham, and Japheth, represent the three-dimensional consciousness that we are here on earth, for we do have a spirit (Shem), a physical body (Ham), and a mind of a mental nature (Japheth).

Since the name Tubal comes from the son of Japheth, it signifies the intellect or reasoning of man, the logic that comes from the mental part of our consciousness, as does free will. Therefore, the name Tubal signifies expanding possibilities of our defiant ego consciousness that could result from increased understanding.

Bible scholars believe that Gog is a nation of people that will battle against Israel and be defeated (Ezek. 38:2–18). But here in Revelation, Gog and Magog symbolize the worshipping of self-absorbed thought patterns of dogmatic beliefs within our consciousness, which means we battle against our "I AM" Christ spirit all the time (the real God-Goddess).

Yeshua taught us that we are a God (John 10:34), and if we are a God, then deep within our memories, we have the understanding of being more than just light and dark, good and evil. Because of our war-like conflicts regarding our religious training in a lifetime past, we move our human consciousness more toward the mind (free will), which is the mental perception of polarity and our self-absorbed religious beliefs (Gog and Magog). Thus, we create much turmoil in our lives, which prevents us from letting go of the many past ego-personalities (lifetimes) and reach for an awakening consciousness that will allow us to let it all go.

In Revelation 20:9, the *"invasion of the breath of the earth and surrounded the camp of the holy ones and the beloved city"* is referring to Jerusalem in Israel. Jerusalem is the city of David, which symbolizes the great nerve center in the back of the heart. It is from this point the "I AM" sends its radiance to all parts of the physical body. The metaphysical meaning is that Jerusalem is a city with peace in developing memories coming from the "I AM." In man, it is the abiding consciousness of spiritual awakening, which will cause those old memories of a dogmatic nature and how we in lifetimes past vowed to keep them as part of our soul forever. This is why the Jews do not believe in Yeshua, the Christ.

However, when Yeshua went up to Jerusalem (Mathew 20:17), it means taking the last step in the unfoldment of old memories to find that peace. Thus, those ego-personalities that made these vows and commitments to a God of polarity, sin, and punishment, therefore, must be crucified (sow and reap) before the "I AM" Christ spirit can come into our heart to lift us to higher consciousness. By Yeshua riding out near Bethphage into Jerusalem, it signifies those progressive memories of old in the fulfillment of time (reincarnation on earth to rid ourselves of those old memories) before the "I AM" takes control and lifts away those earth forces of man into the "I AM" realm of mastery, purity, and peace.

This is why in Revelation 20:9, *"fire came down from heaven and consumed them,"* as this is a profound statement because it is telling us that we have to cleanse those old memories about our oaths, vows, and commitments (commandments) that we made to different religions in other lifetimes. We humans, without realizing it, have some deep-rooted vows and oaths where we have been creating our idea of heaven on earth. The ascension we all have long waited for has come, but we keep ignoring the signs because we are too committed to pray to a God to rescue us.

When we hold to the belief that we live only one lifetime and that there is a mythical, all-powerful God outside of us who must be reckoned with and feared, then we destine ourselves to live in an illusion of shortages and needs. Many of us believe that power, health, and abundance come to us from outside of ourselves and not from within ourselves. We are the God, Goddess, and the Christ, and all energy comes from within the self, as each of us owns our energy. But we keep on giving it away to others because we continue to hold onto our old vows and commitments to a God of polarity, taught to us by religions.

Mostly all of us here on earth have kept our promise not to interfere with our creations and have fulfilled that promise by experiencing the full range of our choices, good and bad, and we all have paid the price doing it. However, some of us have come to the point where it is time to take the veil off our soul and let go of those old vows and promises.

There is no more need to look upon our defiant ego nature (the beast/Satin) as something we must hide from or push away. In fact, our defiant ego nature is not something we should hate or fear, because we were the ones from a higher level that sent our defiant ego forth to create separation to help with our wisdom. And, these defiant ego-personality aspects have served us well. It comes down to this; if we choose not to trust in the self as a Christ also, and we refuse to contend with our stubborn nature because of our vows and commitments to religions, then more than likely, we will experience more cycles of lifetimes.

Look at where you were born and the family you joined. Are your beliefs based on the traditions of your family, which have been handed down through generations, or are they based on your research? Most people let their reality just grow up around them, and it never occurs to them that they have a choice in how they want to live. They allow the system and family to dictate to them what their life should be like, how they should think, what they should believe, even things like how they should dress and talk. Then, when things go wrong in their lives, they say it was destiny, or God was testing them, or it is just the way it is.

Look at Revelation 20:10, *"the Devil who had led them astray was thrown into the pool of fire and sulfur."* Know that this "Devil" is the same "Devil" that was thrown out of heaven a long time, which of course, was us or you, not the "I AM" you, but the defiant ego you. According to the Bible, Satan was thrown out of Heaven to a place where it would be tormented forever and ever at the end of days.

My friends, the end of days, is for those that are now coming into an awakening where they now understand they were the "beast" (ego) of long ago that left higher consciousness to explore all facets of polarity. Yes, we were the ones that invited our defiant ego to take the bite of life and polarity (apple) that caused us to split our consciousness into many layers to the point that we forgot who we are at our core essence.

The story of Yeshua overcoming Satan in the wilderness symbolizes our experience in facing our demonic creations by journeying through many lifetimes sowing and reaping. And now, like Yeshua, some of us have purified ourselves with the justice of polarity energy (fire). Thus, there are no places in memory where our defiant ego nature can come and haunt us again. By using polarity energy, our testing grounds of learning wisdom, we transform polarity into the whole new energy of four that can expand in every direction.

The *"large white throne,"* Revelation 20:11, is referring to one's purified consciousness once they have integrated all that one is from their many ego personalities, good and bad, to their mind-soul and current ego into accepting full responsibility for being the creator of all their choices.

"The earth and the sky fled from his presence," Revelation 20:11, is referring to the old concepts, ideas, beliefs, thoughts of polarity, and our intelligence that we harbored within our soul and how we played them out here on earth. And now, these things of polarity have no place within our integrated consciousness because some of us have learned to purify ourselves of them. When Yeshua was dying on the cross, he asked God had he forsaken him. This symbolizes that many of us, in this lifetime is the last one, and now we can overcome polarity without heavenly help. Yeshua has already proved that it can be done.

The *"dead, the great and lowly, standing before the throne,"* Revelation 20:12, refers to our many light and dark personality aspects (other lifetimes) opening up to us, the human self, in this lifetime if we are ready to receive them. By allowing our "I AM" Christ-spirit to integrate with our human self, we not only move into a new, expansional energy of four; we also open ourselves up to all the secret memories (scrolls) of our soul, including all of what we have judged to be good and evil *("and the scrolls were opened")*.

As John sees the dead "standing before the throne," Revelation 20:12, it symbolizes us in our human ego body standing before our own "I AM"

Christ-spirit and recalling all that we have ever done and paid the price for. How could I write what I am writing here if not for my own "I AM" Christ-spirit, opening up to me the memories of my soul? This also means there is no such thing as death or a final judgment day, for this is just our old way of thinking.

"Another scroll" (memory) was opened," Revelation 20:12 is referring to our own "the Book of Life," which signifies those old beliefs in external, religious thought patterns and the many ego-personality aspects that are asking the self to forgive them and set them free. We have the capacity right now to expand our mind and consciousness beyond polarity and receive our "I AM" Christ-spirit, thus translating our memories of old into where the old book of life that everyone fears and God keeps in heaven to record our sins is replaced by a New Book of Life that is the essence of the self working out of their "I AM" Christ spirit.

"The dead were judged according to their deeds." Revelation 20:12 refers to what was written in the "scrolls" or our memories. The "dead" symbolizes the state of mind where we played out many lifetimes on earth, unwilling to listen to our "I AM" Christ-spirit. Thus, we "judged" ourselves. Our soul recorded (written) what we would do and put it all to memory (scrolls), and then we acted everything out in the flesh as we did as spirits in the etheric realms before coming to earth.

Death is always the result of our failure to recognize our "I AM" Christ-spirit as the source of our creations. All wisdom comes from our "I AM" because it is associated with our dark side in storing all of what we have done and put to memory. When we fall short of this understanding, we commit to what we call "sin" because we believe in it. Therefore, we experience what the Bible calls sowing and reaping (the Son of Man on the cross) until we awaken to us being the God, Goddess, and the Christ who created every experience up to the present.

My friends, we will remain "dead" to our "I AM," even though we are walking around and breathing, saying we are alive. Although we think we are alive and have a little understanding about ourselves being more than human, there is always the possibility that, if we are not willing to let go of our old, dogmatic beliefs about light and dark, we may experience a second death because of our stubbornness.

In conjunction with our journey of lifetimes from the previous chapters, Revelation 20:13, *"the sea gave up its dead; then death and Hades gave up their dead,"* all pertain to our subconsciousness (the sea) and how it will reveal all those forgotten memories about our most deviant and merciless lifetimes that we have played out on earth. When we finally awaken to some understanding about being a Christ also, our subconsciousness will reveal to us our most ruthless memories where we experienced death and hell on a scale of unforgiveness.

Once we chose death and hell as our experiences, we developed a very strong belief in wickedness, which we felt was the best way to obtain power and control over others. This belief affected that part of our subconsciousness that created our reactions to it in an appalling way. Thus, after many lifetimes playing with our first memories of a devilish nature, we had to review these appalling choices, *"according to their deed,"* Revelation 20:13. And, once we came to the understanding that we created them, we concluded that we have to judge them.

According to the *Metaphysical Bible Dictionary,* by Charles Fillmore, the word "Hades" is a Greek word, and the Hebrew word for "Hades" is "Sheol." In the English version (King James) of the New Testament, it is translated as "hell." Hades refers to the "netherworld" or the "house of the dead." Sheol refers to the "grave" or the "pit" in the Old Testament and therefore has the same meaning as Hades (Gen. 37:35; 42:38; I Sam. 2:6; I Kings 2:6; Job 14:13).

Hades, Sheol, Grave, Pit, Netherworld, or House of the Dead all refer to the outer realm of the physical senses and the descent of our physical consciousness into the illusion that there was such a thing as light and dark, or good and evil. Therefore, to focus on and live in the outer world is to live outside of the "I AM." Hence, Hades (house of the dead) represents the realm of incarnate souls living in an illusionary world of light and dark, good and evil, and being dead to the real, inner, spiritual senses of the "I AM."

"Hades" was us souls withdrawing and retreating from our own "I AM" Christ spirit in favor of carrying on with a strong belief in polarity, good and evil, light and dark. Thus, our outer masculine mental mind (Adam) became silenced and dead to any thought of its misunderstanding of energy and how it works with the feminine soul consciousness of responsibility (Eve). This misunderstanding by our mind took away our authority as a God, Goddess, and a Christ. It gave it to our ego-personality of defiance where, in the end, this created even more ego aspects of self to see how far we could go with that power.

When we rejected our own "I AM" Christ spirit as to whom we indeed are in favor of seeing ourselves as an ego-personality, because of it having us feel separate and independent from our "I AM," we became vulnerable and susceptible to the forces of polarity. This created within us a feeling of being someone to reckon with, which then created a belief within us to seek out more power for ourselves. Therefore, "Hades" signifies burying or putting out of sight, though, and mind our own "I AM" Christ spirit as something separate.

However, this unforgiveness of some of our first memories of our ego's most deviant and merciless lifetimes found the pathway to redemption through *"Death and Hades being thrown into the pool of fire,"* Revelation 20:14, since those ego personalities of old lost sight of the mind and the "I AM" Christ spirit. Once those power-hungry ego personalities of ours moved into the *"pool of fire,"* sowing and reaping, in what we created in those horrific lifetimes, some of us in this lifetime are awakening to them all because of working out karma for many, many lifetimes as if hell was real.

Note: the first death is when we souls became dead to being Christ while we were still part of the astral/physical realms. The second death is when we enter a lifetime where we learn of our "I AM" Christ spirit as the self, and then refuse to forgive our most demonic lifetimes. Once we learn of our "I AM" Christ spirit as to whom we are in any given lifetime, and then fail to forgive ourselves because of feeling some unworthiness deep within, we risk the chance to slip into a second death.

The note that Yeshua and the Ascended Masters just mentioned above is confirmed by presenting to you Revelation 20:15, *"anyone whose name was not found written in the book of life was thrown into the pool of fire."* If you or any of your ego personalities aspects of the past are not accepted as being part of your "I AM" Christ spirit and soul consciousness (your book of life), you then run the risk in experiencing a second death where you will journey through many more lifetimes, sowing and reaping.

When we learn to understand that consciousness is not made of energy and that energy is only there to serve you, the Christ, you begin to understand light and dark, good and evil, as just an illusion put in place for you to feel your choices. Everything outside of the "I AM" Christ spirit is an illusion, and therefore not real. This means that our mental mind-soul, our many ego-personalities aspects that played as good and evil on earth, and the polarity energy we used to manifest our creations feel real.

All that we are at our core essence is consciousness, having no form to us but what we have created as a "universal omnipresent mind field of pure neutralized energy of light." Therefore, we souled beings are only consciousness and light, as consciousness represents the Goddess/Christ feminine spirit and light represents this universal mind field of pure neutralized energy, the masculine, that we use for our creations. Therefore, it is the energy belief in polarity that keeps us weighed down, and compassion, unconditional love, and the forgiveness of self and others is the only remedy that can release the burdens of our guilt, fear, and shame.

To learn that the earth was created by us souled beings working together as the Goddess, and to help resolve our issues with our stuck energy due to belief systems, we had to become limited to a world of polarity. Earth was not only created for us to release ourselves from stuck polarity energy. It also became a place to launch this new, expansional energy (New Earth) to a whole new level of understanding once we stepped off the old road of polarity and karma.

This new, expansional energy of four makes you multidimensional to the point of separation from the old, dogmatic beliefs, and the letting goes of the old, karmic path of suffering. It fulfills our journey that began when we all left the first creation (garden) to understand our true identity as a Christ also. It has always been a great potential to understand that our "I AM" has creator abilities. And now, because of our many experiences in the flesh, we humans have inherited the throne, being a sovereign God-Goddess in our own right. This is why we came to earth and why we created all of what we have experienced.

We all chose what we wanted to experience, good and evil, and our "I AM" Christ-spirit agreed to let us do as we pleased. We have issues with our body, life, and others, but what we don't realize is that we cause everything we are feeling and experiencing, even though we may feel and believe otherwise. This is meant by the call of Gabriel, for he calls out to us, asking, "What are you choosing?" Are you ready to let yourself be the creator, or are you just going to stick to blaming others for your problems?

Remember, we can fear God and Satan so much that we will take on another cycle of lifetimes (second death), even though we may be expressing to ourselves, what we are reading may have some legitimacy to it.

Are you ready to come out of your sleep state and become an actual creator, God, Goddess, and Christ in your own right? Don't just think about these things as something far off. Take full responsibility for everything in your life, and you will see your "I AM" Christ-spirit come in to help you manage all that you are.

Chapter 40

THE NEW HEAVEN AND NEW EARTH

This chapter brings out the consciousness of the Son of Man, more known as our ego personality in human form, teaming up with our mind-soul and our "I AM in attaining Christhood after numerous lifetimes of experiences. The "bride of the Lamb" is not the church or those who worship Yeshua as their God. The human body is the church where we meet up our own "I AM" Christ spirit. Therefore, the new church is you integrated with all that you created since the time you left higher consciousness (Garden).

It is also you to accept the truth about light and dark, good and evil, as joined together as one, merging to create a whole new energy of four and a higher consciousness filled with the wisdom of everything that you have done since the beginning. And, with this acceptance, we ascend to a whole new expansional consciousness and energy where we no longer see ourselves as a masculine (male) or feminine (female), or that good and evil, right and wrong, and light and dark but it has to be one or the other.

The earth realm and the physical body was the densest of all realms, and it allowed us, as divine humans, to play with polarity in a way that couldn't have been more challenging. Also, the vibrational slow-down of our energy was never a mistake. It was a way for us to become a conscious creator and discover who we are, part of a massive soul-group of angels, together, representing the Godhead.

Many of us have forgotten that Yeshua looked at himself as equal to God and was killed for it. Therefore, many of us denied our Godhood as well a long time ago, and we were also killed, like Yeshua, and now, we can awaken from our sleep. So, stop delaying your ascension! You have only to let go of those beliefs coming from the system and take full responsibility for all of your creations.

Once you learn to take full responsibility, no matter what you are experiencing right now, then trust becomes the ultimate achievement in bringing about your ascension. And, ascension is not about disappearing, as portrayed by religions. However, it may turn your life upside down because of balancing. However, know that you can remain on earth but live and walk as an ascended Master in your own right. All that you need to do is let go of the old belief that some God created you.

This chapter will show that, even though we may reach a certain level of spiritual awareness, we are still subject to that last argument with ourselves that is keeping us asleep. Thus, this chapter warns of such a possibility. So, keep focused on what you are reading, and if you feel that the messages and the book seem overwhelming, then please reread it. When John was shown the foundation of Christ, it represents us, humans, learning to take full responsibility for our life. So, take time for the study of why you are here on earth.

When we read in Revelation 21:1, *"then I saw a new heaven and new earth,"* the Ascended Masters are speaking about some of us here on earth who are moving into a new awareness and a new ego consciousness that is beginning to have insights into our memories of old (book of life). It is this new human ego consciousness that sets the foundation for this new expansion energy of four to come into our lives where we will find ourselves one with "all that we are in consciousness." This means our old memories of polarity are now in the process of coming into harmony with the newly awakened ego-self, while we are still in the flesh.

Therefore, *"the former heaven and former earth had passed away, and the sea was no more,"* Revelation 21:1. This refers to our former ego-consciousness of misunderstanding that has now accepted our darkest ego personalities and has now integrated them with our new awakened ego-consciousness of today. Thus, washing away all that was of old polarity energy, cleansing our subconsciousness from any more defiant ego personalities that seek resolution. All of our dark secrets that we considered as our judgments for hell and damnation have now been transmuted into eternal wisdom that we can now tap into at well.

When the *"former heaven and earth"* are gone, our subconsciousness and ego personality of today are cleansed of all memories based on old beliefs in polarity. Thus, leaving us to open up to only unconditional love where we move from a three-density consciousness to a four-density consciousness. Ever since we have been coming to earth in physical form, we have often gone through near dimensional realms of an etheric nature, designed and created by group-consciousness (the system).

And, when we leave earth in what is called death, it is not that we go to some heaven or hell. We take with us everything that we have experienced from the beginning, including all of our beliefs and that of group belief systems. The only thing we shed is the physical body, and this is why most of us become very confused when we pass over and see ourselves still alive on the other side of the veil.

Religions say that we humans are losing our spirituality because we believe that we, as humanity, are evil in nature, and therefore need guidance more than ever from the church. It is not so much that we are losing our spirituality; we are becoming more spiritual today than ever before. Because of the awakening going on today here on earth, we humans are causing a quantum leap in consciousness to take place. It is not about a church building or some God living in it, or about us having to worship in it. It is about releasing the concept of destiny (karma) and coming to a place in consciousness where we become a conscious creator in our own right. It is about honoring our past because it took many lifetimes to get where we are today.

The *"new Jerusalem,"* Revelation 21:2, is about the joy and freedom we all can experience just by inviting in our "I AM" Christ-spirit (Oversoul- the feminine) to unite with our outer, masculine mind. And, in doing so, our underlying ideas, truths, and beliefs about unconditional love are then greatly enhanced. Thus, expanding the awareness of our outer, ego consciousness to further acknowledge our "I AM" Christ authority in bringing about our neutrality, self-trust, and great confidence.

In reference to what I mentioned before on the City of Jerusalem is the City of David, and was said to represent the great nerve center just in the back of the heart; Our Christ-spirit sends its joy, energy, intelligence, and health to all parts of our body. Then, the way to Jerusalem, the city of peace and love, is through Christ and the perfect expression of the mental faculties (disciples) and their position under the dominion of our "I AM" Christ consciousness" (Luke 17:11).

Paul's visit to the holy city to redeem it (Acts 21:13–22:1) signifies that love focuses on the center of religious thoughts that are given over to bigotry, bias, narrow-mindedness, racism, and political extremes. Only unconditional love can enter the temple (physical body) and speak the words that will free us. We all want love, truth, and the freedom that comes from the holy city, but when unconditional love and truth are presented to us, we object to the universal spirit that it proclaims.

Here is an example: The Jews are taught that they are the chosen ones. Muslims believe that Allah is the one God, having no equal the purpose of life is to worship him; thus, all other religions are considered of no significance. When man believes himself to be better than any other, even within his religion, he makes a place in his heart where he is superior over others. This type of belief extends to our physical nature, and then we build temples that create divisions among us. Then anyone who dares to go astray meets with great opposition. This leads to conditional love, which then brings conflict, disagreements, and misunderstanding among families, friends, neighbors, and nations, finally leading to hostility.

When people are confronted with new truths about God or Christ, they first reject them, which then creates great turmoil in the mind and in the ego and physical body. This rejection also generates great fear within people, where they believe their customs and traditions are being threatened. So, it becomes very important for them to resist these new truths because they see their teachings, customs, and past beliefs as more important than any new truths.

Any act, thought, or process that introduces new energy, or suggests that we are children of ignorance, is automatically resisted, which then sets us up to disregard any new truths that come into our consciousness. And this is why people cannot feel the divine love that comes from their "I AM" Christ-spirit because they build walls of beliefs and customs that prevent them from experiencing true freedom.

When we open up our eyes and hearts to new truths and let go of old, dogmatic concepts about who God is, we cheer in a "loud voice," Revelation 21:3, because we are entering into a new ego consciousness and a new expansional energy of four. And, when we reach the throne of higher understanding of spirit, where we know that God is the self, we learn to invite our "I AM" Christ spirit in with our human ego and become Christ in physical form, as Yeshua did.

Our old mental and physical consciousness had a talent for putting words (choices) into our mouths, where we expressed only polarity as the foundation of our existence. But now that we know we are God and Christ in physical form, we are in a position (mentally and physically) to speak the same language, speak our truths, and to put them across in words with a smile, and in our love and compassion for others. It is about acknowledging the Christ in the self and acknowledging the Christ in others. (This paragraph refers to Revelation 21:3)

Of course, *"tears, death, pain, and suffering,"* Revelation 21:4, can feel very real to us, but once we understand that the outer mind (Anti-Christ) has been trying to control our every thought and belief and that the mind (Anti-Christ) creates rules for us to follow, then we can see why we feel limited and confused. The mind cannot understand the ways of our "I AM" Christ-spirit, as our Christ-spirit truly doesn't understand the ways of our mind. However, when we invite in our "I AM" Christ-spirit to dwell with our human ego, we move past our Anti-Christ like mind and go directly to our "I AM" Christ-spirit for answers and solutions.

Therefore, the *"one who sat on the throne,"* Revelation 21:5, is that of our "I AM" Christ spirit now occupies the seat of our authority as a God-Goddess also. *"Behold, I make all things new,"* Revelation 21:5, refers to our new expansional human ego self making *"all thing new,"* because now we understand things in a whole new light. It is through this new awareness and understanding that we learn to re-balance and rejuvenate our physical body, even as some of us flush away our old, dogmatic beliefs and step into a new consciousness.

And, when we look at Revelation 21:5, *"Write these words down, for they are trustworthy and true,"* means the word of God is you in your truest essence, adding power to the mind, your choices, desires, and expressions, giving them the gift of life and unconditional love. And, when you speak your words as a God (Christ also), those words are written within your memory as to your truths, possibilities, and the qualities of your "I AM," thereby making you completely trustworthy. Every word, thought, and expression coming from you when in your Christ state, carries your authority according to your realization of oneness.

The most frightening thing I faced in this lifetime, as it may be for you, was letting go of a God of judgment and my perception that he and Yeshua were beyond my reach. It helped when I asked myself, "what reason do I have for even being here on earth if everything I have done is for the benefit of some God I don't even know?" I make the choices, I take on the beliefs, I generate the action, and then I pay the price, and not Yeshua, my parents, brothers, or sisters, just me. Life, my friends, is about meeting yourself, and sooner or later, everyone will meet themselves and their idea of God.

When we integrate all parts of ourselves, while in the flesh, including our "I AM" Christ-spirit, we become awakened to the real God, Goddess, and Christ. For we are the Lord of Lords (alpha) who left the garden long ago, and we are the Christ (omega) that we have long been awaiting, Revelation 21:6. When we finally master the energy of polarity, we set ourselves free from both the light and the dark, good and evil, because now we know we are neither.

When this understanding comes to us with no doubt, we come to a place in consciousness where we witness the transformation where we join together our human ego consciousness with our mind and "I AM" Christ consciousness. This is when we learn that God is not a mystery, that he has a name and feelings that make this God unique because he is *you* in human form. Know that our Christ-spirit honors the human identity and all of what it has created.

We have been locked into a small part of our consciousness, and other parts of us have been working out as many potentials as they could to learn the wisdom of their choices. This is why our "I AM" Christ-spirit is so filled with unconditional love and compassion for everything that each part of our soul has accomplished. Therefore, our "I AM" Christ spirit gives us the gift of infinite life and the authority of our throne.

We are the *"victor who will inherit these gifts,"* Revelation 21:7, of higher awareness, unconditional love, expansion of consciousness, our sovereignty as a Christ, our gnost consciousness of solutions, and in the knowing that everything outside of us is an illusion because we dared to let go of the old, dogmatic beliefs tied to polarity. Our physical body is the chalice, our "I AM" Christ spirit is the Goddess and Oversoul, and our mind is the Son through whom we created and gave life to experience our creations (*and I shall be his God, and he will be my son"* (Revelation 21:7).

The more we worship polarity energy, judgment, sin, and a God who teaches it, the more we categorize and define our reality as real, even though it is not real. It may feel real to us because our mind is telling us it is real. But we may not realize that we are living in a consciousness that resembles physicalness and that our mind keeps telling us that this physicalness is real. Our mind has a playing area made up of duality, and it cannot see beyond this compartmentalized consciousness, thus creating doubt and suffocating those natural life forces that flow through us.

This encourages us to move more into the mind and back into a three-density analytical thinking, as we choke off the flow of any new energy coming into our mind. And, because of this, we create a virus (perhaps Covid-19) within us that sets up a whole chain of doubts and suffering. This then creates a feeling of not being worthy of God, thinking that we are only human, believing that suffering is the gateway to our salvation and many other restrictions and limitations that keep us away from learning the real truth.

Therefore, it takes courage to move past our minds, the doubts and fears it creates, and the limits that we have placed on it because we are afraid of a God who keeps us from receiving our own "I AM" Christ spirit. We may be at the point of stressing out because of everything going on around us, like losing a job, a house, a vehicle, or contracting a disease. Because of what we are experiencing, we try to build our life on prayers, thus fortifying our faith in a God of sin and punishment who cannot help us because we see ourselves less than a God.

When duality and polarity energy is all that we know, and things go bad in our lives, it is natural for us to call upon a God who judges us for sin, and we become more restricted. And this is why many who are reading this book right now have done their bit trying to figure out God. Many of us have prayed and have concluded that God is a mystery. But these barriers have all been the revelation of the mind-soul, ego, and our physical body. Therefore, at our deepest level, we feel there is more to us than what we perceive.

My fellow angels, we have paid our debt to spirit, and now our own "I AM" Christ spirit wants to come in and welcome us home to a new consciousness of sovereignty. There are many of us here on earth who are not ready at this time to move toward integrating all aspects of themselves, let alone their own "I AM" Christ-spirit. There are many devoted people of the earth who believe they are part of God, but lack faith in themselves as God. These people only see themselves as a creation of God, and they only understand God as someone higher and grander than they are.

Therefore, my awakened friends, these many devoted people who refuse to awaken in this lifetime, *"the unfaithful, the depraved, murderers, the unchaste, sorcerers, idol worshipers, and deceivers of every sort,"* Revelation 21:8, who claim right is good and wrong is evil. Because of their fear, they will continue to fall into the *"burning pool of fire and sulfur,"* Revelation 21:8, (many more incarnations sowing and reaping) to work out their belief in it.

The *"angel who held the seven bowls and the last seven plagues,"* Revelation 21:9-10, is about those of us in human form that are ready and have the courage to open up our mind and ego to new truths, letting go of old, dogmatic concepts about God and Satan. When our "I AM" Christ spirit may join our mind and ego humanness in this lifetime, then *"the holy city of Jerusalem coming down out of heaven from God,"* Revelation 21:9-10, refers to our transfiguration to being only a human to a Christ in the flesh, as Yeshua did in his day.

The marriage of the Lamb (Son of Man) is depicted here in Revelation 21: 9-10, as a re-enactment of our marriage in higher consciousness (garden), except that our Revelation through many lifetimes undid our original separation from God and placed us back into our higher consciousness. However, with the exception that this new higher consciousness is filled with wisdom.

Perhaps the deep sleep of Adam is the deep sleep of humanity here on earth, forgetting his own "I AM" Christ spirit. It is about our outer, conscious mind and ego (Adam/human self) having a great deal of trouble learning how to communicate with our "I AM" Christ spirit because the vibratory frequency rate of our spirit is much higher than our mind and ego human consciousness. This is why John, the symbol of our human self/body consciousness, saw it descending out of heaven.

For example, the *"gleaming with splendor,"* Revelation 21:11, is our outer, human consciousness in the early stages attempting to integrate with our "I AM" Christ spirit. Why do we say this? It is that our "I AM" Christ spirit that is measured by its wisdom and what we humans learn through our many lifetimes. Therefore, the *"radiance like that of a precious stone,"* Revelation 21:11, refers to our outer human consciousness, and the intellectual capacity of our mind that is really a rare and extraordinary achievement.

With all that we have accomplished and worked out in our many past lifetimes and including this one, these experiences have become the greatest importance to our "I AM" Christ spirit, for we are indeed a *"precious stone."* If we would just learn to quiet our mind and ego and fall under the influence of our "I AM," we would feel that unconditional love. Thus, we all would become much kinder, gentler, more tolerant, more approachable, and not so judgmental toward our fellow man.

We, humans, fail to understand that we would not be giving up our mind or ego because our intellectual consciousness and human ego form will always be a valuable servant to our "I AM." The only thing that would happen no longer is that our mind and ego would not rule our consciousness, where we would lose sight about who we indeed are. It is our higher wisdom that should always be given precedence over our mind and ego because *"the wisdom from above is always unadulterated, peaceable, gentle, compliant, and full of mercy and good fruits, without inconsistency or artificial"* (James 3:17).

Just in words *"jasper, clear as a crystal,"* Revelation 21:11, pertains to our evolution and how we have grown from being a disaster to being an ornamental soul where we (while in the flesh) now sense our progress by way of the real truth, light, color, and becoming very intuitive to the wisdom (treasures) of spirit. From the vibrational energy of "two," the color of the rainbow transforms our split consciousness of positive and negative, male and female, into a multidimensional consciousness filled with wisdom (color). Thus, moving us beyond our five physical senses and far beyond the limits of time, space, and matter.

By opening up our eyes, heart, and mind and allow grace to enter, it becomes *"crystal clear"* that our multidimensional consciousness will learn to integrate with our outer ego physical consciousness, as they both become Christ-like. For example, Revelation 21:12-27 is all about the relevancy about our physical body, our mind-soul, ego, and our "I AM" Christ spirit.

The "massive *high wall*" pertains to the structure of our physical body, which in this case is the human skin. The *"twelve gates," the "twelve angels, and the "twelve tribes of Israel,"* Revelation 21:12, all refer to the twelve openings of the physical body, the seven endocrine glands, plus the five physical senses, and the twelve left-brain activities for which the names are inscribed. Thus, allow the Ascended Masters and I to illustrate:

Twelve Openings of the Physical Body (Gates)

1. Right Eye
2. Left Eye
3. Right Nostril
4. Left Nostril
5. Right Ear
6. Left Ear
7. Mouth
8. Sweat Glands
9. Anus
10. Urethra
11. Vagina
12. Nipples

Seven Endocrine Systems, Plus the Five Physical Senses and the Twelve Major System of the Physical Body (Angels)

1. Gonads
2. Leydig
3. Adrend
4. Thymus
5. Thyroid
6. Pineal
7. Pituitary
8. Tates
9. Smell
10. Touch
11. Sight
12. Hearing

Twelve Left Brain Activities (Tribes of Israel)

1. Understanding (Reuben)
2. Follower (Simeon)
3. Love/Service (Levi)
4. Spiritual Intelligence (Judah)
5. Forgetfulness (Manasseh)
6. Elimination (Naphtali)
7. Power (Gad)
8. Spiritual Ideals (Asher)
9. Hidden Wisdom (Issachar)
10. Abundance (Zebulun)
11. Authority (Joseph)
12. Faith/Trust (Benjamin)

Remember that Dan, the son of Jacob, was also named one of the Tribes of Israel. And yet, Dan was not mentioned in the Book of Revelation, and for that reason, man's judgments are part of both the left and right brain activity.

The *"three gates facing east, north, south, and west,"* Revelation 21:13, are referring to the twelve openings of the physical body, and they are as follows:

	East	North	South	West
1.	Right Eye	Mouth	Anus	Left Eye
2.	Right Ear	Nipples	Urethra	Left Ear
3.	Right Nostril	Sweat Glands	Vagina	Left Nostril

The work of Yeshua and what he laid out to his Disciples about the foundation of his ministry can be found in Revelation 21:14, as the essence found in the "twelve stumbling blocks" within humanity while incarnated on earth. It is through these stumbling blocks that introduce us to our customs, practices, and the twelve right-brain activities of the mind *("twelve apostles of the Lamb")*. These twelve right-brain activities relate to the twelve major systems of the physical body *("twelve courses of stone")*, and they are as follows:

Twelve Major Systems of the Physical Body and How They Associate with the Zodiac Ways of Seeking Experiences (Twelve Courses of Stones)

1. Endocrine, Aries (fire), rules the head: action personality
2. Immune, Taurus (earth), rules the neck: dependable personality
3. Respiratory, Gemini (air), rules the arms, lungs, and shoulders: communicating personality
4. Digestive, Cancer (water), rules the breast and stomach: sensitive personality
5. Muscular (front & rear), Leo (fire), rules the heart and back: proud personality
6. Nervous, Virgo (earth), rules the nervous system and intestines: detailed personality
7. Urinary, Libra (air), rules the skin, kidneys, and buttocks: balanced personality

8. Reproductive (male/female), Scorpio (water), rules the bladder and genitals: passionate personality
9. Lymphatic, Sagittarius (fire), rules the brain, heart, and blood: responsible personality
10. Integumentary, Capricorn (earth), rules the bones, knees, and skin: practical personality
11. Circulatory, Aquarius (air), rules the shins, ankles, and circulatory system: creative personality
12. Skeletal, Pisces (water), rules the feet: imaginative personality

Twelve Right-Brain Activities (Disciples/Apostles)

1. Justice/emotion (James Zebedee)
2. Desires/suffering/form (Judas)
3. Reasoning/intellect (Thomas)
4. Free Will/expression (Matthew)
5. Courage/responsibility (Andrew)
6. Choices/substance (James Alphaeus)
7. Power/passion/words (Philip)
8. Polarity/growth (John)
9. Purging (Jude/Thaddeus)
10. Universal Intelligence (Simon)
11. Imagination (Bartholomew)
12. Compassion/belief (Peter)

The Bible, especially Genesis and Revelation, are filled with numbers and is a mathematical formula to show the sacred geometry of humanity and why we are here on a three-dimensional earth. When we use numerology and the study of sacred geometry, we begin to understand the science of numbers and how they are reduced to their lowest value, except for 11 and 22, for these are known as master numbers.

It was our "I AM" Christ consciousness that caused and turned "nothingness" into "somethingness," and this was all done by us souled beings manipulating (arousing) the "universal omnipresent mind field of pure absolute neutral energy of light (Father-God)." As this is descriptive of the masculine part of all souled beings, through what is called sacred geometry. Without sacred geometry, there would be no physical body, earth, stars, planets, universes, rocks, trees, animals, or anything else that has form. Thus, the building blocks of space, time, earth, and physical manifestation, including the physical body, come from the geometric configurations of the "I AM" Christ spirit.

Channeling of the Ascended Masters on the Apocalypse

If we look into where materialism came from, we will find that mathematics is the key to everything. According to Tobias, who is one of our most extraordinary teachers, known as Tobit in the apocryphal Book of Tobit, and has since been reincarnated on earth, gave an informative session on the principles of sacred geometry. In that session, Tobias talked about sacred geometry as the "map" of the physical universe. He stated that "by understanding how the infinite God-Goddess is translated into mathematics and geometry, we would have a full understanding of how ideas are manifested into physical reality.

Tobias spoke of the four steps of creation as they apply to sacred geometry: (i) desire, (ii) ideas, (iii) attraction, and (iv) manifestation. As Tobias mentions, we first have nothingness, which is represented by zero (0). Then creation begins, and we have a dot (.), which defines nothingness as somethingness, and is represented by the number one (1). We add another dot (.) and create a line (.__.), which then defines energy and is represented by the number two (2).

Creation continues by adding another dot (.), which equals a dimension, and then we have a triangle Δ, which gives the first true definition of space and is signified by the number three (3). Add one more dot (.), and we have a square , which defines solidity, such as earth (matter), and completeness and balance. It is represented by the number and energy of four (4).

When we look at these "five sacred geometric building blocks," the zero (o) of nothing, the dot (.), the line (_), the triangle (Δ), and the square (□), we can see that everything that has a form of any kind, including time, space, man, and earth, are patterned with these five symbols. Of course, math is multidimensional as well, which means we can have a number from 0 through 9 in the positive as well as the negative, and in many interdimensional sides.

Therefore, when we apply the numbers of the 12 gates, 12 angels, 12 tribes of Israel, 12 courses of stones, and the 12 apostles of the Lamb, we have 12 X 5, which equals sixty (60). When we break down the number 60 to 6 + 0, it equals 6, and this 6 represents the last digit of the Beast's number 66(6). Thus, the number of humanity while on earth!

The first 6 of the number (6)66 represents the "six divine attributes of spirit" found in Revelation 1:4; 4:4 and Genesis 1:1-31, (the six days of creation). This first 6 is what makes us all a living God-Goddess, and a Christ. When we take the first six found in Revelation 13:18, and since it is also part of our mind-soul body, we add the "seventh attribute of silence" to it, and we come up with a total of seven (7). This is why the *"first six wings,"* in Revelation 4:8, is associated with the *"seven spirits before the throne"* found in Revelation 1:4.

When we take the seven subtle bodies of the mind in Revelation 2:1, known as the *"seven stars,"* and add these seven (7) subtle bodies to the six divine attributes (6), plus the day of silence as one (1), along with our polarity factor (positive and negative) like a number 1, we have 7 + 6 + 1 + 1, giving us a total of 15. Once we break down the number 15 to its primary value of 1 + 5, it equals the number of the second 6 in 6(6)6 found in Revelation 13:18. Thus, the number of the beast of 666 represents humanity here on earth.

The *"one who spoke,"* Revelation 21:15, is our own "I AM" Christ spirit telling us that we humans hold the authoritative power of Christ. Man has always considered the *"rod,"* Revelation 21:15, as a symbol of power, and we can see this throughout the Bible. Therefore, the power of the Christ is within and is expressing itself through us humans while we are in physical form. This gives us humans the mastery of understanding *(measuring)* our thoughts, beliefs, strengths, experiences, and our physical body. This also gives us a new life and a new body where we can go out and discover ourselves as a sovereign "I AM" God, Goddess, and a Christ in our own right.

We, humans, hold the *"golden measuring rod,"* Revelation 21:15, of the city (our memories), which is why our newly evolved physical body becomes one with our mind-soul and "I AM" Christ spirit. And, we also have the wisdom and understanding of the twelve openings (gates) of the physical body. Thus, confirming why we souled beings enclosed (wall) our "I AM" Christ spirit within a physical form to learn that wisdom.

And, once we understand the wisdom and our purpose in the flesh, we then come to a new choice where we become a standard to a new calling where one knows that one is Christ. Thus, letting go of this God of the earth and all that is external to the Christ consciousness. This would be like ridding ourselves of God to detach ourselves from any earthly concepts of some God speaking to us from an external level.

Let us remember that the word of the divine always comes from within ourselves. The acceptance of responsibility (our soul record and who is symbolized by Eve), has now overcome the projection of us working in a rebellious nature and has become the bride to our human self. Thus, the return to our own "I AM" Christ spirit is the *"golden measuring rod"* of understanding, responsibility, and wisdom.

After many incarnations, there are some of us here on earth now who are ready to evolve into a new light physical body that is in oneness with our "I AM" Christ spirit. And, *"the city being square"* describes the quality *(length)* of our mental level *(width/breath)* and our journey through the depths *(height)* of darkness *(bottom)* and back again to the light of remembering who we are *(top)*. We created such a journey for ourselves, and we became a grand angel where other souls that did not take the plunge into matter they look upon us like movie stars (Revelation 21:16).

This is confirmed by the word *"miles"* in Revelation 21:16, as it refers to our journey through many lifetimes not being aware of what was going on around us or how much was being expressed with thoughts of polarity. This kept our mind and ego preoccupied with something we are not.

The *"fifteen hundred miles (1500) in length, width, and height,"* Revelation 21:16, refers to our completeness in this lifetime because of our journey through physical form. Using sacred geometry, we have 1500 X 3 = 4500, and when broken down to its lowest value of 4 + 5 + 0 + 0 = 9, there is completeness because the only thing after nine (9) is ten (10). We achieve patience, wisdom, knowledge, understanding, and, most of all, responsibility by which we become a true creator God-Goddess in our own right. The number nine (9) is significant because:

1. It is the number for our completion in polarity energy.
2. The only thing that comes after 9 is 10, which means we come back to our original Oneness, but this time with a new oneness of understanding that we are a sovereign God, Goddess, and Christ in our own right.

Yes, when awakened, we do become the Alpha and the Omega, the first and the last, for we are the Father-Mother God-Goddess, and the Christ we have been seeking. The first zero (0), as we know, is about our "original Oneness" in higher understanding (garden), not understanding polarity, and that self is a Christ also. The second zero again is about us moving outside of the self and into nothingness, creating "all there is" today.

From studying Revelation 21:17, we can find this verse very interesting as it is reflecting us souled beings, in the beginning, moving outside of our "I AM" Christ spirit and into a three-dimensional consciousness, and then after many lifetimes, sowing and reaping, we move into a four-density consciousness. This brings us to a whole new meaning of the *"one hundred and forty and four cubits"* mentioned in Revelation 21:17 compared to the "one hundred and forty-four thousand marked from every tribe of Israel."

A *"cubit"* is an ancient unit of measure where the distance of something was measured from a person's elbow to the tip of the middle finger. Thus, the measurement of a cubit is approximately a foot and a half. The measurement of 144 is broken down to its lowest value, and since the 100,

40, and 4 are separated here in Revelation 21:17, they equate to the Beast found in Revelation.

When you take the first 100 cubits X 1.5 feet, its measurement is 1,500 feet. The 40 cubits X 1.5 feet comes in at a measurement of 600 feet, and the 4 cubits X 1.5 feet comes in at 60 feet. When we look at the first 1,500 feet using sacred geometry, it equals 1 + 5 + 0 + 0, which equals to the first 6 mentioned as the number of the beast. When you look at the 600 feet (40 cubits), it equals 6 + 0 + 0, thus equals to the second 6 found in the number of the beast. And, when you look at the last 60 feet (4 cubits), it equals to 6 + 0, which then equals the third 6 mentioned in the number of the beast.

It is through this formula from Revelation 21:17 where the confirmation comes to all numbers found in Revelation about the beast equals to humanity here on earth playing in a consciousness of a three-dimensional perception where our ego is in control of our creations. Thus, we are a slave to our ego beliefs and how our mind-soul carries those beliefs as if "all that we are is human." Once we get to understand who the beast is here on earth, then as you break down the beast number, 666 to 6 + 6 + 6, it equals 18, which then equates to 1 + 8 = 9, which is the number of completion.

When we awaken to this wisdom, because in metaphysical terms, "cubits" represents the "measurement of one's wisdom and understanding," this is when we integrate "all parts and pieces" of ourselves and enter into a new cycle, and we enter into the fourth and fifth-dimensional consciousness where we meet up with the Christ within ourselves. Please note: when the ascended masters speak of the fourth-density consciousness, they are speaking of the fourth and fifth-dimensional consciousness.

When we awaken to the New World of a fifth-dimensional consciousness, we leave behind the polarity pull of just dealing with positive and negative and into a new energy of "four." Thus, completeness and expansional understanding come into where we have completed our many incarnations paying off our debt to the Earth. Thus, instead of having the resistance of positive and negative playing on our consciousness acts, we begin working with a New Body of memories (the new city) and expansional energy of (i) positive, (ii) negative, (iii) Neutrality, and (iv) the Christ-Gnost or Crystalline Energy.

According to the measurement of humanity equaling to the number of the beast (666), the Masters have shown the measurement of how we humans have worked with the elements of fire, water, air, and earth (physical form); and with our spirit, mind-soul, and ego, all because of how we tied "free will" to our mental mind. In our fifth dimensional consciousness, there is the use of "free will," but it comes through as our "divine plan (will) in carrying out our choices to eventually become awakened to whom we truly are. Thus, it is best to learn to give up our "free will" of the mind and pass it on to our "divine plan" (will) of the Christ consciousness that we hold as our true identity.

This wisdom and understanding bring in the meaning behind Revelation 21:17, *"standard unit of measurement the angel used"* to describe humanity in our newly fifth-dimensional body here on earth, as the angel is our "free will" giving way to our "divine will."

This wisdom then explains the many incarnations, sowing, and reaping, giving us a whole new state of beingness where the *"gates of heaven (wall),"* Revelation 21:18, becomes a prototype or pattern and model *(jasper)* for others, just as Yeshua did over two thousand years ago. The prototype and the meaning of "jasper" are about those of us who are moving into a new understanding, wisdom, and an upgraded physical body that can hold the energy frequency of a fifth-dimensional earth.

The *"city being of pure gold,"* Revelation 21:18, represents you as God, Goddess, the Christ, and the creator, builder, and the maker of yourself and your physical body and experiences. Thus, you are filled with breathtaking wisdom that lifts you to a full new understanding of who you indeed are. If you will let go of the old, dogmatic system and open yourself up to your "I AM" Christ spirit, and allow this New Energy of Four (New Earth) to come into your life, while here on earth, you will become a Master, as Yeshua did, in your own right.

And this is confirmed with Revelation's *"clear as glass,"* as this represents you in your last days playing in a three-dimensional consciousness using polarity energy as your source in what you create to experience. It is you coming into a realization to let go of the belief that some God outside of you created you to follow his rules according to good and evil. It is about you allowing your wisdom to shine through, while in human form, showing your completeness as "I AM That I AM" God, Goddess, and Christ.

Chapter 41

WE ARE ETERNAL, INDESTRUCTIBLE AND UNCHANGEABLE

Why are we absolute, eternal, indestructible, and unchangeable? It is that we are the "I AM" God, Goddess, and the Christ that carries *"the foundation of the city wall"* spoken about in Revelation 21:19-20. We have a foundation of memories filled with breathtaking wisdom because of our many light and dark lifetimes. And, we are the most *"decorated"* human *with every precious stone,"* indicating and confirming that we are a God, Goddess, and Christ in our own right that is absolute, eternal, indestructible, and unchangeable. It is, and always has been, impossible to destroy our "I AM" Christ spirit no matter how far we fall into the pit of hell.

The *"twelve precious stones,"* Revelation 21:19-20, are symbolic of the "twelve active principles" of our basic divine patterns in being a Christ also, and they are as follows:

1. *Jasper:* Associated with the color of red. We all move through patterns of emotions such as anger and sexual activities that, in the end, move us into a whole new balance energy and in a new understanding of life.
2. *Sapphire:* Associated with the color of deep blue. This represents our intuitive understanding of our inner memories and the pattern of our soul journey through time and space, learning the results of those memories.

3. *Chalcedony:* Associated with the color of gray. This is a combination of black and white. This represents good and evil, right and wrong, positive and negative, male and female, polarity at its best. It is about seeing the light and dark, God and Satan, as two different energies, and yet they are one, like our outer, human consciousness evolving to a higher understanding where one's shadow (dark side) is part of our Oversoul, the "I AM" Christ.
4. *Emerald:* Associated with the color green. It is also associated with vegetation and therefore represents our evolutional growth patterns playing in polarity, which have allowed us to learn about energy and life. Green can also symbolize a hard, bluish, metallic element that represents a resistant, sickly green, thus symbolizing our jealousy, judgment, and fear.
5. *Sardonyx:* Associated with the colors of light orange, brown, and white chalcedony. This represents our power to perceive impressions through the five physical senses and the endocrine system. In the end, it brings enlightenment, self-knowledge, wisdom, and our "I AM" Christ spirit (the bride) into understanding our creations.
6. *Carnelian:* Associated with the color of reddish translucence. It represents us, humans, allowing some light to pass through from our Christ spirit. But, only in a scattered way that lacks organization so our purpose and the answering of the question: "Who am I?" cannot be answered until we are ready.
7. *Chrysolite:* Associated with yellow or green. It is a silicate of magnesium and iron found in lava, thus representing self-confidence and the perceptiveness toward the external and how everything evolves.
8. *Beryl:* Associated with white, yellow, pink-red, green, and blue. It represents our intuition in being self-confident and perceptive (yellow), having emotional feelings of love and anger (pink-red), having the vitality of life and how we evolve (green), and being self-preoccupied by being shy and quiet around groups (blue).
9. *Topaz:* Associated with the colors of transparent brown with a yellowish variety of quartz. Being colorless or transparent represents wisdom, knowledge, great understanding, and being very intelligent.
10. *Chrysoprase:* Associated with bright green quartz that is a variety of grayish stones. It represents us humans moving our consciousness past the illusion of polarity (grayish stones) to where we understand our greener pastures of heaven here on earth.

11. *Hyacinth:* Associated with fragrant, cultivated plants or flowers of pink, white, or blue. This represents our cultivated consciousness carrying within it, even though everything is understood as illusionary, a rosy outlook that will bring in our "I AM" Christ spirit and our realization.
12. *Amethyst:* Associated with the colors of violet and purple. It represents our human importance here on earth and how we have the authority (power) and the wisdom to see ourselves free of our union with playing opposites.

The *"twelve gates"* shown previously in Revelation 21:12 are those of the "twelve openings" of our physical body. Therefore, they are the *"twelve pearls"* here for Revelation 21:21, as each of them represents the wholeness of the self, spirit, mind-soul, and ego-personality behavior patterns, as described in Revelation 21:19:20 above.

The *"street of the city was of pure gold, transparent as glass,"* Revelation 21:21 is symbolic of how our journey of many lifetimes playing with the forces of polarity has brought to us a whole new expansional energy where we have the wisdom, understanding, and knowledge to become a sovereign God, Goddess, and Christ in our own right. Thus, *"transparent of the glass,"* Revelation 21:21, has the same meaning as Revelation 21:18 above.

While reviewing Revelation 21:22-23, we can see that our "I AM" Christ spirit can now speak to us, while in human form, at this time, and clarifying that our multi-expansional consciousness needs no direction or control by others in expressing the glory of who we indeed are at our core.

The *"no temple in the city,"* Revelation 21:22-23, is those of us coming into memory, while in the flesh, no longer needing artificial intelligence (sun), or that of our outer mind (moon) to shed light upon the idea of polarity energy as being all that is. The *"glory of our "I AM" Christ spirit (God)"* will always bring us the light of a universal intelligence that far surpasses the idea of polarity and sin. This causes an understanding to come through where we are now of pure spirit and neutrality. This means we can now create any desire, idea, or belief without the description of polarity is our purpose.

When we overcome our ego personality aspects and integrate them with our "I AM" Christ spirit, we become open to multitudes of memory cells (nations) that are now evolving (walking) to a higher understanding (light) of our first cause and the reason we separated ourselves from our true essence. Therefore, those of us who are awakened, and to our many personality aspects of the past (kings of the earth, Revelation 21:24), have completed the promise to our "I AM" to become one with the influences of our mind-soul, ego, and the New Earth. And, because of this new understanding about who we are, all parts and pieces of us will bring us the wisdom of their experiences. What a *"treasure"* this is!

The *"gates,"* in Revelation 21:25, relates again to our physical body openings through which we all receive the motivation and the act of experiencing our ideas, beliefs, and choices. These "gates" can act as building blocks or memory openings in receiving the impulses necessary for us to respond in an awakening state. We have two choices! We can shut these memories off by not accepting the truth that we are Christ, or we can accept ourselves as a Christ.

However, we can never shut out those memory ego aspects where we are a Christ also because sooner or later, we (in some lifetime) will remember them. If we accept the latter, then there can be no more ignorance (no night) in which to receive the prompting of our "I AM" Christ spirit to act on our behalf. Once awakened to our Christ spirit, we will experience and possess *(wealth)* wisdom, understanding, and knowledge *(treasures)* because of our memories *(nations)* and how they have served and honored us; therefore, the opportunity to become one with our new expansional consciousness is high.

And, once we are awakened to this new energy of four (new earth), nothing of polarity (unclean), good or bad, right or wrong, positive or negative, will ever be allowed to enter our manifestations other than what we create with our multi-expansional consciousness. *"Only those will enter whose names are written in the Lamb's book of life,"* Revelation 21:26-27, and as discussed in Revelation 3:5, are our memories of the lessons and wisdom we have learned journeying through many lifetimes now being understood from our conscious level. Therefore, the name we hold in this lifetime will never be erased from our memory (Book of Life), and therefore will be acknowledged forevermore in the presence of our own "I AM" Christ-spirit.

Once awakened to whom we are, our outer mind and ego, symbolized by the false prophet (our unawakened mind) and the Beast (our ego), will no longer be part of our Book of Life (our soul record), for they will have died (integrated). This becomes amazing to us, even though we are still part of the earth, for the *"end times"* are only about us putting an end to our rebellious nature and those old, dogmatic beliefs about good and evil that we have held for so long. Our new beginning is the awakening to being a Christ, just like our brother Yeshua did.

Chapter 42

THE CHRIST RETURN IS NOW FULFILLED

Can we trust that the prophecy of Christ's second coming is being fulfilled today because it has? A story might help us understand the wisdom behind the second coming of Christ. The story is about Archangel Michael and us humans. When I first read this story, channeled by Tobias through Geoffrey Hoppe of Crimson Circle in a Shroud dated June 1, 2002, "the Ascension Series," I was surprised when Tobias made it known that we humans go from a "no identity to a new identity." However, the more I thought about it, the more I realized it made good sense.

According to Master Tobias, when we souled beings first left our oneness of consciousness long ago, Archangel Michael gave us the "sword of truth." To elaborate: Michael is the archangel that we humans work with at many levels of our lives because, when the "Order of the Arc" was formed for us souls to enter physical earth, it was Michael who helped train and prepares us for our journey on earth.

First, to keep the story straight, Archangel Michael has never taken on human form. Michael is an archetypical angel, meaning that he is an angel who came from the collectiveness of many souls. Therefore, Archangel Michael, along with other soul group consciousnesses, helped create the template of earth and our human body. Therefore, Michael became our training instructor before we left the Order of the Arc to come to earth.

Since Archangel Michael is the angel of truth, then his name became synonymous with the "sword of truth" that Michael used on Satan. This "sword of truth" became the symbol of our journey to carry out our belief in polarity, good and bad, through many lifetimes. Therefore, the "sword of truth" became part of everyone's consciousness and biology before we even embarked on our journey to find the truth. Even though we play out our belief in good and evil in the flesh, the "sword of truth" has been with us ever since we left the Order of the Arc, disguised by what we all call "the law of cause-and-effect," or what we find in the Bible as "sowing and reaping."

According to the Bible and religion, Archangel Michael fought Satan in a big battle in heaven that finally led to him throwing Satan out along with his troubled followers. However, according to Tobias' story about Archangel Michael, the teachings are somewhat mixed up because the account of Satan being kicked out of heaven is really about us humans who left the Order of the Arc by agreement, and not because we were kicked out for disobeying God.

What has been called heaven and the garden in the Bible is nothing more than us souled beings, in the beginning, working out of a consciousness of oneness. However, this oneness we all were experiencing wasn't enough to learn who we were or our purpose to learn wisdom. So, we souled beings split our consciousness into two parts, a mental-soul and an ego-consciousness to feel independent from our "I AM" consciousness.

We souls wanted to experience both sides of the coin, one side being a Christ and the other side playing with polarity energy where we could play the opposite of being Christ. Thus, the "order of the arc" came into existence where 144,000 Archangels became the major influencer for each of the 144,000 souled group families. Thus, Archangel Michael became the archetypical angel that got the job to prepare us souls that wanted to incarnate on earth to play with polarity energy where we could experience opposites, good and evil.

However, when we souls were ready to enter earth for the very first time, Michael gave us the "sword of truth," which is symbolic of karma, or sowing and reaping, to learn the wisdom of our choices. Therefore, no one was thrown out of heaven. We souls chose to leave heaven (the oneness of consciousness) and come to earth in a physical body to find the answer to the question, "Who am I?" And, to experience our choices to learn wisdom.

The battle with Satan was not real because Satan is not real. He just symbolizes our rebellious ego-consciousness at work studying and learning responsibility for our choices. The real story is about our departure from the "Order of the Arc" and coming to earth in a physical form to learn the wisdom of our choices. It is each of our responsibility to find the real truth behind the belief patterns of polarity, and how those patterns have cut us off from our own "I AM" Christ spirit.

The story will conclude once we awaken, after many lifetimes playing with polarity energy that cut ourselves off from our own "I AM" Christ spirit, by using sowing and reaping as the method to find our way back to our true identity. Once we came to earth, and after many lifetimes experiencing with polarity energy, Archangel Michael, with his sword of truth (us humans sowing and reaping), send Archangel Gabriel, the angel of awakening, to help us become ready to release the old ways of polarity living, and then come to an energetic moment in finding the truth that we are God, Goddess, and the Christ.

When we learn to let go of the old, dogmatic ways of polarity living, we come into a realization that there was no darkness or avoid (abys) that we fell into; it was just us souls passing through experiences to learn wisdom. Therefore, it is time to pause and feel this polarity energy of positive and negative that has been around us since the time we left the Order of the Arc.

And to feel our real identity, the energy of "two" needs to change to an energy of "four." As we humans are the second coming of Christ, coming into the flesh body and claiming our sovereignty and our freedom as a Christ also. There are many here on earth who are fighting this second coming of Christ, as most of them are the ones who claim to be the most religious. This is easily seen because we can see it through human consciousness and the way they want to hang onto the old ways while others want to let go and move forward.

According to Tobias, the chaos we are seeing is "polarity flipping back and forth between wanting to be free and wanting to hang on." Just by being conscious of what is going on around us, we can see how people are trying to maintain their old, false identities instead of allowing their new identities to come in. This happens because people feel deep within their hearts that they are losing something when all that's happening is that they are losing who they thought they were.

The time has come to trust ourselves as being divine, for we carry the "sword of truth" within our consciousness. It has always been there, waiting for us to open up to it. Man continues to wait for some great sign about Yeshua's second coming, not realizing Christ is already at the front door of their consciousness. Therefore, you either see Christ and feel it, or you don't! Most people do not want to see Christ or feel it because it means taking full responsibility for themselves and everything they are experiencing.

The sword of truth (symbolized by karma) will always guide us in the steps we need to take to achieve our freedom and sovereignty as a God, Goddess, and a Christ in our own right. This means we may go through some physical issues, wondering what is going on. However, the panic we may be feeling is nothing more than the beginning of remembering that we can free ourselves from what we are experiencing. No one can relieve us from our suffering but the self!

Master Tobias said, "The more we continue to look at our image in the mirror, the more it will not feel like us. The image in the mirror will begin to not resonate with us anymore." So, I took Tobias's advice and researched this out for myself. And, I found this, before retiring to my bed one night, I looked at myself in the mirror, and the more I looked, the more I felt strange about the image not being me, just as Tobias had said!

I noticed that the image I was looking at did not echo the same beliefs that I instinctively aspire to know. And, since then, I have done it several times. And now, I see no reflection of my old self, because my identity has changed where I only see the Christ within me. I have noticed that people who used to be close no longer seem to be part of my life anymore. And, out of nowhere, other people have become part of my life.

Why did these people stay away? It is because these people who ignore me now represent some of the energies that came from my old identity, the one that believed in a person being good or evil. This is when I went from seeing myself in the mirror as I thought I was to a new identity that I hardly recognized. The only thing I can attribute this to is the fact that my old identity is leaving or has left, indeed disappearing, and yet I am not disappearing. I am only going through a change in energy, consciousness, and identity.

Now, when I look in the mirror, all that I see is the real me. So, like Master Tobias, I challenge you to look in the mirror, and when you do, look intently at yourself. See and feel whether it seems like you in the mirror. If it does not, then you, too, are moving from "no identity" to a "new identity." Perhaps it is the rapture that everyone seems to seek. This means that the image is reflected "no identity" because it is an illusion. The real identity (true self) is the one creating the image (human lifetime).

Once we realize the falseness of our human identity, a human with intellect and an ego that gives us a feeling that we are only human, we build on the real identity that knows it is the creator (mirror) without an image (reflection), as this is seen in Revelation 22:1-2, *"river of life-giving water."* This signifies the inspiration of our "I AM" Christ spirit giving life, sovereignty, and complete authority back to the true self in the flesh.

This also means that our true identity is neither light nor dark, good or evil, male or female, but is of a Christ spirit and consciousness only. The *"water of life"* (our "I AM" Christ spirit) has cleansed our soul memories through the baptism of material life, thus washing away our belief in an external God who judges us based on polarity living and who only caters to those that worship him. Therefore, the water of baptism symbolizes letting go of our erroneous thinking about polarity and our unworthiness to being a Christ also. This, my friends, is the first step in recognizing the "sword of truth" (the sowing and reaping) is the method to return to our real identity.

Because many of us have come into an awareness and a realization that we are the individualized portion of the whole (throne of God, Revelation 22:1-2), our separated ego (Lamb) is now one with our mind and our "I AM" Christ. Even with this oneness, we feel deep within; we still remain a spirit bound to our physical body to finish our old way of thinking. And, once this occurs, our mind and our ego learn of this New Expansional Truth that flows from the "river of life," and that is when we understand everything in a whole new light.

And, when we read in Revelation 22:1-2, *"down the middle of its street,"* it means that our own "I AM" Christ spirit is in the middle of every lifetime we have had, including all our created acts that we have manifested and experienced since leaving the first creation (the Oder of the Arc) long ago. And, in Revelation 22:1-2, *"on either side of the river grew the tree of life that produces fruit twelve times a year,"* the tree appears to mean that now, because of some of us coming into an awakening in this lifetime, the "I AM" Christ within can show up in either side of the mind, the left or right brain hemisphere, and then act as one with the mind.

The number "twelve" refers to spiritual fulfillment, just as the twelve stones in 1 Kings 18:31 represent the twelve most important nerve centers in the physical body. The "tree" signifies the connecting link between our earthly body and our "I AM" Christ spirit, the formless and the formed. The "tree of life" is in the midst of our physical body, and the roots of the "tree of life" are centered in the solar plexus region, symbolized by the twelve divisions of the body functions shown in Revelation 7. This means our body functions are now spiritualized to yield one fruit, the love for the self, which means that the split consciousness or brain activity has been healed.

The *"leaves of the trees serve as medicine for the nations,"* Revelation 22:1-2, as the "leaves" are the many belief patterns that we inherited genetically while journeying through many lifetimes playing with the "Tree of Knowledge of Good and Evil," or polarity. And now, the wisdom (medicine) accumulated because of these belief patterns (leaves) has become part of our memories (nations) for discerning the real truth in this lifetime.

Remember the branch (the outer, ego personality) that separates itself from the "Tree of Life" (our Christ-spirit or the real self) will wither away and die (closed off from knowing one is Christ). This means that the belief coming from our defiant ego-personalities of old do cut us off from the real source of supply (the Tree of Life). That is why we revolve in a mental whirlpool of rising water, where dominant thoughts are always based on good and evil, birth and death, and our emotions.

The "Tree of Life" is the inherent life of the physical body, and it is symbolized by the nerves and the spinal column. The spinal column represents the tree trunk. The nerves, which carry the living waters, are the branches, and the leaves are the tree's history (memories). Every month, a change of the living waters takes place under divine order; thus, the twelve divisions of the body functions are becoming spiritualized. Most of us are kept from this precious healing and life-giving fruit only because we (through the mind) look at polarity as being our truth.

As one can see in Revelation 22:3-4, the presence of our "I AM" Christ spirit is putting us in a perfect state of consciousness because our memories of past lifetimes are now ready to open up to us about polarity thinking and believing. Thus, the declaration, *"nothing accursed will be found,"* relates to the union between our ego physical consciousness and our "I AM" Christ spirit.

Also mentioned in Revelation 22:3-4, the conflict between our Cain (Ego) and Abel (higher awareness) consciousness, as well as our many ego aspects of the past, becomes a burden to us because it keeps us asleep to the truth. However, if we have been paying attention, our Abel consciousnesses have opened the door for those ego aspects of us to integrate with our "I AM." Yeshua and the Ascended Masters say this because the *"throne of God and the Lamb,"* Revelation 22:3-4, is about our mental mind and our many past ego-personality aspects that have already returned. At least enough of them where some of us can now sit with our "I AM" (throne) and become a sovereign God and Goddess in our own right.

And, once we realize that sin and polarity were created by us to learn wisdom and not some God above us, then the prophecy of Christ coming to earth has been fulfilled. The fulfillment is with Revelation 22:3-4, *"his servants will worship him,"* as this reminds us that many of our ego personalities of the past are now ready to listen (*worship*) to us, as our superego of realization today has become the forefront of our light and dark ego-personality aspects of the past; where we have no more memory of doing bad things because they all have been forgiven and cleansed of their sins, via sowing and reaping.

And now, these ego personality aspects of our past "*will look upon his* (or our) *face, and our name*" of today and will be written on their (our) "*foreheads*" (or our consciousness) as the coming savior. Once your super ego-personality aspect in this lifetime becomes awakened to your own "I AM" Christ spirit, all of your other ego aspects will no longer need to be in ignorance (night) because all that you and your other ego aspects will ever need is to feel your connection to this universal intelligence. That is where we will learn all intelligence comes from "all that is in consciousness," and how you can tap into it, for you are the Lord of Lords and the God and Goddess you seek (Revelation 22:5).

The idea of "*forever and ever,*" Revelation 22:5, refers to the limitations of our outer, human consciousness mind and how the split of consciousness attempts to find a beginning and an end to all things. However, we all know that the mind is said to be the highest level of thinking and intelligence we have on earth. And yes, the mind is incredible in what it can produce. But, as we move into the New Energy of Four (New Earth) and our new identity as a fifth-dimensional being, the desire to move beyond the mind, and the intelligence it holds, becomes stronger. The greatest blockage we all have in meeting up with our "I AM" Christ spirit is our strong belief in polarity, sin, and punishment.

Our "I AM" Christ spirit is wise, delicate, and enduring, and it does not care about our intellect or the occupation we carry out in the flesh. As for myself, I am not what one would call a brilliant person intellectually. But I am brilliant when it comes to knowing my Christ spirit. It is this intellectual stuff that tends to bog us down, and we get stuck in the mind thinking that we are better than another because of education.

For example: "*And he said to me,*" refers to our superego personality of today telling our mental mind to trust ourselves as the "*Lord, the God of prophetic spirits,*" Revelation 22:6. Remember, John was shown, "*what must happen soon,*" Revelation 1:1), which means that John, like ourselves, and from his superego level, was very close to his own "I AM" Christ spirit, as some of us are today. Therefore, John represents a higher version of himself, which means we, too, will learn the mystery of God through the experiences and stories of our many ego-personality aspects of the past ("*prophetic spirits*").

Channeling of the Ascended Masters on the Apocalypse

Everything foretold to us has been from the many ego aspects of our past, symbolized by the old prophets of the Bible. To live life upon the earth is to prophesy because the way we live and look at our belief systems upon the earth determines the way we measure and work with our consciousness. Since we are programmed to get caught in polarity thinking and see ourselves as sinners, we tend to get stuck in the mind. Therefore, we have a hard time moving beyond the mind, not realizing how small the mind is compared to the overall consciousness of our "I AM" Christ consciousness.

The study of the human mind deals with just the human self; it knows only this dimension and how to work with it. The mind tries to relate everything it experiences to the environment, family, friends, and the experiences it encounters along the way. This is why, when we cannot find a solution to our problems, we get very frustrated. And this is why new energy is here, now on earth, because the old system of polarity cannot satisfy the needs of our evolving consciousness.

My friends, we have tried religion, we have prayed, and committed to what is good. We have even tried visualization, but none of it worked because it all came from the limitations of our mind and our view on how we see things. And, this method has held us all in a hypnotic state for a long time. Therefore, the ego aspects of our past must be allowed to come to us through memory, asking us to free them from their stuck energy.

Therefore, *"Behold, I am coming soon,"* Revelation 22:7, as one would think that Yeshua is coming soon. However, according to Yeshua himself, he is not coming in the way our religions have taught us. The deeper meaning here is about our super ego personality ascending to an awareness where some of us, while in the flesh, come into an awakening that we are the Christ coming into our mind and human ego body consciousness to integrate all the parts and pieces of ourselves. When we come to understand and trust ourselves as the God, Goddess, and the Christ, our superego of today ascends into a New Energy of safety, abundance, healing, and joy while still on earth.

This is the very definition of the Harvest! When *"blessed is the one who keeps the prophetic message of this book,"* Revelation 22:7, it is referring to some of us in this lifetime learning that each of us is the whole book. The collectiveness of all parts and pieces of us becomes the message, the whole book, and the one "coming soon." Ever since we came to earth and took up a physical body, everything has been an illusion. Thus, the purpose of our defiant beastly ego nature (symbolized by Satan) has been to keep us from getting too comfortable in our illusions of many lifetimes, because we knew that we could get stuck in them by seeing them as real.

We have gone through many lifetimes cursing Satan for our suffering when all the time, this suffering has been moving us along so we can move past the illusion of polarity being real. We create our riches, and we see ourselves as being devoted to God, and then who comes along and bursts our bubble? It is the energy of Satan (our beastly ego) that is setting a new course for us to follow. We need this Satan energy to come along and push us further along, so we do not get trapped in our illusions.

This is why some people begin life in deprived situations, and then after they seem to get everything right in their life, cancer or some major disease comes along and knocks them down. We try to perfect the illusion without realizing that we are getting deeper and deeper into it, ultimately making it harder to get out of it, which is why Satan (our beastly defiant ego) comes along and shoots us down over and over again until we awaken from to what is happening.

When John falls to worship at the feet of the angel, Revelation 22:8, his action symbolizes that we too can, and most probably will fall under the spell of our mind, free will, and our ego for a while before making the final shift to a higher understanding. Consider how often we say and believe what Yeshua said over two thousand years ago, but our actions demonstrate very little faith in following his example as being a Christ in the flesh. We can see this happening, as John did when most worshipped Yeshua instead of following his example.

As described in Revelation 22:10, *"do not seal up the prophetic words of this book, for the appointed time is near."* Do not seal up the messages coming from your many ego-personality stories and memories of the past, because the time for measuring their deeds (choices) are over. The experiences they have endured have given you an awe-inspiring ego personality that can run havoc if you don't learn to view them as previous lifetimes that had paid their debt by sowing and reaping. Or, if you will integrate them with you in your present state today, they would be willing to come home to you, their creator, and become one with you.

Revelation 22:11 is about accepting yourself for who you indeed are, a Christ in your own right where you now accept others for the way they are, and without judgment or prejudice. It is about accepting everything and everyone, even those who do great harm, with compassion and unconditional love.

Most people are very much absorbed in their daily lives, and they are just trying to survive. They see themselves as victims, and they don't even realize what is going on around them. The religious become more religious, the wicked more wicked, the righteous more righteous, and the rich become richer, as they all are playing with the system (harlot) and the fears it generates. And, because of this fear, they see themselves as needing a savior.

Many of us can see right now how people are colliding with each other because they believe the rich, the church, the government, the businesses, and that God should take care of them. Oh, they pretend to honor each other, but behind closed doors, they curse and make fun of those with beliefs different from their own. These people feel right and righteous, thinking God and their education is behind them; but they don't realize that God and their education, because of time and space, turned into one religion being better than another, or one race being better than another and that politicians being better than common folk because of their intellect.

By honoring people and allowing them to be who they are without judgment or prejudice, we become one of the "haves" that gets more. The world right now is being set up for the "haves" to have more and the "have-nots" to have less because the "have-nots" don't believe in taking responsibility for their own stories. People are afraid they will not be taken care of; therefore, politicians, religion, businesses, and family (the system) intoxicate them, making them feel comfortable and secure with their talk of knowledge.

Because of this, we will see more separation between those who understand their place in the illusion and others who hang on tight to their old ways of doing things. The more the "have-nots" collide with each other, the more interesting things will happen. This clash will cause some to reassess themselves and what they believe to be true. For instance, when people fear the dark and death, and how they refuse to talk about it. It comes from the belief the dark and their death will attract Satan. Thus, they will be taken over by Satan. This type of belief should tell us the fallacy of their beliefs.

There are others who have moved beyond polarity, and those who still believe that Yeshua is their God and will come and save them. The ones who say they are from the light talk about how bad things have become because of the dark, and they want the dark to be wiped out. Those who believe that Yeshua will come and do this for them do not realize that the dark is as much a part of the light as they are part of the dark. Because of this misunderstanding, those who say they are the light of the world will feel a real explosion of energy within themselves that, in the end, allows them to clear some of this old, stuck energy.

Know that sooner or later, the light has to give way to the dark because of the misconception about the dark. The more the light (righteous) concentrates on who is right and who is wrong, the more prominent will be the explosion of energy that will take place within them. This also applies to us humans as a group consciousness on earth. Overlooking this fact that the light and dark are one energy can cause poverty, illness, war, and suffering. Therefore, there is no God of light or Satan of darkness, because all energy is one.

"*Behold, I am coming soon,*" Revelation 22:12 is an expression that comes from our own Christ spirit showing us preference in receiving our "I AM" sooner than later. "*Coming soon*" refers to our "I AM's" desire to be part of our human consciousness. All that we have to do to receive it is open up to the real true self, integrate the pretend ego selves, and then release them with love and respect for what they did in helping us find the real Christ, the self.

Know that we humans are the "*Alpha and the Omega, the first and the last, the beginning and the end,*" Revelation 22:13 because we souled beings were ordained as a Christ before the earth ever existed. We are the savior of the self, not Yeshua. It was our "I AM" that led us to create many ego-personality aspects to come to earth as the first Adam. Therefore, it was us humans that were among the first to leave the Order of the Arc to come to earth. And now, we are the first to take the next step toward becoming a sovereign God, Goddess, and Christ in our own right. However, we must choose it!

Also, know that you today are not the same you that lived in those previous lifetimes. That past, yous were born to play out certain stories for your soul to register and record the wisdom and the experiences in those lifetimes. It did not matter what those other you's from the past experienced, good or evil, because it made no difference to your "I AM" or Oversoul. Therefore, the superego you in this lifetime has no sins to pay for, all that you are simply feeling are the guilt and shame associated with what the other past you's experienced.

We do suffer today because of the good and evil committed by our many past ego personalities. Why? Because mostly they all have sowed and reap for what they did, and therefore we should not be suffering because of our past. So, why are so many of us suffer in this lifetime? We suffer today because of those ego personalities of our past lifetimes still hang onto the belief that they are unworthy of forgiveness because of what they did. And, therefore, feel that they should suffer more.

This then makes us today, in this lifetime, feel alone and separated from our "I AM" Christ spirit. And this is why we are going through our present experience, suffering, and/or healing. For example, I have had hundreds of lifetimes playing out many different characters, and some of those lifetimes, I was a monk, a priest, a rabbi, a Chinese warrior, and many more. But, in one particular lifetime, over two thousand years ago, I was born a fisherman named Simon Bar-Jonah, the son of Jonah. And later, in that same lifetime, I became a disciple to Yeshua Ben-Joseph, more known as Jesus today.

During my lifetime as Simon Peter, the Rock, I had a personality of action, and my actions often lacked a full understanding of Christ. My personality was such that if I believed something had to be said or done, no matter if I understood the situation fully or not, I said and did it anyway. For example: When I proclaimed Yeshua (Jesus) as the Messiah, the Son of God, and also when I appealed to protect Yeshua (Jesus) with my life, it was all based on my lack of understanding of the true meaning behind what Yeshua (Jesus) was trying to do.

As Peter, the disciple, I showed a lot of courage in that lifetime, but to the point of being arrogant with my faith. So, I spoke freely on a lot of things that I did not fully comprehend, especially when it came to Yeshua's (Jesus) intent about presenting Christ. My Peter aspect misunderstood the true meaning of faith despite Yeshua (Jesus) calling him the "rock."

During that lifetime as a disciple of Yeshua, there were many times I lacked faith in myself, and in the Christ Yeshua spoke about. Thus, deep down within my soul, I lacked having faith in Yeshua and the Christ he was presenting. It is the same with all of us who claim they have incredible faith in God, and yet, when we are most desperate and afraid, our faith succumbs to fear.

This fear is known to many of us today, as it did when the character I played as Peter, the rock, and how he lost faith when he denied knowing Yeshua after he was arrested. Thus, Peter's fear that day was shown to be his weakness by way of self-preservation. We all think we know where we stand with our faith and what we believe as our truth, but in a moment of fear, all of what we stand for can disappear very fast all because of not knowing or understanding the real Christ.

Many of our religious leaders today are proud to show off their faith, their intellect, and their understanding of Christ. And, it was the same during Peter's time when Yeshua called him "the rock." Peter, in his days being a disciple of Yeshua, thought that his name represented strength, faith, and leadership, and it made him feel more important and superior to others, even though, in Yeshua's eyes, all of his disciples were considered important.

However, Peter thought he was more important than the others. After all, Peter's thought process was that he was the first to proclaim Yeshua as the true Son of God and the Messiah who was to come. As most can see, during that lifetime as Simon Peter, I placed myself above others, thinking that I was special and incapable of lacking faith. But we all know that Simon Peter, the rock, sank to the bottom when he denied knowing Yeshua to save his own life.

As I look back at my lifetime as Simon Bar-Jonah (Peter), the son of Jonah, today, and what has since happened to me in this lifetime, I can understand now that the actions of my character as Peter has helped me to ascend in this lifetime as a Christ also. Therefore, Peter's failures, successes, an encounter with Yeshua, and his experiences as a disciple, have helped me in this lifetime to gain the wisdom needed to redeem and integrate all that "I AM" as a Christ, as did Yeshua in his day over two thousand years ago.

Because of that lifetime as Simon Peter, I now understand Yeshua's mission was to proclaim to all those that would listen that we, too, are a Christ as much as he was a Christ. And, he showed us all by placing all of his faith in himself being a Christ in the flesh. I have also learned that Yeshua is not my Messiah or is he yours, because together, we humans, are the Messiah coming to an awakening where we know now that we too are Christ, thus equal to God and the Goddess. Thus, having no fear of being called an enemy of Christ (Matt. 16:22–25).

When we have complexities and difficulties in life, the first thing we do is connect to our emotional side of the mind to handle the situation, which means we connect to the "tree of polarity" instead of the "tree of life." And, when most become overwhelmed with fear because of our bills, job, health, children, life, or the world, then the real you, the Christ deep within, disappears. The fear that comes in takes over our outer consciousness and becomes an adversary (Anti-Christ) to the "I AM" Christ within.

However, once we learn to get our bearings straight about who Christ is, after many lifetimes of sowing, reaping, and learning, we are then blessed with the *"washed robes"* (our many past ego-personality lifetimes), as they have helped us *"enter the city"* (our memories) through the physical body. Thus, delivering us to the *"tree of life,"* Revelation 22:14, where we awaken to the self being Christ. Therefore, to obtain this robe, it requires us to trust in the full impact of what Yeshua was trying to achieve over two thousand years ago.

Remember, however, that adverse energy comes from polarity thinking and the Tree of Knowledge of Good and Evil. And, the only way to overcome it is to realize that it has all been part of a divine plan for us to understand life and all the light and dark, good and evil, that comes with it. Now, here we are today, and our own "I AM" Christ spirit wants to integrate with us, even though, after all that we had done throughout our many lifetimes, our "I AM" Christ spirit had forgiven them and us when we left higher consciousness eons ago. But, because of fear and the shame we feel deep within because of what we did, most of us continue to reject, misunderstand, and deny the real Christ, as I did as Peter.

Therefore, we continue to look outside of ourselves for Christ to come and heal us, help with our abundance, give us joy and freedom, and, most of all, forgive and save us. Because of this belief, our mind-soul, ego, and physical body believe that anything outside of us must be foreign. Thus, our ego of today keeps out the real Christ and Messiah because of fearing to follow a false prophet.

Perhaps now you see that although Simon Peter failed in faith, his wisdom in that lifetime came through and helped me in this lifetime to integrate all that I am as a Christ also instead of me looking for Yeshua, the Christ, to come and save me. Hence, my friends, all my other ego aspects, fulfilled their destinies in each of their lifetimes, as did Simon Peter. And, because they were never created to ascend in those particular lifetimes, it is for me in this lifetime that will bring together all my parts and pieces of me, including my aspect as Simon Peter, and become Christ in the flesh. However, in truth, none of these aspects are me today; even the super aspect of "Terry" is not me. And yet, they are all me!

Most of us have been taught that the way to heaven is to follow the guidelines set by our religious leaders who declare themselves to be the official interpreters between man, God, and Christ. Hence, the word *"dogs, sorcerers, the murderers, idol-worshipers, and who love to practice deceit,"* Revelation 22:15, refers to one who is faithful and devoted to group-consciousness and individuals, such as religions, priests, ministers, scholars, evangelists, and some shrewd intellectuals who claim to understand the supernatural forces and how they relate to God, Goddess, and Christ's miracles.

From my understanding, religion follows certain doctrines about God, Jesus, the disciples, and how the prophets have come to be spokespersons for God. Religious collaborators and shrewd intellectuals mentioned in the previous paragraph claim to know what people need and what is good for them because they believe they understand the thought process of God and Christ, all because of their faith and expertise. The drawback to this belief, as it was for Simon Peter, is that one can become stuck in thought, believing that everything can be explained with the mind and with his/her intellect (arrogance).

Because we perceive things subjectively through the outer senses, including God, Goddess, and Christ, we turn to an emotional mind to explain the material instead of looking beyond the emotional mind for the real truth. Most scientists, religions, and intellectuals believe that emotions, reason, thought, and desire can eventually be explained as physical or mental functions of the body. By keeping us in fear, this then allows them to keep us a slave to them.

Even certain religions call for self-sacrifice, obedience, and suffering, and they promote the belief that humanity is nothing more than helpless humans because of our natural instinct to be evil. By teaching doctrines that require suffering and sacrifice to get to heaven, we humans will always see ourselves as a hopeless victim who will never be worthy of Yeshua, let alone God endorsing us to enter heaven. We all can see this in the teaching that man is born with an original sin, which places us at a disadvantage just by being born.

Doctrines like this are incorporated within rigid, dogmatic opinions relating to rules or principles we all must follow. They will always lead us to join like-minded people to find truth and heaven in a very limited and narrow viewpoint. It is like trying to attract the magic needed for happy and comfortable living by using someone of a scholarly intellectual understanding of God and Christ to keep us in fear, and in a mind frame to trust only in them. Please, I do not place judgment on these approaches, because every person has the right and choice to find their path to Christ and the life they desire to experience.

It is okay to honor Yeshua Ben Joseph (Jesus) for what he did for us, but never worship him. Even Yeshua himself has told me not to ever worship him, but only to follow his example in becoming a Christ in our own right. My friends, do you worship your brother or sister, or do you just love them unconditionally? Remember, Yeshua was crucified because he did not follow the traditional ways of the church during his time on earth.

My friends know that consciousness is changing, and we can know it only if we take the time to go within ourselves and feel the change. Finding the real truth is not about denying our Christhood or praying to a God who we believe created us. It is about loving, enjoying, and experiencing life while we are here on earth and not about suffering or sacrificing ourselves to become a martyr for God. As Yeshua gave me in a channel, there are no points given when we choose to suffer. It is about us integrating all of our many ego personality aspects with our mind-soul, spirit, and the "I AM" Christ spirit as one.

Yeshua not only symbolizes the Christ within us all, but he also represents us as the *"root and the offspring of David and the morning star,"* Revelation 22:16-17, as this refers to us humans becoming a perfect man, and therefore the forerunner in becoming a Christ in our own right while in human form.

David was the youngest son of Jesse and was anointed king of Israel in Saul's stead (1 Sam. 17:12; 1 Kings 2:10; Matt. 1:1). David is often referred to as a forerunner of being a perfect man where he, because of his style of ruling, represented divine love as being part of the human consciousness. This means that we humans can integrate this divine unconditional love with all our created ego-personality aspects. And, when we awaken to do so, we will see the promise of the throne become our wisdom in the knowing that we are the *"morning star."*

Therefore, *"let the one who thirsts come forward and the one who wants to receive the gift of life-giving water,"* Revelation 22:17, speaks for itself. If we are ready to receive our own "I AM" Christ-spirit *(life-giving water)* and our soul consciousness of responsibility *(bride)* as being part of our human ego (groom), and invite them in and become one body of consciousness, then we become the Christ in the flesh.

This *"warning,"* in Revelation 22:18-19, is about being cautious with what we have learned about a God that hates, is jealous, commands, says we sin, and is ready to punish us for what we do because the old, dogmatic beliefs *(prophetic words)* coming from our memories *(book)* that are now offering us to *"hear"* the real truth about how we all have been misled when it comes to whom we indeed are in the scheme of things. The *"book"* is symbolic of the recorded accounts of all our past lifetimes, stories, and experiences, and how we kept our truth tied to polarity teachings.

This is seen by our own "I AM" Christ spirit today, trying to get our attention through this extravagant symbolism of the Book of Revelation. And, if we ignore the rightful meaning behind the text, then we will most likely have to experience more lifetimes playing with the forces of polarity energy, positive and negative. It all equates to more sowing and reaping *(plagues)*. In effect, Revelation 22:18-19, is warning us against overlooking or ignoring the wisdom behind the text found in the Book of Revelation.

Over many lifetimes we have added to our story (book), let go of some, and integrated our stories, even as we created more lifetimes and experiences playing with the forces of polarity, good and bad, sowing, and reaping (plagues). However, if we are ready to take full responsibility for ourselves and give thanks to our own "I AM," then we can reap the wisdom of those plagues (experiences) and establish them within our outer, physical consciousness as something grand instead of seeing them as good and evil.

When we read that God seems to take away our share, it is nothing more than us humans not owning up to our responsibilities as an actual creator. And, if we do not take full responsibility for our choices and our many stories, we will experience the results of those choices over and over, again and again, until we become aware of the wisdom contained within them all.

Therefore, the one who gives the testimony is indeed our own "I AM" Christ spirit, and it declares to us while we are in the flesh, that polarity and the forces of positive and negative have led us back home to our oneness again. Even from reading Revelation 22:20-21, it shows, if we allow our "I AM" in our lives, our spirit will give us evidence of its existence, and that we were the ones, at the beginning who create our divine plan in discovering life, via using polarity energy. And now, some of us are aware of how vibrational polarity energy works with our mind, ego, and physical body.

My friends, some of us here on earth, are among the first to complete the full range of the earth's forces of polarity operating through us. Consequently, we will never have to be incarnated on earth ever again, unless one desires to be. Therefore, are you paying attention to the workings of polarity energy, or are you among those who still the belief that polarity energy is all that there is, thus must be real? Are you ready to consider the real truth about your purpose and let go of those beliefs that do not serve you any longer? Are you ready to become a Christ in your own right?

The *"grace of the Lord Jesus"* mentioned in Revelation 22:21 indicates the end of our story (book) of playing irresponsibly with polarity, which can be in this lifetime if we will bring in a new story and a new awareness, and if we are willing to step into our own Christhood. Since some of us have prepared the way through the earth realm by accepting whatever happened to us throughout our many lifetimes, then by the grace of our own "I AM" Christ-spirit, we become the standard for others to follow.

ACKNOWLEDGMENT

I give special thanks to Yeshua (Jesus), Lord Melchizedek, Mother Mary, Mary Magdalene, Tobias, Moses, Abraham, Methuselah, Adamus Saint-Germain (also known as Samuel in the Old Testament), Kuthumi Lal Singh (also known as Balthazar, one of the wise men who came to honor the birth of Jesus), and Saint Dominic. I also give thanks to John the Apostle, who wrote the Book of Revelation.

These wonderful Ascended Masters have gone beyond the confines of human beliefs and incarnations, giving them a broader outlook of God, Goddess, Christ, the Anti-Christ, the Beast, and Satan, which they have shared with me. And now, I am pleased, honored, and content to share the message with you. These Grand Masters from the other side of the veil are eager and overjoyed for those that choose to read the message in this book, because it could end their suffering.

I give honor, respect, thanks, and love to my wife Dianna for her patience, support, devotion, and love, giving me space, time, and trust to stay committed to my support of the angelic realm and their objective to awaken those that are ready for a whole new life.

I want to give a special thanks to an exceptional lady, Nancy Salminen, Surry, Maine. Through Nancy's editing and her contribution of endless hours of hard work proved invaluable as she patiently, and with unconditional love and determination, gave of herself in making the production of this book possible. Nancy, I am deeply blessed and honored to have you as a friend and a spiritual companion. It was you who set the stage for me to express my work in a clear and precise manner. Therefore, I give my gratitude, unconditional love, and thanks.

www.ingramcontent.com/pod-product-compliance
Lightning Source LLC
Chambersburg PA
CBHW030900080526
44589CB00010B/86